JOHN CALVIN

*Selections
from His Writings*

American Academy of Religion
Aids for the Study of Religion

edited by
Gerald J. Larson

John Dillenberger

was Professor of Historical Theology in the Graduate Theological Union, Berkeley, California. He has taught at Princeton, Columbia and Harvard, and his writings include *God Hidden and Revealed; Protestant Christianity* (with Claude Welch); *Protestant Thought and Natural Science; Contours of Faith.*

He is editor of the Doubleday-Anchor volume, *Martin Luther, Selections from His Writings*, a companion to the present volume on John Calvin.

He is now serving as president of the Hartford Seminary Foundation in Hartford, Connecticut.

Number 2
JOHN CALVIN
Selections From His Writings

SCHOLARS PRESS
Missoula, Montana

JOHN CALVIN

Selections from His Writings

EDITED AND WITH AN INTRODUCTION

by John Dillenberger

Published by
SCHOLARS PRESS
for
The American Academy of Religion

JOHN CALVIN

Edited by
John Dillenberger

Copyright © 1975
by
American Academy of Religion

Anchor Books Edition: 1971
Copyright © 1971 by John Dillenberger
All Rights Reserved

Library of Congress Cataloging in Publication Data

Calvin, Jean, 1509-1564.
    John Calvin: selections from his writings.

    (American Academy of Religion aids for the study of religion ; 2)
    Bibliography: p.
    Includes index.
    1. Reformed Church—Collected works. 2. Theology—Collected works—16th
century. I. Dillenberger, John. II. Title. III. Series: American Academy of Religion.
American Academy of Religion aids for the study of religion ; 2.
BX9420.A32D54 1975   230'.4'208   75-26875
ISBN 0-9130-025-2

Material from *Calvin: Institutes of the Christian Religion*, The Library of Christian
Classics, edited by John T. McNeill and translated by Ford Lewis Battles. Published
simultaneously in the U.S.A. by The Westminster Press, Philadelphia, and in Great
Britain by S.C.M. Press, Ltd., London. Copyright © 1960, by W. L. Jenkins. Used by
permission.

Material from *Calvin: Theological Treatises, Vol. XXII*, The Library of Christian
Classics, translated with introductions and notes by The Rev. J. K. S. Reid. Published
simultaneously in the U.S.A. by The Westminster Press, Philadelphia, and in Great
Britain by S.C.M. Press, Ltd., London. First published in 1954. Used by permission.

Material from *Commentary Upon the Acts of the Apostles. Vol. I*, edited from the
original English translation of Christopher Fetherstone by Henry Beveridge, pp. 72-
92, Wm. B. Eerdmans Publishing Company, Grand Rapids, Michigan, 1949. Used by
permission of the publishers.

Material from *The Deity of Christ and Other Sermons*, translated from the French and
Latin by LeRoy Nixon, pp. 243-57, Wm. B. Eerdmans Publishing Company, Grand
Rapids, Michigan, 1950. Used by permission of the publishers.

Printed in the United States of America

5

Edwards Brothers, Inc.
Ann Arbor, MI 48104

CONTENTS

IV
The Institutes

V
Three Forms of Exposition

A NOTE TO THE READER

This volume, like its companion one on Martin Luther, is meant for the general reader. A variety of texts has been chosen to show the range of John Calvin's life and writings—commentaries, sermons, letters, catechisms, tracts, broad-based theological works. The materials cover his major ideas; but the particular text in which an issue is developed may not always be the fullest or the classical expression it has received by Calvin. It seemed more important to show the diversity of his writings. This can be safely done because Calvin's ideas did not change to an extent which would make the present process of selection distorting of his views. Moreover, it has the advantage of showing that Calvin should not be exclusively identified with the *Institutes of the Christian Religion*. While recognizing the importance of the *Institutes*, it is equally necessary to see that this theological work represents a fraction of Calvin's life and work and that, as the introduction shows, the *Institutes* needs to have the halo removed which history has put around it.

The materials are arranged in groupings of allied content, but the style of writing in any grouping may vary considerably. The Table of Contents provides a clue to the context for each section. For the general reader, the order of the present selections is recommended, but no difficulty should be experienced in choosing another order.

The selections are frequently chosen from within larger documents, not only among documents. But whatever sections are included have been taken intact, that is, within the selected material, no omissions have been made. These selections are all taken from existing texts and hence the work of the whole is entirely dependent upon the translation and editorial work of others. Obviously, a definite view of Calvin is evident in what has been selected, as well as in the Introduction.

Brief introductory notes have been provided for each selection. The footnotes and Biblical references which remain are largely those of the translators and editors of the respective volumes from which the materials are taken. But the footnotes have been mainly eliminated because of considerations of space. Those wishing to use the notes are referred to the document sources from which they have been taken. Biblical references have been standardized in the texts. Brackets, i.e., square brackets—indicate editorial comments and additions throughout. Although both brackets and parentheses are used within the texts from which this volume is selected, brackets have been changed to parentheses in all such instances. Hence, brackets refer to my work; parentheses to previous work.

For the reader who wishes an account of the activities of John Calvin, either as an introduction to the selections or as a sequel, an introduction to the man, his life and thought follows. Because his life and thought forms such a unity and each aspect is necessary to understand the other, the introduction may serve a purpose for the general reader beyond what would ordinarily be the case.

J.D.

AN INTRODUCTION
TO JOHN CALVIN

I. The Man and His Life

The year in which Calvin was born, 1509, Luther took a baccalaureate degree in Bible and was already giving lectures. Before Calvin reached his teens, the Reformation in Germany had already reached a zenith in Luther's ideas and actions. When Calvin published his first edition of the *Institutes* in 1536, at the age of twenty-seven, Luther was already fifty-three and within a decade of his death. In 1541, five years before Luther's death, Calvin was to settle in Geneva for the second time for a twenty-three-year ministry, until the day of his death. Thus Calvin is definitely among the second generation reformers, though second to none.

The first fourteen years of Calvin's life were spent in Noyon, approximately 65 miles to the northeast of Paris, where his father was a staff official in the second oldest Gothic Cathedral.[1] Reared in a circle of students and associations beyond his own social heritage, Calvin early acquired an upper-class demeanor of aloof involvement, of being above the fray while being in it, punctuated on occasion by a loss of temper followed by remorse. But thoroughness and determination marked his life throughout, and even the unplanned intervals were used to full advantage.

At fourteen, Calvin applied himself to study at the staid Arts and Theological Colleges of the University of Paris. He excelled in Latin under the aegis of Cordier and received his Master of Arts in 1528. In the same year, Calvin's father, estranged from the Cathedral chapter over his staff responsibilities and accepting the promising place of the legal profession in society, directed Calvin to study law, which he did at Orléans and Bourges. But when his father died in 1531, Calvin felt himself freed from this responsibility. After finish-

[1] Charles Seymour, Jr., *Notre-Dame of Noyon in the Twelfth Century* (New Haven, 1939).

ing his law course,[2] he returned to Paris, enamored with the
thought of becoming a classical scholar. While Calvin had
done well enough at law, he had become interested in classical languages and writings in his associations with Wolmar
and Alciati at Bourges. In the excitement of this interest,
Calvin published his first book, *A Commentary on Seneca*, in
1532 in Paris. It did not have a wide circulation.

While Calvin undoubtedly had knowledge of Luther during this period, either directly or through friends, there is no
evidence that it occupied or preoccupied him in the least.
The theological-student-turned-lawyer now was interested in
being a classical scholar. But somewhere between 1532–34,
Calvin was led from general humanist interests to what he
himself in the preface to the *Commentary on the Psalms*[3]
describes as a sudden conversion. But like most conversions,
it was prepared, the result being the dramatic recastings of
elements which now re-form themselves. Knowledge of individuals whose dissent was suppressed, an association in
common danger and alliance with Nicholas Cop and his rec-
toral address calling for a more spiritual church, conversations
and associations with du Tillet, a meeting with Lefèvre—all
may have played their part. In the spring of 1534, Calvin
surrendered the clerical benefices from whose income he had
carried on his studies, surely a sign that the conversion had
happened. Like other conversions to the Protestant cause, it
signified the conviction that reform was no longer possible
in the Catholic Church as then constituted. The logic of that
position is retrospectively given in words ascribed to someone else, but the statement is probably Calvin writing about
himself. The material is in his *Reply to Cardinal Sadolet*,
written in 1539.[4]

It is interesting that the two great reformers, Luther and
Calvin, have left such uncertain clues about the circumstances and dates of the conversions which established their
historic roles. Their life thrusts were so directed to involvements and the issues about them that self-involvement was
only retrospectively registered.[5]

[2] Here following: McNeill, J. T., *The History and Character of
Calvinism* (New York: Oxford University Press, 1954), p. 104.

[3] Included in this volume, pp. 21 ff.

[4] This text is included in this volume, pp. 81 ff. The particular
statement recurs on pp. 108 ff.

[5] In both instances, it is my judgment that the dramatic changes
must be placed later than most scholars assume.

The convert Calvin was interested in changing badges from classical to theological scholar, but not in the least in changing his style of life as student and writer. But the history of his life is his inability to do just that. After wandering associations with the religiously awakened and concerned in Paris, Poitiers, Angoulême, and Orléans, Calvin found his way to Basel, probably both to escape the danger of persecution and to settle down to study. It was in Basel that Calvin extensively read the Church Fathers, mastered Hebrew, and published the first edition of the *Institutes* in 1536,[6] with a preface to the French King Francis I. Apparently, Calvin had some hope that Francis I would grant freedom of religious expression to views shared in France similar to his own, perhaps even total reform.

The first edition is a plea for the new views as well as their elaboration in the form of what is believed, and what is to be believed. It is the scholar Calvin believing in the power of the Gospel to have its way, hopefully with the support of the King, but if not, in spite of him. Calvin was French to the core and it was a lifelong disappointment to him that the reform was culturally and politically so unsuccessful in spite of his own efforts and the sacrifice of life and limb of many in its behalf. But the book itself, judged by publishing standards, was a success, as were the successively enlarged editions.

The book was no more than published when Calvin went to Italy where he conferred with the Duchess of Ferrara, whose sympathy and association with those interested in reform was well known. If Calvin went to Italy partly because every educated man was supposed to, one can only report that it did not take, for as he said, he entered Italy only to leave it. Perhaps the fact that the Duchess could successfully influence the reform neither in Italy nor among her friends and relatives in France conditioned Calvin negatively.

After two short months, Calvin was back in Paris and Noyon, settling the estate in the latter, and planning to travel to Strassbourg, to settle down as a scholar who influenced the life of the reform movement. But the war between Francis I and Charles V was responsible for the road being blocked, and Calvin, via a detour, found himself in Geneva overnight, only to have a friend disclose his presence. It was the fateful

[6] Sections of the 1536 edition and of the 1559 edition are included in this volume, pp. 267 ff.

night in which Farel, the passionate leader of reform in
Geneva, knocked on Calvin's door and verbally bludgeoned
Calvin into accepting a position in Geneva by threatening
God's condemnation on one who would retreat to a study
when the reform needed his active services. Shortly thereafter, in September 1536, Calvin returned to Geneva, was
given the title of "Professor of Sacred Scripture," and several
months thereafter became one of the pastors, apparently
through some ceremony which qualified him as ordained.

Geneva had just come through two developments, a grow-
ing self-government freed of outside domination except for
pressure from Bern, and the beginning stages of the Reformation. Farel had been given the assurance of support by the
political powers of Geneva for the total reform of the religious
and moral life of the community, Geneva having been known
in its own time as a free-swinging city.

Thus Farel and Calvin set about to reorient the life of the
city. But while the Little Council (comprised of four syndics
and a treasurer elected by the citizens and an additional
sixteen elected by the Council of Two Hundred) and the
Council of Two Hundred (elected by the Little Council) had
authorized the plans of Calvin and Farel, they hardly expected them to be as serious and adamant as they were. Calvin prepared a Confession of Faith, to be accepted by all who
wished to be citizens, planned an educational program for
all, and invoked the discipline of excommunication, particularly exclusion from the Sacrament, for those whose life and
thought did not correspond to the rule of life and faith delineated in the Scripture. It was not that men's lives were to
be beyond all traces of sin, but rather that their life was only
worthy if they believed in and exhibited in their behavior
signs of relying on the continuing mercies manifest in the
Holy Supper. Hence, the Communion was to be frequent,
indeed available each week in one of the parishes, but with
the appropriate expectations, lest the Sacrament be profaned.
Hence, the right of excommunication residing in the church,
not among the magistrates, was to be the rule.

After over a year of struggle the issue finally came to a
head, partly under pressure upon the Geneva magistrates
from Bern. In January of 1538 the Council of Two Hundred
forbade the ministers to preach and to keep anyone from the
Supper. Farel and Calvin preached anyway and refused to
administer the Sacraments under the circumstances. In April
of that year Farel and Calvin were ordered to leave the city

within three days. Calvin, glad to be rid of Geneva, attempted again to settle down to a life of scholarship in Basel. But this time Bucer threatened the divine wrath and Calvin accepted a call to the French refugee church in Strassbourg.

In Strassbourg, too, Calvin had a teaching and pastoral position, and he was able to have implemented the patterns of church life and discipline rejected in Geneva. But Geneva did not forget Calvin. When the moderate Catholic reformer Cardinal Sadolet of Modena in North Italy wrote to the governing authorities in Geneva, subsequent to Calvin's departure, in the hope that they would return to the Roman fold, Calvin was asked to reply, which he did in a document that sets forth Calvin's views on reform and indicates that the reformed churches belong to the ancient traditions. But Calvin's *Reply to Sadolet,* written in six days in the early fall of 1539, was obviously only a part of his literary activity. The first of his Biblical commentaries, the *Commentary on Romans,* was also published in 1539 and in 1540 appeared his *Short Treatise on the Holy Supper of Our Lord,*[7] a clear statement of his views as well as the Zwinglian and Lutheran positions. A greatly enlarged Latin edition of the *Institutes* appeared in 1539 and a French translation of the same in 1541. During these years, Calvin also attended various meetings—Frankfurt, Hagenau, Worms, Regensburg—and at one of these had an extensive conversation with Melanchthon, whom he found too willing, as the letters to him included in this volume also show, to make concessions to opponents where matters of truth were at stake. Moreover, in August of 1540 Calvin, then thirty-one, married a widow with two children, Idelette de Bure.

The relatively idyllic years at Strassbourg gave way as Calvin reluctantly bowed again to increasing pressure from Geneva to the effect that his God-given responsibilities lay in return to the city. In September 1541 Calvin took up residence in Geneva, where he was to serve until his death in 1564.

With little enthusiasm, considerable determination, and the conviction that his return was a form of "sacrifice to the Lord," he used his personal and pastoral influence to the utmost for the religious and moral transformation of the city. For the next decade and a half that task was to demand all his resources of spirit and body. The secure though uneven

[7] Included in this volume, pp. 507 ff.

victory of the following years was marred—though Calvin
would not have had delight in victory—by his failing health.
Indeed, Calvin, under the tutelage of the Word, had learned
to live in trouble to the discomfort of those who could not.

In the attempt to secure a church consonant with its ancient period and with the Word, Calvin involved the Geneva
Councils in a process which resulted in the Ecclesiastical Ordinances of the Church of Geneva.[8] Four offices were said
to belong to the church: (1) pastors who preached, taught,
administered the sacraments, admonished and, with the elders, corrected the erring; (2) teachers who had theological
expertise and who were responsible for correct theological
views and for an educational task, ranging from regular
schools to the theological equipping of prospective pastors;
(3) elders, appointed by and from the magistrates, whose
responsibility was the oversight of the moral and religious
life of the community; and (4) deacons who had responsibility for the poor and the ill and for the financial affairs of
the church. The twelve elders in Geneva together with the
ministers formed the Consistory, responsible for offences referred to them. These ranged from non-attendance at services,
attempts to reestablish medieval religious practices, disruption of services, to drinking, adultery, gambling, dancing.

To understand Geneva at this time, as most places in Europe of the period, it is necessary to assume the interrelated
responsibilities shared by governing bodies and the church.
Religion was assumed to be the business of governments with
the church concerned that it be supported and protected by
the magistrates but left free to delineate religious truth
within the church and, if necessary, against the government.
The notion of religious freedom from both government and
church was only inchoately and sporadically evident in the
Reformation period. Hence, in Calvin's Geneva the moral issues involved both government and church, sometimes in alliance, sometimes in opposition. Indeed, what Calvin so
seriously pursued was largely an ethical code already on the
books but certainly not enforced.

Calvin encountered a series of episodes on the religious
and moral level, some of which threatened the Reformation
and his role in Geneva. Castellio, a humanist who joined the
Protestant fold and was appointed head of the school in
Geneva, was discovered to have unacceptable notions on Bib-

[8] Included in this volume, pp. 229 ff.

lical books, having declared the Song of Solomon to consist of love stories, and subsequently having attacked Calvin and his associates in an uncharitable way. So he was exiled from Geneva. Several years later, Jerome Bolsec attacked Calvin's views on predestination, and the Council also banished him. But the most remembered historic incident in which Castellio figures again is the case of Servetus. Physician and theologian, competent in his time in both, Servetus vigorously rejected the Trinity and was universally considered a heretic in both Catholic and Protestant circles. He had the habit of getting his views known, yet of eluding persecution and inevitable death by his secret maneuvers. But he made a daring, open appearance in the church in Geneva. Only the hunch that he would win sufficient support in Geneva makes such a sudden switch intelligible.

In the decade preceding the appearance of Servetus in Geneva in 1553, Calvin had frequent encounters with a series of fairly prominent individuals in Geneva on moral issues. There was the wife of Pierre Ameux, who apparently proposed, and set about practicing, free love. There was François Favre, his son Gaspard and his daughter Franchequine, who was married to Ami Perrin—all of whom affronted Calvin in what certainly was considered immoral conduct by both church and state alike. They belonged to an increasing number known as the Libertines, who in 1537 challenged the Council of Two Hundred, and who in a threatening episode, were quieted by Calvin as he rushed headlong into the armed crowd. Berthelier organized a political party from among the opponents to Calvin, and he also supported Servetus.

For the most part, the opposition to Calvin was less interested in repudiating him as such or in supporting Servetus than it was in establishing its own freedom of life and morals. Servetus was a convenient pawn and one, in turn, who felt that the Libertines could be used to his advantage. Apparently, the Libertines, Servetus, and Calvin alike recognized the situation as a crisis of power and control.

But in spite of the stakes, Calvin was given the best hand. No person had made himself less acceptable, personally and theologically, throughout Europe than Servetus, and no one had a greater price on his head. Hence, in spite of the power of the Libertines, the verdict outside and in Geneva would have the support of those who in other circumstances might be inclined to be more lenient or to exonerate him.

Although Calvin had counseled decapitation as a form of mercy, Servetus was nevertheless burned at the stake and died with great dignity. Calvin then too vigorously defended putting Servetus to death, and Castellio rejected Calvin's position in his volume *Whether Heretics Ought to be Persecuted*. Indeed, it was his liberal defense of the freedom of religious convictions in this tract which became the basis for the historic negative consciousness about Calvin and the Servetus affair.

However, for the period, Calvin's attitude toward divergent religious opinion showed considerable latitude. He had given a letter of recommendation to Castellio when he was first banished from Geneva, and he had friendly conversations with Blandrata and Lelio Sozzini, both doubting Trinitarians from North Italy. But like other Protestants and Catholics of the time, Calvin was responsible for death penalties for divergencies less acute than those represented by Servetus. Calvin and his time are infinitely more guilty than the facts of the Servetus case would indicate. But Servetus came to symbolize the victims of the intolerance of that age; and Calvin became the symbol of the persecutors of that age.

Throughout this period Calvin also lived through personal tragedy in his own household. In 1542, a son died in infancy, and Calvin's wife never regained her health. After eight and a half years of marriage, she died, and Calvin, though never romantic, grieved deeply as his letters indicate. Throughout the Genevan period Calvin's household was not without inhabitants and problems. Calvin's youngest brother, Antoine, had lived in the household since the original flight to Geneva. Antoine's wife was found guilty of adultery with Calvin's manservant. Divorced as a result, Antoine again married and Calvin's house was filled with children from both marriages. Calvin's step-daughter, who had lived with Calvin and his wife in Geneva prior to her marriage, was also found guilty of adultery.

Beyond the problems within his own household, Calvin was occupied in finding a place for the refugees who came to Geneva in increasing numbers. Most came from France, but also a considerable number from England and northern Italy. Indeed, approximately one-third of Geneva's inhabitants at one time were refugees, and while the greatest number came after Calvin's victory, the refugees who became citizens tipped the voting balance, assuring Calvin's role at the time of, and in the light of, the Servetus affair. It is interesting that Calvin himself did not become a citizen until 1559, that is, until five years before his death, and that John Knox, the Scottish reformer, was one of the refugees who became a citizen and referred to Geneva as "the most perfect school of Christ that ever was in the earth since the days of the apostles."

Calvin considered these involvements as the arena of his ministry. But it also involved him in counseling, visitation of the sick, marriage and baptisms, preaching, writing of tracts and letters, the revisions of the *Institutes*. During the plague, the Council, against Calvin's wishes, forbade him to visit the sick. T. H. L. Parker records that for the period between 1550 and 1559 approximately 270 weddings and 50 baptisms were recorded as performed by Calvin.[9] Calvin, too, took his regular stint at preaching, which usually meant twice each Sunday and every day of alternate weeks. Preaching meant the exposition of Biblical books, taking phrases, clauses, sentences as they give themselves to be elaborated in their own right and as their meaning for faith broke in on the contemporary believer. Calvin believed that God's lively encounter with people came through the nexus of such Biblical exposition, vivified by the Spirit. But the form of preaching was essentially an instructional mode, in faith, and in faith's meaning and form for life.

The regularity of this concern with Scripture left in its wake a stupendous array of sermons, taken down by a writer designated by the community for the purpose (many still unpublished), inasmuch as Calvin spoke deliberately out of a context of preparation that had neither text nor note. The written commentaries were more background material for preaching, the clarification of the text and its meaning in ways which show considerable independence on Calvin's part over against authorities of the stature of Erasmus. Calvin wrote commentaries on every New Testament book except the Book of Revelation, which he confessed he did not understand, and on all but eleven of the books of the Old Testament.

He also found time to write tracts on the controversial issues of the time—predestination, Trinity, the Lord's Supper. Once an extensive traveler, Calvin, upon his return to Geneva in 1542, relied more on correspondence and occasional tracts

[9] T. H. L. Parker, *Portrait of Calvin* (London, S.C.M. Press), p. 81.

for his contact with the wider world than upon visits. His written contact is extensive, covering the major countries of Europe.

Reference has already been made to the 1536 and 1539 Latin editions and to the 1541 French edition of the *Institutes*. In 1543 another Latin edition with new material appeared. In 1545 the same edition was re-issued and also appeared in French. The Latin edition of 1550 has only minor changes, but the Latin edition of 1559 is the one Calvin himself felt best about, particularly because the form of ordering of the material was finally the one he wanted. A French translation of this edition, in which Calvin had a major hand, appeared in 1560.

It is obvious that Calvin had little leisure, and even his diversions were planned. He enjoyed companionship, games if not gaming, and had no scruples about a glass of wine, having declared that it was used in the Lord's Supper as an analog to the Holy Spirit because of the lively quality it imparted. Calvin had intense discipline in the midst of forces and powers that bore in on him from every side. But Puritan he was not; Puritanism was a subsequent development.

Toward the end of his life, Calvin's health increasingly deteriorated. For a time, he was carried to the Cathedral to preach, which he did until the sixth of February 1564. With death near at hand, he asked to speak both to the magistrates and to the pastors, and did so respectively on April 27 and April 28. Both of these documents are included in this volume. On the 27th of May he died, and Beza, his colleague, successor, and biographer said that on Calvin's death bed "nothing seemed left but his spirit."[10] At his own instructions, Calvin was buried in an unmarked grave.

II. The Man and His Thought

If ever the thought and the life of a man are of one piece, they are so in the case of Calvin. Yet the man seems to stand apart from both as if one had a portrait of him unmoved in all his involvement. Perhaps that is what vexes one so—his appearing so unmoved. It is as if he were never in need or want, nor were ever unfulfilled. He has friends but no friendships. He gives praise but not with generosity, and he is inclined to be moved more by negative things around him than by positive ones.

[10] *Ibid.,* p. 123.

In the portraits of Calvin, the eyes look out with a fixed but unfocused stare as if anything in his way would be ignored. He is a man who is set in a direction from which he will not be deflected. He is, to use the phrase Jean Cadier used, "a man God mastered," but at the price of such human foibles as incongruity. He delineates his sufferings without anxiety and hardly a complaint. He is almost too God-like in the traditional sense of that term for us to be comfortable with him. That is why he seems so self-righteous, though self-righteousness is indeed foreign to his being. He wrestles with the world, but never with God.

Wherever Calvin set his direction, he pushed ahead. More than most people, he stood on principle and never wavered not because compromise was unintelligible, but because he saw truth so clearly that any compromise was error to him. That is why Melanchthon vexed him so, and why Calvin would not leave their differences alone. This doggedness made Calvin a difficult adversary for his followers.

Such singlemindedness ignores aspects of humanity and limits sensibilities. For Calvin, the artistic world is so circumscribed that only God is the great artist, and the arts as a result lose much of the vibrancy that makes them appealing. There is no evidence that poetry or art were media which stirred his sensibilities. Even his letters are like mannerist paintings, suffering a certain lack of warmth and compassion. They pile reason upon reason, and have an overbearing insistence upon off-centered issues. Calvin's artistic imagination is confined to his prose writing. He saw the whole world through a creative prose style. Born of the classical and scriptural tradition, he was a master of the word with all the strength and limitation that implies.

Calvin was a man carried along by the work before him. He would have chosen a different role, but having accepted Strassbourg and Geneva as the pastoral role God had assigned him, he pushed along doing everything with consistency and singleness of purpose. This does not mean that he always got everything straightened out. He exhibits a dogged persistence at every point and is not upset when plans do not work out. He simply tries again as is evident in the case of the *Institutes*, which he finally succeeded in putting in a form that was acceptable to him.

Theologically, Calvin is most remembered for the *Institutes of the Christian Religion*, the first draft of which grew fivefold in a series of editions which extended well over two decades. But this fixation on the *Institutes* distorts both the man and his theological work. Successive editions were revised and expanded in the midst of administrative, pastoral and other writing activities. It is hard to believe that Calvin ever had a sustained period of time in which the *Institutes* could have received the attention theological work requires. The fact that it is finally organized in four books, various chapters and subsections does not make it either theological or systematic. It simply means that it received Calvin's organizational push. Indeed, the organizational aspects of the *Institutes*, like the traditional three points of a sermon, pose the problem of inconsistencies and the incapacity to make adequate, coherent transitions.

The first edition of the *Institutes* is a beautiful book, organized along themes which flow in form and substance. Later organization, in terms of the two major theological motifs of God as Creator and God as Redeemer—under which rubrics everything else is subsumed—is an adequate theological conception. But, as executed, it does not always work. The inconsistencies, particularly in the sections on God the Creator, may be due as much to Calvin's own inability (largely because of pressures of time) to work matters out as to our inability to understand what he is doing. The overpraising of the *Institutes* as a systematic work has even robbed Calvin of his humanity in this failure of organization. It is nevertheless theologically superb.

But if there are problems about how various facets of what Calvin says relate to each other in any given work, particularly the *Institutes*, it must also be said that Calvin seldom changed his mind. That is why one can give a picture of Calvin's theological work by drawing themes from any documents—letters, commentaries, sermons,[11] catechisms,[12] Institutes—and find no difference in thought. There is considerable diversity in the prose medium which Calvin employed, a variety, depending upon the settings in which he exercised his pen. The thought changes only in slight variations or nuances, and occasionally in further elaboration.

No attempt will be made here to give a full picture of Calvin's thought. The texts included in this volume have

[11] A sample of both commentary and sermons is included as part of this volume, pp. 542 ff.

[12] A selection from the catechism of the Church of Geneva is included in this volume, pp. 245 ff.

been selected to be reasonably comprehensive, despite the variety of their form. The focus of both is to show aspects particularly central and unique to Calvin, with occasional reference to differences and likenesses with respect to individuals such as Luther, Melanchthon, and Zwingli.

For Calvin, theological work is essentially the exposition and elaboration of Scripture through which one attains a lively knowledge of God. Scriptures provide the spectacles which give everything its true shape for the beholder. Therefore, to be true to Scripture is the task of the preacher and the theologian. Indeed, Calvin is so interested in being true to Scripture that he will accept Scriptural inconsistencies when he has no other alternative but will try to reconcile them wherever he can. Where Luther is willing to set James and Paul against each other, to the detriment of the former, Calvin gives "doing works" their due in the context of James without retreating one bit from the centrality of justification in Paul. If Luther is willing to think of a Bible within the Bible because of the centrality of justification by faith and of the way in which Gospel is set against law, Calvin without retreating from justification, nevertheless sees the totality of Scripture as a book which makes manifest the benefits of God for men. He even goes so far as to suggest that there must be a divine original of Scripture behind the received documents. But Calvin was not a fundamentalist, for the authority of Scripture did not rest upon the words being the word of God but upon the conjunction of word and spirit by which the knowledge of God through Scripture becomes self-authenticating. The superior wisdom of Scripture, its great antiquity, miracles, fulfillment in terms of prophetic prediction—, Calvin, contrary to his orthodox Calvinist successors, considers secondary matters subservient to the fundamental principle.

"Therefore, Scripture will ultimately suffice for a saving knowledge of God only when its certainty is founded upon the inward persuasion of the Holy Spirit. Indeed, these human testimonies which exist to confirm it will not be vain if, as secondary aids to our feebleness, they follow that chief and highest testimony. But those who wish to prove to unbelievers that Scripture is the word of God are acting foolishly, for only by faith can this be known."[13]

[13] *Institutes* I, viii, 13.

Calvin's sections on Scripture in Book I of the *Institutes*, essential as they are, are actually an intrusion at that point made necessary by the fact that he can no longer proceed to discuss the knowledge of God the Creator without having recourse to Scripture. Indeed, it would have been better had he put the section on Scripture first; but it is perhaps best that he did not, for Biblicist he was not. He assumed that his whole theological labor was the exposition of Scripture. Calvin had discussed the knowledge of God the Creator in the light of Scripture without having said so. From Scripture one knows that all men have a sense of God, that they feel an awesome response but fill it with manageable conceptions, that is, they make idols. There is enough of God manifest in creation for man to be "without excuse," but every attempt to do something about it exacerbates the problem. Calvin even has a section on man as if Adam had not sinned. He treats this apart from Scripture but certainly in the light of it. Indeed, because man needs the spectacles of Scripture to see God the Creator, Calvin accordingly inserts the section on Scripture. Indeed, from Scripture alone comes the knowledge of God the Creator on such issues as Trinity and Providence. In discussing God the Creator, Calvin already assumes the section on faith and the knowledge of God the Redeemer, which he does not actually discuss until Book III.

The organizational problem of the *Institutes* which Calvin never solved—though he felt better about the last edition than the previous ones—should not blind us to what he was doing. The essential structure of his thought is evident in a series of parallels which run throughout—God the Creator and God the Redeemer, law and Gospel, the Old Israel and the New Israel, Providence and election. Indeed, all the pairs can be put under God the Redeemer and God the Creator. Creation anticipates redemption and redemption assumes creation. Therefore, even law and Gospel are not different. The Gospel is a clearer manifestation of law, which for Calvin is identical with the religion of Israel. Essentially, the lively faith of Israel is already the faith of the New Testament community, though now faith takes on its true colors. The Old Covenant and the New Covenant are the same covenant, though under a different administration. The Old Covenant is built on mercy, not merit. Patriarchs and the prophets knew Christ in some sense, for they saw the promises fulfilled from afar. Both deal with the benefits of God.

This exceptionally positive role of Israel is already essentially akin to what comes to fuller disclosure in the New Testament. The harmony between the old and the new is more pronounced than is the case in Luther, for whom the major accent sets the two against each other. While in Luther the law as a schoolmaster that drives one to Christ is considered to be the "alien work" of God, for Calvin it certainly belongs to his "proper work." Law as the schoolmaster that drives one to mercy and as the restraining force which makes community possible, is in both instances already in the service of the religion of Israel. But the law under the old dispensation is the guide to the believers in Israel and now, under the new dispensation, to the Christians. While the forms of the ceremonial law have been abandoned, the law is not abolished but finds its true setting in the context of believers. Indeed, for Calvin it is surprising but crucial to his thought that the law is not basically considered in its negative form. Hence, the Ten Commandments are interpreted not with respect to what they prohibit, but rather to what they enjoin upon the believer.

What has happened in the Gospel is that the benefits of God the Redeemer in Christ have flooded in upon us. What has been there all along has been made clear and its fullness is now manifest at one point—Jesus Christ.

The fullness of these benefits are evident in Calvin's conception of faith and justification in the Christian life. The ingredients in each instance should not be missed. Calvin defines faith as "a firm and certain knowledge of God's benevolence toward us, founded upon the truth of the freely given promise in Christ, both revealed to our minds and sealed upon our hearts through the Holy Spirit."[14] The appellation that faith is a lively knowledge of God is certainly correct. For Calvin, Biblical history and logic make clear that God's beneficent dealing with the world has some standing as knowledge; that it is built upon a discerning apprehension; that its benefits, anchored in Christ, are not ephemeral because they are known to our minds; nor simply for assent, for they are known in our depths by the activity of the Spirit.

While faith is a comprehensive category, justification, the Reformation slogan, has to do with the precise situation of men before God. Hence, Calvin says, "we explain justification simply as the acceptance with which God receives us into

[14] *Institutes* III, ii, 7.

His favor as righteous men. And it consists of the remission of sins and the imputation of Christ's righteousness."[15] The news of being received in God's favor, of being forgiven, and of having righteousness ascribed to one as one finally stands before God includes all the elements which had been so central to Luther. But in Calvin's own thinking, justification now takes its appropriate place in the wider setting of the total dimensions of faith. That is because the role of justification has been won and now each aspect can take its appropriate place.

Nevertheless, the justification aspect remains more central than its place in the *Institutes* might suggest. Faith makes a difference, and Calvin tries to delineate the difference it makes. He can even suggest a compendium of Scriptural texts as a kind of guide to the believer's life. Works are a confirmation of faith. But while it is clear that one is justified not without works, it is not by works. Calvin never successfully solved the problem of how one can know that the works, which are meant to confirm faith, actually do so. He never understood the psychological tailspin this could engender and the frenzied activity of works that might result, in part because he came to the problem from another angle, mainly one of trying to encourage believers not to despair of their small progress:

"Let each one of us, then, proceed according to the measure of his puny capacity and set out upon the journey we have begun. No one shall set out so inauspiciously as not daily to make some headway, though it be slight. Therefore, let us not cease so to act that we may make some unceasing progress in the way of the Lord. Let us not despair at the slightness of our success; for even though attainment may not correspond to desire, when today outstrips yesterday the effort is not lost."[16]

Indeed, the security for Calvin lies not in works, which for him as for Luther would never be acceptable, but in the God-given, apprehended faith. Faith, too, has its comforts in the lively knowledge of what God is about, namely, that to the believer his benefits are sure. Calvin makes this point in the *Institutes* by placing the section on election in the setting of faith. It is the believer who knows the comforts of

[15] *Institutes* III, ix, 2.
[16] *Institutes* III, vii, 5.

election and its correlate, predestination. The notion that God controls all things, as Calvin delineated it in his concept of Providence under the knowledge of God the Creator and in predestination under the knowledge of God the Redeemer, was the positive rock of consolation to the believer. That it should be an oppressive idea had hardly entered the level of consciousness, certainly not for Luther or Calvin, believing as they did that powers, not man's freedom, controlled the world. He found emancipation and joy in the fact that the world was securely in the hands of God and that the believer who had received the gift of faith could believe that God had destined him for the present and for the future. To Calvin the notion of double predestination, which includes the rejection of those who are not among the elect, is the obverse side of election; it is an idea from which Calvin could not retreat because he found Scriptural bases for it. But he counseled every believer to accept that he was among the elect and to look upon others as the same. The completely deterministic mode in his analysis of Providence and predestination has a jarring effect for us, for we see it in the context of the dynamics of faith. But for him this is only inchoately the case. The logic of his argument leads him to make God the cause of evil, but he denies this conclusion, escaping only by a verbal declaration that this is not the case.

Surely it is obvious that such theological thinking is formed in the parish and in the church. Luther was a professor of theology, who from that base of operation changed the form of the church by everything that came in the wake of his major breakthrough. Calvin, the pastor-preacher-churchman, fashioned the church in a city which for generations was regarded as the beacon set on the hill, the model for all to follow. Calvin, the second generation reformer, needed to be less critical than Luther, though his positive statements are interlaced by still longer sections giving critiques of his own contemporaries. But Calvin can calmly and assuredly repeat with Cyprian and Augustine that "for those to whom he is father, the church may also be mother. . . . God, therefore, in his wonderful providence accommodating himself to our capacity has prescribed a way for us, though still far off, to draw near to him."[17] The church is the community of faith, where God has accommodated himself to men, for grace runs through in all the imperfections that continue. A certain char-

[17] *Institutes* IV, i, 1.

ity of judgment therefore is necessary among those who are recognized as members of the church, provided that "by confession of faith and example of life, by partaking of the Sacraments, (they) profess the same God and Christ with us."[18] Hence, "where we see the word of God clearly preached and heard, and the Sacraments administered according to Christ's institution, there, it is not to be doubted, a church of God exists."[19] Calvin's context suggests that his accent is that we are not to doubt that there is a genuine church where certain marks are evident. It was his successors who overzealously spelled out the content of the signs of the church.

The double character of proclamation and Sacrament should not be overlooked, for to Calvin the benefits of Christ are to be received in both forms. For Calvin, baptism is the initiation or the ingrafting into Christ, the mark and sign of our total involvement as believers—mortification, renewal, union. It is our entrance into the New Covenant, just as circumcision was the entrance into the old. Calvin is, of course, acutely aware that infants cannot comprehend the sign which they carry. Thus, he argues that while hearing in a comprehending sense is the ordinary arrangement by which God calls people, he has called many, "giving them true knowledge of Himself by inward means, that is, by the illumination of the Spirit apart from the medium of preaching."[20] Moreover, he adds, "this objection can be solved without difficulty: infants are baptized into future repentance and faith, and even though these have not yet been formed in them, the seed of both lies hidden within them by the secret working of the Spirit."[21]

Indeed, here Calvin calls upon the Spirit to rescue him in this dilemma. In one sense his conception of Spirit is his escape hatch, but from another standpoint it is the pivot upon which everything turns. For Calvin, every apprehension of God depends upon the activity of the Spirit, upon the way in which God becomes alive and lively to the depths of man. At the edges and limits of Calvin's thought, the Spirit takes over. The Spirit is so self-evidently the pivot of his apprehensions that it frequently operates as a *deus ex machina* in his thinking.

[18] *Institutes* IV, i, 8.
[19] *Institutes* IV, i, 9.
[20] *Institutes* IV, xvi, 19.
[21] *Institutes* IV, xvi, 20.

Baptism is administered once. But its reality lives on. In turmoil and tribulation of spirit, its promises are to be remembered and banked upon. The Lord's Supper is to be understood as the sheer liberality of God, who like a provident householder wishes continually to sustain us, this time in figures and images adapted to our capacity, making Christ's presence as certain as if we had seen it with our own eyes. While the union of Christ with us remains a mystery, here in the Lord's Supper we receive it in more tangible form in ways that refresh, strengthen and gladden us."[22] While the tangible presence is a marvelous accommodation for us, it is not to be overstressed. It is not the seeing, but the eating and drinking *in faith* which enjoins the signs and the mysteries.

For Calvin there is a presence in the Lord's Supper, though he cannot accept the Lutheran view of the ubiquity of Christ's body in the elements nor in the traditional views of transubstantiation. The meal as a memorial is not adequate, Calvin insisting that our "souls are fed by the flesh and blood of Christ in the same way that bread and wine keep and sustain physical life."[23] Hence, Calvin again calls upon the Spirit to solve his problems. Christ sits at the right hand of God; He is present in the Sacraments:

"Even though it seems unbelievable that Christ's flesh, separated from us by such great distance, penetrates to us, so that it becomes our food, let us remember how far the sacred power of the Holy Spirit towers above all our senses, and how foolish it is to wish to measure his immeasureableness by our measure. What, then, our mind does not comprehend, let faith conceive: that the Spirit truly unites things separated in space."[24]

In a subsequent passage Calvin suggested that the Spirit may lift us to Christ as well as Christ descending to us.[25]

Precisely because proclamation is the way in which Christ is present to us verbally and the Lord's Supper is the way under which he is present to us through other sensibilities, Calvin theologically insists upon the frequency of the Supper, suggesting that it should be observed at least once a week. He had considered the agreement with the magistrates of

[22] *Institutes* IV, xvii, 1.
[23] *Institutes* IV, xvii, 10.
[24] *Ibid.*
[25] *Institutes* IV, xvii, 31.

Geneva to the effect that the Lord's Supper was to be offered four times a year as a temporary expedient so that proper discipline could be exercised for worthy participation. But what was to be a temporary expedient has had, and continues to have, an incredibly long history in the Reformed tradition!

It often has been said of Calvin's thought that it illumines the benefits of God in Christ for the believer. It would not be too much to call it a religious functionalism, for his religious exposition serves the life and understanding of the believer. Only the sections on Trinity and Christology seem less vibrant and real, though Calvin there, too, takes on his opponents. That is because here Calvin, like Luther, follows a traditional path, for no critical faith issues were being reborn or reformed, only defended. Perhaps that is why he was personally offended when he was accused of heresy on the trinitarian issue.

His statements on political theory were less traditional. While he shared the traditional assumption of the times, to the effect that government existed for the sake of maintaining true religion as well as genuine civil order, he had enunciated these in such a way that the constituted authority could be subverted under specific circumstances. In commenting on the Fifth Commandment, he suggests that if our parents lead us to transgress the law, we have a right not to regard them as parents; and he then goes on to add that the same obtains with respect to princes, lords and every kind of superior.[26] In elaborating on civil government, he suggests that the role of resistance to tyranny is lodged in the lesser magistrates who have a definite responsibility to oppose the unjust ruler, and he proceeds to cite several ancient precedents.[27] He, too, comments on the forms of government, stating that government is best which checks the vices of men, and therefore has power distributed and checked.[28] It is conceivable that the Constitution of the United States, drafted by Madison, who studied under John Witherspoon, a Calvinist divine at Princeton, owes as much to John Calvin as it does to the artificial checks and balances of Montesquieu.

[26] *Institutes* II, viii, 38.
[27] *Institutes* IV, xx, 31.
[28] *Institutes* IV, xx, 8.

I

The Man and His Life

THE AUTHOR'S PREFACE TO
THE COMMENTARY
ON THE BOOK OF PSALMS[1]

[*Calvin's preface to the Commentary on the Book of Psalms, written in 1557, bears a role similar to Luther's Preface to the Complete Edition of his Latin writings in that it provides a retrospective look at his own life and work. Moreover, it is one of the few places in which Calvin speaks about himself. He feels a particular kinship to David and his tribulations.*]

THE AUTHOR'S PREFACE

JOHN CALVIN

TO THE GODLY AND INGENUOUS READERS,

GREETING

If the reading of these my *Commentaries* confer as much benefit on the Church of God as I myself have reaped advantage from the composition of them, I shall have no reason to regret that I have undertaken this work. Having expounded here, in our small school, the Book of Psalms, about three years ago, I thought I had by this means sufficiently discharged my duty, and had resolved not to publish to the

[1] [The text here reprinted is taken from the *Commentary on the Book of Psalms*, Vol. I, translated from the original Latin and collated with the author's French version by the Rev. James Anderson. (Edinburgh: Printed for the Calvin Translation Society, 1845), pp. xxxv–xlix.]

world what I had familiarly taught those of my own household. And, in fact, before I had undertaken to expound this
book in my lectures, at the request of my brethren, I said
what was true, that I had kept away from this subject, because that most faithful teacher of the Church of God, Martin Bucer, had laboured in this field with such singular learning, diligence, fidelity, and success, that at least there was
not so great need that I should put my hand to the work.
And had the Commentaries of Wolphangus Musculus at that
time been published, I would not have omitted to do them
justice, by mentioning them in the same way, since he too,
in the judgment of good men, has earned no small praise by
his diligence and industry in this walk. I had not yet come to
the end of the book, when, lo! I am urged by renewed solicitations not to suffer my lectures, which certain persons had
carefully, faithfully, and not without great labour, taken
down, to be lost to the world. My purpose still remained unaltered; only I promised what for a long time I had been
thinking of, to write something on the subject in the French
language, that my countrymen might not be without the
means of being enabled to understand so useful a book when
perusing it. Whilst I am thinking of making this attempt,
suddenly, and contrary to my first design, it occurred to me,
by what impulse I know not, to compose in Latin, only as it
were in the way of trial, an exposition of one Psalm. When I
found that my success corresponded to my desire far beyond
what I had ventured to anticipate, I was encouraged, and
accordingly began to make the same attempt in a few other
Psalms. On perceiving this, my intimate friends, as if in this
way they held me bound, urged me with the greater confidence not to desist from my course. One reason which made
me comply with their solicitations, and which also had from
the commencement induced me to make this first attempt,
was an apprehension that at some future period what had
been taken down from my lectures, might be published to
the world contrary to my wishes, or at least without my
knowledge. I can truly say, that I was drawn to execute this
work rather from such an apprehension, than led to it from
my own free will. At the same time, as I continued to prose-
cute the work, I began to perceive more distinctly that this
was by no means a superfluous undertaking, and I have also
felt from my own individual experience, that to readers who
are not so exercised, I would furnish important assistance in
understanding The Psalms.

The varied and resplendid riches which are contained in this treasury it is no easy matter to express in words; so much so, that I well know that whatever I shall be able to say will be far from approaching the excellence of the subject. But as it is better to give to my readers some taste, however small, of the wonderful advantages they will derive from the study of this book, than to be entirely silent on the point, I may be permitted briefly to advert to a matter, the greatness of which does not admit of being fully unfolded. I have been accustomed to call this book, I think not inappropriately, "An Anatomy of all the Parts of the Soul;" for there is not an emotion of which any one can be conscious that is not here represented as in a mirror. Or rather, the Holy Spirit has here drawn to the life all the griefs, sorrows, fears, doubts, hopes, cares, perplexities, in short, all the distracting emotions with which the minds of men are wont to be agitated. The other parts of Scripture contain the commandments which God enjoined his servants to announce to us. But here the prophets themselves, seeing they are exhibited to us as speaking to God, and laying open all their inmost thoughts and affections, call, or rather draw, each of us to the examination of himself in particular, in order that none of the many infirmities to which we are subject, and of the many vices with which we abound, may remain concealed. It is certainly a rare and singular advantage, when all lurking places are discovered, and the heart is brought into the light, purged from that most baneful infection, hypocrisy. In short, as calling upon God is one of the principal means of securing our safety, and as a better and more unerring rule for guiding us in this exercise cannot be found elsewhere than in The Psalms, it follows, that in proportion to the proficiency which a man shall have attained in understanding them, will be his knowledge of the most important part of celestial doctrine. Genuine and earnest prayer proceeds first from a sense of our need, and next, from faith in the promises of God. It is by perusing these inspired compositions, that men will be most effectually awakened to a sense of their maladies, and, at the same time, instructed in seeking remedies for their cure. In a word, whatever may serve to encourage us when we are about to pray to God, is taught us in this book. And not only are the promises of God presented to us in it, but oftentimes there is exhibited to us one standing, as it were, amidst the invitations of God on the one hand, and the impediments of the flesh on the other, girding and preparing himself for prayer: thus

teaching us, if at any time we are agitated with a variety of
doubts, to resist and fight against them, until the soul, freed
and disentangled from all these impediments, rise up to God;
and not only so, but even when in the midst of doubts, fears,
and apprehensions, let us put forth our efforts in prayer, until
we experience some consolation which may calm and bring
contentment to our minds. Although distrust may shut the
gate against our prayers, yet we must not allow ourselves to
give way, whenever our hearts waver or are agitated with
inquietude, but must persevere until faith finally come forth
victorious from these conflicts. In many places we may perceive the exercise of the servants of God in prayer so fluctuat-
ing, that they are almost overwhelmed by the alternate hope
of success and apprehension of failure, and gain the prize
only by strenuous exertions. We see on the one hand, the
flesh manifesting its infirmity; and on the other, faith putting
forth its power; and if it is not so valiant and courageous
as might be desired, it is at least prepared to fight until by
degrees it acquire perfect strength. But as those things
which serve to teach us the true method of praying aright
will be found scattered through the whole of this Commentary, I will not now stop to treat of topics which it will be
necessary afterwards to repeat, nor detain my readers from
proceeding to the work itself. Only it appeared to me to be
requisite to show in passing, that this book makes known to
us this privilege, which is desirable above all others—that not
only is there opened up to us familiar access to God, but
also that we have permission and freedom granted us to lay
open before him our infirmities, which we would be ashamed
to confess before men. Besides, there is also here prescribed
to us an infallible rule for directing us with respect to the
right manner of offering to God the sacrifice of praise, which
he declares to be most precious in his sight, and of the sweet-
est odour. There is no other book in which there is to be
found more express and magnificent commendations, both of
the unparalleled liberality of God towards his Church, and
of all his works; there is no other book in which there is recorded so many deliverances, nor one in which the evidences
and experiences of the fatherly providence and solicitude
which God exercises towards us, are celebrated with such
splendour of diction, and yet with the strictest adherence to
truth; in short, there is no other book in which we are more
perfectly taught the right manner of praising God, or in
which we are more powerfully stirred up to the performance

of this religious exercise. Moreover, although The Psalms are replete with all the precepts which serve to frame our life to every part of holiness, piety, and righteousness, yet they will principally teach and train us to bear the cross; and the bearing of the cross is a genuine proof of our obedience, since by doing this, we renounce the guidance of our own affections, and submit ourselves entirely to God, leaving him to govern us, and to dispose of our life according to his will, so that the afflictions which are the bitterest and most severe to our nature, become sweet to us, because they proceed from him. In one word, not only will we here find general commendations of the goodness of God, which may teach men to repose themselves in him alone, and to seek all their happiness solely in him; and which are intended to teach true believers with their whole hearts confidently to look to him for help in all their necessities; but we will also find that the free remission of sins, which alone reconciles God towards us, and procures for us settled peace with him, is so set forth and magnified, as that here there is nothing wanting which relates to the knowledge of eternal salvation.

Now, if my readers derive any fruit and advantage from the labour which I have bestowed in writing these Commentaries, I would have them to understand that the small measure of experience which I have had by the conflicts with which the Lord has exercised me, has in no ordinary degree assisted me, not only in applying to present use whatever instruction could be gathered from these divine compositions, but also in more easily comprehending the design of each of the writers. And as David holds the principal place among them, it has greatly aided me in understanding more fully the complaints made by him of the internal afflictions which the Church had to sustain through those who gave themselves out to be her members, that I had suffered the same or similar things from the domestic enemies of the Church. For although I follow David at a great distance, and come far short of equalling him; or rather, although in aspiring slowly and with great difficulty to attain to the many virtues in which he excelled, I still feel myself tarnished with the contrary vices; yet if I have any things in common with him, I have no hesitation in comparing myself with him. In reading the instances of his faith, patience, fervour, zeal, and integrity, it has, as it ought, drawn from me unnumbered groans and sighs, that I am so far from approaching them; but it has, notwithstanding, been of very great advantage to me to behold in him as in a mirror, both the commencement of my calling, and the continued course of my function; so that I know the more assuredly, that whatever that most illustrious king and prophet suffered, was exhibited to me by God as an example for imitation. My condition, no doubt, is much inferior to his, and it is unnecessary for me to stay to show this. But as he was taken from the sheepfold, and elevated to the rank of supreme authority; so God having taken me from my originally obscure and humble condition, has reckoned me worthy of being invested with the honourable office of a preacher and minister of the gospel. When I was as yet a very little boy, my father had destined me for the study of theology. But afterwards, when he considered that the legal profession commonly raised those who followed it to wealth, this prospect induced him suddenly to change his purpose. Thus it came to pass, that I was withdrawn from the study of philosophy, and was put to the study of law. To this pursuit I endeavoured faithfully to apply myself, in obedience to the will of my father; but God, by the secret guidance of his providence, at length gave a different direction to my course. And first, since I was too obstinately devoted to the superstitions of Popery to be easily extricated from so profound an abyss of mire, God by a sudden conversion subdued and brought my mind to a teachable frame, which was more hardened in such matters than might have been expected from one at my early period of life. Having thus received some taste and knowledge of true godliness, I was immediately inflamed with so intense a desire to make progress therein, that although I did not altogether leave off other studies, I yet pursued them with less ardour.

I was quite surprised to find that before a year had elapsed, all who had any desire after purer doctrine were continually coming to me to learn, although I myself was as yet but a mere novice and tyro. Being of a disposition somewhat unpolished and bashful, which led me always to love the shade and retirement, I then began to seek some secluded corner where I might be withdrawn from the public view; but so far from being able to accomplish the object of my desire, all my retreats were like public schools. In short, whilst my one great object was to live in seclusion without being known, God so led me about through different turnings and changes, that he never permitted me to rest in any place, until, in spite of my natural disposition, he brought me forth to public notice. Leaving my native country, France, I in fact retired into Germany, expressly for the purpose of being able there to enjoy in some obscure corner the repose which I had always desired, and which had been so long denied me. But lo! whilst I lay hidden at Basle, and known only to a few people, many faithful and holy persons were burnt alive in France; and the report of these burnings having reached foreign nations, they excited the strongest disapprobation among a great part of the Germans, whose indignation was kindled against the authors of such tyranny. In order to allay this indignation, certain wicked and lying pamphlets were circulated, stating, that none were treated with such cruelty but Anabaptists and seditious persons, who, by their perverse ravings and false opinions, were overthrowing not only religion but also all civil order. Observing that the object which these instruments of the court aimed at by their disguises, was not only that the disgrace of shedding so much innocent blood might remain buried under the false charges and calumnies which they brought against the holy martyrs after their death, but also, that afterwards they might be able to proceed to the utmost extremity in murdering the poor saints without exciting compassion towards them in the breasts of any, it appeared to me, that unless I opposed them to the utmost of my ability, my silence could not be vindicated from the charge of cowardice and treachery. This was the consideration which induced me to publish my Institutes of the Christian Religion. My objects were, first, to prove that these reports were false and calumnious, and thus to vindicate my brethren, whose death was precious in the sight of the Lord; and next, that as the same cruelties might very soon after be exercised against many unhappy individuals, foreign nations might be touched with at least some compassion towards them and solicitude about them. When it was then published, it was not that copious and laboured work which it now is, but only a small treatise containing a summary of the principal truths of the Christian religion; and it was published with no other design than that men might know what was the faith held by those whom I saw basely and wickedly defamed by those flagitious and perfidious flatterers. That my object was not to acquire fame, appeared from this, that immediately after I left Basle, and particularly from the fact that nobody there knew that I was the author.

Wherever else I have gone, I have taken care to conceal that I was the author of that performance; and I had resolved to continue in the same privacy and obscurity, until at length

William Farel detained me at Geneva, not so much by counsel and exhortation, as by a dreadful imprecation, which I felt to be as if God had from heaven laid his mighty hand upon me to arrest me. As the most-direct road to Strasburg, to which I then intended to retire, was shut up by the wars, I had resolved to pass quickly by Geneva, without staying longer than a single night in that city. A little before this, Popery had been driven from it by the exertions of the excellent person whom I have named, and Peter Viret; but matters were not yet brought to a settled state, and the city was divided into unholy and dangerous factions. Then an individual who now basely apostatised and returned to the Papists, discovered me and made me known to others. Upon this, Farel, who burned with an extraordinary zeal to advance the gospel, immediately strained every nerve to detain me. And after having learned that my heart was set upon devoting myself to private studies, for which I wished to keep myself free from other pursuits, and finding that he gained nothing by entreaties, he proceeded to utter an imprecation that God would curse my retirement, and the tranquillity of the studies which I sought, if I should withdraw and refuse to give assistance, when the necessity was so urgent. By this imprecation I was so stricken with terror, that I desisted from the journey which I had undertaken; but sensible of my natural bashfulness and timidity, I would not bring myself under obligation to discharge any particular office. After that, four months had scarcely elapsed, when, on the one hand, the Anabaptists began to assail us, and, on the other, a certain wicked apostate, who being secretly supported by the influence of some of the magistrates of the city, was thus enabled to give us a great deal of trouble. At the same time, a succession of dissensions fell out in the city which strangely afflicted us. Being, as I acknowledge, naturally of a timid, soft, and pusillanimous disposition, I was compelled to encounter these violent tempests as part of my early training; and although I did not sink under them, yet I was not sustained by such greatness of mind, as not to rejoice more than it became me, when, in consequence of certain commotions, I was banished from Geneva.

By this means set at liberty and loosed from the tie of my vocation, I resolved to live in a private station, free from the burden and cares of any public charge, when that most excellent servant of Christ, Martin Bucer, employing a similar kind of remonstrance and protestation as that to which Farel had recourse before, drew me back to a new station. Alarmed by the example of Jonas which he set before me, I still continued in the work of teaching. And although I always continued like myself, studiously avoiding celebrity; yet I was carried, I know not how, as it were by force to the Imperial assemblies, where, willing or unwilling, I was under the necessity of appearing before the eyes of many. Afterwards, when the Lord having compassion on this city, had allayed the hurtful agitations and broils which prevailed in it, and by his wonderful power had defeated both the wicked counsels and the sanguinary attempts of the disturbers of the Republic, necessity was imposed upon me of returning to my former charge, contrary to my desire and inclination. The welfare of this church, it is true, lay so near my heart, that for its sake I would not have hesitated to lay down my life; but my timidity nevertheless suggested to me many reasons for excusing myself from again willingly taking upon my shoulders so heavy a burden. At length, however, a solemn and conscientious regard to my duty, prevailed with me to consent to return to the flock from which I had been torn; but with what grief, tears, great anxiety and distress I did this, the Lord is my best witness, and many godly persons who would have wished to see me delivered from this painful state, had it not been that that which I feared, and which made me give my consent, prevented them and shut their mouths.

Were I to narrate the various conflicts by which the Lord has exercised me since that time, and by what trials he has proved me, it would make a long history. But that I may not become tedious to my readers by a waste of words, I shall content myself with repeating briefly what I have touched upon a little before, that in considering the whole course of the life of David, it seemed to me that by his own footsteps he showed me the way, and from this I have experienced no small consolation. As that holy king was harassed by the Philistines and other foreign enemies with continual wars, while he was much more grievously afflicted by the malice and wickedness of some perfidious men amongst his own people, so I can say as to myself, that I have been assailed on all sides, and have scarcely been able to enjoy repose for a single moment, but have always had to sustain some conflict either from enemies without or within the Church. Satan has made many attempts to overthrow the fabric of this Church; and once it came to this, that I, altogether feeble and timorous as I am, was compelled to break and put a stop to his deadly assaults by putting my life in danger, and opposing my person to his blows. Afterwards, for the space of five years, when some wicked libertines were furnished with undue influence, and also some of the common people, corrupted by the allurements and perverse discourse of such persons, desired to obtain the liberty of doing whatever they pleased, without control, I was under the necessity of fighting without ceasing to defend and maintain the discipline of the Church. To these irreligious characters and despisers of the heavenly doctrine, it was a matter of entire indifference, although the Church should sink into ruin, provided they obtained what they sought,—the power of acting just as they pleased. Many, too, harassed by poverty and hunger, and others impelled by insatiable ambition or avarice and a desire of dishonest gain, were become so frantic, that they chose rather, by throwing all things into confusion, to involve themselves and us in one common ruin, than to remain quiet by living peaceably and honestly. During the whole of this lengthened period, I think that there is scarcely any of the weapons which are forged in the workshop of Satan, which has not been employed by them in order to obtain their object. And at length matters had come to such a state, that an end could be put to their machinations in no other way than cutting them off by an ignominious death; which was indeed a painful and pitiable spectacle to me. They no doubt deserved the severest punishment, but I always rather desired that they might live in prosperity, and continue safe and untouched; which would have been the case had they not been altogether incorrigible, and obstinately refused to listen to wholesome admonition.

The trial of these five years was grievous and hard to bear; but I experienced not less excruciating pain from the malignity of those who ceased not to assail myself and my ministry with their envenomed calumnies. A great proportion of them, it is true, are so blinded by a passion for slander and detraction, that to their great disgrace, they betray at once their impudence, while others, however crafty and cunning, cannot so cover or disguise themselves as to escape being shamefully convicted and disgraced; yet when a man has been a hundred times found innocent of a charge brought against him, and when the charge is again repeated without any cause or occasion, it is an indignity hard to bear. Because I affirm and maintain that the world is managed and governed by the se-

cret providence of God, a multitude of presumptuous men
rise up against me, and allege that I represent God as the author of sin. This is so foolish a calumny, that it would of itself
quickly come to nothing, did it not meet with persons who
have tickled ears, and who take pleasure in feeding upon such
discourse. But there are many whose minds are so filled with
envy and spleen, or ingratitude, or malignity, that there is
no falsehood, however preposterous, yea, even monstrous,
which they do not receive, if it is spoken to them. Others endeavour to overthrow God's eternal purpose of predestination, by which he distinguishes between the reprobate and
the elect; others take upon them to defend free will; and
forthwith many throw themselves into their ranks, not so
much through ignorance as by a perversity of zeal which I
know not how to characterise. If they were open and avowed
enemies, who brought these troubles upon me, the thing
might in some way be borne. But that those who shroud
themselves under the name of brethren, and not only eat
Christ's sacred bread, but also administer it to others, that
those, in short, who loudly boast of being preachers of the
gospel, should wage such nefarious war against me, how detestable is it? In this matter I may very justly complain with
David, "Yea, mine own familiar friend, in whom I trusted,
who did eat of my bread, hath lifted up his heel against me,"
(Ps. 41:9.) "For it was not an enemy that reproached me;
but it was thou, a man mine equal, my guide, and mine
acquaintance. We took sweet counsel together, and walked
unto the house of God in company," (Ps. 55:12, 13, 14.)
Others circulated ridiculous reports concerning my treasures;
others, of the extravagant authority and enormous influence
which they say I possess; others speak of my delicacies and
magnificence. But when a man is content with scanty food
and common clothing, and does not require from the humblest
more frugality than he shows and practises himself, shall it be
said that such an one is too sumptuous, and lives in too high
a style? As to the power and influence of which they envy me,
I wish I could discharge this burden upon them; for they
estimate my power by the multitude of affairs, and the vast
weight of labours with which I am overwhelmed. And if there
are some whom I cannot persuade whilst I am alive that I am
not rich, my death at length will prove it. I confess, indeed,
that I am not poor; for I desire nothing more than what I
have. All these are invented stories, and there is no colour
whatever for any one of them; but many nevertheless are

very easily persuaded of their truth, and applaud them; and
the reason is, because the greatest part judge that the
only means of cloaking their enormities is to throw all things
into disorder, and to confound black and white; and they
think that the best and shortest way by which they can obtain
full liberty to live with impunity just as they please, is to
destroy the authority of Christ's servants.

In addition to these, there are "the hypocritical mockers
in feasts," of whom David complains, (Ps. 35:16;) and I
mean by these not only lick-dish characters, who seek a meal
to fill their belly, but all those who by false reports seek to
obtain the favour of the great. Having been long accustomed
to swallow such wrongs as these, I have become almost
hardened; yet when.the insolence of such characters increases,
I cannot but sometimes feel my heart wounded with bitter
pangs. Nor was it enough that I should be so inhumanly
treated by my neighbours. In addition to this, in a distant
country towards the frozen ocean, there was raised, I know
not how, by the frenzy of a few, a storm which afterwards
stirred up against me a vast number of persons, who are too
much at leisure, and have nothing to do but by their bickering
to hinder those who are labouring for the edification of the
Church. I am still speaking of the internal enemies of the
Church—of those who, boasting mightily of the gospel of
Christ, nevertheless rush against me with greater impetuosity
than against the open adversaries of the Church, because I
do not embrace their gross and fictitious notion concerning
a carnal way of eating Christ in the sacrament; and of whom
I may protest, after the example of David, "I am for peace;
but when I speak, they are for war," (Ps. 120:7.) Moreover,
the cruel ingratitude of all of them is manifest in this, that
they scruple not to assail both in flank and rear a man who
strenuously exerts himself to maintain a cause which they
have in common with him, and whom therefore they ought to
aid and succour. Certainly, if such persons were possessed of
even a small portion of humanity, the fury of the Papists
which is directed against me with such unbridled violence,
would appease the most implacable animosity which they
may bear towards me. But since the condition of David was
such, that though he had deserved well of his own people,
he was nevertheless bitterly hated by many without a cause,
as he complains in Ps. 69:4, "I restored that which I took
not away," it afforded me no small consolation when I was
groundlessly assailed by the hatred of those who ought to

have assisted and solaced me, to conform myself to the example of so great and so excellent a person. This knowledge and experience have been of much service in enabling me to understand The Psalms, so that in my meditations upon them, I did not wander, as it were, in an unknown region.

My readers, too, if I mistake not, will observe, that in unfolding the internal affections both of David and of others, I discourse upon them as matters of which I have familiar experience. Moreover, since I have laboured faithfully to open up this treasure for the use of all the people of God, although what I have done has not been equal to my wishes, yet the attempt which I have made deserves to be received with some measure of favour. Still I only ask that each may judge of my labours with justice and candour, according to the advantage and fruit which he shall derive from them. Certainly, as I have said before, in reading these Commentaries, it will be clearly seen that I have not sought to please, unless in so far as I might at the same time be profitable to others. And, therefore, I have not only observed throughout a simple style of teaching, but in order to be removed the farther from all ostentation, I have also generally abstained from refuting the opinions of others, although this presented a more favourable opportunity for plausible display, and of acquiring the applause of those who shall favour my book with a perusal. I have never touched upon opposite opinions, unless where there was reason to fear, that by being silent respecting them, I might leave my readers in doubt and perplexity. At the same time, I am sensible that it would have been much more agreeable to the taste of many, had I heaped together a great mass of materials which has great show, and acquires fame for the writer; but I have felt nothing to be of more importance than to have a regard to the edification of the Church. May God, who has implanted this desire in my heart, grant by his grace that the success may correspond thereto!

GENEVA, *July 22*, 1557.

CALVIN'S WILL AND ADDRESSES
TO THE MAGISTRATES
AND MINISTERS[1]

[*Calvin's will, as well as his parting addresses to the magistrates and ministers on April 27 and 28, 1564, respectively provide additional information on how Calvin saw his life work. The will and address to the magistrates are taken from Beza's* Life of Calvin, *with Beza's comments given in parentheses. An abbreviated address to the ministers is also included by Beza, Calvin's colleague and successor. A fuller text of this address was prepared by one of the pastors, Jean Pinault, from his own notes. The latter text is included in this volume and Pinault's own comments are given in parentheses.*]

(On the 25th of April, he made his will in the following terms:—)

THE TESTAMENT OF JOHN CALVIN

In the name of God, Amen. On the 25th day of April, in the year of our Lord 1564, I, Peter Chenalat, citizen and notary of Geneva, witness and declare that I was called upon by that admirable man, John Calvin, minister of the Word of God in this church at Geneva, and a citizen of the same

[1] [The text of the will and the addresses for the magistrates is reprinted from *Tracts Relating to the Reformation*, Vol. I, translated from the original Latin by Henry Beveridge (Edinburgh: Printed for the Calvin Translation Society, 1844), pp. xix–c. The text of the address to the ministers is reprinted from the *Letters of John Calvin*, Vol. IV, compiled from the original manuscripts and edited with historical notes by Dr. Jules Bonnet (Philadelphia: Presbyterian Board of Education, 1858), pp. 372–77. The translation is by Marcus Robert Gilchrist.]

State, who, being sick in body, but of sound mind, told me
that it was his intention to execute his testament, and explain
the nature of his last will, and begged me to receive it, and
to write it down as he should rehearse and dictate it with his
tongue. This I declare that I immediately did, writing down
word for word as he was pleased to dictate and rehearse;
and that I have in no respect added to or subtracted from his
words, but have followed the form dictated by himself.

In the name of the Lord, Amen. I, John Calvin, minister of
the Word of God in this church of Geneva, being afflicted
and oppressed with various diseases, which easily induce me
to believe that the Lord God has determined shortly to call
me away out of this world, have resolved to make my testament, and commit my last will to writing in the manner
following:—First of all, I give thanks to God, that taking
mercy on me, whom he had created and placed in this world,
he not only delivered me out of the deep darkness of idolatry
in which I was plunged, that he might bring me into the
light of his Gospel, and make me a partaker in the doctrine
of salvation, of which I was most unworthy; and not only,
with the same mercy and benignity, kindly and graciously
bore with my faults and my sins, for which, however, I deserved to be rejected by him and exterminated, but also
vouchsafed me such clemency and kindness that he has
deigned to use my assistance in preaching and promulgating
the truth of his Gospel. And I testify and declare, that it is
my intention to spend what yet remains of my life in the same
faith and religion which he has delivered to me by his Gospel; and that I have no other defence or refuge for salvation
than his gratuitous adoption, on which alone my salvation depends. With my whole soul I embrace the mercy which he
has exercised towards me through Jesus Christ, atoning for
my sins with the merits of his death and passion, that in this
way he might satisfy for all my crimes and faults, and blot
them from his remembrance. I testify also and declare, that
I suppliantly beg of Him that he may be pleased so to wash
and purify me in the blood which my Sovereign Redeemer
has shed for the sins of the human race, that under his
shadow I may be able to stand at the judgment-seat. I likewise declare, that, according to the measure of grace and
goodness which the Lord hath employed towards me, I have
endeavoured, both in my sermons and also in my writings and
commentaries, to preach His Word purely and chastely, and

faithfully to interpret His sacred Scriptures. I also testify and declare, that, in all the contentions and disputations in which I have been engaged with the enemies of the Gospel, I have used no impostures, no wicked and sophistical devices, but have acted candidly and sincerely in defending the truth. But, woe is me! my ardour and zeal (if indeed worthy of the name) have been so careless and languid, that I confess I have failed innumerable times to execute my office properly, and had not He, of His boundless goodness, assisted me, all that zeal had been fleeting and vain. Nay, I even acknowledge, that if the same goodness had not assisted me, those mental endowments which the Lord bestowed upon me would, at his judgment-seat, prove me more and more guilty of sin and sloth. For all these reasons, I testify and declare that I trust to no other security for my salvation than this, and this only, viz., that as God is the Father of mercy, he will show himself such a Father to me, who acknowledge myself to be a miserable sinner. As to what remains, I wish that, after my departure out of this life, my body be committed to the earth, (after the form and manner which is used in this church and city,) till the day of a happy resurrection arrive. As to the slender patrimony which God has bestowed upon me, and of which I have determined to dispose in this will and testament, I appoint Anthony Calvin, my very dear brother, my heir, but in the way of honour only, giving to him for his own the silver cup which I received as a present from Varanius, and with which I desire he will be contented. Every thing else belonging to my succession I give him in trust, begging he will at his death leave it to his children. To the Boys' School I bequeath out of my succession ten gold pieces; as many to poor strangers; and as many to Joanna, the daughter of Charles Constans, and myself by affinity. To Samuel and John, the sons of my brother, I bequeath, to be paid by him at his death, each 400 gold pieces; and to Anna, and Susanna, and Dorothy, his daughters, each 300 gold pieces; to David, their brother, in reprehension of his juvenile levity and petulance, I leave only 25 gold pieces. This is the amount of the whole patrimony and goods which the Lord has bestowed on me, as far as I can estimate, setting a value both on my library and moveables, and all my domestic utensils, and, generally, my whole means and effects; but should they produce a larger sum, I wish the surplus to be divided proportionally among all the sons and daughters of my brother, not excluding David, if, through

the goodness of God, he shall have returned to good be-
haviour. But should the whole exceed the above mentioned
sum, I believe it will be no great matter, especially after my
debts are paid, the doing of which I have carefully committed to my said brother, having confidence in his faith and
good-will; for which reason I will and appoint him executor
of this my testament, and along with him my distinguished
friend, Lawrence Normand, giving power to them to make
out an inventory of my effects, without being obliged to comply with the strict forms of law. I empower them also to sell
my moveables, that they may turn them into money, and
execute my will above written, and explained and dictated
by me, John Calvin, on this 25th day of April, in the year
1564.

After I, the foresaid notary, had written the above testament, the aforesaid John Calvin immediately confirmed it
with his usual subscription and handwriting. On the following day, which was the 26th day of April of same year, the
same distinguished man, Calvin, ordered me to be sent for,
and along with me, Theodore Beza, Raymund Chauvet,
Michael Cop, Lewis Enoch, Nicholas Colladon, and James
Bordese, ministers and preachers of the Word of God in this
church of Geneva, and likewise the distinguished Henry
Scrimger, Professor of Arts, all citizens of Geneva, and in
presence of them all, testified and declared that he had dictated to me this his testament in the form above written;
and, at the same time, he ordered me to read it in their hearing, as having been called for that purpose. This I declare I
did articulately, and with clear voice. And after it was so read,
he testified and declared that it was his last will, which he
desired to be ratified. In testimony and confirmation whereof,
he requested them all to subscribe said testament with their
own hands. This was immediately done by them, month and
year above written, at Geneva, in the street commonly called
Canon Street, and at the dwelling-place of said testator. In
faith and testimony of which I have written the foresaid
testament, and subscribed it with my own hand, and sealed
it with the common seal of our supreme magistracy.

PETER CHENALAT.

(This testament being executed, he sent an intimation to
the four syndics, and all the senators, that, before his departure out of life, he was desirous once more to address
them all in the senate-house, to which he hoped he might

be carried on the following day. The senators replied, that they would rather come to him, and begged that he would consider the state of his health. On the following day, when the whole senate had come to him in a body, after mutual salutations, and he had begged pardon for their having come to him, when he ought rather to have gone to them; first premising that he had long desired this interview with them, but had put it off until he should have a surer presentiment of his decease, he proceeded thus:—)

Honoured Lords,—I thank you exceedingly for having conferred so many honours on one who plainly deserved nothing of the kind, and for having so often borne patiently with my very numerous infirmities. This I have always regarded as the strongest proof of your singular good-will toward me. And though in the discharge of my duty I have had various battles to fight, and various insults to endure, because to these every man, even the most excellent, must be subjected, I know and acknowledge, that none of these things happened through your fault; and I earnestly entreat you, that if, in anything, I have not done as I ought, you will attribute it to the want of ability rather than of will; for I can truly declare that I have sincerely studied the interest of your republic. Though I have not discharged my duty fully, I have always, to the best of my ability, consulted for the public good; and did I not acknowledge that the Lord, on his part, hath sometimes made my labours profitable, I should lay myself open to a charge of dissimulation. But this I beg of you, again and again, that you will be pleased to excuse me for having performed so little in public and in private, compared with what I ought to have done. I also certainly acknowledge, that on another account also I am highly indebted to you, viz., your having borne patiently with my vehemence, which was sometimes carried to excess; my sins, in this respect, I trust, have been pardoned by God also. But in regard to the doctrine which I have delivered in your hearing, I declare that the Word of God, entrusted to me, I have taught, not rashly or uncertainly, but purely and sincerely; as well knowing that His wrath was otherwise impending on my head, as I am certain that my labours in teaching were not displeasing to Him. And this I testify the more willingly before God, and before you all, because I have no doubt whatever that Satan, according to his wont, will stir up wicked, fickle, and giddy men, to corrupt the pure doctrine which you have heard of me.

(Then referring to the great blessings with which the Lord had favoured them,) [he says] "I am the best witness from how many and how great dangers the hand of Almighty God hath delivered you. You see, moreover, what your present situation is. Therefore, whether in prosperity or adversity, have this, I pray you, always present before your eyes, that it is He alone who establishes kings and states, and on that account wishes men to worship him. Remember how David declared, that he had fallen when he was in the enjoyment of profound peace, and assuredly would never have risen again, had not God, in his singular goodness, stretched out his hand to help him. What then will be the case with such diminutive mortals as we are, if it was so with him who was so strong and powerful? You have need of great humbleness of mind, that you may walk carefully, setting God always before you, and leaning only on his protection; assured, as you have often already experienced, that, by his assistance, you will stand strong, although your safety and security hang, as it were, by a slender thread. Therefore, if prosperity is given you, beware, I pray you, of being puffed up as the wicked are, and rather humbly give thanks to God. But if adversity befalls you, and death surrounds you on every side, still hope in Him who even raises the dead. Nay, consider that you are then especially tried by God, that you may learn more and more to have respect to Him only. But if you are desirous that this republic may be preserved in its strength, be particularly on your guard against allowing the sacred throne on which he hath placed you to be polluted. For He alone is the supreme God, the King of kings, and Lord of lords, who will give honour to those by whom He is honoured, but will cast down the despisers. Worship Him, therefore, according to his precepts; and study this more and more, for we are always very far from doing what it is our duty to do. I know the disposition and character of each of you, and I know that you need exhortation. Even among those who excel, there is not one who is not deficient in many things. Let every one examine himself, and wherein he sees himself to be defective, let him ask of the Lord. We see how much iniquity prevails in the counsels of this world. Some are cold; others, negligent of the public good, give their whole attention to their own affairs; others indulge their own private affections; others use not the excellent gifts of God as is meet; others ostentatiously display themselves, and, from overweening confidence, insist that all their opinions shall be approved of by others. I admonish the old not to envy their younger brethren, whom they may see adorned, by God's goodness, with some superior gifts. The younger, again, I admonish to conduct themselves with modesty, keeping far aloof from all haughtiness of mind. Let no one give disturbance to his neighbour, but let every one shun deceit, and all that bitterness of feeling which, in the administration of the Republic, has led many away from the right path. These things you will avoid, if each keeps within his own sphere, and all conduct themselves with good faith in the department which has been entrusted to them. In the decision of civil causes let there be no place for partiality or hatred; let no one pervert justice by oblique artifices; let no one, by his recommendations, prevent the laws from having full effect; let no one depart from what is just and good. Should any one feel tempted by some sinister affection, let him firmly resist it, having respect to Him from whom he received his station, and supplicating the assistance of his Holy Spirit. Finally, I again entreat you to pardon my infirmities, which I acknowledge and confess before God and his angels, and also before you, my much respected Lords." (Having thus spoken, and prayed to Almighty God, that he would crown them more and more with his gifts, and guide them by his Holy Spirit, for the safety of the whole Republic, giving his right hand to each, he left them in sorrow and in tears, all feeling as if they were taking a last farewell of their common parent.)[2]

(On the 28th of April, when all of us in the ministry of Geneva had gone to him at his request, he says,) Brethren, inasmuch as I have had something to say to you, which concerns not only this church, but also several others, which in a certain manner depend on it, it will be good to begin with prayer, in order that God may give me grace to say every thing without ambition, always having a respect to his glory, and also that every one may retain and profit by what shall be said.

It may be thought that I am too precipitate in concluding my end to be drawing near, and that I am not so ill as I persuade myself; but I assure you, that though I have often felt myself very ill, yet I have never found myself in such a state,

[2] The preceding is from the text supplied by Beza; what follows is from the text prepared by Pinault.

nor so weak as I am. When they take me to put me in bed, my head fails me and I swoon away forthwith. There is also this shortness of breathing, which oppresses me more and more. I am altogether different from other sick persons, for when their end is approaching their senses fail them and they become delirious. With respect to myself, true it is that I feel stupefied, but it seems to me that God wills to concentrate all my senses within me, and I believe indeed that I shall have much difficulty and that it will cost me a great effort to die. I may perhaps lose the faculty of speech, and yet preserve my sound sense; but I have also advertised my friends of that and told them what I wished them to do for me, and it is for this very reason I have desired to speak with you before God call me away; not that God may not indeed do otherwise than I think; it would be temerity on my part to wish to enter into his counsel.

When I first came to this church, I found almost nothing in it. There was preaching and that was all. They would look out for idols it is true, and they burned them. But there was no reformation. Everything was in disorder. There was no doubt the good man Master William [Farel], and then blind Courant (not born blind, but he became so at Bâle). There was besides Master Antony Saulnier, and that fine preacher Froment, who having laid aside his apron got up into the pulpit, then went back to his shop where he prated, and thus gave a double sermon.

I have lived here amid continual bickerings. I have been from derision saluted of an evening before my door with forty or fifty shots of an arquebuse. How think you must that have astonished a poor scholar timid as I am, and as I have always been, I confess?

Then afterwards I was expelled from this town and went away to Strasbourg, and when I had lived there some time I was called back hither, but I had no less trouble when I wished to discharge my duty than heretofore. They set the dogs at my heels, crying, Here! here! and these snapped at my gown and my legs. I went my way to the council of the two hundred when they were fighting, and I kept back the others who wanted to go, and who had nothing to do there; and though they boast that it was they who did everything, like M. de Saulx, yet I was there, and as I entered, people said to me, "Withdraw, sir, we have nothing to say to you." I replied, "I will do no such thing—come, come, wicked men that you are; kill me, and my blood will rise up against you, and these very benches will require it." Thus I have been amid combats, and you will experience that there will be others not less but greater. For you are a perverse and unhappy nation, and though there are good men in it the nation is perverse and wicked, and you will have troubles when God shall have called me away; for though I am nothing, yet know I well that I have prevented three thousand tumults that would have broken out in Geneva. But take courage and fortify yourselves, for God will make use of this church and will maintain it, and assures you that he will protect it.

I have had many infirmities which you have been obliged to bear with, and what is more, all I have done has been worth nothing. The ungodly will greedily seize upon this word, but I say it again that all I have done has been worth nothing, and that I am a miserable creature. But certainly I can say this that I have willed what is good, that my vices have always displeased me, and that the root of the fear of God has been in my heart; and you may say that the disposition was good; and I pray you, that the evil be forgiven me, and if there was any good, that you conform yourselves to it and make it an example.

As to my doctrine, I have taught faithfully, and God has given me grace to write what I have written as faithfully as it was in my power. I have not falsified a single passage of the Scriptures, nor given it a wrong interpretation to the best of my knowledge; and though I might have introduced subtle senses, had I studied subtilty, I cast that temptation under my feet and always aimed at simplicity.

I have written nothing out of hatred to any one, but I have always faithfully propounded what I esteemed to be for the glory of God.

As to our internal state, you have elected M. Beza to hold my place. Advise how to relieve him, for the charge is great, and so weighty that he might well sink under the load. But advise how to support him. Of him I know that he has a good will and will do what he can.

Let every one consider the obligation which he has not only to this church but also to the city, which you have promised to serve in adversity as well as in prosperity; thus let each keep by his vocation and not endeavour to retire from it nor enter into cabals. For when people go under ground to seek for shifts, they may say indeed that they did not reflect, and that they did aim at this or that. But let them consider the obligation that they have here contracted before God.

And study too that there be no bickerings or sharp words among you, as sometimes biting gibes will be bandied about. This will take place, it is true, in laughing, but there will be bitterness in the heart. All that is good for nothing, and is even contrary to a Christian disposition. You should then guard against it, and live in good accord and all friendship and sincerity.

I had forgotten this point: I pray you make no change, no innovation. People often ask for novelties. Not that I desire for my own sake out of ambition that what I have established should remain, and that people should retain it without wishing for something better, but because all changes are dangerous and sometimes hurtful.

On my return from Strasbourg, I composed the catechism and in haste, for I would never accept the ministry till they had taken an oath respecting these two points: namely, to preserve the catechism and discipline; and while I was writing it, they came to fetch bits of paper as big as my hand and carry them to the printing office. Though Master Peter Viret was then in this town, do you think I ever showed him a word of it? I never had leisure; I have sometimes indeed thought of putting a finishing hand to it if I had had leisure.

As to the prayers for the Sabbath I adopted the form of Strasbourg, and borrowed the greater part of it. Of the other prayers, I could not take any part from that formulary, for it contained nothing of the kind; but I took the whole from the Holy Scriptures.

I was also obliged to compose a formulary of baptism when I was at Strasbourg, where people brought me the children of Anabaptists from five or six leagues off to have them baptized. I then composed this unpolished formulary, which I would not advise you, notwithstanding, to change.

The Church of (Berne) has betrayed this one, and they have always feared me more than they loved me. I am desirous they should know that I died in the opinion that they feared rather than loved me, and even now they fear me more than they love me, and have always been afraid lest I should disturb them about their [eucharist].

(This remark ought to have been introduced before in some place of which I have not a distinct recollection.)

(He made use of the aforesaid words. I have not set them

down in doubt or uncertainty. I doubt not but he himself would have set them down better, and would have said more. But what I did not recollect with the most perfect distinctness I have left out. He took a courteous leave of all the brethren who shook him by the hand, one after the other, all melting into tears.)

(Written the 1st day of May, 1564, on the 27th day of which month he died.)

LETTERS OF JOHN CALVIN[1]

[*Since Calvin disclosed so little of himself in his theological writings, the letters reveal clues about the man Calvin not otherwise available. The letters reprinted here provide glimpses of Calvin's view of other Reformation figures, particularly Luther and Melanchthon, and they show him writing about his failing health.*]

TO BUCER

(Unsuccessful results of the Colloquy of Berne—Sacramentarian discord—Remarkable judgment concerning Luther)

GENEVA, 12*th January*, 1538.

I have a good many things to write to you about, things too by no means agreeable, had I a little more leisure; write however I must, as much as my very limited time will permit, since to me it will be no slight consolation, to confide to your friendly bosom, the evils which oppress us. In the letter which I wrote to Capito from Berne, I exulted as if matters had been terminated to our satisfaction; and who would have entertained any doubts about the success of so good a cause? For our confession, which was then the point in question, was judged by the ministers to be a devout production, and an oath in confirmation of it was with the highest propriety exacted by the people; what remained but that a deputation should be named to cure the wound which had been inflicted by the former deputies of Berne? That was not obtained without the greatest difficulty, but when even those who were

[1] [The letters here reprinted are taken from the *Letters of John Calvin*, Vols. III and IV, compiled from the original manuscripts and edited with historical notes by Dr. Jules Bonnet (Philadelphia: Presbyterian Board of Education, 1858). The translation is by Marcus Robert Gilchrist. Vol. IV, pp. 382–86; 400–4; Vol. III, pp. 57–58; 59–60; 61–63; 157–58; 159–60; 219–20; 293–94; 335–38; 399–400; 410–12; 461–63; 481–84; Vol. IV, pp. 31–33; 148–50; 300–23; 358–60; 362–63; 364.]

actuated by the most iniquitous sentiments could not oppose our demand, deputies were appointed to settle this question, who it was very sure would never undertake the task for which they had been selected. As soon as they refused, the duty was entrusted to those among whom the evil had arisen; but that you may understand how little seriousness there was in this measure, the moment that the feeblest rumor of public report indicated to what issue things so well prepared were tending, these new deputies were immediately recalled.

I dare not give way to too malignant suspicions, but all declare that those who take such delight in disturbances and seditions are watching for an opportunity of making innovations. A short time after that, it was announced that Megander had left the country by a sentence of banishment. This news was as great a blow to us as if we had heard that the Church of Berne had for the most part fallen off. I begin to fear, my dear Bucer, that we are aiming at an agreement which will have to be sanctioned by the sacrifice and blood of many pious men, nor is this the phrase of a man who wishes to draw back, but of one who desires such an agreement as all good men could join us in. And if we have this at heart, all those perplexing difficulties which it seems might restrain the more timid, will be swept away. But these, which we ourselves thought were to be opposed, are that Luther should not give scope to his wild fancy, about our flesh being as it were a graff into that of Christ's, or that of Christ's into ours, nor feign that Christ's body is of infinite extension, nor impose upon us a local presence: for there is hardly any one of those who have hitherto protested who does not suspect something of this kind. If Luther can cordially accept of us along with our confession, there is nothing which I could more willingly desire; but in the mean time he is not the only one in the church of God to be looked up to. For we should be cruel and barbarous if we made no account of the many thousands who are cruelly domineered over under pretext of that agreement.

What to think of Luther I know not, though I am thoroughly convinced of his piety; but I wish it were false, what is commonly said by most people, who in other respects would be very unwilling to be unjust to him, that with his firmness there is mixed up a good deal of obstinacy. His conduct affords us no slight grounds for entertaining this suspicion. If that is true which I understood to be rumored about lately in the churches of Wurtemberg, that they had compelled nearly all the churches to recognize error, how much vainglory, pray, is there in such conduct? If we were not afflicted with the malady of ambition, would it not have been enough for us that Christ should be deemed veracious, and that his truth should shine forth in the hearts of men? I see indeed what will come of all this. Nothing can be safe as long as that rage for contention shall agitate us. All recollections of past times must then be buried in oblivion, if we look for a solid peace. For the contest was so keen and so much embittered, that it is not possible to bring it to mind without kindling at least some sparks of strife; and if Luther has so great a lust of victory, he will never be able to join along with us in a sincere agreement respecting the pure truth of God. For he has sinned against it not only from vainglory and abusive language, but also from ignorance and the grossest extravagance. For what absurdities he pawned upon us in the beginning, when he said the bread is the very body! And if now he imagines that the body of Christ is enveloped by the bread, I judge that he is chargeable with a very foul error. What can I say of the partisans of that cause? Do they not romance more wildly than Marcion respecting the body of Christ? If the Swiss should take upon them to inveigh against such mistakes, how would this pave the way for an agreement?

Wherefore if you have any influence or authority over Martin, use it to dispose him to prefer subduing to Christ, rather than to himself, those with whom he has hitherto wrangled in the most inauspicious of strifes; nay, that he himself submit to the truth which he is now manifestly attacking. Here what should have been done was that every one should ingenuously confess of his own accord his own error, and I could not help protesting to you as I think you yourself recollect, that those wily insinuations by which you attempted to excuse yourself and Zwingli displeased me. It is not in the mean time by any means becoming to insult one another. Would that all these reproaches might fall upon my head, and yet I am fully convinced in my own mind that I have never been so abandoned by God since I began to taste of his word, as not to preserve a pious sense of the use of the sacraments and of our participation of the body of Christ. There is nothing certainly in my introduction to contradict this; and even should we grant that there was an absurd shame in one party of confessing their fault, who would not after all excuse this feeling compared with what is said of the insolent fury of Martin?

Wherefore, my dear Bucer, you must strive that all things be properly adjusted on both sides. A difficult task, you will say; I admit it, certainly; but since you have taken it upon you, you must labour seriously, I do not say to fulfil it, but to endeavour to do so. How intolerable do you think it appears that so many, and by no means contemptible churches of the whole of Saxony, when they have shown their readiness to come to an equitable agreement, should be kept so long in suspense! If then you ask of the Swiss to lay aside their obstinacy, contrive that Luther in his turn cease to bear himself so imperiously. . . .

To Zebedee

(Pressing invitations to concord—Apology for Bucer—Judgment respecting Zwingli, Luther, Carlostadt—Necessity of union.)

STRASBOURG, 19th May, 1539.

Your letter gave me uneasiness for other reasons, but greatly agitated my mind, because I see that you still entertain so great an aversion to the agreement which I imagined had been duly established in your parts. As you do not seem, however, to have taken up your views of the subject without some reasons, I shall first endeavour to satisfy you as well as I can respecting the things which you object to, then I shall slightly touch on the cause itself. You say that those men whose talents and hearts I so highly commend, have diminished their own authority among most persons whom you know, both men of small and of great importance. I confess it indeed. But whose fault is it? "I wish it were not their own," you say.

Take care, lest you do injustice to the servants of Christ, whom you suspect so maliciously when they themselves have given you no grounds for doing so. Bucer conducted himself in such a manner in the affair of the agreement, that while many exclaim that his actions displease them, no one can point out the slightest point in which he did wrong. I know what complaints are everywhere heard about him among those who cry out against the agreement. But if you examine a little more closely, it will be clear to you that they are mere invectives. If we condemn, with so much facility, a man

endowed with so many excellent gifts, and whose services
the Lord has made use of for such excellent things, what,
pray, shall we say of those who have hitherto approved themselves by no notable action? But should you persist in flattering yourself by depreciating men who do not deserve it,
you shall never, for all that, persuade me not to feel and declare those to be sincere men whose sincerity I see with my
eyes. It is to no purpose you recur to that commonplace remark, we should not from admiration of men let ourselves
be led away from the certain truth of religion. For I am not
enslaved by so preposterous and blind an admiration of any
man, as to be detached by it from a sound judgment, much
less from the authority of the faith; and I know that Farel
has too much firmness to leave me any room for fearing that
he could in this manner be turned aside from the word of
God. But as I know that all who stand up for the opinions of
Luther are suspected of too much wiliness by the men of our
party, I was unwilling to allow Farel to be tormented by a
needless mistrust. But to what purpose dread the astuteness
of that man of whose candour you can be assured? I shall
not cease then loudly to proclaim that virtue which I think
I perceive in Melanchthon. Meanwhile there are certain
things in which I myself confess him to be deficient, so far am
I from wishing to subject any one to his opinions. For this is
my purpose, that banishing all suspicions which are an obstacle to us, we should confidingly on the one side and the
other listen to each other's reasons, reserving for our own
judgment the question itself intact till the truth be discovered.
I know that there is an immense fear of the Gorgon as far as
Bucer is concerned. But it vexes you, that he has overthrown
a doctrine, which lately (1537, Sept.), was so well established there, and you think it to be the more dishonourable,
that he himself should bring into doubt a doctrine, which
formerly he defended with the greatest firmness against most
obstinate opponents. What kind of a truth it is we are wavering in, I do not preceive; but I venture to say, that we
perfectly and firmly agree with Bucer, so that no part of
sound doctrine is abandoned by us. What is there repugnant
to the plain meaning of the Scripture in the formula I drew
up some time ago? What is there in my articles, which could
in any way give you offence? Nevertheless nothing prevents
an agreement, but that those men, who wish to appear very
conservative, entirely reject this doctrine. If we think that
Martin dissembles, why do we not thoroughly draw him out?

Let us simply assent to the teaching of the Scripture, and we shall either win him over, with or against his will, to the light; or he certainly will not be able to use evasion, but will disclose whatever poison may be in his heart. But since we have not fully found out his opinion, we even shrink from confessing the truth, lest we may seem to assent to his views. What harm could result from drawing up a clear confession of the participation of the body and blood of the Lord, which is the privilege of the faithful in the holy supper? Surely Martin would be compelled to accept it, or we would justly bid him farewell. You have no cause to take so great offence at the retractations of Bucer. Since his teaching concerning the use of the sacraments was erroneous, he justly retracted it. I would that Zwingli had made up his mind to do the same. For his opinion on this subject was both wrong and pernicious. When I saw that our friends eagerly accepted it with great applause, I did not hesitate to oppose it, while I was still working in France. I confess, he (Bucer) commits a mistake by endeavouring to soften the sentiments of Œcolampadius and Zwingli, because he makes them almost agree with Luther. But those men, who most spitefully censure him in every other respect, do not blame him for this. For they have nothing more at heart, but that Zwingli should remain untouched. But I wish, that they would cease to defend him so urgently, and would with singleness of mind give glory to God by a bare confession of the truth. I am very far from conceding to you that there was no rigidity in the doctrine of Zwingli. Indeed one can see at a glance that, too much absorbed with overturning the superstition of a carnal presence, he at the same time set aside the true efficacy of our participation, or at least threw an obscurity over it. So that what we required was that greater light should have been thrown on that point. You have reason to be offended that Luther retracts nothing, palliates nothing, but stubbornly maintains all his opinions.

But what could Bucer do? He might have waited, you will say. But it was better by his example to incite Luther and others to their duty. To what end that holy obtestation? For after he had retracted his own errors, he also adjures them in God's name to correct in their turn whatever mistakes they have committed. What Luther's book against the Arians contains, I know not, except that from the title I guess the main points of the subject. If in handling it he has given Carlostadt a good drubbing, it is not without reason. Wherefore they cannot feel wroth with him, except that it is matter of sorrow that by the unnecessary ripping up of old quarrels, minds should be exasperated. It is more certain than certainty itself, that the Church of Wittemberg has been pestered with that foolish dogma by Carlostadt. We have not Bucer's Latin book. If such are their acts of conciliation it is with reason they displease you, and I should not consider them in a more favourable light if I saw them. But it does not follow that every difference of opinion should immediately break out into an open rupture. Wherefore, though your conscience compel you to oppose in some respects his opinion, it is your duty to do your endeavour that the fraternal union between you and him be maintained. For it behoves us not rashly to break up our connection with those whom the Lord has joined with us in the fellowship of his work. And this alone I ask of you, that you constantly retain that faith in which you have hitherto stood, but in such a manner as that you may not appear of your own free will to seek for a rupture with those to whom you cannot refuse the right of being esteemed both by you and all pious men as among the leading servants of Christ. Good God, to what a point have we come. We ought to consider a separation from the ministers of Christ, with the same disposition as if our own bowels were torn out. Now it is almost a sort of sport not only to cut off certain members, but to retrench the most vital parts from their connection with us. These things, as I have thrown them together at random and without any arrangement, you will reflect on, and endure patiently the just liberty I have taken. Moreover you have no occasion to be under any apprehensions from me. The things you have written I will keep by me as religiously as I should wish them to be kept, if it were my own life that was at stake.

<hr>

To John Sleidan

(Marks of fraternal confidence—blame pronounced on Melanchthon—persecutions in France and Italy.)

GENEVA, 27th August 1554.

When I learned lately from a letter of our brother N., that of the three whom the senate had set at the head of the French Church you are one, I was, as you may well suppose, greatly delighted, and this joy, I hope, will be lasting. For

I conclude that it is rather by divine direction than by human counsels that this task has devolved on you, that by your good faith and prudence you might compose all the differences which Satan has hitherto stirred up. You will do well then to take precautions beforehand not to afford the wicked any pretext for raising disturbances. Thus, to my heart's desire, the interests of this little flock have been consulted for. And if I do not exhort you to do your duty, it is no timidity on my part which occasions this omission, but because I deem such exhortation superfluous. I know not how much I ought to congratulate myself on Philip's agreement with me in one thing, since in the most important matters, catching at the approbation even of the philosophers, he openly opposes sound doctrine; or lest he should provoke the resentment of certain persons, he cunningly, or at least, with but little manliness, disguises his own opinion. May the Lord endow him with a more courageous spirit, lest posterity suffer great detriment from his timidity. Within the last three months, five or six persons have been burnt in Gascony, in whose death the Lord has sublimely triumphed. Lately, also, in a town of the Venetian dominions, a pious man, with whom I was well acquainted, confessed Christ with admirable constancy to his last breath. Here we have nothing new, but what is equally known to you. Farewell, most distinguished and ever respected man, may the Lord protect and bless you and your family. Of the Turkish fleet more certain intelligence has been brought us, that having burned certain towns, laid waste the sea coast, and taken five thousand men prisoners, it has sailed back to Greece.

To Peter Martyr

(He engages him to defend the sound doctrine on the question of the Sacraments, and gives him an account of the steps he has taken in favour of the French Church at Strasbourg.)

Geneva, *27th August* 1554.

Though our common friend Sturm, when giving me his advice respecting the dedication of the commentaries, had added that you entirely coincided with him, yet it has given me much greater pleasure to learn the fact from your own letter. One thing I fear is that my labour, about which you shew yourself so anxious, shall not have the good fortune to be much esteemed. But how comes it, that you say not a word about your own commentaries on the same work? From the answer you had given to Robert Etienne, while you were yet in England, I expected that they would be published in a short time. Wherefore I am dissatisfied that the Church should be any longer defrauded of the fruits of them, which I am confident will be abundant. For in the present heterogeneous mass of books, it is especially necessary that we should be able to lay our hands on the grave, learned, and solid lucubrations of pious and orthodox men, who are endowed with equal judgment and authority, both for the purpose of asserting purity of doctrine, and of having this doctrine transmitted to our posterity sound and entire, as also for the purpose of confuting the foolish levity of those who embroil everything. I am truly grieved on account of Philip.[2] It is not enough for him then, either to be wavering from suppleness of temper to the side where the favour of men impels him, or by his silence to be betraying the truth, unless he can at the same time endeavour to incline, to his own timid inaction, men of understanding whom he had better strive to imitate. But you have acted nobly in professing that you would be the voluntary defender of the true doctrine. For thus by your example a rule has been prescribed to him up to what point peace is to be cherished, that he may at length learn to emit some sparks of manly virtue. He was disposed to pay too servile a court to your colleague, to whom, by the advice of M. Sturm, I have written that I might reconcile him to N. Whatever turn the affair may take, I shall never repent of having attempted something. But if any have fallen away, your duty is to bear the more courageously on that account the burden imposed on you; which when I plainly perceive that you do, I am more and more confirmed in the opinion that you have been detained where you are by a wonderful providence of God, in order to succour an afflicted church. I beg of you to salute M. Zanchi in my name; the Marquis sends you his kindest respects. Farewell, most excellent man, and my truly honoured brother; may the Lord always stand by you, govern you, and bless your labours. If your letter had been put into my hands earlier, my exhortation to the princes would have been, according to your advice, more copious; but I received it after the middle of August. My colleagues salute you.—Yours,

[2] The reference to Philip in these letters is to Melanchthon.

To Melanchthon

(He deplores the silence of Melanchthon, and urges him to apply himself to the controverted questions of Election and the Lord's Supper.)

GENEVA, 27*th August* 1554.

Though I am sorry and much surprised, that you did not answer my last letter, yet I can by no means bring myself to suspect that this occurred from any haughtiness or contempt on your part, feelings which I know to be most alien to your temper and manners. For that reason, having chanced on this messenger, who has offered me his services in conveying a letter to you, I have thought that I should make a second attempt to see whether I might not be able to draw something from you. I do not express myself thus, as doubting of your friendship towards me, which indeed has always been unbounded, but because your silence, as I esteem it to be detrimental to the Church of God, cannot for that reason but be painful and annoying to me. I wrote to you lately respecting that article of doctrine, in which you rather dissemble your own opinion than dissent from us. For what else can I suppose of a man of the most penetrating judgment, and profoundly learned in heavenly doctrine, when what you conceal as a thing unknown to you, cannot but force itself on the observation of every one, who is, however superficially, versed in the sacred scriptures? And yet the doctrine of the gratuitous mercy of God is entirely destroyed, unless we hold that the faithful, whom God has thought fit to choose out for salvation, are distinguished from the reprobate by the mere good pleasure of God; unless this also be clearly established as a consequence, that faith flows from the secret election of God, because he enlightens, by his Spirit, those whom it seemed good to him to elect before they were born, and by the grace of adoption grafts them into his family. Weigh well in your wisdom, how absurd it is that this doctrine should be impugned by the greatest of theologians. You see that the manifest discordance which is certainly remarked between our writings has a pernicious tendency. Nor do I prescribe this law for the removal of our discrepancy that you should assent to me, but at least let us not be ashamed to subscribe to the sacred oracles of God. And, indeed, whatever method of reconciling our differences it shall please you to adopt, that I will gladly embrace. Behold how illiterate and turbulent men are renewing the Sacramentarian quarrel from your quarter. All good men lament and complain, that these same individuals are encouraged by your silence. For however audacious ignorance is, still nobody doubts, if you could bring your mind to speak out openly what you think, but that it would be an easy task for you to appease, at least in part, their violence. Nor indeed am I so forgetful of what is due to human feelings, as not to revolve in my own mind, and also to point out to others, with what sort of men you will have to deal; in what anxiety and perplexity the troubled state of affairs must keep you; and how necessary it will be for you to have an eye in all directions, to discover what obstacles impede and retard your course. But no consideration should have such weight with you, as to induce you by your dissimulation, to give a loose to frantic men to trouble and disperse the churches. Not to mention, moreover, how precious a thing we should deem an undisguised profession of sound doctrine. You know that, for upwards of thirty years, the eyes of an innumerable multitude of men have been fixed upon you, who desire nothing more than to prove their docility to you. What! are you ignorant to-day what numbers are held floating in doubts in consequence of the ambiguous manner of teaching, to which you too timidly adhere? But if you are not at liberty to declare, candidly and fully, what it would be advantageous to have made known, at least you should make an effort to bridle the fury of those who brawl unseasonably about nothing. For what, I would fain ask, do they aim at? Luther, during his whole life, loudly proclaimed that all he contended for, was but to assert the efficacy inherent in the sacraments. It is admitted that they are not empty figures, but that what they typify is in reality imparted to us—that there is present in baptism an efficacy of the Spirit which cleanses and regenerates us—that the Lord's Supper is truly a spiritual banquet, in which we feed on the flesh and blood of Christ. In calming then the tumults which these absurd men have stirred up anew, the cause seems too favourable to permit you from fear of odium to hang back, and in the distinguished position which you occupy, you cannot moreover, if you would, escape from its various fluctuations. Endeavour only that the brazen wall of a good conscience may enable you to stand up courageously against these, and whatever violent attacks the whole world may bring against you. For when, by the partisans of Osiander, I hear you described both as versatile and more devoted to profane philosophy than heavenly wisdom, the reproach wounds me more deeply, than if malevolent or wanton men upbraided you with what it would be not only honourable to avow, but glorious to exult in. Farewell, my very dear sir, and highly respected brother. May the Lord continue to shield you with his protection, and govern you by his Spirit, even unto the end.—Yours,

---

To Melanchthon

(Thanks him for his approbation of the condemnation of Servetus—urgent entreaties to determine Melanchthon to pronounce with more firmness in the question of the sacraments.)

Geneva, 5th March 1555.

Your letter, most renowned sir, was grateful to me, not only because whatever comes from you is dear to me, and because it let me know that the affection, which you entertained for me in the commencement of our intercourse, still remains unaltered; but above all because in it I find a magnificent eulogium, in which you commend my zeal in crushing the impiety of Servetus. Whence also I conjecture that you have not been offended with the honest freedom of my admonitions. In this they were defective, that I could have wished them to have been more ample. And yet I do not urge them too importunately; still as much as with your permission I may venture to do, I would again and again entreat you at least to weigh well silently in your own mind, the points on which I have written. For so I am confident, you will endeavour, that respecting the gratuitous election of the pious, a more orthodox manner of teaching may be mutually agreed upon between us. About the worship of the bread, (περὶ τῆς ἀρτολατρείας) your most intimate opinion has long been known to me, which you do not even dissemble in your letter. But your too great slowness displeases me, by which not only is kept up, but from day to day increased, the madness of those whom you see rushing on to the destruction of the church. And though it should not be easy for you to bridle such wild beasts, which however I think is a groundless fear, would you only set boldly about it, you know however that our duties by no means depend on our hopes of success, but that it behoves us to accomplish what God requires of us, even when we are in the greatest despair respecting the results. Nor indeed does that excuse satisfy me that malevolent men, who wish to crush you, may hence find a feasible pretext. For what are we to expect from the servants of Christ, unless, in despite of ill-will, and contemning malicious rumours, they overcome by their victorious constancy whatever obstacles Satan may raise up against them? Certainly, however madly they may rage against you, nothing more cruel threatens you on their part than to be forced to abandon that part of the world where you now are; which thing in my judgment is what for many reasons you should spontaneously desire. But should you have to fear the worst extremes, still it is necessary that you should determine once for all what you owe to Christ, lest, by suppressing a candid confession of the truth, you should lend to wicked men a kind of implied patronage to oppress the church. That I might restrain their tumults, I have again comprised the summary of our doctrine in a short compendium. All the Swiss churches have subscribed to it. Those of Zurich gave it their unqualified approbation. Now I long to have your opinion; what also the rest of your countrymen think and say I am very desirous to know. But if those cease not to breed disturbances, who defame us so hostilely, we shall endeavour to make the whole world hear our complaints. Farewell, most renowned and my ever honoured sir. May the Lord govern you by his Spirit, defend you with his protection, sustain you by his power, and may he always keep us in holy union, till at length he gather us into his heavenly kingdom.

To Martin Sidemann[3]

(He congratulates him on his moderation in the midst of the theological fury of Germany—comparison of Luther with his ˇdisciples.)

Geneva, 14th March 1555.

I am delighted indeed that this messenger luckily presented himself to you, as by his favour you have become known to me. With your letter, as it was full of courtesy, I

[3] Professor at Erfurt.

have been exceedingly gratified. But what afforded me particular satisfaction, was to learn that you are not at all one of those who are so hurried away by their own violence, or enchained as it were by their obstinacy and captiousness, that they cannot assent to any thing that comes from this quarter, because we do not chime in with all the opinions of the Saxons. The wider this contagion has spread, so much more praiseworthy is your moderation; since devoting yourself to truth alone, exempt from silly prejudices, honestly, and without antipathies, you esteem only what is true. Would that Luther were alive now. For though his vehemence in the conduct of the Sacramentarian cause, always exceeded the bounds of moderation, yet it was nothing to their violence and phrensy. If however they continue to the last to be implacable, the result will be that they will at length, by their intolerable contumacy, conciliate favour to us among all sane and moderate persons, who, intimidated for a time, did not dare to form an impartial judgment on the subject. But when forsooth they do not possess a single one of Luther's virtues, by their lusty bawling they give themselves out for his genuine disciples. As if indeed to *ape*, and to *imitate*, any person, were not very different things. But amid so much ignorance and barbarity, nothing is more disgusting than their arrogance, since they do not spare even Philip. The blame of this is partly to be attributed to himself, because hitherto he has not manfully repelled their attacks. Now, though the remedy will come late, he will be compelled to assume a more courageous attitude, and this will be the most efficacious method of crushing their knavery. I have just tried in a short tract, whether it were possible to calm their fervour. If I do not succeed, we must, as I predict, come more vigorously to the combat. It is to be deplored, indeed, that in the very bosom of the church there should be such ebullitions of strife, but when people will raise disturbances without a motive, our contention for the defence of truth is excusable. Farewell, distinguished sir, and respected brother. May the Lord stand always by you, govern, and protect you.—Yours,

To Melanchthon

(He exhorts him to prefer the approbation of God to that of men, in pronouncing frankly against the adversaries of sound doctrine and the disturbers of the church.)

GENEVA, 23d *August* 1555.

You justly and wisely remark, most accomplished sir, that our antagonists have no other object in view, than to shew themselves off on a public stage. But though their expectations, as I trust and as is probable, will be frustrated, nevertheless, even if they should gain the plaudits of the whole world, it becomes us to direct all our attention with so much the more zeal to the heavenly prize-giver under whose eyes we combat. What! Shall the sacred assembly of the angels, who animate us by their favour, and strenuously point out to us by their example the manner of acting, permit us to grow sluggish or advance with hesitating steps? And the whole band of the holy fathers! Do they not also stimulate us to exertion? In fine, the church of God which is present to our view in the world! When we know that its prayers combat on our side, and that it is animated by our example, shall its suffrages in our favour be lost upon us? No, let this be my theatre, and satisfied with its approbation, though the whole world should hiss me, I shall never want courage. I am very far from envying these silly and noisy players. Let them enjoy for a brief space and in an obscure corner their barren little sprig of triumph. What the world deems worthy of its applause or hatred does not escape me. But far more important I hold it to follow the rule prescribed by our Master. Nor have I any doubt that this ingenuousness will in the end prove more agreeable to all pious and rational minds, than a complaisant and wavering manner of teaching, which is always swayed by some empty terror. I entreat you to discharge as soon as you can, the debt which you acknowledge you owe to God and the church. Nor do I insist on this subject, because I trust that by discharging on you a part of the odium which attaches to me, I may be proportionably relieved. Much rather on the contrary, if the thing were possible, from the affection and respect I bear to you, would I shift from your shoulders to my own, whatever burden presses heavily upon you. But it is your duty attentively to consider that I should never have presented myself to you in the shape of an adviser, but that you might early deliver pious men, who look up to you, from a doubt which they entertain of your ever entirely fulfilling your promise. Reflect moreover that if this warning, like a cock crowing rather late and out of season, do not awaken you, all will cry out with justice, that you are a sluggard. Farewell, most distinguished sir, whom I venerate

from the heart. May Christ, the faithful keeper of his followers, stand always by you, and govern and protect you.
Amen. Salute in my name, M. Camerarius, and whatever
other friends I have in your part of the world.

To Melanchthon

(Necessity of a conference to terminate the religious differences of Germany.)

FRANKFORT, 17th September 1556.

I have been dragged hither by the dissensions with which
Satan has rent, for nearly two years, the little French church
established here, and reduced to such extremities that it must
have disappeared, unless some remedy had been very
promptly applied. Since I entered the town I have not had a
moment's repose, and as if I had not had sufficient occupation
in this affair, a madman called Velsius, to whom you had
written twice, involved us in new fooleries. But we have devoted only two days to this importunity. I am continually
distracted up to this moment, in appeasing those dissensions
which, from the long lapse of time, have struck deep root.
You will therefore excuse the brevity of my letter, for when
I came in to supper I was told that the messenger was to
leave this the following morning. Though indeed I am less
anxious about soliciting your pardon, because from your silence I conclude that you feel no great desire to receive a
letter from me. And yet I am so convinced, not only of your
equity, but also of your true and sincere affection for me,
that I cannot doubt but my courtesy in this respect is agreeable to you. Since I have been here I have learned from some
letters of yours to your friends, how much you are tormented
by the savage ferocity of those men who feed upon quarrels
and contentions, not without deadly detriment to the church.
But though certain individuals put your patience to the proof
in private, yet in consideration of your piety and the prevailing evils, I am of opinion that you should be more deeply
affected, and preserve your anguish of mind much longer.
Lest then so much fury should assail us any longer with impunity, the remedy which I am overjoyed to think pleases
you must be applied. And a convention is so much the more
to be desired by us, as these men more obstinately reject it,
or rather as they with greater rage recoil from it. It was in-

deed the business of the princes to drag them to it, since they will not of their own accord accede to it. But while some of the princes, perhaps too much occupied with other matters, procrastinate, and the fear of incurring odium keeps back others, you judge well and wisely that the assembly should be set on foot by private counsels, provided we put in execution what you have written with so much good sense, nor should we wait till a great many join us. But when you have raised the standard, those who have the tranquillity of the church at heart will flock round it. I wish you had gone to the Palatine, for it would have been highly expedient that he had been directed in the beginning by good and sound counsels. But should an opportunity present itself, it is better late than never. Whatever you shall decide upon, I beg and entreat of you, let me know.

Farewell, most accomplished sir, whom I respect with all my heart. May the Lord always support you by his power, govern you by his Spirit, and shield you with his protection. Salute my friends, if I have any, in your quarter of the world. —Yours,

To Melanchthon

(He complains of the long silence of Melanchthon, in exhorting him to shew more firmness than he has hitherto done.)

GENEVA, 3d *August* 1557.

How it has happened that for more than a space of three years, you have not given me one word in reply to my letters, I know not. As moreover from so long a silence I might well conclude that they were not very agreeable to you, and even that my affection for you was repudiated by you, I should not have ventured at present to write to you, were I not informed by this excellent old man that you still entertain the same disposition of mind towards me, a thing I should otherwise have had some difficulty in believing. Now having recovered more confidence, because I trust that during this month you will be at Worms, where my letter will come earlier and more safely into your hands, I was unwilling to let slip the present opportunity. I could wish only that I had a more agreeable subject to write on. And yet if you retain a spark of your old affection for me, you will easily get over the uneasy feeling, should you experience any, arising from

my unburdening myself familiarly of my cares and sorrows
into your bosom. That your neighbours have broken out on
me with so intemperate a rage, is, I doubt not, when I consider your moderation and courteousness, exceedingly displeasing to you; nay, when they make war not only on one
individual, but on all pious men, not on the doctrine of a
single person, but on the common faith; this ought to occasion
you no common sorrow. But as it is no longer in the power
of him who has once been dragged into this arena speedily
to withdraw from thence, and as it would be absurd to treat
these savage wild beasts in the manner of men, you will
grant some indulgence to my vehemence which, amid so
much indignity, I have not been able to bridle in. If I have
given you any personal cause of offence, I do not think that
I shall need to make a long apology. Because from time to
time I perceived that my adversaries made use of your name
to give a plausible colour to the representations which they
employed to deceive the ignorant, that I might not seem in
so clear a matter to tergiversate, (which would have been
far from candid,) I did not hesitate more than once to appeal to your testimony. I am so far from recognizing that in
so doing I was guilty of any fault of which it would be worth
while for me to exonerate myself, that I think I have the very
best right to complain of your hesitation. Though you shrink
from noisy contests, yet you know what Paul prescribes by
his example to all the servants of Christ. Certainly you cannot desire praise for greater moderation than that which was
evidenced in him. When he then, who was endowed with so
much forbearance, passed intrepidly through seditions, we
cannot give way where the circumstances in our times are
by no means so painful. But, in one word, you should
maturely consider whether your too obstinate a silence may
not leave a stain on your reputation in the eyes of posterity.
If you wait till these hippocentaurs pierce you from all sides
with their darts, it is to be feared that your confession will
not appear very seasonable, or rather it will seem wrung
from you by urgent necessity. What if death should anticipate your wishes? That you may be stripped of all authority
and that all confidence in you may be destroyed, will they
not call out that you were slavishly timid? I do not think you
need to be reminded in many words how necessary it is for
you to hasten to wipe out this blot from your character. If
a means of pacification is sought for, our only hope lies in
a conference; which I doubt not but you desire, but which I

could wish that you called for more courageously. For when you perceive that the princes not only are loitering, but that they are even dragged by their doctors in a contrary direction, you no doubt conclude that every avenue has been closed, unless your authority should serve as a rein to some, and a spur to others. I learned lately, what I was far from expecting, that the Duke of Wurtemberg was of his own accord inclined to this measure, nay, had there only been that common politeness which there ought to have been, we were presented with that opportunity which we constantly wished for; but as there lurks in many minds a perverse suspicion that the sentiments of the princes were too much alienated from us to admit of our being listened to, all stand in fear of the conference. They add, moreover, that with the single exception of yourself, none but intractable men would come to them, who would imperiously prescribe that there should be no departure from the opinions they had thought fit to lay down. Nor is the sourness of temper, on the part of those who hold this language, such as would prevent them from coming with good will if they were called. Reflect then that this task now depends on you, viz., that influenced by your discourse the princes should invite the men of our party to a conference, and a convenient place for assembling might be either at Strasbourg, or Tubingen, or Heidelberg, or even at Frankfort. If you could only obtain this, that both parties would come forward prepared for a peaceable discussion, I trust there would be a better result than many suspicious men conjecture. But if you betake yourself again to Saxony before the accomplishment of this business, I fear me you will repent too late that a remedy had not been applied by your efforts to those fatal disturbances. Moreover remember that in the present case you must enter upon the work, not with mere wishes, but with a vigorous solicitude that, for the accomplishment of your task, you must set about it with greater fervour than is compatible with your natural character. And now, even if the princes shall not be gained over, you must not neglect what you wrote to some friends last year, namely, that you would do your endeavour to come yourself to the colloquy with some pious, upright, and moderate men. If you class me in the number of such men, no necessity, however urgent, will prevent me from putting up this as my chief vow, that before the Lord gather us into his heavenly kingdom, I may yet be permitted to enjoy on earth a most delightful interview with you, and feel some alleviation of my grief by deploring along with you the evils which we cannot remedy.

Farewell, most excellent sir and brother, whom from the heart I honour. May the Lord always govern you by his Spirit, shield you with his protection, furnish you for this undertaking with holy prudence and unshaken fortitude, and bless all your efforts.

To Francis Othman[4]

(Ecclesiastical affairs of Germany—complaints against Melanchthon—renewal of the alliance between Berne and Geneva.)

GENEVA, 10*th January* 1558.

Crispin affirms that he does not know who it can be to whom you delivered your letter. You have done well then not to hesitate to repeat to me the principal points of its contents. Though the Zurichers fear, as much as we desire, a conference, it will not for all that be of less utility. This astonishes me, that it should be made a pretext for avoiding it, that we shall have to do with captious men, since the defence of the truth and of the good cause will at least be open to us. It will rouse the princes and make them more attentive for the future. Nevertheless I am afraid lest Philip should now shrink back, who has lately by his last act sullied whatever renown he had acquired. And assuredly, when in the person of Zwingli he has condemned the Swiss, the desponding feeling is increased which already produced an aversion for conferences. Do you nevertheless persevere as long as any hope of obtaining one remains. And certainly those persons are too little actuated by humane sentiments who can witness the sad dissensions which prevail without being stimulated to seek a remedy. I have no need to write separately to M. Sturm, because I trust you will be my interpreter with him, or rather this letter will be common to both of you. After many bickerings, at length a perpetual league with the Bernese was yesterday confirmed by a solemn oath. This, however, will not, I fancy, remove all the grounds of our

4 [Friend in the law.]

contention; it is nevertheless an advantage that if any controversies shall still subsist, they will be settled by equitable arbiters. On this occasion, your brother, of whose presence at Lausanne I was not yet aware, paid us a visit. He scarcely spent, however, two full days among us; thus amid so much bustle, he had but twice some conversation with me. I exhorted him, as the opportunity permitted, to a more decided progress, but I shall have a better opportunity if I go to Lausanne. The moderation which his conduct breathed gives me good hopes.

Farewell, distinguished sir, and respected brother; you will present my kindest respects to M. Sturm and the others. May the Lord bless you along with your wife and children. Our friends most affectionately salute you.—Yours,

To Bullinger

(Dissolution of the conference of Worms—complaints against Melanchthon—sad state of the brethren in France.)

GENEVA, 23d *February* 1558.

At length I have learned from your letter to our friend Beza, most accomplished sir and respected brother, how unworthily you have been deceived by that Englishman to whom you had entrusted your letter, unless perhaps he died on his journey, which is not very probable. Perhaps also to gain your confidence he told you a falsehood, in saying that he was the bearer of letters from John Laski. Now, though I am sorry to have missed the opportunity of reading a letter from you; yet what gives me greater anxiety is the apprehension, lest he be one of those vagabonds, who by giving publicity to our secrets, strive to gain importance among the ill-disposed. The unfortunate issue of the conference at Worms does not so much distress me, as the inconstancy of Philip moves both my anger and detestation. For though I had not forgotten how pliant and weak he has always been, and knew that on the present occasion also he is too timid and indolent, nevertheless he has exceeded himself far beyond what I could ever have suspected. What is more, I did not think that even Brentz would have acted with so much hostility. But whatever may have dropped from them, it is fortunate that our liberty in the defence of sound doctrine is restrained by none of their prejudices. Even if the conflict were to be renewed to-morrow, they are mistaken if they think they have gained an inch of ground; nay, I feel much more ardently disposed to re-demand a conference, that a free discussion may teach them to conduct themselves with greater moderation.

In the mean time I have written to James André, that they have acted neither rightly, nor politely, nor considerately, that they may be made aware that all our churches have been justly offended. Beza and Budé will gain more information at the courts of the princes, for they have been obliged to undertake a third expedition; partly because Michael Dicer informed us that the cause of the brethren had been betrayed among them by a bribed knave, who had insinuated himself into the favour of the Palatine; partly because the implacable rage of the king urges us to look out for some remedy; for if out of a crowd of individuals several were dismissed, that was owing neither to compassion nor clemency, but because seven of the martyrs who had been burned shook to such a degree, by their constancy, the courage of the judges, that these were of opinion that some new plan should be adopted. They made choice then on purpose of two youths, of whom the one had scarcely entered on his sixteenth year, and who they were in hopes would be unequal to the task of resisting. When they were deceived in their expectations, they distributed about a hundred of them among the convents, with the intention that the monks should serve as their daily tormentors. Many of these made their escape, both because it was desirable for the monks that their cloisters should be purged from such pests for fear the contagion might spread wider, and also because it was burdensome to them to maintain gratis so many needy persons. The more robust of those who were apprehended were shut up in loathsome cells, whence they were dragged forth to execution on the first opportunity. The remissness of the judges was in the meantime reprimanded by many and often repeated insults and threats, as if they had conducted themselves in too effeminate a manner. The king then humbly begged through his ambassador of the Roman Antichrist (for the words of the bull suggest this expression), that he should appoint for this investigation three Cardinals, to whom is granted an unrestrained licence of butchery and destruction. The king himself also promulgated a new edict in which absolute power of life and death is entrusted to the bishops, nor are any other duties left to the royal judges except to serve the bishops as their executioners. These are the magnificent promises with which he inveigled your countrymen. These things I have thought proper to place in their proper light, lest you should suppose that we busy ourselves but lukewarmly in their affairs, when our brethren are every where trembling and terror-struck by menacing edicts.

Farewell, most distinguished sir and venerable brother; be careful to salute in my name M. Peter Martyr and your fellow-pastors. May God preserve you all in safety, direct, and bless you.—Yours,

To Venceslas Zeuleger[5]

(Organization of the Academy of Deux Ponts—letter of Melanchthon—progress of the Gospel in France.)

That you have been received into the family of the most illustrious prince of Deux Ponts, I congratulate you on your own account and mine, both because you will be nearer us, and because, as I hope, you will have an opportunity and the means of illustrating the glory of God. But as experience will teach you with how many temptations the courts of princes abound, you will have to be sedulously on your guard, not to contract therefrom any contamination. This I am confident you will do, even without being reminded of it. I had already heard something of the prince's pious zeal in establishing a school. Up to this moment I was ignorant that Doctor Marbach had been charged with this duty. I hope the others who are joined with him do not resemble him. For, if he does not entertain different views from you—so much the worse, that without any reason he shews himself so bitter an enemy. I perceive that you are deceived by his false appearance of kindness. He has been accustomed to retain the favour of all by his bland manners, but he afterwards secretly lets out his venom. If I shall hear that any good proceeds from him, I shall reckon it among those advantages that have fallen out contrary to my expectation. If you think that the regulations of our consistory will be of any service to you, I shall make it my business to have an abstract of them written out for you as soon as it shall be con-

[5] [Protestant clergyman and scholar.]

venient. This it has not been in my power to do from want of time, for your letter came to hand only a short time before the departure of our friend Crispin. With regard to the letter of Philip, whom you would like to see approving of our unanimity in regard to the Lord's Supper, I know not if it will be proper that it should pass through the hands of men of whom we are not quite sure, for he has made complaints that those things which he wrote to me in confidence have been spread abroad. You know how timid he is. But, though I see him agitated by vain fears, yet I desire to shew indulgence to his advanced age. It would be a much better method if the prince should ask him how far he agrees with us, for if he suspects no craft he will freely profess his opinion. I am also sorry that among us the Lord's Supper is not administered to the sick. Nor is it my fault, that those who are about to depart from this life should be deprived of this consolation. But as a contrary practice had so long prevailed that a change could not be effected without much contention, I have preferred to consult peace; especially as I saw that there would be not only dissensions in the city, but we should be forced into a hostile conflict with our neighbours, and a load of infamy would be brought on me as if I attached salvation to an external symbol. Only it has been my wish that an attestation of what I wished on that subject should go down to posterity. We shall see whether it will be possible to gratify the wishes of Michael Peuther. Two things form our principal obstacle, viz., that false rumours are often disseminated, and that almost all men are blind to the remarkable proofs of God's judgment.

God protects in a miraculous manner the little churches which are scattered up and down France; nay, amid the atrocious threats of our enemies, he gives an increase which no one would ever have dared to hope. Our brother Macaire is at Paris, and persists vigorously in the discharge of his duty, nor will he depart thence unless he be expelled by some overpowering force. His three colleagues are animated by the same courage. We have sent another pastor to Bourget, not to succeed Martin, but to take a part of the burden off his shoulders, for one man was already unequal to so great a task. The number of the faithful is every where increasing, and already in very many places secret meetings are held. I am apprehensive, lest ere long you will hear that the fury of the enemy has been more violently kindled, because now in certain towns of Gascony the common people have opened temples for the pure doctrine, but commissaries sent by the parliament of Bordeaux have closed their doors. You know the impetuosity of the Gascon character, and therefore I dread more disturbances from that cause, unless God send down among them a spirit of moderation. It is for us then to implore the King of peace to temper the constancy of his followers with gentleness, to restrain the fury of their enemies, and defeat their obstinate cruelty.

Farewell, most accomplished sir and respected brother. May the Lord always stand by you, govern you by his Spirit, and bless your labours. Our friends salute you.—Yours,

---

To Melanchthon

(Malady of Calvin—formidable coalition of the kings of France and Spain against Geneva—exhortations to fraternal union.)

GENEVA, 19*th* *November* 1558.

I am aware, most distinguished sir and reverend brother, that as you are yourself an indolent correspondent, you very good-naturedly overlook a similar want of punctuality on the part of your friends. I had, therefore, determined to plead the excuse of bad health for not writing to you, but, that it gives me pleasure to pour into your bosom the annoyances, of which the burden weighs me down. As, thank God, I have up to these years never been visited by a quartan ague, it required a fourth attack to cure me of my ignorance of it, and reveal to me what kind of malady I had to deal with. Now, though I am ashamed of this indolence, you will perhaps be inclined to excuse me when you are made aware of what obstacles I had to contend with. At first, when the fit came upon me, as I was asleep or in a dozing mood, it was no difficult thing for it to steal a march on me without my perceiving it, especially as it was accompanied with very troublesome and acute pains, to which I am but too well accustomed from a long familiarity with them. But when the shivering fit once seized me, at supper time, I thought it quite sufficient to rid myself in my usual manner of my dyspepsy by a rigid fasting. The following day as I was lying with my strength quite prostrate, but relieved, however, and almost entirely delivered from the violence of my pain, I came to my fourth attack, still a novice and perfectly ignorant of the enemy I had to grapple with. Nearly six weeks have now elapsed since I became acquainted with the nature of my complaint, during which I have been in the hands of the doctors, who keep me shut up in my bed-room and pretty generally confine me to bed in which I am protected by a double coverlet, while every now and then they keep dinning in my ears the verse of Sophocles, "the belly has become so hard bound that it will not relax unless aided by a clyster," which is a state very alien to my usual habits. They prescribe to me all the best and most digestible kinds of food, none of which flatter my taste, so that my strength gets gradually more and more feeble. I struggle against my illness, nevertheless, and recruit my exhausted stomach with the most insipid of food, nor do I either allow my loathing to get the better of me, nor like most people, do I coax myself into an appetite by employing stimulants that are pernicious to my complaint. Nay, in everything I take care not to deviate one hair-breadth from the doctor's prescription, except that in my burning thirst I allow myself to drink a little more copiously. And even this excess I impute to their fault, for they most pointedly exact of me to drink Burgundy wine, which I am not allowed to temper with water or any more common beverage. Nay, unless I had obstinately protested, they wanted to kill me outright with the heating fumes of Malmsey and Muscat wine. But as I know that they are men of no common skill in their profession, persons of sound good sense moreover, and experienced from a long practice of their art, I not only from motives of politeness pay implicit attention to their orders, but even willingly permit myself to be guided by such masters. They mix my wine with spleenwort or wormwood. They fortify my stomach by fomenting it with syrups of hyssop, or elecampane, or citron bark, at the same time applying to it a certain pressure, that the novelty of the sensation may give greater energy to the remedy and cause it to act more speedily. They only once attempted to expel the bilious humours from my spleen. But though I seem now to be abusing your leisure moments with too much indifference, and in dictating these details during the heat of the fever, I was not very judiciously consulting my own health; yet, as the issue of my complaint is still doubtful, I wished to

assure you that I am now making it the principal subject of
my meditation, how at a moment's warning I may be prepared to meet any lot which God intends for me. Meanwhile,
that you may not be ignorant of what my dangers are, know
that it is currently reported, that peace being concluded between the two kings, the whole brunt of the war will be
directed against us, that whatever expiation has been judged
necessary may be ratified by our blood. Know also, that we
are not better protected, either by the distance of the locali-
ties or by fortifications, than if we had to engage in a conflict in the open field. Philip's territories are only two days
march from our gates. The king is still nearer, whose troops
could reach our city in the space of half-an-hour. Whence
you may conclude that we have not only exile to fear, but
that all the most cruel varieties of death are impending over
us, for in the cause of religion they will set no bounds to their
barbarity. Wherefore your lot should appear to you less bitter
if disciples, who ought to have repaid to your old age what
they owed to you, now hostilely attack you, a man who had
discharged with the highest fidelity and diligence the functions of a teacher, and also deserved the highest honours
from the whole church; when you see that the treatment
you experience is common to you with others, and particularly with myself; for it is scarcely to be believed how
petulantly and unworthily certain brawlers assail me. The
partisans of Westphal, though they hurl their darts from a
distance, nevertheless, in their wickedness, take far more impudent liberties with me. I shall not for all that cease to press
towards the mark at which I had begun to aim; in the controversy respecting the Lord's Supper, not only your enemies
traduce what they calumniously style your weakness, but
your best friends also, and those who cherish you with the
pious feelings which you deserve, would wish that the flame
of your zeal burned more brightly, of which we behold but
some feeble sparks, and thus it is that these pigmies strut
like giants. Whatever happen, let us cultivate with sincerity
a fraternal affection towards each other, of which no wiles of
Satan shall ever burst asunder the ties. I confess, indeed,
that about six months ago, when I read a letter of your acquaintance, Hubert Languet, I was slightly piqued because
he reported you as having spoken in no friendly, or rather in
a contemptuous manner of my doctrine. But it was his design
to flatter Castalio, and to have his ravings approved of by

your suffrage—ravings which are the greatest pest of our times. But by no slight shall my mind ever be alienated from that holy friendship and respect which I have vowed to you.

To PETER MARTYR

(Calvin's illness—Death of Lactanzio Ragnone—Troubles of the Italian Church.)

GENEVA, 2nd March, 1559.

Respecting myself, most accomplished sir and respected brother, I have nothing to write, except that the violence of my fever has abated. But my bodily strength as well as my vigour of mind has been so much shattered that I do not seem greatly relieved by this mitigation. Nay, I even feel a greater degree of lassitude than when I had to struggle against more violent attacks. The debility of my stomach is especially a cause of suffering to me, and it is increased by a catarrh which brings along with it its accompaniment a cough. For as vapours arising from indigestion trouble my brain, the evil reacts in its turn upon my lungs. To all this has been added for the last eight days a pain occasioned by hemorrhoids from which it is not possible to force the blood, as they are of that kind which are commonly termed blind. If any dependence is to be placed on the order of the seasons, the only remaining hope I have lies in the near approach of spring, but the Lord in whose hand are life and death will direct the issue.

Of the death of our most excellent brother Lactanzio, others have no doubt written to you, and it is with reluctance that I awaken a sorrowful recollection. In him the Italian church has certainly sustained no common loss, but what is worse, I fear that God will avenge the ingratitude and arrogance of certain persons by the difficulty of finding a good and fitting pastor. You would hardly believe with what unworthy contempt he was treated, and how little account was made of those remarkable virtues which made him an object of well merited respect among all right minded persons; and though I have sternly and openly denounced them with the punishment which they have deserved, yet I wish to have the benefit of your assistance and counsels lest the goodly structure which God has built up should fall to ruin. Another wound has been inflicted by one Sylvester, whose name probably is not unknown to you; for he lived in England, and is I believe a countryman of your own. Since he had given many indications that he had participated in the impiety of George, and as he had been rather roughly handled by Simon the catechist of the church who had exposed his perfidy, he turned round on Simon and accused him of a disgraceful and abominable crime. At last we discovered that boys had been suborned by him to bear false witness. He himself absconded. One of the witnesses in the case who had obstinately persisted in his false testimony was banished. Simon was acquitted in presence of the Italian congregation by our sentence and that of the elders, but only of what related to the infamous charge brought against him; for he was censured for not having maintained the dignity becoming a minister, and also because he had positively denied all the things laid to his charge, some of which were nevertheless true, though not involving a grave accusation. How atrociously the Bernese have vented their rage and fulminated against the poor brethren, as it pains me to hear it, I shall not write to you concerning it. It is better that the whole matter with all its circumstances should be explained to you, which it will be I trust ere long. Other details you will learn from our excellent brother, who in returning to his own country has resolved to take your town in his way for the purpose of visiting you.

Farewell, most accomplished sir. May the Lord extend his protection to you and all your colleagues, govern you with his Spirit and enrich you with his blessings. Amen.—Yours,

To Bullinger

(Unsuccessful issue of Beza's mission to the King of Navarre —Scruples respecting the communication of Melanchthon's letter—Intolerance of the German Theologians.)

GENEVA, 4th December, 1560.

I made a brief reply to your last letter, honoured brother, because our most excellent friend, John Liner, came to me when exhausted with a multiplicity of cares I was sitting down to supper, and told me that he was urged by his companions to take leave of us the following day. Our brother Beza will touch upon the principal points of his expedition.

Those whom we wished to save would listen to no counsels, though, indeed, we took all this trouble, not so much for their sake as for that of the church. The King of Navarre, as I wrote to you, had of his own accord implored my assistance, and begged in a very courteous manner that Beza should be sent to him. If he had met with a refusal, what clamours would have been raised by everybody, that it was all our fault, if things had turned out unfortunately! We should have been reproached, not only with timidity, but with perfidiousness and cruelty. Beza accomplished every thing which his duty required of him, not only with fidelity but incredible constancy. A hundred times they changed their resolutions. Finally, that fell out, which is now a secret to nobody, that the King of Navarre and his brother were resolved to rush on their ruin. If our advice had been attended to, without a drop of blood being shed, they would have effected their purpose. This was what we always aimed at. Now everybody is plunged in despair, because the soldiery are everywhere let loose, as in a conquered country. And yet our neighbours, who blew the flames of sedition, now cast all the blame on us. But I will pass them by for the present.

I cannot, for sundry reasons, comply with your demand to have sent to you those letters of Philip's, in which he undisguisedly professes himself to be of our opinion. They are not numerous, and are written in such a spirit that you yourself will perceive that they contain things which he poured confidentially into my bosom, but which would afford matter of ridicule to certain, that is, to unfriendly persons; to others, again, who were less intimately acquainted with him, they would hardly be intelligible. Some consideration for the memory of the dead should also have weight with us, which would certainly suffer by the revelation of some things which he wrote to me. Mixed up with them are others which it would certainly do me honour to have made public, but they would be obnoxious at the same time to the malicious carpings of Flaccius, and such like fellows. And that reminds me that when your letter was delivered to me I had already dispatched one-half of my reply to Heshusius. In it I determined to confute him, not so much by dispassionate argument as by an irrepressible burst of indignation. His baseness is so intolerable that it might well call for a lapidation. We are very sorry to learn that the population of Glaris is still kept in suspense. But Moab, in his pride, will dash himself to pieces, and beyond all doubt, God is driving headlong these Cyclops, that while they plot mischief against others they may compass their own destruction. Let them fall into their own snares, but let us stand firm on our own foundation. I abstain from writing any thing about the troubles in France, lest I should give uncertain intelligence. Ere long you will learn something.

Farewell, most accomplished and honoured brother. Best wishes for the health of M. Peter Martyr, M. Gualter, and your other fellow pastors. May the Lord protect, govern, and bless you all. We are in such jeopardy every moment that many despair, many are anxious, and others laugh. We, therefore, commend ourselves to your prayers.—Yours,

To Bullinger

(Sufferings of Calvin—News of the court and kingdom of France—Precautions against the Confession of Augsburg.)

Geneva, 2d July, 1563.

The inconsiderateness of a worthy but thoughtless man obliges me to dictate these words in a hurry. Being about to send his sons to your city he did not apprise me of his intention till the moment of their departure. At present, I am relieved from very acute suffering, having been delivered of a calculus about the size of the kernel of a filbert. As the retention of urine was very painful to me, by the advice of my physician, I got upon horseback that the jolting might assist me in discharging the calculus. On my return home I was surprised to find that I emitted discoloured blood instead of urine. The following day the calculus had forced its way from the bladder into the urethra. Hence still more excruciating tortures. For more than half an hour I endeavoured to disengage myself from it by a violent agitation of my whole body. I gained nothing by that, but obtained a slight relief by fomentations with warm water. Meanwhile, the urinary canal was so much lacerated that copious discharges of blood flowed from it. It seems to me now that I begin to live anew for the last two days since I am delivered from these pains.

Of the state of France, I should have written to you with more details if I had been at leisure. At Lyons the churches have been restored to the priests. Four only have been left to us, of which one was obtained by craft, and under a false pretext. The former governor of the city has been recalled, a man of a peaceable and mild character, detested by the Papists, because he is favourable to us. The godly are everywhere recovering their courage. The enemies are still raising disturbances in many places, and their fury breaks out in fires and massacres. It will proceed, at last, to such lengths that even their protectors will feel that they are implacable. The Constable grows milder every day. Though the queen caresses the Prince of Condé, yet the versatile and crafty woman inspires us with but very little or no confidence. But though she is entirely destitute of sincerity, she would nevertheless comply with the prince, if she saw in him a prudent and magnanimous man. Though the Parliament of Paris has, at length, readmitted those counsellors who had taken to flight, many have nevertheless abdicated their functions. The chancellor is much offended at that, because he would wish to see in it as many persons as possible favourable to our party. He therefore severely represses these resignations as much as it depends on him. The Admiral hitherto remains quiet. His brother is at court. It is with great difficulty that the Constable has been at length induced to lead an army against the English. Either the faint-heartedness and cowardice of Condé outstrips all belief, or we shall have some favourable change ere long.

Farewell, most accomplished sir and honoured brother. May the Lord prosper you and yours. Carefully salute all your fellow pastors. My colleagues, who are now present with me, also salute you. I have retired for a moment from their society to dictate this letter to you.—Yours,

I am carefully on the watch that Lutheranism gain no ground, nor be introduced into France. The best means, believe me, for checking the evil would be that the confession written by me in the name of the Prince of Condé and the other nobles should be published, by which Condé would pledge his good faith and reputation, and endeavour to draw over the German princes to our party. I am waiting for his answer. The Admiral is urging him. If we could bring people to subscribe it, this proceeding would procure us some pleasant sport. Meanwhile, the condition of the churches is better than you imagine. They are permitted to make use of the confession presented to the king, as well as the catechism.

In one word, things are strangely mixed up. There is no reason to fear, however, that the Papists will admit the Confession of Augsburg, should it be offered to them a hundred· times. As my commentaries on Jeremiah will be published about the time of the next fair, I have resolved to dedicate them to the Prince Palatine. In my preface I have introduced an abstract of our whole controversy. So there is no doubt Brentz will have at me.

The father of the boys who will deliver to you this letter begs me to recommend them to you. But he does not wish you to be put to any inconvenience on their account, only when an opportunity may present itself he would be delighted if you inquired whether they behaved modestly, and that you should make it your business that they be kept to their studies.

To the Physicians of Montpellier

(Medical consultation.)

Geneva, 8th February, 1564.

When the physician Sarrazin, on whose directions I principally rely for the re-establishment of my health, presented me not long ago some remedies which you prescribed for the relief of my complaints, I asked him, who had without my knowledge taken that task upon him. He replied that at the request of one of my colleagues, who is at present resident among you, he had drawn up a short abstract of matters connected with my case, in order that you might give me the benefit of your advice. On my part, I cannot but recognize from the very minute answers you have transmitted, how much interest you take in my life, about the prolongation of which you have spontaneously shown yourselves so solicitous. If to have given yourselves that trouble at my demand would have been no small token of kindness on your part, how much more must I feel indebted to you for thus anticipating my desires by your unsolicited benevolence! Moreover, I have no other means of testifying my gratitude to you, besides that of recommending you to draw in your turn from my writings what may afford you a spiritual medicine. Twenty years ago I experienced the same courteous services from the distinguished Parisian physicians, Acatus, Tagant, and Gallois. But at that time I was not attacked by arthritic pains, knew nothing of the stone or the gravel—I was not tormented with the gripings of the cholic, nor afflicted with hemorrhoids, nor threatened with expectoration of blood. At present all these ailments as it were in troops assail me. As soon as I recovered from a quartan ague, I was seized with severe and acute pains in the calves of my legs, which after being partially relieved returned a second and a third time. At last they degenerated into a disease in my articulations, which spread from my feet to my knees. An ulcer in the hæmorrhoid veins long caused me excruciating sufferings, and intestinal ascarides subjected me to painful titillations, though I am now relieved from this vermicular disease, but immediately after in the course of last summer I had an attack of nephritis. As I could not endure the jolting motion of horseback, I was conveyed into the country in a litter. On my return I wished to accomplish a part of the journey on foot. I had scarcely proceeded a mile when I was obliged to repose myself, in consequence of lassitude in the reins. And then to my surprise I discovered that I discharged blood instead of urine. As soon as I got home I took to bed. The nephritis gave me exquisite pain, from which I only obtained a partial relief by the application of remedies. At length not without the most painful strainings I ejected a calculus which in some degree mitigated my sufferings, but such was its size, that it lacerated the urinary canal and a copious discharge of blood followed. This hemorrhage could only be arrested by an injection of milk through a syringe. After that I ejected several others, and the oppressive numbness of the reins is a sufficient symptom that there still exist there some remains of uric calculus. It is a fortunate thing, however, that minute or at least moderately sized particles still continue to be emitted. My sedentary way of life to which I am condemned by the gout in my feet precludes all hopes of a cure. I am also prevented from taking exercise on horseback by my hemorrhoids. Add to my other complaints that whatever nourishment I take imperfectly digested turns into phlegm, which by its density sticks like paste to my stomach. But I am thoughtlessly tasking your patience, giving you double labour as the reward of your previous kindness, not indeed in consulting you, but in giving you the trouble to read over my vain complaints.

Farewell, most accomplished sirs whom I sincerely honour. May the Lord always direct you by his Spirit, sustain you by his power, and enrich you more and more with his gifts.

To Bullinger

(Sufferings of Calvin and the inefficacy of the healing art to relieve them—News of France and Germany.)

GENEVA, *6th April,* 1564.

I do not claim your indulgence for my long silence, respected brother, because you must have learned from others how just an excuse I have had for my delay, and which excuse I may in a great measure still allege. For though the pain in my side is abated, my lungs are nevertheless so charged with phlegmatic humours that my respiration is difficult and interrupted. A calculus in my bladder also gives me very exquisite pain for the last twelve days. Add to that the anxious doubts we entertain about the possibility of curing it, for all remedies have hitherto proved ineffectual; exercise on horseback would have been the best and most expeditious method of getting rid of it, but an ulcer in my abdomen gives me excruciating pain even when seated or lying in bed, so that the agitation of riding is out of the question. Within the last three days the gout has also been troublesome. You will not be surprised then if so many united sufferings make me lazy. It is with much ado I can be brought to take any food. The taste of wine is bitter. But while I wish to discharge my duty in writing to you, I am only tiring out your patience with my insipid details.

Respecting the affairs of France, Beza has promised to write to you. I dispense then with saying anything, not to repeat a twice told tale. I shall only allude to one subject however. You have heard long ago that the king has gone to Lorraine. The cause of his journey was a secret to the courtiers themselves, but it was revealed to me lately by the person who was charged to convey instructions backwards and forwards. The envoy of the king to the emperor, and who formerly was among you at the time he was Abbot of St. Laurence, is holding out to the queen mother great and dazzling prospects from King Maximilian. But in the mean time he stipulates that the queen should not openly declare that she entertains any hopes. I make no doubt, therefore, but he will sell himself to the cardinal of Lorraine. For after having failed in all his projects, he conceives that his only remaining resource is to gain time by giving out these ambiguous intimations. I see no other fraud or treachery concealed in this mission, except to amuse the queen with false expectations, and bring himself forward by his insinuations, to undertake affairs which he will never bring to any conclusion. For it is evident that Roschetelle has made a false use of King Maximilian's name, since he childishly advises the queen to dissemble and keep everything a profound secret. But my cough and a difficulty of breathing leave me no voice to dictate any more. Farewell, then, venerable brother, along with Mr. Gualter, your other colleagues, and your whole family. May the Lord protect you all, enrich you more and more with his benefits, and sustain you by his power. I am unwilling to lose my pains in writing to you about the state of our city.—Yours,

To Farel

(Last adieus.)

GENEVA, *2nd May*, 1564.

Farewell, my most excellent and upright brother; and since it is the will of God that you should survive me in the world, live mindful of our intimacy, which, as it was useful to the church of God, so the fruits of it await us in heaven. I am unwilling that you should fatigue yourself for my sake. I draw my breath with difficulty, and every moment I am in expectation of breathing my last. It is enough that I live and die for Christ, who is to all his followers a gain both in life and death. Again I bid you and your brethren Farewell.

II

On Reform

REPLY TO LETTER BY CARDINAL
SADOLET TO THE SENATE
AND PEOPLE OF GENEVA[1]

[*Cardinal Sadolet, a reform-interested Catholic of North Italy who wanted the Bishops to reform the church, was asked to convince Geneva to return to the Roman Church after Calvin's departure to Strassbourg. Calvin, in spite of his exile from Geneva, was asked to compose a reply. The reply was prepared by Calvin in a short period of time and exhibits his conception of reform.*]

REPLY BY CALVIN

TO

CARDINAL SADOLET'S LETTER

John Calvin to James Sadolet, Cardinal,—Health

In the great abundance of learned men whom our age has produced, your excellent learning and distinguished eloquence having deservedly procured you a place among the few whom all, who would be thought studious of liberal arts, look up to and revere, it is with great reluctance I bring forward your name before the learned world, and address to

[1] [Reprinted from *Tracts Relating to the Reformation*, Vol. I, translated from the original Latin by Henry Beveridge (Edinburgh: Printed for the Calvin Translation Society, 1844), pp. 25–68.]

you the following expostulation. Nor, indeed, would I have done it if I had not been dragged into this *arena* by a strong necessity. For I am not unaware how reprehensible it would be to show any eagerness in attacking a man who has deserved so well of literature, nor how odious I should become to all the learned were they to see me stimulated by passion merely, and not impelled by any just cause, turning my pen against one whom, for his admirable endowments, they, not without good reason, deem worthy of love and honour. I trust, however, that after explaining the nature of my undertaking, I shall not only be exempted from all blame, but there will not be an individual who will not admit that the cause which I have undertaken I could not on any account have abandoned without basely deserting my duty.

You lately addressed a Letter to the Senate and People of Geneva, in which you sounded their inclination as to whether, after having once shaken off the yoke of the Roman Pontiff, they would submit to have it again imposed upon them. In that letter, as it was not expedient to wound the feelings of those whose favour you required to gain your cause, you acted the part of a good pleader; for you endeavoured to soothe them by abundance of flattery, in order that you might gain them over to your views. Any thing of obloquy and bitterness you directed against those whose exertions had produced the revolt from that tyranny. And here (so help you) you bear down full sail upon those who, under pretence of the gospel, have by wicked arts urged on the city to what you deplore as the subversion of religion and of the Church. I, however, Sadolet, profess to be one of those whom with so much enmity you assail and stigmatise. For though religion was already established, and the form of the Church corrected, before I was invited to Geneva, yet having not only approved by my suffrage, but studied as much as in me lay to preserve and confirm what had been done by Viret and Farel, I cannot separate my case from theirs. Still, if you had attacked me in my private character, I could easily have forgiven the attack in consideration of your learning, and in honour of letters. But when I see that my ministry, which I feel assured is supported and sanctioned by a call from God, is wounded through my side, it would be perfidy, not patience, were I here to be silent and connive.

In that Church I have held the office first of Doctor, and then of Pastor. In my own right, I maintain, that in undertaking these offices I had a legitimate vocation. How faithfully and religiously I have performed them, there is no occasion for now showing at length. Perspicuity, erudition, prudence, ability, not even industry, will I now claim for myself, but that I certainly laboured with the sincerity which became me in the work of the Lord, I can in conscience appeal to Christ, my Judge, and all his angels, while all good men bear clear testimony in my favour. This ministry, therefore, when it shall appear to have been of God, (as it certainly shall appear, after the cause has been heard,) were I in silence to allow you to tear and defame, who would not condemn such silence as treachery? Every person, therefore, now sees that the strongest obligations of duty—obligations which I cannot evade—constrain me to meet your accusations, if I would not with manifest perfidy desert and betray a cause with which the Lord has entrusted me.

For though I am for the present relieved of the charge of the Church of Geneva, that circumstance ought not to prevent me from embracing it with paternal affection—God, when he gave it to me in charge, having bound me to be faithful to it for ever. Now, then, when I see the worst snares laid for that Church, whose safety it has pleased the Lord to make my highest care, and grievous peril impending if not obviated, who will advise me to await the issue silent and unconcerned? How heartless, I ask, would it be to wink in idleness, and, as it were, vacillating at the destruction of one whose life you are bound vigilantly to guard and preserve? But more on this point were superfluous, since you yourself relieve me of all difficulty. For if neighbourhood, and that not very near, has weighed so much with you, that while wishing to profess your love towards the Genevese, you hesitate not so bitterly to assail me and my fame, it will, undoubtedly, by the law of humanity, be conceded to me, while desiring to consult for the public good of a city entrusted to me by a far stronger obligation than that of neighbourhood, to oppose your counsels and endeavours, which I cannot doubt tend to its destruction. Besides, without paying the least regard to the Genevan Church, (though assuredly I cannot cast off that charge any more than that of my own soul,) supposing I were not actuated by any zeal for it, still, when my ministry (which, knowing it to be from Christ, I am bound, if need be, to maintain with my blood) is assailed and falsely traduced, how can it be lawful for me to bear it as if I saw it not?

Wherefore, it is easy not only for impartial readers to

judge, but for yourself, also, Sadolet, to consider how numerous and valid the reasons are which have compelled me to engage in this contest, if the name of contest should be given to a simple and dispassionate defence of my innocence against your calumnious accusations. I say *my* innocence, although I cannot plead for myself without, at the same time, including my colleagues, with whom all my measures in that administration were so conjoined, that whatever has been said against them I willingly take to myself. What the feelings are which I have had toward yourself in undertaking this cause, I will study to testify and prove by my mode of conducting it. For I will act so, that all may perceive that I have not only greatly the advantage of you in the goodness and justice of the cause, in conscientious rectitude, heartfelt sincerity, and candour of speech, but have also been considerably more successful in maintaining gentleness and moderation. There will doubtless be some things which will sting, or, it may be, speak daggers to your mind, but it will be my endeavour, *first*, not to allow any harsher expression to escape me than either the injustice of the accusations with which you have previously assailed me, or the necessity of the case may extort; and, *secondly*, not to allow any degree of harshness which may amount to intemperance or passion, or which may, by its appearance of petulance, give offence to ingenuous minds.

And, first, if you had to do with any other person, he would, undoubtedly, begin with the very argument which I have determined altogether to omit. For, without much ado, he would discuss your design in writing, until he should make it plain that your object was anything but what you profess it to be. For, were it not for the great credit you formerly acquired for candour, it is somewhat suspicious that a stranger, who never before had any intercourse with the Genevese, should now suddenly profess for them so great an affection, though no previous sign of it existed, while, as one imbued, almost from a boy, with Romish arts, (such arts as are now learned in the Court of Rome, that forge of all craft and trickery,) educated, too, in the very bosom of Clement, and now, moreover, elected a cardinal, you have many things about you which, with most men, would in this matter subject you to suspicion. Then as to those insinuations by which you have supposed you might win your way into the minds of simple men, any one, not utterly stupid, might easily refute them. But things of this nature, though many will, perhaps, be disposed to believe them, I am unwilling to ascribe to you, because they seem to me unsuitable to the character of one who has been polished by all kinds of liberal learning. I will, therefore, in entering into discussion with you, give you credit for having written to the Genevese with the purest intention as becomes one of your learning, prudence, and gravity, and for having, in good faith, advised them to the course which you believed conducive to their interest and safety. But whatever may have been your intention, (I am unwilling, in this matter, to charge you with anything invidious,) when, with the bitterest and most contumelious expressions which you can employ, you distort, and endeavour utterly to destroy what the Lord delivered by our hands. I am compelled, whether I will or not, to withstand you openly. For then only do pastors edify the Church, when, besides leading docile souls to Christ, placidly, as with the hand, they are also armed to repel the machinations of those who strive to impede the work of God.

Although your Letter has many windings, its whole purport substantially is to recover the Genevese to the power of the Roman Pontiff, or to what you call the faith and obedience of the Church. But as, from the nature of the case, their feelings required to be softened, you preface with a long oration concerning the incomparable value of eternal life. You afterwards come nearer to the point, when you show that there is nothing more pestiferous to souls than a perverse worship of God; and again, that the best rule for the due worship of God is that which is prescribed by the Church, and that, therefore, there is no salvation for those who have violated the unity of the Church unless they repent. But you next contend, that separation from your fellowship is manifest revolt from the Church, and then that the gospel which the Genevese received from us is nothing but a large farrago of impious dogmas. From this you infer what kind of divine judgment awaits them if they attend not to your admonitions. But as it was of the greatest importance to your cause to throw complete discredit on our words, you labour to the utmost to fill them with sinister suspicions of the zeal which they saw us manifest for their salvation. Accordingly, you captiously allege that we had no other end in view than to gratify our avarice and ambition. Since, then, your device has been to cast some stain upon us, in order that the minds of your readers, being preoccupied with hatred, might give us no credit, I will, before proceeding to other matters, briefly reply to that objection.

I am unwilling to speak of myself, but since you do not permit me to be altogether silent, I will say what I can consistent with modesty. Had I wished to consult my own interest, I would never have left your party. I will not, indeed, boast that there the road to preferment had been easy to me. I never desired it, and I could never bring my mind to catch at it; although I certainly know not a few of my own age who have crept up to some eminence—among them some whom I might have equalled, and others outstripped. This only I will be contented to say, it would not have been difficult for me to reach the summit of my wishes, viz., the enjoyment of literary ease with something of a free and honourable station. Therefore, I have no fear that any one not possessed of shameless effrontery will object to me, that out of the kingdom of the Pope I sought for any personal advantage which was not there ready to my hand.

And who dare object this to Farel? Had it been necessary for him to live by his own industry, he had already made attainments in literature, which would not have allowed him to suffer want, and he was of a more distinguished family than to require external aid. As to those of us to whom you pointed as with the finger, it seemed proper for us to reply in our own name. But since you seem to throw out indirect insinuations against all who in the present day are united with us in sustaining the same cause, I would have you understand, that not one can be mentioned for whom I cannot give you a better answer than for Farel and myself. Some of our Reformers are known to you by fame. As to them, I appeal to your own conscience. Think you it was hunger which drove them away from you, and made them in despair flee to that change as a means of bettering their fortunes? But not to go over a long catalogue, this I say, that of those who first engaged in this cause, there was none who with you might not have been in better place and fortune than require on such grounds to look out for some new plan of life.

But come and consider with me for a little what the honours and powers are which we have gained. All our hearers will bear us witness that we did not covet or aspire to any other riches or dignities than those which fell to our lot. Since in all our words and deeds they not only perceived no trace of the ambition with which you charge us; but, on the contrary, saw clear evidence of our abhorring it with our whole heart, you cannot hope that by one little word their minds are to be so fascinated as to credit a futile slander in opposition to the many certain proofs with which we furnished them. And to appeal to facts rather than words,—the power of the sword, and other parts of civil jurisdiction, which bishops and priests, under the semblance of immunity, had wrested from the magistrate and claimed for themselves, have not we restored to the magistrate? All their usurped instruments of tyranny and ambition have not we detested, and struggled to abolish? If there was any hope of rising, why did we not craftily dissemble, so that those powers might have passed to us along with the office of governing the Church? And why did we make such exertion to overturn the whole of that dominion, or rather butchery, which they exercised upon souls, without any sanction from the Word of God? How did we not consider that it was just so much lost to ourselves? In regard to ecclesiastical revenues, they are still in a great measure swallowed up by these whirlpools. But if there was a hope that they will one day be deprived of them, (as at length they certainly must,) why did we not devise a way by which they might come to us? But when with clear voice we denounced as a thief any bishop who, out of ecclesiastical revenues, appropriated more to his own use than was necessary for a frugal and sober subsistence; when we protested that the Church was exposed to a deadly poison, so long as pastors were loaded with an affluence under which they themselves might ultimately sink, when we declared it inexpedient that these revenues should fall into their possession; finally, when we counselled that as much should be distributed to ministers as might suffice for a frugality befitting their order, not superabound for luxury, and that the rest should be dispensed according to the practice of the ancient Church; when we showed that men of weight ought to be elected to manage these revenues, under an obligation to account annually to the Church and the magistracy, was this to entrap any of these for ourselves, or was it not rather voluntarily to shake ourselves free of them? All these things, indeed, demonstrate not what we are, but what we wished to be. But if these things are so plainly and generally known, that not one iota can be denied, with what face can you proceed to upbraid us with aspiring to extraordinary wealth and power, and this especially in the presence of men to whom none of those things are unknown? The monstrous lies which persons of your order spread against us among their own followers we are not surprised at, (for no man is present who can either reprimand or venture to refute them,) but where men have been eye-witnesses of all the things which we have above mentioned, to try to persuade them of the contrary is the part of a man of little discretion, and strongly derogates from Sadolet's reputation for learning, prudence, and gravity. But if you think that our intention must be judged by the result, it will be found that the only thing we aimed at was, that the kingdom of Christ might be promoted by our poverty and insignificance. So far are we from having abused His sacred name to purposes of ambition.

I pass in silence many other invectives which you thunder out against us, (open mouthed,) as it is said. You call us crafty men, enemies of Christian unity and peace, innovators on things ancient and well established, seditious, alike pestiferous to souls, and destructive both publicly and privately to society at large. Had you wished to escape rebuke, you either ought not, for the purpose of exciting prejudice, to have attributed to us a magniloquent tongue, or you ought to have kept your own magniloquence considerably more under check. I am unwilling, however, to dwell on each of these points; only I would have you to consider how unbecoming, not to say illiberal, it is, thus in many words to accuse the innocent of things, which by one word can be instantly refuted; although to inflict injury on man is a small matter, when compared with the indignity of that contumely, which, when you come to the question, you offer to Christ and his word. When the Genevese, instructed by our preaching, escaped from the gulf of error in which they were immersed, and betook themselves to a purer teaching of the gospel, you call it defection from the truth of God; when they threw off the tyranny of the Roman Pontiff, in order that they might establish among themselves a better form of Church, you call it a desertion from the Church. Come, then, and let us discuss both points in their order.

As to your preface, which, in proclaiming the excellence of eternal blessedness, occupies about a third part of your Letter, it cannot be necessary for me to dwell long in reply. For although commendation of the future and eternal life is a theme which deserves to be sounded in our ears by day and by night, to be constantly kept in remembrance, and made the subject of ceaseless meditation, yet I know not for what reason you have so spun out your discourse upon it here, unless it were to recommend yourself by giving some

indication of religious feeling. But whether, in order to remove all doubt concerning yourself, you wished to testify
that a life of glory seriously occupies your thoughts, or
whether you supposed that those to whom you wrote required to be excited and spurred on by a long commendation of it, (for I am unwilling to divine what your intention
may have been,) it is not very sound theology to confine
a man's thoughts so much to himself, and not to set before
him, as the prime motive of his existence, zeal to illustrate
the glory of God. For we are born first of all for God, and
not for ourselves. As all things flowed from him, and subsist in
him, so, says Paul, (Rom. 11:36,) they ought to be referred
to him. I acknowledge, indeed, that the Lord, the better to
recommend the glory of his name to men, has tempered
zeal for the promotion and extension of it, by uniting it indis-
solubly with our salvation. But since he has taught that this
zeal ought to exceed all thought and care for our own good
and advantage, and since natural equity also teaches that God
does not receive what is his own, unless he is preferred to all
things, it certainly is the part of a Christian man to ascend
higher than merely to seek and secure the salvation of his own
soul. I am persuaded, therefore, that there is no man imbued
with true piety, who will not consider as insipid that long and
laboured exhortation to zeal for heavenly life, a zeal which
keeps a man entirely devoted to himself, and does not, even
by one expression, arouse him to sanctify the name of God.
But I readily agree with you that, after this sanctification,
we ought not to propose to ourselves any other object in life
than to hasten towards that high calling; for God has set
it before us as the constant aim of all our thoughts, and
words, and actions. And, indeed, there is nothing in which
man excels the lower animals, unless it be his spiritual communion with God in the hope of a blessed eternity. And,
generally, all we aim at in our discourses is to arouse men to
meditate upon it, and aspire to it.

I have also no difficulty in conceding to you, that there
is nothing more perilous to our salvation than a preposterous and perverse worship of God. The primary rudiments,
by which we are wont to train to piety those whom we wish
to gain as disciples to Christ, are these; viz., not to frame
any new worship of God for themselves at random, and
after their own pleasure, but to know that the only legitimate worship is that which he himself approved from the
beginning. For we maintain, what the sacred oracle declared,

that obedience is more excellent than any sacrifice, (1 Sam.
15:22.) In short, we train them, by every means, to be contented with the one rule of worship which they have received
from his mouth, and bid adieu to all fictitious worship.

Therefore, Sadolet, when you uttered this voluntary confession, you laid the foundation of my defence. For if you
admit it to be a fearful destruction to the soul, when, by
false opinions, divine truth is turned into a lie, it now only
remains for us to inquire which of the two parties retains
that worship of God which is alone legitimate. In order that
you may claim it for your party, you assume that the most
certain rule of worship is that which is prescribed by the
Church, although, as if we here opposed you, you bring the
matter under consideration, in the manner which is usually
observed in regard to doubtful questions. But, Sadolet, as I
see you toiling in vain, I will relieve you from all trouble on
this head. You are mistaken in supposing that we desire to
lead away the people from that method of worshipping God
which the Catholic Church always observed. You either labour under a delusion as to the term Church, or, at least,
knowingly and willingly give it a gloss. I will immediately
show the latter to be the case, though it may also be that
you are somewhat in error. First, in defining the term, you
omit what would have helped you, in no small degree, to the
right understanding of it. When you describe it as that which
in all parts, as well as at the present time, in every region of
the earth, being united and consenting in Christ, has been
always and every where directed by the one Spirit of Christ,
what comes of the Word of the Lord, that clearest of all
marks, and which the Lord himself, in pointing out the
Church, so often recommends to us? For seeing how dangerous it would be to boast of the Spirit without the Word, he
declared that the Church is indeed governed by the Holy
Spirit, but in order that that government might not be vague
and unstable, he annexed it to the Word. For this reason
Christ exclaims, that those who are of God hear the word
of God—that his sheep are those which recognise his voice
as that of their Shepherd, and any other voice as that of a
stranger, (John 10:27.) For this reason the Spirit, by the
mouth of Paul, declares, (Eph. 2:20,) that the Church is
built upon the foundation of the Apostles and Prophets. Also,
that the Church is made holy to the Lord, by the washing of
water in the word of life. The same thing is declared still
more clearly by the mouth of Peter, when he teaches that

people are regenerated to God by that incorruptible seed, (1 Pet. 1:23.) In short, why is the preaching of the gospel so often styled the kingdom of God, but because it is the sceptre. by which the heavenly King rules his people?

Nor will you find this in the Apostolical writings only, but whenever the Prophets foretell the renewal of the Church, or its extension over the whole globe, they always assign the first place to the Word. For they tell that from Jerusalem will issue forth living waters, which being divided into four rivers, will inundate the whole earth, (Zech. 14:8.) And what these living waters are, they themselves explain when they say, "That the law will come forth from Zion, and the word of the Lord from Jerusalem," (Is. 2:3.) Well, then, does Chrysostom admonish us to reject all who, under the pretence of the Spirit, lead us away from the simple doctrine of the gospel—the Spirit having been promised not to reveal a new doctrine, but to impress the truth of the gospel on our minds. And we, in fact, experience in the present day how necessary the admonition was. We are assailed by two sects, which seem to differ most widely from each other. For what similitude is there in appearance between the Pope and the Anabaptists? And yet, that you may see that Satan never transforms himself so cunningly, as not in some measure to betray himself, the principal weapon with which they both assail us is the same. For when they boast extravagantly of the Spirit, the tendency certainly is to sink and bury the Word of God, that they may make room for their own falsehoods. And you, Sadolet, by stumbling on the very threshold, have paid the penalty of that affront which you offered to the Holy Spirit, when you separated him from the Word. For, as if those who seek the way of God were standing where two ways meet, and destitute of any certain sign, you are forced to introduce them as hesitating whether it be more expedient to follow the authority of the Church, or to listen to those whom you call the inventors of new dogmas. Had you known, or been unwilling to disguise the fact, that the Spirit goes before the Church, to enlighten her in understanding the Word, while the Word itself is like the Lydian Stone, by which she tests all doctrines, would you have taken refuge in that most perplexing and thorny question? Learn, then, by your own experience, that it is no less unreasonable to boast of the Spirit without the Word, than it would be absurd to bring forward the Word itself without the Spirit. Now, if you can bear to receive a truer definition of the

Church than your own, say, in future, that it is the society
of all the saints, a society which, spread over the whole
world, and existing in all ages, yet bound together by the one
doctrine, and the one Spirit of Christ, cultivates and observes unity of faith and brotherly concord. With this Church
we deny that we have any disagreement. Nay, rather, as we
revere her as our mother, so we desire to remain in her bosom.

But here you bring a charge against us. For you teach
that all which has been approved for fifteen hundred years
or more, by the uniform consent of the faithful, is, by our
headstrong rashness, torn up and destroyed. Here I will not
require you to deal truly and candidly by us, (though this
should be spontaneously offered by a philosopher, not to say
a Christian.) I will only ask you not to stoop to an illiberal
indulgence in calumny, which, even though we be silent,
must be extremely injurious to your reputation with grave
and honest men. You know, Sadolet, and if you venture to
deny, I will make it palpable to all that you knew, yet cunningly and craftily disguised the fact, not only that our
agreement with antiquity is far closer than yours, but that
all we have attempted has been to renew that ancient form
of the Church, which, at first sullied and distorted by illiterate men of indifferent character, was afterwards flagitiously
mangled and almost destroyed by the Roman Pontiff and
his faction.

I will not press you so closely as to call you back to that
form which the Apostles instituted, (though in it we have the
only model of a true Church, and whosoever deviates from
it in the smallest degree is in error,) but to indulge you so far,
place, I pray, before your eyes, that ancient form of the
Church, such as their writings prove it to have been in the
age of Chrysostom and Basil, among the Greeks, and of
Cyprian, Ambrose, and Augustine, among the Latins; after so
doing, contemplate the ruins of that Church, as now surviving
among yourselves. Assuredly, the difference will appear as
great as that which the Prophets describe between the famous Church which flourished under David and Solomon,
and that which under Zedekiah and Jehoiakim had lapsed
into every kind of superstition, and utterly vitiated the
purity of divine worship. Will you here give the name of an
enemy of antiquity to him who, zealous for ancient piety and
holiness, and dissatisfied with the state of matters as existing
in a dissolute and depraved Church, attempts to ameliorate
its condition, and restore it to pristine splendour?

Since there are three things on which the safety of the
Church is founded, viz., doctrine, discipline, and the sacraments, and to these a fourth is added, viz., ceremonies, by
which to exercise the people in offices of piety, in order that
we may be most sparing of the honour of your Church, by
which of these things would you have us to judge her? The
truth of Prophetical and Evangelical doctrine, on which the
Church ought to be founded, has not only in a great measure perished in your Church, but is violently driven away
by fire and sword. Will you obtrude upon me, for the Church,
a body which furiously persecutes everything sanctioned
by our religion, both as delivered by the oracles of God, and
embodied in the writings of holy Fathers, and approved by
ancient Councils? Where, pray, exist among you any vestiges
of that true and holy discipline, which the ancient bishops
exercised in the Church? Have you not scorned all their
institutions? Have you not trampled all the Canons under
foot? Then, your nefarious profanation of the sacraments I
cannot think of without the utmost horror.

Of ceremonies, indeed, you have more than enough, but,
for the most part, so childish in their import, and vitiated by
innumerable forms of superstition, as to be utterly unavailing
for the preservation of the Church. None of these things, you
must be aware, is exaggerated by me in a captious spirit.
They all appear so openly, that they may be pointed out with
the finger wherever there are eyes to behold them. Now, if
you please, test us in the same way. You will, assuredly, fall
far short of making good the charges which you have
brought against us.

In the Sacraments, all we have attempted is to restore the
native purity from which they had degenerated, and so enable them to resume their dignity. Ceremonies we have in a
great measure abolished, but we were compelled to do so,
partly because by their multitude they had degenerated into
a kind of Judaism, partly because they had filled the minds
of the people with superstition, and could not possibly remain without doing the greatest injury to the piety which it
was their office to promote. Still we have retained those
which seemed sufficient for the circumstances of the times.

That our discipline is not such as the ancient Church professed we do not deny. But with what fairness is a charge
of subverting discipline brought against us by those who
themselves have utterly abolished it, and in our attempts to
re-instate it in its rights have hitherto opposed us? As to our

doctrine, we hesitate not to appeal to the ancient Church. And since, for the sake of example, you have touched on certain heads, as to which you thought you had some ground for accusing us, I will briefly show how unfairly and falsely you allege that these are things which have been devised by us against the opinion of the Church.

Before descending to particulars, however, I have already cautioned you, and would have you again and again consider with what reason you can charge it upon our people, as a fault, that they have studied to explain the Scriptures. For you are aware, that by this study they have thrown such light on the Word of God, that, in this respect, even envy herself is ashamed to defraud them of all praise. You are just as uncandid when you aver that we have seduced the people by thorny and subtle questions, and so enticed them by that philosophy of which Paul bids Christians beware. What? Do you remember what kind of time it was when our Reformers appeared, and what kind of doctrine candidates for the ministry learned in the schools? You yourself know that it was mere sophistry, and sophistry so twisted, involved, tortuous, and puzzling, that scholastic theology might well be described as a species of secret magic. The denser the darkness in which any one shrouded a subject, the more he puzzled himself and others with preposterous riddles, the greater his fame for acumen and learning. And when those who had been formed in that forge wished to carry the fruit of their learning to the people, with what skill, I ask, did they edify the Church?

Not to go over every point, what sermons in Europe then exhibited that simplicity with which Paul wishes a Christian people to be always occupied? Nay, what one sermon was there from which old wives might not carry off more whimsies than they could devise at their own fireside in a month? For, as sermons were then usually divided, the first half was devoted to those misty questions of the schools which might astonish the rude populace, while the second contained sweet stories, or not unamusing speculations, by which the hearers might be kept on the alert. Only a few expressions were thrown in from the Word of God, that by their majesty they might procure credit for these frivolities. But as soon as our Reformers raised the standard, all these absurdities, in one moment, disappeared from amongst us. Your preachers, again, partly profited by our books, and partly compelled by shame and the general murmur, conformed to our example, though they still, with open throat, exhale the old absurdity. Hence, any one who compares our method of procedure with the old method, or with that which is still in repute among you, will perceive that you have done us no small injustice. But had you continued your quotation from Paul a little farther, any boy would easily have perceived that the charge which you bring against us is undoubtedly applicable to yourselves. For Paul there interprets "vain philosophy" (Col. 2:8) to mean that which preys upon pious souls, by means of the constitutions of men, and the elements of this world: and by these you have ruined the Church.

Even you yourself afterwards acquit us by your own testimony; for among those of our doctrines which you have thought proper to assail, you do not adduce one, the knowledge of which is not essentially necessary for the edification of the Church.

You, in the first place, touch upon justification by faith, the first and keenest subject of controversy between us. Is this a knotty and useless question? Wherever the knowledge of it is taken away, the glory of Christ is extinguished, religion abolished, the Church destroyed, and the hope of salvation utterly overthrown. That doctrine, then, though of the highest moment, we maintain that you have nefariously effaced from the memory of men. Our books are filled with convincing proofs of this fact, and the gross ignorance of this doctrine, which even still continues in all your churches, declares that our complaint is by no means ill founded. But you very maliciously stir up prejudice against us, alleging that, by attributing every thing to faith, we leave no room for works.

I will not now enter upon a full discussion, which would require a large volume; but if you would look into the Catechism which I myself drew up for the Genevese, when I held the office of Pastor among them, three words would silence you. Here, however, I will briefly explain to you how we speak on this subject.

First, We bid a man begin by examining himself, and this not in a superficial and perfunctory manner, but to sist his conscience before the tribunal of God, and when sufficiently convinced of his iniquity, to reflect on the strictness of the sentence pronounced upon all sinners. Thus confounded and amazed at his misery, he is prostrated and humbled before God; and, casting away all self-confidence, groans as if given up to final perdition. Then we show that the only haven of safety is in the mercy of God, as manifested in Christ, in whom every part of our salvation is complete. As all mankind are, in the sight of God, lost sinners, we hold that Christ is their only righteousness, since, by his obedience, he has wiped off our transgressions; by his sacrifice, appeased the divine anger; by his blood, washed away our stains; by his cross, borne our curse; and by his death, made satisfaction for us. We maintain that in this way man is reconciled in Christ to God the Father, by no merit of his own, by no value of works, but by gratuitous mercy. When we embrace Christ by faith, and come, as it were, into communion with him, this we term, after the manner of Scripture, the righteousness of faith.

What have you here, Sadolet, to bite or carp at? Is it that we leave no room for works? Assuredly we do deny that, in justifying a man, they are worth one single straw. For Scripture everywhere cries aloud, that all are lost; and every man's own conscience bitterly accuses him. The same Scripture teaches, that no hope is left but in the mere goodness of God, by which sin is pardoned, and righteousness imputed to us. It declares both to be gratuitous, and finally concludes that a man is justified without works, (Rom. 4:7.) But what notion, you ask, does the very term Righteousness suggest to us, if respect is not paid to good works? I answer, if you would attend to the true meaning of the term *justifying* in Scripture, you would have no difficulty. For it does not refer to a man's own righteousness, but to the mercy of God, which, contrary to the sinner's deserts, accepts of a righteousness for him, and that by not imputing his unrighteousness. Our righteousness, I say, is that which is described by Paul, (2 Cor. 5:19,) that God hath reconciled us to himself in Jesus Christ. The mode is afterwards subjoined—by not imputing sin. He demonstrates that it is by faith only we become partakers of that blessing, when he says that the ministry of reconciliation is contained in the gospel. But faith, you say, is a general term, and has a larger signification. I answer, that Paul, whenever he attributes to it the power of justifying, at the same time restricts it to a gratuitous promise of the divine favour, and keeps it far removed from all respect to works. Hence his familiar inference—if by faith, then not by works. On the other hand—if by works, then not by faith.

But, it seems, injury is done to Christ, if, under the pretence of his grace, good works are repudiated; he having come to prepare a people acceptable to God, zealous of good

works, while, to the same effect, are many similar passages
which prove that Christ came in order that we, doing good
works, might, through him, be accepted by God. This
calumny, which our opponents have ever in their mouths,
viz., that we take away the desire of well-doing from the
Christian life by recommending gratuitous righteousness, is
too frivolous to give us much concern. We deny that good
works have any share in justification, but we claim full authority for them in the lives of the righteous. For, if he who
has obtained justification possesses Christ, and, at the same
time, Christ never is where his Spirit is not, it is obvious that
gratuitous righteousness is necessarily connected with regeneration. Therefore, if you would duly understand how inseparable faith and works are, look to Christ, who, as the
Apostle teaches, (1 Cor. 1:30,) has been given to us for
justification and for sanctification. Wherever, therefore, that
righteousness of faith, which we maintain to be gratuitous, is,
there too Christ is, and where Christ is, there too is the
Spirit of holiness, who regenerates the soul to newness of
life. On the contrary, where zeal for integrity and holiness is
not in vigour, there neither is the Spirit of Christ nor Christ
himself; and wherever Christ is not, there is no righteousness, nay, there is no faith; for faith cannot apprehend Christ
for righteousness without the Spirit of sanctification.

Since, therefore, according to us, Christ regenerates to a
blessed life those whom he justifies, and after rescuing them
from the dominion of sin, hands them over to the dominion
of righteousness, transforms them into the image of God, and
so trains them by his Spirit into obedience to his will, there
is no ground to complain that, by our doctrine, lust is left
with loosened reins. The passages which you adduce have
not a meaning at variance with our doctrine. But if you will
pervert them in assailing gratuitous justification, see how un-
skilfully you argue. Paul elsewhere says (Eph. 1:4) that we
were chosen in Christ, before the creation of the world, to be
holy and unblameable in the sight of God through love. Who
will venture thence to infer, either that election is not
gratuitous, or that our love is its cause? Nay, rather, as the
end of gratuitous election, so also that of gratuitous justification is, that we may lead pure and unpolluted lives before
God. For the saying of Paul is true, (1 Thess. 4:7,) we have
not been called to impurity, but to holiness. This, meanwhile,
we constantly maintain, that man is not only justified freely
once for all, without any merit of works, but that on this

gratuitous justification the salvation of man perpetually depends. Nor is it possible that any work of man can be accepted by God unless it be gratuitously approved. Wherefore, I was amazed when I read your assertion, that love is the first and chief cause of our salvation. O, Sadolet, who could ever have expected such a saying from you? Undoubtedly the very blind, while in darkness, feel the mercy of God too surely to dare to claim for their love the first cause of their salvation, while those who have merely one spark of divine light feel that their salvation consists in nothing else than their being adopted by God. For eternal salvation is the inheritance of the heavenly Father, and has been prepared solely for his children. Moreover, who can assign any other cause of our adoption than that which is uniformly announced in Scripture, viz., that we did not first love him, but were spontaneously received by him into favour and affection?

Your ignorance of this doctrine leads you on to the error of teaching that sins are expiated by penances and satisfactions. Where, then, will be that one expiatory victim, from which, if we depart, there remains, as Scripture testifies, no more sacrifice for sin? Search through all the divine oracles which we possess; if the blood of Christ alone is uniformly set forth as purchasing satisfaction, reconciliation, and ablution, how dare you presume to transfer so great an honour to your works? Nor have you any ground for ascribing this blasphemy to the Church of God. The ancient Church, I admit, had its satisfactions, not those, however, by which sinners might atone to God and ransom themselves from guilt, but by which they might prove that the repentance which they professed was not feigned, and efface the remembrance of that scandal which their sin had occasioned. For satisfactions were not regularly prescribed to all and sundry, but to those only who had fallen into some heinous wickedness.

In the case of the Eucharist, you blame us for attempting to confine the Lord of the universe, and his divine and spiritual power, (which is perfectly free and infinite,) within the corners of a corporeal nature with its circumscribed boundaries. What end, pray, will there be to calumny? We have always distinctly testified, that not only the divine power of Christ, but his essence also, is diffused over all, and defined by no limits, and yet you hesitate not to upbraid us with confining it within the corners of corporeal nature! How so? Because we are unwilling with you to chain down his body to earthly elements. But had you any regard for sincerity, as-

suredly you are not ignorant how great a difference there is
between the two things—between removing the local presence
of Christ's body from bread, and circumscribing his spiritual
power within bodily limits. Nor ought you to charge our
doctrine with novelty, since it was always held by the
Church as an acknowledged point. But as this subject alone
would extend to a volume, in order that both of us may escape so toilsome a discussion, the better course will be for
you to read Augustine's Epistle to Dardanus, where you will
find how one and the same Christ more than fills heaven and
earth with the vastness of his divinity, and yet is not everywhere diffused in respect of his humanity.

We loudly proclaim the communion of flesh and blood,
which is exhibited to believers in the Supper; and we distinctly show that that flesh is truly meat, and that blood truly
drink—that the soul, not contented with an imaginary conception, enjoys them in very truth. That presence of Christ,
by which we are ingrafted in him, we by no means exclude
from the Supper, nor shroud in darkness, though we hold
that there must be no local limitation, that the glorious
body of Christ must not be degraded to earthly elements;
that there must be no fiction of transubstantiating the bread
into Christ, and afterwards worshipping it as Christ. We
explain the dignity and end of this solemn rite in the loftiest
terms which we can employ, and then declare how great the
advantages which we derive from it. Almost all these things
are neglected by you. For, overlooking the divine beneficence which is here bestowed upon us, overlooking the legitimate use of so great a benefit, (the topics on which it were
becoming most especially to dwell,) you count it enough that
the people gaze stupidly at the visible sign, without any understanding of the spiritual mystery. In condemning your
gross dogma of transubstantiation, and declaring that stupid
adoration which detains the minds of men among the elements, and permits them not to rise to Christ, to be perverse
and impious, we have not acted without the concurrence of
the ancient Church, under whose shadow you endeavour in
vain to hide the very vile superstitions to which you are here
addicted.

In auricular confession we have disapproved of that law of
Innocent, which enjoins every man once a year to pass all his
sins in review before his priest. It would be tedious to enumerate all the reasons which induced us to abrogate it. But that
the thing was nefarious is apparent even from this, that pious

consciences, which formerly boiled with perpetual anxiety, have at length begun, after being freed from that dire torment, to rest with confidence in the divine favour; to say nothing, meanwhile, of the many disasters which it brought upon the Church, and which justly entitle us to hold it in execration. For the present, take this for our answer, that it was neither commanded by Christ, nor practised by the ancient Church. We have forcibly wrested from the hands of the sophists all the passages of Scripture which they had contrived to distort in support of it, while the common books on ecclesiastical history show that it had no existence in an earlier age. The testimonies of the Fathers are to the same effect. It is, therefore, mere deception when you say, that the humility therein manifested was enjoined and instituted by Christ and the Church. For though there appears in it a certain show of humility, it is very far from being true, that every kind of abasement, which assumes the name of humility, is commended by God. Accordingly, Paul teaches, (Col. 2:18,) that that humility only is genuine which is framed in conformity to the Word of God.

In asserting the intercession of the saints, if all you mean is, that they continually pray for the completion of Christ's kingdom, on which the salvation of all the faithful depends, there is none of us who calls it in question. Accordingly, you have lost your pains in labouring this part so much, but, no doubt, you were unwilling to lose the opportunity of repeating the false asseveration which charges us with thinking that the soul perishes with the body. That philosophy we leave to your Popes and College of Cardinals, by whom it was for many years most faithfully cultivated, and ceases not to be cultivated in the present day. To them also your subsequent remark applies, viz., to live luxuriously, without any solicitude concerning a future life, and hold us miserable wretches in derision, for labouring so anxiously in behalf of the kingdom of Christ. But, in regard to the intercession of the saints, we insist on a point which it is not strange that you omit. For here innumerable superstitions were to be cut off, superstitions which had risen to such a height, that the intercession of Christ was utterly erased from men's thoughts, saints were invoked as gods, the peculiar offices of Deity were distributed among them, and a worship paid to them which differed in nothing from that ancient idolatry which we all deservedly execrate.

As to purgatory, we know that ancient churches made

some mention of the dead in their prayers, but it was done seldom and soberly, and consisted only of a few words. It was, in short, a mention in which it was obvious that nothing more was meant than to attest in passing the affection which was felt toward the dead. As yet, the architects were unborn, by whom your purgatory was built; and who afterwards enlarged it to such a width, and raised it to such a height, that it now forms the chief prop of your kingdom. You yourself know what a hydra of errors thence emerged; you know what tricks superstition has at its own hand devised, wherewith to disport itself; you know how many impostures avarice has here fabricated, in order to milk men of every class; you know how great detriment it has done to piety. For, not to mention how much true worship has in consequence decayed, the worst result certainly was, that while all, without any command from God, were vying with each other in helping the dead, they utterly neglected the congenial offices of charity, which are so strongly enjoined.

I will not permit you, Sadolet, by inscribing the name of Church on such abominations, both to defame her against all law and justice, and prejudice the ignorant against us, as if we were determined to wage war with the Church. For though we admit that in ancient times some seeds of superstition were sown, which detracted somewhat from the purity of the gospel, still you know, that it is not so long ago since those monsters of impiety with which we war were born, or, at least, grew to such a size. Indeed, in attacking, breaking down, and destroying your kingdom, we are armed not only with the energy of the Divine Word, but with the aid of the holy Fathers also.

That I may altogether disarm you of the authority of the Church, which, as your shield of Ajax, you ever and anon oppose to us, I will show, by some additional examples, how widely you differ from that holy antiquity.

We accuse you of overthrowing the ministry, of which the empty name remains with you, without the reality. As far as the office of feeding the people is concerned, the very children perceive that Bishops and Presbyters are dumb statues, while men of all ranks know by experience, that they are active only in robbing and devouring. We are indignant, that in the room of the sacred Supper has been substituted a sacrifice, by which the death of Christ is emptied of its virtues. We exclaim against the execrable traffic in masses, and we complain, that the Supper of the Lord, as to one of its halves, has been stolen from the Christian people. We inveigh against the accursed worship of images. We show that the sacraments are vitiated by many profane notions. We tell how indulgences crept in with fearful dishonour to the cross of Christ. We lament, that by means of human traditions, Christian liberty has been crushed and destroyed. Of these and similar pests, we have been careful to purge the churches which the Lord has committed to us. Expostulate with us, if you can, for the injury which we inflicted on the Catholic Church, by daring to violate its sacred sanctions. The fact is now too notorious for you to gain anything by denying it, viz., that in all these points, the ancient Church is clearly on our side, and opposes you, not less than we ourselves do.

But here we are met by what you say, when, in order to palliate matters, you allege that though your manners should be irregular, that is no reason why we should make a schism in the holy Church. It is scarcely possible that the minds of the common people should not be greatly alienated from you by the many examples of cruelty, avarice, intemperance, arrogance, insolence, lust, and all sorts of wickedness, which are openly manifested by men of your order, but none of those things would have driven us to the attempt which we made under a much stronger necessity. That necessity was, that the light of divine truth had been extinguished, the word of God buried, the virtue of Christ left in profound oblivion, and the pastoral office subverted. Meanwhile, impiety so stalked abroad, that almost no doctrine of religion was pure from admixture, no ceremony free from error, no part, however minute, of divine worship untarnished by superstition. Do those who contend against such evils declare war against the Church, and not rather assist her in her extreme distress? And yet you would take credit for your obedience and humility in refraining, through veneration for the Church, from applying your hand to the removal of these abominations. What has a Christian man to do with that prevaricating obedience, which, while the word of God is licentiously contemned, yields its homage to human vanity? What has he to do with that contumacious and rude humility, which, despising the majesty of God, only looks up with reverence to men? Have done with empty names of virtue, employed merely as cloaks for vice, and let us exhibit the thing itself in its true colours. Ours be the humility, which, beginning with the lowest, and paying respect to each in his degree, yields the highest honour and respect to the Church, in subordination, however, to Christ the Church's head; ours the obedience, which, while it disposes us to listen to our elders and superiors, tests all obedience by the word of God; in fine, ours the Church, whose supreme care it is humbly and religiously to venerate the word of God, and submit to its authority.

But what arrogance, you will say, to boast that the Church is with you alone, and to deny it to all the world besides! We, indeed, Sadolet, deny not that those over which you preside are Churches of Christ, but we maintain that the Roman Pontiff, with his whole herd of pseudo-bishops, who have seized upon the pastor's office, are ravening wolves, whose only study has hitherto been to scatter and trample upon the kingdom of Christ, filling it with ruin and devastation. Nor are we the first to make the complaint. With what vehemence does Bernard thunder against Eugenius and all the bishops of his own age? Yet how much more tolerable was its condition then than now? For iniquity has reached its height, and now those shadowy prelates, by whom you think the Church stands or perishes, and by whom we say that she has been cruelly torn and mutilated, and brought to the very brink of destruction, can bear neither their vices nor the cure of them. Destroyed the Church would have been, had not God, with singular goodness, prevented. For in all places where the tyranny of the Roman Pontiff prevails, you scarcely see as many stray and tattered vestiges as will enable you to perceive that there Churches lie half buried. Nor should you think this absurd, since Paul tells you (2 Thess. 2:4) that antichrist would have his seat in no other place than in the midst of God's sanctuary. Ought not this single warning to put us on our guard against tricks and devices which may be practised in the name of the Church?

But whatever the character of the men, still you say it is written, "What they tell you, do." No doubt, if they sit in the chair of Moses. But when, from the chair of verity, they intoxicate the people with folly, it is written, "Beware of the leaven of the Pharisees," (Matt. 16:6.) It is not ours, Sadolet, to rob the Church of any right which the goodness of God not only has conceded to her, but strictly guarded for her by numerous prohibitions. For, as pastors are not sent forth by Him to rule the Church with a licentious and lawless authority, but are astricted to a certain rule of duty which they must not exceed, so the Church is ordered (1

Thess. 5:21; 1 John 4:1) to see that those who are appointed over her on these terms faithfully accord with their vocation. But we must either hold the testimony of Christ of little moment, or must hold it impious to infringe in the least degree on the authority of those whom he has invested with such splendid titles! Nay, it is you who are mistaken in supposing that the Lord set tyrants over his people to rule them at pleasure, when he bestowed so much authority on those whom he sent to promulgate the gospel. Your error lies here, viz., in not reflecting that their power, before they were furnished with it, was circumscribed within certain limits. We admit, therefore, that ecclesiastical pastors are to be heard just like Christ himself, but they must be pastors who execute the office entrusted to them. And this office, we maintain, is not presumptuously to introduce whatever their own pleasure has rashly devised, but religiously and in good faith to deliver the oracles which they have received at the mouth of the Lord. For within these boundaries Christ confined the reverence which he required to be paid to the Apostles; nor does Peter (1 Pet. 4:11) either claim for himself or allow to others anything more than that, as often as they speak among the faithful, they speak as from the mouth of the Lord. Paul, indeed, justly extols (2 Cor. 13:10) the spiritual power with which he was invested, but with this proviso, that it was to avail only for edification, was to wear no semblance of domination, was not to be employed in subjugating faith.

Let your Pontiff, then, boast as he may of the succession of Peter: even should he make good his title to it, he will establish nothing more than that obedience is due to him from the Christian people, so long as he himself maintains his fidelity to Christ, and deviates not from the purity of the gospel. For the Church of the faithful does not force you into any other order than that in which the Lord wished you to stand, when it tests you by that rule by which all your power is defined—the order, I say, which the Lord himself instituted among the faithful, viz., that a Prophet holding the place of teacher should be judged by the congregation, (consessu,) (1 Cor. 14:29.) Whoever exempts himself from this must first expunge his name from the list of Prophets. And here a very wide field for exposing your ignorance opens upon me, since, in matters of religious controversy, all that you leave to the faithful is to shut their own eyes, and to submit implicitly to their teachers. But since it is certain that every soul which depends not on God alone is enslaved to Satan, how miserable must they be who are imbued with such rudiments of faith? Hence, I observe, Sadolet, that you have too indolent a theology, as is almost always the case with those who have never had experience in serious struggles of conscience. For, otherwise, you would never place a Christian man on ground so slippery, nay, so precipitous, that he can scarcely stand a moment if even the slightest push is given him. Give me, I say not some unlearned man from among the people, but the rudest clown, and if he is to belong to the flock of God, he must be prepared for that warfare which He has ordained for all the godly. An armed enemy is at hand, on the alert to engage—an enemy most skilful and unassailable by mortal strength; to resist him, with what guards must not that poor man be defended, with what weapons armed, if he is not to be instantly annihilated? Paul informs us, (Eph. 6:17,) that the only sword with which he can fight is the word of the Lord. A soul, therefore, when deprived of the word of God, is given up unarmed to the devil for destruction. Now, then, will not the first machination of the enemy be to wrest the sword from the soldier of Christ? And what the method of wresting it, but to set him a doubting whether it be the word of the Lord that he is leaning upon, or the word of man? What will you do for this unhappy being? Will you bid him look round for learned men on whom reclining he may take his rest? But the enemy will not leave him so much as a breathing time in this subterfuge. For when once he has driven him to lean upon men, he will keep urging and repeating his blows until he throws him over the precipice. Thus he must either be easily overthrown, or he must forsake man, and look directly to God. So true it is, that Christian faith must not be founded on human testimony, not propped up by doubtful opinion, not reclined on human authority, but engraven on our hearts by the finger of the living God, so as not to be obliterated by any colouring of error. There is nothing of Christ, then, in him who does not hold the elementary principle, that it is God alone who enlightens our minds to perceive his truth, who by his Spirit seals it on our hearts, and by his sure attestation to it confirms our conscience. This is, if I may so express it, that full and firm assurance commended by Paul, and which, as it leaves no room for doubt, so not only does it not hesitate and waver among human arguments as to which party it ought to adhere, but maintains its consistency though the whole world should oppose.

Hence arises that power of judging which we attribute to the Church, and wish to preserve unimpaired. For how much soever the world may fluctuate and jar with contending opinions, the faithful soul is never so destitute as not to have a straight course to salvation. I do not, however, dream of a perspicacity of faith which never errs in discriminating between truth and falsehood, is never deceived, nor do I figure to myself an arrogance which looks down as from a height on the whole human race, waits for no man's judgment, and makes no distinction between learned and unlearned. On the contrary, I admit that pious and truly religious minds do not always attain to all the mysteries of God, but are sometimes blind in the clearest matters—the Lord, doubtless, so providing, in order to accustom them to modesty and submission. Again, I admit that they have such a respect for all good men, not to say the Church, that they do not easily allow themselves to be separated from any man in whom they have discovered a true knowledge of Christ; so that sometimes they choose rather to suspend their judgment than to rush, on slight grounds, into dissent. I only contend, that so long as they insist on the word of the Lord, they are never so caught as to be led away to destruction, while their conviction of the truth of the word of God is so clear and certain, that it cannot be overthrown by either men or angels. Away, then, with that nugatory simplicity (which you say becomes the rude and illiterate) of looking up and yielding to the beck of those who are more learned! For, besides that the name of faith is undeservedly bestowed on any religious persuasion, however obstinate, which rests any where but in God, who can give such a name to some (I know not what) wavering opinion, which is not only easily wrested from them by the arts of the devil, but fluctuates of its own accord with the temper of the times, and of which no other end can be hoped for than that it will at length vanish away?

As to your assertion, that our only aim in shaking off this tyrannical yoke was to set ourselves free for unbridled licentiousness after, (so help us!) casting away all thoughts of future life, let judgment be given after comparing our conduct with yours. We abound, indeed, in numerous faults, too often do we sin and fall; still, though truth would, modesty will not, permit me to boast how far we excel you in every respect, unless, perchance, you are to except Rome, that famous abode of sanctity, which having burst asunder the cords of pure discipline, and trodden all honour under foot, has so overflowed with all kinds of iniquity, that scarcely any thing so abominable has ever been before. We behoved, forsooth, to expose our heads to so many perils and dangers that we might not, after her example, be placed under too severe constraint! But we have not the least objection that the discipline which was sanctioned by ancient canons should be in force in the present day, and be carefully and faithfully observed; nay, we have always protested that the miserable condition into which the Church had fallen was owing to nothing more than to its enervation by luxury and indulgence. For the body of the Church, to cohere well, must be bound together by discipline as with sinews. But how, on your part, is discipline either observed or desired? Where are those ancient canons with which, like a bridle, bishops and presbyters were kept to their duty? How are your bishops elected? after what trial? what examination? what care? what caution? How are they inducted to their office? with what order? what solemnity? They merely take an official oath that they will perform the pastoral office, and this apparently for no other end than that they may add perjury to their other iniquities. Since, then, in seizing upon ecclesiastical offices they seem to enter upon an authority astricted by no law, they think themselves free to do as they please, and hence it is that among pirates and robbers there is apparently more justice and regular government, more effect given to law, than by all your order.

But since, towards the end, a person has been introduced to plead our cause, and you have cited us as defenders to the tribunal of God, I have no hesitation in calling upon you there to meet me. For such is our consciousness of the truth of our doctrine, that it has no dread of the heavenly Judge, from whom, we doubt not, that it proceeded. But it dwells not on those frivolities with which it has pleased you to amuse yourself; certainly very much out of place. For what more unseasonable than after you had come into the presence of God, to set about devising I know not what follies, and framing for us an absurd defence which must instantly fail. In pious minds, as often as that day is suggested, the impression made is too solemn to leave them at leisure so to disport themselves. Therefore, frivolity aside, let us think of that day, in expectation of which the minds of men ought ever to be on the watch. And let us remember, that while it is a day to be desired by the faithful, it is also one at which the ungodly and profane, and those who are despisers of God, may well be alarmed. Let us turn our ears to the clang of that trumpet which even the ashes of the dead shall hear in their tombs. Let us direct our thoughts and minds to that Judge who, by the mere brightness of his countenance, will disclose whatever lurks in darkness, lay open all the secrets of the human heart, and crush all the wicked by the mere breath of his mouth. Consider, now, what serious answer you are to make for yourself and your party: Our cause, as it is supported by the truth of God, will be at no loss for a complete defence. I speak not of our persons, whose safety will be found not in defence, but in humble confession and suppliant deprecation; but in so far as our ministry is concerned, there is none of us who will not be able thus to speak:—

"O Lord, I have, indeed, experienced how difficult and grievous it was to bear the invidious accusations with which I was harassed on the earth; but with the same confidence with which I then appealed to thy tribunal, I now appear before thee, because I know that in thy judgment truth always reigns—that truth by whose assurance supported I first ventured to attempt—with whose assistance provided I was able to accomplish whatever I have achieved in thy Church. They charged me with two of the worst of crimes—heresy and schism. And the heresy was, that I dared to protest against dogmas which they received. But what could I have done? I heard from thy mouth that there was no other light of truth which could direct our souls into the way of life, than that which was kindled by thy Word. I heard that whatever human minds of themselves conceive concerning thy Majesty, the worship of thy Deity, and the mysteries of thy religion, was vanity. I heard that their introducing into the Church instead of thy Word, doctrines sprung from the human brain, was sacrilegious presumption. But when I turned my eyes towards men, I saw very different principles prevailing. Those who were regarded as the leaders of faith neither understood thy Word, nor greatly cared for it. They only drove unhappy people to and fro with strange doctrines, and deluded them with I know not what follies. Among the people themselves, the highest veneration paid to thy Word was to revere it at a distance, as a thing inaccessible, and abstain from all investigation of it. Owing to this supine state of the pastors, and this stupidity of the people, every place was filled with pernicious errors, falsehoods, and superstition. They, indeed, called thee the only God, but it was while transferring to others the glory which thou hast claimed for thy Majesty.

They figured and had for themselves as many gods as they had saints, whom they chose to worship. Thy Christ was indeed worshipped as God, and retained the name of Saviour; but where he ought to have been honoured, he was left almost without honour. For, spoiled of his own virtue, he passed unnoticed among the crowd of saints, like one of the meanest of them. There was none who duly considered that one sacrifice which he offered on the cross, and by which he reconciled us to thyself—none who ever dreamed of thinking of his eternal priesthood, and the intercession depending upon it—none who trusted in his righteousness only. That confident hope of salvation which is both enjoined by thy Word, and founded upon it, had almost vanished. Nay, it was received as a kind of oracle, that it was foolish arrogance, and, as they termed it, presumption for any one trusting to thy goodness, and the righteousness of thy Son, to entertain a sure and unfaltering hope of salvation. Not a few profane opinions plucked up by the roots, the first principles of that doctrine which thou hast delivered to us in thy Word. The true meaning of Baptism and the Lord's Supper, also, were corrupted by numerous falsehoods. And then, when all, with no small insult to thy mercy, put confidence in good works, when by good works they strove to merit thy favour, to procure justification, to expiate their sins, and make satisfaction to thee, (each of these things obliterating and making void the virtue of Christ's cross,) they were yet altogether ignorant wherein good works consisted. For, just as if they were not at all instructed in righteousness by thy law, they had fabricated for themselves many useless frivolities, as a means of procuring thy favour, and on these they so plumed themselves, that, in comparison of them, they almost contemned the standard of true righteousness which thy law recommended—to such a degree had human desires, after usurping the ascendancy, derogated, if not from the belief, at least from the authority, of thy precepts therein contained. That I might perceive these things, thou, O Lord, didst shine upon me with the brightness of thy Spirit; that I might comprehend how impious and noxious they were, thou didst bear before me the torch of thy Word; that I might abominate them as they deserved, thou didst stimulate my soul. But in rendering an account of my doctrine, thou seest (what my own conscience declares) that it was not my intention to stray beyond those limits which I saw had been fixed by all thy servants. Whatever I felt assured that I had learned from thy mouth,

I desired to dispense faithfully to the Church. Assuredly, the thing at which I chiefly aimed, and for which I most diligently laboured, was, that the glory of thy goodness and justice, after dispersing the mists by which it was formerly obscured, might shine forth conspicuous, that the virtue and blessings of thy Christ (all glosses being wiped away) might be fully displayed. For I thought it impious to leave in obscurity things which we were born to ponder and meditate. Nor did I think that truths, whose magnitude no language can express, were to be maliciously or falsely declared. I hesitated not to dwell at greater length on topics on which the salvation of my hearers depended. For the oracle could never deceive which declares, (John 17:3,) 'This is eternal life, to know thee the only true God, and Jesus Christ, whom thou has sent.'

"As to the charge of forsaking the Church, which they were wont to bring against me, there is nothing of which my conscience accuses me, unless, indeed, he is to be considered a deserter, who, seeing the soldiers routed and scattered, and abandoning the ranks, raises the leader's standard, and recalls them to their posts. For thus, O Lord, were all thy servants dispersed, so that they could not, by any possibility, hear the command, but had almost forgotten their leader, and their service, and their military oath. In order to bring them together, when thus scattered, I raised not a foreign standard, but that noble banner of thine whom we must follow, if we would be classed among thy people.

"Then I was assailed by those who, when they ought to have kept others in their ranks, had led them astray, and when I determined not to desist, opposed me with violence. On this grievous tumults arose, and the contest blazed and issued in disruption. With whom the blame rests it is for thee, O Lord, to decide. Always, both by word and deed, have I protested how eager I was for unity. Mine, however, was a unity of the Church, which should begin with thee and end in thee. For as oft as thou didst recommend to us peace and concord, thou, at the same time, didst show that thou wert the only bond for preserving it. But if I desired to be at peace with those who boasted of being the heads of the Church and pillars of faith, I behoved to purchase it with the denial of thy truth. I thought that any thing was to be endured sooner than stoop to such a nefarious paction. For thy Anointed himself hath declared, that though heaven and earth should be confounded, yet thy word must endure for ever, (Matth. 24:35.) Nor did I think that I dissented from

thy Church, because I was at war with those leaders; for
thou hast forewarned me, both by thy Son and by the apostles, that that place would be occupied by persons to whom
I ought by no means to consent. Christ had predicted not of
strangers, but of men who should give themselves out for
pastors, that they would be ravenous wolves and false
prophets, and had, at the same time, cautioned to beware of
them. Where Christ ordered me to beware, was I to lend my
aid? And the apostles declared that there would be no enemies of thy Church more pestilential than those from within,
who should conceal themselves under the title of pastors,
(Matth. 7:15; Acts 20:29; 2 Pet. 2:1; 1 John 2:18.) Why
should I have hesitated to separate myself from persons whom
they forewarned me to hold as enemies? I had before my eyes
the examples of thy prophets, who I saw had a similar contest
with the priests and prophets of their day, though these were
undoubtedly the rulers of the Church among the Israelitish
people. But thy prophets are not regarded as schismatics,
because, when they wished to revive religion which had fallen
into decay, they desisted not, although opposed with the utmost violence. They still remained in the unity of the Church,
though they were doomed to perdition by wicked priests, and
deemed unworthy of a place among men, not to say saints.
Confirmed by their example, I too persisted. Though denounced as a deserter of the Church, and threatened, I was
in no respect deterred, or induced to proceed less firmly and
boldly in opposing those who, in the character of pastors,
wasted thy Church with a more than impious tyranny. My
conscience told me how strong the zeal was with which I
burned for the unity of thy Church, provided thy truth were
made the bond of concord. As the commotions which followed
were not excited by me, so there is no ground for imputing
them to me.

"Thou, O Lord, knowest, and the fact itself has testified to
men, that the only thing I asked was, that all controversies
should be decided by thy word, that thus both parties might
unite with one mind to establish thy kingdom; and I declined
not to restore peace to the Church at the expense of my
head, if I were found to have been unnecessarily the cause of
tumult. But what did our opponents? Did they not instantly,
and like madmen, fly to fires, swords, and gibbets? Did they
not decide that their only security was in arms and cruelty?
Did they not instigate all ranks to the same fury? Did they
not spurn at all methods of pacification? To this it is owing

that a matter, which might at one time have been settled amicably, has blazed into such a contest. But although, amidst
the great confusion, the judgments of men were various, I am
freed from all fear, now that we stand at thy tribunal, where
equity, combined with truth, cannot but decide in favour of
innocence."

Such, Sadolet, is our pleading, not the fictitious one which
you, in order to aggravate our case, were pleased to devise,
but that the perfect truth of which is known to the good even
now, and will be made manifest to all creatures on that day.

Nor will those who, instructed by our preaching, have adhered to our cause, be at a loss what to say for themselves,
since each will be ready with this defence:—

"I, O Lord, as I had been educated from a boy, always professed the Christian faith. But at first I had no other reason
for my faith than that which then every where prevailed.
Thy word, which ought to have shone on all thy people like a
lamp, was taken away, or at least suppressed as to us. And lest
any one should long for greater light, an idea had been instilled into the minds of all, that the investigation of that
hidden celestial philosophy was better delegated to a few,
whom the others might consult as oracles—that the highest
knowledge befitting plebeian minds was to subdue themselves into obedience to the Church. Then, the rudiments in
which I had been instructed were of a kind which could
neither properly train me to the legitimate worship of thy
Deity, nor pave the way for me to a sure hope of salvation,
nor train me aright for the duties of the Christian life. I had
learned, indeed, to worship thee only as my God, but as the
true method of worshipping was altogether unknown to me, I
stumbled at the very threshold. I believed, as I had been
taught, that I was redeemed by the death of thy Son from
liability to eternal death, but the redemption I thought of
was one whose virtue could never reach me. I anticipated a
future resurrection, but hated to think of it, as being an event
most dreadful. And this feeling not only had dominion over
me in private, but was derived from the doctrine which was
then uniformly delivered to the people by their Christian
teachers. They, indeed, preached of thy clemency towards
men, but confined it to those who should show themselves
deserving of it. They, moreover, placed this desert in the
righteousness of works, so that he only was received into thy
favour who reconciled himself to thee by works. Nor, mean-

while, did they disguise the fact, that we are miserable sinners, that we often fall through infirmity of the flesh, and that to all, therefore, thy mercy behoved to be the common haven of salvation; but the method of obtaining it, which they pointed out, was by making satisfaction to thee for offences. Then, the satisfaction enjoined was, first, after confessing all our sins to a priest, suppliantly to ask pardon and absolution; and, secondly, by good to efface from thy remembrance our bad actions. Lastly, in order to supply what was still wanting, we were to add sacrifices and solemn expiations. Then, because thou wert a stern judge and strict avenger of iniquity, they showed how dreadful thy presence must be. Hence they bade us flee first to the saints, that by their intercession thou mightest be rendered exorable and propitious to us.

"When, however, I had performed all these things, though I had some intervals of quiet, I was still far off from true peace of conscience; for, whenever I descended into myself, or raised my mind to thee, extreme terror seized me—terror which no expiations nor satisfactions could cure. And the more closely I examined myself, the sharper the stings with which my conscience was pricked, so that the only solace which remained to me was to delude myself by obliviousness. Still, as nothing better offered, I continued the course which I had begun, when, lo, a very different form of doctrine started up, not one which led us away from the Christian profession, but one which brought it back to its fountain head, and, as it were, clearing away the dross, restored it to its original purity. Offended by the novelty, I lent an unwilling ear, and at first, I confess, strenuously and passionately resisted; for (such is the firmness or effrontery with which it is natural to men to persist in the course which they have once undertaken) it was with the greatest difficulty I was induced to confess that I had all my life long been in ignorance and error. One thing, in particular, made me averse to those new teachers, viz., reverence for the Church. But when once I opened my ears, and allowed myself to be taught, I perceived that this fear of derogating from the majesty of the Church was groundless. For they reminded me how great the difference is between schism from the Church, and studying to correct the faults by which the Church herself was contaminated. They spoke nobly of the Church, and showed the greatest desire to cultivate unity. And lest it should seem they quibbled on the term Church, they showed it was no new thing for Antichrists to preside there in place of pastors. Of this they produced not a few examples, from which it appeared that they aimed at nothing but the edification of the Church, and in that respect were similarly circumstanced with many of Christ's servants whom we ourselves included in the catalogue of saints. For inveighing more freely against the Roman Pontiff, who was reverenced as the Vicegerent of Christ, the Successor of Peter, and the Head of the Church, they excused themselves thus: Such titles as those are empty bugbears, by which the eyes of the pious ought not to be so blinded as not to venture to look at them, and sift the reality. It was when the world was plunged in ignorance and sloth, as in a deep sleep, that the Pope had risen to such an eminence; certainly neither appointed Head of the Church by the word of God, nor ordained by a legitimate act of the Church, but of his own accord, self-elected. Moreover, the tyranny which he let loose against the people of God was not to be endured, if we wished to have the kingdom of Christ amongst us in safety.

"And they wanted not most powerful arguments to confirm all their positions. First, they clearly disposed of every thing that was then commonly adduced to establish the primacy of the Pope. When they had taken away all these props, they also, by the word of God, tumbled him from his lofty height. On the whole, they made it clear and palpable, to learned and unlearned, that the true order of the Church had then perished—that the keys under which the discipline of the Church is comprehended had been altered very much for the worse—that Christian liberty had fallen—in short, that the kingdom of Christ was prostrated when this primacy was reared up. They told me, moreover, as a means of pricking my conscience, that I could not safely connive at these things as if they concerned me not; that so far art thou from patronising any voluntary error, that even he who is led astray by mere ignorance does not err with impunity. This they proved by the testimony of thy Son, (Matth. 15:14,) 'If the blind lead the blind, both shall fall into the ditch.' My mind being now prepared for serious attention, I at length perceived, as if light had broken in upon me, in what a stye of error I had wallowed, and how much pollution and impurity I had thereby contracted. Being exceedingly alarmed at the misery into which I had fallen, and much more at that which threatened me in the view of eternal death, I, as in duty bound, made it my first business to betake myself to thy way, condemning my past life, not without groans and tears.

And now, O Lord, what remains to a wretch like me, but,
instead of defence, earnestly to supplicate thee not to judge
according to its deserts that fearful abandonment of thy word,
from which, in thy wondrous goodness, thou hast at last delivered me."

Now, Sadolet, if you please, compare this pleading with
that which you have put into the mouth of your plebeian.
It will be strange if you hesitate which of the two you ought
to prefer. For the safety of that man hangs by a thread whose
defence turns wholly on this—that he has constantly adhered
to the religion handed down to him from his forefathers. At
this rate, Jews, and Turks, and Saracens, would escape the
judgment of God. Away, then, with this vain quibbling at
a tribunal which will be erected not to approve the authority
of man, but to condemn all flesh of vanity and falsehood,
and vindicate the truth of God only.

But were I disposed to contend with you in trifles, what
picture might I paint, I say not, of a Pope, or a Cardinal,
or any reverend Prelate whatsoever of your faction, (in what
colours almost every man of them might, without any great
stretch of ingenuity, be exhibited, you well know,) but of
any, even the most select among your doctors? For his condemnation, there would, assuredly, be no need either to
adduce doubtful conjectures against him, or devise false accusations. He would be burdened heavily enough with such
as are certainly just. But that I may not seem to imitate what
I blame in you, I decline this mode of pleading. I will only
exhort these men to turn for once to themselves, and consider with what fidelity they feed the Christian people, who
cannot have any other food than the Word of their God. And
that they may not flatter themselves too much, because they
now act their part with great applause, and for the most part,
amid favourable acclamations, let them remember, that they
have not yet come to the conclusion; at which, assuredly,
they will not have a theatre on which to vend their smoke
with impunity, and, by their tricks, ensnare credulous minds,
but will stand or fall by the decision of God himself, whose
judgment will not be regulated by the popular gale, but by
his own inflexible justice; and who will not only inquire into
each man's deeds, but put to proof the hidden sincerity or
iniquity of his heart. I dare not pronounce on all without
exception; and yet, how many of them feel in their consciences, that, in contending against us, they are hiring out
their services to men, rather than (giving them) to God?

While, throughout your Letter, you treat us without mercy, towards its conclusion, you pour out the venom of your bitterness upon us with open mouth. But though your invectives by no means hurt us, and have already been partly answered, I would yet ask, what could make you think of accusing us of avarice? Think you our Reformers were so dull as not to perceive from the very outset, that they were entering on a course most adverse to gain and lucre? And, when they charged you with greediness, did they not see that they were necessarily binding themselves to temperance and frugality, if they were not to become ridiculous even to children? When they showed that the method of correcting that greediness was to disburden pastors of their excessive wealth, in order that they might be more at liberty to care for the Church, did they not spontaneously shut against themselves the avenue to wealth? For what riches now remained to which they might aspire? What! Would not the shortest road to riches and honours have been to have transacted with you at the very first, on the terms which were offered? How much would your Pontiff then have paid to many for their silence? How much would he pay for it, even at the present day? If they are actuated in the least degree by avarice, why do they cut off all hope of improving their fortune, and prefer to be thus perpetually wretched, rather than enrich themselves without difficulty, and in a twinkling? But ambition, forsooth, withholds them! What ground you had for this other insinuation I see not, since those who first engaged in this cause could expect nothing else than to be spurned by the whole world, and those who afterwards adhered to it exposed themselves knowingly and willingly to endless insults and revilings from every quarter. But where is this fraud and inward malice? No suspicion of such things cleaves to us. Talk of them rather in your sacred Consistory, where they are in operation every day.

As I hasten to a conclusion, I am compelled to pass by your calumny, that, leaning entirely to our own judgment, we find not in the whole Church one individual to whom we think deference is due. That it is a calumny, I have already sufficiently demonstrated. For, although we hold that the Word of God alone lies beyond the sphere of our judgment, and that Fathers and Councils are of authority only in so far as they accord with the rule of the Word, we still give to Councils and Fathers such rank and honour as it is meet for them to hold, under Christ.

But the most serious charge of all is, that we have attempted to dismember the Spouse of Christ. Were that true, both you and the whole world might well regard us as desperate. But I will not admit the charge, unless you can make out that the Spouse of Christ is dismembered by those who desire to present her as a chaste virgin to Christ,—who are animated by a degree of holy zeal to preserve her spotless for Christ,—who, seeing her polluted by base seducers, recall her to conjugal fidelity,—who unhesitatingly wage war against all the adulterers whom they detect laying snares for her chastity. And what but this have we done? Had not your faction of a Church attempted, nay, violated her chastity, by strange doctrines? Had she not been violently prostituted by your numberless superstitions? Had she not been defiled by that vilest species of adultery, the worship of images? And because, forsooth, we did not suffer you so to insult the sacred chamber of Christ, we are said to have lacerated his Spouse! But I tell you that that laceration, of which you falsely accuse us, is witnessed not obscurely among yourselves;—a laceration not only of the Church, but of Christ himself, who is there beheld miserably mangled. How can the Church adhere to her Spouse, while she has him not in safety? For where is the safety of Christ, while the glory of his justice, and holiness, and wisdom, is transferred elsewhere?

But it seems, before we kindled the strife, all was tranquillity and perfect peace! True! among pastors, and also among the common people, stupor and sloth had caused, that there were almost no controversies respecting religion. But in the schools, how lustily did sophists brawl? You cannot, therefore, take credit for a tranquil kingdom, when there was tranquillity for no other reason than because Christ was silent. I admit, that, on the revival of the gospel, great disputes arose, where all was quietness before. But that is unjustly imputed to our Reformers, who, during the whole course of their proceedings, desired nothing more than that religion being revived, the Churches, which discord had scattered and dispersed, might be gathered together into true unity. And not to go back upon old transactions, what sacrifices did they, on a late occasion, decline to make, merely that they might procure peace to the Churches? But all their efforts are rendered vain by your opposition. For, while they desire peace, that along with it the kingdom of Christ may flourish, and you, on the other hand, think that all which is gained to Christ is lost to you, it is not strange that you strenuously resist. And you have arts by which you can in one day overturn all that they accomplish for the glory of Christ in many months. I will not overwhelm you with words, because one word will make the matter clear. Our Reformers offered to render an account of their doctrine. If overcome in argument, they decline not to submit. To whom, then, is it owing that the Church enjoys not perfect peace, and the light of truth? Go now, and charge us as seditious, in not permitting the Church to be quiet!

But, (that you might not omit any thing which might tend to prejudice our cause,) since, during these few years, many sects have sprung up, you, with your usual candour, lay the blame upon us. See with what fairness, or even with what plausibility! If we deserve hatred on that account, the Christian name also must, in times of old, have deserved it from the ungodly. Therefore, either cease to molest us on this subject, or openly declare that the Christian religion, which begets so many tumults in the world, ought to be banished from the memory of man! It ought not to hurt our cause in the least, that Satan has tried in all ways to impede the work of Christ. It were more to the point to inquire which party has devotedly opposed itself to all the sects which have arisen. It is plain, that while you were idle and fast asleep, we alone bore all the brunt.

The Lord grant, Sadolet, that you and all your party may at length perceive, that the only true bond of Ecclesiastical unity would exist if Christ the Lord, who hath reconciled us to God the Father, were to gather us out of our present dispersion into the fellowship of his body, that so, through his one Word and Spirit, we might join together with one heart and one soul.

Basle, September 1, 1539.

ANTIDOTE TO THE COUNCIL OF TRENT[1]

[The reformers had called for the reform of the Church. The antidote, published the year after Luther's death in 1547, marks the first major Protestant response to the reforming activity of the Roman Catholic Church undertaken since the start of the Reformation. It discloses that the issues which divided the two groups were wider than the concept of reform as originally envisaged. Calvin's general comments on various sessions are clear enough without reference to what the Council of Trent said. When Calvin comments on particular canons of the Council of Trent, they are included in parentheses so that the contrast and context is clear to the reader.]

CALVIN'S PREFACE TO THE ANTIDOTE

The name of SACRED COUNCIL is held in such reverence in the Christian Church, that the very mention of it produces an immediate effect not only on the ignorant but on men of gravity and sound judgment. And doubtless, as the usual remedy which God employed from the beginning in curing the disease of his Church was for pious and holy pastors to meet, and, after invoking his aid, to determine what the Holy Spirit dictated, Councils are deservedly honoured by all the godly. There is this difference, however,— the vulgar, stupified with excessive admiration, do not afterwards make any use of their judgment, whereas those of sounder sense allow themselves, step by step, and modestly, indeed, but still allow themselves to inquire before they absolutely assent. And so it ought to be, in order that our faith, instead of rashly subscribing to the naked decisions of men, may submit to God only.

[1] [Reprinted from *Tracts, containing Antidote to the Council of Trent, . . . ,* Vol. III, translated from the original Latin and French by Henry Beveridge (Edinburgh: Printed for the Calvin Translation Society, 1851), pp. 30–54, 57–60, 67–77, 85–91, 108–62, 171–88.]

This is objected to by those who are persuaded, or at least would persuade others, that no Council whatever, provided it have been duly called, can err—inasmuch as it is guided by the Holy Spirit. Accordingly they insist that everything proceeding from it shall be received, like an oracle, without controversy. How much wiser is Augustine who, from his singular modesty, indeed bestows no small honour upon Councils, and yet ceases not to observe the moderation which I have described. Writing against the Arian, Maximinus, he says: "I ought neither to adduce the Council of Nice, nor you that of Ariminum, as if to prejudge the question. I am not determined by the authority of the latter, nor you by that of the former. Founding on the authority of Scripture not peculiar to either, but the common witness of both, fact contends with fact, plea with plea, reason with reason." So much liberty does this holy man concede to himself and others, that he will not allow the Council of Nice to operate as a previous judgment, unless the truth of the case be plainly established from Scripture.

But there is no occasion at present to dwell longer on these Ancient Councils. I have to treat of THE COUNCIL OF TRENT, which was of a very different description. When many corruptions were seen in the Church, when grave disputes on doctrine had arisen, a Council was long and ardently desired by many who hoped that by this means all evils would be ended. In this, indeed, they erred. For as matters are at present constituted, those possessed of any discernment easily perceive that no alleviation of evils is to be hoped from those who have the power of calling and holding a Council. Still as no better method appeared, very many persons not ill-disposed, who wished well to the Church, anticipated some good from a Council. Accordingly, being desired by many, it was at length demanded, as it were, by the common voice of Christendom.

Of the causes which delayed it for a considerable time, the more discerning are aware. For as to those causes which the Roman Pontiff alleges in his Bull, whosoever does not see them to be impudent fictions is more than blind. The causes which induced him to weave all possible delays, he himself best knows; and yet we can in some measure conjecture. Some think he was afraid lest the Council might as a kind of vulgar thing be held cheap, both by princes and people, if it were at once so easily obtained. For long expectation, provided it does not tire out men's patience, usu-

ally adds a new value to things. I think, however, that there
was a different reason. Although he knew that the Council
which he would give would be nothing else than a hired
crew of his own followers, among whom he himself alone
would be eminent; still, such is the power of an evil conscience, that he trembled at the very mention of a Council.
For with such dissolute and unbridled license is the Papal
tyranny exercised, that those who are most desirous to preserve it in being, have no doubt as to the necessity of curbing
it. Hence, not without cause, he endeavoured by spinning
out the time to escape from any diminution of his power.
This afterwards appeared still more clearly; for all the steps
which he took in ordering his Council, contrary to the received custom, are so many proofs of the distrust which I
have mentioned. To omit an infinite number of other things,
why were three legates sent but just that they might operate
as mutual checks, and each prevent the other from attempting anything? In his own band, though they are all his sworn
serfs, he found none whom he could trust.

Such were the private views of the Pope. A different view
was taken by those who are unwilling that the present state
of the Church, be it what it may, should be disturbed. They
held that anything was better than to enter on a regular
discussion of the subjects debated in the present day. Why
so? Partly because it seems to them unbecoming to raise
discussion, in any form, as to human decrees which have
once been received; partly because violent possession delights them more than free government in any shape. For
how few are those who now defend the Papacy under the
pretext of zeal for the Church, who do not desire the liberty
of the Christian people to be so crushed, that no one may
dare a whisper about correcting the vices of the Church,
or who do not clamour that a Council is needless, and that
atrocious injustice is done to prior decisions, if they are not
adhered to without any mention of a Council. What else is
this, they ask, but to do what has been already done? And
what license will be given in future to innovation and disturbance, if we do not acquiesce in things once decided? If
the decisions already given are oracles of the Holy Spirit,
what can be gained by new discussion? All this is easily refuted. Questions are agitated in the present day which were
never before duly discussed; and it is plain that both the
doctrine and the whole administration of the Papacy are so
much at variance with the majority of ancient Councils, that

nothing more opposite can be imagined. Moreover, the diseases under which the Church labours are so various and deadly, that at no period was it ever more necessary to hold a Council, if indeed there were any hope that a lawful Council could be obtained. It is apparent, therefore, that those who thus speak have not the least sense of true piety, but at ease, and almost with joy, contemplate the miserable distraction of the Church. Their assertion, that matters which have once been decided cannot again be lawfully agitated, is too absurd. For in this view, wherein does the Holy Word of God differ from the decrees of man? If they would go back for their authorities to those purer ages which were distinguished for learning and piety, they might perhaps be listened to; but the Councils by whose decisions they wish to fetter us are those in which nothing but the grossest ignorance appears, united to barbarian ferocity. That this is strictly true will be made plain in its proper place. It furnishes the true reason for their talking so loudly of final judgments already pronounced.

Moreover, if hitherto there was any doubt how great the difference is between a Council and the tribunal of the Holy Spirit, from which there is no appeal, a striking illustration has been given us in THE COUNCIL OF TRENT. They contend that a Council cannot err, because it represents the Church. What if the latter position be denied to be true? But in order to determine the point we must, I presume, see who the men are that compose it. Perhaps forty Bishops or so are present. I do not keep to a number, nor much care about it, as it is of little consequence. Let the advocates of Councils answer me in good faith. Were any one to review them all in order, how many of them would he not contemn? Nay, when the venerable Fathers look in each other's faces, it must be impossible for them not to feel ashamed; for they know themselves, and are not ignorant of the opinion which they have of each other. Hence, if you take away the name of Council, the whole Papacy will confess that all the bishops who attended were nothing but dregs.

I am willing, however, to let other nations keep their ornaments untouched. I will only ask my French countrymen what price they set on the portion which they contributed? They doubtless hold the kingdom of France to be one of the leading branches of the Church. Why, then, it sent but two bishops, one from Nantes, and another from Clermont, both equally dull and unlearned. The latter was not long ago deemed as ridiculous as a buffoon, and so libidinous, that he was wont to track out dens of infamy with the scent of a pointer, till he placed himself under the discipline of a notorious Parisian, Sosia. After this he became suddenly wise, if men can so easily be made wise by a lady of the school of Francis Picart. It is clear that the master is completely devoid of brains, belongs to the class of fanatics, and is little better than a madman. The Archbishop of Aix I scarcely count a Frenchman. He of Asti, however, as is usual with curious men, was present as an idle spectator. I ask you, my countrymen, who among you can persuade himself that anything which even a countless multitude of such men could have vented proceeded from the Holy Spirit? The two of whom I speak never had a taste of even the first rudiments of theology. How miserable, then, will the condition of the Christian Church be, if everything which pleased them, and a few no better than they, is to be held oracular! And yet very many are so thoughtless, that when they hear of the publication of the Decrees of the Holy Council, they reflect not that the authors of them are persons to whom they would not give the least credit in the paltriest question. Did this occur to them they would instantly reject with indignation and trample under foot what they now inconsiderately kiss. Why? Is there anything which their judgment approves? Not at all. But reverence for the Council blinds them. What folly, when you know the ass to tremble at his lion's skin!

But here it may be objected by the opposite party, that the decision did not rest with the bishops alone. I am aware. And this I particularly wished to observe. For there are certain garrulous and audacious monks, some of whom hunt after mitres, and others after cardinals' hats, while all of them sell their prattle to the Roman Pontiff. Let us assume, however, that they are excellent persons, and theologians of no common erudition. This, however, I know, that the venerable Fathers, on whose nod all religion depends, are preceded verbally by a set of sophists whose *dicta* they afterwards chant. What end then does it serve for them to mount a lofty seat, and then like demigods give out what a lower bench has dictated? Where is that representation of the Church to which they bind the Holy Spirit, if they are compelled precariously to borrow elsewhere what they need—if they would not be silent or speak in error? Your axiom is, that whatever be the meeting to which you give the name of UNIVERSAL COUNCIL, there the Holy Spirit presides, and nothing can proceed from it that is not heavenly and divine. Meanwhile, you appoint hungry, venal-tongued monks, to whom this fancied spirit of yours must listen. They, in long and formal discussions, debate whatever is to be defined by the fathers: so I have heard; they keep quarrelling and croaking away like the frogs of Aristophanes. At length those famous decrees are concocted and afterwards given out as the responses of the Holy Spirit. And why should I misrepresent in a matter which is perfectly notorious? It is certain that there is no school so obscure as not to look down with contempt on anything coming from the theologians of Trent. What then? Shall we think that the moment they have changed their place, they receive a sudden afflatus, as if, like the priestesses of Apollo, they had entered the Delphian cauldron? Absurd! Were it to be announced to-day to the Sorbonne at Paris, that the Fathers of Trent differed in one iota from their decisions, the brains of its doctors would instantly warm, and they would rush forth to the combat. Not only would they set the authority of the Council at nought, but assail every man of them by name with the fiercest invectives. But here, if they give a white ball in support of their absurdest dreams, all the schools of France, Spain, Germany, and Italy will vie in applause. How dishonest then to obtrude and call upon the Christian world to worship that which they in their hearts utterly disregard!

But suppose we assume that those disputants who sweat in forging decrees are not only wondrously acute and learned, but are angels just come down from heaven; and suppose we also pardon our opponents the great absurdity of holding that a Council, which they proudly affirm to be guided by the immediate inspiration of the Spirit, goes a begging to a few individuals for that which it sends over the whole world as of divine origin—not even thus will the Council of Trent obtain a particle of credit. For nothing is determined there save at the nod of the Roman Pontiff. In future, then, let them have done with their bombast, that he who rejects the decrees of the Council fights not with men but with God—that they are nothing but instruments, while he is the President who guides their minds and tongues by his Spirit. Were it so, I hold that they themselves insult the Holy Spirit by reprimanding him through their Pope, to whose decision and censure everything is subjected. I speak of what is perfectly notorious. As soon as any decree is framed, couriers flee off to Rome, and beg pardon and peace at the feet of their idol.

The holy father hands over what the couriers have brought to
his private advisers for examination. They curtail, add, and
change as they please. The couriers return, and a sederunt
is appointed. The notary reads over what no one dares to disapprove, and the asses shake their ears in assent. Behold the
oracle which imposes religious obligations on the whole
world! Why do they not openly confess the thing as it is—
that ten or twenty monks, whose labours they have hired,
concoct the decrees—that the Pope puts his censorial pen
through whatever does not please him, and approves of the
rest—that nothing is left to the Council but the burden of
publishing? In ancient times, after the Roman Senate had
deliberated, the plebeians examined; but the Pope, by no
means contented with examining, arrogates right, moreover,
to correct anything that does not please him in the deliberation of the Council. Presumptuously does he so act, if he
thinks that the Holy Spirit is presiding there. We, however, I
presume, may with impunity despise it, because we are
aware of its being composed by such doctors, and corrected
by such an Aristarchus. The proclamation of the Council is
entitled to no more weight than the cry of an auctioneer.

But not to preface longer, should I, while trusting to the
sure testimony of the Word of God, call the decrees of a
Council in question, methinks I have proved that there is no
reason why sober readers should charge me with presumption. But now, who that is not more than fatuous can be angry with me, when compelled by the necessity of maintaining
the truth, I hesitate not to expose an ape though adorned
with purple, and let all see him to be the ape he is? I have
already amply shewn that those Neptunian fathers are not
so formidable with their Trident as that one may not boldly
flagellate them with the Word of God, nor so sacred as to
make it impious to touch them. But to my view that is not
now the question. The mask which the Roman Pontiff has
placed on the eyes of men is one by which no seeing man
can be deceived. When, ten years ago, a Council was everywhere talked of, and the belief accordingly was, that the
Pope could no longer by equivocation escape from collecting
his flocks in good earnest, and bulls of citation had begun to
fly about, I for my part conjectured that the summonses
founded on the bulls would gradually go off into smoke. For
I remembered another bull of Mantua, under the pontificate
of Pius II., which, after much swelling talk, had instantly
vanished. But if a Council were at length to be assembled,

I considered with myself that the Roman Pontiff would use every means to dazzle the eyes of the simple with no ordinary splendour: and, to confess the truth, this thought made me exceedingly anxious. As to one thing there was no doubt, viz., that whoever should be allowed to sit and give their opinion, all of them, some ensnared by ambition, others blinded by avarice, others inflamed with rage, would be mortal enemies to sound doctrine, and being bound together in secret conspiracy to establish the tyranny of the Pope, would exert themselves to destroy the kingdom of Christ. There might, perhaps, be a very few unaffected by this cruel and impious feeling, but still without the manliness to resist it in others. I therefore immediately concluded, that under such unjust judges, the truth would be oppressed without being heard. For it was not even to be hoped that any one pious and right-hearted man would venture, at the expense of his life, to purchase one hour's audience. Meanwhile many unskilful, though otherwise honest persons would be imposed upon, by the plausible axiom that the decision of the Church must be acquiesced in. Thanks to the Pope for furnishing us with a display which our very children will hold in derision! I ask nothing of my readers, however, but to lay prejudice in favour of either party aside, and come unbiassed to the discussion. This they can only do by withdrawing their eye from persons, and fixing it on the subject.

ON THE PREFATORY DISCOURSE BY THE LEGATES
IN THE FIRST SESSION, AND OTHER
PRELIMINARY MATTERS OF THE COUNCIL

It is well! At length the Romanists confess, that the fearful distraction of the Church at present, which all good men deplore, is in a great measure attributable to themselves. Any one, not very shrewd, on hearing this candid confession, will forthwith conceive good hopes. And the exhortations which follow exhibit no ordinary zeal for the renovation of the Church. Thus, that part in which they declare that none can succour their falling affairs save Christ the only Shepherd, that therefore they must implore and listen to him alone; that all will go prosperously if he guides all their actions and presides over them; that all other counsels, other arts, are but leaky cisterns which let out water; that the wisdom of man does nought but further provoke the anger of God, and increase evils rather than cure them—of all that part, I say—how strongly it breathes of piety! But it is apparent from the acts which followed, that those were vain words given to the winds. Nay, they do not wait till a judgment is formed from their acts. For in regard to the doctrine of salvation, which they have wholly adulterated by their impious and abominable fictions; in regard to the sacraments which they have utterly vitiated, and which they prostitute to a vile and shameless trafficking, they find nothing in themselves to correct. How little aid, then, do they bring to ruined affairs! And truly we can expect nothing from the Tridentines who serve under Neptune but what is of a watery nature, when the business to be undertaken is the Reformation of the Church. But when persecution is to rage against the innocent, and impious tyranny is to be confirmed by the blood of the godly, they at once blaze into flame. Indeed, something resembling this may be seen within the realm of Neptune, when with roaring noise he lashes the waves into foam. Soon, however, it bursts by its own tumescence, and the uproar immediately subsides. They, in like manner, as soon as the smoke has cleared away from their forehead, shew without disguise what the nature of their conduct is to be in regard to the principal head. They are to cling with a death-grasp to all their impieties, while we who desire nothing but the reign of Christ, and maintain the pure doctrine of the Gospel, are to be judged heretics. For thus, before cognisance is taken, they declare all heretical who have dared at this time to move a whit against the received doctrine of the Roman Church. What is this? The whole Christian world was in expectation of a Council in which controverted points might be regularly discussed. These men avow that they sit for no other end than to condemn whatever is not to their mind. Therefore, let no man any longer deceive himself: From their own mouths we hear that this pompous Council is held not for inquiry, but to establish that kind of doctrine, be it what it may, with which monks and sophists have imbued the world; that all rites shall remain by whatever superstition they may have crept in; and all the fetters of conscience be drawn into a tighter knot.

Can any one still be so stupid as to think of seeking any alleviation of our evils from a Council? We complain that the whole doctrine of godliness is adulterated by impious dogmas; that the whole worship of God is vitiated by foul and disgraceful superstitions; that the pure institution of the sacraments has been supplanted by horrible sacrilege; that their use has been converted into a profane trafficking; that poor souls, which ought to have been ruled by the doctrine of Christ, are oppressed by cruel bondage; that nothing is seen in the Christian Church that is not deformed and debased; that the grace of Christ not only lies half-buried, but is partly torn to pieces, partly altogether extinguished. All these complaints, which we have made for many years, and in published books, and which we make in our daily sermons, we are prepared to prove well founded, whenever a freedom of utterance is given. Such is the goodness of our cause, that it does not at all fear the light. And many are the tens of thousands so firmly persuaded of it, that they desired no farther investigation. Still, lest the Christian world might lay aside dissension, and unite in holy concord, a Council is summoned. Ought not its members to have discussed controverted points before they prejudged either themselves or others? They allow nothing of the kind. Nay, should any one have attempted to change one tittle of their customs, they hold him as already condemned.

Behold the specious Reformation, with the promise of which they have hitherto amused the world! The many portentous idolatries by which the Church of God is deformed—the many defilements of superstitions—the many profanations of sacred things—the vast sink of errors must not be touched. There is to be no diminution of the tyrannical yoke of impious laws by which miserable consciences have been ensnared; but all who desire any change are to be judged heretics. Where is that hearing which many were simple enough to promise themselves? If religion had any hold of their minds, nay, if they had any belief of a God, would they so confidently, and, as it were, in jest, skip over matters of so much moment? The glory of God is in question, the everlasting kingdom of Christ, the safety of the whole Church. They are compelled, in compliance so far with the common wishes of the Christian people, to hold a Council. They, however, premise, that they come for the very purpose of cutting off all hope of reform. For these words are the same in effect as if they had plainly and distinctly declared that the future would be no better than the past. And yet in thus acting they exhibit nothing foreign to their character. For in the overthrow of piety and the corruptions of sacred things, which in the present day all good men deplore, there is nothing of which those men who sit as judges do not deserve the blame. Do we wonder, then, if, while they themselves are the accused parties, they proceed forthwith, without touching the cause, to pass sentence in their own favour? It is more than absurd to leave the power of judging to those whose criminality is under discussion. And yet, what do they gain, but just to make all who have eyes aware that they do not in the least repent of their crimes while they pertinaciously defend everything of which we accuse them? They will not succeed, however, in getting a sanction to their impiety, because they are themselves obstinate.

Some one will now ask, What then do they hold forth as the benefits to be derived from a Council? To put an end to wars among Christian princes and give tranquillity to the Church. Folly! For who knows not that the Romanists are bellows which fan the flame of warlike commotions wherever their blast is applied? The only thing remaining, therefore, is to restore lapsed discipline, especially in their own clergy. With what faith they have exerted themselves in this direction is apparent from their acts; for they there, as we shall see, open up a way by which everything which has been allowed in time past is to be allowed in future. But to prevent it being thought that after all this costly show nothing has been done, there will, perhaps, be some reformation in caps and shoes, and other parts of dress. While they in this way mock God and men, they are not ashamed to personate the Prophets, as if the three Legates of Antichrist were the three intercessors of whom Ezekiel speaks, who first threw themselves into the breach to appease the anger of God. They make an humble confession of sins—they mention groans and tears, the signs of repentance. I believe the person employed as their reader on this occasion must have found it difficult to keep from laughing.

But while they wish to act as players, one expression escapes from them, which I think should be regarded as a divine prediction; for, like Caiaphas of old, what is to prevent the enemies of Christ from prophesying? They declare that the Holy Spirit is not present with them if they do not accuse themselves; they say that he will not be present so long as they refuse to listen to their sins. I receive the oracle. Afterwards, indeed, to give eclat to their assembly, they falsely state that they see tears. But while the case itself proclaims that they remained obstinate in establishing the kingdom of impiety, we believe, according to their prediction, that nothing governed them less than the Holy Spirit. And who sees not that they were forced, against their inclination, by the secret impulse of God, as if they had been put to the question, to make this confession? They adduce Ezekiel as a witness, who declares that God will not answer the people if they do not first acknowledge their own abominations and those of their fathers. Where, then, is such an acknowledgment on their part? Let them be silent, then, or confess that they send forth the figments of their own brain at random. But if I have not yet convinced all men of this, at least let the reader remember, that when we come to discussion, truth itself must decide whether their decrees proceeded from the inspiration of the Holy Spirit. Formerly they gave out, that all decisions of a Council were, without exception, divine responses. Now, God has extorted this confession from them as if they had been malefactors on the wheel. Whether the Spirit of God presided over the Council must be decided by this test—Did they condemn their own and their fathers' abominations, and turn to true repentance? Let any one who would not be voluntarily deceived try the following canons by this rule. If I do not make it clearer than day that there was not a whit more of repentance in them than in the worst of the Israelites, let it be, as they insist, that it was the voice of God, and not of man. Therefore, as they choose to compare their crew with Ezra, Nehemiah, and the other leaders of the ancient people, and say, by the mouth of their reader, that in the spirit of sorrow they duly lamented their own sins and those of the people, let them, I say, be forgiven for their insolence in putting an atrocious affront on the holy servants of God, by comparing them to a filthy herd of swine, and let them with dry eyes impudently boast of their tears; for what is it that they may not do? Still they cannot deprive us of the liberty of forming our decision from facts rather than words. Herein, indeed, they are very ridiculous. After declaring that they have abundantly wept over their sins in godly sorrow, they exhort themselves and others to open fountains of tears. The rhetorician must surely have been oblivious when he composed this declaration for them: or what if he wished to expose them to derision, as they deserved? The latter may be the true explanation, but I pass it as a matter with which I have no concern.

It were irksome to follow out every single point, nor is it necessary; for they so mingle praise and exhortation, that there is nothing in either but fiction and sheer falsehood. When they accuse our churches of expelling their pastors, substituting laymen in their stead, confounding orders, plundering ecclesiastical property, impeding the course of the word of God, our answer to their accusations is at hand. First, they give the name of pastors to those of whose expulsion they complain. How long will this title be usurped by men who have nothing pastoral but the badge of a silver staff? The confounding of orders which they deplore is nothing else than a moderate restoration of discipline. They insist that they themselves shall be counted sacred in consequence of having been anointed. Fortified with this privilege, they hold that their vices cannot be touched. Hence, provided they may do as they please, everything will be duly ordered. If this sacred order is violated, all things are in their judgment as much confounded as if the heavens were falling. As to the plundering of property, I wish our people were as well prepared to give satisfaction to God as we are to make a candid and true defence against our accusers. That idle-bellies have been deprived of the means which they were swallowing up, I admit. Let us see whether anything was taken by robbery from the Church. It is certain that that which the venerable Legates now dedicate to the Church had been seized by robbers. It is certain that it was not only spent in stuffing their gullet, but basely squandered on debauchery, gaming, theatrical indecencies, and in other ways not a whit better. The poor were neglected. They more frequently squeezed something out of the teachers of schools than aided them with salaries. Now, on the other hand, if the administration is not yet so pure and holy as were to be wished, at least godly pastors are maintained to feed souls with the doctrine of salvation; something is expended on schools; the poor have ten times more distributed to them than they used to get. Some portion also is bestowed on other uses, neither profane nor liable to censure. See why they charge our adherents with plunder! But what have I to say to the charge of impeding the course of the word of God? It is a very serious charge. I am altogether at a loss how to meet it. Nefarious extinguishers of pure doctrine! dare you impute to us the very sacrilege of which you are guilty before God and his angels and the whole world? Yet I wonder not that they spoke so in such a meeting—a meeting to which they knew nothing would be palatable but what was villanously said.

But there were other monitors whose business it was to

correct any omission or error of the Legates. There are extant some speeches delivered by monks who, we are to believe, were a kind of channels through which the Holy Spirit flowed out of the mouths of the fathers. There is also one by a bishop, I know not who, than which nothing can be imagined more absurd. The sum of the whole is, that we are to be put down by brief decisions, because it must remain a settled point, that before our friends appeared everything in their doctrine was good and pure. Because Isaiah promises that the Lord will be a wall and rampart to Jerusalem, one Sotus (which in French means stupid and fatuous) devises a twofold bulwark for the Church—one of divine, and another of human laws; and in this foolish imagination he exults as if he were heading a magnificent triumph over us. Could I lose labour and time in hunting down such a creature? To me it is more than enough to have pointed to it with the finger. Because cities are fortified with a wall and rampart, the Lord declares that he alone will serve for both. But the interpretation of Sotus transfers the rampart to human laws, and teaches that the ruins of the Church cannot be restored in any other way than by filling up the breach which we have made.

Another, named Marinarius, exhales smoke from his Carmelite kitchen, and says that our gospel liberty is a pretext for all kinds of corruption; and to give his oration a sprinkling of elegance, he exclaims,—O, impure and vile! Although they have no shame, they will not dare to deny that vice stalks among them with greater freedom than with us. That with us, assuredly, there is more real and chaste severity and a stricter discipline, our daily sermons testify; and yet this dog, just emerged from the mire of a fetid cloister, is not ashamed thus to bark at us. But, after abolishing vows, throwing off celibacy, contemning holy prayers, treading fasting under our feet, and rejecting the customs of our fathers, we have seized on the opportunity of sinning as the leading principle of our life! What kind of life, then, did the Apostles lead? They knew nothing of the celibacy for which the Papists contend; under them there was no mention of vows; they laid no burden on the conscience as to the choice of meats. Contented with the rule which their Lord had prescribed, they attempted not to fetter any by laws and traditions. There is nothing of which we are calumniously accused which might not be equally charged against the Apostles. The kind of vows of which we disapprove is evident from our writings. Into

what a sink of impurity the whole world has been plunged
by their celibacy, which we desire to change for holy marriage, is but too well known. When Paul censured celibacy
in younger widows, his reason was because some of them
had gone over to Satan. At the present day it is well ascertained that there is more obscenity in the cloisters of monks
and nuns than in common dens of infamy. Wherever priests
penetrate they leave some impress of their unchastity; as if
they had been prohibited from marriage solely for the purpose of giving free scope to their lust in any quarter. And
shall all this experience not have the effect of inducing us
to relieve them from the necessity of celibacy? He falsely
asserts that we condemn Christian fasting and holy prayer;
but he does it securely, because he knew that he would receive the more applause the more bacchanalian rage he
vented against us. Meanwhile, this worthy vindicator of gospel liberty describes all the servile superstitions of the papacy
as its proper fruits, solace, delight, and nourishment! It is
strange he did not also call them celestial nectar and am-
brosia! What can you make of an animal like this? Paul
teaches that Christian liberty consists in the free use of things
indifferent; and though, as is becoming, he makes the external
use subordinate to charity, he allows no fetters to be laid on
the conscience, and carefully admonishes us to beware of
being entangled with the yoke of bondage. This gentle son
of Venus (for both his names smack of the sea) affirms that
liberty will not be safe unless it be buried under an infinite
load of laws and ceremonies; and at length exclaims, that
we execrate the approved sayings of the fathers, the sacraments, the honour due to saints, and all that is sacred. By
these fictions Papists were formerly wont to stir up the
blinded populace against us. Now, it is easy to infer what
opinion they have of each other, when this illiberal license
of lying catches applause in their most sacred convention.

In what respect, pray, do we impair the honour of the
saints, unless it be in forbidding idols to be made of them?
Is it honour to the saints to rob God of his honour and transfer it to them, that they may be worshipped promiscuously
with God? They will deny that they do so, by bringing in
their distinction of *dulia* and *latria*. An excellent method,
forsooth, of avoiding idolatry when they distinguish between
kinds of worship altogether similar by employing two voca-
bles, just as horses in a stall are kept separate by their
tethers. Meanwhile, they allow the saints to be worshipped

indifferently with God. What is it that the prophets everywhere condemn in the people of Israel, but just that they
give incense to their idols, provide sacred feasts, pay gifts,
dedicate altars, and prostrate themselves before them? In all
these things the Papists go beyond the Israelites. For they
kindle lamps and tapers at the dead images of the dead,
sprinkle incense, celebrate their memory in solemn feasts,
place them on altars, make oblations to them, carry them
about on their shoulders in procession, undertake long pil-
grimages to visit them, bow down before them and pray to
them. Nay, illiterate females and almost all the peasantry,
in praying to Hugo and Lubin, use the very form of prayer
which was given us by the Son of God. Thus a block of wood
will be our Father in heaven. So far is any one from opposing
this horrid sacrilege, that priests and monks sing out, Well
done! Well done! And it is made a serious charge against us
that we have studied to purify the holy worship of God from
all these profanations. Hence we are styled enemies of all
that is sacred! And yet no new thing has happened to us;
for the same was said of the Prophets and Apostles.

I say nothing of those charges which will be better discussed in their own place. Only there is one which ought
not to be omitted, viz., that all we aim at is under the pretext
of the primitive and apostolic Church, to set up the carnal
daughter of old Adam and the spouse of Satan, instead of a
pious Reformation, is to introduce confusion into the Christian
commonwealth, and procure license for all kinds of vice; and
to leave us no defence, he adds, that all this has been proved
by the event. What kind of Church we long for, God well
knows and is our witness, while numerous proofs bear ample
testimony to the world. A judgment cannot be more truly or
rightly formed than from our doctrine and the case itself. Let
any one, who will, compare our writings with theirs, and
then let him turn his eye and survey the reality. I say nothing
more than that it will at once be plain how just our grounds
are for bewailing the destruction of the Church, and calling
for the restitution of its fallen state; and how in prescribing
the method we mingle nothing of carnal prudence or zeal, but
refer all our feelings, counsels, wishes, and endeavours to the
true and only rule. What agreement or affinity is there between their whole hierarchy which they proudly extol, and
the government of Christ and the Apostles? Nay, in what
point are they not utterly opposed to each other? But we
must pardon Marinarius, who, while he beholds the faces of

the Fathers of Trent, is ravished with admiration at the splendid sight, and thinks he sees and hears Christ. Hence, it is not strange that the man in his ecstasy sends forth torrents of froth instead of words! He says: While I contemplate you, Fathers, preeminent in ecclesiastical dignity, and distinguished for all kinds of learning, you the lights and ornaments of the world, methinks I see Christ walking on the water, and also hear him saying, Fear not: it is I! The reason why he inveighs so fiercely against us is because we set no more value on that divine splendour of the Council of Trent, at which he gazes in amazement, than on a children's show. In what terms shall I rebuke his sordid adulation? But anything from a Carmelite scarcely deserves rebuke, since the world has long been accustomed not to require anything like ingenuousness in that begging fraternity.

Next, Ambrosius Catharinus, of the order of the Dominicans, the old antagonist of Luther, blows out his cheeks. I thought that under the confusion to which he was put twenty years ago, he had gone into some obscure corner to hide himself. So disgracefully was he prostrated by Luther, when yet a young soldier, so thoroughly was he hissed by the consent of all classes, that if he were wise he would never have appeared again in public. But now, I presume, aroused by the published bull of the Council, as if a jubilee had been proclaimed, he again comes to light a kind of new man. He is the same, however, as before. Those who formerly read the absurdities of Catharinus would not know that that putrid carcase is still breathing, did they not read his harangues delivered in the Council, in which the mother of Christ is called his most faithful associate, and represented as sitting on his throne to obtain grace for us! Many before him have given loose reins to their impudence, but none I believe was found, while seeking to deck the blessed Virgin with fictitious titles, to call her the associate of Christ. And that this blasphemous expression was uttered in such an assembly, and received with no small favour, posterity never would have believed had not the oration been published. What is meant by dividing Christ, if this is not? Therefore, when he says that she has been appointed by God to be our advocate, it is just equivalent to saying that half of what the Apostles declare of Christ is applicable to her. And this fellow dares to compare himself to Simeon, though the venerable old man had his whole soul intent on the one salvation of God, even not yet revealed, whereas to Catharinus Christ is only one among a crowd of advocates. After making this beautiful arrangement in heaven, he descends to the terrestrial hierarchy, and declares that whoso refuses to submit to Paul III. is an alien from the body of Christ! What! even though he hold a primacy only like that of the devil among his angels?

He says, that he who holds the See of Rome cannot but be the Vicar of Christ. Are these triflers not yet ashamed to sport their futile inanities, which they know to have been refuted a thousand times to weariness? At the period when there was still a Church and a bishopric at Rome, there was no mention of any such primacy as the Romanists now arrogate to themselves. To Christ alone belongs the universal bishopric, while each single pastor, as Cyprian tells us, possesses part of the undivided whole. The appellation of Universal Bishop, if conferred on a man, Gregory everywhere testifies to be blasphemous, nefarious, accursed, and the forerunner of Antichrist. What! were the Africans cut off from the body of Christ when they would not even concede the title of first or highest bishop to the bishop of Rome? Did Cyprian discard himself from the communion of the Church, when he not only called Stephen the Roman bishop to order, and taught him to be docile to his colleagues, but charged him with error, ignorance, and mulish obstinacy? Was Jerome the author of schism from the flock of Christ, when he declared that no bishop was made superior by the pride of riches, nor inferior by the humility of poverty,—whether he were the bishop of Rome or of Eugubium? But though with one assent the Roman See were raised to the third heaven, how ridiculous is it to make a primate of bishops of one who is no more like a bishop than a wolf is like a lamb! It is little to say that there is nothing episcopal in him, but while he is the declared enemy of Christ and the Church, it is surely too much to insist on our acknowledging him to be also The Vicar of Christ? At present, however, it is not our purpose to carry this discussion farther. It is better to consult our books on this subject. The words of Catharinus himself remind us that we must not stay longer here. For after swearing that the last thing he would do would be to curry favour by flattery, he immediately adds,—"But to the subject,"—intimating that he had wandered and spoken away from the subject. It is hopeless, however, to expect that he will bring us back to the subject, unless he previously return to a sound mind.

If we may judge a lion by his claws, our readers now have the means of knowing what they ought to think of the Council of Trent. For it is to be supposed, that of the monks present, those to whom chiefly the task of discoursing was given, were deemed the first and as it were the flower. Let it be understood that they are also the persons who concocted the Canons, and dictated to the horned Fathers what they, like dumb persons, were to approve by a silent nod. To what have we fallen! Are we to give the honour of Divine oracles to whatever such creatures might growl with obstreperous voice into other ears? Although I am not so ignorant of matters as to believe that the orations published in their name, be they what they may, were their own composition; for they have their speech-makers, to whom they hand their absurdities, and get them glossed over with some colour of words, lest even children should laugh! But let us assume that the whole was polished by their own industry, still it is a great point gained to have such a specimen of the awful wisdom of the Papacy.

We must not pass over some bishop or other named Cornelius, who, as he surpassed his superiors in dignity, far surpasses them also in folly. Had there been anything like gravity and seriousness in the Acts of the Council, one might have said that the part assigned to him was that of the fool in the play; but there is no doubt that he was a chosen one among the bishops, though the whole flower of the order was displayed; and therefore I only say, that if they were not sorry for him and ashamed of him, I very much pity them. Their eyes indeed may have been dazzled by one circumstance— his gathering flowers from every quarter, and thrusting into his oration every elegant expression he had ever learnt, that he might pass himself off as an orator. And I for one am perfectly willing that he should think himself most eloquent, and seem so to his party. He must, indeed, have been very familiar with Cicero, from whom he with so much confidence borrows patches of sentences, which he huddles into his discourse. But that, while thus playing the buffoon, he should employ his borrowed garrulity to oppress the kingdom of Christ and profane Scripture at will, is not on any account to be borne. It were an endless work to specify every point, but the reader may take the following as a specimen. The joyous orator, after pouring upon his audience his threefold joy, congratulates himself and his associates that they now see with their eyes and handle with their hands that blessed hope which many desired to see but were not able. These words once spoken, partly of the former advent of Christ, and partly of the final revelation for which we still look, what pious man can, without indignation, hear transferred by this madman to such a sink as Trent? And that nothing might be wanting to crown his impudence, he tags to it a third clause from the eleventh chapter of Hebrews, on the final perfection of believers.

After this prelude, what might he not think himself at liberty to do? Accordingly, he hesitates not to strip Christ in order that he may deck his Pope with the spoils. The Pope, he says, came a light into the world. Blasphemous mouth! will you apply to that fetid monster of yours sacred terms applicable to none but the Son of God? Had you believed in a God, must not the very sound of your nefarious voice have struck you with sudden horror and amazement? Had there been any feeling of piety in that famous Council, must not this great profanation of Scripture, and more especially this insult to the Son of God, have inflamed all with indignation? And will they still pretend that the Holy Spirit presides where our Redeemer is with such impunity mocked? For what is more peculiar to Christ than the honour which the evangelist renders to him when, excluding the Baptist by name, or rather under his name excluding all mortals, he asserts of Christ alone, and proclaims that the Son of God came as our light from heaven? It is one of those sentences which must produce the highest reverence in all pious minds. The Council, however, receive it as if it were mere gaudy verbiage. What words of rebuke could be strong enough for such impiety? But it is well that my readers have no need of many words to form a just estimate of it; for which reason I shall merely glance at the remainder.

When he breaks forth in praise of Paul III., one would say that he has drawn his water from a full fountain, there is such a flow of words. He is, he says, the bravest and best in the memory of man; he will be celebrated by the tongues of all nations; no age will be silent in his praise! He had read these things in Cicero. He thought them elegantly expressed —as indeed they are—provided they be aptly applied. How well they apply to Paul III. let the consciences even of those who are most devoted to his tyranny bear witness. I were more than foolish were I to detail the encomiums in the thundering out of which this trifler exercises his lungs. After saying that he was preserved by the wondrous providence of God to bless us with his faith, wisdom, and power, he bids the venerable Fathers, as sitting on a kind of tripod, exclaim,

Long life to the Holiest—Long life to the Œcumenical—
Long life to the Apostolical! O good father, how much better
were it for you to be a man of sense than to sing out your
vivat in favour not only of a dead man, but of a fatal pestiferous monster! As to your proclaiming him worthy of heaven,
I don't know if you are aware of the universal belief that he
was unworthy of the earth! Here you certainly made a most
grievous mistake; you ought to have assigned him a station
far removed from heaven. Of the remaining bundle of praises
with which this elegant eulogist loads his idol, I will only
say this much: He had perhaps heard the old adage, Praise is
a pleasant song—but mistook its meaning. Accordingly, that
he might shew himself a pleasant orator, his whole oration is
devoted to praise. He next passes to the Council; and of the
three Legates makes one a celestial, viz., Cardinal de Monti,
whom all know to be truculent in temper and rude in manners; the second he makes a strict exacter of Christian policy,
(I wish he would begin with his own bed-chamber!) and the
third he makes an angel, (I wish he would lay aside his ambition, a principal part of the flesh!) At length the Council
appears to him like the New Jerusalem, and what not. This
no doubt was in compliance with the grave obtestation of the
Legates, that no man should be praised. But the amusing
part is, that though he intended to say all these things, he
deprecates their indignation. Let none of you, he says, be
offended with me; for better are the wounds of a friend than
the treacherous kisses of an enemy. They must surely be
cruel, ravenous beasts if such soft handling irritates them.
What would they do under harder provocation?

Afterwards, as if he had appeased them, he gives way to
exultation, exclaiming, We came, and saw, and conquered!
Cæsar indeed might thus boast. But how ridiculous are these
pæans in the shade of the valley of Trent, out of sight of an
enemy! I should like to know what they saw to conquer?
But I am afraid he may charge me with misrepresenting;
since he immediately adds the reason, viz., that the gates of
the Council being opened, the gates of heaven were opened
also, as if it were not palpable to all how wide the difference
is between heaven and the Council. But we must pardon a
delirious man when he wanders out of bounds. He next congratulates them on the restoration of the Church, which was
nodding to destruction, when the new light of God, and of
him who makes the nearest approach to God—Paul III.—
arose! What! is Paul III. superior to angels, and Prophets,

and Apostles? I see how it is. He had read that Cicero (whom he imitates not quite so well as a monkey does a man) had on one occasion thus flattered the Roman people, and he was unwilling to lose the fine sentence. Meanwhile, what pious mind does not abominate such blasphemy?

Who can say that the Spirit was absent from a Council which was blown up by such bellows? And yet this bishopling does make a glowing harangue about the clemency of Paul III. and the Fathers. For he declares that Paul, forgetful of himself, and mindful of us, aimed solely at what was humane and fatherly. We will believe that the mind of Paul was thus mild, whenever it shall appear that he forgot himself. This colouring, however, is far more tolerable than the cruel instigation of a rhetorician, I say not who, (for from respect I suppress his name.) Afraid, perhaps, that the men of Trent would not be bold enough in issuing sanguinary decrees, he exhorts them to dare, and promises that the moment they order, hands will be ready to execute. Is it thus that you, who are not ignorant of their disposition, and ought rather, if conscience had any weight with you, to have exposed your own head—is it thus that to subject the innocent to unworthy treatment, you hesitate not to whet the fury of men already possessed by cruel and brutish rage? Has the Italian air so debased all your feelings, as to make you forget that the Son of God, whose cause is discussed, will one day be a just Judge? Have you forgotten how great value he sets upon his kingdom, which is comprehended under the preaching of the Word? Do you not bear in mind how strict an avenger he declares himself to be, when his Father's glory is infringed? By what figures of rhetoric will you efface the fearful judgments which he fulminates against perfidious dissimulation? What madness has so blinded you, that you fear not to trample under foot the sacred blood of martyrs, which he declares, and not in vain declares, to be precious in his sight? Does not this single sentence strike you with terror,— Woe to those who call light darkness? I tremble on your account, while I think of that fearful vengeance which must shortly overtake you, if you return not to the right path. I therefore spare you not, in order that God may spare. But so it is. The tongues of rhetoricians must become meretricious when they begin to speak for hire. But if they are so eloquent in cursing, we must not be dumb in repressing their virulence. It were base cowardice if, while they pour all possible approbrium on the memory of the martyrs, (which the Lord hath with his own lips declared would be blessed among the righteous,) we should tamely allow it; it were flagitious perfidy if, while they defame the eternal truth of God, we should in a manner betray it by our silence! But let us now come to the decree of the Second Session, as the first act of the play.

ON THE DECREE OF THE SECOND SESSION

As they know that the name of Council is held in honour, they use it for the purpose of procuring respect to themselves from good men, to whom they are unknown; for while they keep using such swelling words as Sacred, Œcumenical, and Universal Council, lawfully met in the Holy Spirit, they dazzle the eyes of the simple. But as it is a part of Christian modesty to reverence the authority of the Church, so it is the part of prudence to take heed that Satan do not delude us by a fallacious pretext. Here, indeed, there is no necessity for such careful prudence; for we have not to guard against spiritual imposture, or some more hidden subtlety. Let us only open our eyes, and we shall see that what they clothe in such splendid titles is nothing. When they published this Canon, perhaps twenty bishops were present. This is what they call an Universal Council, and the more to overawe the ignorant, they use a Greek term, as if an unknown word were to have the power of a magical charm! But what is meant by calling it an Œcumenical Council? It is the same as if it were said that all the bishops throughout the habitable globe had flocked to Trent. Had it been only a Provincial Council they should have been ashamed of the fewness of its members. Why, then, or on what ground shall we regard this as a Holy Council? How long, pray, will they think that they are dealing with children, and can add to their dignity by pomposities fit only to excite laughter? How can they make us believe that they are duly met in the Holy Spirit, unless it be that they were summoned by bull? As if they held men's minds fascinated by the absurd idea, that the Holy Spirit is brought down from heaven by the nod of a Pope. At the time when those Councils were held, to which they themselves are obliged to give pre-eminence, the Roman bishop did not possess the right of calling them. The Emperor, along with others, summoned them by his edict. That this was the

case not only with what are called the four great Councils,
but also with very many others, is attested by ancient acts
still extant, and by all history. Let them not here allege that
the validity of such summoning was questionable. This is dis-
proved by the letters of Leo, in which he humbly begs the
Emperors Theodosius, Valentinian, and Marcion, that they
would be pleased, of their imperial authority, to intimate a
day and place for the bishops. Gregory long after begged
the same of Mauricius.

But, perhaps, the three Legates of the Apostolic See
brought the Holy Spirit. If so, the Council of Nice was not
duly assembled, since it only gave the Legates of the Roman
Church the fourth place. What is to be said of the Council
of Aquila, which, though it was held in Italy, and was a general Council, makes no mention of the Roman bishop? If a
Council is not duly constituted unless the Legates of the
Pope preside, what answer will the African bishops give who
assigned the last place to Philip and Asellus, the two Legates
of Boniface, because they were only presbyters and not of
the episcopal order? Now, if a deacon of the Roman Church
is only distinguished by a red cloak, he will carry his head
over those of all the bishops. However, it is of no consequence
to me what rank each of them holds. I will give them no
trouble on that head. Nay, I will readily allow the mitres
to be vanquished by the hats, provided they do not bind
the Holy Spirit to their masks of recent invention, and maintain, that wherever the purple glare is seen, the Council is
duly assembled. But if they lay down this as the law, why
do they refuse to hold the Council at Basle to have been a
lawful Council? Who can tolerate the insolent pretence, that
a man can send forth the Spirit and recall him when he
pleases? If they would convince us by a sound argument that
the Spirit of God is their President, they must first prove that
they are assembled in the name and under the auspices of
Christ.

Their acts proclaim that it is far otherwise. First, their lofty
preamble is not followed up by anything worthy of the occasion; and, secondly, as soon as they enter upon business,
the very best they have is drawn from the veriest dregs of
superstition. At the very commencement, how flat and lifeless
they are, and devoid of all spiritual energy in their first Canon,
I will leave to the judgment of my readers. There is no man
possessed of moderate intelligence who does not see this for
himself. It is sufficient to touch on what follows. One simple

fact will enable us to give judgment. They exhort the bishops and priests holding the Council, in other words, themselves, to perform the sacrifice of the Mass at least every Lord's day. Behold the beginning of their famous Reformation! We loudly maintain that the sacrifice of the Mass is nothing else than an impious profanation of the Lord's Supper. This we make plain by the clear words of our Lord. For in instituting the sacred Supper, he does not enjoin us to sacrifice, but invites us to partake of the sacrifice which he himself once offered. He commands distribution to be made, and orders all alike to communicate in both symbols. And there is no obscurity in the words; Take, distribute among yourselves; drink ye all of this cup. What resemblance is there between the observance which corresponds to our Lord's command and the Papal Mass, in which they pretend that Christ offers himself to the Father to expiate the sins of the world by the sacrifice of himself, and not only so, but also to obtain redemption for the dead—in which no invitation is given to partake, but one individual sets himself apart from the whole flock—and where, if any one comes forward to partake, the half is withheld from him?

Anciently, when the people were remiss in their attendance, Chrysostom said, In vain stand we at the altar. He said this at a time when he had been used to many corruptions. What will our Lord say when his ordinance is not only corrupted but altogether subverted? Let them go then, and anew, by their sacrilege, provoke the anger of the Lord, already too much awakened. Next, they exhort all to fast every Friday in remembrance of our Lord's passion, etc. Is this what Paul teaches concerning the observance of days? Is this his admonition regarding the choice of meats, in the same Epistle, where he calls it εθελοθρησκεια, *i.e.*, a factitious worship, which, however it may have a show of wisdom, being founded only on the decisions of men, vanishes along with the meats which perish in the using? Where, pray, have they read that the Lord commanded such a commemoration of his death? Nay, rather by his death, everything of the kind was abolished. What then is to be said of those preparatory steps by which they wish to bring the Holy Spirit down from heaven? What, but just that they are fatuous superstitions fit for old women to talk of when sitting with the wool and distaff. To these they add litanies, that is, chants consisting of as many blasphemies as words. With what gloss will they excuse their passing by the intercession of Christ in perfect silence, and choosing hundreds of advocates for themselves at will from among the dead? What resemblance has the doctrine of Scripture, or the primitive customs of the godly, to their conduct in omitting the one Mediator of God and man, fixing by name or mediations which they have assumed at their own hand, and at length invoking the whole body of the saints, as if they were all bound up in one bundle? However they permit themselves to depart from the pure doctrine of the Gospel, it is certain that at a time when superstition had so far prevailed, that holy pastors could not hold the straight course, it was prohibited in distinct terms by the Council of Carthage, to invoke saints at the altar, or the priest was forbidden to use the expression, "St. Peter or St. Paul, pray for us." What reformation is to be hoped from those whose degeneracy so much outstrips even a degenerate eye?

ON THE FOURTH SESSION

There is an old proverb,—The Romans conquer by sitting. Trusting to this, those degenerate and bastard sons of the Roman See, *i.e.*, the great harlot, sat down to conquer when they appointed the third session. For what hinders them from raising a trophy, and coming off victorious to their hearts' content, if we concede to them what they have comprehended in one decree? There are four heads: First, they ordain that in doctrine we are not to stand on Scripture alone, but also on things handed down by tradition. Secondly, in forming a catalogue of Scripture, they mark all the books with the same chalk, and insist on placing the Apocrypha in the same rank with the others. Thirdly, repudiating all other versions whatsoever, they retain the Vulgate only, and order it to be authentic. Lastly, in all passages either dark or doubtful, they claim the right of interpretation without challenge. These four things being established, who can deny that the war is ended? Wherefore, their after discussions were more for ostentation than from any necessity for them; for whatever they produce, if supported by no authority of Scripture, will be classed among traditions, which they insist should have the same authority as the Law and the Prophets. What, then, will it be permitted to disapprove? for there is no gross old wife's dream which this pretext will not enable them to defend; nay, there is no superstition, however monstrous, in front of which they may not place it like a shield of Ajax. Add to this, that they provide themselves with new supports when they give full authority to the Apocryphal books. Out of the second of the Maccabees they will prove Purgatory and the worship of saints; out of Tobit satisfactions, exorcisms, and what not. From Ecclesiasticus they will borrow not a little. For from whence could they better draw their dregs? I am not one of those, however, who would entirely disapprove the reading of those books; but in giving them an authority which they never before possessed, what end was sought but just to have the use of spurious paint in colouring their errors? But as the Hebrew or Greek original often serves to expose their ignorance in quoting Scripture, to check their presumption, and so keep down their thrasonic boasting, they ingeniously meet this difficulty also by determining that the Vulgate translation only is to be held authentic. Farewell, then, to those who have spent much time and labour in the study of languages, that they might search for the genuine sense of Scripture at the fountainhead! At least it has been amply provided by this decree that they shall give no farther trouble to the Romanists. Is not this to subdue Greece and all the East? One thing still was wanting; for disagreeable men were always springing up, who, when anything was brought into question, could not be satisfied without Scripture proof! There are others too clearsighted, since even in the Vulgate translation they find weapons wherewith to annoy the Papacy. That they may not sustain loss from this quarter, they devise a most excellent remedy, when they adjudge to themselves the legitimate interpretation of Scripture. Who can now imagine any improvidence in them? By one article they have obtained the means of proving what they please out of Scripture, and escaping from every passage that might be urged against them. If Confession is to be proved, they are ready with— "Shew yourselves to the priests." If it be asked, Whether recourse should be had to the intercession of the dead? the passage will immediately occur, "Turn to some one of the saints;" also, "For this every holy man will pray to thee." Nor will Purgatory be left without a sure foundation, for it is written, "He shall not come out thence till he shall have paid the uttermost farthing." In short, anything may be made of anything! When they formerly produced such passages they made themselves ridiculous even to children. Now, if credit is given them, the right of authorized interpretation will remove every doubt. For what passage can be objected to them so clear and strong that they shall not evade it? Any kind of quibble will at once relieve them from difficulty. Against opposing arguments they will set up this brazen wall —Who are you to question the interpretation of the Church? This, no doubt, is what they mean by a saying common among them, in that Scripture is a nose of wax, because it can be formed into all shapes. If postulates of this kind were given to mathematicians, they would not only make an ell an inch, but prove a mile shorter than an ell, till they had thrown everything into confusion.

What, then, are we to do with this victorious and now, as it were, triumphal Session? Just stand and let the smoke clear away. In regard to Traditions, I am aware that not unfrequent mention of them is made by ancient writers, though not with the intention of carrying our faith beyond the Scriptures, to which they always confine it. They only say that certain customs were received from the Apostles. Some of them appear to have that origin, but others are unworthy of it. These touch only upon a few points, and such as might be tolerated. But now we are called to believe, that whatever the Romanists are pleased to obtrude upon us, flowed by tradition from the Apostles; and so shameless are they, that without observing any distinction, they bring into this class things which crept in not long ago, during the darkness of ignorance. Therefore, though we grant that the Apostles of the Lord handed down to posterity some customs which they never committed to writing; still, *first,* this has nothing to do with the doctrine of faith, (as to it we cannot extract one iota from them,) but only with external rites subservient to decency or discipline; and *secondly,* it is still necessary for them to prove that everything to which they give the name is truly an apostolical tradition. Accordingly they cannot, as they suppose, find anything here to countenance them either in establishing the tyranny of their laws, by which they miserably destroy consciences, or to cloak their superstitions, which are evidently a farrago gathered from the vicious rites of all ages and nations. We especially repudiate their desire to make certainty of doctrine depend not less on what they call αγραφα, (unwritten,) than on the Scriptures. We must ever adhere to Augustine's rule, "Faith is conceived from the Scriptures."

Of their admitting all the Books promiscuously into the

Canon, I say nothing more than it is done against the consent of the primitive Church. It is well known what Jerome states as the common opinion of earlier times. And Ruffinus, speaking of the matter as not at all controverted, declares with Jerome that Ecclesiasticus, the Wisdom of Solomon, Tobit, Judith, and the history of the Maccabees, were called by the Fathers not canonical but ecclesiastical books, which might indeed be read to the people, but were not entitled to establish doctrine. I am not, however, unaware that the same view on which the Fathers of Trent now insist was held in the Council of Carthage. The same, too, was followed by Augustine in his Treatise on Christian Doctrine; but as he testifies that all of his age did not take the same view, let us assume that the point was then undecided. But if it were to be decided by arguments drawn from the case itself, many things beside the phraseology would shew that those Books which the Fathers of Trent raise so high must sink to a lower place. Not to mention other things, whoever it was that wrote the history of the Maccabees expresses a wish, at the end, that he may have written well and congruously; but if not, he asks pardon. How very alien this acknowledgment from the majesty of the Holy Spirit!

In condemning all translations except the Vulgate, as the error is more gross, so the edict is more barbarous. The sacred oracles of God were delivered by Moses and the Prophets in Hebrew, and by the Apostles in Greek. That no corner of the world might be left destitute of so great a treasure, the gift of interpretation was added. It came to pass—I know not by what means, but certainly neither by judgment nor right selection—that of the different versions, one became the favourite of the unlearned, or those at least who, not possessing any knowledge of languages, desired some kind of help to their ignorance. Those, on the other hand, who are acquainted with the languages perceive that this version teems with innumerable errors; and this they make manifest by the clearest evidence. On the other hand, the Fathers of Trent contend, that although the learned thus draw the pure liquor from the very fountain, and convict the infallible Vulgate of falsehood, they are not to be listened to. No man possessed of common sense ever presumed to deprive the Church of God of the benefit of learning. The ancients, though unacquainted with the languages, especially with Hebrew, always candidly acknowledge that nothing is better than to consult the original, in order to obtain the true and genuine meaning.

I will go further. There is no man of ordinary talent who, on comparing the Vulgate version with some others, does not easily see that many things which were improperly rendered by it are in these happily restored. The Council, however, insists that we shall shut our eyes against the light that we may spontaneously go astray.

Who could have imagined they would be so senseless as thus boldly to despise the judgments of good men, and hesitate not to make themselves odious and detestable to all? Those who were aware that they had nothing useful in view, were yet persuaded that they would make some show of it to the world, and assign to some of their sworn adherents the task of executing a new version. In this instance, however, they use no deceit. They not only order us to be contented with a most defective translation, but insist on our worshipping it, just as if it had come down from heaven; and while the blemishes are conspicuous to all, they prohibit us from desiring any improvement. Behold the men on whose judgment the renovation of the Church depends!

It were tedious beyond measure to mark the passages erroneously and absurdly rendered. So far is there from being an entire page, that there are scarcely three continuous verses without some noted blunder. As a specimen, let the Book of Psalms suffice, in which I will touch on a few examples in passing, more to give my readers a sample which may dispose them to ascertain for themselves, than to give full information. In the second Psalm is the well-known exhortation, "Kiss the Son." For this the Vulgate has, "Lay hold of discipline!" There is no resemblance. While the former is clearly correct, why should the latter be held the more authentic? The Vulgate interpreter has, "Sons of man, how long will you with a heavy heart?" while the Hebrew has nothing like this, but, "How long will ye turn my glory into shame?" (Ps. 4:3.) Where David complains that his sap was turned into the drought of summer, (Ps. 32:4,) the translator has substituted, "I am turned in my sorrow till the thorn is fixed." Again, in another verse, "In their mouths is bit and bridle to prevent them from approaching thee;" but the translator says, "With hook and rein curb the jaws of those who do not draw near unto thee." And what are we to understand by "lungs filled with illusions," in Ps. 38?

But I act imprudently in entering a boundless forest; I will therefore confine myself to a single Psalm. It will be the sixty-eighth. There David, among the other praises of

God, mentions this also, that he makes the single to dwell in a house, *i.e.*, enriches the solitary and childless with a family. The translator substitutes, that he makes them "of one manner." The next words are, "He places the rebellious in a dry parched place." For this the translator has, "In like manner those who exasperate; who dwell in the tombs." Afterward, where the meaning is perfectly obvious in the words of David, the translator makes a riddle fit to puzzle an Œdipus. David says, "The kings of armies have fled, have fled, and the dwellers of the house, *i.e.*, the women who remained at home, have divided the spoil." The translator says, "The king, the virtue of the beloved, beloved, and houses of appearance, have divided the spoil." A little further on, "Though ye have slept among the pots;" translator, "among the clergy!" "To look up to the piled mountains" he substitutes for, "To envy the fertile mountains." Where the Hebrew original has, "Even the rebellious, that God the Lord may dwell," the translator has, "Even those not believing that God the Lord dwells." Again, when the literal meaning is, "I will bring back from Bashan, I will bring back from the depths of the sea," the translator gives the very opposite, "I will turn from Bashan, I will turn into the depth of the sea." Again, "There is little Benjamin their ruler." The translator (I know not what he was thinking of) says, "In excess of mind." I have gone over the half of the Psalm or rather more. What monstrosities do my readers already perceive!

And yet, to confess the truth, there is an excuse for the Latin translator, who gave the meaning of the Greek version as exactly as he could. But who can tolerate those blunderers, who would rob the Church of the gift of interpretation, and thus, as it were, close up the entrance, that none might have access to the pure meaning of David? Add, that they not only prefer the ignorance and blunders of their interpreters to the true renderings of others, but there is no hallucination, however gross, to which they will not give the power of a divine oracle. There is an example of this in Psalm 132. The Lord there promises that he will bless the food of his people. Some luscious priestling, reading the *c* and *t* as one letter, makes the word *vidum;* but as there is no such word, the insertion of a letter introduced a new reading, which prevails throughout the Papacy, and hence there is no church in Italy, France, Spain, and Germany, in which they do not with loud voice bawl out, "His widow blessing, I will bless." And so attentive and clear-sighted are they, that none of them has observed the ridiculous corruption. But it is not strange that, when they rob us of the word for bread, they introduce the mention of widowhood, since the object on which they are wholly bent is cruelly to bereave souls of the bread of heavenly life. What! are they not ashamed to make the Vulgate version of the New Testament authoritative, while the writings of Valla, Faber, and Erasmus, which are in everybody's hands, demonstrate with the finger, even to children, that it is vitiated in innumerable places? In the first chapter of the Romans the translator calls Christ "the pre-destinated Son of God." Those not acquainted with Greek are at a loss to explain this term, because, properly speaking, only things which do not yet exist are predestinated; whereas Christ is the eternal Son of God. There is no difficulty in the Greek word, which means "*declared.*" I have given one example. It were needless labour to give others. In one word, were this edict of the Council sanctioned, the simple effect would be, that the Fathers of Trent would make the world look with their eyes open, and yet not see the light presented to them.

I come to the right of interpreting, which they arrogate to themselves whenever the meaning is doubtful. It is theirs, they say, to give the meaning of Scripture, and we must acquiesce. For everything which they bestow upon the Church they bestow upon themselves. I acknowledge, indeed, that as Scripture came not by the private will of man, (2 Pet. 1:21,) it is unbecoming to wrest it to the private sense of any man. Nay, in the case of an obscure passage, when it is doubtful what sense ought to be adopted, there is no better way of arriving at the true meaning than for pious doctors to make common inquiry, by engaging in religious discussion. But that is not now the question. They wish, by their tyrannical edict, to deprive the Church of all liberty, and arrogate to themselves a boundless license; for, be the meaning which they affix to Scripture what it may, it must be immediately embraced. Except themselves, moreover, no man will be permitted to prove anything out of Scripture. Would that they were equal to the performance of so great a task. But oxen usurp the reins, or rather asses the lyre. In short, their aim is to make all revere a Scripture hidden in darkness like the mysteries of Ceres, and let none presume to aspire to the understanding of it.

There would be no end were I to collect all the examples which would make it plain to my readers what fetters of iniquitous and intolerable slavery are forged by this decree. I will therefore give a specimen, in the case of only one Council. About the year 800 was held a Council of Nice, which both restored Images that had been overthrown under Leo and decreed that they were to be worshipped. That Council, because it supports idolatry, the Papists deem holy and lawful. Hence, according to their axiom, it cannot have erred in the exposition of Scripture. But if such interpreters of sacred things are to be listened to, (it is abominable to say they are,) the religion of the Egyptians will be preferable to the Christian. To prove from Scripture that churches were properly adorned with images and pictures, the following passages were adduced:—"God created man after his own image and likeness;" "Joshua erected twelve stones;" "No man lighteth a candle and putteth it under a bushel;" whence they inferred that images were to be placed upon altars! Again, "The light of thy countenance has been stamped upon us:" "as we have heard, so have we also seen;" "O Lord, I have loved the beauty of thy house;" "Shew me thy face, for it is lovely." In support of adoration, they wrested the following passages:—"Abraham worshipped the people of the land;" "Jacob set up an inscription, and blessed." Again, "He worshipped the top of the staff of his son Joseph;" "All the rich among the people will deprecate thy countenance;" "Worship his footstool;" "God is to be admired in his saints." And that nothing might be wanting to crown their effrontery, they appended out of another psalm, "His saints who are on the earth." This they applied to images!

I am aware that the narrative I now give will scarcely seem credible. I was myself amazed when I read it, though our ears should long ago have been trained by them to any absurdities, however enormous. Were I to collect all their interpretations, which even children would laugh at, and not even all, but those which are distinguished by some notable absurdity, I would require to form a volume thrice as large as the Bible.

The sum is, that the spirit of Trent wished, by this decree, that Scripture should only signify to us whatever dreaming monks might choose. For what else do they mean by the Church? Though the Roman bishops, I mean all who serve under the banner and auspices of that Anti-Christian See, were to assemble from every quarter of the world, how, pray, could they, by laying their heads together, frame a proper version for us? Many of them hardly knew the elements of grammar. At least, they will not venture to deny that there is scarcely one in a hundred who has read an entire book of the Prophets, or one of the Apostolical Epistles, or one of the Gospels. They are too much occupied with other cares to have any leisure for sacred literature. The only resource is, to reserve the privilege for the Apostolic See, and say that the interpretation of Scripture must be sought from the holy lips of Paul Farnese! Otherwise, let them shew us a Church which may justly be deemed able to sustain so great a burden. For, how highly soever they may extol the Roman See, they can never persuade some men either that Cephas is its head, or that chaste and holy marriage is the carnal life which is accursed in the sight of God. Both of these have been asserted in Papal responses. They cry out that the whole authority of the Church must fall if it is denied the right of interpreting Scripture—that a door would thus be thrown open to lascivious minds, allowing them to break through every restraint. Nay, in order to cast obloquy upon us, they are wont to charge us with arrogating the interpretation of Scripture to ourselves, in order that there may be no check on our licentiousness. Modesty will not allow me to speak of ourselves as fact would justify; and yet I will most truly declare that we have thrown more light upon the Scriptures than all the doctors who have appeared under the Papacy since its commencement. This praise even they themselves dare not deny us. Still there is none of us who does not willingly submit his lucubrations to the judgment of the Church. Therefore we neither contemn nor impair the authority of the Church; nor do we give loose reins to men to dare what they please. I wish they would shew us such a Church as Scripture itself pourtrays; we should easily agree as to the respect due to it. But when, falsely assuming the name of Church, they seize upon the spoils of which they have robbed it, what else can we do than protest?

ON THE FIRST DECREE OF THE FIFTH SESSION

That there may be somewhat in this Decree in accordance with the Preface, they borrow the first four heads from the ancient and approved doctrine of the Church. As to these there will be no dispute, and therefore it was obviously mali-

cious in them to premise that their object was to settle the
dissensions which have arisen at this time. Of what use was
it, pray, to thunder out so many anathemas? Just to make
the unskilful believe that there really was some ground for
it; though, in fact, there was not. In the fifth head, where
they introduce something of their own, they begin to act in
their own way, that is, to inculcate the futilities of their
sophists, and pertinaciously defend them. They pronounce
anathema on any one who denies that everything which has
the proper nature of sin is taken away by baptism, and
who holds that it is only erased or not imputed. Here they
craftily introduce the term *erase*, which they know to be in
bad odour, as the Pelagians annoyed Augustine with it. Let
them, therefore, have it their own way, as far as erasing
goes. We assert that the whole guilt of sin is taken away in
baptism, so that the remains of sin still existing are not imputed. That this may be more clear, let my readers call to
mind that there is a twofold grace in baptism, for therein
both remission of sins and regeneration are offered to us.
We teach that full remission is made, but that regeneration
is only begun and goes on making progress during the whole
of life. Accordingly, sin truly remains in us, and is not instantly in one day extinguished by baptism, but as the guilt is
effaced it is null in regard to imputation.

Nothing is plainer than this doctrine. Let us see then
why it is anathematised by the Council. There is nothing in
the regenerate which God hates; so say the venerable Fathers.
Were I to grant them this, does it follow that there is nothing
deserving of hatred—or is it not rather true that he hates
nothing because he pardons what he might justly hate? The
passage from the Apostle which they lay hold of plainly
supports our view—"There is no condemnation to them who
are in Christ Jesus." By these words he does not exempt
believers from blame, as if they were pure and free from all
sin. He only frees them from guilt, so that while groaning
under the burden of sin they are supported by the consolation which he had formerly mentioned, and of which he
afterwards discourses more at large, as we shall shortly see.
They add, moreover, that there is nothing to stand in the way
of their entering heaven. I admit this, not indeed because
there is no impediment, but because nothing can hurt those
who are clothed with the innocence of Christ. These horned
fathers assign a very different reason, viz., because putting off
the old man and putting on the new man, who is created

after God, they are pure and harmless. Who would not say
that they are quibbling? Surely those who are still in the act
have not reached the effect. There is therefore a palpable
inconsistency in calling those pure and harmless who are still
in course of putting off the old man. If they reply, that
though they used the present tense they were speaking of the
past, I will give them up. For Paul is addressing believers
when he bids the Ephesians put off the old man, thereby
intimating that the change by which we are renewed from
the flesh into the spirit is not the work of one day merely.
What have sound readers yet observed in the words quoted
by the men of Trent which aids them in the least; nay, where
is the quotation that is not utterly opposed to them?

Let us proceed, however, in sifting their decree. They
affirm that concupiscence, or the tendency to sin, which they
acknowledge to remain in the regenerate, cannot hurt those
who do not consent to it, seeing it is left for trial. In other
words, it does not hurt, because God perfects his strength in
their weakness. But if they insist on its being only a whet-
stone to sharpen their virtue, Paul erroneously complains that
on this very account he was wretched.

But I am foolish in arguing against them from use of the
term *wretched*, while the names of concupiscence, vice, and
sin cannot move them. When it is said that pravity in the
will is not sin, it might as well be said that man is not an
animal; or when it is said that vice is free from blame before
God, it might as well be said that the sun is not a shining
body. What shall I say of the term *sin*? They quibble and
say that Paul here used the term for the cause and punishment of sin: as if this were not clearly at variance with the
context. After mentioning sin he immediately adds, "I find a
law, that when I would do good evil is present with me."
Do they think that this is also spoken improperly? If it were
only a verbal question, still they ought no more to be listened
to than those who affirm that infants cannot properly be said
to be born with sin. Both interpret sin in the same way. There
is this difference, that the latter speak thus of original sin
generally, whereas these venerable Fathers maintain that
after baptism a thing is no longer the same thing it was,
though it remains the same. If they would better their case,
they must first of all shew that there is such a conversion in
the nature of things that what is the same becomes unlike
itself. But the slightest consideration of the matter removes all
dispute. It cannot be denied without effrontery, that repug-

nance to the law of God is truly sin. But the Apostle affirms this of a disease remaining in the regenerate. It follows, therefore, that of its own nature it is sin, although it is not imputed, and the guilt is abolished by the grace of Christ. If the true standard of righteousness is to love God with the whole heart, and mind, and strength, it is clear that the heart cannot incline otherwise without declining from righteousness. Paul complains that he is hindered from doing the good which he would do. The law, I say, requires perfect love: we do not yield it. Our duty was to run, and we go on slowly limping. In this defect the venerable fathers find nothing which ought to be considered sin.

With the same dishonesty they declare that the Church never understood otherwise. But Ambrose, as Augustine testifies, distinctly calls it "unrighteousness." What says Augustine himself? There are many passages in which his acknowledgment of this appears without obscurity. As when he says, in the second book against Julian, that "in baptism the law of sin is remitted, not ended." Again, "The guilt is loosed, the thing remains." Again, "Sin is dead in the guilt by which it held us, but the dead rebels until cured by the finished work of sepulture." Again, in the homily on John, on the first of Lent, "As long as you live sin must be in your members. At Lent let it be deprived of dominion: do not as it bids." But of many passages it will be sufficient to adduce one which seems to have been written for the express purpose of refuting their folly. In the fifth book against Julian he names three reasons why it is called sin, even in the regenerate. The words are, "As blindness of heart is the sin by which we believe not in God, and the punishment of sin by which the proud heart receives condign chastisement, and the cause of sin when through the error of a blind heart any offence is committed, so the concupiscence of the flesh, which the Good Spirit resists, is also sin, because there is disobedience in it against the dominion of the mind, and the punishment of sin because inflicted on the demerits of the disobedient, and the cause of sin from defect of will or corruption of nature." A meaning, which the Council declares to have been unknown to the early Church, every one here sees set down as the primary meaning by the most competent witness of antiquity. The definition of the Council will be mighty indeed if it can make darkness out of this clear light, and so fascinate the eyes of men as to make them think they are looking at one thing when they see another.

ON THE SECOND DECREE OF THE FIFTH SESSION

I should like first to know what approved Councils there are which they join with Sovereign Pontiffs? For at the time when lawful Councils of good fame were held no man was acknowledged as sovereign pontiff, nor even as first bishop; for this was expressly forbidden in the Council of Carthage. Accordingly we see that the Councils to which this specious colouring is given, are no other than six or seven spurious Councils held after the light of sound doctrine was extinguished, and discipline had decayed, and when the merest dolts were present—Councils which exhibit no appearance of ancient dignity, but smack of the Gothic tyranny of the Roman See. Fine Reformers, truly! See how things which the Lateran Council raked together from the foul dregs of a most corrupt age, and which posterior Councils made even worse, are here brought forward to claim new honours! But I mistake, for they distinctly avow that they will make I know not what additions to them. To know the quality of these additions we must look at the decrees.

They enjoin, that those who hold prebends intended for lecturers on sacred theology shall perform the office of teaching either themselves or by others if they are unfit. The Council thus leaves men who are unlearned and utterly unfit in possession of the place which they have usurped by fraud, injustice, and sacrilege, without any appearance of law, provided they bestow some small portion of the stipend on substitutes. But they carefully provide that in future none but fit persons shall be admitted! By whose judgment? To whom could they assign the task but to the canonical authorities of the districts? A bishop therefore is to elect any kind of reader he pleases. What Chapter will be so harsh as not to be satisfied with any person, whatever his qualifications? But if he happens to be disapproved, litigation will arise. Unless something miraculous occur the nomination of the bishop will be sustained. Then what is to be the course of lectures? what the time? what the auditory? As to all these things the venerable fathers are prudently silent, in order to persuade the simple they were doing something when they were doing nothing. What! is not the thing which they prescribe already common? The lecturer, in order merely to preserve the emolument, every week invites two or three of his boon companions, and makes a mere show of lecturing.

In the second chapter they appoint new lectures. Where? In Metropolitan or Episcopal Churches, but only if the city be of note and populous. No doubt they were afraid lest the audience should freeze if the places were less distinguished. This, however, is just as much as saying nothing; but they wish the same rule to be observed in distinguished towns. They say this, but what plan do they propose? That either the bishop assign a stipend out of a simple benefice, or the clergy of the diocese contribute, or some other plan be adopted by the canons. These alternatives can have no other effect than to put the thing off for ages.

To the same effect is their enactment about teachers; for there is no ground to hope that the incomes of priests will be employed in that way; far less that the bishops will curtail their table in the least. The third plan remaining is for the bishop to devise some method. But before the litigation between him and the clergy on the subject of contribution is ended, the memory of the Council of Trent will be buried in oblivion. The worthy decretists are not ignorant of this; but it was necessary to adopt some fiction, so as not to leave it perfectly apparent that nothing was done.

If the fourth chapter be read cursorily, it might cause no little alarm to the monks, lest they should be sent back to theological studies. But there are two exceptions which rid them of their fear. First, they ordain lectures only when it will be convenient. But there is no monastery which is not as inhospitable to all kinds of liberal study as if it were a den of Cyclops. The second exception makes them still safer. Command is given to the bishops to use compulsion with the abbots if they are negligent. And they are to do this as if they were delegates of the Apostolic See. Therefore, whenever any bishop proves troublesome to an abbot, an appeal will be taken, and the cause will be pleaded at Rome. What will the issue be? The monks will sooner swallow the whole volume of Scripture than be forced to hear one lecture!

Moreover, that no celebrated School may be without a theological lecture, they exhort sovereigns and states to contribute the expense; as if this perfunctory recommendation were to have much weight, especially when it is clear enough that an hundred times more is swallowed up by lazy-bellies than would serve the purpose. Why, then, do they not command it to be taken from that quarter, but just because their real intention is that nothing shall be done?

As the rest are of the same description, there is no use in wasting good time in the discussion of such trifling. It is quite certain that they wished by a profusion of words to blind the eyes of the simple, and make them believe that they were something to the purpose, until experience should teach them how they had been deluded. Every one who has an ounce of sound judgment will acknowledge with me, that the whole is nothing better than a mere sound of words, which they who use them have no wish to be heard.

ON THE SIXTH SESSION
OF THE COUNCIL OF TRENT

The doctrine of man's Justification would be easily explained, did not the false opinions by which the minds of men are preoccupied, spread darkness over the clear light. The principal cause of obscurity, however, is, that we are with the greatest difficulty induced to leave the glory of righteousness entire to God alone. For we always desire to be somewhat, and such is our folly, we even think we are. As this pride was innate in man from the first, so it opened a door for Satan to imbue them with many impious and vicious conceits with which we have this day to contend. And in all ages there have been sophists exercising their pen in extolling human righteousness, as they knew it would be popular. When by the singular kindness of God, the impiety of Pelagius was repudiated with the common consent of the ancient Church, they no longer dared to talk so pertly of human merit. They, however, devised a middle way, by which they might not give God the whole in justification, and yet give something.

This is the moderation which the venerable Fathers adopt to correct the errors on Justification, which, they say, have arisen in our day. Such indeed is their mode of prefacing, that at the outset they breathe nothing but Christ; but when they come to the subject, far are they from leaving him what is his own. Nay, their definition at length contains nothing else than the trite dogma of the schools: that men are justified partly by the grace of God and partly by their own works; thus only shewing themselves somewhat more modest than Pelagius was.

This will easily be shewn to be the fact. For under the *second* head, where they treat of Original Sin, they declare that free-will, though impaired in its powers and biassed, is not however extinguished. I will not dispute about a name, but since they contend that liberty has by no means been extinguished, they certainly understand that the human will has still some power left to choose good. For where death is not, there is at least some portion of life. They themselves remove all ambiguity when they call it impaired and biassed. Therefore, if we believe them, Original Sin has weakened us, so that the defect of our will is not pravity but weakness. For if the will were wholly depraved, its health would not only be impaired but lost until it were renewed. The latter, however, is uniformly the doctrine of Scripture. To omit innumerable passages where Paul discourses on the nature of the human race, he does not charge free-will with weakness, but declares all men to be useless, alienated from God, and enslaved to the tyranny of sin; so much so, that he says they are unfit to think a good thought. (Rom. 3:12; 2 Cor. 3:5.) We do not however deny, that a will, though bad, remains in man. For the fall of Adam did not take away the will, but made it a slave where it was free. It is not only prone to sin, but is made subject to sin. Of this subject we shall again speak by and bye.

The *third* and *fourth* heads I do not touch. Towards the end of the *fifth* head they affirm that no transference to a state of grace takes place without Baptism, or a wish for it. Would it not have been better to say, that by the word and sacraments Christ is communicated, or, if they prefer so to speak, applied to us, than to make mention of baptism alone? But they have been pleased to exclude infants from the kingdom of God, who have been snatched away before they could be offered for baptism. As if nothing were meant when it is said that the children of believers are born holy. (1 Cor. 7:14.) Nay, on what ground do we admit them to baptism unless that they are the heirs of promise? For did not the promise of life apply to them it would be a profanation of baptism to give it to them. But if God has adopted them into his kingdom, how great injustice is done to his promise, as if it were not of itself sufficient for their salvation! A contrary opinion, I admit, has prevailed, but it is unjust to bury the truth of God under any human error, however ancient. The salvation of infants is included in the promise in which God declares to believers that he will be a God to them and to their seed. In this way he declared, that those deriving descent from Abraham were born to him. (Gen. 17:7.) In virtue of this promise they are admitted to baptism, because they are considered members of the Church. Their salvation, therefore, has not its commencement in baptism, but being already founded on the word, is sealed by baptism. But these definition-mongers thrust forward the passage, "Unless a man be born of water and of the Spirit." (John 3:3.) First, assuming with them that water means baptism, who will concede to them that it moreover means a wish to receive baptism? But were I to say that the passage has a different meaning, and were I following some ancient expositors to take the term *water* for *mortification,* they would not, I presume, be so bitter as therefore to judge me heretical. I interpret it, however, as added by way of epithet to express the nature and power of the Spirit. Nor can they make out that water here means baptism, any more than that fire means some sacrament, when it is said, "In the Holy Spirit and fire." (Matt. 3:11.) See on what grounds they arrogate to themselves supreme authority in interpreting Scripture!

In the *sixth* head, they assert that we are prepared by the grace of God for receiving Justification, but they assign to this grace the office of exciting and assisting, we ourselves freely co-operating; in other words, we are here treated with the inanities which the sophists are wont to babble in the schools. But I ask, Is it the same thing to excite a will, and aid it when in itself weak, as to form a new heart in man, so as to make him willing? Let them answer, then, whether creating a new heart, and making a heart of flesh out of a heart of stone, (both of which the Scripture declares that God does in us,) is nothing else than to supply what is wanting to a weak will. But if they are not moved by these passages, let them say whether he who makes us to be willing simply assists the will. Paul claims the whole work for God; they ascribe nothing to him but a little help. But for what do they join man as an associate with God? Because man, though he might repudiate it, freely accepts the grace of God and the illumination of the Holy Spirit. How greatly do they detract from the work of God as described by the Prophet!—"I will put my law," says he, "in your hearts, and make you to walk in my precepts." (Jer. 32:39; Ezek. 36:27; Heb. 8:10; 10:16.)

Is this the doctrine delivered by Augustine, when he says, "Men labour to find in our will some good thing of our own not given us of God; what they can find I know not?" (Aug. Lib. de Precator. Merit. et Remiss. 2.) Indeed, as he elsewhere says, "Were man left to his own will to remain under the help of God if he chooses, while God does not make him willing, among temptations so numerous and so great, the will would succumb from its own weakness. Succour, therefore, has been brought to the weakness of the human will by divine grace acting irresistibly and inseparably, that thus the will however weak might not fail." (Aug. de Corruptione et Gratia.) But the Neptunian fathers, in a new smithy, forge what was unknown to Augustine, viz., that the reception of grace is not of God, inasmuch as it is by the free movement of our own will we assent to God calling. This is repugnant to Scripture, which makes God the author of a good will. It is one thing for the will to be moved by God to obey if it pleases, and another for it to be formed to be good. Moreover, God promises not to act so that we may be able to will well, but to make us will well. Nay, he goes farther when he says, "I will make you to walk;" as was carefully observed by Augustine. The same thing is affirmed by Paul when he teaches, that "it is God that worketh in us both to will and to do of his good pleasure." The hallucination of these Fathers is in dreaming that we are offered a movement which leaves us an intermediate choice, while they never think of that effectual working by which the heart of man is renewed from pravity to rectitude. But this effectual working of the Holy Spirit is described in the thirty-second chapter of Jeremiah, where he thus speaks in the name of God, "I will put the fear of my name into their hearts, that they decline not from my commandments." In short, their error lies in making no distinction between the grace of Regeneration, which now comes to the succour of our wretchedness, and the first grace which had been given to Adam. This Augustine carefully expounds. "Through Christ the Mediator," he says, "God makes those who were wicked to be good for ever after. The first man had not that grace by which he could never wish to be bad; for the help given him was of that nature that he might abandon it when he would, and remain in it if he would, but it was not such as to make him willing. The grace of the second Adam is more powerful. It makes us will,

will so strongly and love so ardently, that by the will of the
spirit we overcome the will of the flesh lusting against it." A
little farther on he says, "Through this grace of God in receiving good and persevering therein, there is in us a power not
only to be able to do what we will, but to will what we are
able." (Aug. Lib. ad Bonif. 2, c. 8.) Although the subject is
too long to be despatched thus briefly, I feel confident that
my statement, though short, will suffice with readers of sense
to refute these fancies.

But they pretend that they have also the support of Scripture. For when it is said, "Turn thou me, O Lord, and I shall
be turned," (Jer. 31:18,) they infer that there is a preventing grace given to men: and, on the other hand, out of the
words, "Turn ye unto me, and I will turn unto you," they extract the power of free-will. I am aware that Augustine uses
this distinction, but it is in a very different sense: For he
distinctly declares, and that in numerous passages, that the
grace of God so works in us as to make us willing or unwilling, whence he concludes that man does no good thing which
God does not do in him. (Aug. Lib. ad Bonif. 3, c. 8.) What
then, you will ask, does Augustine mean when he speaks of
the freedom of the will? Just what he so often repeats, that
men are not forced by the grace of God against their will,
but ruled voluntarily, so as to obey and follow of their own
accord, and this because their will from being bad is turned
to good. Hence he says, "We therefore will, but God works in
us also to will. We work, but God causes us also to work."
Again, "The good which we possess not without our own
will we should never possess unless he worked in us also to
will." Again, "It is certain that we will when we are willing, but he makes us to be willing. It is certain that we do
when we do, but he makes us to do by affording most effectual strength to the will." (Aug. Lib. ii. de Bon. Persev. cap.
13; Lib. ii. 23, de Grat. et Liber. Arbit.) The whole may be
thus summed up—Their error consists in sharing the work
between God and ourselves, so as to transfer to ourselves
the obedience of a pious will in assenting to divine grace,
whereas this is the proper work of God himself.

But they insist on the words of the Prophet, that in requiring conversion from us he addresses free-will, which he would
do in vain (that is, in their opinion) unless free-will were
something. I admit that expressions of this kind would be
absurd if there were not some will in man, but I do not
therefore concede that the free faculty of obeying may be

thence inferred. Those venerable Fathers must be the merest of novices if they form their estimate of what man is able to do from the commandments given him, seeing that God requires of us what is above our strength for the very purpose of convincing us of our imbecility, and divesting us of all pride. Let us remember, therefore, that will in man is one thing, and the free choice of good and evil another: for freedom of choice having been taken away after the fall of the first man, will alone was left; but so completely captive under the tyranny of sin, that it is only inclined to evil.

Moreover, not to dwell longer here, I say that the doctrine here delivered by the Fathers of Trent is at open war with our Saviour's words, "Whosoever hath heard of the Father, cometh unto me." (John 6:45.) For as Augustine wisely observes, it hence follows, that no man hears and learns of God without at the same time believing on Christ; and that the motion of the Holy Spirit is so efficacious that it always begets faith. They, on the contrary, place it in the option of man to listen to the inspiration of God, if he will! It is impossible to reconcile the two things—that all who have learned of God believe in Christ, and that the inspiration of God is not effectual and complete unless men of themselves assent to it. We have the Son of God, who is never at variance with himself, for the author of the former. To whom shall we ascribe the latter, which is utterly contrary to it, but to the father of lies?

After treating, under the *seventh* head, of The Mode of Preparation, so frigidly that every one but a savourless Papist must feel ashamed of such senselessness, they at length, under the *eighth* head, when they come to define, set out with cautioning us against supposing that the justification of man consists in faith alone. The verbal question is, What is Justification? They deny that it is merely the forgiveness of sins, and insist that it includes both renovation and sanctification. Let us see whether this is true. Paul's words are, "David describeth the blessedness of the man to whom God imputeth righteousness without works, saying, Blessed are they whose iniquities are forgiven." (Rom. 4:6; Psalm 32:1.) If, from this passage of David, Paul duly extracts a definition of gratuitous righteousness, it follows that it consists in the forgiveness of sins. Paul interprets thus—David calls him righteous to whom God imputeth righteousness by not imputing sin; and the same Apostle, without appealing to the testimony of another, elsewhere says, "God was in Christ reconciling the world unto himself, not imputing unto men their trespasses." Immediately after, he adds, "He made him who knew no sin to be sin for us, that we might be the righteousness of God in him." (2 Cor. 5:19.) Can anything be clearer than that we are regarded as righteous in the sight of God, because our sins have been expiated by Christ, and no longer hold us under liability?

There is no room for the vulgar quibble that Paul is speaking of the beginning of Justification; for in both places he is shewing, not how men who had hitherto been unbelievers begin to be righteous, but how they retain the righteousness which they have once procured during the whole course of life; for David speaks of himself after he had been adopted among the children of God; and Paul asserts that this is the perpetual message which is daily heard in the Church. In the same sense also he says, "Moses describeth the righteousness of the law, that he who doeth these things shall live in them, (Lev. 18:5;) but the righteousness of faith thus speaketh, He that believeth," etc. (Rom. 10:5.) We thus see that the righteousness of faith, which by no means consists of works, is opposed to the righteousness of the law, which so consists. The words have the same meaning as those which, as Luke tells us, Paul used to the people of Antioch, "By this man is preached unto you the forgiveness of sins, and every one who believeth in him is justified from all the things from which ye could not be justified by the law of Moses." (Acts 13:38.) For justification is added to forgiveness of sins by way of interpretation, and without doubt means *acquittal.* It is denied to the works of the law; and that it may be gratuitous, it is said to be obtained by faith. What! can the justification of the publican have any other meaning (Luke 17.) than the imputation of righteousness, when he was freely accepted of God? And since the dispute is concerning the propriety of a word, when Christ is declared by Paul to be our righteousness and sanctification, a distinction is certainly drawn between these two things, though the Fathers of Trent confound them. For if there is a twofold grace, inasmuch as Christ both justifies and sanctifies us, righteousness does not include under it renovation of life. When it is said, "Who shall lay anything to the charge of God's elect?—It is God that justifieth"—it is impossible to understand anything else than gratuitous acceptance.

I would be unwilling to dispute about a word, did not the whole case depend upon it. But when they say that a man is justified, when he is again formed for the obedience of God, they subvert the whole argument of Paul, "If righteousness is by the law, faith is nullified, and the promise abolished." (Rom. 4:14.) For he means, that not an individual among mankind will be found in whom the promise of salvation may be accomplished, if it involves the condition of innocence; and that faith, if it is propped up by works, will instantly fall. This is true; because, so long as we look at what we are in ourselves, we must tremble in the sight of God, so far from having a firm and unshaken confidence of eternal life. I speak of the regenerate; for how far from righteousness is that newness of life which is begun here below?

It is not to be denied, however, that the two things, Justification and Sanctification, are constantly conjoined and cohere; but from this it is erroneously inferred that they are one and the same. For example:—The light of the sun, though never unaccompanied with heat, is not to be considered heat. Where is the man so undiscerning as not to distinguish the one from the other? We acknowledge, then, that as soon as any one is justified, renewal also necessarily follows: and there is no dispute as to whether or not Christ sanctifies all whom he justifies. It were to rend the gospel, and divide Christ himself, to attempt to separate the righteousness which we obtain by faith from repentance.

The whole dispute is as to The Cause of Justification. The Fathers of Trent pretend that it is twofold, as if we were justified partly by forgiveness of sins and partly by spiritual regeneration; or, to express their view in other words, as if our righteousness were composed partly of imputation, partly of quality. I maintain that it is one, and simple, and is wholly included in the gratuitous acceptance of God. I besides hold that it is without us, because we are righteous in Christ only. Let them produce evidence from Scripture, if they have any, to convince us of their doctrine. I, while I have the whole Scripture supporting me, will now be satisfied with this one reason, viz., that when mention is made of the righteousness of works, the law and the gospel place it in the perfect obedience of the law; and as that nowhere appears, they leave us no alternative but to flee to Christ alone, that we may be regarded as righteous in him, not being so in ourselves. Will they produce to us one passage which declares that begun newness of life is approved by God as righteousness either in whole or in part? But if they are devoid of authority, why may we not be permitted to repudiate the figment of partial justification which they here obtrude?

Moreover, how frivolous and nugatory the division of causes enumerated by them is, I omit to shew, except that I neither can nor ought to let pass the very great absurdity of calling Baptism alone the instrumental cause. What then will become of the gospel? Will it not even be allowed to occupy the smallest corner? But baptism is the sacrament of faith. Who denies it? Yet, when all has been said, it must still be granted me that it is nothing else than an appendage of the gospel. They, therefore, act preposterously in assigning it the first place, and act just as any one who should call a mason's trowel the instrumental cause of a house! Unquestionably, whosoever postponing the gospel enumerates baptism among the causes of salvation, by so doing gives proof that he knows not what baptism is, what its force, its office, or its use. What else I wish to say of the formal cause will be said on the tenth Canon. Here I wish only to advert to what belongs to the present place. For they again affirm that we are truly righteous, and not merely counted so. I, on the contrary, while I admit that we are never received into the favour of God without being at the same time regenerated to holiness of life, contend that it is false to say that any part of righteousness (justification) consists *in quality*, or in the habit which resides in us, and that we are righteous (justified) only by gratuitous acceptance. For when the Apostle teaches that "by the obedience of one many were made righteous," (Rom. 6:19,) he sufficiently shews, if I mistake not, that the righteousness wanting in ourselves is borrowed elsewhere. And in the first chapter to the Ephesians, where he says that we are adopted to the predestination of sons of God, that we might be accepted in the Beloved, he comprehends the whole of our righteousness. For however small the portion attributed to our work, to that extent faith will waver, and our whole salvation be endangered. Wherefore, let us learn with the Apostle to lay aside our own righteousness, which is of the law, as a noxious impediment, that we may lay hold of that which is of the faith of Jesus Christ. (Phil. 3:9.) Of what nature this is we have abundantly shewn; and Paul intimates in a single sentence in the third chapter to the Galatians, that the righteousness of the law, because it consists of works, has no congruity with the righteousness of faith.

But what can you do with men like these? For after they

have enumerated many causes of Justification, forgetting that
they were treating of the cause of justification, they infer
that righteousness partly consists of works, because no man
is reconciled to God by Christ without the Spirit of regeneration. How gross the delusion! It is just as if they were to say,
that forgiveness of sins cannot be dissevered from repentance, and therefore repentance is a part of it. The only point
in dispute is, how we are deemed righteous in the sight of
God, and where our faith, by which alone we obtain righteousness, ought to seek it? Though they should repeat a thousand times, that we cannot share in the merit of Christ's
passion, without being at the same time regenerated by his
Spirit, they will not make it cease to be a fundamental principle; that God is propitious to us because he was appeased
by the death of Christ; and that we are counted righteous in
his sight, because by that sacrifice our transgressions were
expiated. "We have propitiation," says Paul, "through faith
in the blood of Christ." (Rom. 3:25; 5:11.) In fine, when the
cause is inquired into, of what use is it to obtrude an inseparable accident? Let them cease then to sport with trifles,
or trifle with quibbles such as—man receives faith, and along
with it hope and love; therefore it is not faith alone that justifies. Because if eyes are given us, and along with them ears
and feet and hands, we cannot therefore say that we either
hear with our feet or walk with our hands, or handle with
our eyes. Of the erroneous application of a passage of Paul
I shall speak elsewhere.

Next follows their approbation of the worse than worthless
distinction between an informal and a formed Faith. The
venerable Fathers, indeed, are ashamed to use the very terms,
but while they stammer out that man is not united to Christ
by faith alone, unless hope and charity are added, they are
certainly dreaming of that faith, devoid of charity, which is
commonly called by the sophists informal. They thus betray
their gross incapacity. For if the doctrine of Paul is true,
that "Christ dwells in our hearts by faith," (Eph. 3:17,)
they can no more separate faith from charity than Christ from
his Spirit. If "our hearts are purified by faith," as Peter affirms,
(Acts 15:9,) if "whosoever believeth hath eternal life," as
our Saviour so often declares, (John 3:16; 5:24; 6:40; 20:31,)
if the inheritance of eternal life is obtained by faith, (Rom.
5:14,) faith is something very different from all forms of dead
persuasion. They deny that we are made living members of
Christ by faith. How much better Augustine, who calls faith

the life of the soul, as the soul is the life of the body? (Aug. in Joan. c. 11,) although Augustine is not so much the authority to be quoted here as Paul, who acknowledges that he lives by the faith of Christ. (Gal. 2:20.) They should perhaps be pardoned this error, because they talk about faith as they might do of fabulous islands, (for who among them knows by the slightest experience what faith is?) were it not that they drag the miserable world along with them in the same ignorance to destruction!

Let us remember that the nature of Faith is to be estimated from Christ. For that which God offers to us in Christ we receive only by faith. Hence, whatever Christ is to us is transferred to faith, which makes us capable of receiving both Christ and all his blessings. There would be no truth in the words of John, that faith is the victory by which we overcome the world, (1 John 5:4,) did it not ingraft us into Christ, (John 16:33,) who is the only conqueror of the world. It is worth while to remark their stupidity. When they quote the passage of Paul, "Faith which worketh by love," (Gal. 5:6,) they do not see that they are cutting their own throats. For if love is the fruit and effect of faith, who sees not that the informal faith which they have fabricated is a vain figment? It is very odd for the daughter thus to kill the mother! But I must remind my readers that that passage is irrelevantly introduced into a question about Justification, since Paul is not there considering in what respect faith or charity avails to justify a man, but what is Christian perfection; as when he elsewhere says, "If a man be in Christ he is a new creature." (2 Cor. 5:17.)

It were long and troublesome to note every blunder, but there is one too important to be omitted. They add, "that when catechumens ask faith from the Church, the answer is, 'If you will enter into life, keep the commandments.'" (Matt. 19:17.) Wo to their catechumens, if so hard a condition is laid upon them! For what else is this but to lay them under an eternal curse, since they acknowledge with Paul, that all are under the curse who are subject to the law? (Gal. 3:10.) But they have the authority of Christ! I wish they would observe to what intent Christ thus spake. This can only be ascertained from the context, and the character of the persons. He to whom Christ replies had asked, What must I do to have eternal life? Assuredly, whosoever wishes to merit life by works, has a rule prescribed to him by the law, "This do, and thou shalt live." But attention must be paid to the

object of this as intimated by Paul, viz., that man experiencing
his powers, or rather convinced of his powerlessness, may
lay aside his pride, and flee all naked to Christ. There is no
room for the righteousness of faith until we have discovered
that it is in vain that salvation is promised us by the law. But
that which the law could not do in that it was weak through
the flesh, God performed by his own Son, by expiating our
sins through the sacrifice of his death, so that his righteousness is fulfilled in us. But so preposterous are the Fathers of
Trent, that while it is the office of Moses to lead us by the
hand to Christ, (Gal. 3:24,) they lead us away from the
grace of Christ to Moses.

Lest they should not be liberal enough in preaching up
the powers of man, they again repeat, under this head, that
the Spirit of God acts in us according to the proper disposedness and co-operation of each. What disposedness, pray,
will the Spirit of God find in stony hearts? Are they not
ashamed to feign a disposedness, when the Spirit himself
uniformly declares in Scripture that all things are contrary?
For the commencement of grace is to make those willing
who were unwilling, and therefore repugnant; so that faith,
as well in its beginnings as its increase, even to its final perfection, is the gift of God; and the preparation for receiving
grace is the free election of God, as Augustine says, (Lib. i.
de Prædest., Sanct. c. 9–11.) And the words of Paul are
clear, "God hath blessed us with all spiritual blessings, according as he hath chosen us in Christ, according to the good
pleasure of his will." (Eph. 1:3.) By these words he certainly
restrains us, while receiving so great a blessing from God,
from glorying in the decision of our will, as Augustine again
says. (Ibid. c. 8.) This which man ought to receive as at
the hands of God, is he to oppose to him as a merit of his
own? For whence is there a first disposition, unless because
we are the sheep of Christ! And who dare presume so far as
to say he makes himself a sheep? Accordingly, when Luke
speaks of effectual calling, he tells us that not those who were
disposed of themselves, but those who were pre-ordained to
eternal life, believed. (Acts 13:48.) And Paul acquaints us
whence a right disposition is, when he teaches that the good
works in which we walk were prepared by God. (Eph. 2:10.)
Let us hear Augustine, whose doctrine is very different, rather
than those babblers. "After the fall of man," he says, (Lib. ii.
de Bono Persev., c. 9,) "God was pleased that man's approach to him should be the effect only of his grace, and

that man's not withdrawing from him should also be the effect only of his grace." For it is he himself who promises that he will give us a heart that we may understand, and ears that we may hear. Wherefore it is His grace alone which makes the difference, as Paul reminds us. Let me conclude by again using the words of Augustine, "The human will obtains not grace by freedom, but freedom by grace, and in order that it may persevere, delectable perpetuity and insuperable fortitude." (Lib. de Corrupt. et Grat. c. 8.)

In the *ninth* chapter, while they desire to shew some signs of modesty, they rather betray their effrontery. Seeing that the doctrine of Scripture was obviously repugnant to their decrees, they, to prevent this from being suspected, first explain what it is for a man to be justified by faith, saying, that faith is the beginning of salvation, and the foundation of justification. As if they had disentangled themselves by this solution, they immediately fly off to another—that the Apostle teaches that we are justified freely, because all the things which precede justification, whether faith or works, do not merit it. Did they think they are engaged in a serious matter, would they perform it as giddily as if they were playing at see-saw? I say nothing of their disregard of the judgments of mankind, as if they had expected to put out the eyes of all by such a sacred dogma as this—Faith justifies, since it begins justification. First, this comment is repugnant to common sense. For what can be more childish than to restrict the whole effect to the mere act of beginning?

But let us see for a little whether the words of Paul allow themselves to be so easily wrested. "The gospel," he says, (Rom. 1:16,) "is the power of God to every one believing unto salvation; for therein is the righteousness of God revealed from faith to faith." Who sees not that here the beginning and the end are alike included? Were it otherwise, it would have been said, from "faith to works," as they would finish what faith begins. To the same effect is the testimony of Habakkuk, "The just shall live by faith." (Hab. 2:4.) This would be improperly said did not faith perpetuate life. In the person of Abraham the chief mirror of justification is held forth. Let us see, then, at what time faith is declared to have been imputed to him for righteousness. (Gen. 15:6; Gal. 3:6.) He was certainly not a novice, but having left his country, had for several years followed the Lord, so that he was no common exemplar of holiness and all virtue. Faith therefore does not open up an access to him to righteousness, in order that his justification may afterwards be completed elsewhere. And Paul at length concludes that we stand in the grace which we have obtained by faith. (Rom. 5:2.) As far as a fixed and immovable station is from a transient passage, so far are they in this dogma of theirs from the meaning of Paul. To collect all the passages of Scripture were tedious and superfluous. From these few, I presume, it is already superabundantly clear, that the completion, not less than the commencement of justification, must be ascribed to faith.

The second branch is, that Justification is said by Paul to be gratuitous, because no merit precedes it. What then? When Paul also exclaims that all glorying of the flesh is excluded by the law of faith, is he looking only to the merits of past life, and does he not rather remind us that men justified by faith have nothing in which they can glory to the very end of life? For when he asserts after David that righteousness is imputed without works, he declares what is the perpetual state of believers. (Rom. 3:27; 4:2.) In like manner David exclaims, that himself and all the other children of God are blessed by the remission of sins, not for one day, but for the whole of life. (Psalm 32:1.) Nor does Peter, in the Acts, speak of the justification of a single day, when he says, "We believe that through the grace of Jesus Christ we are saved, as did also our fathers." (Acts 15:11.) The question under discussion was, whether observance of the law was to be exacted of the Gentiles. He says it ought not, because there is no other salvation in the Christian Church than through the grace of Christ, and there never was any other. (Acts 4:12.) And justly; for, as Paul says, the promise will not be secure unless it depends on the grace of God and on faith. (Rom. 4:16.) Will they pretend that he is here, too, speaking of preceding merits? Nay, he declares that the greatest saints can have no assurance of salvation, unless it repose on the grace of Christ. He therefore abolishes faith who does not retain his as the only righteousness, which exists even until death.

We are justified freely, they say, because no works which precede justification merit it. But when Paul takes away all ground of glorying from Abraham, on the ground that faith was imputed to him for righteousness, he immediately subjoins by way of proof—where works are, there a due reward is paid, whereas what is given to faith is gratuitous. Let us observe that he is speaking of the holy Patriarch. Paul

affirms, that at the time when he renounced the world to
devote himself entirely to God, he was not justified by any
works. If these spurious Fathers object, that it was then only
he began to be justified, the quibble is plainly refuted by the
context of the Sacred History. He had for many years exercised himself in daily prayer to God, and he had constantly
followed the call of God, wherein was contained the promise
of eternal life. Must they not therefore be thrice blind who
see no gratuitous righteousness of God, except in the very
vestibule, and think that the merit of works pervades the
edifice? But it is proper to attend to the gloss by which
they attempt to cloak this gross impiety, viz., that in this
way they satisfy the Apostle's sentiment, "If it be of grace,
then it is no more of works." (Rom. 11:5.) But Paul ascribes it to Divine grace that a remnant is left, and that they
are miraculously preserved by God from the danger of eternal
destruction, even unto the end. Far, therefore, is he from re-
stricting it to so small a portion, *i.e.*, to the beginning alone.

It was indeed an absurd dream, but they are still more
grossly absurd when they give it as their opinion, that none
of all the things which precede Justification, whether faith
or works, merit it. What works antecedent to Justification
are they here imagining? What kind of order is this in which
the fruit is antecedent in time to the root? In one word, that
pious readers may understand how great progress has been
made in securing purity of doctrine, the monks dunned into
the ears of the reverend Fathers, whose part was to nod assent, this old song, that good works which precede justification are not meritorious of eternal salvation, but preparatory only. If any works precede faith, they should also be
taken into account. But there is no merit, because there are
no works; for if men inquire into their works, they will
find only evil works.

Posterity will scarcely believe that the Papacy had fallen
into such a stupor as to imagine the possibility of any work
antecedent to justification, even though they denied it to be
meritorious of so great a blessing! For what can come from
man until he is born again by the Spirit of God? Very different is the reasoning of Paul. He exhorts the Ephesians to
remember (chap. 2.) that they were saved by grace, not by
themselves nor by their own works. He subjoins a proof, not
the one which these insane Fathers use, that no works which
precede suffice, but the one which I have adduced, that we
are possessed of no works but those which God hath pre-

pared, because we are his workmanship created unto a holy and pious life. Faith, moreover, precedes justification, but in such a sense, that in respect of God, it follows. What they say of faith might perhaps hold true, were faith itself, which puts us in possession of righteousness, our own. But seeing that it too is the free gift of God, the exception which they introduce is superfluous. Scripture, indeed, removes all doubt on another ground, when it opposes faith to works, to prevent its being classed among merits. Faith brings nothing of our own to God, but receives what God spontaneously offers us. Hence it is that faith, however imperfect, nevertheless possesses a perfect righteousness, because it has respect to nothing but the gratuitous goodness of God.

In the *tenth* chapter, they inveigh against what they call The Vain Confidence of Heretics. This consists, according to their definition, in our holding it as certain that our sins are forgiven, and resting in this certainty. But if such certainty makes heretics, where will be the happiness which David extols? (Psalm 32.) Nay, where will be the peace of which Paul discourses in the fifth chapter to the Romans, if we rest in anything but the good-will of God? How, moreover, have we God propitious, but just because he enters not into judgment with us? They acknowledge that sins are never forgiven for Christ's sake, except freely, but leaving it in suspense to whom and when they are forgiven, they rob all consciences of calm placid confidence. Where, then, is that boldness of which Paul elsewhere speaks, (Eph. 3:12,) that access with confidence to the Father through faith in Christ? Not contented with the term confidence, he furnishes us with boldness, which is certainly something more than certainty. And what shall we say to his own occasional use of the term certainty? (Rom. 8:37.) This certainty he founds upon nothing but a mere persuasion of the free love of God. Nay, they overthrow all true prayer to God, when they keep pious minds suspended by fear which alone shuts the door of access against us. "He who doubts," says James, (James 1:6,) "is like a wave of the sea driven by the wind." Let not such think that they shall obtain anything of the Lord. "Let him who would pray effectually not doubt." Attend to the antithesis between faith and doubt, plainly intimating that faith is destroyed as soon as certainty is taken away.

But that the whole of their theology may be more manifest to my readers, let them weigh the words which follow under the same head. It ought not to be asserted, they say, that those who have been truly justified ought to entertain an unhesitating doubt that they are justified. If it be so, let them teach how πληροφορία (full assurance) can be reconciled with doubt. For Paul makes it the perpetual attendant of faith. I say nothing as to their laying down as a kind of axiom what Paul regards as a monstrous absurdity. "If the inheritance is by the law," he says, (Rom. 4:14,) "faith is made void." He argues that there will be no certainty of faith if it depends on human works—a dependence which he hesitates not to pronounce most absurd. And justly; seeing he immediately infers from it that the promise also is abolished.

I am ashamed to debate the matter, as if it were doubtful, with men who call themselves Christians. The doctrine of Scripture is clear. "We know," says John, (1 John 4:6,) "that we are the children of God." And he afterwards explains whence this knowledge arises, viz., from the Spirit which he hath given us. In like manner Paul, too, reminds us, (1 Cor. 2:12,) "That we have not received the spirit of the world but the Spirit which is of God, that we may know the things which are given us of God." Elsewhere it is said still more explicitly, "We have not received the spirit of bondage again to fear, but the Spirit of adoption, whereby we cry, Abba, Father." (Rom. 8:15.) Hence that access with confidence and boldness which we mentioned a little ago. And, indeed, they are ignorant of the whole nature of faith who mingle doubt with it. Were Paul in doubt, he would not exult over death, and write as he does in the eighth of the Romans, when he boasts of being so certain of the love of God that nothing can turn him from the persuasion. This is clear from his words. And he assigns the cause, "Because the love of God is shed abroad in our hearts by the Holy Spirit which is given to us." By this he intimates that our conscience, resting in the testimony of the Holy Spirit, boldly glories in the presence of God, in the hope of eternal life. But it is not strange that this certainty, which the Spirit of God seals on the hearts of the godly, is unknown to sophists. Our Saviour foretold that so it would be. "Not the world, but you alone in whom he abideth, will know him." (John 14:17.) It is not strange that those who, having discarded the foundation of faith, lean rather on their works, should waver to and fro. For it is a most true saying of Augustine, (in Psalm 88,) "As the promise is sure, not according to our merits, but according to his grace, no man ought to speak with trepidation of that of which he cannot doubt."

They think, however, that they ingeniously obviate all objections when they recommend a general persuasion of the grace of Christ. They prohibit any doubt as to the efficacy of Christ's death. But where do they wish it to be placed? In the air, so as to be only in confused imagination. For they allow none to apply grace to themselves with the firm assurance of faith, as if we had to no purpose received such promises as these, "Behold your king cometh;" "Ye are the heirs of promise;" "The Father is pleased in thee;" "The righteousness of God is unto all and upon all them that believe." (Matt. 21:5; Zech. 9:9; Acts 2:39; Luke 12:32; Rom. 3:22.) Surely, if they admit that by faith we apprehend what God offers to us, Christ is not set before me and others, merely that we may believe him to have been the Redeemer of Abraham, but that every one may appropriate the salvation which he procured. And how improper is it to assert that "no man can know with certainty of faith that he has obtained the grace of God." Paul and John recognise none as the children of God but those who know it. Of what knowledge can we understand them to speak, but that which they have learned by the teaching of the Holy Spirit? Admirably says Bernard, (Serm. v. in Dedicat. Temp.,) "Faith must here come to our aid; here truth must lend us succour; that that which lies hid in the heart of the Father respecting us may be revealed by the Spirit, or the Spirit may persuade our hearts that we are the children of God; and persuade by calling and justifying us freely by faith." But if Paul, when he exhorts the Corinthians to prove themselves whether they be in the faith, (2 Cor. 13:5,) pronounces all reprobate who do not know Christ dwelling in them, why should I hesitate to pronounce them twice reprobate, who, not allowing the Church to enter on any such proof, abolish all certainty concerning the grace of God?

Under the *eleventh* head, when they describe Increase of Righteousness, they not only confound the free imputation of righteousness with the merit of works, but almost exterminate it. Their words are, "Believers increase in righteousness by good works, through the observance of the commandments of God and the Church, and are thence more justified." They ought at least to use the exception of Augustine. (De Civit. xix. c. 27.) "The righteousness of believers, while they live in the world, consists more in the forgiveness of sins than the perfection of virtues." He teaches that no dependence at all is to be placed on righteousness of works, which he names with contempt. For he declares that the only hope of all the godly who groan under the weakness of the flesh is, that they have a mediator, Christ Jesus, who is the propitiation for their sins. (Lib. ad Bonif., v. c. 5.) On the contrary, the Fathers of Trent, or rather the hireling monks, who, as a kind of Latin pipers, compose for them whatever tune they please, doing their utmost to call their disciples away from the view of grace, blind them by a false confidence in works. We, indeed, willingly acknowledge, that believers ought to make daily increase in good works, and that the good works wherewith they are adorned by God, are sometimes distinguished by the name of righteousness. But since the whole value of works is derived from no other fountain than that of gratuitous acceptance, how absurd were it to make the former overthrow the latter! Why do they not remember what they learned when boys at school, that what is subordinate is not contrary? I say that it is owing to free imputation that we are considered righteous before God; I say that from this also another benefit proceeds, viz., that our works have the name of righteousness, though they are far from having the reality of righteousness. In short, I affirm, that not by our own merit but by faith alone, are both our persons and works justified; and that the justification of works depends on the justification of the person, as the effect on the cause. Therefore, it is necessary that the righteousness of faith alone so precede in order, and be so pre-eminent in degree, that nothing can go before it or obscure it.

Hence it is a most iniquitous perversion to substitute some kind of meritorious for a gratuitous righteousness, as if God after justifying us once freely in a single moment, left us to procure righteousness for ourselves by the observance of the law during the whole of life. As to the observance of the Divine Commandments, they must, whether they will or not, confess this much, that all mortals are very far from accomplishing it perfectly. Let them now answer, and say whether any part of it whatever be righteousness, or a part of righteousness? They will strenuously maintain the latter. But it is repugnant to Scripture, which gives this honour to none but perfect obedience. "The man who doeth these things shall live in them;" "Cursed is he that continueth not in all things written in the book of the law to do them." (Gal. 3:10.) Again, "He who fails in one point is guilty of all." (James

2:10.) There is no man who does not acknowledge, without one word from me, that we are all subject to the curse while we keep halting at the observance of the law, and that righteousness, since works cannot procure it, must be borrowed from some other quarter. Of the commandments of the Church, which they mix up with those of God, we shall speak elsewhere. My readers, however, must be informed in passing, that no kind of impiety is here omitted. Who can excuse their profanity in not hesitating to claim a power of justifying for their own inventions? Never did even Pelagius attempt this. He attempted to fascinate miserable men by the impious persuasion that they could, by the observance of the Divine law, acquire righteousness for themselves; but to attribute this merit to human laws never entered his mind. It is execrable blasphemy against God for any mortal to give way to such presumption as to award eternal life to the observance of his own traditions.

But whither shall I turn? It is a Sacred Council that speaks, and it cannot err in the interpretation of Scripture. And they have passages of Scripture, the first out of Ecclesiasticus, "Fear not to be justified even until death." I believe there is one way of getting myself out of the difficulty. Let my readers look at the passage, and they will find that the worthy Fathers have impudently corrupted it; for the writer says, "Be not forbidden, *i.e.*, prevented until death," although it ought rather to be rendered *defer not;* for this the Greek word means. He is inveighing against the slothfulness of those who put off their conversion to God. What was thus spoken of the commencement, these religious Fathers, not only in gross ignorance, but open malice, apply to progress. In the passage of James there is more plausibility. (James 2:24.) But any one who has read our writings knows well enough that James gives them no support, inasmuch as he uses justification to signify, not the cause of righteousness, but the proof of it. This plainly appears from the context. But they become more ridiculous when they infer that a man is justified by good works because the Church prays for increase of faith, hope, and charity. Who, if he is not too old to be a child, is not frightened at this thunder?

Under the *twelfth* head they renew the old anathema:— Let none say that the Commandments of God are impossible to be observed by a justified man. It serves no purpose to dispute about the term *impossible*. It is enough for me, and should be enough for all who are pious, and not at all con-

178 JOHN CALVIN

tentious, that no man ever lived who satisfied the law of God, and that none ever can be found. What! shall we accuse the Holy Spirit of falsehood, when he charges all men with the guilt of transgression, not those of our age only, but all who shall ever exist to the end of the world? "There is not a man upon earth," saith Solomon, "who sinneth not." (1 Kings 8:46.) And David had said, "In thy sight shall no man living be justified." (Psalm 143:2.) If it be possible to find any one who can fulfil the law, let the Holy Spirit retract. But far from us be the devilish pride of making the eternal Author of truth a liar. Nay, even Paul's argument would fail:—"It is written, Cursed is every one that continueth not in all things written in the book of the law. Therefore, whosoever are under the law are under curse." (Gal. 3:10.) It will be easy to object, that the law can be fulfilled. But the Apostle assumes as an acknowledged principle what these men stigmatize with anathema. Accordingly in another place, when deploring the bondage in which himself, in common with all saints, was held, he could find no other remedy than that of being freed from the body. (Rom. 7:24.)

The Pelagians annoyed Augustine with the same quibble. He admits that God may, if he pleases, raise men to this pitch of perfection, but that he never had, and never would, because the Scriptures teach otherwise. I go farther, and assert, that what the Scriptures declare never shall be, is impossible; although, if we are to debate about a word, the very thing was expressed by Peter, (Acts 15) when he spoke of the yoke of the law as that which none of their fathers could bear. It is an error to suppose that this refers only to ceremonies: for what so very arduous was there in ceremonies as to make all human strength fail under the burden of them? He undoubtedly means that all mankind from the beginning were, and still are, unequal to the observance of the law, and that therefore nothing remains but to flee to the grace of Christ, which, loosing us from the yoke of the law, keeps us as it were under free custody. And it is to be observed that he is speaking of the regenerate, lest the Fathers of Trent quibble, and say that he spoke of the weakness of the flesh when the assistance of the Spirit is wanting. For he affirms that prophets and patriarchs, and pious kings, however aided by the Spirit of God, were unable to bear the yoke of the law, and declares, without ambiguity, that the observance of the law was impossible.

But they also produce Scripture as a witness on the other

side: for John says, that "his commandments are not grievous." (1 John 5:3.) I admit it, provided you exclude not the
doctrine of the remission of sins, which he places before all
the commandments. If it be not grievous to perform the law,
you will find me several men without sin to make God a liar;
as is said also by John. (1 John 1:8.) But these fools consider not that the facility of which John speaks depends on
this, that the saints have a remedy in readiness to supply their
defects—they flee for pardon. Hence, too, it is that Christ's
yoke is easy and his burden light, because the saints feel an
alacrity in their liberty while they feel themselves no longer
under the law. Paul applies to them this best stimulus of exhortation. (Rom. 6:12.) And David also teaches, "With thee
is forgiveness, that thou mayest be feared." (Psalm 130:4.)
Take that hope of pardon from me, and the least commandment of the law will be a heavier load than Ætna. But what
is this to idle monks, who have here touched with the little
finger that observance of the commandments of the facility
of which they so confidently prattle. Nay, they openly betray
their irreligion by this one dogma. How? This admirable
Apostle laments that he is held captive from inability to obey
the law as is meet, and he cries out that the disease cannot
be cured till death cure it. (Rom. 7:23.) These sturdy doctors superciliously smile, and sing out that such complaints
are causeless, because Christ's burden is light. They afterwards add, "The disciples of Christ love him, and those who
love him do his commandments." (John 14:23.) This is all
true. But where is the perfect love of Christ—love, I mean,
with the whole heart, and mind, and strength? There only
where the flesh lusteth not against the spirit, and therefore
not in the world at all. The disciples of Christ love him with
sincere and earnest affection of heart, and according to the
measure of their love keep his commandments. But how small
is this compared with that strict perfection in which there is
no deficiency?

Let readers of sense now attend to the consistency of the
dicta of these Fathers. After boldly asserting that the Law
can be fulfilled by believers, they admit that even the most
holy sometimes fall into light and daily sins. First I ask,
whether there be any sin, however light, that is not incon-
sistent with the observance of the law? For what vicious
thought will creep into the mind of man if it be wholly occupied with the love of God? The law is not satisfied unless
God is loved with the whole heart. That men do not there-

fore cease to be righteous I admit. But why so, but just because they are blessed to whom sin is not imputed? If they insist on being righteous by works, on which their consciences can repose in the sight of God, they, in the first place, subvert faith, and do an insufferable wrong to the grace of God; and, in the second place, they bring no support to their impious doctrine as to possible observance of the law. If they consider what they call lighter lapses as nothing, the dreadful sentence of the Supreme Judge thunders forth, "He who shall despise one of these least commandments shall be called the least in the kingdom of heaven." Although I should like to know what sins they call light, (for so they speak by way of extenuation,) and why they say that the righteous fall into them sometimes rather than constantly, or ever and anon; for scarcely a moment passes in which we do not contract some new guilt. In their eyes all kinds of concupiscence which prompt us to evil are light sins, and also all kinds of temptations which urge us to blasphemy against God. Be this as it may, they are here placed in a manifest dilemma.

What afterwards follows under the same head is no more applicable than if one were to attempt to prove from the movement of the feet that the hands do not feel. They gather some exhortations to a pious life. What, pray, will they force out of these except what may be learned a hundred times better, and with very different effect, from our writings and discourses, and even daily conversation, viz., that "we are not called to uncleanness but to holiness," that "the mercy of God hath appeared, that denying the lusts of the flesh, we may live piously and holily in the world," that "we have risen with Christ to set our affections on things above." (1 Thess. 4:7; Tit. 2:11; Col. 3:12.) But they seem to think they have done some great thing when they infer that it is in vain for those who are unwilling to be partakers of the sufferings of Christ, to glory in the heavenly inheritance. How much better we explain the matter let our readers judge. There is one difference, however: we teach that we are to share in the sufferings of Christ in order that we may attain to the fellowship of his blessed resurrection; (Rom. 8:17;) we do not separate Christ from himself. They erroneously infer what does not at all follow—that men by suffering merit eternal life, and that part of their righteousness consisting therein, they do not depend entirely on the grace of God.

But they are still more absurd in their conclusion. For they infer that all are enemies to the Christian religion who teach that the righteous sin in every good work, at least venially. I should like to know what logic taught them to draw such an inference as this: "So run that you may obtain the reward" —*ergo*, In the good works of saints there is nothing that deserves blame. Must not men be thrice stupid when such fellows can persuade them that such follies proceeded from the Holy Spirit? But, passing this absurdity, let us look at the substance.

They must of necessity admit that works are to be judged from the internal affection of mind from which they emanate, and the end at which they aim, rather than from the external mask under which they appear to men: for God looketh on the heart, as was said to Samuel, and his eyes behold the truth, as Jeremiah reminds us. It is too plain, however, that we are never animated and actuated by a perfect love to God in obeying his just commands. Various passions withdraw us from our course, so that we scarcely walk when God enjoins us to hasten on with the greatest speed; we are scarcely lukewarm when we ought to be all ardour. Though from self-deception we are not sensible of this defect, God sees and judges: in his sight the stars are dim, and the sun shineth not. In short, the seventh chapter of the Romans disposes of this controversy. There Paul, in his own person and that of all the godly, confesses that he is far from perfection, even when his will is at its best. Wherefore let a man flatter himself as he may, the best work that ever was, if brought by God to judgment, will be found stained by some blemish. But these works are approved by God. Who denies it? We only maintain that they cannot please without pardon. But what is it that God pardons except sin? Hence it follows that there is nothing so very censurable in saying, that all good works whatever, if judged with strict rigour, are more deserving of eternal damnation than of the reward of life; for wherever sin, in however slight a degree, is found, no man of sound judgment will deny that there too the materials of death are found. Owing, however, to the boundless mercy of God, works have a recompense in heaven, though they not only merited nothing of the kind, but would have the reward of eternal death were not the impurity with which they are otherwise defiled wiped away by Christ. I have moreover shewn in many places how absurd the reasoning is which infers dignity or merit from the use of the term *reward*. The reason is obvious. The very recompense which the sophists assert to be founded on merit, depends on gratuitous acceptance.

Under the *thirteenth* head, if they only did what the title professes, I would give them my subscription. But since, while professing to obviate rashness and presumption, they make it their whole study to efface from the minds of the pious all confidence in their election, I am forced to oppose them, because they are plainly opposed by Scripture. For to what end does Paul discourse at such length in the first chapter to the Ephesians, on the eternal election of God, unless to persuade them that they were chosen by it unto eternal life? And there is no need of conjecture; for he repeatedly enjoins the Ephesians to hold it fixed in their minds, that they have been called and made partakers of the gospel, because they were elected in Christ before the foundation of the world. Likewise in the eighth chapter to the Romans, he expressly conjoins the doctrine of election with the assurance of faith.

I acknowledge, indeed, and we are all careful to teach, that nothing is more pernicious than to inquire into the secret council of God, with the view of thereby obtaining a knowledge of our election—that this is a whirlpool in which we shall be swallowed up and lost. But seeing that our Heavenly Father holds forth in Christ a mirror of our eternal adoption, no man truly holds what has been given us by Christ save he who feels assured that Christ himself has been given him by the Father, that he may not perish. What! are the following passages mere verbiage? "The Father who has placed us under the protection and faith of his Son is greater than all." "The Son will not allow anything to be lost." (John 6:39; 10:28.) These things are said that all who are the sons of God may trust in such a guardian of their salvation, and feel safe in the midst of danger; nay, when beset with infinite perils, may trust that their salvation is secure because in the hand of God.

But they affirm, that it is impossible to know whom God has chosen except by special revelation. I admit it. And, accordingly, Paul says that we have not received the spirit of this world, but the Spirit which is of God, that we may know the things which are given us of God. The gift he elsewhere interprets as meaning the adoption, by which we are classed among his children, and which he holds to be so certain that we may with loud voice glory in it. But I am not unaware of what they intend by special revelation. I, however, mean that which our Heavenly Father specially deigns to bestow on his own children. Nor is this any fancy of my own. The words of Paul are well known, "Those things which are hidden from human sense God hath revealed unto us by his Spirit, who also searcheth the deepest things of God." Again, "Who hath known the mind of God, or who hath been his counsellor? But we have the mind of Christ."

On the whole, then, we see that what the venerable Fathers call rash and damnable presumption, is nothing but that holy confidence in our adoption revealed unto us by Christ, to which God everywhere encourages his people.

Under the *fourteenth* head they prohibit any one from feeling absolutely certain that God will bestow upon him the gift of Final Perseverance, and yet they do not disapprove of entertaining the strongest hope of it in God. But let them first shew us by what kind of cement they can glue together things so opposed to each other as the strongest hope and a doubtful expectation. For certainly, he whose expectation of eternal life is not founded on absolute certainty, must be agitated by various doubts. This is not the kind of hope which Paul describes, when he says that he is certainly persuaded that neither life nor death, nor things present, nor things to come, will dissolve the love with which God embraces him in Christ. He would not speak thus did not the certainty of Christian hope reach beyond the last hour of life. And what language do the promises speak? The Spirit not only declares that the just lives by faith, but that he shall live. (Hab. 2:4.) Thus far must hope reach. Paul even shews this when he describes hope as patiently waiting for things which are yet concealed.

But, it may be said, they do not take away hope, but only absolute certainty. What! is there any expression of doubt or uncertainty when Paul boldly asserts that a crown of righteousness is laid up for him? (1 Tim. 4:8.) Is there anything conditional in the words, when he declares that an earnest of our adoption has been given us, so that we can dare with loud voice to call God our Father? They take refuge in the frivolous quibble out of which I have already driven them, viz., that Paul had this by special revelation. But he claims nothing so special for himself as not to share it with all believers, when in their name as much as his own, he boldly exults over death and life, the present and the future. Nor does John claim for himself alone that knowledge in which he glories, when he says, "We know that we shall be like

God, for we shall see him as he is." (1 John 3:2.) Nor Paul, when he says, "We glory in hope of the glory of God;" and again, "We know that when this earthly tabernacle falls, a mansion is prepared for us in heaven." (Rom. 5:2; 2 Cor. 5:1.)

They make a gloss of what is said in the tenth chapter of First Corinthians, "Let him who standeth take heed lest he fall." Of this there is a twofold solution. Paul there only checks carnal arrogance, which has nothing to do with the assurance of hope; nor does he address believers only, but all of the Gentiles who had assumed the name of Christ, among whom there might be many puffed up with vain confidence. For the comparison which is there made between Jews and Gentiles, is not confined to the elect only, but comprehends all who belonged to the Church by name. I will be satisfied, however, with this one reply, as it is quite sufficient, viz., that the fear enjoined is not that which in the smallest degree impairs the certainty of faith or hope, but only that which keeps us solicitous in the fear of God.

The regenerate are not yet in glory, but only in the hope of glory, and much of the contest still remains. Hence did they infer that torpor must be shaken off, and no overweening security indulged, there is no man of sense who would not subscribe to them. But when they employ the passage as a battering-ram to shake the firmness of our hope, and drive us headlong, their conduct is on no account to be tolerated. In qualifying Paul's sentiment, and making it mean that the work of salvation which God has begun will be perfected in us only if we are not wanting to his grace, they act very ignorantly, not observing that one part of grace consists in having God present with us so as to prevent our being wanting to his grace. This doctrine ought not to give occasion to sloth; it ought only to make them recognise what they have received of God, and what they expect from him.

I could like, if I durst, to pass many things without affixing a stigma to them. But what can I do? There is scarcely one line which does not contain some notable error or give indications of dishonest dealing. On the *fifteenth* head, where they treat of recovery after the fall, they say that Jerome gave an appropriate definition of repentance, when he called it the second plank after shipwreck. Were I disposed to criticise the *dictum* of Jerome, I would ask why he calls it the second plank, and not the third or fourth? for how few are there who do not during life make more than one ship-

wreck. Nay, what man was ever found whom the grace of
God has not rescued from daily shipwrecks? But I have no
business with Jerome at present.

The Fathers of Trent do not treat of Repentance, but of
the Sacrament of Penitence, which they pretend to have been
instituted by Christ. When? When he said, Receive ye the
Holy Spirit; whose sins ye remit, they shall be remitted. (John
20:22.) First, because Christ gave the Apostles this authority,
is it therefore a sacrament? Where is the sign? where the
form? Secondly, who knows not that this office was assigned
to the Apostles that they might perform it towards strangers?
How asinine the Fathers must be to allow the absurd trifling
of a dreaming monk thus to pass without opposition! Christ
confirms the testimony which the Apostles were to bear to
the world concerning the remission of sins. Such is the message which is conveyed by the gospel, and that, too, to those
who are not yet chosen into the Church. Some babbler among
the monks who rule the Council having never perhaps looked
at the passage, certainly never pondered it, read out his own
commentary that there a formula is prescribed by which
those who had fallen after baptism were to be restored to a
state of grace. The stupid Fathers nodded assent. The passage itself, however, proclaims that it was shamelessly
wrested. They infer that the penitence of a Christian man
after a lapse, is very different from baptismal penitence: as
if Christ had only referred to one species, and not expressly
required, as the twenty-fourth chapter of Luke informs us,
that repentance as well as remission of sins should be
preached in his name.

They go farther, and say, that this Penitence with which
they trifle consists not only in contrition of heart, but the
confession of the mouth and the satisfaction of works: although not to appear unmerciful, they mitigate the rigour of
their law when they allow themselves to be appeased by a
wish to confess. Why should I begin a long discussion here?
The point is the remission of sins: which is the knowledge
of salvation. (Luke 1:77.) God promises it to us free in the
blood of Christ: of auricular confession he says not a word.
These new lawgivers tie down forgiveness to a formula of confession, contrary to the command of God, and assert that it
is redeemed by satisfaction. What will remain for miserable
consciences, if they are forced to abandon the word of God
and acquiesce in the decrees of men?

I am desirous to be assured of my salvation. I am shewn

in the word of God a simple way, which will lead me straight
to the entire and tranquil possession of this great boon. I will
say no more. Men come and lay hands on me, and tie me
down to a necessity of confession from which Christ frees
me. They lay upon me the burden of satisfaction, ordering
me to provide at my own hand that which Christ shews me
is to be sought from his blood alone. Can I long doubt what
it is expedient to do? Nay, away with all hesitation, when
attempts are made to lead us away from the only author of
our salvation. Search as they may, not a syllable will be found
by which Christ orders us to confess our sins into a human
ear. All the promises relating to the remission of sins make
not the smallest mention of such a thing. The law was wholly
unknown to the Apostles. Throughout the Eastern Church it
was scarcely ever used. Nay, the observance was everywhere
free for more than a thousand years, till Innocent III., with
a few of his horned crew, entangled the Christian people
in this net, which the Fathers of Trent would now make fast.
What I say is abundantly testified by ancient history. Our
books are filled with proofs. None of them are unknown to
those who dictated this famous formula to the Council; and
yet so impudent are they, that they would persuade us by
one word that the door of salvation is closed, and can only
be opened by the key of a fictitious confession. But who will
grant them a license to restrict the promises of Christ, by
imposing any condition they please?

I do not say at present how cruel an executioner to torture
and excruciate consciences is that law of Innocent which they
anew promulgate; how many it has driven headlong to despair; what a narcotic of hypocrisy it has been to lull others
asleep; how many monstrous iniquities have sprung from it!
Nay, let us even imagine, as they themselves falsely give out,
that some advantage flows from it: it is nothing to the purpose. The question is asked, How are those who have fallen
from divine grace restored to it? Scripture everywhere shews
the method, but makes no reference to confession, which
was long afterwards coined in human brains. What effrontery!
to preclude access to the hope of obtaining pardon, unless
the confession which they have been pleased to prescribe
precedes. The question relates to repentance. Its whole force
and nature are so frequently, so copiously, so clearly de-
picted by the Holy Spirit in the law, the Prophets, and the
Gospel, that no doctrine is more lucidly explained. Of confession, such as they pretend, there is throughout a profound

silence. Who, then, will believe them when they affirm that no repentance is genuine without that appendage, nay, unless it be included in it?

It is enough for me to know the two following things—first, that they devise a Repentance altogether different from that which is recommended to us in Scripture; and secondly, that they enact a condition for obtaining the remission of sins, from which he, to whom alone the power of remitting belongs, wished us to be free. The latter is just as if they were forbidding God to promise salvation without their permission, or at least were opposing his performance of the promise of salvation which he has given. For they do not permit him to pardon our sins, unless it be on the condition of our performing an observance which they alone make binding.

With regard to Satisfaction, they think they make a subtle distinction when they collect the dregs of the vile comments of the sophists,—that not eternal punishment, indeed, but temporal, is to be compensated by satisfaction. Who knew not that such was the prattle of the sophists? And yet, when they pretend that eternal punishment, together with guilt, is remitted to us by confession, or the wish to confess, what else do they mean than that we merit by works what God promises to give freely?

But let us now see the force of the distinction. When the Prophets mention the gratuitous remission of sins, it is true they usually refer to its other effect, viz., that God would be appeased, and no longer avenge the sins of his people or visit them with his rod. Whoever is moderately versed in Scripture will acknowledge the strict accuracy of my statement, that the punishments which we deserved are mitigated, loosed, in fine, abolished, because God pardons us, not for any merit of our own, as if he were appeased by compensation, but because he is moved solely by his own mercy. The Babylonish captivity was a temporal punishment. Its termination in seventy years, when the Israelites deserved it much longer, God ascribes to his own free mercy. Whenever the chastisements which God had threatened are withdrawn, it is uniformly represented as the result of gratuitous reconciliation. It is certainly a relaxation of temporal punishment which God promises in these words, "Not on your account will I do it, but for my name's sake." And Isaiah, when he states, that the satisfaction or price of our peace was laid upon Christ, reminds us that we have not only been freed from punishment by his interposition, but that he bore on our account all the pains by which God is wont to avenge or chastise our sins, in order that we may, however unworthy, enjoy all the blessings of the present life also. (Isaiah 48:9; 53:5.) But God nevertheless still chastises believers. I admit it. But to what end? Is it that he, by inflicting punishment, may pay what is due to himself and his own justice? Not at all; but that he may humble them, by striking them with a dread of his anger, that he may produce in them an earnest feeling of repentance, and render them more cautious in future. But there are means by which they may avert these punishments; I mean, when they anticipate them of their own accord, there is no reason why God should as it were drag them violently. When is there occasion for the rod but just when voluntary correction is wanting? Accordingly, the Apostle tells us that those who shall have judged themselves shall not be judged by the Lord. (1 Cor. 11:31.)

But how preposterous to infer satisfaction from this? The greater part of believers have, by prayer, warded off the chastisement to which they had made themselves liable. Nay, even Ahab, when he humbles himself spontaneously, feels the hand of God fall lighter upon him. (1 Kings 21:29.) The deprecatory petitions which the saints employed are the most decisive witnesses to gratuitous satisfaction. But these Fathers, it seems, adduce nothing which they cannot prove by passages of Scripture; for Paul teaches, that the sorrow which is agreeable to God worketh repentance unto salvation not to be repented of. (2 Cor. 7:10.) What! does Paul here call us back to satisfaction? I hear no word of it. They are dishonestly deluding us. They do so still more in what follows, when they tell us that John must be understood to refer to the same penitence in saying, "Repent, and bring forth fruits meet for repentance." (Luke 3:8.) But whom did John address in these terms? Was it not persons who offered themselves for baptism while not yet imbued with the faith of Christ? Somewhat different from this, and yet not less absurd, is their quotation from the second chapter of the Revelations, "Remember whence thou art fallen, and first do works;" whereas the proper reading is, *"do the first works,"* or the former works. The writer exhorts the Ephesians to return to their former state of life. With what face is this stretched to satisfaction? When they so pertly called black white, did they think there would be no eyes to detect their fraud? Lysander once said to deputies who had spoken in a meeting of allies more imperiously than they ought, that they had need of a city which would be very indulgent to them. These masters would need a herd of oxen if they wish to have an audience which they can persuade to believe what they please. Let them go and boast of being guided immediately by the Holy Spirit, while they are palpable falsifiers of holy writ.

To sum up the whole—Though believers ought to be constantly thinking of Repentance, these Holy Fathers imagine it to be an indescribable something of rare occurrence—though Scripture declares repentance to be a renewal of the whole man—though it points out its very source, fear excited by a true sense of the Divine judgment—though it enumerates its parts, self-denial, which consists in a hatred of sin and dissatisfaction with our own depravity, and renewal of life or regeneration of the spirit, which is nothing else than the restoration of the Divine image—though it carefully marks its effects, and explicitly defines its whole nature,—the venerable Fathers produce nothing but the flimsy inanities by which the doctrine of repentance has been corrupted under the Papacy. What was said by ecclesiastical writers concerning external discipline, which referred to the formal profession of repentance, they ignorantly wrest to the spiritual renovation which formed the subject of their discourse. Not to be tedious in reviewing each point, let any one compare their lucubrations with our writings, and he will find and acknowledge that they have turned light into darkness.

I have hitherto endeavoured to censure without accusing; and impartial readers will observe, that I censure nothing unless compelled to do so. But there is not a sentence which does not extort more of it from me than I could wish. Of this nature is the assertion under the *sixteenth* head, that the grace of Justification is lost, not only by unbelief, but by any mortal sin. If they meant that we are ejected from the possession (enjoyment) of this great blessing by an evil conscience, I would not at all gainsay them, I mean as far as regards ourselves. For although God does not cast us off, yet an evil conscience is such a separation from him as excludes us from the enjoyment of a lively and justifying knowledge of his paternal love towards us. But they are preposterous, *first*, in recognising no sin as mortal that is not gross and palpable, whereas most inward sins wound the mind more grievously and even fatally; and, *secondly*, in not perceiving how a good conscience is the inseparable attendant of faith. Were it not so, how could it be said that our hearts are purified by faith, that Christ dwells in our hearts by faith, that it is the victory by which we overcome the world, the shield for repelling the assaults of the devil, and that we are kept by faith through the power of God unto salvation? (Acts 15:9; Eph. 3:17; 1 John 5:4; Eph. 6:16; 1 Peter 5:9; 1:5.) There is no doubt, therefore, that faith is overwhelmed and buried in a man whenever he has been overcome by any temptation so as to abandon the fear of God. For the Spirit of holiness cannot be separated from faith any more than can Christ himself. I do not assert, however, that when we forsake the fear of the Lord faith is altogether extinguished in us. But as the fear of God is oppressed by depraved lusts, so I say that faith is stifled, and for the time exerts its power no more than if it were in a manner dead. The holy Fathers craftily endeavour to burrow out a hole in which they may hide their impious dogma, that we are not justified by faith alone. Not succeeding in this they attempt another method.

We come now to the *last* head, which treats of The Merit of Works. Here there is no dispute between us as to the necessity of exhorting believers to good works, and even stimulating them by holding forth a reward. What then? First, I differ from them in this, that they make eternal life the reward; for if God rewards works with eternal life, they will immediately make out that faith itself is the reward which is paid, whereas Scripture uniformly proclaims that it is the inheritance which falls to us by no other right than that of free adoption. But there is still greater ground for contradicting, when they are not ashamed to affirm that nothing is to prevent believers from satisfying the Law, at least in a degree proportioned to the present state, and meriting eternal life. Where then will be the blessedness of which David speaks, (Psalm 32,) and without which we are all thrice wretched? Wo to those miserable men who perceive not that he who has come nearest to perfection has not yet advanced half-way! All who have their conscience exercised feel the strict truth of Augustine's sentiment, "The righteousness of saints in this life consists more in the forgiveness of sins than the perfection of virtues." (Lib. de Civit. Dei, xix, c. 27.) Still more accurate is another passage which I quoted, that, "so long as they groan under the infirmity of the flesh, the only hope left them is, that they have a mediator in Christ by whom they are reconciled to God." (Lib. ad Bon., iii, c. 5.)

It is not strange, however, that addle-pated monks who, having never experienced any struggle of conscience, and who, moreover, being intoxicated with ambition, or surfeiting and drunkenness, only desire to raise themselves in the estimation of their idol, should thus prate of the perfection of the Law. With the same confidence do they talk of a heaven for hire, while they themselves meanwhile continue engrossed with the present hire, after which they are always gaping. But in vain do they attempt to dazzle eyes not wholly blind with those fair colours which they afterwards employ when they prohibit any one from glorying or confiding in works, because they are the gifts of God. Not to mention that what they now confess to be gifts of God, they previously claimed in a greater degree for human ability, there are three errors in their decree which are not to be tolerated. Though they mention incidentally that the good works of the pious are meritorious by the merit of Christ, they omit the most necessary part, viz., that there is no work untainted with impurity, until it be washed away by the blood of Christ. Nay rather, they annex a false dignity to works, as if they could please without pardon. There is, indeed, a speciousness in the gloss that they all flow from the Spirit of Christ. But where will the absolute power of the Holy Spirit be found? Is it not distributed to every one in measure? (1 Cor. 12:11.) They ought, therefore, to have observed, that it is always mixed with dross of ours which taints its purity. But while our inherent depravity renders every kind of work which proceeds from us vicious in the sight of God, the only thing left for our works is to recover the grace which they have not in themselves, by a gratuitous acceptance. This is done when works acknowledged to have no value in themselves borrow, and, as it were, beg their value from Christ.

It is, indeed, a gross and impious delusion, not to acknowledge that every work which proceeds from us has only one way of obtaining acceptance, viz., when all that was vicious in it is pardoned by paternal indulgence. Another delusion almost similar to this is their not reflecting, that even if we should have merited anything by any one work, the whole of the merit, be it what it may, is lost by contrary transgression. "He who offends in one point is guilty of all." (James 2:10.) What reward do you promise yourself when nothing is produced but liability to eternal death? They are also in error when they do not flee to the only remedy, and assuming that there is some good thing in them, ask God of his goodness to regard it with favour, by not imputing the evil things which far exceed it both in weight and number.

The third error, however, is by far the worst, I mean their making assurance of salvation depend on the view of works. At one time, indeed, they prohibit us from trusting in ourselves, but when they again tell us to look to our works that we may have a sure hope of salvation, what grounds of hope can we find in them? Do they not plainly place our whole trust in ourselves? Accordingly, they add a clause which is fit only for such a doctrine. It is, that in this life we carry on a warfare of doubtful issue, and cannot attain certainty, until God render to every one according to his works. By this they overthrow all confidence in our faith, or to use Paul's expression, make faith itself void. (Rom. 4:14.) But Paul declares that he is not justified, because he is not conscious of anything in himself. (1 Cor. 4:4.) This is true, and therefore, in order that our possession of righteousness may be stable and tranquil, our part is to omit all mention of works, and beseech our Judge not to enter into judgment with us. (Psalm 143:2.) We reach the haven of security only when God lays aside the character of Judge, and exhibits himself to us as a Father.

And yet those swinish men are not ashamed to thunder out a cruel denunciation to terrify the simple, that no man is capable of receiving righteousness who does not firmly adhere to whatever they prescribe. What! has a new method of Justification lately appeared? Or rather, as salvation is one, do we not all come to it by one way? What will become of the Prophets and Apostles who gave no heed to such masters? Therefore, paying no regard to the Council of Trent, let us hold that fixed faith which the Prophets and Apostles, by the Spirit of Christ, delivered to us, knowing whence we have learned it. But the venerable Fathers, as if to make it impossible for any man to doubt that they are of the number of those whose mouth, as David exclaims, (Psalm 4:7,) is full of cursing and bitterness, proceed, with truculent bluster, to send forth almost as many anathemas as there are individuals among them, and give these the plausible and honourable name of Canons! Yet that I may not seem to act maliciously, as if I had forgotten the moderation I have hitherto observed, I willingly subscribe to the three first. To the rest I will affix brief censures.

ANTIDOTE TO THE CANONS OF THE
COUNCIL OF TRENT

(ON JUSTIFICATION)[2]

(CANON I.—If any one saith, that man may be justified before God by his own works, whether done through the teaching of human nature, or that of the law, without the grace of God through Jesus Christ: let him be anathema.)

(CANON II.—If any one saith, that the grace of God, through Jesus Christ, is given only for this, that man may be able more easily to live justly, and to merit eternal life, as if, by free-will without grace, he were able to do both, though hardly indeed and with difficulty: let him be anathema.)

(CANON III.—If any one saith, that without the prevenient inspiration of the Holy Ghost, and without his help, man can believe, hope, love, or be penitent as he ought, so that the grace of Justification may be bestowed upon him: let him be anathema.)

To Canons I, II, and III, I say, Amen.

(CANON IV.—If any one saith, that man's free-will moved and excited by God, by assenting to God exciting and calling, nowise co-operates towards disposing and preparing itself for obtaining the grace of Justification; that it can not refuse its consent, if it would, but that, as something inanimate, it does nothing whatever and is merely passive: let him be anathema.)

This was answered above, when I explained how free-will assents to God calling and exciting it. We certainly obey God with our will, but it is with a will which he has formed in us. Those, therefore, who ascribe any proper movement

---

[2] Material in parentheses is from the Council of Trent and is supplied in order to show the material to which Calvin is responding. The Council of Trent canons are reprinted from *Creeds of Christendom*, with a history and critical notes by Philip Schaff, Vol. II (New York: Harper & Brothers, 1877, 1905), pp. 110–26.

to free-will, apart from the grace of God, do nothing else than rend the Holy Spirit. Paul declares, not that a faculty of willing is given to us, but that the will itself is formed in us, (Phil. 2:13,) so that from none else but God is the assent or obedience of a right will. He acts within, holds our hearts, moves our hearts, and draws us by the inclinations which he has produced in us. So says Augustine. (Lib. de Corrupt. et Grat., c. 14.) What preparation can there be in a heart of iron, until by a wondrous change it begins to be a heart of flesh? This, as the Prophet declares, is entirely the work of God. The will of man will, indeed, dissent from God, so long as it continues contrary, but when it has been framed for obedience, the danger of dissenting is removed. But that the efficacy of divine grace is such, that all opposition is beaten down, and we who were unwilling are made obedient, it is not we who assent, but the Lord by the Prophet, when he promises that he will make us to walk in his precepts; and Christ also, when he says, "Whosoever hath heard of my Father cometh unto me." (John 6:45.)

(CANON V.—If any one saith, that, since Adam's sin, the free-will of man is lost and extinguished; or, that it is a thing with only a name, yea a name without a reality, a figment, in fine, introduced into the Church by Satan: let him be anathema.)

Let us not raise a quarrel about a word. But as by Free-will they understand a faculty of choice perfectly free and unbiassed to either side, those who affirm that this is merely to use a name without a substance, have the authority of Christ when he says, that they are free whom the Son makes free, and that all others are the slaves of sin. Freedom and slavery are certainly contrary to each other. As to the term itself, let them hear Augustine, who maintains that the human will is not free so long as it is subject to passions which vanquish and enthral it. (Epist. 144, ad Anastas.) Elsewhere he says, "The will being vanquished by the depravity into which it has fallen, nature is without freedom." (Hom. 3, in Joann.) Again, "Man making a bad use of free-will lost both himself and it." Again, "Man received great powers of free-will when he was created, but lost them by sinning. Foolish men consider not that in the term free-will freedom is implied. But if they are the slaves of sin, why do they boast of free-will? For of whom a man is overcome, to the same is he bound a slave." Nay, in another place he openly derides the

name. "The will," says he, "is free, not freed—free to righteousness, the slave of sin! Why, then, do they so much inflame miserable men by reminding them of their slavery, but
just that they might learn to flee to the deliverer?" (Aug.
de Perfect. Justit. Lib. de Verb. Apost. Serm. 3; De Spiritu et
Litera, c. 30; De Corrupt. et Grat., c. 13.)

(CANON VI.—If any one saith, that it is not in man's power to
make his ways evil, but that the works that are evil God worketh
as well as those that are good, not permissively only, but properly,
and of himself, in such wise that the treason of Judas is no less his
own proper work than the vocation of Paul: let him be anathema.)

As I abhor paradox, I readily repudiate the saying that
the treachery of Judas is as properly the work of God as the
calling of Paul. But they never will convince any man that
God only acts permissively in the wicked, except it be one
who is ignorant of the whole doctrine of Scripture. When it
is said that the reprobate are set apart to execute the work
of God; that his are the snares, swords, and axes which are
directed by his hand; that his hiss arouses them to execute
what his hand and counsel have decreed; that Christ was
slain by the Jews by the determinate counsel of God, (Isaiah
10:5; Ezek. 17:20; 32:2; Psalm 17:13; Acts 2:4, 23,) the
words are too strong to be evaded by the subterfuge of permission. Augustine interprets better. After quoting the passages of Scripture in which the Father is said to have delivered up the Son, and Christ to have delivered himself; he
immediately adds, "What, then, did Judas do but sin." Nor
can he be justly blamed for saying elsewhere, that "God
worketh in the hearts of men to incline their wills as he
pleaseth, whether to good, of his mercy, or to evil, according
to their deservings, and that by his judgment, sometimes
open, sometimes hidden, but always just;" for he immediately adds the qualification, that "the malice is not his." (De
Verb. Dom. Serm. 63.) In like manner he had said a little
before, "He does not command the wicked by ordering, in
which case obedience would be laudable, but by his secret
and just judgment he bends their will, already bad by their
own depravity, to this misdeed or that." (Aug. de Gr. et
Lib. Arb. c. 21.) For there is nothing here but what the
Scriptures teach almost in the same words when they speak
of *inclining* and *turning, hardening* and *doing.*

(CANON VII.—If any one saith, that all works done before Justification, in whatsoever way they be done, are truly sins, or merit the hatred of God; or that the more earnestly one strives to dispose himself for grace, the more grievously he sins: let him be anathema.)

Assuredly a bad tree can only produce bad fruit. But who will be so shameless as to deny that we are bad trees until we are ingrafted into Christ? Therefore, if any good fruit is praised in man, let the root of it be sought in faith, as Augustine admonishes, (in Psalm 31, Serm. 1.) There God so often declares that he regards not the outward appearance, but looketh on the heart. This is said expressly by Jeremiah. (Jer. 55.) But what can be the cleanness or sincerity of a heart which Peter tells us is purified only by faith? (Acts 15:9.) Admirably, therefore, does Augustine say to Boniface, "Our religion distinguishes the just from the unjust, not by the law of works, but by the law of faith, without which the works which seem good turn to sin." He adds, "Therefore unbelievers sin in whatever they do, because they do not refer their doings to a lawful end." (Lit. ad Bonif., Lib. 3, c. 5.) He treats copiously of the same subject in his tract against Julian. Hence, also, in another place he describes theirs as a wandering course, inasmuch as the more active they are, the farther they are carried from the goal, and the more therefore their condition becomes hopeless. At last he concludes, that "it is better to limp in the course than keep running out of it." (Praef. in Psalm 31.) And what more would we have? Let them anathematize the Apostle, who declares that without faith it is impossible to please God! (Heb. 11:6.) Let them anathematize Christ and Paul, who declare that all unbelievers are dead, and are raised from death by the gospel! (John 5; Eph. 2:1.)

(CANON VIII.—If any one saith, that the fear of hell,—whereby, by grieving for our sins, we flee unto the mercy of God, or refrain from sinning,—is a sin, or makes sinners worse: let him be anathema.)

I answer: AMEN. Nor do I think that the thing ever came into any man's mind. For being such as is described by them, it comprehends true repentance and is conjoined with faith. On the subject of the servile fear of hell, which to some degree restrains unbelievers from rushing with such furious and headlong impetus into wicked courses, we are of the same sentiments as Augustine, whose words are, (Ad. Anast. Ep. 144,) "What man is found innocent before God, who, if fear were withdrawn, would do what God forbids? He is guilty in his will by wishing to do what cannot lawfully be done. As far as he is concerned, he would rather that there was no justice prohibiting and punishing sin. And hence, if he would rather that there was no justice, who can doubt that he would take it away if he could? How then is he righteous who is such an enemy to righteousness, that if power were given him he would take it away when commanding, and not bear it when threatening or judging? He, therefore, is the enemy of righteousness who does not sin, because he is afraid of punishment. And, indeed, when all the progress made is that the sinner curbed by terror murmurs against God, who can deny that by such contumacy he aggravates his sin?"

(CANON IX.—If any one saith, that by faith alone the impious is justified, in such wise as to mean, that nothing else is required to co-operate in order to the obtaining the grace of Justification, and that it is not in any way necessary, that he be prepared and disposed by the movement of his own will: let him be anathema.)

This Canon is very far from being canonical; for it joins things which are utterly at variance. They imagine that a man is justified by faith without any movement of his own will, as if it were not with the heart that a man believeth unto righteousness. Between them and us there is this difference, that they persuade themselves that the movement comes from the man himself, whereas we maintain that faith is voluntary, because God draws our wills to himself. Add, that when we say a man is justified by faith alone, we do not fancy a faith devoid of charity, but we mean that faith alone is the cause of justification.

(CANON X.—If any one saith, that men are just without the justice of Christ, whereby he merited for us to be justified; or that it is by that justice itself that they are formally just: let him be anathema.)

Could these anathemas take effect, all who are not versed in the sophistical art would pay dearly for their simplicity. They formerly asserted in their decrees that the righteousness of God was the only formal cause of Justification; now

they anathematize those who say that we are formally righteous by the obedience of Christ. But it is in another sense.
I see it or scent it. But how few are there who will not be
misled by the ambiguity? Although it may be that having
met with the sentiment somewhere and not understood it,
they boldly condemn it. For as it were impious to say that
the righteousness of Christ is only an exemplar or type to us,
so if any one were to teach that we are righteous formally,
i.e., not by quality but by imputation, meaning that our righteousness is in relation merely, there would be nothing worthy
of censure. The adverb *formally* is used in both senses.

(CANON XI.—If any one saith, that men are justified, either by the
sole imputation of the justice of Christ, or by the sole remission
of sins, to the exclusion of the grace and *the charity which is
poured forth in their hearts by the Holy Ghost,* and is inherent
in them; or even that the grace, whereby we are justified, is only
the favor of God: let him be anathema.)

I wish the reader to understand that as often as we mention Faith alone in this question, we are not thinking of a
dead faith, which worketh not by love, but holding faith to
be the only cause of justification. (Gal. 5:6; Rom. 3:22.)
It is therefore faith alone which justifies, and yet the faith
which justifies is not alone: just as it is the heat alone of the
sun which warms the earth, and yet in the sun it is not alone,
because it is constantly conjoined with light. Wherefore we
do not separate the whole grace of regeneration from faith,
but claim the power and faculty of justifying entirely for
faith, as we ought. And yet it is not us that these Tridentine
Fathers anathematize so much as Paul, to whom we owe the
definition that the righteousness of man consists in the forgiveness of sins. The words are in the fourth chapter to the
Romans, "David speaketh of the blessedness of the man to
whom God imputeth righteousness without works, saying,
Blessed are those whose iniquities are forgiven." (Psalm
32:1.) We see that in Paul's view blessedness and righteousness mean the same thing. And where does he place both
but solely in the remission of sins? His meaning is the same
as in the fifth chapter of the Second Epistle to the Corinthians, "God was in Christ reconciling the world unto himself,
not imputing unto men their trespasses." For he immediately
explains how that reconciliation comes to us: "We are ambassadors beseeching you as in the name of Christ. He made

him who knew no sin to be sin for us, that we might be the righteousness of God in him." See how being reconciled to God by the sacrifice of Christ, we both are accounted and are righteous in him. But why quote one passage after another, while this is the doctrine uniformly inculcated by Prophets and Apostles?

It is worth while to observe how dexterously they accommodate Scripture to their purpose. They say that the love which is shed abroad in our hearts by the Holy Spirit must not be excluded. Thus they corrupt one passage by another. The context shews that Paul does not there speak of our own love, but of the paternal love of God toward us; for he holds it forth as ground of consolation in all circumstances of adversity, that the Spirit suggests proof of the divine benevolence towards us. This swinish herd, on the contrary, twist it to mean, that we are not ashamed of hoping because we love God. And the moment they have given utterance to the words they insist on being regarded as oracles! With similar perversion they make justifying grace a habit, and deny that it proceeds from the free favour of God. The words of Scripture are clear as day against them. For when Paul says, that to believers reward is imputed not as of debt but of grace; and again, that the inheritance is of faith that it may be of grace, (Rom. 4:4,) how is it possible in expounding it to give it any other meaning than that of free favour? What else is meant by a purpose of grace? One of the most striking passages is the first chapter to the Ephesians, where, going on word by word, he tells us that the Father hath made us acceptable to himself in the Son.

(CANON XII.—If any one saith, that justifying faith is nothing else but confidence in the divine mercy which remits sins for Christ's sake; or, that this confidence alone is that whereby we are justified: let him be anathema.)

The venerable Fathers will not allow Justifying Faith to be defined as the confidence with which we embrace the mercy of God as forgiving sin for Christ's sake. But it pleases the Holy Spirit, who thus speaks by the mouth of Paul, "We are justified freely by the grace of God, through the redemption which is in Christ, whom God hath appointed a propitiation through faith in his blood for the remission of sins which are past." (Rom. 3:24.) Nor is it possible to give a different exposition to what he afterwards says, viz., that "being justified by faith we have peace with God." (Rom. 5:1.) How so, but just that our consciences are never at ease until they rest in the mercy of God? This he distinctly expresses immediately after, when he adds the reason, that the love of God is shed abroad in our hearts by the Holy Spirit, as being the witness of our free adoption, and not the witness only, but also the earnest and seal. Again, "We have boldness and access with confidence through faith in him." For the same reason he calls the gospel, rather than the law, "the doctrine of faith." He moreover declares, that the gospel is "the message of reconciliation."

(CANON XIII.—If any one saith, that it is necessary for every one, for the obtaining the remission of sins, that he believe for certain, and without any wavering arising from his own infirmity and indisposition, that his sins are forgiven him: let him be anathema.)

That, however, is Paul's meaning when he concludes, that if Faith is made void the promise is abolished. (Rom. 4:14.) That too is the meaning of the term πληροφορία, which Paul also sometimes uses. Accordingly he regards the eyes of our mind as not duly enlightened unless we perceive what is the hope of our inheritance. It is also sufficiently obvious from the above passages, that faith is not right unless we dare with tranquil minds to sist ourselves into the divine presence. For, as Bernard admirably expresses it, (Super Cantic. Serm. xvi. c. 3, 10,) "If conscience is troubled, it will not be troubled out of measure, because it will remember the words of our Lord. Therein the infirm have firm rest and security." To the same effect are the words of Zechariah, "Each one will come to his own vine, and dwell safely under his own fig-tree, when the iniquity of the land shall have been forgiven."

(CANON XIV.—If any one saith, that man is truly absolved from his sins and justified, because that he assuredly believed himself absolved and justified; or, that no one is truly justified but he who believes himself justified; and that, by this faith alone, absolution and justification are effected: let him be anathema.)

I see not why they should condemn the same thing twice, unless it be they were afraid that their first thunderbolt had fallen scatheless! But though they should fulminate a hundred times they will not be able to prevail in the least degree against this clear truth of God. Christ says, "Son, be of good cheer, thy sins are forgiven thee." This sentence the horned Fathers abominate, whenever any one teaches that acquittal is completed by faith alone. And yet the pious reader ought to remember that we do not exclude repentance, which is altogether necessary, but mention faith only when the inquiry relates to the cause of acquittal. And justly do we so. For how can any one begin truly to fear God unless he is persuaded that God is propitious to him? And whence this persuasion but from confidence in acquittal?

(CANON XV.—If any one saith, that a man, who is born again and justified, is bound of faith to believe that he is assuredly in the number of the predestinate: let him be anathema.)

It is indeed true that to pry too minutely into this matter is hurtful, and therefore to be avoided; but that knowledge of Predestination which Paul recommends dreads neither the stern trident of Neptune, nor all the blasts of Æolus, nor the thunders of the Cyclops, nor any violence of tempests. For he wishes the Ephesians to know and be assured that 'they have been made partakers of heavenly grace in Christ, as they had been chosen in him before the foundation of the world. (Eph. 1:4.) Thus therefore it becomes all believers to be assured of their election, that they may learn to behold it in Christ as in a mirror. Nor is it to no purpose that Christ animates his followers by this consoling reflection—that not one of those whom the Father hath given him shall perish. (John 6:39.) What else, good Sirs, is a certain knowledge of our Predestination than that testimony of adoption which Scripture makes common to all the godly?

(CANON XVI.—If any one saith, that he will for certain, of an absolute and infallible certainty, have that great gift of perseverance unto the end,—unless he have learned this by special revelation: let him be anathema.)

That I may not be forced often to repeat the same thing, what they here condemn is nothing else than what I have previously shewn to have been delivered by the same oracles of the Holy Spirit.

(CANON XVII.—If any one saith, that the grace of Justification is only attained to by those who are predestined unto life; but that all others who are called, are called indeed, but receive not grace, as being, by the divine power, predestined unto evil: let him be anathema.)

The words of Luke are, "All who had been pre-ordained to life believed." (Acts 13:48.) He intimates whence it was that in one audience such a difference existed that some believed, and others persisted in their obstinacy. In like manner Paul asserts, that those are called whom God has previously chosen. (Rom. 8:29.) Are not also the reprobate called? Not effectually. For there is this difference in the calling of God, that he invites all indiscriminately by his word, whereas he inwardly calls the elect alone, as Christ says, "All that the Father hath given me will come to me." (John 6:37.) In short, if any man is ignorant that the Spirit of regeneration is given to none but the regenerate, I know not what part of Scripture he holds.

(CANON XVIII.—If any one saith, that the commandments of God are, even for one that is justified and constituted in grace, impossible to keep: let him be anathema.)

Were Regeneration perfected in this life the observance of the law would be possible. But seeing that believers as long as they live here only perceive the goal at a distance, and with much difficulty keep panting towards it, where is the perfection of obedience, of which those men dream, to be found? But there is no wonder that they prate so boldly of things they know not. War is pleasant to those who never tried it.

(CANON XIX.—If any one saith, that nothing besides faith is commanded in the Gospel; that other things are indifferent, neither commanded nor prohibited, but free; or, that the ten commandments nowise appertain to Christians: let him be anathema.)

AMEN.

(CANON XX.—If any one saith, that the man who is justified and how perfect soever, is not bound to observe the commandments of God and of the Church, but only to believe; as if indeed the Gospel were a bare and absolute promise of eternal life, without the condition of observing the commandments: let him be anathema.)

While no sane man will strike off the yoke of God from the shoulders of believers, as if they behoved not to keep his Commandments, it must still be understood that assurance of salvation by no means depends on the observance of them. For the words of Paul always hold true, that the difference between the Law and the Gospel lies in this, that the latter does not like the former promise life under the condition of works, but from faith. What can be clearer than the antithesis—"The righteousness of the law is in this wise, The man who doeth these things shall live in them. But the righteousness which is of faith speaketh thus, Whoso believeth," etc. (Rom. 10:5.) To the same effect is this other passage, "If the inheritance were of the law, faith would be made void and the promise abolished. Therefore it is of faith that in respect of grace the promise might be sure to every one that believeth." (Rom. 4:14.) As to ecclesiastical laws, they must themselves see to them: we acknowledge one Legislator, to whom it belongs to deliver the rule of life, as from him we have life.

(CANON XXI.—If any one saith, that Christ Jesus was given of God to men, as a redeemer in whom to trust, and not also as a legislator whom to obey: let him be anathema.)

No one says so. The Fathers, therefore, are anathematizing their own figments, unless perhaps they are offended because we deny that Christ as a lawgiver delivered new laws to the world. That he did so they imagined foolishly. Neither did Moses testify in vain that the Law which he had brought was the way of life and death, (Dcut. 30:19;) and again, "This is the way, walk ye in it;" nor in vain do the Prophets and Apostles, whenever they discourse of the true and entire perfection of righteousness, call us back to the law; nor in vain did Christ reply to the Pharisee, "If thou wouldst enter into life, keep the commandments." (Matt. 19:17; Luke 18:20.) Accordingly, when Paul charges the law with weakness, he does not place the defect in its teaching, as if it could not bestow life but in our flesh. (Rom. 7, 8.)

(CANON XXII.—If any one saith, that the justified, either is able to persevere, without the special help of God, in the justice received; or that, with that help, he is not able: let him be anathema.)

AMEN.

(CANON XXIII.—If any one saith, that a man once justified can sin no more, nor lose grace, and that therefore he that falls and sins was never truly justified; or, on the other hand, that he is able, during his whole life, to avoid all sins, even those that are venial,—except by a special privilege from God, as the Church holds in regard of the Blessed Virgin: let him be anathema.)

We condemn those who affirm that a man once justified cannot sin, and likewise those who deny that the truly justified ever fall: those in like manner who assert that a man regenerated by the Spirit of God is able to abstain even from the least sins. These are the delirious dreams of fanatics, who either with devilish arrogance deceive, or with hypocrisy fascinate the minds of men, or plot to lead them to the precipice of despair. As to the special privilege of the Virgin Mary, when they produce the celestial diploma we shall believe what they say: for to what do they here give the name of the Church, but just to the Council of Clermont? Augustine was certainly a member of the Church, and though he in one passage chooses, in order to avoid obloquy, rather to be silent respecting the blessed Virgin, he uniformly, without making her an exception, describes the whole race of Adam as involved in sin. Nay, he even almost in distinct terms classes her among sinners, when writing to Marcellinus, he says, They err greatly who hold that any of the saints except Christ require not to use this prayer, "Forgive us our debts." In so doing, they by no means please the saints whom they laud. Chrysostom and Ambrose, who suspect her of having been tempted by ambition, were members of the Church. All these things I mention for no other end but to let my readers understand that there is no figment so nugatory as not to be classed by these blockheads among the Articles of Faith.

(CANON XXIV.—If any one saith, that the justice received is not preserved and also increased before God through good works; but that the said works are merely the fruits and signs of Justification obtained, but not a cause of the increase thereof: let him be anathema.)

That God visits the good works of the godly with reward, and to former adds new and ampler grace, we deny not. But whosoever asserts that works have the effect of increasing justification, understands neither what is the meaning of justification nor its cause. That we are regarded as righteous when we are accepted by God, has already been proved. From this acceptance, too, works derive whatever grace they had.

(CANON XXV.—If any one saith, that, in every good work, the just sins venially at least, or—which is more intolerable still— mortally, and consequently deserves eternal punishments; and that for this cause only he is not damned, that God does not impute those works unto damnation: let him be anathema.)

Solomon is correct when he says that "the ways of a man seem right in his own eyes, but God weigheth the heart." (Prov. 16:2.) For how comes it that the horned men of Trent pour forth this execration, but just because they try things by the false balance of their own opinion, not by the weights of God? In the judgment of God nothing is genuine and good, save what flows from perfect love to Him. If the heart of man is never reformed so far in this life, as not to labour un- der many defects, and to be distracted by various passions, and often tickled by worldly allurements, works must of ne- cessity carry some taint along with them. There is no work, therefore, which is not sin, unless it acquires a value in con- sequence of a gratuitous estimate.

(CANON XXVI.—If any one saith, that the just ought not, for their good works done in God, to expect and hope for an eternal recom- pense from God, through his mercy and the merit of Jesus Christ, if so be that they persevere to the end in well doing and in keeping the divine commandments: let him be anathema.)

Such boldness is not strange in men who have never felt any serious fear of the Divine judgment. Let them, if they will, expect eternal life for their good works; only let us on the authority of Paul hope for it from the grace of God. But it may be said that in thus speaking of grace they do not overthrow it. Although they leave the name of grace to a certain extent, yet so long as consciences in seeking out the cause of salvation look around for works, wo to them! If they waver with trepidation, they have fallen from the certainty of faith: and wo again if they dare to promise themselves any certainty, for they are inflated with devilish presumption! Let the saying of Paul then stand fast—that "the inheritance is not of the law but of faith, that the promise according to grace may be sure to every one that believeth." (Rom. 4:14.)

(CANON XXVII.—If any one saith, that there is no mortal sin but that of infidelity; or, that grace once received is not lost by any other sin, however grievous and enormous, save by that of infidelity: let him be anathema.)

As we acknowledge and feel that every sin, inasmuch as it is condemned by the law of God, is mortal, so the Holy Spirit teaches that all sins flow from unbelief, or, at least, from deficiency of faith. Eternal death is indeed the curse which God denounces against adulterers, thieves, and false witnesses; but wherever faith reigns it expels all sin, and so averts the Divine anger in the same way in which one extinguishes a fire by withdrawing the fuel.

(CANON XXVIII.—If any one saith, that, grace being lost through sin, faith also is always lost with it; or, that the faith which remains, though it be not a lively faith, is not a true faith; or, that he who has faith without charity is not a Christian: let him be anathema.)

I deny not that, even during the most grievous lapses, some seed of Faith remains, though in a smothered state. However small it is, I admit that it partakes of the nature of true faith: I add, living faith, since otherwise no fruit could come from it. But since it does not appear for a time, nor exhibit itself by the usual signs, it is, in respect of our sense, as if it were dead. But nothing of this kind entered the minds of the Fathers or their dictatorial monks. All they wished was to establish their absurd dogma of an informal and a formal faith. Hence they maintain that faith to be true which is manifestly dead; as if faith could be the life of the soul, (as Augustine, in accordance with the uniform doctrine of Scripture, elegantly terms it,) and yet not be itself alive. To the same purpose they contend that men are Christians though they have no charity, and anathematize those who think otherwise; in other words, according to them, we anathematize the Holy Spirit if we deride a false profession of Christianity, and set it at nought. Paul pronounced them no Israelites who were not truly the children of Abraham. He moreover defines true Christianity as consisting in "the putting off of the old man;" and he declares that God is denied by those "who do not live godly."

(CANON XXIX.—If any one saith, that he who has fallen after baptism is not able by the grace of God to rise again; or, that he is able indeed to recover the justice which he has lost, but by faith alone without the sacrament of Penance, contrary to what the holy Roman and universal Church—instructed by Christ and his Apostles—has hitherto professed, observed, and taught: let him be anathema.)

The first article, along with its author, Novatus, we also execrate. As to the second, if the lapsed can only be reinstated in grace by the Sacrament of Penance, what will become of Peter, who, after his dreadful fall, had no access to the remedy which they require as of absolute necessity? Nay, what will become of the tens of thousands in those ages which know nothing of that Auricular Confession which they now represent as the gate of salvation? As to their glorying in the teaching of Christ and his Apostles, their effrontery is extreme, seeing it is clear, from their own historians, that for four hundred years there was no law on the subject of Confession. Therefore, if they would obtain credit for their wicked figments, it will be necessary for them not only to exterminate all the monuments of antiquity, but also to deprive mankind of all sense and judgment!

(CANON XXX.—If any one saith, that, after the grace of Justification has been received, to every penitent sinner the guilt is remitted, and the debt of eternal punishment is blotted out in such wise that there remains not any debt of temporal punishment to be discharged either in this world, or in the next in Purgatory, before the entrance to the kingdom of heaven can be opened [to him]: let him be anathema.)

They think that, after the guilt is remitted, the liability to punishment remains. But Scripture everywhere describes, as the fruit of forgiven guilt, that God withdraws his chastisements, and, forgetting his wrath and revenge, blesses us. And when David proclaims those blessed "to whom the Lord imputeth not sin," he not only refers to the remission of guilt, but speaks chiefly of punishment. And what, pray, will be the end or limit, should God begin to exact punishment for sins which are both in number infinite and in weight so heavy, that the hundredth part would sink us to the lowest hell? It is easy indeed for Fathers intoxicated with devilish presumption to call for temporal punishment. To them scarcely any-

thing short of murder is a sin; whoredom is a trivial mistake
—the foulest lusts praiseworthy trials of virtue, a hidden
wound of the conscience, a mere bagatelle. But to us, who,
after long examination, feeling as it were confused and overwhelmed, are forced at length to break out into these words
with David, "Who can understand his errors?" the mode of
escape is not so easy. Still we deny not, that sometimes after
the guilt is forgiven, God chastises us, but it is in the way of
admonition and correction—not vengeance. Their idea that
punishment is exacted by the justice of God is therefore a
profane fiction. All are not punished in the same way, nor in
proportion to their faults; but just according as God knows
the application of the rod to be necessary, in order that each,
under the training of discipline, may act more wisely in
future.

The Fathers, however, here demonstrate what industrious
architects they are. Out of one little word they construct a
labyrinth composed of a thousand labyrinths. The abyss
which they say swallowed up all souls must surely be of
immense extent. We see indeed that all the riches of the
world are engulfed in it! They ought at least to have spent
a little more labour in the construction. There is no mention
of Purgatory at all in any part of Scripture. But, as Augustine
says, (Ep. 157, ad Optat.,) when a matter naturally obscure cannot be comprehended by us, and Scripture does
not come distinctly to our aid, human conjecture is presumptuous in giving any decision. What then must our conclusion
be, but that these men act presumptuously in daring, out of
their own brains, to make a fabric of that which has no foundation in the word of God? unless, perhaps, they would have
us to receive their device of Purgatory as a kind of vaticina-
tion vented by ventriloquism; for there is nothing which
serves so well to fill their bellies! But what of this? Purgatory
cannot stand without destroying the whole truth of Scripture.
The demonstration of this would be long, but it is clearly
given in our writings. In short, when satisfactions are overthrown, Purgatory of necessity tumbles along with them.

(Canon XXXI.—If any one saith, that the justified sins when he
performs good works with a view to an eternal recompense: let
him be anathema.)

I acknowledge that he who is truly justified will not forget
that a reward is laid up for him, but be incited by it as the

best stimulus to well-doing. And yet he will not look to this alone; for seeing that God requires an ingenuous obedience from his children, he will not only repudiate slavish observance of this description, but utterly reject it. Accordingly, the Holy Spirit, in every part of Scripture, as well as in those words which he puts into the mouth of Paul in the first chapter of the Ephesians, assigns a very different motive to a pious and holy life.

(CANON XXXII.—If any one saith, that the good works of one that is justified are in such manner the gifts of God, that they are not also the good merits of him that is justified; or, that the said justified, by the good works which he performs through the grace of God and the merit of Jesus Christ, whose living member he is, does not truly merit increase of grace, eternal life, and the attainment of that eternal life,—if so be, however, that he depart in grace, —and also an increase of glory: let him be anathema.)

By what right or in what sense the Good Works which the Spirit of Christ performs in us are called ours, Augustine briefly teaches when he draws an analogy from the Lord's Prayer: saying, that the bread which we there ask is called "ours" on no other ground than simply that it is given to us. Accordingly, as the same writer elsewhere teaches, no man will embrace the gifts of Christ till he has forgotten his own merits. He sometimes gives the reason: because, what is called merit is nought else but the free gift of God. Let us therefore allow these Fathers to bawl out, that by separating merit from grace, we are wickedly lacerating what is truly one. He who has learned from our former observations wherein it is that the merit of works consists, will not be greatly dismayed at the sound of the present anathema.

(CANON XXXIII.—If any one saith, that, by the Catholic doctrine touching Justification, by this holy Synod set forth in this present decree, the glory of God, or the merits of our Lord Jesus Christ are in any way derogated from, and not rather that the truth of our faith, and the glory in fine of God and of Jesus Christ are rendered [more] illustrious: let him be anathema.)

A very ingenious caution! no man is to see what every man sees! They almost go the length of making void both the glory of God and the grace of Christ. Meanwhile they hurl a dire execration at any one who presumes to think that they derogate in any respect from either. It is just as if a man were to murder another in the open market-place before the eyes of the public, and yet prohibit any one from believing that the murder thus manifest to all has been really committed. Moreover, the rats here turn informers against themselves, by holding out an anathema *in terrorem* against all who shall dare to perceive the impiety of which they themselves are conscious.

ANTIDOTE TO THE SEVENTH SESSION

How much sweat must be spent in any contest where a bad cause is pleaded, the venerable Fathers had experienced in last Session. Therefore, that they might not over-fatigue themselves by a second conflict, they preferred to return to their compendious method of settling the matter by fulmination. And, indeed, it was unbecoming their dictatorial style to undergo the trouble of rendering a reason. What then! The Corybantes sound their brass and redouble the clang. Tremble, boys! Whoever possesses a spark of manly courage will despise their futile crepitations, and boldly, with unruffled mind, inquire into the contents of their decrees. How they teem with stupid absurdities I engage to demonstrate with my finger.

(ON THE SACRAMENTS IN GENERAL.)

(CANON I.—If any one saith, that the sacraments of the New Law were not all instituted by Jesus Christ, our Lord; or, that they are more, or less, than seven, to wit, Baptism, Confirmation, the Eucharist, Penance, Extreme Unction, Order, and Matrimony; or even that any one of these seven is not truly and properly a sacrament: let him be anathema.)

They insist that Seven Sacraments were instituted by Christ. Why, then, did they not order him to institute them? The number Seven which they place under the sanction of an anathema has not only no support from Scripture, but none even from any approved author. This is little. Of the Sacraments which they enumerate we shew that some were temporary, as the anointing of the sick, and others, falsely so called, as matrimony. The arguments by which we evince this are plain and strong. What! will they boast that they have the gift of healing? If anointing is the symbol of that gift, are they not apes when they use it without the reality? Again, what promise is there in this ceremony that has any application to us? If a sacrament consists of spiritual grace and an external sign, where will they find anything of the kind in penance? For giving marriage this name they have no other reason than the gross ignorance of the monks, who reading in the Epistle to the Ephesians (Eph. 5:32) the word *sacrament* used instead of *mystery,* and that concerning the secret union between Christ and his Church, transferred it to marriage. Of all these things our writings contain clear and copious demonstrations, which the good Fathers refute by the one vocable *anathema.* This is to conquer without a contest, or rather to triumph without a victory!

(CANON II.—If any one saith, that these said sacraments of the New Law do not differ from the sacraments of the Old Law, save that the ceremonies are different, and different the outward rites: let him be anathema.)

Since the Sacraments of both Testaments have the same Author, the same promises, the same truth, and the same fulfilment in Christ, we justly say that they differ from each other in external signs, but agree in those things which I have mentioned, or, in one word, in the reality. For as they are appendages of doctrine, but the substance of the doctrine is the same, so the same rule holds in regard to the Sacraments. My readers perhaps would not understand the object of the Fathers of Trent in launching this thunderbolt, did I not briefly explain. There is a vulgar dogma of the sophists, that the Sacraments of the Mosaic law figured grace, but that ours exhibit it. We maintain that God was always true in his promises, and from the beginning figured nothing which he did not exhibit to the ancient Church in reality; for the reality of circumcision was evident under Moses. Paul testifies that they then partook of the same spiritual food and the same spiritual drink. (1 Cor. 10:3.) What answer do they give but just that it is otherwise taught in the schools? I only touch in a few words on matters which my readers will, if they please, learn fully from our writings. Let this be the sum. From the Word of God, not from the decrees of Romanists, are we to learn what difference or resemblance there is between the Sacraments. Still we deny not that a more exuberant grace is received under the kingdom of Christ, and accordingly we are wont to note a twofold difference. *First,* that our Sacraments do not point out Christ at a distance, as if he were absent, but exhibit him as with the finger. *Secondly,* as the mode of revelation is more ample, so the communication of grace is more exuberant.

(CANON III.—If any one saith, that these seven sacraments are in such wise equal to each other, as that one is not in any way more worthy than another: let him be anathema.)

Who would not face the Neptunian bolt sooner than put the inventions of men on a footing with the ordinances of Christ? We read that Baptism was recommended by Christ: we read in like manner that the Lord's Supper was recommended. (Matth. 27, 28.) Of the others we read nothing of the kind: nay, for many ages after, the doctrine of these men was unknown. There can be no doubt as to the aim and force of our Saviour's question, "The baptism of John, was it from heaven or of men?" For he means that it would not be legitimate if it had not come down from heaven. Wherefore let us decide in all safety on the authority of Christ, that there is no danger in repudiating whatever has emanated merely from human authority. Not contented, however, with claiming equal authority for all, they prefer the chrism of their confirmation to the baptism of Christ! For their making one of more dignity than another is not for the purpose of placing those which have no support from Scripture in an inferior grade, but they renew those execrable blasphemies which the Council of Aurelium first vented—that we are made only half Christians by baptism, and are finished by confirmation!—and other things there delivered to the same effect.

(CANON IV.—If any one saith, that the sacraments of the New Law are not necessary unto salvation, but superfluous; and that, without them, or without the desire thereof, men obtain of God, through faith alone, the grace of justification;—though all [the sacraments] are not indeed necessary for every individual: let him be anathema.)

I will readily allow that the use of those things which Christ gave us as helps to salvation is necessary, that is, when an opportunity is given: although believers are always to be reminded that there is no other necessity for any sacrament than that of an instrumental cause, to which the power of God is by no means to be tied down. Every pious person must with his whole heart shudder at the expression that the things are superfluous. But here the worthy Fathers, with their usual stupidity, perceive not that whatever grace is conferred upon us by the Sacraments, is nevertheless to be ascribed to faith. He who separates faith from the Sacraments, does just as if he were to take the soul away from the body. Therefore, as we exclude not the doctrine of the gospel when we say that we obtain the grace of Christ by faith alone, so neither do we exclude the Sacraments, the nature of which is the same, as they are seals of the gospel.

(CANON V.—If any one saith, that these sacraments were instituted for the sake of nourishing faith alone: let him be anathema.)

We acknowledge that the Sacraments are intended, not only to maintain but to increase faith. But these horned gentry mean something else; for they pretend that the Sacraments have a magical power, which is efficacious without faith. This error destroys the relation which the Scriptures uniformly establish between the Sacraments and faith. That my readers may perceive this more clearly, they must always call to mind, that the Sacraments are nothing but instrumental causes of bestowing grace upon us, and are beneficial, and produce their effect only when they are subservient to faith.

(CANON VI.—If any one saith, that the sacraments of the New Law do not contain the grace which they signify; or, that they do not confer that grace on those who do not place an obstacle thereunto; as though they were merely outward signs of grace or justice received through faith, and certain marks of the Christian profession, whereby believers are distinguished amongst men from unbelievers: let him be anathema.)

Here these preposterous men mix dross with silver. Wherefore we must make a distinction:—First, then, if there are any who deny that the Sacraments contain the grace which they figure, we disapprove of them. But when the horned Fathers add that the Sacraments of themselves confer grace on those not opposing any obstacle to it, they pervert the whole force of Sacraments. For they always relapse into the old delirium of the sophists, that even unbelievers receive the grace which is offered in the Sacraments, provided they do not reject it by opposing other obstacles—as if unbelief were not in itself obstacle enough. Let us hold, therefore, that we cannot obtain the grace offered in the Sacraments, unless we are capacitated by faith. What immediately follows they have appended either very maliciously, or very absurdly. They say, "as if they were only external signs;" nay, they speak as if there was no alternative between these two things. As we repudiate the monkish fiction, that the Sacraments are available in any other way than by faith, so we willingly conjoin with the signs a true exhibition of the reality, holding that they have no effect without faith, and yet that they are not empty and naked signs of a distant grace.

(Canon VII.—If any one saith, that grace, as far as God's part is concerned, is not given through the said sacraments, always, and to all men, even though they receive them rightly, but [only] sometimes, and to some persons: let him be anathema.)

The first thing was to define what it is duly to receive the Sacraments. For this swinish herd, passing by faith, and placing repentance in the back-ground—not indeed that ceremonial repentance which they loudly extol, but that inward repentance of the heart, by which the whole man turns to God—think that the due receiving of the Sacraments consists in some sort of simulate devotion, as they term it. But if we were agreed as to what constitutes a legitimate disposition, there would be no farther dispute as to efficacy. For who doubts that the grace which God promises is exhibited to those who make a due approach? Hence, every one moderately instructed in the pure use of the Sacraments, will perceive that they make an absurd distinction when they say, that in so far as relates to God, grace is given, for, be the unworthiness of man what it may, God must always remain true. In respect of God, therefore nothing is withheld or deducted from the efficacy of the Sacraments, however unbecoming the profanation of them in respect of the evil conscience of man. The effect only is lost, or at least intercepted from coming to us.

(Canon VIII.—If any one saith, that by the said sacraments of the New Law grace is not conferred through the act performed, but that faith alone in the divine promise suffices for the obtaining of grace: let him be anathema.)

Here, indeed, they disclose their impiety, not only more clearly, but also more grossly. The device of *opus operatum* is recent, and was coined by illiterate monks, who had never learned anything of the nature of Sacraments. For in Sacraments God alone properly acts; men bring nothing of their own, but approach to receive the grace offered to them. Thus, in Baptism, God washes us by the blood of his Son, and regenerates us by his Spirit; in the Supper he feeds us with the flesh and blood of Christ. What part of the work can man claim, without blasphemy, while the whole appears to be of grace? The fact of the administration being committed to men, derogates no more from the operation of God than the hand does from the artificer, since God alone acts by them, and does the whole. But those blockheads, to say nothing of their finding human merit in the free gifts of God, pretend that we, in doing nothing, merit from God, and lay him under liability to us; and not contented with this, give vent to monstrous words to extort a confession from God, that he is not to be regarded as acting alone in the Sacraments,—hence their additional inference necessarily follows, viz., that grace is not received by faith alone. For if we grant their postulate—that grace is procured in the Sacraments *opere operato*—a part of merit is separated from faith, and the use of the Sacraments is in itself effectual for salvation. But if the same thing is to be affirmed of the Sacraments as of the word, then the Apostle is a witness that they are of no avail unless received by faith.

(CANON IX.—If any one saith, that, in the three sacraments, to wit, Baptism, Confirmation, and Order, there is not imprinted in the soul a character, that is, a certain spiritual and indelible sign, on account of which they can not be repeated: let him be anathema.)

Their fable of an indelible character is the product of the same forge. It was altogether unknown to the Primitive Church, and is more suited to magical charms than to the sound doctrine of the gospel! Therefore it will be repudiated with the same facility with which it was devised. That Baptism is not to be repeated the pious are sufficiently agreed. This, which was true of Baptism, they afterwards rashly transferred to their Confirmation and Orders. The curious

sought for a reason. That they might not seem to say nothing, they contrived this fictitious impression, and now they
denounce anathema against all who assent not to their figment.

(CANON X.—If any one saith, that all Christians have power to
administer the word, and all the sacraments: let him be anathema.)

No sound Christian makes all men equal in the administration of Word and Sacraments, not only because all things
ought to be done in the Church decently and in order, but
also because, by the special command of Christ, Ministers
are ordained for that purpose. Therefore, as a special call is
required, no man who is not called may take the honour
upon himself. Moreover, where do they find the office of
baptizing enjoined on women, as they permit them to do?

(CANON XI.—If any one saith, that, in ministers, when they effect,
and confer the sacraments, there is not required the intention at
least of doing what the Church does: let him be anathema.)

The lavishness with which they pour out their anathemas
shews that they set little value upon them. Their prattle
about the intention of consecrating was produced by the
sophists without any show of reason. This, though not tolerable, would be less grievous, if it did not utterly overthrow
whatever solid comfort believers have in the Sacraments,
and suspend the truth of God on the will of man: for if the
intention of the minister is necessary, none of us can be certain of his Baptism—none approach the Holy Supper with
sure confidence. I was baptized—if it so pleased the priest,
whose good faith is no more known to me than that of any
Ethiopian! Whether the promise of Christ in the Holy Supper
is to be good to me, depends on the nod of a man whom I
do not know. What kind of faith can it be that depends on
the secret will of another? And yet this herd [sic] fear not to
threaten us with windy anathemas, if we do not on the instant
subscribe to such blasphemies. Such is my deference for the
holy ordinance of Christ, that if some epicurean, inwardly
grinning at the whole performance, were to administer the
Supper to me according to the command of Christ and the
rule given by him, and in due form, I would not doubt that
the bread and the cup held forth by his hand are pledges to
me of the body and the blood of Christ. It is painful to dis-

cuss such silliness, as when they say, "at least of doing what the Church does." Here they re-echo the dictates of their masters. Who that has his eyes sees not that this is just equivalent to enjoining in one word all that monks have ever dreamed in their dens or sophists babbled in their quarrels? How stupid and absurd soever they may be, they must nevertheless be held firm and sure.

(CANON XII.—If any one saith, that a minister, being in mortal sin,—if so be that he observe all the essentials which belong to the effecting, or conferring of, the sacrament,—neither effects, nor confers the sacrament: let him be anathema.)

AMEN.

(CANON XIII.—If any one saith, that the received and approved rites of the Catholic Church, wont to be used in the solemn administration of the sacraments, may be contemned, or without sin be omitted at pleasure by the ministers, or be changed, by every pastor of the churches, into other new ones: let him be anathema.)

What they mean by the received and approved Rites of the Church every one is aware. Hence by this *caveat* they establish whatever superstitions human presumption has superinduced on the pure ordinances of the Lord. The genuine rite of Baptism is simple, and the administration of the Supper simple, if we look to what the Lord has enjoined. But under how many, and how various and discordant additions has this simplicity been buried? They will say, that if there is any excess, it behoves to be rescinded—only, however, if they think so. But what hope do they give us, when with bacchanalian fury they belch forth their anathemas against whosoever permits himself to omit one little ceremony? All the godly complain, or at least regret, that in Baptism more is made of the chrism, the taper, the salt, the spittle in fine, than the washing with water, in which the whole perfection of Baptism consists. They deplore that the Supper has not only been vitiated by impure additions, but converted into a kind of spurious show. According to the Fathers of Trent, nothing can be so monstrous as not to find a place among the approved rites of the Catholic Church. Augustine, even in his time, complained that the Church was burdened with a Jewish bondage, though the rites then in use were scarcely a tenth part of those the observance of which is now more rigidly required than that of any human or divine law. The men of Trent deliberate as to what should be done, and then, without holding out any hope of relief, launch curses and imprecations at all who will not submit to every iota of the usages prescribed!

(ON BAPTISM.)

(CANON I.—If any one saith, that the baptism of John had the same force as the baptism of Christ: let him be anathema.)

A great matter certainly to determine, that when the doctrine is the same, the grace offered the same, and the rites observed the same, there is a similitude. If in these three things the Baptism of Christ differs in any respect from that of John, I admit that they have gained the day; but if they are all common to both, in vain do they vent their bile. Nobody of composed mind will be frightened. Had they thought that reason was to decide, they would have been far more moderate.

(CANON II.—If any one saith, that true and natural water is not of necessity for baptism, and, on that account, wrests, to some sort of metaphor, those words of our Lord Jesus Christ: *Unless a man be born again of water and the Holy Ghost:* let him be anathema.)

Why they raise a question on the former point I know not, unless perhaps this is the one only method in which they wish to be wise in checking the frivolous subtleties of the Sorbonists. But they are too passionate in fulminating against all who differ from them in the exposition of a single passage, especially when no ancient writer can be quoted who gives a metaphorical meaning to the words, "Unless men be born of water and of the Spirit." But as I said at the beginning, having a rich storehouse of execration, there is no wonder that they are liberal in dealing them out.

(CANON III.—If any one saith, that in the Roman Church, which is the mother and mistress of all churches, there is not the true doctrine concerning the sacrament of baptism: let him be anathema.)

Why did they not rather begin with this, since on this, as the foundation, they might raise any superstructure? For if all they teach is true, why are we still fighting? But our writings clearly shew that the whole doctrine of Baptism, as taught by them, is partly mutilated, partly vicious. Now, while they are unable to refute our arguments, it is vain to think of hiding themselves under the flash of an anathema! When they proudly call Rome the mother and witness of all Churches, what effrontery? Did she beget in Christ the Greek and Eastern Churches, by which rather she was begotten? What teaching of hers could reach other Churches which had far more learned Bishops? Let them bring forward all the most distinguished men they have ever had, will they out of the whole catalogue produce one equal either to Cyprian, or Ambrose, or Augustine?

(CANON IV.—If any one saith, that the baptism which is even given by heretics in the name of the Father, and of the Son, and of the Holy Ghost, with the intention of doing what the Church doth, is not true baptism: let him be anathema.)

What the Minister intends to do is of little consequence to us, provided the action itself corresponds to the genuine ordinance of Christ, both in doctrine and ritual. Let it suffice us then to have been baptized in the name of the Father, and the Son, and the Holy Spirit, whatever may have been the ignorance or impiety of those who administered Baptism to us. Man is merely the hand; it is Christ alone who truly and properly baptizes.

(CANON V.—If any one saith, that baptism is free, that is, not necessary unto salvation: let him be anathema.)

That the unskilful may not be imposed upon, we must tell them that there is a middle place between *free* and *necessary*, in the sense in which the Romanists use the latter term. We, too, acknowledge that the use of Baptism is necessary —that no one may omit it from either neglect or contempt. In this way we by no means make it free (optional.) And not only do we strictly bind the faithful to the observance of it, but we also maintain that it is the ordinary instrument of God in washing and renewing us; in short, in communicating to us salvation. The only exception we make is, that the hand of God must not be tied down to the instrument. He may of himself accomplish salvation. For when an opportunity of Baptism is wanting, the promise of God alone is amply sufficient. But of this subject something was said on a former Session.

(Canon VI.—If any one saith, that one who has been baptized can not, even if he would, lose grace, let him sin ever so much, unless he will not believe: let him be anathema.)

The paradox which they condemn we also repudiate, were it only for this one reason, that it extinguishes the life of faith.

(Canon VII.—If any one saith, that the baptized are, by baptism itself, *made debtors* but to faith alone, and not to the observance of *the whole law* of Christ: let him be anathema.)

Did they understand what the law of Christ is, they would without difficulty agree as to the rest; but from the way in which they are wont to speak of the law of Christ, they demonstrate by this one head how far they are from the true knowledge of Baptism. Nor am I unaware what it is that has misled them. For as Paul teaches, that by circumcision a man was bound to keep the law of Moses, (Gal. 5:3,) so they make out a similar obligation in Baptism in respect of the law of Christ. And the comparison would be apt did they not stumble, so to speak, on the very threshold: for they err exceedingly in thinking that Paul is there discoursing of the use and not rather of the abuse of circumcision. For if all who were circumcised were debtors to keep the whole law, it follows that they were liable to the curse. But Paul teaches very differently when he calls circumcision a seal of the righteousness of faith. (Rom. 4:11.) Those who pretended that working was meritorious made a profession of keeping the law. What is Baptism to us in the present day? Although it is a deed of mutual obligation between us and God, it has this as its special property, viz., to make us certain of the free forgiveness of sins, and the perpetual gift of adoption. This is as repugnant to the affirmation of Trent as freedom is contrary to slavery.

(Canon VIII.—If any one saith, that the baptized are freed from all the precepts, whether written or transmitted, of holy Church, in such wise that they are not bound to observe them, unless they have chosen of their own accord to submit themselves thereunto: let him be anathema.)

There is one Lawgiver, says James, who is able to save and to destroy. When they have demonstrated this to be false, we will not refuse to bind ourselves by their laws. But so long as it shall appear that God has taken the consciences of the godly under the government of his word, and claims this as his right, we may safely conclude that there is no Holy Church which will attempt to fetter consciences by other laws.

(CANON IX.—If any one saith, that the remembrance of the baptism which they have received is so to be recalled unto men, as that they are to understand that all vows made after baptism are void, in virtue of the promise already made in that baptism; as if, by those vows, they both derogated from that faith which they have professed, and from that baptism itself: let him be anathema.)

The first thing to have determined was, What are lawful vows? This being fixed, little or no dispute would remain. But now the vows under which wretched souls are put, or rather strangled, are not only full of superstition, but altogether at variance with the right rule of Christian life. Wherefore, to make any vow binding, it ought to be required at the profession of Baptism. If this be so, there is not one of the vows used in the Papacy at the present day that will not be void.

(CANON X.—If any one saith, that by the sole remembrance and the faith of the baptism which has been received, all sins committed after baptism are either remitted, or made venial: let him be anathema.)

Those who hold that sins are effaced by the mere remembrance of Baptism, do not mean a bare or frigid remembrance, but are conjoined with faith and repentance. Such also is the primary view of Baptism. For we ought to turn our thoughts not only to the sprinkling of water, but to the spiritual reality which begets the confidence of a good conscience by the resurrection of Christ, as Peter speaks. (1 Pet.

3:21.) Such remembrance, I say, not only makes sins venial, but altogether obliterates them. Whenever the question relates to the forgiveness of sins, we must flee to Baptism, and from it seek a confirmation of forgiveness. For as God reconciles us to himself by the daily promises of the gospel, so the belief and certainty of this reconciliation, which is daily repeated even to the end of life, he seals to us by Baptism. We were indeed baptized once, but there is a perpetual testimony of pardon and free propitiation in Christ.

What do the venerable Fathers say? Out of the trite rhapsodies of the sophists they restrict the promises of Baptism to the past, and the moment any one has sinned, burying all remembrance of Baptism, they enjoin him to rest in the fictitious Sacrament of Penance—as if Baptism were not itself a proper Sacrament of Penance. And still they will boast that they hold sound doctrine on the subject of Baptism, although they comprehend all its force in a momentary and evanescent promise of grace.

To the next three heads I not unwillingly subscribe [Canons XI, XII, XIII]. On the fourth [Canon XIV] I agree with them so far, but would wish my readers to observe what a deluge of anathemas they have poured forth. What they disapprove dropt on some occasion from Erasmus, perhaps, without much consideration. This I deny not, and yet a candid interpreter would only desire some correction in the terms, and conclude that the author of them was not fully versant in the government of the Church. No man of equity and moderation will fly at once to the terrors of an anathema.

(CANON XI.—If any one saith, that baptism, which was true and rightly conferred, is to be repeated, for him who has denied the faith of Christ amongst Infidels, when he is converted unto penitence: let him be anathema.)

(CANON XII.—If any one saith, that no one is to be baptized save at that age at which Christ was baptized, or in the very article of death: let him be anathema.)

(CANON XIII.—If any one saith, that little children, for that they have not actual faith, are not, after having received baptism, to be reckoned amongst the faithful; and that, for this cause, they are to be rebaptized when they have attained to years of discretion; or, that it is better that the baptism of such be omitted, than that,

while not believing by their own act, they should be baptized in the
faith alone of the Church: let him be anathema.)

(CANON XIV.—If any one saith, that those who have been thus
baptized when children, are, when they have grown up, to be
asked whether they will ratify what their sponsors promised in
their names when they were baptized; and that, in case they
answer that they will not, they are to be left to their own will; and
are not to be compelled meanwhile to a Christian life by any other
penalty, save that they be excluded from the participation of the
Eucharist, and of the other sacraments, until they repent: let him
be anathema.)

(ON CONFIRMATION.)

(CANON I.—If any one saith, that the confirmation of those who
have been baptized is an idle ceremony, and not rather a true and
proper sacrament; or that of old it was nothing more than a kind of
catechism, whereby they who were near adolescence gave an account of their faith in the face of the Church: let him be anathema.)

As this anathema has two edges, I hasten, in order to
avoid being smitten with the former one, to declare that I
am certainly not of the number of those who think that Confirmation, as observed under the Roman Papacy, is an idle
ceremony, inasmuch as I regard it as one of the most deadly
wiles of Satan. Let us remember that this pretended Sacrament is nowhere recommended in Scripture, either under
this name or with this ritual, or this signification. Let us now
hear with what titles they adorn their figment. In the name
of Pope Melciades, (De Consecrat. Dist. 5,) they declare
that the Spirit is given in Baptism for innocence, in Confirmation for increase of grace—that Baptism is sufficient for those
who were instantly to die, but by Confirmation, those who
are to prove victorious are armed so as to be able to sustain
the contest. Thus one half of the efficacy of Baptism is lopt
off, as if it were said in vain, that in Baptism the old man
is crucified, in order that we may walk in newness of life.
(Rom. 6:6.) They add, besides, that though neither of the
two is perfect without the other, yet Confirmation must be
regarded with higher veneration than Baptism. For there is
a decree of the Council of Aurelium, that no man should be
deemed a Christian who has not been anointed by Episcopal

unction. These words are fit to be propounded to children in sport. Sacrilege so replete with execrable blasphemy does indeed differ much from an idle ceremony.

Of the second branch of this head, what shall I say but that they have no mean idea of the effect which their anathemas are to have: they pour them forth as readily as if they thought they are immediately to make white black. But the truth is, that from the wonder or rather stupor with which they have seen their mysteries hitherto regarded by the vulgar, they have imagined that all their babble will be similarly received. Hence their exceeding confidence. Never would they have ventured to expose their absurdities to the judgment of the rudest hind had they not hoped that the mask of Council would hoodwink all eyes.

(CANON II.—If any one saith, that they who ascribe any virtue to the sacred chrism of confirmation, offer an outrage to the Holy Ghost: let him be anathema.)

The question is, whether oil, the moment after they have been pleased to call it Chrism, receives, at the will of man, a new and secret virtue of the Spirit? Oil is not mentioned by any ancient Christian writer, nay, not even by any one of that middle age wherein numerous errors abounded. Let them do what they may, therefore, they will gain nothing by denying that they insult the Spirit of God when they transfer his virtue to filthy oil.

(CANON III.—If any one saith, that the ordinary minister of holy confirmation is not the bishop alone, but any simple priest soever: let him be anathema.)

Of a truth the horned and mitred herd are worthy of such a privilege. For what could they do, seeing they are no fitter to execute the Episcopal office than hogs are to sing? Verily I do not envy them; only let them confine their impurities to their taverns, and keep them out of the Church of God. But how, pray, will they prove that this office is more befitting Bishops than other priests, unless that it hath so pleased some unknown authors? If a reason be sought from Scripture, all confess that it makes no distinction between a Bishop and a Presbyter. Then Paul is enjoined to receive imposition of hands from Ananias who was one of the disciples. (Acts 9:17.) If imposition of hands is their Confirmation, why do they not charge God with violating orders, and so profaning a mystery by confounding Presbyter and Bishop? In short, their doctrine is sanctioned either by a law of God or by human decree. If by a law of God, why are they not afraid to violate it? For they give Presbyters a right to confirm on extraordinary occasions. While they thus thunder away in behalf of a human decree, who will be afraid?

ANTIDOTE TO THE SUBSEQUENT CANONS

ON RESIDENCE

I sometimes wonder how it happens that, in such light of the gospel, they are just as absurd as they were wont to be in the thickest darkness. But I immediately turn to reflect on the admirable judgment of God, by which it is certain that they are so blinded and stupified, that, lost both to sight and feeling, they cast away all shame, and glory unblushingly in their own disgrace. Since the provisions of the Church, which were destined for the maintenance of pastors long ago, have begun to be the revenues of idle men, and those who are maintained at the expense of the Church think that no obligation lies upon them, they profess to have prepared themselves for the correction of this great iniquity. When they enter upon the subject they seem to say something. Where corruption is so rampant, it is, I admit, no small matter that two bishoprics are not to be held by one man. And there are other things of a similar nature, framed to curb the licentiousness which now stalks abroad, although in any reformation which they attempt, they are far, I say not from the primitive and austerer discipline which flourished a thousand years ago, but from any tolerable state of pious and well ordered government. They forbid a Bishop to absent himself from his diocese for more than half a year. The leave is liberal enough which gives six months' vacation out of twelve to those who ought to watch continually over the flock, both day and night. But even here a reservation is added—unless they have a just excuse for absence. When will they be without such excuse? And yet, supposing they most strictly observe what is here prescribed, what benefit will result, unless, perhaps, that they will not be able to carry out of the district all the money which the living yields?

If they love the city, they will have their palaces where, away from all noise, they will drink, play, and sleep as usual; if they prefer the country, they will have pleasant retreats in their seats and castles. Thus they will perform their office doing nothing, and yet giving actual residence.

As to parishes, they confirm schools in their privileges, so that the pretext of studying will excuse absence. Meanwhile, while the young and raw tyro learns to act the pastor, will he nevertheless draw the milk of the flock which will be left without a pastor. Grant that this may be tolerated, yet who knows not that lazy scullions alone enjoy the privileges of the Schools? The consequence will be, that the miserable churches will be forced to rear two wolves, one at home and another abroad. The resolution not to give effect in future to dispensations *de non promovendo,* beyond a year, was, I shrewdly guess, suggested by the granters. For what an addition will be made to their gains, if a new prerogative shall require to be purchased every year? In short, their only care seems to have been to exhibit some show of justice in a state of universal confusion.

But even if their regulations had been perfect to a title, good men could not congratulate themselves on the prospect of a better state of matters. For before they enact any law they abrogate all laws together, by one word, or at least point out a method by which they may all be abrogated: for they promise that none of the things which they may say are to hinder the Apostolic See from maintaining its authority unimpaired. Now, let any one consider with himself by what limits that authority is bounded, or how far it extends. Does not a preliminary of this kind just mean, that the Popes may order anything to be lawful that they please? What remedy, pray, do they bring by so acting? None of the things which they undertake to correct have hitherto been practised as if permitted by common law, but what the laws prohibited was done with impunity by means of dispensations. Accordingly, those guilty of abuses never alleged that they observed the strict rule, but having been set free from law, they thought they might do what otherwise in itself was not lawful. The Neptunian fathers now provide that the future shall be no better, by making a special proviso that the power of the Roman Court shall suffer no diminution. For though a thousand knots of laws were tied, the sword of Alexander is unsheathed to cut them all at once. Could they more openly mock the Christian world? Why do I say mock? Could they more grossly insult the expectation of the good, than when they deliver thus distinctly, and with barbarian haughtiness, that they will set no bounds to the unbridled tyranny of the Pope?

Callous as those who live under the Papacy have become to all evils, it might be said that on this one matter they had forgotten their bondage, I mean, in not only freely lamenting but crying aloud that the Church was ruined by dispensations. All eyes were turned to the venerable Fathers, sitting like strict and zealous censors to check the abuse. After pondering for eighteen months they declare their approval of ancient discipline, provided the Roman See retain its right of dispensing as before. In other words, the laws are to be so far enforced that liberty to violate them shall not be gratuitous, but may be purchased. And that the Pope may not be prevented by modesty from boldly exercising the power, they confirm him in the title of Universal Bishop, which Gregory calls nefarious, blasphemous, abominable, and the forerunner of Antichrist, while they leave nothing more to the Bishops than to be his Vicars. Where is that equality which Jerome heralds when he compares the Bishop of Rome to the Bishop of Eugubium? (Hierom. ad Evag.) Where is the doctrine of Cyprian that the Bishopric of Christ is one, and part of it is held entire (*in solidum*) by each Bishop? (Cyp. de Simplic. Prelat.) Bernard writes that it was a common complaint in his time, that the Churches were maimed and mutilated, because the Roman Bishop by drawing all power to himself confounded orders. (Bernard. de Consid. ad Eng. lib. 3.) To cure this evil the Holy Council bids Bishops be the Vicars of the Pope.

I will spend no more time in exposing their impudence. But as all see that they are worse than hopeless, every one who is wise will in future disregard their decrees, and be in no dubiety about them. It were indeed most desirable that the dissensions by which the Church is now disturbed should be settled by the authority of a pious Council, but as matters are we cannot yet hope for it. Therefore, since Churches are scattered in a dreadful manner, and no hope of gathering them together appears from man, each cannot do better than hasten to rally round the banner which the Son of God holds out to us. This is not a time to keep waiting for one another. As every one sees the light of Scripture beaming forth, let him instantly follow. In regard to the whole body of the Church, we commend it to the care of its

Lord. Meanwhile, let us not be either slothful or secure. Let each do his best. Let us contribute whatever in us is of counsel, learning, and abilities, to build up the ruins of the Church. But, in affairs so desperate, let us be sustained and animated by the promise that, as none appears from among men to undertake the office with manly and heroic mind, THE LORD, armed with His own justice and with the weight of His own arm, will Himself alone perform all things.

III

The Geneva Church

DRAFT ECCLESIASTICAL ORDINANCES
SEPTEMBER AND OCTOBER 1541[1]

[When Calvin returned to Geneva in 1541, he secured approval, with individuals assigned to help, to work out the pattern of ecclesiastical life in Geneva. The text here reproduced, bearing Calvin's hand in spite of official modification, is the charter of the Genevan Church. Important added modifications are included in the footnotes.]

There are four orders of office instituted by our Lord for the government of his Church.

First, pastors; then doctors; next elders; and fourth deacons.

---

[1] [From *Calvin: Theological Treatises*, Vol. XXII. The Library of Christian Classics, translated with introductions and notes by The Rev. J. K. S. Reid, pp. 58–72.]

Instead of the title, the following: In the Name of Almighty God, we, the Syndics of the Small and the Great Council with our people assembled at the sound of trumpet and great bell, according to our ancient customs, having considered that it is a thing worthy of commendation above all others, that the doctrine of the Holy Church of our Lord be well preserved in purity and the Christian Church be duly maintained, that the youth be in the future faithfully instructed, the hospital kept in good condition for sustaining the poor, all of which cannot be done unless there be a certain rule and manner of life by which each estate attends to the duties of its office: For this reason it appeared good to us that the spiritual government such as our Lord showed and instituted by his Word should be reduced to good order and have place and be observed

Hence if we will have a Church well ordered and maintained we ought to observe this form of government.

As to the pastors, whom Scripture also sometimes calls elders and ministers, their office is to proclaim the Word of God, to instruct, admonish, exhort and censure, both in public and private, to administer the sacraments and to enjoin brotherly corrections along with the elders and colleagues.

Now in order that nothing happen confusedly in the Church, no one is to enter upon this office without a calling. In this it is necessary to consider three things, namely: the principal thing is the examination; then what belongs to the institution of the ministers; third, what ceremony or method of procedure it is good to observe in introducing them to office.

The examination contains two parts, of which the first concerns doctrine—to ascertain whether the candidate for ordination has a good and holy knowledge of Scripture; and also whether he be a fit and proper person to communicate it edifyingly to the people.

Further to avoid all danger of the candidate holding some false opinion, it will be good that he profess his acceptance and maintenance of the doctrine approved by the Church.

To know whether he is fit to instruct, it would be necessary to proceed by interrogation and by hearing him discuss in private the doctrine of the Lord.

The second part concerns life, to ascertain whether he is of good habits and conducts himself always without reproach. The rule of procedure in this matter which it is needful to follow is very well indicated by Paul.

There follows, to whom it belongs to institute Pastors

It will be good in this connection to follow the order of the ancient Church, for it is the only practice which is shown us in Scripture. The order is that ministers first elect such as ought to hold office; afterwards that he be presented to the Council; and if he is found worthy the Council receive and accept him, giving him certification to produce finally to the

---

among us. Hence we have commanded and established to be followed and observed in our city and territory the Ecclesiastical Constitution which follows, seeing that it is taken from the gospel of Jesus Christ.

people when he preaches, in order that he be received by the common consent of the company of the faithful. If he be found unworthy, and show this after due probation, it is necessary to proceed to a new election for the choosing of another.

As to the manner of introducing him, it is good to use the imposition of hands, which ceremony was observed by the apostles and then in the ancient Church, providing that it take place without superstition and without offence. But because there has been much superstition in the past and scandal might result, it is better to abstain from it because of the infirmity of the times.[2]

When he is elected, he has to swear in front of the Seigneury. Of this oath there will be a prescribed form, suitable to what is required of a minister.

Now as it is necessary to examine the ministers well when they are to be elected, so also it is necessary to have good supervision to maintain them in their duty.

First it will be expedient that all the ministers, for conserving purity and concord of doctrine among themselves, meet together one certain day each week, for discussion of the Scriptures; and none are to be exempt from this without legitimate excuse. If anyone be negligent, let him be admonished.

As for those who preach in the villages, throughout the Seigneury, they are to be exhorted to come as often as they are able. For the rest, if they default an entire month, it is to be held to be very great negligence, unless it is a case of illness or other legitimate hindrance.

If there appear difference of doctrine, let the ministers come together to discuss the matter. Afterwards, if need be, let them call the elders[3] to assist in composing the contention. Finally, if they are unable to come to friendly agreement because of the obstinacy of one of the parties, let the case be referred to the magistrate to be put in order.

[2] The article runs: As to the manner of introduction, since the ceremonies of time past have been perverted into much superstition, because of the weakness of the times, it will suffice that a declaration be made by one of the ministers denoting the office to which ordination is being made; then that prayers and petitions be made, in order that the Lord give him grace to discharge it.

[3] and the clerk at the Seigneury.

To obviate all scandals of living, it will be proper that there be a form of correction to which all submit themselves. It will also be the means by which the ministry may retain respect, and the Word of God be neither dishonoured nor scorned because of the ill reputation of the ministers. For as one is to correct those who merit it, so it will be proper to reprove calumnies and false reports which are made unjustly against innocent people.

But first it should be noted that there are crimes which are quite intolerable in a minister, and there are faults which may on the other hand be endured while direct fraternal admonitions are offered.

Of the first sort are:

heresy, schism, rebellion against ecclesiastical order, blasphemy open and meriting civil punishment, simony and all corruption in presentations, intrigue to occupy another's place, leaving one's Church without lawful leave or just calling, duplicity, perjury, lewdness, larceny, drunkenness, assault meriting punishment by law, usury, games forbidden by the law and scandalous, dances and similar dissoluteness, crimes carrying with them loss of civil rights, crime giving rise to another separation from the Church.

Of the second sort are:

strange methods of treating Scripture which turn to scandal, curiosity in investigating idle questions, advancing some doctrine or kind of practice not received in the Church, negligence in studying and reading the Scriptures, negligence in rebuking vice amounting to flattery, negligence in doing everything required by his office, scurrility, lying, slander, dissolute words, injurious words, foolhardiness and evil devices, avarice and too great parsimony, undisciplined anger, quarrels and contentions, laxity either of manner or of gesture and like conduct improper to a minister.[4]

In the case of the crimes which cannot at all be tolerated, if some accusation and complaint arise, let the assembly of ministers and elders investigate it, in order to proceed reason-

[4] The rest of the article reads: If there are civil crimes, that is crimes which should be punished by the laws, should any ministers fall into them, the Seigneury is to take them in hand, and beyond the ordinary penalty they are accustomed to impose on others, deposition from office will be the punishment.

ably and according to whatever is discovered in judging the case, and then report judgment to the magistrate in order that if required the delinquent be deposed.[5]

In the case of the lesser vices which may be corrected by simple admonition, one is to proceed according to the command of our Lord, so that as a last step it come for ecclesiastical judgment.

To keep this discipline in operation, let the ministers every three months take special notice whether there be anything to discuss among themselves, to remedy it as is reasonable.

Of the number, place and time of preachings

Each Sunday, there is to be sermon at St. Peter[6] and St. Gervais at break of day, and at the usual hour at the said St. Peter and St. Gervais.

At midday, there is to be catechism, that is, instruction of little children in all the three churches, the Magdalene, St. Peter and St. Gervais.

At three o'clock second sermon in[7] St. Peter and St. Gervais.

For bringing children to catechism, and for receiving the sacraments, the boundaries of the parishes should as far as possible be observed; that is, St. Gervais embracing what it had in the past, the Magdalene similarly, St. Peter what belonged formerly to St. Germain, St. Cross, Our Lady the New, and St. Legier.

Besides the two preachings which take place, on working days there will be a sermon at St. Peter three times a week, on Monday, Tuesday and Friday[8] one hour before beginning is made at the other places.

[5] As to the other crimes of which the first investigation belongs to the ecclesiastical Consistory, the clerks or elders with the ministers are to be watchful for them. And if anyone is convicted of them, they are to make a report to the Council with their advice and judgment; thus the final sentence of punishment is to be reserved to the Seigneury.

[6] Add: at the Magdalene

[7] At three o'clock also in all the three parishes

[8] For the end of the article: These sermons are to be heard one after another at such an hour that they can be finished before beginning elsewhere. If some extraordinary prayer for the necessity of the time is to be made, the order for Sunday will be observed.

To maintain these charges and others pertaining to the ministry, it will be necessary to have five ministers and three coadjutors who will also be ministers, to aid and assist as necessity requires.

Concerning the second order, which we have called Doctors

The office proper to doctors is the instruction of the faithful in true doctrine, in order that the purity of the Gospel be not corrupted either by ignorance or by evil opinions. As things are disposed today, we always include under this title aids and instructions for maintaining the doctrine of God and defending the Church from injury by the fault of pastors and ministers. So to use a more intelligible word, we will call this the order of the schools.

The degree nearest to the minister and most closely joined to the government of the Church is the lecturer in theology, of which it will be good to have one in Old Testament and one in New Testament.

But because it is only possible to profit from such lectures if first one is instructed in the languages and humanities, and also because it is necessary to raise offspring for time to come, in order not to leave the Church deserted to our children, a college should be instituted for instructing children to prepare them for the ministry as well as for civil government.

For the first, a proper place ought to be assigned for both doing lessons and accommodating the children and others who would profit. There must be a man learned and expert in arranging both the house and the instruction, who is able also to lecture. He is to be chosen and remunerated on condition that he have under his charge lecturers both in languages and in dialectic, if it can be done. Likewise there should be some matriculated persons to teach the little children; and[9] these we hope shortly to appoint to assist the master.

All who are there will be subject like ministers to ecclesiastical discipline.

There need be no other school in the city for the little children, but let the girls have their school apart, as has hitherto been the case.

[9] this we wish and order to be done

Let no one be received if he is not approved by the ministers[10] on their testimony, for fear of impropriety.

Concerning the third order which is that of Elders[11]

Their office is to have oversight of the life of everyone, to admonish amicably those whom they see to be erring or to be living a disordered life, and, where it is required, to enjoin fraternal corrections themselves and along with others.

In the present condition of the Church, it would be good to elect two of the Little Council, four of the Council of Sixty, and six of the Council of Two Hundred, men of good and honest life, without reproach and beyond suspicion, and above all fearing God and possessing spiritual prudence. These should be so elected that there be some in every quarter of the city, to keep an eye on everybody.

The best way of electing them seems to be this, that the Little Council suggest the nomination of the best that can be found and the most suitable; and to do this, summon the ministers to confer with them; after this they should present those whom they would commend to the Council of Two Hundred, which will approve them. If it find them worthy, let them take the special oath, whose form will be readily drawn up. And at the end of the year, let them present themselves to the Seigneury for consideration whether they ought to be continued or changed. It is inexpedient that they be changed often without cause, so long as they discharge their duty faithfully.

The fourth order of ecclesiastical government, that is, the Deacons

There were always two kinds in the ancient Church, the one deputed to receive, dispense and hold goods for the poor, not only daily alms, but also possessions, rents and pensions; the other to tend and care for the sick and administer allowances

[10] by the ministers having first informed the Seigneury; and then let him again be presented to the Council along with their testimony, for fear of impropriety. The examination ought always to be conducted in the presence of two gentlemen of the Little Council.

[11] who are to be sent or deputed by the Seigneury to the Consistory

to the poor. This custom we follow again now for we have procurators and hospitallers.

The number of procurators appointed for this hospital seems to us to be proper; but we wish that there be also a separate reception office, so that not only provisions be in time made better, but that those who wish to do some charity may be more certain that the gift will not be employed otherwise than they intend. And if the revenue assigned by their Lordships be insufficient, or should extraordinary necessity arise, the Seigneury will advise about adjustment, according to the need they see.

The election of both procurators and hospitallers is to take place like that of the elders; and in electing them the rule proposed by Paul for deacons is to be followed.

With regard to the office of procurator, we think the rules which have already been imposed on them by us are good, by means of which, in urgent affairs, and where there is danger in deferment, and chiefly when there is no grave difficulty or question of great expense, they are not obliged always to be meeting, but one or two can do what is reasonable in the absence of the others.

It will be their duty to watch diligently that the public hospital is well maintained, and that this be so both for the sick and the old people unable to work, widowed women, orphaned children and other poor creatures. The sick are always to be lodged in a set of rooms separate from the other people who are unable to work, old men, widowed women, orphaned children and the other poor.

Moreover, care for the poor dispersed through the city should be revived, as the procurators may arrange it.

Moreover, besides the hospital for those passing through which must be maintained, there should be some attention given to any recognized as worthy of special charity. For this purpose, a special room should be set aside to receive those who ought to be assisted by the procurators, which is to be reserved for this business.

It should above all be demanded that the families of the hospitallers be honourably ruled in accordance with the will of God, since they have to govern houses dedicated to God.

The ministers[12] must on their side enquire whether there be any lack or want of anything, in order to ask and desire

[12] and the assistants or elders with one of the Lords Syndic

the Seigneury to put it in order. To do this, some of their company with the procurators should visit the hospital every three months, to ascertain if all is in order.

It would be good, not only for the poor of the hospital, but also for those of the city who cannot help themselves, that they have a doctor and a surgeon of their own who should still practise in the city, but meanwhile be required to have care of the hospital and to visit the other poor.

As for the hospital for plague, it should be wholly separate and apart, and especially if it happen that the city be visited by this scourge of God.

For the rest, to discourage mendicancy which is contrary to good order, it would be well,[13] and we have so ordered it, that there be one of our officials at the entrance of the churches to remove from the place those who loiter, and if there be any who give offence or offer insolence to bring them to one of the Lords Syndic. Similarly for the rest of the time, let the Overseers of Tens take care that the total prohibition of begging be well observed.

Of the Sacraments[14]

Baptism is to take place at the time of Sermon, and should be administered only by ministers or coadjutors. The names of children with those of their parents are to be registered, that, if any be found a bastard, the magistrate may be informed.

The stone or baptismal font is to be near the pulpit, in order that there be better hearing for the recitation of this mystery and practice of baptism.

Only such strangers as are men of faith and of our communion are to be accepted as godparents, since others are not capable of making the promise to the Church of instructing the children as is proper.

Of the Supper

Since the Supper was instituted for us by our Lord to be frequently used, and also was so observed in the ancient

[13] The Seigneury should appoint some of its officers, and so we have ordained

[14] Add sub-title: Of Baptism

Church until the devil turned everything upside down, erecting the mass in its place, it is a fault in need of correction, to celebrate it so seldom.[15]

Hence it will be proper that it be always administered in the city once a month, in such a way that every three months it take place in each parish. Besides, it should take place three times a year generally, that is to say at Easter, Pentecost and Christmas, in such a way that it be not repeated in the parish in the month when it should take place by turn.

The ministers are to distribute the bread in proper order and with reverence; and none are to give the chalice except the colleagues or deacons with the ministers. Hence there should not be a large number of vessels.

The tables should be beside the pulpit in order that the mystery be more conveniently set forth beside the tables.

It should be celebrated in the church at the most fitting time.

The Sunday before the celebration, intimation is to be made, in order that no child come before it has made profession of its faith as proved by examination by the Catechism, and also that all strangers and new-comers may be exhorted first to come and present themselves at the church, so that they be instructed and thus none approach to his own condemnation.

Of Marriage

After the announcement of the customary banns, the marriage ceremony is to take place as the parties require, whether Sunday or working day, provided it be at the beginning of Service. It is proper that one abstain from this on the day when the Supper is to be celebrated, in honour of the sacrament.

It will be good to introduce ecclesiastical songs, the better to incite the people to prayer and to praise God.

To begin with, little children are to be instructed; then in time all the Church will be able to follow.

With regard to differences in matrimonial cases, because

[15] Add: For the present, let it be advised and ordained that it always be administered four times in the year.

it is not a spiritual matter but involved with civil affairs,[16] we remit these to their Lordships, desiring them nevertheless to be willing to set up a Consistory without delay to judge in such matters, to which, if it seem good to them, there could be joined some ministers as counsellors. Above all may it please them to appoint men to make ordinances which may be followed forthwith.

Of Burial

The dead are to be buried decently in the place appointed. The attendance and company are left to each man's discretion.

It will be good that the carriers be warned by us[17] to discourage all superstitions contrary to the Word of God, not to do duty at too late an hour, and to make a report in the case of sudden death, in order to obviate all inconvenience that might thereby arise.

Moreover they are to do duty not earlier than twelve hours after death, and not later than twenty-four.

Of the Visitation of the Sick

There are many people negligent in comforting themselves in God by his Word when they are afflicted with sickness, and so many die without the admonition or teaching which is more salutary for a man then than at any other time. It will be good therefore that their Lordships ordain and make public that no one is to be totally confined to bed for three days without informing the minister, and that each be advised to call the ministers when they desire it in good time, in order that they be not diverted from the office which they publicly discharge in the Church. Above all it is to be commanded that parents, friends and attendants do not wait until the patient is about to die, for in this extremity consolation is in most cases hardly useful.

[16] it will remain the business of the Seigneury. Nevertheless we have advised leaving to the Consistory the duty of hearing the parties, in order to report their advice to the Council. For assessing judgment, proper ordinances are to be set up, which will be followed henceforward.

[17] before the Seigneury

Of the Visitation of Prisoners

It will be good that their Lordships ordain a certain day each week on which admonition be given to prisoners, to reprove and exhort them; and if it seem good to them,[18] let them depute someone of their company in order that no fraud be committed. If they have anyone in irons, whom it is not desirable to take out, if it seems good to them, they could give entry to some minister to console him in their presence as above. For if one waits until they are about to die, they are often so preoccupied with fear of death, that they can neither receive nor listen. The day for doing this, it is decided, will be Saturday after dinner.

The Order to be observed in the case of little Children

All citizens and inhabitants are to bring or convey their children on Sundays at midday to Catechism, of which something has been said.

A definite formulary is to be composed by which they will be instructed, and on this, with the teaching given them, they are to be interrogated about what has been said, to see if they have listened and remembered well.

When a child has been well enough instructed to pass the Catechism, he is to recite solemnly the sum of what it contains, and also to make profession of his Christianity in the presence of the Church.

Before this is done, no child is to be admitted to receive the Supper; and parents are to be informed not to bring them before this time. For it is a very perilous thing, for children as for parents, to introduce them without good and adequate instruction; for which purpose this order is to be used.

In order that there be no mistake, let it be ordained that children who come to school assemble there before twelve o'clock, and that the masters conduct them in good order in each parish.

The fathers are to bring the others or have them conducted. In order that there be the less confusion, the distinction of parishes in this connection is to be observed as far as

[18] And two of the Gentlemen of the Council are to be deputed to assist, in order that there be committed

possible, as has been said above concerning the sacraments.

Those who contravene these regulations are to be called before the company of the elders, and, if they will not yield to good advice, they must be reported to their Lordships.[19]

To advise who do their duty and who do not, elders are to keep an eye over all to give warning.

Of the Order which is to be observed in the case of those in authority, for the maintenance of supervision in the Church

The elders, as already said, are to assemble once a week with the ministers, that is to say on Thursday morning, to see that there be no disorder in the Church and to discuss together remedies as they are required.

Because they have no compulsive authority or jurisdiction, may it please their Lordships, to give them one of their officials to summon those whom they wish to admonish.

If anyone refuse with contempt to comply, their office will be to inform their Lordships, in order that remedy be applied.

There follows the list of persons whom the elders ought to admonish, and how one is to proceed.

If there be anyone who dogmatizes against the received doctrine, conference is to be held with him. If he listen to reason, he is to be dismissed without scandal or dishonour. If he be opinionative, he is to be admonished several times, until it is seen that measures of greater severity are needed. Then he is to be interdicted from the communion of the Supper and reported to the magistrate.

If anyone is negligent in coming to church, so that a noticeable contempt of the communion of the faithful is evident, or if any show himself contemptuous of the ecclesiastical order, he is to be admonished, and if he prove [dis]obedient dismissed in friendliness. If he persevere in his evil way, after being three times admonished, he is to be separated from the Church and reported.[20]

As for each man's conduct, for the correction of faults, proceedings should be in accordance with the order which our Lord commands.

[19] let report be made to the Seigneury.
[20] to the Seigneury.

Secret vices are to be secretly admonished; no one is to bring his neighbour before the Church to accuse him of faults that are not in the least notorious or scandalous, unless after having found him contumacious.

For the rest, those who despise particular admonitions by their neighbour are to be admonished anew by the Church; and if they will not at all come to reason or acknowledge their fault when convicted of it, they will be informed that they must abstain from the Supper until such time as they return in a better frame of mind.

As for vices notorious and public which the Church cannot dissimulate, if they are faults that merit admonition only, the duty of the elders will be to summon those who are implicated to make friendly remonstrance to them in order that they make correction, and, if amendment is evident, to do them no harm. If they persevere in doing wrong, they are to be admonished repeatedly; and if even then there is no result, they are to be informed that, as despisers of God, they must abstain from the Supper until a change of life is seen in them.

As for crimes which merit not merely remonstrance in words but correction by chastisement, should any fall into them, according to the needs of the case, he must be warned that he abstain for some time from the Supper, to humble himself before God and to acknowledge his fault the better.

If any in contumacy or rebellion wish to intrude against the prohibition, the duty of the minister is to turn him back, since it is not permissible for him to be received at the Communion.

Yet all this should be done with such moderation, that there be no rigour by which anyone may be injured; for even the corrections are only medicines for bringing back sinners to our Lord.[21]

[21] additional article: All this is to take place in such a way that the ministers have no civil jurisdiction, nor use anything but the spiritual sword of the Word of God, as Paul commands them; nor is the Consistory to derogate from the authority of the Seigneury or ordinary justice. The civil power is to remain unimpaired. Even where there will be need to impose punishment or to constrain parties, the ministers with the Consistory having heard the parties and used such remonstrances and admonitions as are good, are to report the whole matter to the Council, which in their turn will advise sentence and judgment according to the needs of the case.

These regulations are to be not only for the city but also for the villages dependent upon the Seigneury.

Form of Oath prescribed for Ministers, July 17, 1542[22]

The form and fashion of oath and promise which ministers of the gospel, admitted and received in the city of Geneva, are to make before the Lord Syndic and Council of the said city runs as follows:

I promise and swear that in the ministry to which I am called I will serve faithfully before God, setting forth purely his Word for the edification of this Church to which he has bound me; that I will in no way abuse his doctrine to serve my carnal affections nor to please any living man; but that I will employ it with pure conscience in the service of his glory and for the profit of his people to which I am debtor.

I promise also and swear to defend the Ecclesiastical Ordinances as they are approved by the Little, the Great and the General Councils of this City, and, in the measure in which I am given charge of administering those that have come short, to acquit myself loyally, without giving place to hatred, or favour, or vengeance, or any other carnal feeling, and in general to do what is proper to a good and faithful minister.

Thirdly, I swear and promise to guard and maintain the honour and welfare of the Seigneury and the City, to take pains, so far as is possible for me, that the people continue in beneficial peace and unity under the government of the Seigneury, and to consent in no wise to those who would violate it.

Finally, I promise and swear to be subject to the polity and

[22] *C.R.* comments as follows: "The draft proposed by the ministers in September 1541, in demanding that the pastor elected and accepted should take oath before the Seigneury, contented itself with saying that 'there would be a written form, suitable to what is required of a minister.' But the Ordinances as published on November 20 of the same year did not even give this reference: they only spoke as before of it being inserted at the place indicated. Apparently the revision continued to be cautious, as is expressly said of the oath to be exacted from members of the Consistory, whose imposition was decreed. 'They are to take a specific oath whose form will be readily drawn up,' says the draft; 'whose form will be drawn up as for the ministers' says the official text" (X/1, 31).

The document here, by the change it suffered on revision, is proved to be the Draft presented by Calvin to the Little Council.

constitution of this City, to show a good example of obedience to all others, being for my part subject to the laws and the magistracy, so far as my office allows; that is to say without prejudice to the liberty which we must have to teach according to what God commands us and to do the things which pertain to our office. And in conclusion, I promise to serve the Seigneury and the people in such wise, so long as I be not at all hindered from rendering to God the service which in my vocation I owe him.

CATECHISM OF
THE CHURCH OF GENEVA[1]

[*Calvin spent considerable time in writing, translating and
revising a catechism—1536, 1538, 1541, 1546. The complete
text, of which this selection is approximately one-third, was
obviously too long to be committed to memory as such. It
was to be absorbed over a period of fifty-five Sundays. The
reformers revived an ancient tradition of catechetical instruction as a medium of imparting and informing members of
the church in terms of what they were to believe.*]

DEDICATION

JOHN CALVIN TO THE FAITHFUL MINISTERS OF

CHRIST THROUGHOUT EAST FRIESLAND, WHO

PREACH THE PURE DOCTRINE OF

THE GOSPEL

Seeing it becomes us to endeavour by all means that unity
of faith, which is so highly commended by Paul, shine forth
among us, to this end chiefly ought the formal profession of
faith which accompanies our common baptism to have reference. Hence it were to be wished, not only that a perpetual
consent in the doctrine of piety should appear among all, but
also that one CATECHISM were common to all the Churches.
But as, from many causes, it will scarcely ever obtain otherwise than that each Church shall have its own Catechism,
we should not strive too keenly to prevent this; provided,

---

[1] [Reprinted from *Tracts containing Treatises on the Sacraments,
Catechism of the Church of Geneva, Forms of Prayer, and Confessions of Faith,* translated from the original Latin and French by
Henry Beveridge, Vol. II (Edinburgh: Printed for the Calvin Translation Society, 1849), pp. 33–56.]

however, that the variety in the mode of teaching is such, that we are all directed to one Christ, in whose truth being united together, we may grow up into one body and one spirit, and with the same mouth also proclaim whatever belongs to the sum of faith. Catechists not intent on this end, besides fatally injuring the Church, by sowing the materials of dissension in religion, also introduce an impious profanation of baptism. For where can any longer be the utility of baptism unless this remain as its foundation—that we all agree in one faith?

Wherefore, those who publish Catechisms ought to be the more carefully on their guard, lest, by producing anything rashly, they may not for the present only, but in regard to posterity also, do grievous harm to piety, and inflict a deadly wound on the Church.

This much I wished to premise, as a declaration to my readers, that I myself too, as became me, have made it my anxious care not to deliver any thing in this Catechism of mine that is not agreeable to the doctrine received among all the pious. This declaration will not be found vain by those who will read with candour and sound judgment. I trust I have succeeded at least so far that my labour, though it should not satisfy, will be acceptable to all good men, as being in their opinion useful.

In writing it in Latin, though some perhaps will not approve of the design, I have been influenced by many reasons, all of which it is of no use to detail at present. I shall only select such as seem to me sufficient to obviate censure.

First, In this confused and divided state of Christendom, I judge it useful that there should be public testimonies, whereby churches which, though widely separated by space, agree in the doctrine of Christ, may mutually recognise each other. For besides that this tends not a little to mutual confirmation, what is more to be desired than that mutual congratulations should pass between them, and that they should devoutly commend each other to the Lord? With this view, bishops were wont in old time, when as yet consent in faith existed and flourished among all, to send Synodal Epistles beyond sea, by which, as a kind of badges, they might maintain sacred communion among the churches. How much more necessary is it now, in this fearful devastation of the Christian world, that the few churches which duly worship God, and they too scattered and hedged round on all sides by the profane synagogues of Antichrist, should mutually give and receive this token of holy union, that they may thereby be incited to that fraternal embrace of which I have spoken?

But if this is so necessary in the present day, what shall our feelings be concerning posterity, about which I am so anxious, that I scarcely dare to think? Unless God miraculously send help from heaven, I cannot avoid seeing that the world is threatened with the extremity of barbarism. I wish our children may not shortly feel, that this has been rather a true prophecy than a conjecture. The more, therefore, must we labour to gather together, by our writings, whatever remains of the Church shall continue, or even emerge, after our death. Writings of a different class will show what were our views on all subjects in religion, but the agreement which our churches had in doctrine cannot be seen with clearer evidence than from catechisms. For therein will appear, not only what one man or other once taught, but with what rudiments learned and unlearned alike amongst us, were constantly imbued from childhood, all the faithful holding them as their formal symbol of Christian communion. This was indeed my principal reason for publishing this Catechism.

A second reason, which had no little weight with me, was, because I heard that it was desired by very many who hoped it would not be unworthy of perusal. Whether they are right or wrong in so judging is not mine to decide, but it became me to yield to their wish. Nay, necessity was almost laid upon me, and I could not with impunity decline it. For having seven years before published a brief summary of religion, under the name of a Catechism, I feared that if I did not bring forward this one, I should cause (a thing I wished not) that the former should on the other hand be excluded. Therefore if I wished to consult the public good, it behoved me to take care that this one which I preferred should occupy the ground.

Besides, I deem it of good example to testify to the world, that we who aim at the restitution of the Church, are everywhere faithfully exerting ourselves, in order that, at least, the use of the Catechism which was abolished some centuries ago under the Papacy, may now resume its lost rights. For neither can this holy custom be sufficiently commended for its utility, nor can the Papists be sufficiently condemned for the flagrant corruption, by which they not only set it aside, by converting it into puerile trifles, but also basely abuse it to purposes of impure and impious superstition. That spurious Confirmation, which they have substituted in its stead, they deck out like a harlot, with great splendour of ceremonies, and gorgeous shows without number; nay, in their wish to adorn it, they speak of it in terms of execrable blasphemy, when they give out that it is a sacrament of greater dignity than baptism, and call those only half Christians who have not been besmeared with their oil. Meanwhile, the whole proceeding consists of nothing but theatrical gesticulations, or rather the wanton sporting of apes, without any skill in imitation.

To you, my very dear brethren in the Lord, I have chosen to inscribe this work, because some of your body, besides informing me that you love me, and that the most of you take delight in my writings, also expressly requested me by letter to undertake this labour for their sake. Independently of this, it would have been reason sufficient, that what I learned of you long ago, from the statement of grave and pious men, had bound me to you with my whole soul. I now ask what I am confident you will of your own accord do—have the goodness to consult for the utility of this token of my goodwill towards you! Farewell. May the Lord increase you more and more in the spirit of wisdom, prudence, zeal, and fortitude, to the edification of his Church.

GENEVA, 2d December, 1545.

TO THE ' READER

It has ever been the practice of the Church, and one carefully attended to, to see that children should be duly instructed in the Christian religion. That this might be done more conveniently, not only were schools opened in old time, and individuals enjoined properly to teach their families, but it was a received public custom and practice, to question children in the churches on each of the heads, which should be common and well known to all Christians. To secure this being done in order, there was written out a formula, which was called a Catechism or Institute. Thereafter the devil miserably rending the Church of God, and bringing upon it fearful ruin, (of which the marks are still too visible in the greater part of the world,) overthrew this sacred policy, and left nothing behind but certain trifles, which only beget superstition, without any fruit of edification. Of this description is that confirmation, as they call it, full of gesticulations which, worse than ridiculous, are fitted only for apes, and have no foundation to rest upon. What we now bring forward, therefore, is nothing else than the use of things which from ancient times were observed by Christians, and the true worshippers of God, and which never were laid aside until the Church was wholly corrupted.

CATECHISM OF THE CHURCH OF GENEVA

OF FAITH

Master.—What is the chief end of human life?

Scholar.—To know God by whom men were created.

M. What reason have you for saying so?

S. Because he created us and placed us in this world to be glorified in us. And it is indeed right that our life, of which himself is the beginning, should be devoted to his glory.

M. What is the highest good of man?

S. The very same thing.

M. Why do you hold that to be the highest good?

S. Because without it our condition is worse than that of the brutes.

M. Hence, then, we clearly see that nothing worse can happen to a man than not to live to God.

S. It is so.

M. What is the true and right knowledge of God?

S. When he is so known that due honour is paid to him.

M. What is the method of honouring him duly?

S. To place our whole confidence in him; to study to serve him during our whole life by obeying his will; to call upon him in all our necessities, seeking salvation and every good thing that can be desired in him; lastly, to acknowledge him both with heart and lips, as the sole Author of all blessings.

M. To consider these points in their order, and explain them more fully—What is the first head in this division of yours?

S. To place our whole confidence in God.

M. How shall we do so?

S. When we know him to be Almighty and perfectly good.

M. Is this enough?

S. Far from it.

M. Wherefore?

S. Because we are unworthy that he should exert his power in helping us, and show how good he is by saving us.

M. What more then is needful?

S. That each of us should set it down in his mind that God loves him, and is willing to be a Father, and the author of salvation to him.

M. But whence will this appear?

S. From his word, in which he explains his mercy to us in Christ, and testifies of his love towards us.

M. Then the foundation and beginning of confidence in God is to know him in Christ?

S. Entirely so.

M. I should now wish you to tell me in a few words, what the sum of this knowledge is?

S. It is contained in the Confession of Faith, or rather Formula of Confession, which all Christians have in common. It is commonly called the Apostles' Creed, because from the beginning of the Church it was ever received among all the pious, and because it either fell from the lips of the Apostles, or was faithfully gathered out of their writings.

M. Repeat it.

S. I believe in God the Father Almighty, maker of heaven and earth; and in Jesus Christ, his only Son, our Lord, who was conceived by the Holy Ghost, born of the Virgin Mary, suffered under Pontius Pilate, was crucified, dead, and buried: he descended into hell; the third day he arose again from the dead; he ascended into heaven, and sitteth on the right hand of God the Father Almighty, from thence he shall come to judge the quick and the dead. I believe in the Holy Ghost; the holy Catholic Church; the communion of saints; the forgiveness of sins; the resurrection of the body; and the life everlasting. Amen.

M. To understand each point more thoroughly, into how many parts shall we divide this confession?

S. Into four leading ones.

M. Mention them to me.

S. The first relates to God the Father; the second to his Son Jesus Christ, which also embraces the whole sum of man's redemption; the third to the Holy Spirit; the fourth to the Church, and the Divine blessings conferred upon her.

M. Since there is no God but one, why do you here mention three, the Father, Son, and Holy Spirit?

S. Because in the one essence of God, it behoves us to

look on God the Father as the beginning and origin, and the first cause of all things; next the Son, who is his eternal Wisdom; and, lastly, the Holy Spirit, as his energy diffused indeed over all things, but still perpetually resident in himself.

M. You mean then that there is no absurdity in holding that these three persons are in one Godhead, and God is not therefore divided?

S. Just so.

M. Now repeat the first part.

S. "I believe in God the Father Almighty, maker of heaven and earth."

M. Why do you call him Father?

S. Primarily with reference to Christ who is his eternal Wisdom, begotten of him before all time, and being sent into this world was declared to be his Son. We infer, however, that as God is the Father of Jesus Christ, he is our Father also.

M. In what sense do you give him the name of Almighty?

S. Not as having a power which he does not exercise, but as having all things under his power and hand; governing the world by his Providence, determining all things by his will, ruling all creatures as seems to him good.

M. You do not then suppose an indolent power in God, but consider it such that his hand is always engaged in working, so that nothing is done except through Him, and by his decree.

S. It is so.

M. Why do you add "Creator of heaven and earth?"

S. As he has manifested himself to us by works, (Rom. 1: 20,) in these too we ought to seek him. Our mind cannot take in his essence. The world itself is, therefore, a kind of mirror in which we may view him in so far as it concerns us to know.

M. Do you not understand by "heaven and earth" all creatures whatever that exist?

S. Yes, verily; under these two names all are included, because they are either heavenly or earthly.

M. But why do you call God a Creator merely, while it is much more excellent to defend and preserve creatures in their state, than to have once made them?

S. This term does not imply that God created his works at once, and then threw off the care of them. It should rather be understood, that as the world was once made by God, so it is now preserved by him, and that the earth and all other things endure just in as far as they are sustained by his energy, and as it were his hand. Besides, seeing that he has all things under his hand, it follows, that he is the chief ruler and Lord of all. Therefore, by his being "Creator of heaven and earth," we must understand that it is he alone who by wisdom, goodness, and power, guides the whole course and order of nature: who at once sends rain and drought, hail and other storms, as well as calm, who of his kindness fertilizes the earth, and on the contrary, by withholding his hand, makes it barren: from whom come health and disease; to whose power all things are subject, and whose nod they obey.

M. But what shall we say of wicked men and devils? Shall we say that they too are under him?

S. Although he does not govern them by his Spirit, he however curbs them by his power as a bridle, so that they cannot even move unless in so far as he permits them. Nay, he even makes them the ministers of his will, so that unwilling and against their own intention, they are forced to execute what to him seems good.

M. What good redounds to you from the knowledge of this fact?

S. Very much. It would go ill with us could devils and wicked men do any thing without the will of God, and our minds could never be very tranquil while thinking we were exposed to their caprice. Then only do we rest safely when we know that they are curbed by the will of God, and as it were kept in confinement, so that they cannot do any thing unless by his permission: the more especially that God has engaged to be our guardian, and the prince of our salvation.

M. Let us now come to the second part.

S. It is that we believe "in Jesus Christ his only Son our Lord."

M. What does it chiefly comprehend?

S. That the Son of God is our Saviour, and it at the same time explains the method by which he has redeemed us from death, and purchased life.

M. What is the meaning of the name Jesus which you give to him?

S. It has the same meaning as the Greek word Σωτηρ, (*Soter.*) The Latins have no proper name by which its force may be well expressed. Hence the term Saviour (*Salvator*) was commonly received. Moreover, the angel gave this ap-

pellation to the Son of God, by the order of God himself.
(Matt. 1:21.)

M. Is this more than if men had given it?

S. Certainly. For since God wills that he be called so, he
must absolutely be so.

M. What, next, is the force of the name Christ?

S. By this epithet, his office is still better expressed—for
it signifies that he was anointed by the Father to be a King,
Priest, and Prophet.

M. How do you know that?

S. *First,* Because Scripture applies anointing to these three
uses; *secondly,* Because it often attributes the three things
which we have mentioned to Christ.

M. But with what kind of oil was he anointed?

S. Not with visible oil as was used in consecrating ancient
kings, priests, and prophets, but one more excellent, namely,
the grace of the Holy Spirit, which is the thing meant by
that outward anointing.

M. But what is the nature of this kingdom of his which
you mention?

S. Spiritual, contained in the word and Spirit of God,
which carry with them righteousness and life.

M. What of the priesthood?

S. It is the office and prerogative of appearing in the presence of God to obtain grace, and of appeasing his wrath by
the offering of a sacrifice which is acceptable to him.

M. In what sense do you call Christ a Prophet?

S. Because on coming into the world he declared himself
an ambassador to men, and an interpreter, and that for the
purpose of putting an end to all revelations and prophecies
by giving a full exposition of his Father's will.

M. But do you derive any benefit from this?

S. Nay, all these things have no end but our good. For the
Father hath bestowed them on Christ that he may communicate them to us, and all of us thus receive out of his fulness.

M. State this to me somewhat more fully.

S. He was filled with the Holy Spirit, and loaded with a
perfect abundance of all his gifts, that he may impart them
to us,—that is, to each according to the measure which the
Father knows to be suited to us. Thus from him, as the only
fountain, we draw whatever spiritual blessings we possess.

M. What does his kingdom bestow upon us?

S. By means of it, obtaining liberty of conscience to live
piously and holily, and, being provided with his spiritual

riches, we are also armed with power sufficient to overcome the perpetual enemies of our souls—sin, the world, the devil, and the flesh.

M. To what is the office of priest conducive?

S. First, by means of it he is the mediator who reconciles us to the Father; and, secondly, access is given us to the Father, so that we too can come with boldness into his presence, and offer him the sacrifice of ourselves, and our all. In this way he makes us, as it were, his colleagues in the priesthood.

M. There is still prophecy.

S. As it is an office of teaching bestowed on the Son of God in regard to his own servants, the end is that he may enlighten them by the true knowledge of the Father, instruct them in truth, and make them household disciples of God.

M. All that you have said then comes to this, that the name of Christ comprehends three offices which the Father hath bestowed on the Son, that he may transfuse the virtue and fruit of them into his people?

S. It is so.

M. Why do you call him the only Son of God, seeing that God designs to bestow this appellation upon us all?

S. That we are the sons of God we have not from nature, but from adoption and grace only, in other words, because God puts us in that place, (John 1:1;) but the Lord Jesus who was begotten of the substance of the Father, and is of one essence with the Father, (Eph. 1:3,) is by the best title called the only Son of God, because he alone is his Son by nature, (Heb. 1:1.)

M. You mean then, that this honour is proper to him, as being due to him by right of nature, whereas it is communicated to us by gratuitous favour, as being his members?

S. Exactly. Hence with a view to this communication he is called the First-born among many brethren. (Rom. 8:29.)

M. In what sense do you understand him to be "our Lord?"

S. Inasmuch as he was appointed by the Father to have us under his power, to administer the kingdom of God in heaven and on earth, and to be the Head of men and angels. (Col. 1:15, 18.)

M. What is meant by what follows?

S. It shows the manner in which the Son was anointed by the Father to be our Saviour—namely, that having assumed our nature, he performed all things necessary to our salvation as here enumerated.

M. What mean you by the two sentences—"Conceived of the Holy Ghost, born of the Virgin Mary?"

S. That he was formed in the womb of the virgin, of her substance, to be the true seed of David, as had been foretold by the Prophets, and that this was effected by the miraculous and secret agency of the Spirit without human connection. (Ps. 132:11; Matt. 1:1; Luke 1:32.)

M. Was it of consequence then that he should assume our nature?

S. Very much so; because it was necessary that the disobedience committed by man against God should be expiated also in human nature. Nor could he in any other way be our Mediator to make reconciliation between God and man. (Rom. 3:24; 1 Tim. 2:5; Heb. 4:15; 5:7.)

M. You say that Christ behoved to become man, that he might, as it were, in our person accomplish the work of salvation?

S. So I think. For we must borrow of him whatever is wanting in ourselves: and this cannot be done in any other way.

M. But why was that effected by the Holy Spirit, and not by the common and usual form of generation?

S. As the seed of man is entirely corrupt, it was necessary that the operation of the Holy Spirit should interfere in the generation of the Son of God, that he might not be affected by this contagion, but endued with the most perfect purity.

M. Hence then we learn that he who sanctifies us is free from every stain, and was possessed of purity, so to speak, from the original womb, so that he was wholly sacred to God, being unpolluted by any taint of the human race?

S. That is my understanding.

M. How is he our Lord?

S. He was appointed by the Father to rule us, and having obtained the empire and dominion of God both in heaven and on earth, to be recognised as the head of angels and good men. (Eph. 1:21; Col. 1:18.)

M. Why do you leap at once from his birth to his death, passing over the whole history of his life?

S. Because nothing is treated of here but what so properly belongs to our salvation, as in a manner to contain the substance of it.

M. Why do you not say in one word simply "was dead,"

(died,) but also add the name of the governor under whom he suffered?

S. That has respect not only to the credit of the statement, but also to let us know that his death was connected with condemnation.

M. Explain this more clearly.

S. He died to discharge the penalty due by us, and in this way exempt us from it. But as we all being sinners were obnoxious to the judgment of God, he, that he might act as our substitute, was pleased to be sisted in presence of an earthly judge, and condemned by his mouth, that we might be acquitted before the celestial tribunal of God.

M. But Pilate pronounces him innocent, and therefore does not condemn him as a malefactor. (Matt. 27:24.)

S. It is necessary to attend to both things. The judge bears testimony to his innocence, to prove that he suffered not for his own misdeeds but ours, and he is formally condemned by the sentence of the same judge, to make it plain that he endured the sentence which he deserved as our surety, that thus he might free us from guilt.

M. Well answered. Were he a sinner he would not be a fit surety to pay the penalty of another's sin; and yet that his condemnation might obtain our acquittal, he behoved to be classed among transgressors?

S. I understand so.

M. Is there any greater importance in his having been crucified than if he had suffered any other kind of death?

S. Very much greater, as Paul also reminds us, (Gal. 3: 13,) when he says, that he hung upon a tree to take our curse upon himself and free us from it. For that kind of death was doomed to execration. (Deut. 21:23.)

M. What? Is not an affront put upon the Son of God when it is said that even before God he was subjected to the curse?

S. By no means; since by undergoing he abolished it, and yet meanwhile he ceased not to be blessed in order that he might visit us with his blessing.

M. Go on.

S. Since death was the punishment imposed on man because of sin, the Son of God endured it, and by enduring overcame it. But to make it more manifest that he underwent a real death, he chose to be placed in the tomb like other men.

M. But nothing seems to be derived to us from this victory, since we still die?

S. That is no obstacle. Nor to believers is death now any thing else than a passage to a better life.

M. Hence it follows that death is no longer to be dreaded as if it were a fearful thing, but we should with intrepid mind follow Christ our leader, who as he did not perish in death, will not suffer us to perish?

S. Thus should we act.

M. It is immediately added, "he descended into hell." What does this mean?

S. That he not only endured common death, which is the separation of the soul from the body, but also the pains of death, as Peter calls them. (Acts 2:24.) By this expression I understand the fearful agonies by which his soul was pierced.

M. Give me the cause and the manner of this.

S. As in order to satisfy for sinners he sisted himself before the tribunal of God, it was necessary that he should suffer excruciating agony of conscience, as if he had been forsaken of God, nay as it were, had God hostile to him. He was in this agony when he exclaimed, "My God, my God, why hast thou forsaken me?" (Matt. 27:46.)

M. Was his Father then offended with him?

S. By no means. But he exercised this severity against him in fulfilment of what had been foretold by Isaiah, that "he was smitten by the hand of God for our sins and wounded for our transgressions." (Is. 53:4, 5.)

M. But seeing he is God, how could he be seized with any such dread, as if he were forsaken of God?

S. We must hold that it was in respect to the feelings of his human nature that he was reduced to this necessity: and that this might be, his divinity for a little while was concealed, that is, did not put forth its might.

M. How, on the other hand, is it possible that Christ, who is the salvation of the world, should have been subjected to this doom?

S. He did not endure it so as to remain under it. For though he was seized with the terrors I have mentioned, he was not overwhelmed. Rather wrestling with the power of hell he subdued and crushed it.

M. Hence we infer that the torture of conscience which he bore differs from that which excruciates sinners when pursued by the hands of an angry God. For what was temporary in him is perpetual in them, and what was in him only the prick of a sting, is in them a mortal sword, which, so to speak, wounds the heart.

S. It is so. The Son of God when beset by this anguish, ceased not to hope in the Father. But sinners condemned by the justice of God, rush into despair, murmur against him, and even break forth into open blasphemies.

M. May we hence infer what benefit believers receive from the death of Christ?

S. Easily. And, first, we see that it is a sacrifice by which he expiated our sins before God, and so having appeased the wrath of God, restored us to his favour. Secondly, That his blood is a laver by which our souls are cleansed from all stains. Lastly, That the remembrance of our sins was effaced so as never to come into the view of God, and that thus the handwriting which established our guilt was blotted out and cancelled.

M. Does it not gain us any other advantage besides?

S. Yes, indeed. For by its benefit, if we are members of Christ, our old man is crucified, and the body of sin is destroyed, so that the lusts of a depraved flesh no longer reign in us.

M. Proceed with the other articles.

S. The next is, "On the third day he rose again from the dead." By this he declared himself the conqueror of sin and death. By his resurrection he swallowed up death, broke the fetters of the devil, and annihilated all his power.

M. How manifold are the benefits resulting to us from the resurrection?

S. Threefold. For by it righteousness was acquired for us; it is also a sure pledge to us of our immortality; and even now by virtue of it we are raised to newness of life, that by living purely and holily we may obey the will of God.

M. Let us follow out the rest.

S. "He ascended into heaven."

M. Did he ascend so that he is no more on the earth?

S. He did. For after he had performed all the things which the Father had given him to do, and which were for our salvation, there was no need of his continuing longer on earth.

M. What good do we obtain from this ascension?

S. The benefit is twofold. For inasmuch as Christ entered heaven in our name, just as he had come down to earth on our account, he also opened up an access for us, so that the door, previously shut because of sin, is now open. Secondly, he appears in the presence of God as our advocate and intercessor.

M. But did Christ in going to heaven withdraw from us, so that he has now ceased to be with us?

S. Not at all. On the contrary, he has engaged to be with us even to the end of the world. (Matt. 28:20.)

M. When we say he dwells with us, must we understand that he is bodily present?

S. No. The case of the body which was received into heaven is one thing; that of the virtue which is everywhere diffused is another. (Luke 24:51; Acts 1:11.)

M. In what sense do you say that he "sitteth on the right hand of the Father?"

S. These words mean that the Father bestowed upon him the dominion of heaven and earth, so that he governs all things. (Matt. 28:18.)

M. But what is meant by "right hand," and what by "sitteth?"

S. It is a similitude taken from princes, who are wont to place those on their right hand whom they make their vice-gerents.

M. You therefore mean nothing more than Paul says, namely, that Christ has been appointed head of the Church, and raised above all principalities, has obtained a name which is above every name. (Eph. 1:22; Phil. 2:9.)

S. It is as you say.

M. Let us pass on.

S. "From thence he will come to judge the quick and the dead." The meaning of these words is, that he will come openly from heaven to judge the world, just as he was seen to ascend. (Acts 1:11.)

M. As the day of judgment is not to be before the end of the world, how do you say that some men will then be alive, seeing it is appointed unto all men once to die? (Heb. 9:27.)

S. Paul answers this question when he says, that those who then survive will undergo a sudden change, so that the corruption of the flesh being abolished, they will put on incorruption. (1 Cor. 15:51; 1 Thess. 4:17.)

M. You understand then that this change will be like death; that there will be an abolition of the first nature, and the beginning of a new nature?

S. That is my meaning.

M. Does it give any delight to our conscience that Christ will one day be the judge of the world?

S. Indeed singular delight. For we know assuredly that he will come only for our salvation.

M. We should not then tremble at this judgment, so as to let it fill us with dismay?

S. No, indeed; since we shall only stand at the tribunal of a judge who is also our advocate, and who has taken us under his faith and protection.

M. Let us come now to the third part.

S. It relates to faith in the Holy Spirit.

M. What do we learn by it?

S. The object is to let us know that God, as he hath redeemed and saved us by his Son, will also by his Spirit make us capable of this redemption and salvation.

M. How?

S. As we have purification in the blood of Christ, so our consciences must be sprinkled by it in order to be washed. (1 Peter 1:2; 1 John 1:7.)

M. This requires a clearer explanation.

S. I mean that the Spirit of God, while he dwells in our hearts, makes us feel the virtue of Christ. (Rom. 8:11.) For when our minds conceive the benefits of Christ, it is owing to the illumination of the Holy Spirit; to his persuasion it is owing that they are sealed in our hearts. (Eph. 1:13.) In short, he alone makes room in us for them. He regenerates us and makes us to be new creatures. Accordingly, whatever gifts are offered us in Christ, we receive by the agency of the Spirit.

M. Let us proceed.

S. Next comes the fourth part, in which we confess that we believe in one Holy Catholic Church.

M. What is the Church?

S. The body and society of believers whom God hath predestined to eternal life.

M. Is it necessary to believe this article also?

S. Yes, verily, if we would not make the death of Christ without effect, and set at nought all that has hitherto been said. For the one effect resulting from all is, that there is Church.

M. You mean then that we only treated of the cause of salvation, and showed the foundation of it when we explained that by the merits and intercession of Christ, we are taken into favour by God, and that this grace is confirmed in us by virtue of the Spirit. Now, however, we are explaining the effect of all these things, that by facts our faith may be made more firm?

S. It is so.

M. In what sense do you call the Church holy?

S. All whom God has chosen he justifies, and forms to holiness and innocence of life, (Rom. 8:30,) that his glory may be displayed in them. And this is what Paul means when he says that Christ sanctified the Church which he redeemed, that it might be a glorious Church, free from all blemish. (Eph. 5:25.)

M. What is meant by the epithet Catholic or Universal?

S. By it we are taught, that as all believers have one head, so they must all be united into one body, that the Church diffused over the whole world may be one—not more. (Eph. 4:15; 1 Cor. 12:12.)

M. And what is the purport of what immediately follows concerning the communion of saints?

S. That is put down to express more clearly the unity which exists among the members of the Church. It is at the same time intimated, that whatever benefits God bestows upon the Church, have a view to the common good of all; seeing they all have communion with each other.

M. But is this holiness which you attribute to the Church already perfect?

S. Not yet, that is as long as she has her warfare in this world. For she always labours under infirmities, and will never be entirely purged of the remains of vice, until she adheres completely to Christ her head, by whom she is sanctified.

M. Can this Church be known in any other way than when she is believed by faith?

S. There is indeed also a visible Church of God, which he has described to us by certain signs and marks, but here we are properly speaking of the assemblage of those whom he has adopted to salvation by his secret election. This is neither at all times visible to the eye nor discernible by signs.

M. What comes next?

S. I believe in "the forgiveness of sins."

M. What meaning do you give to the word forgiveness?

S. That God of his free goodness forgives and pardons the sins of believers that they may not be brought to judgment, and that the penalty may not be exacted from them.

M. Hence it follows, that it is not at all by our own satisfaction we merit the pardon of sins, which we obtain from the Lord?

S. That is true; for Christ alone gave the satisfaction by paying the penalty.

M. Why do you subjoin forgiveness of sins to the Church?

S. Because no man obtains it without being previously united to the people of God, maintaining unity with the body of Christ perseveringly to the end, and thereby attesting that he is a true member of the Church.

M. In this way you conclude that out of the Church is nought but ruin and damnation?

S. Certainly. Those who make a departure from the body of Christ, and rend its unity by faction, are cut off from all hope of salvation during the time they remain in this schism, be it however short.

M. Repeat the remainder.

S. I believe in "the resurrection of the body and the life everlasting."

M. To what end is this article set down in the Confession of Faith?

S. To remind us that our happiness is not situated on the earth. The utility and use of this knowledge is twofold. First, we are taught by it that we are to live in this world as foreigners, continually thinking of departure, and not allowing our hearts to be entangled by earthly thoughts. Secondly, however the fruit of the grace of Christ bestowed upon us may escape our notice, and be hidden from our eyes, we must not despond, but patiently wait for the day of revelation.

M. In what order will this resurrection take place?

S. Those who were formerly dead will recover their bodies, the same bodies as before, but endued with a new quality, that is, no longer liable to death or corruption. (1 Cor. 15:53.) Those who survive God will miraculously raise up by a sudden change.

M. But will this be common to the righteous and the wicked?

S. There will be one resurrection of all, but the condition will be different: some will rise to salvation and blessedness, others to death and extreme misery.

M. Why then is eternal life only here mentioned, and is there no mention of hell?

S. Because nothing is introduced here that does not tend to the consolation of pious minds; accordingly, only the rewards are enumerated which the Lord hath prepared for his servants, and nothing is added as to the doom of the wicked, whom we know to be aliens from the kingdom of God.

M. As we understand the foundation on which faith ought to rest, it will be easy to extract from it a true definition of faith.

S. It will. It may be defined—a sure and steadfast knowledge of the paternal goodwill of God toward us, as he declares in the gospel that for the sake of Christ he will be our Father and Saviour.

M. Do we conceive faith of ourselves, or do we receive it from God?

S. Scripture teaches that it is the special gift of God, and this experience confirms.

M. What experience do you mean?

S. Our mind is too rude to be able to comprehend the spiritual wisdom of God which is revealed to us by faith, and our hearts are too prone either to diffidence or to a perverse confidence in ourselves or creatures, to rest in God of their own accord. But the Holy Spirit by his illumination makes us capable of understanding those things which would otherwise far exceed our capacity, and forms us to a firm persuasion, by sealing the promises of salvation on our hearts.

M. What good accrues to us from this faith, when we have once obtained it?

S. It justifies us before God, and this justification makes us the heirs of everlasting life.

M. What! are not men justified by good works when they study to approve themselves to God, by living innocently and holily?

S. Could any one be found so perfect, he might justly be deemed righteous, but as we are all sinners, guilty before God in many ways, we must seek elsewhere for a worthiness which may reconcile us to him.

M. But are all the works of men so vile and valueless that they cannot merit favour with God?

S. First, all the works which proceed from us, so as properly to be called our own, are vicious, and therefore they can do nothing but displease God, and be rejected by him.

M. You say then that before we are born again and formed anew by the Spirit of God, we can do nothing but sin, just as a bad tree can only produce bad fruit? (Matt. 7:18.)

S. Altogether so. For whatever semblance works may have in the eyes of men, they are nevertheless evil, as long as the heart to which God chiefly looks is depraved.

M. Hence you conclude, that we cannot by any merits

anticipate God or call forth his beneficence; or rather that all the works which we try or engage in, subject us to his anger and condemnation?

S. I understand so; and therefore mere mercy, without any respect to works, (Titus 3:5,) embraces and accepts us freely in Christ, by attributing his righteousness to us as if it were our own, and not imputing our sins to us.

M. In what way, then, do you say that we are justified by faith?

S. Because, while we embrace the promises of the gospel with sure heartfelt confidence, we in a manner obtain possession of the righteousness of which I speak.

M. This then is your meaning—that as righteousness is offered to us by the gospel, so we receive it by faith?

S. It is so.

M. But after we have once been embraced by God, are not the works which we do under the direction of his Holy Spirit accepted by him?

S. They please him, not however in virtue of their own worthiness, but as he liberally honours them with his favour.

M. But seeing they proceed from the Holy Spirit, do they not merit favour?

S. They are always mixed up with some defilement from the weakness of the flesh, and thereby vitiated.

M. Whence then or how can it be that they please God?

S. It is faith alone which procures favour for them, as we rest with assured confidence on this—that God wills not to try them by his strict rule, but covering their defects and impurities as buried in the purity of Christ, he regards them in the same light as if they were absolutely perfect.

M. But can we infer from this that a Christian man is justified by works after he has been called by God, or that by the merit of works he makes himself loved by God, whose love is eternal life to us?

S. By no means. We rather hold what is written—that no man can be justified in his sight, and we therefore pray, "Enter not into judgment with us." (Ps. 143:2.)

M. We are not therefore to think that the good works of believers are useless?

S. Certainly not. For not in vain does God promise them reward both in this life and in the future. But this reward springs from the free love of God as its source; for he first embraces us as sons, and then burying the remembrance of the vices which proceed from us, he visits us with his favour.

M. But can this righteousness be separated from good works, so that he who has it may be void of them?

S. That cannot be. For when by faith we receive Christ as he is offered to us, he not only promises us deliverance from death and reconciliation with God, but also the gift of the Holy Spirit, by which we are regenerated to newness of life; these things must necessarily be conjoined so as not to divide Christ from himself.

M. Hence it follows that faith is the root from which all good works spring, so far is it from taking us off from the study of them?

S. So indeed it is; and hence the whole doctrine of the gospel is comprehended under the two branches, faith and repentance.

M. What is repentance?

S. Dissatisfaction with and a hatred of sin and a love of righteousness, proceeding from the fear of God, which things lead to self-denial and mortification of the flesh, so that we give ourselves up to the guidance of the Spirit of God, and frame all the actions of our life to the obedience of the Divine will.

M. But this second branch was in the division which was set down at first when you showed the method of duly worshipping God.

S. True; and it was at the same time added, that the true and legitimate rule for worshipping God is to obey his will.

M. Why so?

S. Because the only worship which he approves is not that which it may please us to devise, but that which he hath of his own authority prescribed.

IV

The Institutes

INSTITUTES OF
THE CHRISTIAN RELIGION—1536[1]

[*In order to compare the style and format of the first and last editions of the Institutes, sections from both are included. The first is obviously less fully elaborated. That point is illustrated here in the sections on faith, which is fully included from the 1536 edition, while three chapters are included from the 1559 edition. On other issues, the materials are largely selected to avoid duplication between the two editions. It should be recalled that the last edition is five times the size of the first edition.*]

CHAPTER ONE

CONCERNING THE LAW, WHICH CONTAINS

AN EXPOSITION OF THE DECALOGUE

Sacred doctrine consists almost entirely of these two parts: the knowledge of God and the knowledge of ourselves. Now for the present we must learn these things about God. First,

---

[1] [Institutes, 1536. Reprinted by permission of Walter G. Hards from his "A Critical Translation and Evaluation of the Nucleus of the 1536 edition of *Calvin's Institutes*," 1955. Microfilm made by Princeton University Library, pp. 68–69, 141–235. Since this was a dissertation for Princeton Theological Seminary, this volume is full of valuable notes to the text. Here the apparatus has been dropped and only an occasional note has been kept which would be necessary for the sake of calling attention to matters which could otherwise be misleading. The scholar is referred to his text.]

we must hold with a firm conviction as incontrovertible that God is infinite wisdom, justice, goodness, mercy, truth, virtue and life: so that there is in no sense any other wisdom, justice, goodness, mercy, truth, virtue and life (Baruch 3:12–14; James 1:17). And wherever a particle of these perfections appears it proceeds from God (Proverbs 16:4). Second, all things which are in heaven and earth were created for his glory (Psalm 148:1–14; Daniel 3:59–63). And so it is rightly due to him, that every one according to the law of his nature should serve him, consider his dominion, submit to his majesty, and, by obeying him, recognize him as Lord and King (Romans 1:20). In the third place, he himself is a just judge, and will execute stern vengeance upon those who depart from his precepts, who fail to submit in all things to do his will, and who think, say or do other things than those which pertain to his glory (Psalm 7:9–11; Romans 2:1–16). In the fourth place, he is compassionate and gentle, and ready to receive with kindness the poor and wretched who seek refuge in his benignity, and who place themselves in his trust. He is ready to spare and forgive, if any ask pardon from him; he wills to succour and aid, those who implore his assistance; he will save those who put and make fast their trust in him (Psalm 103:3–4, 8–11; Isaiah 55:6; Psalm 25:6–11 and 85:5–7, 10). In order that we may arrive at a sure knowledge of ourselves, we must hold this point first: that Adam, the parent of us all, was created in the image and likeness of God (Genesis 1:26–27), that is, he was endowed with wisdom, righteousness, and holiness, and by means of these gifts of grace, he thus cleaved to God, so that he would have lived in him forever, had he remained in this integrity of nature which he had received from God.

But as soon as he fell into sin (Genesis 3) this image and likeness of God was erased and obliterated, that is, he lost all the gifts of divine grace, by means of which he could have been led into the way of life. Furthermore, he was cut off from God, and was made a complete stranger. And, as a consequence, he was stripped and divested of all wisdom, righteousness, virtue and life, which cannot be possessed except in God, as was said before, wherefore, nothing remained in him except ignorance, iniquity, impotence, death and judgment (Romans 5:12–21): for these are the fruit of sin. This calamity fell not only upon Adam, but also upon us who are his seed and posterity. Therefore, as all of us are descended from Adam, we are all ignorant and deprived of

God, perverse, corrupt and destitute of all good. Truly our heart is especially inclined toward all evil, and given over to depraved longings, and enthralled by these, and rebellious against God (Jeremiah 17:9). But if we occasionally display any good in our outward appearance, our inmost desire, nevertheless, remains in its own crooked perversity, and the heart is first, or rather, stands for all else, under the judgment of God, who does not judge according to outward appearance, nor values the external magnificence of the great, but considers the secret things of the heart (I Samuel 16:7; Jeremiah 17:10). And so, although a man may have externally noble appearance of sanctity, it is nothing but hypocrisy and even an abomination before God, since the thoughts of his mind remain perverse and corrupt.

Although we are born in such a condition that it is not in our power to do anything that might be acceptable to God, neither is it within our ability to please, nevertheless, we do not cease to owe him that very thing which we cannot pay; for since we are the creatures of God, we are bound to serve his honour and glory, and to regulate our conduct according to his commandments. Nor may we offer the excuse that we lack the ability, and that we are not able to pay, just as if we were bankrupt debtors. For the guilt is ours and from our sin, which holds us in bondage, so that we neither will nor are able to do good (John 8:34–38; Romans 7:15–25). Then, since God is the just avenger of crimes, we must recognize that we are exposed to the curse and that we deserve the judgment of eternal death; since there is not one of us who either wills or is able to do those things for which he is responsible.

For this reason Scripture calls us all "sons of the wrath" of God, and proclaims that we are all going headlong to death and perdition (Ephesians 2:1–3; Romans 3:9–20). Therefore, there is no reason left to man why he should seek in himself his own righteousness, virtue, life, and salvation, all of which does not exist except in God alone, from whom man is estranged and separated by his sin (Hosea 13:4–9). Man will find in himself nothing except unhappiness, impotency, death, and finally hell itself. In order that men may not be ignorant of these things, the Lord inscribed as, as it were, stamped the law on the hearts of all men (Romans 2:15). This law is none other than conscience, which is a witness within us of the things which we owe to God, and which shows to us what is good and what is bad, and thus accuses us and holds us as guilty, while we are conscious in ourselves that we have not performed our duty (as was fitting.) Since, however, man is bloated with arrogance and ambition and blinded by self-love so that he cannot scrutinize himself and, as it were, descend into himself, so that he may learn to humble himself and to lower himself and to confess his own misery, the Lord has laid down a written law for us, by means of which we may be taught about perfect righteousness, what it is, how it is, and of how many parts it consists. For if we are wholly fixed in God, we shall not tend toward, nor aim at, anyone else whatever we think, desire, do, or speak. This doctrine of righteousness clearly shows us how far we are from the right way. This is also the purpose of all the promises and curses proposed to us in the law itself. For in the law the Lord promises that if anyone by his deeds will fulfill perfectly and exactly whatever it commands, the Lord will recompense him with the reward of eternal salvation (Leviticus 18:5). By which he actually shows us that that perfection of life taught in the law is truly righteousness, and that he regards it as such, and that it shall be worthy of such a reward, if it could be found among men. On the other hand, he decrees a curse and pronounces the judgment of eternal death upon all who will not keep fully and without any exception all the righteousness of the law (Deuteronomy 27:26; Galatians 3:10). Certainly, this punishment binds together all men who ever were, are, or shall be. Among these not one can be shown who is not a transgressor of the law. Wherefore, the law, while it teaches us the will of God, which we are bound to fulfill and towards which we are in debt, and while it shows us that we may not accomplish completely any of these things which are prescribed by God (Romans 3:19, 7:7–25), is clearly a mirror for us, in which it is possible to perceive and contemplate our sin and curse, just as in a mirror we commonly look at the dirt and stains of our face. And strictly speaking, this written law is nothing else but the witness of the natural law, which from time to time arouses our memory and impresses on us those things which, taught by the law of nature within our hearts, we have not learned sufficiently. It is easy to understand now what must be learned from the law; namely, that God is our Creator, Lord, and Father; that for this reason we owe him glory, honour and love; yet since not one of us performs his duties, all of us are worthy of malediction, judgment, and finally eternal death. We must, then, seek another way of salvation than through

the righteousness of our works. And this way is the remission
of our sins. Furthermore, since it is not in our power or ability
to pay what we owe to the law, we must despair of ourselves
and ask and hope for help from another quarter. After we
lower ourselves to this humility and submission, then the Lord
shall cause his light to shine upon us, and show himself accessible, merciful, gentle, and indulgent; of whom it is written: "He resisteth the proud and giveth grace to the humble"
(James 4:6; 1 Peter 5:5). And first, if we pray with confidence that his wrath be turned aside and ask pardon, without doubt he will grant it to us; he will remit whatever our
sins merited and receive us in his mercy. Then, if we implore
his helping hand, in the firm persuasion that, armed with his
defense, we can do all things, he will grant us by virtue of
his good will a new heart (Ezekiel 36:26) to will his commandments, and a new strength to be strong to do them.
And, indeed, he grants us all these things for the sake of Jesus
Christ our Lord, who being one God with the Father (John
1:1–14), put on our flesh, that he might enter into a covenant
with us, and bring us close to God, from whom our sins had
separated us for a long time (Isaiah 53:4–11). He, by the
merit of his death, payed our debts to the justice of God,
and caused his wrath to abate from malediction and judgment which were hovering over us, redeeming us, and bearing in his own body the penalty of sin, in order to release us
from it (Ephesians 2:1–6, 11–22; Colossians 1:20–22). Coming down to earth he brought with himself all the riches of
heavenly blessings which he poured out upon us with an open
hand (John 1:14–16, 7:38; Romans 8:32). For these are
the gifts of the Holy Spirit by whom we are born again, extricated from the power and chains of the devil, graciously
adopted among the children of God, and sanctified to do
every good work. By the same Spirit also, as long as we are
held in this mortal body, depraved urges die in us, namely,
the desires of the flesh and whatever the twisted, corrupt
perversity of our nature breeds. By the same Spirit we are
renewed from day to day, so that we may walk and live in
newness of life and justice. These are the gifts which are
offered to us by God and given to us in Christ our Lord:
the free remission of sins, peace, and reconciliation with
God, the gifts and favours of the Holy Spirit, if only we embrace and receive them with firm faith. Firm faith means
leaning, with great trust, on the divine goodness, and, as it
were, resting upon it, and not doubting for a moment that the

word of God which promises all these things to us is strength
and truth (Romans 3:21–26, 5:1–11). Finally, if we com-
mune with Christ, we possess in him all the heavenly treasures and gifts of the Holy Spirit which lead us to salvation.
We never attain these except by a true and living faith. We
likewise recognize that all our good is in him, and that we are
truly nothing except in him. Furthermore, we hold this for
certain that in Christ we are made children of God and heirs
of the heavenly kingdom (John 1:12; Romans 8:14–17). On
the other hand, those who have no part in Christ, whoever
they may be, whatever they may do, however much they
may exert themselves, go out to destruction and confusion
and to the judgment of eternal death, rejected by God and
excluded from every hope of salvation (John 3:18–20; 1 John
5:12). And this knowledge of ourselves and of our need and
calamity, by which we are taught to humiliate our very
selves and to even cast ourselves down before God and to
seek his mercy (Jeremiah 31:18–20), as well as that faith
which offers us a taste of the divine goodness and mercy, by
which he deals with us in Christ himself, are not of us, or
placed within our power. Therefore, we must ask God, not
with simulated penitence, that he lead us to that knowledge
of ourselves, and with real faith to that knowledge of his
kindness and sweetness, which he exhibits in his Christ, so
that we may be led, with him as the leader, to eternal beatitude. He is the only way in which the Father is reached
(Philippians 1:6; John 14:6; Romans 5:1–11).

The ten commandments of the law were logically arranged into two tables (Exodus 32:15, 34:1; Deuteronomy
10:1). The first table consists of the first four commandments,
by which we are taught those things which we owe to God:
namely, that we should acknowledge and confess him alone
as God, that we should love, honour, and fear him above all
and before all, and that we should place in him alone all our
hopes and resources and always seek his help. In the second
table are the remaining six commandments. These commandments explain love, and the services of love which are due to
our neighbour for the sake of God. For this reason (as
the Evangelists recount) (Luke 10:27)[2] our Lord briefly
summed up all the law under two heads: that we should
love God with all our heart, with all our mind, and with all
our strength, and that we should love our neighbour as our-

[2] [added by the translator]

selves. But, although all the law is included under these two heads, our Lord, nevertheless, to remove every pretext of excuse, willed to develop at greater length and more explicitly by means of the Ten Commandments, not only whatever refers to honour, fear and love of God, but also those things which pertain to the love which he commands us to show towards our neighbour for his sake. But before he gives the commandments, he prefaces them in this manner (Exodus 20:7; Deuteronomy 5:6).

I AM THE LORD THY GOD, WHICH BROUGHT THEE OUT OF THE LAND OF EGYPT, AND OUT OF THE HOUSE OF BONDAGE.

With these words he admonishes us that he is the Lord who both has the right to command and who must be obeyed. Besides, he recalls to our memory how magnificently he showed his strength and power when he liberated the Jewish people from the slavery of Pharaoh and the Egyptians. He shows the same power daily, as long as he frees his elect (who are the true Israelites) from the bondage of their sins (which is typified by the name "Egypt"). He manifests his power also when he extricates his elect from the chains of the devil (who in a spiritual sense is Pharaoh, the Lord of the Egyptians, that means the Lord of those who walk in their own lusts). After this he formulates the first commandment. . . .

CHAPTER TWO

CONCERNING FAITH, TOGETHER WITH AN
EXPLANATION OF THE CREED,
WHICH THEY CALL APOSTOLIC

It can be understood sufficiently well from the discussion in the previous chapter what the Lord, by means of the law, has commanded us to do. Furthermore, if we should have fallen in part from the observance of the law, he decrees wrath and the terrible judgment of eternal death. Again, to fulfill the law, as the law requires, is not only difficult, but absolutely above our strength and beyond all our capacities. Wherefore, if we look only at ourselves, and think about what things may be worthy of us, there is nothing left of genuine hope, but, having been rejected by God, death and most certain confusion remain. And it has been explained already that there is but one way of escaping such a calamity, and one way which may restore us to a better condition, namely, the mercy of God which we most certainly experience, if we accept it with firm faith and rest securely in it. It remains for us to state the nature of this faith. This we may easily learn from the creed (which they call apostolic) which consists in a brief digest, and so to speak, as a certain epitome of the faith in which the Catholic Church concurs.

But before we proceed further, we must remember that there are two kinds of faith. The one kind is this: if anyone believes that God exists, or regards as true history that which he is told of Christ. This is as when we pronounce as true past events which are being reported, or present events which we witness. Now this kind of faith is of no importance, and as such is unworthy to be called faith. If any man should boast of such a faith, let him understand that he has it in common with the devils (James 2:19), its only outcome being that the devils are terrified, shaken, and confounded all the more. The other kind of faith is when we believe, not only that God and Christ exist, but also believe in God and in Christ, truly acknowledging God as our God and Christ as our Saviour. This, indeed, is not only to consider true all that which is written or said about God and Christ, but to put all our hope and trust in one God and Christ, and to be made steadfast by this knowledge that we do not doubt at all about the good pleasure of God toward us; that we may be firmly persuaded that whatever is necessary for us, not only in spirit, but also in body, will be given to us by him; that we may certainly expect that he will fulfill whatever the Scriptures promise concerning him; that we should not doubt at all that Christ is for us Jesus, that is, Saviour; that as we obtain the remission of sins and sanctification through him, so also salvation is given to us; that at last we may be led into the kingdom of God which will be revealed at the last day. And so this, indeed, is the capital part and, so to speak, almost the sum of those things which the Lord promises and offers to us in his Holy Word. This is the goal which he sets up in Scripture. This is the target which he places before us.

The word of God, therefore, is the object and target of faith, at which faith ought to take aim. The word of God is the basis upon which faith ought to be supported and sus-

tained, without which it certainly will not stand straight. And
so this true faith, which indeed can be called Christian, is
none other than a firm conviction of the mind, by means of
which we assure ourselves that the truth of God is so certain
that he cannot not perform that which he through his holy
word has taken upon himself to do (Romans 10:9–11). This
is also what Paul (Hebrews 11:1) teaches in his definition.
He calls faith the substance of things hoped for, and the
demonstration of things not seen. By substance or hypostatis
(as the Greeks read) he understands, as it were, a support
upon which we recline and rest; it is as if he had said that
faith is a certain, sure and secure possession of those things
which God has promised to us. Again, in order to signify that
the last day in which the books will be opened will be more
sublime than the things which can be perceived by the
senses, or seen by the eyes, or touched by the hands, and that
in the meantime we cannot possess the promise in any other
way, as if we could exceed all the power of our mind and
direct our vision upon everything which is in the world we
may finally surpass them, he adds that faith is the security of
possessing the things which lie in hope and are therefore not
seen. For (Paul himself writes in another place) "hope which
is seen is not hope, nor does anyone hope for the things which
he sees" (Romans 8:24). For when he calls faith a sign or
test (for in Greek it is elenchus) "of the things which are
not seen," as he says, it is exactly as if he had said: "the evidence of things which do not appear," the vision of things
which are not seen, the clearness of things which are obscure, the presence of things which are absent, the demonstration of things which are hidden. For the mysteries of God,
which are the kind that belong to salvation, cannot be discerned in themselves or in their own nature (as was said)
but we see them, in so far as we see them at all, in his word,
whose truth ought to be for us so persuasive that whatever it
says we consider as good as done and complete.

This kind of faith is very different from the first kind. Whoever has it cannot but be acceptable to God, as also, on the
contrary, it is impossible that anyone should please him without it (Hebrews 11:6). By means of this faith we get whatever we desire and ask from God, as long as he foresees that
it is useful to us. But this faith cannot either have its seat in
a crooked, perverse or hypocritical heart, or be born or preserved without the grace of God. This is the very faith which
God requires of us in the first commandment of his law,

where he, having mentioned beforehand that he alone is the
Lord our God, subjoins that we should not have other gods
before him. He wills, of course, that our hope and trust,
which we owe to him, should not rest in any other than in
him alone. At the same time he suggests that if our hope and
trust belong to another that other is our god. We have built
the following discourse concerning this kind of faith, on account of which the creed was composed as a summary instruction, on the basis of a fourfold division. The first three
parts are devoted to the three persons of the Holy Trinity,
the Father, the Son, and the Holy Spirit, the One, Eternal
and Almighty God in whom we believe. The fourth part deals
with the benefits which we may derive from this faith in
God, and which we ought to expect.

But when certain ungodly persons, intent upon uprooting
our faith, clamour against first principles and hold in derision
our confession of one God in three persons, it is in order that
their blasphemies should be silenced here. But since it is my
purpose here to lead teachable persons by the hand, and not
to come to grips with contentious rebels, I shall not engage
them with a full array of arguments. I shall only indicate in
this part with a few words what should be followed and what
should be avoided, so that they who give their ears easily and
openly to the truth might consider where they may place
with security their foot. The Scripture teaches us that there
is one God, not many. "Israel," he says, "the Lord thy God is
one God" (Deuteronomy 6:4). The Scripture asserts beyond
all obscurity that the Father is God, the Son is God, and
the Holy Spirit is God.

We offer only one argument, but it is worth a thousand.
Paul so connects these three, God, faith and baptism, that
he reasons from one to the other (Ephesians 4:4–5). That
since there is only one faith, he demonstrates from this fact
that there is only one God; since there is only one baptism,
from this he shows that there is only one faith. For since faith
ought not to look here and there, nor run about in various
directions, but ought to look to God alone, unite with him,
and cleave to him, it is easily established from this that if
there are many faiths, there ought also to be many gods.
Again, since baptism is the sacrament of faith, it confirms
unto us the very unity of the faith, because baptism is one.
And so no one can confess faith except in God. Therefore,
as we are baptized into one faith, in the same manner our
faith believes in one God. And so baptism is one and faith

is one, because both are from the one God. Hence it also follows that it is not lawful to baptize except into one God, because we are baptized in the faith of him in whose name we are baptized. Furthermore, since the Scripture prescribes (Matthew 28:19) that we should be baptized in the name of the Father, and of the Son, and of the Holy Spirit, it also demands at the same time that everyone should believe with one faith in the Father, Son, and Holy Spirit. But this, what else is it but to testify clearly that the Father, Son, and Holy Spirit are one God. For if we are baptized in their name, we are baptized into their faith. Therefore, they are one God, if they are worshipped with one faith. Other excellent testimonies exist which assert in part the one divinity of the three and in part the personal distinctions. To the Son is attributed that name which the Jews called ineffable, according to Jeremiah 23:6, 33:16.

This eternal God must be one, who in another place refuses to give his glory to another (Isaiah 42:8). And, nevertheless, when it is said that he was in the beginning with God, and that the Father made the universe through him; besides when he testifies that he had his own glory with the Father before the world was made, a distinction is shown between the two. The distinction is stated more plainly by the fact that the Father did not come and put on our flesh, but the Son came out from the Father in order to descend to us and to be made man (John 1:1–2; Hebrews 1:3; John 17:5; 15:3, 5, 10, 15, 17, 25–28, *et alibi*). Both distinctions are expressed at the same time by another prophet, where the Father calls him an associate or a relative (Zechariah 13:7). He cannot be, however, a relative or an associate to God, except in so far as he is God himself. Again, if he is an associate, he must be distinct, since there is no society except between two persons. Peter states clearly in Acts (Acts 5:3–9) that the Holy Spirit is God. But that the Holy Spirit different from Christ is well known from more than ten places in John's Gospel (John 14:16, 25; 15:26). But Paul explained clearest of all this mystery (Romans 8:11), when he referred to the Spirit as being "the Spirit of Christ" and of him who "raised Jesus from the dead." Now if the Spirit of the Father and of the Son is one, the Father and the Son must of necessity be one. Again, it is fitting that the same Spirit should be one with the Father and with the Son, since no one is separate from his own spirit. Certain people argue that they hear that God is a Spirit; therefore, they do not understand any thing else by Spirit except God the Father. But just as they hear that God is a Spirit, in the same manner they also hear that the Holy Spirit is the Spirit of God. Therefore, there is nothing repugnant in believing that all the essence of God is spiritual, and that in that essence are Father, Son and Spirit. Neither are there lacking persons who say that God is called now Father, now Son, now Holy Spirit, in the same way that he is now called strong, now good, now glorious and now merciful. But these people may easily be refuted since these words appear to be epithets which show God's manner of being, but those names declare who he really is. If only people were not contentious or obstinate they will immediately perceive that the Father, Son and Holy Spirit are one God, because the Father is God, the Son is God and the Holy Spirit is God, and yet there cannot be but one God. Again, three are named, three are described and three are distinguished. And so the one and the three are one God, one essence. Who are these three? They are not three gods, not three essences. The orthodox doctors of old, in order to signify both the "unity and the trinity," said that there is one οὐσία and three ὑποστάσεις, that is, one substance and three subsistences in one substance. The Latin theologians, although they agreed completely with the Greeks, employed another name to express the same meaning in another way. For they said that there is one essence (which name corresponds to the Greek) but there are three persons, by which they wanted to show a certain relationship.

Heretics rail at those who use these terms, saying that οὐσία, ὑποστάσεις, essence, persons, are names invented arbitrarily by men, and are never read or seen in Scripture. But when they are not able to wrest from us the knowledge that three are called God, who are one God, what kind of pedantry is this to find fault with words which do not teach anything else than what is attested in, and authenticated by, the Scriptures? It would be better, they say, to confine not only our opinions but also our words within the limits of the Scripture, rather than to sow exotic words which will become seedbeds of dissensions and altercations. For thus one is sickened by verbal disputes, thus truth is lost in altercations, thus love is dissolved. If they call a word which cannot be found syllable for syllable in Scripture "exotic" they, indeed, impose an iniquitous law upon us, a law which condemns all preaching which is not stitched together by joining texts of Scripture. But if by exotic they mean that which, being curiously devised, is superstitiously defended, that which is worth more for contention than for edification, that which is either used out of season or fruitlessly, that which offends pious ears because of its harshness, that which takes away from the simplicity of the word of God, then I embrace them with all my heart. For I do not think that we ought to speak about God with less piety than we think about him, since whenever and whatever we think of him by ourselves is foolish, and whatever we say is absurd. For we must seek indeed out of Scripture a rule for thinking and speaking to which we are to refer exactly both the thoughts of our mind and the words of our mouth. But, what forbids that, at least, we should explain those things in the Scripture which are obscure and difficult to our understanding by more simple words. These words which yet reverently and faithfully serve the truth of Scripture itself should be used with caution and measure and not without occasion. Examples occur daily. There is often a dispute about the righteousness of faith. Few comprehend that we are justified by faith. We add that the righteousness is not ours but Christ's, that it is in him, not in us, but that it becomes ours by imputation when it is accepted by us. So if we say that we are not actually righteous, but imputatively, or, not that we are righteous, but that by means of imputation we are considered as righteous in so far as we possess the righteousness of Christ through faith, the matter will be clear and simple. It is said that God works in the reprobates whose works are condemned. The question is difficult and involved, namely, whether God is the author of evil? Whether evil may be imputed to God, whether injustice should be regarded as belonging to his work? May we suggest that in the same act one may see both the work of a perverse man and the work of a righteous God. Reprobate men have the root of evil fixed in themselves; by themselves they think evil, they will evil, they strive for evil and achieve evil. Therefore, whatever evil and guilt there is in the works of man must be imputed to man, because by means of his own counsel, his will and his action he strives against God. But God causes the evil will and evil act, by which he wills to move man, sometimes to punish him, sometimes to restrain him, sometimes to give him success and power. But all is done justly. Thus Pharaoh, Nebuchadnezar and Sennacherib fought against the living God, they laughed at his power, they persecuted as much as they could innocent people, they violently and unjustly seized the property of others.

God, however, had raised them all (Exodus 9:16; Jeremiah 5:15), so that they would commit such deeds. Yet these men, bent upon evil and meditating evil, or rather their ill will and criminal purpose against Israel, God turned into benefit, either through chastizing the impiety of his own people or delivering them more magnificently. In the same way, the affliction of Job was the work of God and the work of the devil, and therefore we have to distinguish the unrighteousness of the devil from the righteousness of God. The devil tried to destroy Job; God, however, was testing him (Job 1:12; 2:6). In like manner, Assyria was the rod of the Lord's anger, Sennacherib the axe of the Lord's hand (Isaiah 10:5). All of them were called, raised up, and driven on by him, in short, they were his servants. But why? While they gave themselves up to their wild wantonness they were unconsciously the servants of God's justice (Jeremiah 27:4–8). Behold! God and these men, authors of the same work, but in the same work the righteousness of God shines forth and the iniquity of men. This distinction looses the knot of this intricate problem. If anyone should interrupt and murmur that we have not proved the distinction to them, because the Sophists stuff their disputes full with minute distinctions, who would not be displeased with such rudeness. If anyone should find fault with the newness of our words does he not see that he is judged unworthy to bear the light of truth, as one who finds fault only with this, that the truth is made so plain and clear to discern? But such novelty of words (if it is to be so called) is most necessary, then, as long as the truth which they elude by tergiversation must be maintained against those who slander it. We experience this tergiversation today only too much, so that most of our business consists in defending the truth against its enemies, who escape like slippery eels which twist sideways and turn around, if you do not grasp them and hold them tightly when they are caught. For this reason, the ancients, harassed by various contentions about false doctrine, were obliged to set forth with carefully sought perspicuity what they believed, lest they should leave the impious the twisted subterfuges in which they had hidden their errors under the concealment of words.

Arius confessed that Christ was God and that he was the Son of God, since he could not strive against the clear teaching of Scripture or, as it were, rightly disregard it. Consequently, he feigned a certain agreement with it. But, at the same time, he did not desist from prating that Christ was created and had had a beginning just as the rest of creation. The ancients, so that they might bring out from their hidden places the subtle artfulness of Arius, took a further step and declared that Christ was the eternal Son of the Father, and that he was consubstantial with the Father. At this point the impiety of the Arians flared up, since they began to exceedingly hate and to execrate the term ὁμοούσιος. If from the beginning they had confessed sincerely and from the heart that Christ was God, they would not have denied that he was consubstantial with the Father. Who dare reproach those excellent men, as if they were brawlers and contentious because they got hot with passion in dispute over only one word, and disturbed the peace of the Church? But that small word distinguished the Christians of the true faith from the sacrilegious Arians. Afterwards,[3] Sabellius rose up who affirmed that the names, Father, Son, and Holy Spirit, were mere names, and that there was no reason for any such distinction, but that they referred to several attributes of God, of which he had many more. If he got into a dispute, he confessed that he believed in God the Father, God the Son, and God the Spirit, but then he escaped affirming that he had said no other than if he had called God strong, just and wise. And so he echoed another old song, namely, that the Father was the Son and the Holy Spirit the Father, without distinction. Those who took piety to heart, to crush the depravity of the man, retorted that three properties had to be recognized in the one God. And to defend themselves against his intricate subtleties, by the plain and simple truth, they affirmed that three persons truly subsisted in one God, or (what was the same) that in the unity of God subsisted a trinity of persons. If, therefore, there was no temerity in inventing these terms, there is temerity in rejecting them. Would that the names were buried, provided that this faith would remain among all Christians, namely, that the Father, the Son, and the Holy Spirit are one God, not, however, that the Son is the Father or the Holy Spirit is the Son, but that they are distinct by means of a certain property. As soon, however, as one is to cope, on the other hand with the Arians, on the other with the Sabellians, the very men who impa-

[3] This is a chronological mistake. Sabellius flourished in the third century. Arius died in 336.

tiently would break off the opportunity for disputing with
either of these heretics, lay themselves open to the suspicion
of being disciples either of Arius or of Sabellius. Arius says
that Christ is God, but he whispers under his breath that he
was made and had a beginning; he says that Christ is one
with the Father, but he whispers secretly in the ears of his
disciples, one like the rest of the faithful, although with
unique prerogatives. Say, "consubstantial" and you will have
removed the mask of the werewolf, and, moreover, you do
not add anything to the Scriptures. Sabellius says that the
names, Father, Son, and Holy Spirit, do not signify any distinction in God. Say that there are three and he will vocifer-
ate that you speak about three gods; say that there is a trinity
of persons in the essence of God and you will say with one
word what the Scriptures say, and you will suppress meaning-
less loquacity. And if they will not tolerate these names, let
them admit, at least to us, that they cannot be corrupted,
even if they may be damaged, since when we hear, one, we
must understand the unity of the substance, when we hear,
three, three properties must be distinguished in this one
essence. Indeed, the Scripture distinguishes them in such a
way that it attributes to the Father the principle of action,
and the source and origin of all things; to the Son it assigns
wisdom and counsel in doing; and to the Spirit it refers power
and the efficacy of action. Whence also the Son is called the
Word of the Father, not of the kind that men speak or think
but eternal and incommunicable, proceeding from the Father
in an ineffable manner, as the Holy Spirit is called power,
finger and hand of God. Now let us hear the simple confession of truth.

THE FIRST PART OF THE APOSTLES' CREED

I BELIEVE IN GOD THE FATHER ALMIGHTY,

CREATOR OF HEAVEN AND EARTH

In this first part we confess that we have fixed all our confidence in God the Father, whom we recognize both as the
creator of ourselves and of the universality of things which
were created. He established them with his Word and
eternal Wisdom (this is the Son), and with his power (this

is the Holy Spirit) (Psalm 33:6, 104:24; Acts 17:24; Hebrews 1:2–10). And so as he established them once and for all, so now he maintains, supports, leads, and preserves them by his goodness and power, without which all things would immediately collapse and vanish into nothing. But when we call him omnipotent and creator of all things, we must think of his omnipotence as the kind by which he works all things in all creatures, and his providence as the kind by which he directs all things (1 Corinthians 12:6; Lamentations 3:37–38), not the kind of providence which those Sophists feigned, empty, inert, and inactive. But, let us have the conviction by means of faith that whatever things happen to us, whether joyful or sad, prosperous or adverse, whether they pertain to the body or the soul, come to us from him (with the exception of sin, however, which must be imputed to our wantonness). We are even securely protected, defended, and preserved by his help, so that no inimical power may harm us (Hosea 13:14), nothing, finally (since we receive all things from his hands) comes to us from him which does not lead to our well-being, however prosperous or adverse things may seem to the common people (Romans 8:28). And so, indeed, all things happen to us because of him, not because of any dignity of our own, not by any merit of ours to which this grace is indebted, not because we are able to repay his beneficence with its countervalue, but the sole cause of his goodness is his paternal benignity and clemency with which he does for us what he does (Romans 11:5–6). For this reason, we must see to it that we return an act of thanksgiving for so much goodness, that we consider it with all our hearts, that we proclaim it with our tongue, and that we exalt it with all possible praises. Let us so worship the Father with grateful piety and ardent love, so that we devote ourselves completely to his service, so that we honour him in all things. Let us receive with an equal affection and peace of mind all things, even adverse things, as from his hands, thinking that his providence thus exercises foresight for us and for our well-being, while he afflicts and troubles us. And so, finally, whatever happens to us, we must never doubt or mistrust him, since he is propitious, and we must expect our salvation from him. For it is most certain and true that this is the correct faith, and in order that everyone may have it, it is taught in this first part of the creed.

THE SECOND PART

AND IN JESUS CHRIST, HIS ONLY SON, OUR LORD, WHO
WAS CONCEIVED FROM THE HOLY SPIRIT, BORN OF THE
VIRGIN MARY, SUFFERED UNDER PONTIUS PILATE, WAS
CRUCIFIED, DEAD, AND BURIED: HE DESCENDED INTO
HELL, THE THIRD DAY HE AROSE FROM THE DEAD, HE
ASCENDED INTO HEAVEN, HE SITS ON THE RIGHT SIDE OF
THE FATHER; FROM WHENCE HE SHALL COME TO JUDGE
THE LIVING AND THE DEAD

Here we confess that we believe in Jesus Christ, whom we
hold for certain as the only Son of God the Father, not begotten as the faithful are by means of adoption only and by
grace, but naturally and from all eternity from the Father.
For when we call him unique, we distinguish him in every
way from everyone else. So that, in so far as he is God, he is
one God with the Father, of the same nature and substance
or essence, not distinct in any way from the Father, except in
person, which he possesses peculiar and distinct from the
Father (Psalm 100:3a).[4] Therefore, whatever human wisdom
possesses, here it must be subordinated and held, as it were,
captive, neither arguing at all from curiosity, nor doubting
these mysteries which are to be adored, which surpass every
capacity of human perception. And lest in this second part
we should either conceive anything in the mind, or feel, or
speak anything except what we are taught in the Scripture,
may the example of the heretics, who have been cast headlong because they willed to trust too much in their own understanding, terrify us. When, therefore, we say that God the
Son is one and the same God with the Father, we hold that
he is true God the creator of heaven and earth (Hebrews
1:2, 10). And so as we place all our trust in the Father, so
also we must place it in his Son, since God is one. But here
the Father is called in a special sense the creator of heaven
and earth. We have already said that it is because of the
distinction of the properties by means of which the beginning

---

[4] [added by the translator]

of activity is referred to the Father, so that, indeed, he said properly to act, still it is through his word and Wisdom, and of his own Power. Moreover, that in creating the world there was a common action of the three persons that saying of the Father makes plain (Genesis 1:26): "Let us make man in our own image and likeness." Now here he does not deliberate with angels, nor does he speak to himself, but he summons his Wisdom and Power.

Furthermore, we confess that we believe that Jesus Christ for our sake, to save us from the tyranny of the devil, to whom we were subject; to release us from the chains of sin, by which we were held tight; to free us from the servitude of death, both of the body and of the mind, into which we had been thrown; to release us from the eternal pains, to which we had been condemned (since we could not be freed or extricated from these things by our own power) was sent from the Father by virtue of the divine goodness and mercy. He descended to us to take upon himself our flesh, which he joined to his divinity. Truly, in this manner, it was for our advantage that he is true God and true man, who would be our future mediator. For since all things had been destroyed when our sins put a cloud between us and our God, who could reach up to him (Isaiah 59:2)? Could it be man? But all men, with their father Adam, shivered with fright in the presence of the Lord (Genesis 3:10–12). Could it be angels? But even these had need of a head, through whom they might be closely connected with God (Ephesians 1:21–23; Colossians 1:16–20). What, then? Everything was lost unless the very majesty of God would descend to us, since it was impossible for us to ascend to him. This is why the Son of God was made for us Emmanuel, that is, God with us (Isaiah 7:14). Again, since our abjectness is opposed in every way to the majesty of God, who would still be sufficiently confident to dare to draw near to God, to dwell with him, to be with him? Therefore, no nearness would be yet close enough, no relationship firm enough, if it did not join his divinity to us so that it might also unite our humanity to his divinity. Thus Paul (1 Timothy 2:5) when he proposes him as a mediator for us, expressly said, "man." He says, "The mediator of God and man, the man Jesus Christ." He could have said "God," at least he could as well have omitted this name as well as the name "God," but he knew our weakness. And so, lest any should torment themselves, asking where the mediator should be sought, how they could reach him, he adds immediately, he is man, as if to say, he is near you, yes, he touches you, he is your flesh. He wishes, of course, to point to that which he explained more clearly in another place (Hebrews 4:15): "We have not a high priest who cannot have compassion on our infirmities, since he was tempted in all things after our manner, yet without sin." It was not an ordinary thing which had to be performed by the mediator, since he had to make sons of God out of sons of men, heirs of the heavenly kingdom out of heirs of hell. Who could have done this, if the Son of God had not been made the Son of Man, and thus taken what is ours in order to transfer to us that which is his; because what by nature was his, by grace he made ours. This, therefore, is our hope, that we are sons of God because the Son of God by nature combined in himself body from our body, flesh from our flesh, bones from our bones, that he might be one and the same with us. That which was properly of us, he willed to belong to himself, so that that which was properly his might belong to us, that he might be in common with us both a Son of God and a Son of Man. This is our hope, that the inheritance of the kingdom of heaven is ours because the unique Son of God whose inheritance was probated has adopted us as his brothers. Therefore, if we are brothers, we also partake of the inheritance. Furthermore, it was thus to our advantage that he who would be our redeemer should be true God and man. It was his task to swallow up death. Who could do this except life? It was his task to overcome sin. Who could do this except righteousness itself? But who is life or righteousness, if not God alone? Therefore, the Lord most merciful made himself our redeemer because he wills to have us redeemed. The second point of our redemption was this: that man who has lost himself by his disobedience, should by obedience get rid of his confusion, in order to satisfy the justice of God and to pay the penalties of sin (Romans 5:12–19). Therefore, the true man, our Lord, appeared. He played the part of Adam, took his name, so that by it he might manifest his obedience to the Father, so that he might offer our flesh in satisfaction to the justice of God, so that he might pay the punishment of sin in our flesh. Those, therefore, who strip Christ of his divinity or of his humanity, surely, either blaspheme his majesty or obscure his goodness. And at the same time they destroy and overturn our faith which cannot stand except upon this foundation. And so the Word was made flesh, and he who was God was made man at the same time, in order that man and God might be the same one, not by confusion of substance, but by unity of the person.

This can be understood by the example of man whom we see composed of two parts. Nevertheless, neither of the two parts is mixed with the other in such a way that it does not retain the peculiarity of its nature. For neither the soul is body nor is the body soul. Wherefore, a particular thing is said about the soul which cannot happen at all to the body; and, again, a particular thing is said about the body which would not be fitting to say for any reason about the soul; a particular thing is said about the entire man which could not be accepted about the soul or the body without absurdity. Finally, the things proper to the soul are transferred to the body, and those proper to the body to the soul. He, therefore, who consists of body and soul is one man, not many. But these ways of speaking signify that the nature of man is one, composed of two things which have been united, and that two different natures are behind the things which compose that one. In the same manner also the Scriptures speak of Christ. They attribute to him, sometimes the things which must be particular concern to his humanity, sometimes the things which agree only with his divinity, sometimes they attribute to both natures the things which do not fit sufficiently well either of the two separately. Finally, by means of a communication of properties, they assign to his divinity what was peculiar to his humanity, and to his humanity what they saw belonged to his divinity. This doctrine is not my own invention, but clear examples of it appear in the Scriptures. When Christ said about himself (John 8:58), "Before Abraham was, I am," he was not speaking at all about his humanity. For he was not made man until many ages after Abraham. This saying, therefore, was proper as regards his divinity. When he was called a servant of the Father, when he grew in age and wisdom before God and man, when he did not seek his own glory; these sayings pertain to his humanity alone (Isaiah 42:1, 53:11; Luke 2:52; John 8:50). Since in so far as he is God, he is equal to the Father, he cannot be made greater by anything, and he works all things for his own self (Philippians 2:9-11). It was not peculiar to his divinity nor to his humanity, but at the same time it pertained to both that he received from the Father the power to remit sins, to raise the dead, that he was appointed judge of the living and the dead (Luke 5:20-24; John 5:21, 6:40-

54; Acts 10:42). For the Son of God was endowed with such prerogatives when he was manifested in the flesh. He, together with the Father, possessed these prerogatives before the formation of the world. They could not have been given to any man, if he were nothing more than a man. Expressions of this kind abound in the Gospel of John, which neither suit well his divinity nor his humanity, but which fit well the person of Christ, in which he was manifest, God and man. In this sense also we must accept what was written by Paul (1 Corinthians 15:24) that Christ will give back the kingdom to God and to the Father. This certainly does not mean that the kingdom of the Son of God which had no beginning will have an end, but it means that even as he was crowned with glory and honour after his rejection and appointed above all things, even as, after he had emptied himself and showed himself obedient to the Father even unto death, he was exalted and received a name to which every knee should be bent. Thus, this very name and what ever else he received from the Father, he will present to the Father, that God may be all in all (Philippians 2:8–10). But a *communicatio idiomatum*, or a communication of properties, is what Paul meant when he says that "God by his blood acquired for himself the Church," and when he says that "the Lord of glory was crucified (Acts 20:28; 1 Corinthians 2:8). For God, strictly speaking, does not have blood, nor does he suffer. But Christ, true God and true man, being crucified, poured out his blood for us. The things which were done in his humanity are transferred to his divinity. Again, when Christ said (John 3:13) that "no one had ascended into heaven, except the Son of man who was in heaven," it is clear that at that time he was not in heaven with the body which he took to himself, but because he was both God and man, on account of the unity of the natures, to the one was attributed what belonged to the other. To the above reason, I add some more, for the sake of those who can in no way be persuaded to recognize in the one person of Christ the properties of both natures. Indeed, they confess that Christ is God and man, and the Son of God. If you press the point, you notice that they do not say God and the Son of God for any other reason than that he was conceived by the Holy Spirit in the womb of the Virgin. This is like the Manichean babble of old; they said that man has a soul by reason of a transfusion from God, because they read that God breathed in man the breath of life. And so in defense of their errors they urge tumultuously

that it is said that God "did not spare his own Son,"[5] and because the angel commanded that he, who would be born
of the Virgin, should be called "the Son of the Most High."[6]
And, indeed, we do not make two Christs, but we simply
confess that he who was the eternal Son of God, assumed our
flesh in such a way that the one and same Christ was God
and man, but with two natures united and not confused. But
lest they should still pride themselves with the futile objections with which they contend, saying that Christ is the Son
of God only according to his humanity, since that man was
born of the Virgin and suffered, not another, was called the
Son of God, let us learn the way in which the Scripture
speaks, from one prophetic passage in which the Lord speaks
thus (Micah 5:2): "But, thou, Bethlehem Ephrata, thou art
small among the thousands of Judah, yet out of thee shall be
born to me a leader, who shall govern my people Israel,
whose going forth is from the beginning, from the days of
eternity." Do they not understand this of Christ himself, who
was born in Bethlehem, that he came out from the days of
eternity? And if we look in that eternity of days, Christ was
not yet. This objection is indeed true, but the Son of God is
he who was afterwards made Christ. Then, the author of the
Epistle to the Hebrews (Hebrews 1:2) says: "In the last days
God has spoken to us in his Son, whom he constituted heir
of all things, by whom he also made the world." Certainly, it
was necessary that he should be a Son before he was made
man, if the world was made by him. Therefore, it may be
concluded at this place, that the Word of God is the Son of
God. For when John says (John 1:3) "All things were made
by the Word," the Apostle says, "By the Son." Paul also
distinguishes more clearly both titles, the Son of God and the
Son of man, so that to reject them would be not only a matter
of blindness but of obstinacy. In the first place, as Paul
says, "he was set apart for the Gospel of God (Romans
1:1–4) which God has promised before by the prophets,
concerning his Son who was made of the seed of David according to the flesh, and declared Son of God in power." Why
should the Apostle note distinctly that according to the flesh,
he is the son of David, unless he wanted to indicate that he is
the Son of God, yet not according to the flesh? In another
place (Romans 9:5) he says, "of whom is Christ according

[5] Romans 8:32
[6] Luke 1:32

to the flesh, who is God blessed for ever." Are there any who wish it stated more clearly than this: Christ is called the seed of Abraham according to the flesh, otherwise, beyond the flesh he is God blessed for ever? Furthermore, I wish to assert this: that we should not deny that the unique Christ is true God and true man, and that by this his divinity is not torn asunder from his humanity, but that it is distinguished from it. These things come together beautifully, if they have a prudent interpreter who treats such mysteries as becomes piety. However, there is nothing which furious and frantic spirit do not disturb. They seize upon the attributes of humanity in order to take away the divinity, and those of divinity to take away the humanity, and as for the things which are jointly said of both natures because they do not belong to any one nature, they get hold of them to do away with both together. Now is that anything else but to contend that Christ is not a man because he is God, and that he is not God because he is man, and that he is neither man nor God because he is God and man at the same time? Christ, therefore, in addition to his being God, having taken real flesh, was made man.

Thus we believe that this one is truly Jesus, as he was called by the voice of the Father and the heavenly oracle (Luke 1:30–35). And "this name, and no other, has been given to men by means of which they may be saved" (Acts 4:12). We believe also that he is Christ, that is anointed with all the graces of the Holy Spirit, which graces are described as oil (Psalm 45:7, 89:20), because without them we, arid and sterile, waste away. And so as the Spirit rested upon him and was poured completely upon him, thus we all might receive from his fulness, all of us who through faith are his brethren and comrades (Isaiah 11:1–5, 6:1–3; John 1:16). Finally, by this unction he was appointed King by the Father, who put all power in heaven and in earth under him (Psalm 2:1–6), so that in him we might be kings, having dominion over the devil, sin, death and hell (1 Peter 2:9). Then, he is Priest. He, by means of his sacrifice, appeased the Father and reconciled him to us, so that we might be priests in him, offering by means of intercession and mediation praises to the Father, thanksgiving, ourselves, and all our possessions (Revelation 1:6; Psalm 110:1–4; Hebrews 5:1–10, 13:15–16). And so we acknowledge that he alone is Lord as he was appointed by the Father over us. We believe that he was conceived man for us by a wonderful and in-

describable power of the Holy Spirit in the womb of the
Holy Virgin (Luke 1:26–38, 2:17; Romans 12)[7] of whom he
was born as a mortal man in order to bring about our salvation. For this reason he had come. He gave over his body to
a most cruel death, and shed his blood as the price of
redemption. He suffered, therefore, under Pontius Pilate. He
was condemned by the sentence of the judge as a guilty and
wicked person, so that by means of his condemnation we
might be absolved before the tribunal of the Supreme Judge.
He was crucified, so that on the cross which was cursed by
the law of God he might bear the curse which our sins
merited (Deuteronomy 21:22–23; Galatians 3:10). He died,
so that by his death he might overcome death which
threatened us and might swallow up death which threatened
to swallow us up (Hosea 13:14; 1 Corinthians 15:54). He
was buried, so that by his grace we might be buried to sin
and be liberated from the devil and the dominion of death
(Hebrews 2:14–15; Romans 6:4). He descended to hell. That
signifies that he was afflicted by God, and felt the horror and
severity of the divine judgment, so that he might stand between the wrath of God and satisfy his justice in our name
(Psalm 21;[8] Isaiah 53:4–5). Thus, paying our debts and
expiating our sins, not his own, (there never were any) but
our iniquity. We must not, however, understand at all that
the Father was angry with him (Matthew 3:17). For, how
could he be angry with "his beloved Son in whom he was
well pleased," or how could he appease the Father with his
intercessions, if he considered him to be full of hatred? But
it is said that he bore the weight of the divine severity in this
sense since, wounded and afflicted by the hand of God, he
experienced all the manifestations of the wrath and vengeance of God, so that he was forced to cry out because of his
pressing distress, "Father, Father, why hast thou forsaken
me?" (Matthew 27:46). This is certainly meant by he descended into hell. It does not mean that he passed to a certain
definite place (for which the name "Limbo" has been
fabricated) in which the fathers who lived under the old
covenant were held, as it were, detained in prison, there
awaiting in chains and captivity their liberation. It does not

[7] The text Romans 12 is omitted in C.R. and Barth. It is, however, a mistake. Calvin may have had in mind Acts 10:36.

[8] The reference here is to the Vulgate. The Scripture to which
Calvin refers is Psalm 22:1–2 in the Hebrew Bible.

mean that he by violence broke the gates of this place in order to bring them out from there. For this fable, although it has many authors, and is also seriously defended as true by many persons today, is, nevertheless, nothing more than a fable. Neither ought the passage in Peter to be interpreted in that sense (1 Peter 3:19). Those who want to defend this interpretation always force upon us that "Christ, coming in the Spirit, preached to those spirits who were in prison." For by this Peter only wished to teach that the power of the redemption devised by Christ was exhibited and clearly manifested to the spirits of those who before that time had died. For the faithful who had always waited for their salvation from him then saw with a clear and present look his appearance. The reprobates, on the other hand, perceiving too late that he was the only means of salvation, from which they were excluded, then recognized more clearly that there was no hope left for them. But when Peter says, without any distinction, that the pious and impious were in prison, it must not be understood as if the pious were held bound in certain narrow rooms. It must be understood to mean that they saw Christ, not yet revealed, at a distance, obscurely, and, as it were, under the shadows of the clouds. He calls this anxious expectation of theirs, by means of a certain figure, a prison. But the Scripture bears witness that they were then in the bosom of Abraham as they also are now, that is, in rest and tranquility, which is for them the beginning of blessedness (Luke 16:22; Revelation 6:9–11). For they understand that they live in God and cleave inseparably to him. From this meaning the faithful receive an extraordinary consolation, waiting for the day of the blessed resurrection. But although this article about the descent into hell has been omitted by some, nevertheless it is not at all superfluous since it contains the most significant mysteries of most important things.

Furthermore, we believe that on the third day he arose from the dead, that is, from the same death which all men suffer according to the law of nature, and that he arose again to life a true man, no longer mortal, however, but incorruptible, glorified in the body and soul which he received. And this is the power of his resurrection, that being justified we might be raised from the death of sin to newness of life and righteousness (Romans 6:4); at the same time we may be sure that all men who of old suffered the same death must arise; since his resurrection is the most sure proof and the foundation of the resurrection of men (1 Corinthians 15:13; Acts 1:22).

We believe that he ascended into heaven. By this ascent he opened for us the way into the kingdom of heaven, which in Adam had been shut to all (John 14:1–3). We believe that since he entered heaven in our flesh, as if in our name, that already in him we possess heaven by hope and, what is more, that we in a certain sense, are seated among the celestial beings (Hebrews 2:10, 13; Ephesians 2:6). We believe, likewise, that he is seated there at the right hand of the Father, in the same way that he was manifested in the flesh. This means that he was appointed and declared King, Judge and Lord over all things, without exception of any creature which would not be subject to his dominion, so that he might enrich us with spiritual gifts by means of his power (1 Corinthians 15:27; Hebrews 2:8; Ephesians 4:8). And so he sanctifies us and cleanses us from the defilement of our sin, he governs and leads us until passing through death we encounter him; for death brings us, indeed, to the end of our imperfections and to the beginning of our beatitude which we shall obtain in him, so that his kingdom and glory may be our strength, power and pride against hell. And that he is now with the Father is not without a great benefit to us, inasmuch, namely, as he makes access for us and paves the way to him, he offers us to him, asks grace for us from him, he addresses him continually for us as an advocate and mediator, he intercedes with him for our offenses, and he reconciles him to us constantly (Hebrews 7:25, 9:6–28; Romans 8:26–27; 1 John 2:1). And so, although he was lifted up into heaven, and removed the presence of his body from our sight, nevertheless he does not cease to stand by his people with his help and power, and he does not cease to show the manifest power of his presence, which, indeed, he promised, saying: "Behold, I am with you even to the consummation of the world" (Matthew 28:20).

Finally, we believe that he will descend from there in a visible form, just as he was seen to ascend, namely, at the last day, in which he will appear simultaneously to all in the ineffable majesty of his kingdom to judge the living and the dead (Acts 1:11; Matthew 24:27, 44), that is, both those whom that day will arise alive, and those who have been taken away by death, and he will give to all a reward according to their works (1 Thessalonians 4:14–17; Matthew

16:27–28), so that everyone might prove himself faithful or
unfaithful by his works.

And so when we see the whole of our salvation and, indeed, every part of it is comprehended in Christ, we must
beware lest we think that even the most insignificant part of
our salvation is placed elsewhere. For in him alone are hidden
all the heavenly treasures, from whence those, who with all
their hope depend upon him alone, may draw whatever good
that is necessary for their satiety. All these things, without
any doubt, which are written above, if they are offered to us
in him, whoever we are who expect them with steadfast faith
because of his word, no particle at all of any good thing can
ever be absent from us.

THIRD PART

I BELIEVE IN THE HOLY SPIRIT

Here we confess that we believe that the Holy Spirit is
true God with the Father and the Son, the third Person of
the most holy Trinity, consubstantial and coeternal with the
Father and the Son, omnipotent and creator of all things. For
there are three distinct Persons in one essence, as was said.
These things, as they are high and hidden mysteries, ought
to be adored rather than discussed, as they neither ought to
be reckoned, nor can be, according to our genius or according
to the standards and nature of our language. Wherefore, as
we have placed all our confidence in God the Father and in
his only Son, so also we should have it in the Holy Spirit,
since he is our God, one with the Father and with the Son.
Persuaded that we have no other Leader or Guide to the
Father than the Holy Spirit, in the same manner as there
is no other way than Christ, no particle of grace from God
may come to us except through the Holy Spirit. This very
grace is the power and action of the Spirit by means of which
the Father works in the Son whatever is in any way good; by
means of which God works, sustains, animates and vivifies all
things; by which he justifies us, cleanses us, calls us and
draws us to himself that we might attain to salvation (Romans 8:11–17; Ephesians 2:18; 1 Corinthians 12:1–13). And
so the Holy Spirit, provided that he dwells in us in this way,
enlightens us with his light by which we may learn and
plainly recognize that we may possess in Christ the immense

riches of the divine goodness (1 Corinthians 2:10–16; 2 Corinthians 13:4). He inflames our hearts with the fire of love to God and our neighbour, and daily he more and more burns and refines the imperfections of our concupiscence (Romans 8:13); so that if there are any good works in us they are the fruits and virtues of his grace. But, indeed, without him our endowments are darkness of mind and perversity of heart (Galatians 5:19–21). And so, indeed, all these gifts are not paid for by any of our efforts or merits, but they are given to us freely and liberally from the divine abundance. And so we believe in the Holy Spirit, recognizing him with the Father and with the Son as our one God, and holding as certain and firm that it is his work and power that we have heard the holy word of the Gospel, that we have received it by faith, that we now stand in that faith. A free work, I say, lest anything should be assigned to our merits. Since these things happen alike to all the faithful, this ought to be the faith of all.

FOURTH PART

I BELIEVE IN THE HOLY CATHOLIC CHURCH, THE COMMUNION OF SAINTS, THE REMISSION OF SINS, THE RESURRECTION OF THE FLESH, ETERNAL LIFE

First, we believe in the Holy Catholic Church, that is, the number of the elect, whether they be angels or men (Ephesians 1:9–10; Colossians 1:16); of men, whether dead or now living; of the living, in whichever lands they dwell or wherever they are scattered throughout the world. There is one Church and society and one people of God, of which Christ our Lord is leader and prince and, as it were, the head of one body; according as they have been chosen in him by virtue of the divine goodness before the foundation of the world, they are all gathered together into the kingdom of God. Now this society is catholic, that is, universal, because one may not find two or three such societies. But all the elect of God are thus united and joined together in Christ, so that just as they depend upon one head, so they may grow together as in one body. By means of this arrangement they band together among themselves as members of the same body. Truly, they are made one, who live at the same time in

one faith, hope, love, in the same Spirit of God, having been
called to the same inheritance of eternal life (Romans 12:4–
5; 1 Corinthians 10:16–17, 12:12–27; Ephesians 4:4–6).
The Church is also holy because as many soever as have been
chosen by the eternal providence to be members of the
Church, are sanctified by the Lord (John 17:17–19; Ephesians 5:25–32). And so, indeed, this order of the mercy of
God is described to us by Paul (Romans 8:30), that those
whom he elected from among men, he might call, that those
whom he called, he might justify; that those whom he justified, he might glorify. He calls when he draws to himself his
own, manifesting himself to them to be known as their God
and Father. He justifies, when he clothes them with the righteousness of Christ, by which also they are adorned for their
perfection and they cover their imperfection. And he refreshes them with the blessings of his Holy Spirit by means of
which day after day they are cleansed from the corruption of
the flesh and regenerated to newness of life, until they appear
in his presence entirely holy and immaculate. He will glorify,
when the majesty of his kingdom shall be manifested in all
and by all. And so when the Lord calls, justifies, glorifies
them, he declares nothing else than their eternal election to
which he had determined them to be born. Wherefore, no
one will ever enter into the glory of the celestial kingdom who
has not been called and justified in this way, since, without
any exception he has chosen them out of all men, the Lord
shows forth and manifests in this way their election. The
Scripture quite often comes close to our interpretation when
it designates as the election of God that which has been
manifested already by this calling and justification. And the
reason is this: that he might often number among the people
of God those in whom God had operated his powers, although they were not chosen; on the other hand, those who
are truly chosen he does not enumerate among the people of
God because they have not been declared so yet (Hosea
2:23; Romans 9:25–26, 10:20, 11:7, 24, 28). For here he
does not reflect upon that one and unchangeable providence
of God, but he describes to us the kind of sons of God that
can be known by us, namely, those who are moved by the
Spirit of God (Romans 8:14).

But since the Church is the people of God's chosen ones,
it is not possible that those who truly are members of it should
perish in the end, or should be lost by evil destruction [John
10:28]. For their salvation rests upon a support so certain

and solid that even though all the machinery of the universe should be violently shaken, it could not destroy it or overthrow it. In the first place, it stands with the election of God, and it can neither fail nor change except with that eternal wisdom. Therefore, they can stagger and vacillate, they can even fall, but they cannot be broken, because the Lord interposes his hand: that is what Paul says (Romans 11:29) "The gifts and calling of God are without repentance." Then, those whom the Lord elected he handed over to the faithful protection and care of Christ his Son, so that "he should not lose one of them but raise them all at the last day" (John 6:39–40). Under such good care the elect can both err and fall, but they certainly cannot be lost. Besides, this must be established: there was no period from the foundation of the world in which the Lord did not have his Church upon the earth, and there certainly will be no time, even to the consummation of the world, in which he is not going to have it, just as he himself promised (Joel 3:20; Psalm 89:29, 35–37, 132:12–18). For although immediately from the beginning of the human race, on account of Adam's sin it was corrupted and marred, from it, however, like as from a polluted mass, God always sanctifies certain vessels to honour so that there would not be any generation which would not experience his mercy. Finally, we must believe in the Church in such a way that resting our trust on the divine goodness, we may be certain that we belong to it. We trust that we shall be perfectly justified and glorified with the rest of the elect of God, with whom we have been called and have already been justified in part. We cannot, of course, comprehend the incomprehensible wisdom of God, nor does it belong to us to discuss it that we may ascertain who by his eternal counsel may have been chosen and who may have been rejected (Romans 11:1–36). But this is not the task of our faith which is repaid abundantly with this secure promise, to wit, that God acknowledges as sons those who will receive his only begotten Son (John 1:12). Who could be so depraved by cupidity that he is not content to be a son of God and should desire something else?

And so, when we find in Christ alone the good will of God the Father toward us, life, salvation and, finally, the kingdom of heaven itself, Christ alone for us ought to be enough and more than enough. For this point must be considered: we shall not lack anything at all which may lead to salvation and to our good, if Christ is ours; truly he and everything which belongs to him will be ours, if we recline on him with sure faith, if we rest in him, if we place in him our salvation, life and, ultimately, our all, if we accept with certainty that it will never come to pass that he will abandon us. For he offers himself to us with open hands; only let us receive him by faith. Indeed, those who, not content with Christ, strive to penetrate higher, provoke against themselves the wrath of God, and because they wish to enter into the abyss of his majesty, they cannot but be overcome with his glory (Proverbs 25:2–6). For since Christ our Lord is the one in whom the Father from eternity chose those whom he willed to be his and to be counted among the flock in his Church, we have a sufficiently clear testimony that we are both among the elect of God and of his Church, if we have fellowship with Christ. Furthermore, since this is the same Christ, the constant and immutable truth of the Father, it must not be doubted at all that his word truly tells us the will of the Father as it was from the beginning and always will be (John 1:1, 14:7–11). And so when we possess Christ by faith and whatever is his, one must state with certainty that as he is the beloved Son of the Father, the heir of the kingdom of heaven, so also we have been adopted through him as sons of God, and so we are his brothers and companions that we may be partakers of the same inheritance. For this reason we also may be certain that we are among those whom the Lord has chosen from eternity, those whom he will always protect, those whom he will never allow to perish (Romans 8:31–39).

Otherwise, it would be a mistake and in vain that we should believe that there is a Catholic Church, unless each one should believe that he is a member of it. Moreover, about the others, it does not belong to us to judge with certainty whether they are of the Church or not, or to distinguish the elect from the reprobates. For this is the unique prerogative of the Lord "to know those who are his," as Paul testifies (2 Timothy 2:19). And lest the temerity of men should rush forward to such judgments, we are admonished by daily occurrences how far the judgments of God supercedes our knowledge. For those who seemed completely lost and were completely given up, were called back again by his grace to the way, and those who seemed to stand before the others fall frequently. The eyes of the Lord alone see who shall persevere until the end (Matthew 24:13), which is, indeed, the capital point of our salvation. Indeed, Christ affirmed that whatever the ministers of his word have loosed and bound on earth is loosed and bound in heaven (Matthew 16:19). Yet it does not follow from this that we can discern those who are of the Church and those who are aliens to it. For by this promise he did not will to give us any external judgment which would indicate plainly to us and place before our eyes those who are bound and those who are loosed, but he promised this alone: that those who should have heard the evangelical promise preached by man himself, by which promise Christ offered himself in the earth, that is, in this life, for redemption and liberation, and should have accepted it by faith, these, I say, are truly loosed and freed in heaven, that is, in the sight of God and of his judgment. But for those who have resisted and despised God, for them there is evidence by the same promise that in heaven and before God they should remain in their chains and, therefore, in their condemnation.

But although we cannot know with the certainty of faith who are chosen, nevertheless since the Scripture describes to us certain infallible distinguishing marks, as was said before, by means of which we may distinguish the elect and the sons of God from the reprobates and foreigners, in so far as he wills that we should know, all those who by a confession of faith, an exemplary life, and participation in the sacraments, confess with us the same Christ and God, ought to be considered with a certain charitable consideration as elect and members of the Church. Even though some imperfection should remain in their manners (as no one on earth is seen to be perfect) provided that they do not caress and please themselves too much in their vices and expect something favourable from them, it will happen that under the guidance of God they will continuously make progress until divested of every imperfection they arrive at the eternal blessedness of the elect. For by means of these distinguishing marks and signs the Scripture defines for us the elect of God, the sons of God, the people of God, the Church of God, so that we might know them. But those who do not agree with us in the same faith or, even if they hold the confession with their lips nevertheless deny with their actions the God whom they confess with their mouth (as we see them in every aspect of life accursed and lost, drunk with the desire to be sinning, asleep and unaware of their evil deeds) they thus signify clearly that they are not, for the present, members of the Church. For this purpose excommunications have been established, by which those are disowned and expelled from the community of the faithful who falsely plead the faith of Christ, those who because of the wantonness of their life, and their unbridled passion in sinning, are not anything else than the scandal of the Church and unworthy, therefore, to glory in the name of Christ (1 Corinthians 5:1–5; Matthew 18:15–19; 1 Timothy 1:20). In the first place, it would be outrageous to God, if they were named among Christians; it would be as if his holy Church were all together a conspiracy of evil and reprobate men. In the second place, they must be excommunicated lest by the example of their perverse life they should corrupt others because of frequent intercourse. Finally, that they themselves, confused by this disgrace, may begin to repent of their baseness, and from this repentance learn at last to know themselves.

We can judge such people as outside the Church for the time being, in so far as it is given to us to determine it, and in accordance with the rule of knowledge of which we spoke above. But, indeed, we must not despair of them, as if they had been abandoned beyond the hand of God. And it is wholly unlawful to strike anyone from the number of the elect, or to despair as if he were already lost, except perhaps those of whom it is known that they are condemned already by the word of God, as if, for example, anyone on purpose and with deliberate malice should oppose the truth in order to oppress the Gospel, to extinguish the name of God, to resist the Holy Spirit. For the mouth of the Lord has already pronounced against these, saying, "Sin against the Holy Spirit is not remitted in this world or the next." This we can feel so seldom, if we ever can that it is rather advisable to wait until the day of revelation, and not to rashly forestall God's judgment (Matthew 12:32; Hebrews 6:6, 10:26; John 5:28–29; 1 Corinthians 4:5). Let us not claim an excessive liberty to judge, unless we are willing to limit the power of God or to dictate a law to his mercy. For it pleased him time and time again that bad men should be changed into very good ones, that strangers should be introduced, and foreigners called, into the Church. Thus God baffles the opinion of men and rebukes their temerity, that they dare not take into their hands the right to judge, beyond what is fitting. We must rather endeavour with mutual candour to think well of each other, as far as possible, to mutually put the best construction on the deeds and words of one another so that we do not twist them covertly and unfavourably as suspicious people often do (Matthew 7:1–5; Romans 12:9–10, 21; 14:13, 19; 1 Thessalonians 5:15; Hebrews 12:14). Therefore, if some are so perverse that they do not allow us to think well of them, let us, nevertheless, commit them into the hands of God and commend them to his goodness, hoping better things of these people than we see. For thus it will happen that mutually supporting ourselves with equity and patience, we may cultivate peace and love, and not, stupidly breaking into the most secret judgments of God, surround ourselves in the darkness of error. In order that I may finish with one word, I say, we should not condemn to death the person himself, who is in the hand and under the judgment of God, but we should only judge of what kind are the works of each one according to the law of God which is the standard of good and evil.

This is the way in which excommunications must be understood, not that by means of them those who are disowned before men in the flock of the Church should be deprived of the hope of salvation, but that by excommunication they should be punished until they return from the baseness of their former life to the way. Just as Paul writes (1 Corinthians 5:5) that he "delivered a man to satan for the destruction of his flesh that his spirit might be saved in the day of the Lord. This means (as I interpret the same) that he delivered him to a temporal condemnation, in order that he might be saved in eternity (1 Corinthians 5:6; 2 Thessalonians 3:14–15). And so, although it is not lawful on account of ecclesiastical discipline to live in a friendly manner or to have intimate fellowship with those who have been excommunicated, we ought, nevertheless, to strive by all means at our disposal, whether by exhortations and doctrine, whether by clemency and kindness, whether by our praises to God, so that, converted to a better moral excellence, they may be received into the society and unity of the Church. And not only must they be so treated but also the Turks and the Saracens and the rest of the enemies of the true religion. Far from us that we should approve of the method by which many have thus far undertaken to compel these men to embrace our faith, by refusing them water, fire, and the common elements of this world, denying them every service of humanity and persecuting them with iron and sword.

But although it is not lawful to judge individually who belongs to the Church and who does not, since we do not yet know the judgment of God, nevertheless wherever we see the word of God is sincerely preached and heard and the sacraments instituted by Christ administered, it is not to be doubted in any way that there is a Church of God, since his

promise cannot fail: "Wherever two or three are gathered in
my name there I am in the midst of them" (Matthew 18:20).
We cannot even have on earth a more certain knowledge of
God's Church, nor can we otherwise discern those who are
outside the Church, not by any means! Yes, indeed, not one
of these things is understood except by faith, because we say
that when we say: we believe in the Church. For these things
are believed which cannot be seen by our present eyes.
Wherefore, it is clear that the Church is not a carnal thing
which ought to be present to our senses, or circumscribed in
a certain place, or fixed in any See.

We also believe in the Communion of the Saints, that is,
that in the Catholic Church there is a mutual communication
and participation of all goods by all the elect, who at the
same time worship God with true faith. Wherefore, it is not
denied that the graces of each one are different (as Paul
teaches that the gifts of the Spirit are diverse and distributed
in different ways) (1 Corinthians 12:4–11;)[9] it is not denied
that each one should rightly and orderly hold his own property, because they possess this right from the civil constitution
(as it is necessary under the first principles of the world that
possessions should be distinct among men); but the community of the faithful observe this point: that they share
among themselves, generously and with the love which they
owe to each other, every kind of possessions, whether of the
spirit or of the body, in so far as it is fair and experience demands it. And, indeed, whichever of God's gifts fall to one's
lot, they are truly participants of it, although by the dispensation of God this gift is given particularly to one, not to the
others (Romans 12:4–8; 1 Corinthians 12:12, 26); likewise,
the members of the body share all things among themselves
by a certain mutual participation, nevertheless each one had
its own peculiar gifts and distinct functions; for, as has been
said, they are gathered and fitted together in one body. This
is the Catholic Church, the mystical body of Christ (Ephesians 1:22–23). Thus in the last section we have testified that
we believe in the Church. In this we truly declare that this is
the kind of Church in which we believe. I know, indeed,
that this part has been omitted by some, interpreted in another sense by others; but I have interpreted it with the best
faith and to the best of my ability.

---

[9] The *editio princeps* has "1 Cor. 11." The C.R. has corrected
the mistake without noting the fact.

We believe in the remission of sins, that is, that by virtue of the divine liberality, and the mediating merit of Christ, there is grace and remission of sins for us who have been admitted and inserted into the body of Christ. But the remission of sins is not given either from some other source, or for any other reason, or to any others (Acts 10:43; 1 John 2:1–12; Isaiah 33:24). For outside this Church and this communion of saints there is no salvation. Further, the Church herself stands and subsists by this remission of sins, that is, as it were, supported by this foundation (Hosea 2:18–23). Since the remission of sins is the way to God, the way by which he is approached, and the reason by which he is reconciled to us, this reconciliation, therefore, at the same time opens for us entrance into the Church (which is the city of God and the tabernacle which the Most High has sanctified for his dwelling place), and keeps and defends us in the Church (Psalm 46:4–5, 87:1–3; 1 Timothy 3:15). But the faithful receive this remission when, confused, afflicted and oppressed by the consciousness of their sins, they are terrified by their consciousness of the divine judgment and are disgusted with themselves and, as it were, groan and labour under a heavy burden, and by this hatred of their sin and their confusion, they mortify their flesh and whatever is from themselves. For as they go on constantly repenting (for this is requisite) as long as they live in the prison of their body, so steadily and constantly they obtain that remission itself. Not because their repentance has any merit, but because it pleased the Lord to manifest himself to men in this manner, so that through knowledge of their own poverty they should lay aside all pride, humble themselves completely, become absolutely vile in their own sight, then, at last, they may begin to taste the sweetness of the mercy which he proposes to them in Christ. Having thus obtained mercy they breathe again, and take comfort having a firm assurance in Christ of the remission of sins and the blessed salvation. Again those who do not try to reach God by these steps never attain this remission of sins which is the pivot of our salvation (Luke 16:15, 26). Even though they should excel by the splendid magnificence of their works, even to the point of doing a miracle, still God abominates their works, deeds and thought, especially those works which beguile men with a greater appearance of holiness; the eyes of these men are blinded by the empty splendour of works.

We believe in the resurrection of the flesh, that it shall

come to pass that all the bodies of men shall be raised at the same time from corruption to incorruption, from mortality to immortality (1 Corinthians 15:20–56; 1 Thessalonians 4:13–17; Acts 23:6–9), and, indeed, even those who have departed previously from life shall receive again their own flesh, whether it has been eaten away by worms, or decayed in the earth, or reduced to dust, or wasted in any other way. (John 5:28–32.)[10] As for those who shall be found alive at that time, even they shall lay aside the corruption of their flesh, and shall be transformed by a sudden change to an immortal nature, the pious, indeed, to the glory of life, the reprobates to the condemnation of death (Matthew 25:31–46).

Finally, we believe in eternal life, to wit, it shall come to pass that the Lord will·then receive them, glorified in body and in soul, to beatitude which will remain unchanged for ever, beyond any kind of change or corruption. This beatitude will be a true and genuine perfection unto life, light and justice, when we shall cling inseparably to the Lord, who as an inexhaustible fountain contains in himself the fulness of these blessings (1 Corinthians 15:28–53). Truly, this beatitude will be the kingdom of God, filled with all brightness, joy, virtue and felicity, things most remote now from the understanding of men, and which (as Paul says) (1 Corinthians 2:9), "no ear heard, no eye saw, no human mind perceived." On the contrary, the impious and reprobates who did not seek or worship God with sincere faith, since they will not have any part in God or in his kingdom, will be thrown to eternal death with the devils; so that, beyond the reach of all joy, virtue, and the other blessings of the heavenly kingdom, condemned to eternal darkness and eternal torment, they are gnawed by the eternal worm and burn in unextinguishable fire (Matthew 22:13; Isaiah 66:26;[11] Mark 9:43–49).

And so, indeed, it is fitting that we believe both in the communion of saints, the remission of sins, the resurrection of the flesh, and eternal life, that assured of the goodness of the Lord, we may believe without doubt that all these things are going to happen to us together with all the saints. And so, in order to signify how certain and immovable the truth of these things is, and in order that all may confirm themselves in this faith, establishing for each other the Lord as his God

---

[10] The text is omitted in C.R. and Barth.
[11] The *editio princeps* has "Ies. ult."

and Christ as his Saviour, awaiting the resurrection and eternal life, this entire confession is closed with the word, Amen, which is the mark of a proven certitude.

Wherever this faith is alive, which we have shown above to be trust in one God and in Christ, it certainly cannot be idle; rather, it has as its companions, hope and love. If these are entirely lacking, howsoever much we may speak eloquently about faith, we are convicted of not having any. This is not because faith is born in us out of hope and love, but because it is absolutely impossible for hope and love not to always follow faith let us prove this first with regard to hope. If faith (as we have heard) is a definite conviction of God's truth which cannot lie to us, nor beguile us, nor be invalid, those who grasp this certitude really expect at the same time that God will fulfill his promises, since in their opinion such promises cannot but be true. In short, hope is nothing else than the expectation of those things which faith has believed to be truly promised by God. Thus faith believes in a truthful God; hope expects that he manifest his truth at the right time. Faith believes that he is our Father; hope expects that he conduct himself toward us as such. Faith believes that eternal life is given to us; hope expects that one day it shall be received. Faith is the foundation upon which hope rests; hope nourishes and sustains faith. For as not one can expect anything from God, if he has not first believed in his promises, so again, the weakness of our faith must with patient hope and expectation be nourished and sustained, lest, as if exhausted, it waste away. As regards love, the argument is just as clear. For when faith embraces Christ as he is offered to us by the Father, he truly is not only our remission, righteousness, peace and reconciliation, but also our sanctification and the fount of living water, it undoubtedly discovers in him love which is the gift and fruit of the Holy Spirit and the work of that sanctification (Galatians 5:22–25). Behold! how hope and love are born and grow alike from faith, and have been added to it and interwoven with it by an indivisible connection. However, we must not think about love what we have taught above about hope, to wit, that faith is nourished, preserved and made firm by it. Indeed, this is proper of hope because while it awaits the Lord in silence and patience it restrains faith lest it should hurry along too fast, and it confirms faith lest it should vacillate and doubt about faith in God's promises (Isaiah 28:16). The essence of love is entirely different. It has nothing in common with these two. Those who are accustomed to unduly stress the saying of Paul (1 Corinthians 13:2), "if a man should have all faith, to the point of moving mountains, yet should not have love, he is nothing." From this they claim that there is a certain faith without love (which they call "fides informis"). But they do not realize what it is that the Apostle means by "faith" in this passage. For, in the preceding chapter, Paul treats of the various gifts of the Spirit, among which he enumerates the powers, the gifts of tongues, and prophecy, and he exhorts the Corinthians to strive after the best of these gifts, that is to say, these from which more fruit returns to the Church. Now he goes on to say that he is going to give a still better reason: for all these gifts, no matter how excellent in themselves, are yet nothing unless they are in the service of love, since they were given for the edification of the Church; thus, if they fail to contribute to that edification, they lose their own value. To prove this, Paul resorts to a distributive argument, repeating the very same gifts which he had enumerated above, but under different names. Thus he uses "powers" and "faith" in the same sense, meaning "the gift to do miracles." And since such a gift, be it called "power," or "miraculous faith," is a particular gift of God, liable to be abused, like also the gift of tongues, prophecy, or other charisms, it is obvious that it is far different from the true and Christian faith. This may be observed from the example of Judas, who had charismatic faith, and yet he was anything but faithful. (Luke 10:17–20, 42). From this very passage and from the following statement in the same chapter, that love is greater than faith and hope, our adversaries forcibly claim that therefore we are justified by love rather than by faith, or, as it were, by a power which, so they say, is a more excellent one. But their cavil may be refuted without difficulty. For we hold that what is said in the first passage has nothing to do with true faith. We also interpret the second passage as about true faith, in which it says that love is greater because it is more fruitful, more accessible, more useful to more people, always flourishes, whereas the usefulness of faith has a temporary value. Which person with sound judgment, yes, which one with a totally sound brain, argues from this passage that love justifies more? For the power of justifying does not consist in the dignity of the work. Our justification depends upon the mercy of God alone. When faith apprehends God's mercy, it is said that faith justifies. But if some brawler should interrupt and ask, why I use the concept "faith" in various ways in so small an interval, I would reply that it is not a small reason that makes this interpretation evident. For since these gifts which Paul enumerates are subjected in some way to faith and hope because they have regard for the knowledge of God, all these things κατ' ἀνακεφαλαιωςιν[12] he comprehends under the name of faith and hope, as if he should say, a prophecy and tongues, and the gifts of interpretation, and science have this aim, to lead to the knowledge of God. But we do not know God in this life except by faith and hope. Therefore, when I name "faith" and "hope" I understand all these things at the same time. "And so these three remain faith, hope, and love"[13] that is, howsoever great the variety of the gifts may be, they are all referred back to these three, but among these love is supreme, etc. Therefore, we must think that faith, hope and love are gifts of the Holy Spirit, and not one of them can be introduced or continue except by the mercy of God (1 Corinthians 4:7). And so we all learn, not to seek in ourselves, but to ask from God. And if we feel in ourselves something either of hope, or of love, or of faith, we refer all which is received to God, entreating him with heart and mouth, with the heart principally, and this continually, as he wishes to protect these virtues in us and to promote them more and more day by day. For thus it is necessary for us that we should increase constantly while we are in this life, which (while it is conducted the best for us) is not anything else than a journey and progression, until we attain wholly to God in whom all our perfection is placed.

CHAPTER THREE

CONCERNING PRAYER, TOGETHER WITH AN
EXPLANATION OF THE LORD'S PRAYER

From the things which have been discussed up to the present, we clearly perceive how needy and empty man is of all good things, and how he lacks all the means of his salvation. Wherefore, if he seeks for relief whereby he may aid his neediness he must go outside himself and procure it from somewhere else. Afterwards, this point was explained to us;

---

[12] By way of recapitulation.
[13] 1 Corinthians 13:13a.

that the Lord voluntarily and freely manifests himself to us in his Christ, in whom he offers all kinds of felicity for our unhappiness and riches for our poverty; in whom he opens to us the heavenly treasures, that our whole faith should contemplate that beloved Son of his, that all our expectation should depend upon him, that in him our hope should adhere and rest. This, indeed, is a secret and hidden philosophy and one which cannot be drawn out of syllogisms; but they learn it thoroughly whose eyes God has opened that in his light they may see light. But since we are taught by faith to recognize that whatever is necessary for us, and whatever we lack, the same is in God and in our Lord Jesus Christ, in whom the Father, indeed, has willed that all the fullness of his liberality should reside, in order that we may draw from thence, as from a most abundant fountain (Colossians 1:19; John 1:16), it remains that we should seek in him and ask from him by means of prayers what we have learned is in him. Otherwise, to know God as the Lord and liberal Giver of all good things, who invites us to call upon him, but neither to draw nigh to him nor to call upon him, would be utterly fruitless; it would be just as if someone shown a treasure, buried and hidden in the ground, should disregard it. This last point, because until now it has been mentioned in passing and, as it were, lightly, must now be treated more at length.

Then, let this be the first law of a right prayer: that we give up every thought of our own glory, that we lay aside every notion of our own dignity, that we depart from all our own confidence, giving the glory, in our abjection and humility, to the Lord, as we are admonished by prophetic doctrine (Daniel 9:18–19): "We do not, because of our own righteousness, pour out our prayers before thee, but because of thy mercy; hear us, O Lord; O Lord be gracious unto us; Hear us and do what we ask for thy sake; because thy name is invoked upon the people and upon thy holy place." Another prophet also (Baruch 2:18–20) writes: "A soul sad and desolate because of the magnitude of evil, crooked and weak, a famished soul and failing eyes give glory to thee, O Lord. Not because of the righteousness of our fathers do we pour out our prayers in thy presence, O Lord our God; but because thou art merciful, have mercy upon us, because we have sinned before thee." Let also another rule be that we should truly feel our own indigence, and seriously consider that we stand in need of those things which we ask from God for ourselves and for our benefit, and that we ask them in order to receive them from him. For if we should have another feeling or intention, our prayer would be faked and impure. As if, for example, someone should ask from God the remission of sins, not really and seriously believing that he was a sinner. This person with his pretence would not do anything else except laugh at God. Then, we are only to ask those things which are for the glory of God, in order that we may ask for them with great passionate desire and fervour, as, for example, when we ask that his name be sanctified, we ought (so to say) to ardently long and thirst for that sanctification. And so, provided that we understand that we are pressed and burdened by the weight of our sins, provided that we see ourselves empty of all those things which could procure for us grace before God (so that such a feeling does not terrify us to the extent that we do not flee to him), it is necessary for us to think and to feel such things when we draw nigh to him (Luke 17:7–10). For prayer was not instituted that we may present ourselves arrogantly before God, or that we should esteem too highly anything of ours, but that we may confess our misfortunes and bewail them before him, as children familiarly put their complaints before their parents. Indeed, this feeling ought to serve more like a spur and stimulus by which we are urged on more and more to prayer.

Our very kind Father has added two things to this knowledge of our indigence by means of which he may powerfully incite us to a zeal for prayer: the command, by which he admonishes us to pray; the promise, in which he pledges that we are going to get whatever we shall ask. We have the command repeated many times: "ask," "come to me," "seek me," "return to me," "call me in the day of your need:" and with many other sayings, as well as in the third commandment of the law, in which we are forbidden to take the Lord's name in vain (Luke 11:13; John 16:23–26; Matthew 7:7, 11:28; Zechariah 1:3; Psalm 50:15; Exodus 20:7). For the same reason that we are forbidden to use his name in vain, we are commanded to use it to his glory, attributing to it all the praise of virtue, of good, of wealth, and of help, while we both expect and ask these very things from him. For this reason, if we do not flee to him when any need urges us, if we do not seek him and implore his help, we provoke his wrath, just as if we either made strange gods for ourselves or fabricated idols, indeed, we despise his will equally with contempt for all his precepts. Again, those who invoke him, seek him, offer praise to him, enjoy a great consolation, because they understand that in this way they do the thing agreeable to him and are obedient to his will. The promise is, "Ask and you shall receive," "it shall happen to you," "I shall hear you," "I shall rescue you," "I shall restore you," "I shall comfort you," "I shall feed you abundantly," "you will not be confounded" (Matthew 7:7; Luke 11:10; John 16:23–24; Mark 11:24).

All these things, as they have been promised to us by the Father, so without doubt they will be performed, if we expect them with steadfast faith. For it is not the merit or dignity of prayer which obtains our petitions, but that all the hope of prayer is placed in such a promise and thus depends upon it (Isaiah 65:24; Jeremiah 29:13–14; Psalm 50:15, 91:16; Matthew 11:28). And so we must establish in our hearts that we shall be heard, no less than Peter or Paul or any other of the Saints was heard (although they were endowed with greater sanctity of life than we are) if, however, we implore God with the same and equally firm faith. This is because we have been provided and armed with the same command to pray and with the same promise to prevail. For God does not esteem the value of prayer from the dignity of the person but from faith alone, by which we listen to his precepts and trust in his promises. Again, those who are by no means secure in the promise of God, call his truthfulness in doubt and so, doubtful and perplexed as to whether they are to be heard, they call upon God himself but effect nothing (as James says) (James 1:6), when he compares them with the waves which are variously tossed and driven about by the wind. Then, since the Lord affirms that it will happen to each one according to his faith, it follows that without faith we can obtain nothing (Matthew 8:13, 9:29; Mark 11:24). But since no man is worthy that he should present himself to God and appear in his presence, the heavenly Father himself, to free us from this confusion which used to cast down the mind of us all, has given his own Son, Jesus Christ our Lord for us, so that he may be before him our advocate and mediator, under whose leadership we might safely draw nigh to him (1 Timothy 2:5; 1 John 2:1; Hebrews 8:1–6, 9:15), assured by such an intercessor that nothing which we may have asked in his name will be denied to us, just as nothing can be denied to him by the Father (Hebrews 4:14–16); that the throne of God is not only the throne of his majesty but also of his grace, before which "we dare to appear with all confidence in his name to obtain mercy and to find grace in time of need."

And so there is a law established that we should call upon God, as also a promise is given that those who have called upon him are to be heard, so we are particularly enjoined to call upon him in the name of Christ, and we have the promise set forth that we obtain the things which we have asked in his name (John 14:13; 16:24). Hence, without controversy it is clear that those who call upon God in another name, other than the name of Christ, obstinately transgress his commands and reckon his will as nothing, and do not have any promise that they will receive anything. For (as Paul says) (2 Corinthians 1:20): "All the promises of God in Christ are yea and amen," that is, they are confirmed and fulfilled. Further, since he is the only way and only entrance by which we are given access to God (John 14:6), those who turn away from this way and forsake this entrance, for them there remains no other way and no other entrance to God; there is nothing left on his throne except wrath, judgment and terror. Finally, since the Father has appointed him as our head and leader (John 6),[14] those who shun him or turn aside from him in any way, try, as far as they can, to destroy and to adulterate the mark stamped by God.

As regards the saints who, being dead, live in Christ, let us not dream that for even them there is any other way of praying to God than Christ (who alone is the way) or that they are accepted by God in any other name. Therefore, since Scripture calls us away from all others to the one Christ, since the heavenly Father wishes that all things should be gathered together in him (Colossians 1:20; Ephesians 1:10), it is an error for us to devise access through the saints who cannot stand before him by themselves. Besides, since they refer all their desires solely to the will of God, they contemplate it, they rest in it, he thinks foolishly and carnally, and even insolently about them, who assigns any prayer to them, than the one in which they pray for the coming of the kingdom of God, which is fulfilled in salvation of the pious as well as in the confusion of the reprobates. Wherefore, we must not expect to be helped in any way by their prayers, unless

[14] Calvin is mistaken in this reference. Matthew 2:6 reads "ex te enim exiet dux . . ." and 1 Corinthians 11:3; Ephesians 1:22, 4:15, 5:23 and Colossians 1:18 teach that Christ is our head.

we have a part in Christ and are a part of his kingdom. In
the same manner, again, if we are partakers of Christ we
must resolve firmly that whatever we decide is from God,
and that all the Church, of which the saints are members,
prays for us, while she prays that the kingdom of her Lord
may come. But further, although they pray for us in this
way, still we must not invoke them. Neither does it thereby
follow that they must do so because men who live on earth
can in turn recommend themselves the one to the other in
their prayers (1 Timothy 2:1–7; James 5:13–18). For this
practice serves to nourish love in them, in so far as they, as
it were, divide and mutually assume their needs among themselves. This procedure is absent in relation to the dead, whom
the Lord has withdrawn from our companionship. Although
their love for us always flourishes, so that by faith they are
one with us in Christ, and with us bound to Christ, still no
communion remains whether of tongue or of hearing (1 Corinthians 13:10 f). For to affirm otherwise, what is it, if not
under the influence of a drunken dream of the brain, to wish
to break through and penetrate without his word into the
hidden judgments of God, and to trample under foot the
Scripture which so many times pronounces the wisdom of our
flesh as an enemy of the wisdom of God, totally condemns
the vanity of our understanding, and having prostrated all
our reason wills that we should have regard for the will of
God alone (Deuteronomy 12:8, 32). But Scripture presents
Christ to us in a unique way, it sends us to him, and it establishes us in him. Even Ambrose says, "He is our mouth
with which we speak to the Father, our eyes with which we
see the Father, our right hand with which we offer ourselves
to the Father;" whereby unless he is interceding, there is
neither for us nor for all the saints anything with God.

Further, those who choose and select particular patrons
from among the saints drag them back from that unique will,
which (as we said) they hold fixed and immovable in God
to the end that the kingdom may come. These people attribute to the saints carnal affection which is more favourable to
one or another of their worshippers. Wherefore, they truly
make them their mediators, as if Christ had failed them, or
were too severe with them, dishonouring him and robbing
him of the title The Sole Mediator, which was given to him
by the Father as a unique prerogative, so that it must not
be transferred to anyone else. And by this very thing they
obscure the glory of his birth, make the cross vain, and finally,

strip and defraud from his praise whatever he did or suffered for our salvation, since all these things point to this, that he alone is the mediator and should be held as such. In the same manner they throw away the kindness of God, who manifested himself to them as Father. For he is not a Father to them unless they recognize that Christ is their brother. This they rotundly deny, if they think that he does not have a brotherly feeling toward them, a feeling more tender than which there is nothing. But some are moved by this argument: that one reads often that the prayers of the saints are heard. Why? Certainly because they prayed. "They hoped in thee," says the Prophet (Psalm 22:5), "and were saved; they cried, and were not confounded." Therefore, let us pray according to their example, so that we, like them, may be heard. But we would argue perversely, contrary to what is fitting, if we should say that none shall be heard except those who have once been heard. How much better James! "Elijah," he says, "was a man like us, and he prayed his prayer that it should not rain, and it did not rain upon the earth for three years and six months. Again he prayed, "and the heavens gave rain and the earth gave its fruit." (James 5:17–18). By this statement he does not ascribe to Elijah a prerogative, but he teaches the power of prayer, so that he might exhort us to pray in like manner.

There are two parts of prayer (as we now use this term): petition and thanksgiving. By means of petition we place before God the desires of our heart, asking from his goodness, first those things which are alone in the service of his glory, then also those things which are profitable for our use (1 Timothy 2:1). By means of thanksgiving we recognize and confess with praise his benefits to us, attributing to his goodness whatever good gifts we have received. Both kinds of prayer are comprehended in one verse of David when he writes (Psalm 50:15) in the person of God: "Call upon me in the day of trouble, I will deliver thee, and thou shalt glorify me." We ought to make use of them both constantly (Luke 18:1, 21:36; Ephesians 5:20). But so great is our indigence, so great our anxiety about the things which press us and beset us on all sides, that there is sufficient reason for all, even the holiest, to continually groan and sigh for God and to call upon him as supplicants. In addition to this, the so great and such widespread liberality of God's benefits almost overwhelms us, so many and so great are his miracles, wherever thou mayest look they are evident, so that we may never lack occasion and reason for praise and thanksgiving. And that these things may be explained somewhat more clearly, since all our hope and resources depend upon God in such a way (this was proved above) that neither we nor our things can be prosperous without his blessing, it is necessary that we should recommend ourselves continually to him and commit all our possessions to him (James 4:14–17). Then, whatever we purpose, speak, or do, we should purpose, speak and do under his hand and will, in short, under the help of his hand. For all persons are pronounced cursed by God who, trusting in themselves or in someone else, discuss and decide upon plans, who outside his will or without calling upon him, attempt to strive after or to undertake anything (Isaiah 30:1, 31:1). But since it was said that he is to be recognized as the author of all good things, it follows that all things are to be accepted as from his hand with continuous thanksgiving, and that there is no other right way to use his benefits which flow and proceed to us from his liberality for no other end than that we should be constantly confessing his praise and giving thanks. For Paul, when he testifies (1 Timothy 4:5) that they are "sanctified by the word and prayer," indicates at the same time that they are not sanctified at all without the word and prayer, understanding, of course, metonomically faith by word.

This is the reason why Paul in another place commands us to pray without ceasing (1 Thessalonians 5:17; 1 Timothy 2:1–3), wishing that at all times, at every hour, in all places, in all things, the prayers of all those who expect all things from him and attribute the praise of all things to him, should be raised to God, in order that the reasons for praising and praying might be perpetually set forth by us. However, this constancy in prayer refers to the personal and private prayers of each one and has nothing to do with the public prayers of the Church, which can be neither continuous, nor ought to be made except in the manner which for the sake of order has been established by common consent. Therefore certain hours are appointed and prescribed which are as indifferent to God as necessary for the needs of men, that the convenience of all might be provided for and "everything be administered decently and in an orderly manner," (according to the decision of Paul) "in the Church" (1 Corinthians 14:40). And for this purpose public places have been selected, which we call temples, which do not make prayers more holy or cause God to hear them because of any secret sanctity of their own, but because they accommodate more satisfactorily the congregation of the faithful when they congregate to pray, to hear the preaching of the word and to receive the sacraments. In other respects (as Paul says) (1 Corinthians 3:16, 6:19; 2 Corinthians 6:16), "we ourselves are the true temples of God." Wherefore, if we wish to pray in the temple of God, we pray even in ourselves. But those who believe that the ear of the Lord is drawn closer to them in the temple, or that the sanctity of the place leads to holier prayers, do this grossly as Jews and pagans, worshipping God carnally, contrary to what is commanded, namely, that we should "worship in spirit and in truth," without making any distinction as regards the place (John 4:23).

But since it is the aim of prayer, as we have already said, that our mind be lifted up and carried to God in a confession of praise and a supplication for help, it must be understood from this that the principal part of prayer is placed in the mind and heart or, rather, that prayer itself is in a proper sense the interior disposition of the heart which is poured out and laid before God the searcher of hearts. Wherefore, Christ our Lord, when he willed to state the best law concerning prayer, commanded that "we should enter into a room, and there, the door being shut, to pray to our Father in secret, so that our Father who is in secret might hear us" (Matthew 6:6). For in this way he drew us away from the example of the hypocrites who capture the favour of men by a studious display of prayers. He adds at the same time what is better, to enter a room and, the door being shut, to pray there. In these words (as I understand them) he taught us to descend and to enter with our whole thought into our heart, promising that by virtue of such feelings of our heart God will be near us, whose temples our hearts ought to be. For neither did he intend to deny that it is also useful to pray in other places; but he shows that prayer is a kind of secret thing, which is both principally in the heart, and requires most of all tranquility of heart, far away from all the disturbances of worldly cares. Thereupon, it is more than clear that neither voice nor song (if they be used in prayer) has any value or help a trifle before God, if they have not proceeded from a deep affection of the heart. Rather, they provoke against us God's wrath if they are simply emitted from the lips and throat; since that is to abuse his most holy name and to hold his majesty in derision, as God affirms by the prophet (Isaiah 29:13–14; Matthew 15:8–9). "This people," he says, "draw near to me with their mouth and honour me with their lips, but their heart is far from me." And, "They have feared me with the command and doctrine of men. Behold, therefore, I will do among this people a miracle, great and to be wondered at; for wisdom shall perish from among their wise men and the prudence of their old men shall vanish."

Nor do we condemn here voice or song, as long as they follow the disposition of the mind and serve it. For in this way they exercise the mind and keep it intent on thinking about God (as it is slippery) and is easily relaxed and distracted in various directions. Besides, since the glory of God ought to shine in some way in every part of our body, it is fitting that the tongue should be assigned and devoted to this ministry, whether singing or speaking. The tongue has been created particularly for narrating and proclaiming the praise of God. But the most excellent use of the tongue is in the public prayers which are held in the assembly of the faithful; the design of which is that we all with one common voice, and, as it were, with the same mouth, together glorify God when we worship in one spirit and with the same faith; and that publicly, so that all, each one mutually, may receive the confession of faith of his own brother, and be incited by his example. Wherefore, it is perfectly obvious that public prayers must not be expressed in Greek among the Latins, or in Latin among the French or English (as until now it has been the custom everywhere) but they must be composed in the language of the people which can be understood by the common assemblage. It is fitting that they should be for the edification of the entire Church, who receives no fruit at all from a sound which is not understood. But those who have no regard for love should at least have been somewhat moved by the authority of Paul, whose words are not at all ambiguous (1 Corinthians 14:16–17): "If thou shouldest bless," he says, "in the Spirit, he who occupies the place of the unlearned, how will he say 'amen' to thy blessing, since he does not know what thou sayest? For thou givest thanks, but the other is not edified." But this must be fully admitted: that it is by no means possible, either in public prayer or in private, that the tongue without the heart is accepted by God. Besides, there ought to be such power and ardour in that which the mind thinks that it surpasses by far that which the tongue can articulate when it enunciates it. Lastly, even words are not necessary for private prayer, as the interior feeling itself is sufficient for exciting itself, so that sometimes the best prayers make no use of words, as is seen in the case of Moses and Hannah (Exodus 14;[15] 1 Samuel 1:13). Now we must learn not only a more certain method of prayer, but also its form as well, namely, that form which the heavenly Father gave to us through his beloved Son, in which one can recognize the liberality of his great goodness and kindness (Matthew 6:9–13; Luke 11:2–4). For besides the fact that he warns and exhorts us to seek him in all our needs (as children are wont to betake themselves to the protection of their parents) when oppressed with any anxiety, seeing that we were not fully aware how great our poverty was, or what was right for our own interest to ask, he has provided for this ignorance; that wherein our capacity failed he has fully supplied. For he composed for us a form, in which he put forth, as if on a tablet, everything that it is lawful to beg from him, everything that is conducive to our good, everything which is necessary to ask. From this kindness of his we receive a great benefit of consolation, because we understand that we ask almost in his words, that we ask nothing that is absurd, or foreign to him, or unsuitable, in short, that we ask nothing unacceptable to him. . . .

[15] This reference is a mistake. Calvin dropped it in 1539.

INSTITUTES OF
THE CHRISTIAN RELIGION
1559, 1560[1]

[See the Introduction to the edition of 1536, p. 267]

SUBJECT MATTER OF THE PRESENT WORK

From the French Edition of 1560

In order that my readers may better profit from this present
work, I should like to indicate briefly the benefit they may
derive from it. For, in doing this, I shall show them the purpose to which they ought to bend and direct their intention
while reading it. Although Holy Scripture contains a perfect
doctrine, to which one can add nothing, since in it our Lord
has meant to display the infinite treasures of his wisdom, yet
a person who has not much practice in it has good reason
for some guidance and direction, to know what he ought to
look for in it, in order not to wander hither and thither, but
to hold to a sure path, that he may always be pressing toward
the end to which the Holy Spirit calls him. Perhaps the duty
of those who have received from God fuller light than others
is to help simple folk at this point, and as it were to lend
them a hand, in order to guide them and help them to find
the sum of what God meant to teach us in his Word. Now,
that cannot be better done through the Scriptures than to
treat the chief and weightiest matters comprised in the
Christian philosophy. For he who knows these things will be

---

[1] [From *Calvin: Institutes of the Christian Religion,* Vol. I, The
Library of Christian Classics, edited by John T. McNeill and translated by Ford Lewis Battles. Vol. I, pp. 68, 35–92, 542–92, 725–54,
768–88, Vol. II, pp. 1485–1521] *Institutes* I. i–viii; III. ii, xi, xiv;
IV. xx.

prepared to profit more in God's school in one day than another in three months—particularly as he knows fairly well to what he must refer each sentence, and has this rule to embrace all that is presented to him.

It is very necessary to help in this way those who desire to be instructed in the doctrine of salvation. Consequently, I was constrained, according to the ability that the Lord gave me, to undertake this task. Such was my purpose in composing the present book. First of all I put it into Latin so as to serve all men of learning, to whatever nation they belonged; then afterward, desiring to communicate what could bear fruit for our French nation, I have also translated it into our tongue. I dare not render too favorable testimony concerning it, nor yet declare how profitable the reading of it could be, for I would shrink from seeming to appraise my work too highly. Nevertheless, I can at least promise that it can be a key to open a way for all children of God into a good and right understanding of Holy Scripture. Thus, if henceforth our Lord gives me the means and opportunity of writing some commentaries, I shall use the greatest possible brevity, because there will be no need for long digressions, seeing that I have here treated at length almost all the articles pertaining to Christianity. Since we must recognize that all truth and sound doctrine proceed from God, I shall in all simplicity dare fearlessly to protest what I think of this work; I shall recognize that it is God's more than mine. And, in truth, any praise for it must be rendered to him.

Thus, I exhort all those who have reverence for the Lord's Word, to read it, and to impress it diligently upon their memory, if they wish to have, first, a sum of Christian doctrine, and, secondly, a way to benefit greatly from reading the Old as well as the New Testament. When they will have done this they will recognize, by experience, that I have not at all meant to misuse words. If anyone cannot understand all the contents, he must not therefore despair, but must ever press onward, hoping that one passage will give him a more familiar explanation of another. Above all, I must urge him to have recourse to Scripture in order to weigh the testimonies that I adduce from it.

Book One

THE KNOWLEDGE OF GOD THE CREATOR

CHAPTER I

THE KNOWLEDGE OF GOD AND THAT OF
OURSELVES ARE CONNECTED. HOW THEY
ARE INTERRELATED

1. Without knowledge of self there is no knowledge of God

Nearly all the wisdom we possess, that is to say, true and sound wisdom, consists of two parts: the knowledge of God and of ourselves. But, while joined by many bonds, which one precedes and brings forth the other is not easy to discern. In the first place, no one can look upon himself without immediately turning his thoughts to the contemplation of God, in whom he "lives and moves" (Acts 17:28). For, quite clearly, the mighty gifts with which we are endowed are hardly from ourselves; indeed, our very being is nothing but subsistence in the one God. Then, by these benefits shed like dew from heaven upon us, we are led as by rivulets to the spring itself. Indeed, our very poverty better discloses the infinitude of benefits reposing in God. The miserable ruin, into which the rebellion of the first man cast us, especially compels us to look upward. Thus, not only will we, in fasting and hungering, seek thence what we lack; but, in being aroused by fear, we shall learn humility. For, as a veritable world of miseries is to be found in mankind, and we are thereby despoiled of divine raiment, our shameful nakedness exposes a teeming horde of infamies. Each of us must, then, be so stung by the consciousness of his own unhappiness as to attain at least some knowledge of God. Thus, from the feeling of our own ignorance, vanity, poverty, infirmity, and—what is more—depravity and corruption, we recognize that the true light of wisdom, sound virtue, full abundance of every good, and purity of righteousness rest in the Lord alone. To this extent we are prompted by our own ills to contemplate the good things of God; and we cannot seriously aspire to him before we begin to become displeased with ourselves. For what man in all the world would not gladly remain as he is—what man does not remain as he is—so long as he does not know himself, that is, while content with his own gifts, and either ignorant or unmindful of his own misery? Accordingly, the knowledge of ourselves not only arouses us to seek God, but also, as it were, leads us by the hand to find him.

2. Without knowledge of God there is no knowledge of self

Again, it is certain that man never achieves a clear knowledge of himself unless he has first looked upon God's face, and then descends from contemplating him to scrutinize himself. For we always seem to ourselves righteous and upright and wise and holy—this pride is innate in all of us—unless by clear proofs we stand convinced of our own unrighteousness, foulness, folly, and impurity. Moreover, we are not thus convinced if we look merely to ourselves and not also to the Lord, who is the sole standard by which this judgment must be measured. For, because all of us are inclined by nature to hypocrisy, a kind of empty image of righteousness in place of righteousness itself abundantly satisfies us. And because nothing appears within or around us that has not been contaminated by great immorality, what is a little less vile pleases us as a thing most pure—so long as we confine our minds within the limits of human corruption. Just so, an eye to which nothing is shown but black objects judges something dirty white or even rather darkly mottled to be whiteness itself. Indeed, we can discern still more clearly from the bodily senses how much we are deluded in estimating the powers of the soul. For if in broad daylight we either look down upon the ground or survey whatever meets our view round about, we seem to ourselves endowed with the strongest and keenest sight; yet when we look up to the sun and gaze straight at it, that power of sight which was particularly strong on earth is at once blunted and confused by a great brilliance, and thus we are compelled to admit that our keenness in looking upon things earthly is sheer dullness when it comes to the sun. So it happens in estimating our spiritual goods. As long as we do not look beyond the earth, being quite content with our own righteousness, wisdom, and virtue, we flatter ourselves most sweetly, and fancy ourselves all but demigods. Suppose we but once begin to raise our thoughts to God, and to ponder his nature, and how completely perfect are his righteousness, wisdom, and power—

the straightedge to which we must be shaped. Then, what masquerading earlier as righteousness was pleasing in us will soon grow filthy in its consummate wickedness. What wonderfully impressed us under the name of wisdom will stink in its very foolishness. What wore the face of power will prove itself the most miserable weakness. That is, what in us seems perfection itself corresponds ill to the purity of God.

3. Man before God's majesty

Hence that dread and wonder with which Scripture commonly represents the saints as stricken and overcome whenever they felt the presence of God. Thus it comes about that we see men who in his absence normally remained firm and constant, but who, when he manifests his glory, are so shaken and struck dumb as to be laid low by the dread of death—are in fact overwhelmed by it and almost annihilated. As a consequence, we must infer that man is never sufficiently touched and affected by the awareness of his lowly state until he has compared himself with God's majesty. Moreover, we have numerous examples of this consternation both in The Book of Judges and in the Prophets. So frequent was it that this expression was common among God's people: "We shall die, for the Lord has appeared to us" (Judg. 13:22; Isa. 6:5; Ezek. 2:1; 1:28; Judg. 6:22–23; and elsewhere). The story of Job, in its description of God's wisdom, power, and purity, always expresses a powerful argument that overwhelms men with the realization of their own stupidity, impotence, and corruption (cf. Job 38:1 ff.). And not without cause: for we see how Abraham recognizes more clearly that he is earth and dust (Gen. 18:27) when once he had come nearer to beholding God's glory; and how Elijah, with uncovered face, cannot bear to await his approach, such is the awesomeness of his appearance (I Kings 19:13). And what can man do, who is rottenness itself (Job 13:28) and a worm (Job 7:5; Ps. 22:6), when even the very cherubim must veil their faces out of fear (Isa. 6:2)? It is this indeed of which the prophet Isaiah speaks: "The sun will blush and the moon be confounded when the Lord of Hosts shall reign" (Isa. 24:23); that is, when he shall bring forth his splendor and cause it to draw nearer, the brightest thing will become darkness before it (Isa. 2:10, 19 p.[1]).

[1] [p. refers to changes in the text made by Calvin.]

Yet, however the knowledge of God and of ourselves may be mutually connected, the order of right teaching requires that we discuss the former first, then proceed afterward to treat the latter.

CHAPTER II

WHAT IT IS TO KNOW GOD, AND TO WHAT PURPOSE THE KNOWLEDGE OF HIM TENDS

1. Piety is requisite for the knowledge of God

Now, the knowledge of God, as I understand it, is that by which we not only conceive that there is a God but also grasp what befits us and is proper to his glory, in fine, what is to our advantage to know of him. Indeed, we shall not say that, properly speaking, God is known where there is no religion or piety. Here I do not yet touch upon the sort of knowledge with which men, in themselves lost and accursed, apprehend God the Redeemer in Christ the Mediator; but I speak only of the primal and simple knowledge to which the very order of nature would have led us if Adam had remained upright. In this ruin of mankind no one now experiences God either as Father or as Author of salvation, or favorable in any way, until Christ the Mediator comes forward to reconcile him to us. Nevertheless, it is one thing to feel that God as our Maker supports us by his power, governs us by his providence, nourishes us by his goodness, and attends us with all sorts of blessings—and another thing to embrace the grace of reconciliation offered to us in Christ. First, in the fashioning of the universe and in the general teaching of Scripture the Lord shows himself to be the Creator. Then in the face of Christ (cf. II Cor. 4:6) he shows himself to be the Redeemer. Of the resulting twofold knowledge of God[2] we shall now discuss the first

---

[2] *"Duplex . . . cognitio."* The distinction, "twofold" knowledge, added to the *Institutes* in 1559, is basic to the structure of the completed work. Calvin calls attention to this repeatedly in a striking series of methodological statements, all added in 1559 to clarify the course of the argument. Cf. I. vi. 1, 2; x. 1; xiii. 9, 11, 23, 24; xiv. 20, 21, and II. vi. 1. Hence, nothing in Book I belongs to the knowledge of the Redeemer, although everything after ch. v is based in the *special* revelation of Scripture.

aspect; the second will be dealt with in its proper place.[3]

Moreover, although our mind cannot apprehend God without rendering some honor to him, it will not suffice simply to hold that there is One whom all ought to honor and adore, unless we are also persuaded that he is the fountain of every good, and that we must seek nothing elsewhere than in him. This I take to mean that not only does he sustain this universe (as he once founded it) by his boundless might, regulate it by his wisdom, preserve it by his goodness, and especially rule mankind by his righteousness and judgment, bear with it in his mercy, watch over it by his protection; but also that no drop will be found either of wisdom and light, or of righteousness or power or rectitude, or of genuine truth, which does not flow from him, and of which he is not the cause. Thus we may learn to await and seek all these things from him, and thankfully to ascribe them, once received, to him. For this sense of the powers of God is for us a fit teacher of piety, from which religion is born. I call "piety" that reverence joined with love of God which the knowledge of his benefits induces. For until men recognize that they owe everything to God, that they are nourished by his fatherly care, that he is the Author of their every good, that they should seek nothing beyond him—they will never yield him willing service. Nay, unless they establish their complete happiness in him, they will never give themselves truly and sincerely to him.

2. Knowledge of God involves trust and reverence

What is God? Men who pose this question are merely toying with idle speculations. It is far better for us to inquire, "What is his nature?" and to know what is consistent with his nature. What good is it to profess with Epicurus some sort of God who has cast aside the care of the world only to amuse himself in idleness? What help is it, in short, to know a God with whom we have nothing to do? Rather, our knowl-

---

[3] What is called "the first" makes up the entire remainder of Book I. "The second" broadly corresponds to the whole material of Books II–IV. Strictly speaking, the subject is taken up in II. vi, which is a chapter entirely new in 1559, added to make the transition to the second element of twofold knowledge. The doctrine of sin, II. iv, thus falls between the two books in subject matter, preceding redemption in such a way as to show the occasion for it.

edge should serve first to teach us fear and reverence; secondly, with it as our guide and teacher, we should learn to
seek every good from him, and, having received it, to credit
it to his account. For how can the thought of God penetrate
your mind without your realizing immediately that, since you
are his handiwork, you have been made over and bound to
his command by right of creation, that you owe your life to
him?—that whatever you undertake, whatever you do, ought
to be ascribed to him? If this be so, it now assuredly follows
that your life is wickedly corrupt unless it be disposed to his
service, seeing that his will ought for us to be the law by
which we live. Again, you cannot behold him clearly unless
you acknowledge him to be the fountainhead and source of
every good. From this too would arise the desire to cleave
to him and trust in him, but for the fact that man's depravity
seduces his mind from rightly seeking him.

For, to begin with, the pious mind does not dream up
for itself any god it pleases, but contemplates the one and
only true God. And it does not attach to him whatever it
pleases, but is content to hold him to be as he manifests
himself; furthermore, the mind always exercises the utmost
diligence and care not to wander astray, or rashly and boldly
to go beyond his will. It thus recognizes God because it
knows that he governs all things; and trusts that he is its
guide and protector, therefore giving itself over completely to
trust in him. Because it understands him to be the Author of
every good, if anything oppresses, if anything is lacking,
immediately it betakes itself to his protection, waiting for
help from him. Because it is persuaded that he is good and
merciful, it reposes in him with perfect trust, and doubts not
that in his loving-kindness a remedy will be provided for all
its ills. Because it acknowledges him as Lord and Father, the
pious mind also deems it meet and right to observe his authority in all things, reverence his majesty, take care to advance his glory, and obey his commandments. Because it
sees him to be a righteous judge, armed with severity to
punish wickedness, it ever holds his judgment seat before its
gaze, and through fear of him restrains itself from provoking
his anger. And yet it is not so terrified by the awareness of
his judgment as to wish to withdraw, even if some way of
escape were open. But it embraces him no less as punisher
of the wicked than as benefactor of the pious. For the pious
mind realizes that the punishment of the impious and wicked
and the reward of life eternal for the righteous equally per-

tain to God's glory. Besides, this mind restrains itself from sinning, not out of dread of punishment alone; but, because it loves and reveres God as Father, it worships and adores him as Lord. Even if there were no hell, it would still shudder at offending him alone.

Here indeed is pure and real religion: faith so joined with an earnest fear of God that this fear also embraces willing reverence, and carries with it such legitimate worship as is prescribed in the law. And we ought to note this fact even more diligently: all men have a vague general veneration for God, but very few really reverence him; and wherever there is great ostentation in ceremonies, sincerity of heart is rare indeed.

CHAPTER III

THE KNOWLEDGE OF GOD HAS BEEN NATURALLY IMPLANTED IN THE MINDS OF MEN

1. *The character of this natural endowment*

There is within the human mind, and indeed by natural instinct, an awareness of divinity. This we take to be beyond controversy. To prevent anyone from taking refuge in the pretense of ignorance, God himself has implanted in all men a certain understanding of his divine majesty. Ever renewing its memory, he repeatedly sheds fresh drops. Since, therefore, men one and all perceive that there is a God and that he is their Maker, they are condemned by their own testimony because they have failed to honor him and to consecrate their lives to his will. If ignorance of God is to be looked for anywhere, surely one is most likely to find an example of it among the more backward folk and those more remote from civilization. Yet there is, as the eminent pagan says, no nation so barbarous, no people so savage, that they have not a deep-seated conviction that there is a God. And they who in other aspects of life seem least to differ from brutes still continue to retain some seed of religion. So deeply does the common conception occupy the minds of all, so tenaciously does it inhere in the hearts of all! Therefore, since from the beginning of the world there has been no region, no city, in short, no household, that could do without religion, there lies in this a tacit confession of a sense of deity inscribed in the hearts of all.

Indeed, even idolatry is ample proof of this conception. We know how man does not willingly humble himself so as to place other creatures over himself. Since, then, he prefers to worship wood and stone rather than to be thought of as having no God, clearly this is a most vivid impression of a divine being. So impossible is it to blot this from man's mind that natural disposition would be more easily altered, as altered indeed it is when man voluntarily sinks from his natural haughtiness to the very depths in order to honor God!

2. Religion is no arbitrary invention

Therefore it is utterly vain for some men to say that religion was invented by the subtlety and craft of a few to hold the simple folk in thrall by this device and that those very persons who originated the worship of God for others did not in the least believe that any God existed. I confess, indeed, that in order to hold men's minds in greater subjection, clever men have devised very many things in religion by which to inspire the common folk with reverence and to strike them with terror. But they would never have achieved this if men's minds had not already been imbued with a firm conviction about God, from which the inclination toward religion springs as from a seed. And indeed it is not credible that those who craftily imposed upon the ruder folk under pretense of religion were entirely devoid of the knowledge of God. If, indeed, there were some in the past, and today not a few appear, who deny that God exists, yet willy-nilly they from time to time feel an inkling of what they desire not to believe. One reads of no one who burst forth into bolder or more unbridled contempt of deity than Gaius Caligula; yet no one trembled more miserably when any sign of God's wrath manifested itself; thus—albeit unwillingly—he shuddered at the God whom he professedly sought to despise. You may see now and again how this also happens to those like him; how he who is the boldest despiser of God is of all men the most startled at the rustle of a falling leaf (cf. Lev. 26:36). Whence does this arise but from the vengeance of divine majesty, which strikes their consciences all the more violently the more they try to flee from it? Indeed, they seek out every subterfuge to hide themselves from the Lord's presence, and to efface it again from their minds. But in spite of themselves they are always entrapped. Although it may sometimes seem to vanish for a moment, it returns at once and rushes in with new force. If for these there is any respite from anxiety of conscience, it is not much different from the sleep of drunken or frenzied persons, who do not rest peacefully even while sleeping because they are continually troubled with dire and dreadful dreams. The impious themselves therefore exemplify the fact that some conception of God is ever alive in all men's minds.

3. Actual godlessness is impossible

Men of sound judgment will always be sure that a sense of divinity which can never be effaced is engraved upon men's minds. Indeed, the perversity of the impious, who though they struggle furiously are unable to extricate themselves from the fear of God, is abundant testimony that this conviction, namely, that there is some God, is naturally inborn in all, and is fixed deep within, as it were in the very marrow. Although Diagoras and his like may jest at whatever has been believed in every age concerning religion, and Dionysius may mock the heavenly judgment, this is sardonic laughter, for the worm of conscience, sharper than any cauterizing iron, gnaws away within. I do not say, as Cicero did, that errors disappear with the lapse of time, and that religion grows and becomes better each day. For the world (something will have to be said of this a little later) tries as far as it is able to cast away all knowledge of God, and by every means to corrupt the worship of him. I only say that though the stupid hardness in their minds, which the impious eagerly conjure up to reject God, wastes away, yet the sense of divinity, which they greatly wished to have extinguished, thrives and presently burgeons. From this we conclude that it is not a doctrine that must first be learned in school, but one of which each of us is master from his mother's womb and which nature itself permits no one to forget, although many strive with every nerve to this end.

Besides, if all men are born and live to the end that they may know God, and yet if knowledge of God is unstable and fleeting unless it progresses to this degree, it is clear that all those who do not direct every thought and action in their lives to this goal degenerate from the law of their creation. This was not unknown to the philosophers. Plato meant nothing but this when he often taught that the highest good of the soul is likeness to God, where, when the soul has grasped the knowledge of God, it is wholly transformed into his likeness. In the same manner also Gryllus, in the writings of Plutarch, reasons very skillfully, affirming that, if once religion is absent from their life, men are in no wise superior to brute beasts, but are in many respects far more miserable. Subject, then, to so many forms of wickedness, they drag out their lives in ceaseless tumult and disquiet. Therefore, it is worship of God alone that renders men higher than the brutes, and through it alone they aspire to immortality.

CHAPTER IV

THIS KNOWLEDGE IS EITHER SMOTHERED OR CORRUPTED, PARTLY BY IGNORANCE, PARTLY BY MALICE

1. Superstition

Experience teaches that the seed of religion has been divinely planted in all men. But barely one man in a hundred can be found who nourishes in his own heart what he has conceived; and not even one in whom it matures, much less bears fruit in its season (cf. Ps. 1:3). Now some lose themselves in their own superstition, while others of their own evil intention revolt from God, yet all fall away from true knowledge of him. As a result, no real piety remains in the world. But as to my statement that some erroneously slip into superstition, I do not mean by this that their ingenuousness should free them from blame. For the blindness under which they labor is almost always mixed with proud vanity and obstinacy. Indeed, vanity joined with pride can be detected in the fact that, in seeking God, miserable men do not rise above themselves as they should, but measure him by the yardstick of their own carnal stupidity, and neglect sound investigation; thus out of curiosity they fly off into empty speculations. They do not therefore apprehend God as he offers himself, but imagine him as they have fashioned him in their own presumption. When this gulf opens, in whatever direction they move their feet, they cannot but plunge headlong into ruin. Indeed, whatever they afterward attempt by way of worship or service of God, they cannot bring as tribute to him, for they are worshiping not God but a figment and a dream of their own heart. Paul eloquently notes this wickedness: "Striving to be wise, they make fools of themselves" (Rom. 1:22 f.). He had said before that "they became futile in their thinking" (Rom. 1:21). In order, however, that no one might excuse their guilt, he adds that they are justly blinded. For not content with sobriety but claiming for themselves more than is right, they wantonly bring darkness upon themselves—in fact, they become fools in their empty and perverse haughtiness. From this it follows that their stupidity is not excusable, since it is caused not only by vain curiosity but by an inordinate desire to know more than is fitting, joined with a false confidence.

2. Conscious turning away from God

David's statement that ungodly men and fools feel in their hearts that there is no God (Ps. 14:1; 53:1) must first, as we shall see again a little later, be limited to those who, by extinguishing the light of nature, deliberately befuddle themselves. Accordingly, we see that many, after they have become hardened in insolent and habitual sinning, furiously repel all remembrance of God, although this is freely suggested to them inwardly from the feeling of nature. But to render their madness more detestable, David represents them as flatly denying God's existence; not that they deprive him of his being, but because, in despoiling him of his judgment and providence, they shut him up idle in heaven. Now there is nothing less in accord with God's nature than for him to cast off the government of the universe and abandon it to fortune, and to be blind to the wicked deeds of men, so that they may lust unpunished. Accordingly, whoever heedlessly indulges himself, his fear of heavenly judgment extinguished, denies that there is a God. And it is God's just punishment of the wicked that fatness envelops their hearts, so that after they have closed their eyes, in seeing they see not (Matt. 13:14–15; cf. Isa. 6:9–10 and Ps. 17:10). And David is the best interpreter of his thought when in another place he says that "the fear of God is not before the eyes of the ungodly" (Ps. 36:1 p.). Likewise, because they persuade themselves that God does not see, they proudly applaud their own wrongdoing (Ps. 10:11).

Even though they are compelled to recognize some god, they strip him of glory by taking away his power. For, as Paul affirms, just as "God cannot deny himself," because "he remains" forever like himself (II Tim. 2:13), so they, by fashioning a dead and empty idol, are truly said to deny God. At this point we ought to note that, however much they struggle against their own senses, and wish not only to drive God thence but also to destroy him in heaven, their stupidity never increases to the point where God does not at times bring them back to his judgment seat. But because no fear restrains them from rushing violently against God, it is certain that so long as this blind urge grips them, their own oafish forgetfulness of God will hold sway over them.

3. We are not to fashion God according to our own whim

Thus is overthrown that vain defense with which many are wont to gloss over their superstition. For they think that any zeal for religion, however preposterous, is sufficient. But they do not realize that true religion ought to be conformed to God's will as to a universal rule; that God ever remains like himself, and is not a specter or phantasm to be transformed according to anyone's whim. One can clearly see, too, how superstition mocks God with pretenses while it tries to please him. For, seizing almost solely upon what God has testified to be of no concern to himself, superstition either holds in contempt or else openly rejects that which he prescribes and enjoins as pleasing to himself. Thus all who set up their own false rites to God worship and adore their own ravings. Unless they had first fashioned a God to match the absurdity of their trifling, they would by no means have dared trifle with God in this way. The apostle accordingly characterizes that vague and erroneous opinion of the divine as ignorance of God. "When you did not know God," he says, "you were in bondage to beings that by nature were no gods" (Gal. 4:8 p.). And elsewhere he teaches that the Ephesians were "without God" at the time they were straying away from the right knowledge of the one God (Eph. 2:12). Nor is it of much concern, at least in this circumstance, whether you conceive of one God or several; for you continually depart from the true God and forsake him, and, having left him, you have nothing left except an accursed idol. Therefore it remains for us to assert with Lactantius that no religion is genuine unless it be joined with truth.

4. Hypocrisy

A second sin arises, that they never consider God at all unless compelled to; and they do not come nigh until they are dragged there despite their resistance. And not even then are they impressed with the voluntary fear that arises out of reverence for the divine majesty, but merely with a slavish, forced fear, which God's judgment extorts from them. This, since they cannot escape it, they dread even to the point of loathing. That saying of Statius' that fear first made gods in the world corresponds well to this kind of irreligion, and to this alone. Those who are of a mind alien to God's righteousness know that his judgment seat stands ready to punish transgressions against him, yet they greatly desire its overthrow. Feeling so, they wage war against the Lord, who cannot be without judgment. But while they know that his inescapable power hangs over them because they can neither do away with it nor flee from it, they recoil from it in dread. And so, lest they should everywhere seem to despise him whose majesty weighs upon them, they perform some semblance of religion. Meanwhile they do not desist from polluting themselves with every sort of vice, and from joining wickedness to wickedness, until in every respect they violate the holy law of the Lord and dissipate all his righteousness. Or at least they are not so restrained by that pretended fear of God from wallowing blithely in their own sins and flattering themselves, and preferring to indulge their fleshly intemperance rather than restrain it by the bridle of the Holy Spirit.

This, however, is but a vain and false shadow of religion, scarcely even worth being called a shadow. From it one may easily grasp anew how much this confused knowledge of God differs from the piety from which religion takes its source, which is instilled in the breasts of believers only. And yet hypocrites would tread these twisting paths so as to seem to approach the God from whom they flee. For where they ought to have remained consistently obedient throughout life, they boldly rebel against him in almost all their deeds, and are zealous to placate him merely with a few paltry sacrifices. Where they ought to serve him in sanctity of life and integrity of heart, they trump up frivolous trifles and worthless little observances with which to win his favor. Nay, more, with greater license they sluggishly lie in their own filth, because they are confident that they can perform their duty toward him by ridiculous acts of expiation. Then while their trust ought to have been placed in him, they neglect him and rely upon themselves, his creatures though they be. Finally, they entangle themselves in such a huge mass of errors that blind wickedness stifles and finally extinguishes those sparks which once flashed forth to show them God's glory. Yet that seed remains which can in no wise be uprooted: that there is some sort of divinity; but this seed is so corrupted that by itself it produces only the worst fruits.

From this, my present contention is brought out with greater certainty, that a sense of divinity is by nature engraven on human hearts. For necessity forces from the reprobate themselves a confession of it. In tranquil times they wittily joke about God, indeed are facetious and garrulous in belittling his power. If any occasion for despair presses upon them, it goads them to seek him and impels their perfunctory prayers. From this it is clear that they have not been utterly ignorant of God, but that what should have come forth sooner was held back by stubbornness.

CHAPTER V

THE KNOWLEDGE OF GOD SHINES FORTH IN THE FASHIONING OF THE UNIVERSE AND THE CONTINUING GOVERNMENT OF IT

(*God manifested in his created works, 1–10*)

1. *The clarity of God's self-disclosure strips us of every excuse*

The final goal of the blessed life, moreover, rests in the knowledge of God (cf. John 17:3). Lest anyone, then, be excluded from access to happiness, he not only sowed in men's minds that seed of religion of which we have spoken but revealed himself and daily discloses himself in the whole workmanship of the universe. As a consequence, men cannot open their eyes without being compelled to see him. Indeed, his essence is incomprehensible; hence, his divineness far escapes all human perception. But upon his individual works he has engraved unmistakable marks of his glory, so clear and so prominent that even unlettered and stupid folk cannot plead the excuse of ignorance. Therefore the prophet very aptly exclaims that he is "clad with light as with a garment" (Ps. 104:2 p.). It is as if he said: Thereafter the Lord began to show himself in the visible splendor of his apparel, ever since in the creation of the universe he brought forth those insignia whereby he shows his glory to us, whenever and wherever we cast our gaze. Likewise, the same prophet skillfully compares the heavens, as they are stretched out, to his royal tent and says that he has laid the beams of his chambers on the waters, has made the clouds his chariot, rides on the wings of the wind, and that the winds and lightning bolts are his swift messengers. (Ps. 104:2–4.) And since the glory of his power and wisdom shine more brightly above, heaven is often called his palace (Ps. 11:4). Yet, in the first place, wherever you cast your eyes, there is no spot in the universe wherein you cannot discern at least some sparks of his glory. You cannot in one glance survey this most vast and beautiful system of the universe, in its wide expanse, without being completely overwhelmed by the boundless force of its brightness. The reason why the author of The Letter to the Hebrews elegantly calls the universe the appearance of things invisible (Heb. 11:3) is that this skillful ordering of the universe is for us a sort of mirror in which we can contemplate God, who is otherwise invisible. The reason why the prophet attributes to the heavenly creatures a language known to every nation (Ps. 19:2 ff.) is that therein lies an attestation of divinity so apparent that it ought not to escape the gaze of even the most stupid tribe. The apostle declares this more clearly: "What men need to know concerning God has been disclosed to them, . . . for one and all gaze upon his invisible nature, known from the creation of the world, even unto his eternal power and divinity" (Rom. 1:19–20 p.).

2. The divine wisdom displayed for all to see

There are innumerable evidences both in heaven and on earth that declare his wonderful wisdom; not only those more recondite matters for the closer observation of which astronomy, medicine, and all natural science are intended, but also those which thrust themselves upon the sight of even the most untutored and ignorant persons, so that they cannot open their eyes without being compelled to witness them. Indeed, men who have either quaffed or even tasted the liberal arts penetrate with their aid far more deeply into the secrets of the divine wisdom. Yet ignorance of them prevents no one from seeing more than enough of God's workmanship in his creation to lead him to break forth in admiration of the Artificer. To be sure, there is need of art and of more exacting toil in order to investigate the motion of the stars, to determine their assigned stations, to measure their intervals, to note their properties. As God's providence shows itself more explicitly when one observes these, so the mind must rise to a somewhat higher level to look upon his glory. Even the common folk and the most untutored, who have been taught only by the aid of the eyes, cannot be unaware of the excellence of divine art, for it reveals itself in this innumerable and yet distinct and well-ordered variety of the heavenly host. It is, accordingly, clear that there is no one to whom the Lord does not abundantly show his wisdom. Likewise, in regard to the structure of the human body one must have the greatest keenness in order to weigh, with Galen's skill, its articulation, symmetry, beauty, and use. But yet, as all acknowledge, the human body shows itself to be a composition so ingenious that its Artificer is rightly judged a wonder-worker.

3. Man as the loftiest proof of divine wisdom

Certain philosophers, accordingly, long ago not ineptly called man a microcosm because he is a rare example of God's power, goodness, and wisdom, and contains within himself enough miracles to occupy our minds, if only we are not irked at paying attention to them. Paul, having stated that the blind can find God by feeling after him, immediately adds that he ought not to be sought afar off (Acts 17:27). For each one undoubtedly feels within the heavenly grace that quickens him. Indeed, if there is no need to go outside ourselves to comprehend God, what pardon will the indolence of that man deserve who is loath to descend within himself to find God? For the same reason, David, when he has briefly praised the admirable name and glory of God, which shine everywhere, immediately exclaims: "What is man that thou art mindful of him?" (Ps. 8:4). Likewise, "Out of the mouths of babes and sucklings thou hast established strength." (Ps.

8:2.) Indeed, he not only declares that a clear mirror of God's works is in humankind, but that infants, while they nurse at their mothers' breasts, have tongues so eloquent to preach his glory that there is no need at all of other orators. Consequently, also, he does not hesitate to bring their infant speech into the debate, as if they were thoroughly instructed, to refute the madness of those who might desire to extinguish God's name in favor of their own devilish pride. Consequently, too, there comes in that which Paul quotes from Aratus, that we are God's offspring (Acts 17:28), because by adorning us with such great excellence he testifies that he is our Father. In the same way the secular poets, out of a common feeling and, as it were, at the dictation of experience, called him "the Father of men." Indeed, no one gives himself freely and willingly to God's service unless, having tasted his fatherly love, he is drawn to love and worship him in return.

4. But man turns ungratefully against God

Here, however, the foul ungratefulness of men is disclosed. They have within themselves a workshop graced with God's unnumbered works and, at the same time, a storehouse overflowing with inestimable riches. They ought, then, to break forth into praises of him but are actually puffed up and swollen with all the more pride. They feel in many wonderful ways that God works in them; they are also taught, by the very use of these things, what a great variety of gifts they possess from his liberality. They are compelled to know—whether they will or not—that these are the signs of divinity; yet they conceal them within. Indeed, there is no need to go outside themselves, provided they do not, by claiming for themselves what has been given them from heaven, bury in the earth that which enlightens their minds to see God clearly.

Even today the earth sustains many monstrous spirits who, to destroy God's name, do not hesitate to misdirect all the seed of divinity spread abroad in human nature. How detestable, I ask you, is this madness: that man, finding God in his body and soul a hundred times, on this very pretense of excellence denies that there is a God? They will not say it is by chance that they are distinct from brute creatures. Yet they set God aside, the while using "nature," which for them is the artificer of all things, as a cloak. They see such exquisite workmanship in their individual members, from mouth and eyes even to their very toenails. Here also they substitute nature for God. But such agile motions of the soul, such excellent faculties, such rare gifts, especially bear upon the face of them a divinity that does not allow itself readily to be hidden—unless the Epicureans, like the Cyclopes, should from this height all the more shamelessly wage war against God. Do all the treasures of heavenly wisdom concur in ruling a five-foot worm while the whole universe lacks this privilege? First, to establish that there is something organic in the soul that should correspond to its several parts in no way obscures God's glory, but rather illumines it. Let Epicurus answer what concourse of atoms cooks food and drink, turns part of it into excrement, part into blood, and begets such industry in the several members to carry out their tasks, as if so many souls ruled one body by common counsel!

5. The confusion of creature with Creator

But now I have no concern with that pigsty; rather, I take to task those given to fanciful subtleties who willingly drag forth in oblique fashion that frigid statement of Aristotle both to destroy the immortality of the soul and to deprive God of his right. For, since the soul has organic faculties, they by this pretext bind the soul to the body so that it may not subsist without it, and by praising nature they suppress God's name as far as they can. Yet the powers of the soul are far from being confined to functions that serve the body. Of what concern is it to the body that you measure the heavens, gather the number of the stars, determine the magnitude of each, know what space lies between them, with what swiftness or slowness they complete their courses, how many degrees this way or that they decline? I confess, indeed, that astronomy has some use; but I am only showing that in this deepest investigation of heavenly things there is no organic symmetry, but here is an activity of the soul distinct from the body. I have put forth one example, from which it will be easy for my readers to derive the rest. Manifold indeed is the nimbleness of the soul with which it surveys heaven and earth, joins past to future, retains in memory something heard long before, nay, pictures to itself whatever it pleases. Manifold also is the skill with which it devises things incredible, and which is the mother of so many marvelous devices. These are unfailing signs of divinity in man. Why is it that the soul not only vaguely roves about but conceives many useful things, ponders concerning many, even divines the future—all while man sleeps? What ought we to say here except that the signs of immortality which have been implanted in man cannot be effaced? Now what reason would there be to believe that man is divine and not to recognize his Creator? Shall we, indeed, distinguish between right and wrong by that judgment which has been imparted to us, yet will there be no judge in heaven? Will there remain for us even in sleep some remnant of intelligence, yet will no God keep watch in governing the world? Shall we think ourselves the inventors of so many arts and useful things that God may be defrauded of his praise even though experience sufficiently teaches that what we have has been unequally distributed among us from another source?

Some persons, moreover, babble about a secret inspiration that gives life to the whole universe, but what they say is not only weak but completely profane. Vergil's famous saying pleases them:

"First of all, an inner spirit feeds
Sky, earth, and watery fields, the shining orb
Of moon, and Titan's star; and mind pervades
Its members, sways all the mass, unites
With its great frame. Thence come the race of man
And beast, the life of winged things, strange shapes
That ocean bears beneath his glassy floor.
Of fire the vigor, and divine the source
Of those life-seeds."[4]

As if the universe, which was founded as a spectacle of God's glory, were its own creator! For thus the same author has elsewhere followed the view common to Greeks and Latins alike:

"The bees, some teach, received a share of mind,
Divine, ethereal draught. For God, men say,
Pervades all things, the earth, expanse of seas
And heaven's depth. From him the flocks and herds,
Men and beasts of every sort, at birth
Draw slender life; yea, unto him all things

[4] Vergil, *Aeneid* VI. 724-30.

Do then return; unmade, are then restored;
Death has no place; but still alive they fly
Unto the starry ranks, to heaven's height."[5]

See, of what value to beget and nourish godliness in men's
hearts is that jejune speculation about the universal mind
which animates and quickens the world! This shows itself
even more clearly in the sacrilegious words of the filthy dog
Lucretius which have been deduced from that principle. This
is indeed making a shadow deity to drive away the true
God, whom we should fear and adore. I confess, of course,
that it can be said reverently, provided that it proceeds from
a reverent mind, that nature is God; but because it is a harsh
and improper saying, since nature is rather the order prescribed by God, it is harmful in such weighty matters, in
which special devotion is due, to involve God confusedly in
the inferior course of his works.

6. The Creator reveals his lordship over the creation

Let us therefore remember, whenever each of us contemplates his own nature, that there is one God who so governs all
natures that he would have us look unto him, direct our faith
to him, and worship and call upon him. For nothing is more
preposterous than to enjoy the very remarkable gifts that
attest the divine nature within us, yet to overlook the Author
who gives them to us at our asking. With what clear manifestations his might draws us to contemplate him! Unless perchance it be unknown to us in whose power it lies to sustain
this infinite mass of heaven and earth by his Word: by his
nod alone sometimes to shake heaven with thunderbolts, to
burn everything with lightnings, to kindle the air with flashes;
sometimes to disturb it with various sorts of storms, and then
at his pleasure to clear them away in a moment; to compel
the sea, which by its height seems to threaten the earth with
continual destruction, to hang as if in mid-air; sometimes to
arouse it in a dreadful way with the tumultuous force of
winds; sometimes, with waves quieted, to make it calm again!
Belonging to this theme are the praises of God's power from
the testimonies of nature which one meets here and there
especially indeed in The Book of Job and in Isaiah. These I
now intentionally pass over, for they will find a more appro-

[5] Vergil, *Georgics* IV. 219–27.

priate place where I shall discuss from the Scriptures the creation of the universe. Now I have only wanted to touch upon the fact that this way of seeking God is common both to strangers and to those of his household, if they trace the outlines that above and below sketch a living likeness of him. This very might leads us to ponder his eternity; for he from whom all things draw their origin must be eternal and have beginning from himself. Furthermore, if the cause is sought by which he was led once to create all these things, and is now moved to preserve them, we shall find that it is his goodness alone. But this being the sole cause, it ought still to be more than sufficient to draw us to his love, inasmuch as there is no creature, as the prophet declares, upon whom God's mercy has not been poured out (Ps. 145:9; cf. Ecclus. 18:11; 18:9, Vg.).

7. God's government and judgment

In the second kind of works, which are outside the ordinary course of nature also, proofs of his powers just as clear are set forth. For in administering human society he so tempers his providence that, although kindly and beneficent toward all in numberless ways, he still by open and daily indications declares his clemency to the godly and his severity to the wicked and criminal. For there are no doubts about what sort of vengeance he takes on wicked deeds. Thus he clearly shows himself the protector and vindicator of innocence, while he prospers the life of good men with his blessing, relieves their need, soothes and mitigates their pain, and alleviates their calamities; and in all these things he provides for their salvation. And indeed the unfailing rule of his righteousness ought not to be obscured by the fact that he frequently allows the wicked and malefactors to exult unpunished for some time, while he permits the upright and deserving to be tossed about by many adversities, and even to be oppressed by the malice and iniquity of the impious. But a far different consideration ought, rather, to enter our minds: that, when with a manifest show of his anger he punishes one sin, he hates all sins; that, when he leaves many sins unpunished, there will be another judgment to which have been deferred the sins yet to be punished. Similarly, what great occasion he gives us to contemplate his mercy when he often pursues miserable sinners with unwearied kindness, until he shatters their wickedness by imparting benefits and by recalling them to him with more than fatherly kindness!

8. God's sovereign sway over the life of men

To this end, the prophet is mindful that in their desperate straits God suddenly and wonderfully and beyond all hope succors the poor and almost lost; those wandering through the desert he protects from wild beasts and at last guides them back to the way (Ps. 107:4–7); to the needy and hungry he supplies food (v. 9); the prisoners he frees from loathsome dungeons and iron bands (vs. 10–16); the shipwrecked he leads back to port unharmed (vs. 23–30); the half dead he cures of disease (vs. 17–20); he burns the earth with heat and dryness, or makes it fertile with the secret watering of grace (vs. 33–38); he raises up the humblest from the crowd, or casts down the lofty from the high level of their dignity (vs. 39–41). By setting forth examples of this sort, the prophet shows that what are thought to be chance occurrences are just so many proofs of heavenly providence, especially of fatherly kindness. And hence ground for rejoicing is given to the godly, while as for the wicked and the reprobate, their mouths are stopped (v. 42). But because most people, immersed in their own errors, are struck blind in such a dazzling theater, he exclaims that to weigh these works of God wisely is a matter of rare and singular wisdom (v. 43), in viewing which they who otherwise seem to be extremely acute profit nothing. And certainly however much the glory of God shines forth, scarcely one man in a hundred is a true spectator of it!

In no greater degree is his power or his wisdom hidden in darkness. His power shows itself clearly when the ferocity of the impious, in everyone's opinion unconquerable, is overcome in a moment, their arrogance vanquished, their strongest defenses destroyed, their javelins and armor shattered, their strength broken, their machinations overturned, and themselves fallen of their own weight; and when their audacity, which exalted them above heaven, lays them low even to the center of the earth; when, conversely the humble are raised up from the dust, and the needy are lifted up from the dung heap (Ps. 113:7); the oppressed and afflicted are rescued from their extreme tribulation; the despairing are restored to good hope; the unarmed, few and weak, snatch victory from the armed, many and strong. Indeed, his wisdom manifests his excellence when he dispenses everything at the best opportunity; when he confounds all wisdom of the world (cf. I Cor. 1:20); when "he catches the crafty in their own craftiness" (I Cor. 3:19 p.; cf. Job 5:13). In short, there is nothing that he does not temper in the best way.

9. We ought not to rack our brains about God; but rather, we should contemplate him in his works

We see that no long or toilsome proof is needed to elicit evidences that serve to illuminate and affirm the divine majesty; since from the few we have sampled at random, whithersoever you turn, it is clear that they are so very manifest and obvious that they can easily be observed with the eyes and pointed out with the finger. And here again we ought to observe that we are called to a knowledge of God: not that knowledge which, content with empty speculation, merely flits in the brain, but that which will be sound and fruitful if we duly perceive it, and if it takes root in the heart. For the Lord manifests himself by his powers, the force of which we feel within ourselves and the benefits of which we enjoy. We must therefore be much more profoundly affected by this knowledge than if we were to imagine a God of whom no perception came through to us. Consequently, we know the most perfect way of seeking God, and the most suitable order, is not for us to attempt with bold curiosity to penetrate to the investigation of his essence, which we ought more to adore than meticulously to search out, but for us to contemplate him in his works whereby he renders himself near and familiar to us, and in some manner communicates himself. The apostle was referring to this when he said that we need not seek him far away, seeing that he dwells by his very present power in each of us (Acts 17:27–28). For this reason, David, having first confessed his unspeakable greatness (Ps. 145:3), afterward proceeds to mention his works and professes that he will declare his greatness (Ps. 145: 5–6; cf. Ps. 40:5). It is also fitting, therefore, for us to pursue this particular search for God, which may so hold our mental powers suspended in wonderment as at the same time to stir us deeply. And as Augustine teaches elsewhere, because, disheartened by his greatness, we cannot grasp him, we ought to gaze upon his works, that we may be restored by his goodness.

10. The purpose of this knowledge of God

Knowledge of this sort, then, ought not only to arouse us to the worship of God but also to awaken and encourage us to the hope of the future life. For since we notice that the examples that the Lord shows us both of his clemency and of his severity are inchoate and incomplete, doubtless we must consider this to presage even greater things, the manifestation and full exhibition of which are deferred to another life. On the other hand—since we see the pious laden with afflictions by the impious, stricken with unjust acts, overwhelmed with slanders, wounded with abuses and reproaches; while the wicked on the contrary flourish, are prosperous, obtain repose with dignity and that without punishment—we must straightway conclude that there will be another life in which iniquity is to have its punishment, and righteousness is to be given its reward. Furthermore, since we observe that believers are often chastised by the Lord's rods, we may with full assurance believe that one day the wicked must no less suffer his lash. Indeed, Augustine's remark is well known: "If now every sin were to suffer open punishment, it would seem that nothing is reserved for the final judgment. Again, if God were now to punish no sin openly, one would believe that there is no providence."

We must therefore admit in God's individual works—but especially in them as a whole—that God's powers are actually represented as in a painting. Thereby the whole of mankind is invited and attracted to recognition of him, and from this to true and complete happiness. Now those powers appear most clearly in his works. Yet we comprehend their chief purpose, their value, and the reason why we should ponder them, only when we descend into ourselves and contemplate by what means the Lord shows in us his life, wisdom, and power; and exercises in our behalf his righteousness, goodness, and mercy. For even though David justly complains that unbelievers are foolish because they do not ponder the deep designs of God in the governance of mankind (Ps. 92: 5–6), yet what he says elsewhere is very true: that God's wonderful wisdom here abounds more than the hairs of our head (cf. Ps. 40:12). But because this argument is to be treated more amply below, I now pass over it.

(Man nevertheless, failing to know and worship him, falls into superstition and confusion, 11–12)

11. The evidence of God in creation does not profit us

But although the Lord represents both himself and his everlasting Kingdom in the mirror of his works with very great clarity, such is our stupidity that we grow increasingly dull toward so manifest testimonies, and they flow away without profiting us. For with regard to the most beautiful structure and order of the universe, how many of us are there who, when we lift up our eyes to heaven or cast them about through the various regions of earth, recall our minds to a remembrance of the Creator, and do not rather, disregarding their Author, sit idly in contemplation of his works? In fact, with regard to those events which daily take place outside the ordinary course of nature, how many of us do not reckon that men are whirled and twisted about by blindly indiscriminate fortune, rather than governed by God's providence? Sometimes we are driven by the leading and direction of these things to contemplate God; this of necessity happens to all men. Yet after we rashly grasp a conception of some sort of divinity, straightway we fall back into the ravings or evil imaginings of our flesh, and corrupt by our vanity the pure truth of God. In one respect we are indeed unalike, because each one of us privately forges his own particular error; yet we are very much alike in that, one and all, we forsake the one true God for prodigious trifles. Not only the common folk and dull-witted men, but also the most excellent and those otherwise endowed with keen discernment, are infected with this disease.

In this regard how volubly has the whole tribe of philosophers shown their stupidity and silliness! For even though we may excuse the others (who act like utter fools), Plato, the most religious of all and the most circumspect, also vanishes in his round globe. And what might not happen to others when the leading minds, whose task it is to light the pathway for the rest, wander and stumble! It is the same where the governance of human affairs shows providence so manifestly that we cannot deny it; yet we profit no more by it than if we believed that all things were turned topsy-turvy by the heedless will of fortune—so great is our inclination toward vanity and error! I always speak of the most excellent, not of those vulgar folk whose madness in profaning God's truth is beyond measure.

12. The manifestation of God is choked by human superstition and the error of the philosophers

Hence arises that boundless filthy mire of error wherewith the whole earth was filled and covered. For each man's mind is like a labyrinth, so that it is no wonder that individual nations were drawn aside into various falsehoods; and not only this—but individual men, almost, had their own gods. For as rashness and superficiality are joined to ignorance and darkness, scarcely a single person has ever been found who did not fashion for himself an idol or specter in place of God. Surely, just as waters boil up from a vast, full spring, so does an immense crowd of gods flow forth from the human mind, while each one, in wandering about with too much license, wrongly invents this or that about God himself. However, it is not necessary here to draw up a list of the superstitions with which the world has been entangled, because there would be no end to it, and so without a word of them it is sufficiently clear from so many corruptions how horrible is the blindness of the human mind. I pass over the rude and untutored crowd. But among the philosophers who have tried with reason and learning to penetrate into heaven, how shameful is the diversity! As each was furnished with higher wit, graced with art and knowledge, so did he seem to camouflage his utterances; yet if you look more closely upon all these, you will find them all to be fleeting unrealities. The Stoics thought themselves very clear when they said that one could elicit from all parts of nature various names for God, yet without on this account destroying the unity of God—as if, indeed, we were not already more than prone to vanity, without being drawn farther and more violently into error by the multiplicity of gods foisted upon us! Even the mystic theology of the Egyptians shows all have sedulously brooded upon this so as not to appear to rave without reason. And perchance even at first glance something that seemed probable would deceive the simple and careless; but no mortal ever contrived anything that did not basely corrupt religion.

And this very confused diversity emboldened the Epicureans and other crass despisers of piety to cast out all awareness of God. For when they saw the wisest persons contending with contrary opinions, from the disagreements of these—and even from their frivolous or absurd teaching—they did not hesitate to gather that men vainly and foolishly bring torments upon themselves when they seek for a god that is not. And this they thought to do with impunity because it would be preferable to deny outright God's existence than to fashion uncertain gods, and then stir up endless quarrels. But these folk pass a purely foolish judgment, or, rather, they conjure up a cloud out of men's ignorance to conceal their own impiety; in such ignorance there is not the least justification for departing from God. But since all confess that there is nothing concerning which the learned and the unlearned at the same time disagree so much, hence one may conclude that the minds of men which .thus wander in their search after God are more than stupid and blind in the heavenly mysteries. Some praise the reply of Simonides, who, asked by the tyrant Hiero what God was, begged to be given a day to ponder. When on the following day the tyrant asked the same question, he asked for two days more, and after having frequently doubled the number of days, finally answered, "The longer I consider this, the more obscure it seems to me." He wisely indeed suspended judgment on a subject so obscure to himself. Yet hence it appears that if men were taught only by nature, they would hold to nothing certain or solid or clear-cut, but would be so tied to confused principles as to worship an unknown god (cf. Acts 17:23).

(Persistent in error, we are without excuse, 13–15)

13. The Holy Spirit rejects all cults contrived by men

Now we must also hold that all who corrupt pure religion —and this is sure to happen when each is given to his own opinion—separate themselves from the one and only God. Indeed, they will boast that they have something else in mind; but what they intend, or what they have persuaded themselves of, has not much bearing on the matter, seeing that the Holy Spirit pronounces them all to be apostates who in the blindness of their own minds substitute demons in place of God (cf. I Cor. 10:20). For this reason, Paul declares that the Ephesians were without God until they learned from the gospel what it was to worship the true God (Eph. 2:12–13). And this must not be restricted to one people, since elsewhere he states generally that all mortals "became vain in their reasonings" (Rom. 1:21) after the majesty of the Creator had been disclosed to them in the fashioning of the universe. For this reason, Scripture, to make place for the true and only God, condemned as falsehood and lying whatever of divinity had formerly been celebrated among the heathen; nor did any divine presence remain except on Mt. Zion, where the proper knowledge of God continued to flourish (Hab. 2:18, 20). Certainly among the pagans in Christ's lifetime the Samaritans seemed to come closest to true piety; yet we hear from Christ's mouth that they knew not what they worshiped (John 4:22). From this it follows that they were deluded by vain error.

In short, even if not all suffered under crass vices, or fell into open idolatries, yet there was no pure and approved religion, founded upon common understanding alone. For even though few persons did not share in the madness of the common herd, there remains the firm teaching of Paul that the wisdom of God is not understood by the princes of this world (I Cor. 2:8). But if even the most illustrious wander in darkness, what can we say of the dregs? It is therefore no wonder that the Holy Spirit rejects as base all cults contrived through the will of men; for in the heavenly mysteries, opinion humanly conceived, even if it does not always give birth to a great heap of errors, is nevertheless the mother of error. And though nothing more harmful may result, yet to worship an unknown god (cf. Acts 17:23) by chance is no light fault. Nevertheless, by Christ's own statement all who have not been taught from the law what god they ought to worship are guilty in this matter (John 4:22). And surely they who were the best legislators did not progress farther than to hold that religion was founded upon public agreement. Nay, according to Xenophon, Socrates praises the oracle of Apollo, which commanded that every man worship the gods after the manner of his forefathers and according to the custom of his own city. But whence comes this law to mortals that they may by their own authority define what far surpasses the world? Or who could so acquiesce in decrees of his ancestors, or enactments of the people, as to receive without hesitation a god humanly taught him? Each man will stand upon his own judgment rather than subject himself to another's decision. Therefore, since either the custom of the city or the agreement of tradition is too weak and frail a bond of piety to follow in worshiping God, it remains for God himself to give witness of himself from heaven.

14. The manifestation of God in nature speaks to
us in vain

It is therefore in vain that so many burning lamps shine for us in the workmanship of the universe to show forth the glory of its Author. Although they bathe us wholly in their radiance, yet they can of themselves in no way lead us into the right path. Surely they strike some sparks, but before their fuller light shines forth these are smothered. For this reason, the apostle, in that very passage where he calls the worlds the images of things invisible, adds that through faith we understand that they have been fashioned by God's word (Heb. 11:3). He means by this that the invisible divinity is made manifest in such spectacles, but that we have not the eyes to see this unless they be illumined by the inner revelation of God through faith. And where Paul teaches that what is to be known of God is made plain from the creation of the universe (Rom. 1:19), he does not signify such a manifestation as men's discernment can comprehend; but, rather, shows it not to go farther than to render them inexcusable. The same apostle also, even if he somewhere denies that God is to be sought far off, inasmuch as he dwells within us (Acts 17:27), in another place teaches of what avail that sort of nearness is, saying: "In past generations the Lord let the nations follow their own ways. Yet God did not leave himself without witness, sending benefits from heaven, giving rain and fruitful seasons, filling men's hearts with food and gladness" (Acts 14:16–17; vs. 15–16, Vg.). Therefore, although the Lord does not want for testimony while he sweetly attracts men to the knowledge of himself with many and varied kindnesses, they do not cease on this account to follow their own ways, that is, their fatal errors.

15. We have no excuse

But although we lack the natural ability to mount up unto the pure and clear knowledge of God, all excuse is cut off because the fault of dullness is within us. And, indeed, we are not allowed thus to pretend ignorance without our conscience itself always convicting us of both baseness and ingratitude. As if this defense may properly be admitted: for a man to pretend that he lacks ears to hear the truth when there are mute creatures with more than melodious voices to declare it; or for a man to claim that he cannot see with his eyes what eyeless creatures point out to him; or for him to plead feebleness of mind when even irrational creatures give instruction! Therefore we are justly denied every excuse when we stray off as wanderers and vagrants even though everything points out the right way. But, however that may be, yet the fact that men soon corrupt the seed of the knowledge of God, sown in their minds out of the wonderful workmanship of nature (thus preventing it from coming to a good and perfect fruit), must be imputed to their own failing; nevertheless, it is very true that we are not at all sufficiently instructed by this bare and simple testimony which the creatures render splendidly to the glory of God. For at the same time as we have enjoyed a slight taste of the divine from contemplation of the universe, having neglected the true God, we raise up in his stead dreams and specters of our own brains, and attribute to anything else than the true source the praise of righteousness, wisdom, goodness, and power. Moreover, we so obscure or overturn his daily acts by wickedly judging them that we snatch away from them their glory and from their Author his due praise.

CHAPTER VI

SCRIPTURE IS NEEDED AS GUIDE AND TEACHER
FOR ANYONE WHO WOULD COME
TO GOD THE CREATOR

1. God bestows the actual knowledge of himself upon us
only in the Scriptures

That brightness which is borne in upon the eyes of all men both in heaven and on earth is more than enough to withdraw all support from men's ingratitude—just as God, to involve the human race in the same guilt, sets forth to all without exception his presence portrayed in his creatures. Despite this, it is needful that another and better help be added to direct us aright to the very Creator of the universe. It was not in vain, then, that he added the light of his Word by which to become known unto salvation; and he regarded as worthy of this privilege those whom he pleased to gather more closely and intimately to himself. For because he saw the minds of all men tossed and agitated, after he chose the Jews as his very own flock, he fenced them about that they might not sink into oblivion as others had. With good reason he holds us by the same means in the pure knowledge of himself, since otherwise even those who seem to stand firm before all others would soon melt away. Just as old or bleary-eyed men and those with weak vision, if you thrust before them a most beautiful volume, even if they recognize it to be some sort of writing, yet can scarcely construe two words, but with the aid of spectacles will begin to read distinctly; so Scripture, gathering up the otherwise confused knowledge of God in our minds, having dispersed our dullness, clearly shows us the true God. This, therefore, is a special gift, where God, to instruct the church, not merely uses mute teachers but also opens his own most hallowed lips. Not only does he teach the elect to look upon a god, but also shows himself as the God upon whom they are to look. He has from the beginning maintained this plan for his church, so that besides these common proofs he also put forth his Word, which is a more direct and more certain mark whereby he is to be recognized.

(Two sorts of knowledge of God in Scripture)

There is no doubt that Adam, Noah, Abraham, and the rest of the patriarchs with this assistance penetrated to the intimate knowledge of him that in a way distinguished them from unbelievers. I am not yet speaking of the proper doctrine of faith whereby they had been illumined unto the hope of eternal life. For, that they might pass from death to life, it was necessary to recognize God not only as Creator but also as Redeemer, for undoubtedly they arrived at both from the Word. First in order came that kind of knowledge by which one is permitted to grasp who that God is who founded and governs the universe. Then that other inner knowledge was added, which alone quickens dead souls, whereby God is known not only as the Founder of the universe and the sole Author and Ruler of all that is made, but also in the person of the Mediator as the Redeemer. But because we have not yet come to the fall of the world and the corruption of nature, I shall now forego discussion of the remedy. My readers therefore should remember that I am not yet going to discuss that covenant by which God adopted to himself the sons of Abraham, or that part of doctrine which has always separated believers from unbelieving folk, for it was founded in Christ. But here I shall discuss only how we should learn from Scripture that God, the Creator of the universe, can by sure marks be distinguished from all the throng of feigned gods. Then, in due order, that series will lead us to the redemption. We shall derive many testimonies from the New Testament, and other testimonies also from the Law and the Prophets, where express mention is made of Christ. Nevertheless, all things will tend to this end, that God, the Artificer of the universe, is made manifest to us in Scripture, and that what we ought to think of him is set forth there, lest we seek some uncertain deity by devious paths.

2. The Word of God as Holy Scripture

But whether God became known to the patriarchs through oracles and visions or by the work and ministry of men, he put into their minds what they should then hand down to their posterity. At any rate, there is no doubt that firm certainty of doctrine was engraved in their hearts, so that they were convinced and understood that what they had learned proceeded from God. For by his Word, God rendered faith unambiguous forever, a faith that should be superior to all opinion. Finally, in order that truth might abide forever in the world with a continuing succession of teaching and survive through all ages, the same oracles he had given to the patriarchs it was his pleasure to have recorded, as it were, on public tablets. With this intent the law was published, and the prophets afterward added as its interpreters. For even though the use of the law was manifold, as will be seen more clearly in its place, it was especially committed to Moses and all the prophets to teach the way of reconciliation between God and men, whence also Paul calls "Christ the end of the law" (Rom. 10:4). Yet I repeat once more: besides the specific doctrine of faith and repentance that sets forth Christ as Mediator, Scripture adorns with unmistakable marks and tokens the one true God, in that he has created and governs the universe, in order that he may not be mixed up with the throng of false gods. Therefore, however fitting it may be for man seriously to turn his eyes to contemplate God's works, since he has been placed in this most glorious theater to be a spectator of them, it is fitting that he prick up his ears to the Word, the better to profit. And it is therefore no wonder that those who were born in darkness become more and more hardened in their insensibility; for there are very few who, to contain themselves within bounds, apply themselves teachably to God's Word, but they rather exult in their own vanity. Now, in order that true religion may shine upon us, we ought to hold that it must take its beginning from heavenly doctrine and that no one can get even the slightest taste of right and sound doctrine unless he be a pupil of Scripture. Hence, there also emerges the beginning of true understanding when we reverently embrace what it pleases God there to witness of himself. But not only faith, perfect and in every way complete, but all right knowledge of God is born of obedience. And surely in this respect God has, by his singular providence, taken thought for mortals through all ages.

3. Without Scripture we fall into error

Suppose we ponder how slippery is the fall of the human mind into forgetfulness of God, how great the tendency to every kind of error, how great the lust to fashion constantly new and artificial religions. Then we may perceive how necessary was such written proof of the heavenly doctrine, that it should neither perish through forgetfulness nor vanish through error nor be corrupted by the audacity of men. It is therefore clear that God has provided the assistance of the Word for the sake of all those to whom he has been pleased to give useful instruction because he foresaw that his likeness imprinted upon the most beautiful form of the universe would be insufficiently effective. Hence, we must strive onward by this straight path if we seriously aspire to the pure contemplation of God. We must come, I say, to the Word, where God is truly and vividly described to us from his works, while these very works are appraised not by our depraved judgment but by the rule of eternal truth. If we turn aside from the Word, as I have just now said, though we may strive with strenuous haste, yet, since we have got off the track, we shall never reach the goal. For we should so reason that the splendor of the divine countenance, which even the apostle calls "unapproachable" (1 Tim. 6:16), is for us like an inexplicable labyrinth unless we are conducted into it by the thread of the Word; so that it is better to limp along this path than to dash with all speed outside it. David very often, therefore, teaching that we ought to banish superstitions from the earth so that pure religion may flourish, represented God as regnant (Ps. 93:1; 96:10; 97:1; 99:1; and the like). Now he means by the word "regnant" not the power with which he is endowed, and which he exercises in governing the whole of nature, but the doctrine by which he asserts his lawful sovereignty. For errors can never be uprooted from human hearts until true knowledge of God is planted therein.

4. Scripture can communicate to us what the revelation in the creation cannot

Accordingly, the same prophet, after he states, "The heavens declare the glory of God, the firmament shows forth the works of his hands, the ordered succession of days and nights proclaims his majesty" (Ps. 19:1–2 p.), then proceeds to mention his Word: "The law of the Lord is spotless, converting souls; the testimony of the Lord is faithful, giving wisdom to little ones; the righteous acts of the Lord are right, rejoicing hearts; the precept of the Lord is clear, enlightening eyes" (Ps. 18:8–9, Vg.; 19:7–8, EV). For although he also includes other uses of the law, he means in general that, since God in vain calls all peoples to himself by the contemplation of heaven and earth, this is the very school of God's children. Psalm 29 looks to this same end, where the prophet—speaking forth concerning God's awesome voice, which strikes the earth in thunder (v. 3), winds, rains, whirlwinds and tempests, causes mountains to tremble (v. 6), shatters the cedars (v. 5)—finally adds at the end that his praises are sung in the sanctuary because the unbelievers are deaf to all the voices of God that resound in the air (vs. 9–11). Similarly, he thus ends another psalm where he has described the awesome waves of the sea: "Thy testimonies have been verified, the beauty and holiness of thy temple shall endure forevermore" (Ps. 93:5 p.). Hence, also, arises that which Christ said to the Samaritan woman, that her people and all other peoples worshiped they knew not what; that the Jews alone offered worship to the true God (John 4:22). For, since the human mind because of its feebleness can in no way attain to God unless it be aided and assisted by his Sacred Word, all mortals at that time—except for the Jews—because they were seeking God without the Word, had of necessity to stagger about in vanity and error.

CHAPTER VII

SCRIPTURE MUST BE CONFIRMED BY THE WITNESS OF
THE SPIRIT. THUS MAY ITS AUTHORITY BE ESTABLISHED
AS CERTAIN; AND IT IS A WICKED FALSEHOOD THAT
ITS CREDIBILITY DEPENDS ON THE JUDGMENT OF THE
CHURCH

1. Scripture has its authority from God, not from the church

Before I go any farther, it is worth-while to say something about the authority of Scripture,[6] not only to prepare our hearts to reverence it, but to banish all doubt. When that which is set forth is acknowledged to be the Word of God, there is no one so deplorably insolent—unless devoid also both of common sense and of humanity itself—as to dare impugn the credibility of Him who speaks. Now daily oracles are not sent from heaven, for it pleased the Lord to hallow his truth to everlasting remembrance in the Scriptures alone (cf. John 5:39). Hence the Scriptures obtain full authority among believers only when men regard them as having sprung from heaven, as if there the living words of God were heard. This matter is very well worth treating more fully and weighing more carefully. But my readers will pardon me if I regard more what the plan of the present work demands than what the greatness of this matter requires.

But a most pernicious error widely prevails that Scripture has only so much weight as is conceded to it by the consent of the church. As if the eternal and inviolable truth of God depended upon the decision of men! For they mock the Holy Spirit when they ask: Who can convince us that these writings came from God? Who can assure us that Scripture has come down whole and intact even to our very day? Who can

[6] Chapters vii–ix form an excursus on Biblical authority. Both the doctrines of the deity of the Spirit (I. xiii. 14–15) and the redemptive work of the Spirit (Book III, throughout, especially chs. i–ii) form the immediate theological context of the doctrine of the "inner testimony." Calvin refers the reader "elsewhere" (I. vii. 5), but this has often been overlooked.

persuade us to receive one book in reverence but to exclude
another, unless the church prescribe a sure rule for all these
matters? What reverence is due Scripture and what books
ought to be reckoned within its canon depend, they say,
upon the determination of the church. Thus these sacrilegious
men, wishing to impose an unbridled tyranny under the cover
of the church, do not care with what absurdities they ensnare
themselves and others, provided they can force this one idea
upon the simple-minded: that the church has authority in
all things. Yet, if this is so, what will happen to miserable
consciences seeking firm assurance of eternal life if all promises of it consist in and depend solely upon the judgment of
men? Will they cease to vacillate and tremble when they receive such an answer? Again, to what mockeries of the impious is our faith subjected, into what suspicion has it fallen
among all men, if we believe that it has a precarious authority dependent solely upon the good pleasure of men!

2. The church is itself grounded upon Scripture

But such wranglers are neatly refuted by just one word
of the apostle. He testifies that the church is "built upon the
foundation of the prophets and apostles" (Eph. 2:20). If the
teaching of the prophets and apostles is the foundation, this
must have had authority before the church began to exist.
Groundless, too, is their subtle objection that, although the
church took its beginning here, the writings to be attributed
to the prophets and apostles nevertheless remain in doubt
until decided by the church. For if the Christian church was
from the beginning founded upon the writings of the prophets
and the preaching of the apostles, wherever this doctrine is
found, the acceptance of it—without which the church itself
would never have existed—must certainly have preceded the
church. It is utterly vain, then, to pretend that the power of
judging Scripture so lies with the church that its certainty
depends upon churchly assent. Thus, while the church receives and gives its seal of approval to the Scriptures, it does
not thereby render authentic what is otherwise doubtful or
controversial. But because the church recognizes Scripture to
be the truth of its own God, as a pious duty it unhesitatingly
venerates Scripture. As to their question—How can we be assured that this has sprung from God unless we have recourse
to the decree of the church?—it is as if someone asked:
Whence will we learn to distinguish light from darkness, white

from black, sweet from bitter? Indeed, Scripture exhibits
fully as clear evidence of its own truth as white and black
things do of their color, or sweet and bitter things do of their
taste.

3. Augustine cannot be cited as counterevidence

Indeed, I know that statement of Augustine is commonly
referred to, that he would not believe the gospel if the authority of the church did not move him to do so. But it is easy to
grasp from the context how wrongly and deceptively they
interpret this passage. Augustine was there concerned with
the Manichees, who wished to be believed without controversy when they claimed, but did not demonstrate, that
they themselves possessed the truth. Because in fact they
used the gospel as a cloak to promote faith in their Mani,
Augustine asks: "What would they do if they were to light
upon a man who does not even believe in the gospel? By what
kind of persuasion would they bring him around to their opinion?" Then he adds, "Indeed, I would not believe the gospel,"
etc., meaning that if he were alien to the faith, he could not
be led to embrace the gospel as the certain truth of God unless constrained by the authority of the church. And what
wonder if someone, not yet having known Christ, should have
respect for men! Augustine is not, therefore, teaching that
the faith of godly men is founded on the authority of the
church; nor does he hold the view that the certainty of the
gospel depends upon it. He is simply teaching that there
would be no certainty of the gospel for unbelievers to win
them to Christ if the consensus of the church did not impel
them. And this he clearly confirms a little later, saying: "When
I praise what I believe, and laugh at what you believe, how
do you think we are to judge, or what are we to do? Should
we not forsake those who invite us to a knowledge of things
certain and then bid us believe things uncertain? Must we
follow those who invite us first to believe what we are not
yet strong enough to see, that, strengthened by this very
faith, we may become worthy to comprehend what we believe (Col. 1:4-11, 23)—with God himself, not men, now
inwardly strengthening and illumining our mind?"

These are Augustine's very words. From them it is easy for
anyone to infer that the holy man's intention was not to make
the faith that we hold in the Scriptures depend upon the assent or judgment of the church. He only meant to indicate

what we also confess as true: those who have not yet been illumined by the Spirit of God are rendered teachable by reverence for the church, so that they may persevere in learning faith in Christ from the gospel. Thus, he avers, the authority of the church is an introduction through which we are prepared for faith in the gospel. For, as we see, he wants the certainty of the godly to rest upon a far different foundation. I do not deny that elsewhere, when he wishes to defend Scripture, which they repudiate, he often presses the Manichees with the consensus of the whole church. Hence, he reproaches Faustus for not submitting to the gospel truth —so firm, so stable, celebrated with such glory, and handed down from the time of the apostles through a sure succession. But it never occurs to him to teach that the authority which we ascribe to Scripture depends upon the definition or decree of men. He puts forward only the universal judgment of the church, in which he was superior to his adversaries, because of its very great value in this case. If anyone desires a fuller proof of this, let him read Augustine's little book *The Usefulness of Belief*. There he will find that the author recommends no other inducement to believe except what may provide us with an approach and be a suitable beginning for inquiry, as he himself says; yet we should not acquiesce in mere opinion, but should rely on sure and firm truth.

4. The witness of the Holy Spirit: this is stronger than all proof

We ought to remember what I said a bit ago: credibility of doctrine is not established until we are persuaded beyond doubt that God is its Author. Thus, the highest proof of Scripture derives in general from the fact that God in person speaks in it. The prophets and apostles do not boast either of their keenness or of anything that obtains credit for them as they speak; nor do they dwell upon rational proofs. Rather, they bring forward God's holy name, that by it the whole world may be brought into obedience to him. Now we ought to see how apparent it is not only by plausible opinion but by clear truth that they do not call upon God's name heedlessly or falsely. If we desire to provide in the best way for our consciences—that they may not be perpetually beset by the instability of doubt or vacillation, and that they may not also boggle at the smallest quibbles—we ought to seek our conviction in a higher place than human reasons, judgments, or conjectures, that is, in the secret testimony of the Spirit. True, if we wished to proceed by arguments, we might advance many things that would easily prove—if there is any god in heaven—that the law, the prophets, and the gospel come from him. Indeed, ever so learned men, endowed with the highest judgment, rise up in opposition and bring to bear and display all their mental powers in this debate. Yet, unless they become hardened to the point of hopeless impudence, this confession will be wrested from them: that they see manifest signs of God speaking in Scripture. From this it is clear that the teaching of Scripture is from heaven. And a little later we shall see that all the books of Sacred Scripture far surpass all other writings. Yes, if we turn pure eyes and upright senses toward it, the majesty of God will immediately come to view, subdue our bold rejection, and compel us to obey.

Yet they who strive to build up firm faith in Scripture through disputation are doing things backwards. For my part, although I do not excel either in great dexterity or eloquence, if I were struggling against the most crafty sort of despisers of God, who seek to appear shrewd and witty in disparaging Scripture, I am confident it would not be difficult for me to silence their clamorous voices. And if it were a useful labor to refute their cavils, I would with no great trouble shatter the boasts they mutter in their lurking places. But even if anyone clears God's Sacred Word from man's evil speaking, he will not at once imprint upon their hearts that certainty which piety requires. Since for unbelieving men religion seems to stand by opinion alone, they, in order not to believe anything foolishly or lightly, both wish and demand rational proof that Moses and the prophets spoke divinely. But I reply: the testimony of the Spirit is more excellent than all reason. For as God alone is a fit witness of himself in his Word, so also the Word will not find acceptance in men's hearts before it is sealed by the inward testimony of the Spirit. The same Spirit, therefore, who has spoken through the mouths of the prophets must penetrate into our hearts to persuade us that they faithfully proclaimed what had been divinely commanded. Isaiah very aptly expresses this connection in these words: "My Spirit which is in you, and the words that I have put in your mouth, and the mouths of your offspring, shall never fail" (Isa. 59:21 p.). Some good folk are annoyed that a clear proof is not ready at hand when the impious, unpunished, murmur against God's Word. As if the Spirit were not called both "seal" and "guarantee" (II Cor. 1:22) for confirming the faith of the godly; because until he illumines their minds, they ever waver among many doubts!

5. Scripture bears its own authentication

Let this point therefore stand: that those whom the Holy Spirit has inwardly taught truly rest upon Scripture, and that Scripture indeed is self-authenticated; hence, it is not right to subject it to proof and reasoning. And the certainty it deserves with us, it attains by the testimony of the Spirit. For even if it wins reverence for itself by its own majesty, it seriously affects us only when it is sealed upon our hearts through the Spirit. Therefore, illumined by his power, we believe neither by our own nor by anyone else's judgment that Scripture is from God; but above human judgment we affirm with utter certainty (just as if we were gazing upon the majesty of God himself) that it has flowed to us from the very mouth of God by the ministry of men. We seek no proofs, no marks of genuineness upon which our judgment may lean; but we subject our judgment and wit to it as to a thing far beyond any guesswork! This we do, not as persons accustomed to seize upon some unknown thing, which, under closer scrutiny, displeases them, but fully conscious that we hold the unassailable truth! Nor do we do this as those miserable men who habitually bind over their minds to the thralldom of superstition; but we feel that the undoubted power of his divine majesty lives and breathes there. By this power we are drawn and inflamed, knowingly and willingly, to obey him, yet also more vitally and more effectively than by mere human willing or knowing!

God, therefore, very rightly proclaims through Isaiah that the prophets together with the whole people are witnesses to him; for they, instructed by prophecies, unhesitatingly held that God has spoken without deceit or ambiguity (Isa. 43:10). Such, then, is a conviction that requires no reasons; such, a knowledge with which the best reason agrees—in which the mind truly reposes more securely and constantly than in any reasons; such, finally, a feeling that can be born only of heavenly revelation. I speak of nothing other than what each believer experiences within himself—though my words fall far beneath a just explanation of the matter.

I now refrain from saying more, since I shall have opportunity to discuss this matter elsewhere. Let us, then, know that the only true faith is that which the Spirit of God seals in our hearts. Indeed, the modest and teachable reader will be content with this one reason: Isaiah promised all the children of the renewed church that "they would be God's disciples" (Isa. 54:13 p.). God deems worthy of singular privilege only his elect, whom he distinguishes from the human race as a whole. Indeed, what is the beginning of true doctrine but a prompt eagerness to hearken to God's voice? But God asks to be heard through the mouth of Moses, as it is written: "Say not in your heart, who will ascend into heaven, or who will descend into the abyss: behold, the word is in your mouth" (conflation of Deut. 30:12, 14 and Ps. 107:26; 106:26, Vg.). If God has willed this treasure of understanding to be hidden from his children, it is no wonder or absurdity that the multitude of men are so ignorant and stupid! Among the "multitude" I include even certain distinguished folk, until they become engrafted into the body of the church. Besides, Isaiah, warning that the prophetic teaching would be beyond belief, not only to foreigners but also to the Jews who wanted to be reckoned as members of the Lord's household, at the same time adds the reason: "The arm of God will not be revealed" to all (Isa. 53:1 p.). Whenever, then, the fewness of believers disturbs us, let the converse come to mind, that only those to whom it is given can comprehend the mysteries of God (cf. Matt. 13:11).

CHAPTER VIII

SO FAR AS HUMAN REASON GOES, SUFFICIENTLY FIRM PROOFS ARE AT HAND TO ESTABLISH THE CREDIBILITY OF SCRIPTURE

(*The unique majesty and impressiveness, and the high antiquity, of Scripture, 1–4*)

1. Scripture is superior to all human wisdom

Unless this certainty, higher and stronger than any human judgment, be present, it will be vain to fortify the authority of Scripture by arguments, to establish it by common agreement of the church, or to confirm it with other helps. For unless this foundation is laid, its authority will always remain in doubt. Conversely, once we have embraced it devoutly as its dignity deserves, and have recognized it to be above the common sort of things, those arguments—not strong enough before to engraft and fix the certainty of Scripture in our minds—become very useful aids. What wonderful confirmation ensues when, with keener study, we ponder the economy of the divine wisdom, so well ordered and disposed; the completely heavenly character of its doctrine, savoring of nothing earthly; the beautiful agreement of all the parts with one another—as well as such other qualities as can gain majesty for the writings. But our hearts are more firmly grounded when we reflect that we are captivated with admiration for Scripture more by grandeur of subjects than by grace of language. For it was also not without God's extraordinary providence that the sublime mysteries of the Kingdom of Heaven came to be expressed largely in mean and lowly words, lest, if they had been adorned with more shining eloquence, the impious would scoffingly have claimed that its power is in the realm of eloquence alone. Now since such uncultivated and almost rude simplicity inspires greater reverence for itself than any eloquence, what ought one to conclude except that the force of the truth of Sacred Scripture is manifestly too powerful to need the art of words? Therefore the apostle rightly contends that the faith of the Corinthians was founded "upon God's power, not upon human wisdom" (I Cor. 2:5 p.) because his own preaching among them commended itself "not in persuasive words of human wisdom but in demonstration of the Spirit and of might" (ch. 2:4 p.). For truth is cleared of all doubt when, not sustained by external props, it serves as its own support.

Now this power which is peculiar to Scripture is clear from the fact that of human writings, however artfully polished, there is none capable of affecting us at all comparably. Read Demosthenes or Cicero; read Plato, Aristotle, and others of that tribe. They will, I admit, allure you, delight you, move you, enrapture you in wonderful measure. But betake yourself from them to this sacred reading. Then, in spite of yourself, so deeply will it affect you, so penetrate your heart, so fix itself in your very marrow, that, compared with its deep impression, such vigor as the orators and philosophers have will nearly vanish. Consequently, it is easy to see that the Sacred Scriptures, which so far surpass all gifts and graces of human endeavor, breathe something divine.

2. Not style but content is decisive

Indeed, I admit that some of the prophets had an elegant and clear, even brilliant, manner of speaking, so that their eloquence yields nothing to secular writers; and by such examples the Holy Spirit wished to show that he did not lack eloquence while he elsewhere used a rude and unrefined style. But whether you read David, Isaiah, and the like, whose speech flows sweet and pleasing, or Amos the herds-man, Jeremiah, and Zechariah, whose harsher style savors of rusticity, that majesty of the Spirit of which I have spoken will be evident everywhere. And I am not unaware that Satan is in many ways an imitator of God, in order by a false likeness to insinuate himself into the minds of simple folk. He has thus cleverly sowed, by uncultivated and even barbarous language, impious errors and by them has deceived miserable men. He has often made use of obsolete forms of speech, that under this mask he may cloak his impostures. But all men endowed with moderate sense see how empty and loathsome is this affectation. As far as Sacred Scripture is concerned, however much froward men try to gnaw at it, nevertheless it clearly is crammed with thoughts that could not be humanly conceived. Let each of the prophets be looked into: none will be found who does not far exceed human measure. Consequently, those for whom prophetic doctrine is tasteless ought to be thought of as lacking taste buds.

3. The great antiquity of Scripture

Others have dealt with this argument at length; it will therefore be enough to select for the present only a few main details that summarize the whole matter. Besides those points which I have already touched upon, the very antiquity of Scripture has no slight weight. For however much Greek writers may talk about the Egyptian theology, no monument of any religion is extant that is not far later than the age of Moses. And Moses devised no new god, but rather set forth what the Israelites had accepted concerning the eternal God handed down by the patriarchs age after age. For what else does he do but call them back to the covenant begun with Abraham (Gen. 17:7)? Had he, however, brought forward something unheard of, it would not have been approved. But their liberation from the slavery in which they were held must have been a matter of such common knowledge that the very mention of it would immediately arouse the minds of all. Indeed, it is likely that they had been taught concerning the four-hundred-year period (Gen. 15:13; Ex. 12:40; Gal. 3:17). Now, if Moses (who nevertheless is so much earlier in time than all other writers) traced the transmission of his doctrine back to such a remote source, we must ponder how much Sacred Scripture outstrips all other writings in antiquity.

4. The truthfulness of Scripture shown by Moses' example

Unless, perhaps, one chooses to believe the Egyptians, who extend their antiquity to six thousand years before the creation of the world! But since their garrulity was always held in derision, even by every secular writer, there is no reason for me to toil in refuting it. Moreover, Josephus cites, in his *Against Apion*, testimonies out of very ancient writers worth recalling, from which one may conclude that by the agreement of all nations the doctrine set forth in the law was renowned from the remotest ages, even though it was neither read nor truly known.

Now to prevent any suspicion from persisting among the malicious, and to remove any occasion for the wicked to quibble, God meets both dangers with the best of remedies. While Moses recalls what Jacob almost three hundred years before had declared under heavenly inspiration concerning his posterity, does he in any way ennoble his tribe? No—he brands it with eternal infamy in the person of Levi! "Simeon and Levi," says he, "are vessels of iniquity: may my soul not enter into their counsel, nor my tongue into their secret place." (Gen. 49:5–6 p.) Surely he could have remained silent about that shame, not only to spare his father, but also not to besmirch himself and his whole family with part of the same ignominy. How could Moses be suspected, who first preached to the family from which he had sprung that their progenitor was utterly detestable to the oracle of the Holy Spirit, and who did not think of his own personal interests or refuse to suffer the odium of his relations for whom this was doubtless an annoyance? Also, when he recalls the wicked murmuring of his brother Aaron and his sister Miriam (Num. 12:1), shall we say that he speaks from the feeling of his flesh, or that he is obedient to the command of the Holy Spirit? Moreover, since his was the highest authority, why did he not at least leave the right of the high priest to his sons, but instead relegate them to the lowest place? I select only a few instances out of many; but in the law itself, here and there, we will meet many proofs that vindicate the full assurance that Moses undoubtedly came forth like an angel of God from heaven.

(*Refutation of objections regarding miracles and prophecy, 5–10*)

5. Miracles strengthen the authority of God's messengers

Now these very numerous and remarkable miracles which he relates are so many confirmations of the law that he has delivered, and of the doctrine that he has published. For—that he was borne up into the mountain in a cloud; that there he was without human fellowship for forty days (Ex. 24:18); that in the very promulgation of the law his face shone like the rays of the sun (Ex. 34:29); that lightnings flashed round about, thunders and crashes were heard throughout the heavens, and a trumpet blown by no human mouth resounded (Ex. 19:16); that the entrance to the Tabernacle, covered by a cloud, was hidden from the people's view (Ex. 40:34); that by the dreadful death of Korah, Dathan, and Abiram, and their whole wicked faction, his authority was most marvelously vindicated (Num. 16:24); that the rock struck by his rod straightway brought forth a river (Num. 20:10–11; Ex. 17:6; cf. I Cor. 10:4); that manna rained from heaven at his prayer (Num. 11:9; Ex. 16:13; cf. I Cor. 10:3)—by these was not God, from heaven, commending Moses as his undoubted prophet? If anyone should object that I am taking as fact what is controversial, this subtle objection is easy to answer. Inasmuch as Moses published all these things before the congregation, among eyewitnesses of the events what opportunity was there for fraud? Moses would, of course, have appeared before the people, rebuked them for their unfaithfulness, obstinacy, ungratefulness, and other offenses, and then would have boasted that under their very eyes his doctrine had been authenticated by miracles that they had never seen!

6. Moses' miracles are incontestable

For this is also worth noting: every time he tells of miracles, at the same time there are disagreeably conjoined things that could stir up the whole people to contradict loudly if the slightest occasion had presented itself. From this it is clear that they have been led to assent solely because they were quite enough convinced by their own experience. But since the matter was too manifest for secular writers to be free to deny that Moses performed miracles, the father of lies slanderously attributed them to magic arts (cf. Ex. 7:11 or 9:11). Moses shrank so much from this superstition as to order that anyone who merely consulted magicians and soothsayers should be stoned to death (Lev. 20:6). By what conjecture then do they make him out to have been a magician? Surely any impostor plies his legerdemain in an effort to overwhelm the minds of the multitude to snatch renown. But what about Moses? Proclaiming that he and his brother Aaron are nothing but only following what God has laid down (Ex. 16:7), he sufficiently wipes away every mark of reproach. Now if the events themselves be considered, what sort of incantation could cause manna daily raining from heaven to provide sufficient food for the people: if anyone had more than his due measure stored up, to teach him from its very putrefaction that his unbelief was divinely punished (Ex. 16:19–20)? Besides, God allows his servant so to be tested by many severe proofs that the wicked may now have no success in clamoring against him. Sometimes the whole people rose up in their pride and insolence; sometimes certain ones among them conspired in an attempt to overthrow God's holy servant. How, then, could Moses by legerdemain have escaped this fury of theirs? And the outcome plainly bears out that in this way his doctrine was sanctioned for all time.

7. Prophecies that are fulfilled contrary to all human expectation

In addition, who can deny that the prophetic spirit, in the person of the patriarch Jacob, caused the primacy to be assigned to the tribe of Judah (Gen. 49:10)—especially if we take the act itself into account, as its outcome has proved? Picture Moses as the first author of this prophecy. Yet from the time that this writing was recorded, four hundred years passed during which there was no mention of a scepter in the tribe of Judah. After the consecration of Saul (I Sam. 11:15), the royal power seems to have resided in the tribe of Benjamin. When David was anointed by Samuel (I Sam. 16:13), what visible reason was there for the transference of the kingly power? Who would have anticipated that a king was to come forth from the lowly house of a herdsman? And since there were seven brothers in the family, who would have marked the youngest for the honor? How could he have any hope of the Kingdom? Who would say that his anointing had been determined by human art or effort or prudence, and was not rather the fulfillment of heavenly prophecy? Similarly, Moses foretells things, albeit obscurely, concerning the election of the Gentiles into God's covenant (Gen. 49:10), which actually took place almost two thousand years later. Is this not plain proof that he spoke by divine inspiration? I omit other predictions, which so clearly breathe the divine revelation as to convince sane men that it is God who speaks. In brief, Moses' one song (Deut., ch. 32) is a bright mirror in which God is manifest.

8. God has confirmed the prophetic words

But in the remaining prophets it is now discerned even more clearly. I will select only a few examples, for to gather all of them together would be too toilsome. Although in the time of Isaiah the Kingdom of Judah was at peace, and perhaps even regarded itself as somewhat under the Chaldeans' protection, Isaiah spoke publicly of the fall of the city and the exile of the people (Isa. 39:6–7). Let us grant that to predict, long before, what at the time seemed incredible but at last actually came to pass was not yet a clear enough token of divine inspiration. Yet from what source but God shall we say have come those prophecies which Isaiah at the same time utters concerning release? He names Cyrus (Isa. 45:1) through whom the Chaldeans had to be conquered and the people set free. More than a hundred years elapsed from the time the prophet so prophesied and the time Cyrus was born; for the latter was born about a hundred years after the prophet's death. No one could have divined then that there was to be a man named Cyrus who would wage war with the Babylonians, would subdue such a powerful monarchy, and terminate the exile of the people of Israel. Does not this bare narrative, without any verbal embellishment, plainly show the things Isaiah recounts to be undoubted oracles of God, not the conjectures of a man? Again, when Jeremiah, some time before the people were led away into exile, set the duration of the captivity at seventy years and indicated the return and liberation (Jer. 25:11–12; 29:10), must not his tongue have been under the guidance of the Spirit of God? How shameless will it be to say that the authority of the prophets has not been confirmed by such proofs, and that what they boast, to claim credibility for their own words, has not so far been fulfilled! "Behold, the former things have come to pass, . . . new things I declare; before they spring forth I point them out to you." (Isa. 42:9, Comm.) I pass over the fact that Jeremiah and Ezekiel, far apart yet prophesying at the same time, in all their statements commonly agreed as if each had dictated the other's words. What of Daniel? Did he not so clothe his prophecies of future events almost to the six hundredth year as if he were writing a history of past events generally known? If godly men take these things to heart, they will be abundantly equipped to restrain the barking of ungodly men; for this is a proof too clear to be open to any subtle objections.

9. *The transmission of the law is to be trusted*

I know what certain rascals bawl out in corners in order to display the keenness of their wit in assailing God's truth. For they ask, Who assures us that the books that we read under the names of Moses and the prophets were written by them? They even dare question whether there ever was a Moses. Yet if anyone were to call in doubt whether there ever was a Plato, an Aristotle, or a Cicero, who would not say that such folly ought to be chastised with the fist or the lash? The law of Moses was wonderfully preserved by heavenly providence rather than by human effort. And although by priests' negligence the law lay buried for a short time, after godly King Josiah found it (II Kings 22:8; cf. II Chron. 34:15), it continued to be read age after age. Indeed, Josiah did not put it forward as something unknown or new, but as something that had always been of common knowledge, the memory of which was then famous. The archetypal roll was committed to the Temple; a copy was made from it and designated for the royal archives (Deut. 17:18–19). What had happened was merely this: the priests had ceased to publish the law itself according to the solemn custom, and the people themselves also had neglected the habit of reading it. Why is it that almost no age goes by in which its sanction is not confirmed and renewed? Was Moses unknown to those who were versed in David? But, to generalize concerning all sacred authors, it is absolutely certain that their writings passed down to posterity in but one way: from hand to hand. Some had heard their actual words; others learned that they had so spoken from hearers whose memories were still fresh.

10. God has marvelously preserved the Law and the Prophets

Indeed, the passage in the history of the Maccabees that they put forth in order to detract from the authenticity of Scripture is such that nothing more appropriate could be thought of to establish it. Yet first let us wipe away their pretenses; then we shall turn back upon them the siege engine they are erecting against us. Since Antiochus (they say) ordered all books to be burned (I Macc. 1:56–57), where did the copies that we now have come from? But I, in turn, ask, In what workshop could they have been fabricated so quickly? For it is well known that directly after the persecutions had ceased, the books were extant, and were acknowledged without controversy by all the godly, who were brought up on their doctrine and knew them intimately. But even though all wicked men, as if conspiring together, have so shamelessly insulted the Jews, no one has ever dared charge them with substituting false books. For whatever, in their opinion, the Jewish religion may be, they confess Moses to be its author. What but their own more than canine shamelessness do these babblers betray when they utter the lie that these books (whose sacred antiquity is confirmed by the agreement of all histories) are spurious? But not to expend further effort uselessly in refuting such filthy calumnies, let us rather ponder here how much care the Lord has taken to preserve his Word, when, contrary to everybody's expectation, he snatched it away from a most cruel and savage tyrant, as from a raging fire. Let us consider how he armed godly priests and others with so great constancy that they did not hesitate to transmit to their posterity this treasure redeemed, if necessary, at the expense of their own lives; and how he frustrated the whole fierce book hunt of rulers and their minions. Who does not recognize as a remarkable and wonderful work of God the fact that those sacred monuments, which the wicked had persuaded themselves had utterly perished, soon returned and took their former place once more, and even with enhanced dignity? For the Greek translation followed, which published them abroad throughout the world.

The miracle appeared not only in that God delivered the Tables of his covenant from the bloody edicts of Antiochus, but also in that the Jewish people, ground down and wasted by such manifold misfortunes, were soon almost exterminated, yet the writings remained safe and intact. The Hebrew language lay not only unesteemed, but almost unknown; and to be sure, if God had not been pleased to care for their religion, it would have perished completely. For after the Jews were brought back from exile, how much they departed from the true use of the mother tongue appears from the prophets of that age, a fact worth noting because from this comparison one more clearly perceives the antiquity of the Law and the Prophets. And through whom did God preserve for us the doctrine of salvation embraced in the Law and the Prophets, that Christ in his own time might be made manifest (Matt. 22:37–40)? Through the Jews, Christ's most violent enemies, whom Augustine justly calls the "bookmen" of the Christian church, because they have furnished us with reading matter of which they themselves do not make use.

(Simplicity and heavenly character and authority of the New Testament, 11)

11. Next, if one comes to the New Testament, with what solid props its truth is supported! Three Evangelists recount their history in a humble and lowly style; for many proud folk this simplicity arouses contempt. This is because they do not pay attention to the chief divisions of doctrine from which it would be easy to infer that the Evangelists are discussing heavenly mysteries above human capacity. Surely all who are endowed with a drop of sincere modesty, on reading the first chapter of Luke, will be made ashamed. Now Christ's discourses, briefly summarized by those three Evangelists, readily clear their writings of all contempt. But John, thundering from the heights, lays low more mightily than any thunderbolt the obstinacy of those whom he does not impel

to the obedience of faith. Let all those sharp-nosed fault-finders—whose highest desire is to drive the reverence for Scripture from their own and others' hearts—come into the open. Let them read John's Gospel: whether they want to or not, there they shall find a thousand sayings to arouse, at least, their dull minds—nay, I should rather say, to burn a dreadful brand upon their consciences for the restraint of their mockery. The same thing applies to Paul and Peter. Although most men are blind to their writings, yet the very heavenly majesty therein holds all men closely attached and as it were bound to itself. But this one fact raises their doctrine more than enough above the world: Matthew, previously tied to the gain of his table, Peter and John going about in their boats—all of them rude, uneducated men—had learned nothing in the school of men that they could pass on to others. Paul, not only a sworn but fierce and murderous enemy, was converted into a new man; this sudden and un-hoped-for change shows that he was compelled by heavenly authority to affirm a doctrine that he had assailed. Let these dogs deny that the Holy Spirit came down upon the apostles; or even let them discredit history. Yet the truth cries out openly that these men who, previously contemptible among common folk, suddenly began to discourse so gloriously of the heavenly mysteries must have been instructed by the Spirit.

(Consent of the church, and fidelity of the martyrs, 12–13)

12. Unvarying testimony of the church to the Scripture

Besides this, there are other very good reasons why the consent of the church should not be denied its due weight. Since the publication of Scripture, age after age agreed to obey it steadfastly and harmoniously. By countless wondrous means Satan with the whole world has tried either to oppress it or overturn it, to obscure and obliterate it utterly from the memory of men—yet, like the palm, it has risen ever higher and has remained unassailable. Indeed, there has scarcely ever been either a sophist or rhetorician of superior ability who did not try his power against it; yet all were unsuccessful. Such facts as these should be accounted of no slight importance. The whole power of earth has armed itself to destroy it, yet all these efforts have gone up in smoke. How could it, assailed so strongly from every side, have resisted if it had relied upon human protection alone? Rather, by this very fact it is proved to be from God, because, with all human efforts striving against it, still it has of its own power thus far prevailed. Besides this, it is not one state, not one people, that has agreed to receive and embrace it; but, as far and as wide as the earth extends, it has obtained its authority by the holy concord of divers peoples, who otherwise had nothing in common among themselves. Such agreement of minds, so disparate and otherwise disagreeing in everything among themselves, ought to move us greatly, since it is clear that this agreement is brought about by nothing else than the divine will. Yet no little weight is added thereto when we observe the godliness of those who so agree, not of all, indeed, but of those whom the Lord has made to shine as lamps in his church.

13. Martyrs died firmly for Scripture doctrine

Now with what assurance ought we to enlist under that doctrine which we see confirmed and attested by the blood of so many holy men! They, having once received it, did not hesitate, courageously and intrepidly, and even with great eagerness, to suffer death for it. Should we not accept with sure and unshaken conviction what has been handed on to us with such a pledge? It is no moderate approbation of Scripture that it has been sealed by the blood of so many witnesses, especially when we reflect that they died to render testimony to the faith; not with fanatic excess (as erring spirits are sometimes accustomed to do), but with a firm and constant, yet sober, zeal toward God.

There are other reasons, neither few nor weak, for which the dignity and majesty of Scripture are not only affirmed in godly hearts, but brilliantly vindicated against the wiles of its disparagers; yet of themselves these are not strong enough to provide a firm faith, until our Heavenly Father, revealing his majesty there, lifts reverence for Scripture beyond the realm of controversy. Therefore Scripture will ultimately suffice for a saving knowledge of God only when its certainty is founded upon the inward persuasion of the Holy Spirit. Indeed, these human testimonies which exist to confirm it will not be vain if, as secondary aids to our feebleness, they follow that chief and highest testimony. But those who wish to prove to unbelievers that Scripture is the Word of God are acting foolishly, for only by faith can this be known. Augustine therefore justly warns that godliness and peace of mind ought to come first if a man is to understand anything of such great matters.

——————— ——————— ———————

BOOK III, CHAPTER II

FAITH: ITS DEFINITION SET FORTH, AND

ITS PROPERTIES EXPLAINED

(The object of faith is Christ, 1)

1. But it will be easy to understand all these matters after a clearer definition of faith has been presented, to enable our readers to grasp its force and nature. We may well recall here what was explained before: First, God lays down for us through the law what we should do; if we then fail in any part of it, that dreadful sentence of eternal death which it pronounces will rest upon us. Secondly, it is not only hard, but above our strength and beyond all our abilities, to fulfill the law to the letter; thus, if we look to ourselves only, and ponder what condition we deserve, no trace of good hope will remain; but cast away by God, we shall lie under eternal death. Thirdly, it has been explained that there is but one means of liberation that can rescue us from such miserable calamity: the appearance of Christ the Redeemer, through whose hand the Heavenly Father, pitying us out of his infinite goodness and mercy, willed to help us; if, indeed, with firm faith we embrace this mercy and rest in it with steadfast hope.

But now we ought to examine what this faith ought to be like, through which those adopted by God as his children come to possess the Heavenly Kingdom, since it is certain that no mere opinion or even persuasion is capable of bringing so great a thing to pass. And we must scrutinize and investigate the true character of faith with greater care and zeal because many are dangerously deluded today in this respect. Indeed, most people, when they hear this term, understand nothing deeper than a common assent to the gospel history. In fact, when faith is discussed in the schools, they call God simply the object of faith, and by fleeting speculations, as we have elsewhere stated, lead miserable souls astray rather than direct them to a definite goal. For, since "God dwells in inaccessible light" (I Tim. 6:16), Christ must become our intermediary. Hence, he calls himself "the light of the world" (John 8:12), and elsewhere, "the way, the truth, and the life"; for no one comes to the Father, who is "the fountain of life" (Ps. 36:9), except through him (John 14:6) because he alone knows the Father, and afterward the believers to whom he wishes to reveal him (Luke 10:22). On this ground, Paul declares that he considers nothing worth knowing save Christ (I Cor. 2:2). In the twentieth chapter of Acts he relates that he has preached "faith in . . . Christ" (v. 21). And in another passage he has Christ speak as follows: "I shall send you among the Gentiles . . . , that they may receive forgiveness of sins and a place among the saints through faith that is in me" (Acts 26:17–18). And Paul testifies that the glory of God is visible to us in His person, or—what amounts to the same thing—that the enlightening knowledge of the glory of God shines in His face (II Cor. 4:6).

Indeed, it is true that faith looks to one God. But this must also be added, "To know Jesus Christ whom he has sent" (John 17:3). For God would have remained hidden afar off if Christ's splendor had not beamed upon us. For this purpose the Father laid up with his only-begotten Son all that he had to reveal himself in Christ so that Christ, by communicating his Father's benefits, might express the true image of his glory (cf. Heb. 1:3). It has been said that we must be drawn by the Spirit to be aroused to seek Christ; so, in turn, we must be warned that the invisible Father is to be sought solely in this image. Augustine has finely spoken of this matter: in discussing the goal of faith, he teaches that we must know our destination and the way to it. Then, immediately after, he infers that the way that is most fortified against all errors is he who was both God and man: namely, as God he is the destination to which we move; as man, the path by which we go. Both are found in Christ alone. But, while Paul proclaims faith in God, he does not have in mind to overturn what he so often emphasizes concerning faith: namely, that all its stability rests in Christ. Peter, indeed, most effectively connects both, saying that through him we believe in God (I Peter 1:21).

(Faith involves knowledge; the true doctrine obscured by the Scholastic notion of implicit faith, 2–5)

2. Faith rests upon knowledge, not upon pious ignorance

This evil, then, like innumerable others, must be attributed to the Schoolmen, who have, as it were, drawn a veil over Christ to hide him. Unless we look straight toward him, we shall wander through endless labyrinths.

But besides wearing down the whole force of faith and almost annihilating it by their obscure definition, they have fabricated the fiction of "implicit faith." Bedecking the grossest ignorance with this term, they ruinously delude poor, miserable folk. Furthermore, to state truly and frankly the real fact of the matter, this fiction not only buries but utterly destroys true faith. Is this what believing means—to understand nothing, provided only that you submit your feeling obediently to the church? Faith rests not on ignorance, but on knowledge. And this is, indeed, knowledge not only of God but of the divine will. We do not obtain salvation either because we are prepared to embrace as true whatever the church has prescribed, or because we turn over to it the task of inquiring and knowing. But we do so when we know that God is our merciful Father, because of reconciliation effected through Christ (II Cor. 5:18–19), and that Christ has been given to us as righteousness, sanctification, and life. By this knowledge, I say, not by submission of our feeling, do we obtain entry into the Kingdom of Heaven. For when the apostle says, "With the heart a man believes unto righteousness, with the mouth makes confession unto salvation" (Rom. 10:10, cf. Vg.), he indicates that it is not enough for a man implicitly to believe what he does not understand or even investigate. But he requires explicit recognition of the divine goodness upon which our righteousness rests.

3. The Roman doctrine of "implicit" faith is basically false

Indeed, I do not deny—such is the ignorance with which we are surrounded—that most things are now implicit for us, and will be so until, laying aside the weight of the flesh, we come nearer to the presence of God. In these matters we can do nothing better than suspend judgment, and hearten ourselves to hold unity with the church. But on this pretext it would be the height of absurdity to label ignorance tempered by humility "faith"! For faith consists in the knowledge of God and Christ (John 17:3), not in reverence for the church. We see the sort of labyrinth they have constructed with this "implication" of theirs! Anything at all, provided it be palmed off on them under the label "church"—sometimes even the most frightful errors—the untutored indiscriminately seize upon as an oracle. This heedless gullibility, although it is the very brink of ruin, yet is excused by them; only on condition that "such is the faith of the church" does it definitely believe anything. Thus they fancy that in error they possess truth; in darkness, light; in ignorance, right knowledge.

But let us not tarry longer over refuting them; we merely admonish the reader to compare these doctrines with ours. The very clarity of truth itself will of itself provide a sufficiently ready refutation. For they do not ask whether faith is wrapped in many remnants of ignorance, but define right believers as those who go numb in their own ignorance, and even brag about it, provided they give assent to the authority and judgment of the church in things unknown to them. As if Scripture does not regularly teach that understanding is joined with faith!

4. Even right faith is always surrounded by error and unbelief

We certainly admit that so long as we dwell as strangers in the world there is such a thing as implicit faith; not only because many things are as yet hidden from us, but because surrounded by many clouds of errors we do not comprehend everything. The height of wisdom for the most perfect is to go forward and, quietly and humbly, to strive still further. Therefore Paul exhorts believers that, if some disagree with others in any matter, they should wait for revelation (Phil. 3:15). Experience obviously teaches that until we put off the flesh we attain less than we should like. And in our daily reading of Scripture we come upon many obscure passages that convict us of ignorance. With this bridle God keeps us within bounds, assigning to each his "measure of faith" (Rom. 12:3) so that even the best teacher may be ready to learn.

Remarkable examples of this implicit faith may be noted

in Christ's disciples before they attained full enlightenment.
We see how with difficulty they taste even the first rudiments, halting over the slightest matters, and though hanging on their Master's words, making but little progress.
Indeed, when, warned by the women, they rush to the tomb,
the resurrection of their Master seems to them like a dream
(Luke 24:11–12; cf. John 20:8). Since Christ previously bore
witness to their faith, it is wrong to say that they were completely devoid of it. No, unless they had been persuaded
that Christ would rise again, all zeal would have failed them.
Nor was it superstition that prompted the women to anoint
with spices the corpse of a dead man for whose life there
could be no hope. But although they had faith in the words
of him whom they knew to be truthful, the ignorance that
as yet occupied their minds so enveloped their faith in darkness that they were almost dumfounded. Hence, also, it said
that they finally believed after they themselves had discovered the truth of Christ's words through the very fact of
his resurrection. Not that they then began to believe, but
because the seed of hidden faith—which had been dead, as
it were, in their hearts—at that time burst through with renewed vigor! For there was in them a true but implicit faith
because they had reverently embraced Christ as their sole
teacher. Then, taught by him, they were convinced he was
the author of their salvation. And finally, they believed he
came from heaven that, through the Father's grace, he might
gather his disciples thither. We ought not to seek any more
intimate proof of this than that unbelief is, in all men, always
mixed with faith.

5. *"Implicit" faith as prerequisite of faith*

We may also call that faith implicit which is still strictly
nothing but the preparation of faith. The Evangelists relate
that very many believed who, caught up into wonderment
by the miracles only, did not advance farther than to believe
Christ the Messiah who had been promised, although they
had not been imbued with even a trace of the gospel teaching. Such reverent attention, which disposed them to submit
themselves willingly to Christ, is graced with the title "faith";
yet it was only the beginning of faith. Thus, the court official
who believed Christ's promise concerning the healing of his
son (John 4:50), having returned to his house, as the Evan-

gelist testifies, believed anew (John 4:53) because he first
received as an oracle what he had heard from the mouth of
Christ, and then submitted to Christ's authority to receive the
teaching. Yet we must know that he was so teachable and
ready to learn that in the first passage his admission of belief
signifies a particular faith, while in the second passage he is
counted among the disciples who had enlisted with Christ.
John sets forth a like example in the Samaritans who so
believed the word of a woman that they eagerly rushed to
Christ, but spoke to her, when they heard him, as follows:
"Now we do not believe on account of your speaking, but
we have heard him and we know that it is the Savior of
the world" (John 4:42). From these instances it is clear that
even those who are not yet imbued with the first elements
but are still inclined to hearken are called "believers"; not
in an exact sense, indeed, but in so far as God in his kindness
deigns to grace that pious affection with such great honor.
But this teachableness, with the desire to learn, is far different
from sheer ignorance in which those sluggishly rest who are
content with the sort of "implicit faith" the papists invent.
For if Paul severely condemns those who "are always learning but never arrive at a knowledge of the truth" (II Tim.
3:7), how much greater ignominy do those merit who deliberately affect complete ignorance!

(*Relation of faith to the Word and brief definition of faith,
6–7*)

6. Faith rests upon God's Word

This, then, is the true knowledge of Christ, if we receive
him as he is offered by the Father: namely, clothed with his
gospel. For just as he has been appointed as the goal of our
faith, so we cannot take the right road to him unless the gospel goes before us. And there, surely, the treasures of grace
are opened to us; for if they had been closed, Christ would
have benefited us little. Thus Paul yokes faith to teaching, as
an inseparable companion, with these words: "You did not
so learn Christ if indeed you were taught what is the truth in
Christ" (Eph. 4:20–21 p.).

Yet I do not so restrict faith to the gospel without confessing that what sufficed for building it up had been handed
down by Moses and the prophets. But because a fuller mani-

festation of Christ has been revealed in the gospel, Paul justly calls it the "doctrine of faith" (cf. I Tim. 4:6). For this reason, he says in another passage that by the coming of faith the law was abolished (Rom. 10:4; cf. Gal. 3:25). He understands by this term the new and extraordinary kind of teaching by which Christ, after he became our teacher, has more clearly set forth the mercy of the Father, and has more surely testified to our salvation.

Yet it will be an easier and more suitable method if we descend by degrees from general to particular. First, we must be reminded that there is a permanent relationship between faith and the Word. He could not separate one from the other any more than we could separate the rays from the sun from which they come. For this reason, God exclaims in The Book of Isaiah: "Hear me and your soul shall live" (ch. 55:3). And John shows this same wellspring of faith in these words: "These things have been written that you may believe" (John 20:31). The prophet, also, desiring to exhort the people to faith, says: "Today if you will hear his voice" (Ps. 95:7; 94:8, Vg.). "To hear" is generally understood as meaning to believe. In short, it is not without reason that in The Book of Isaiah, God distinguishes the children of the church from outsiders by this mark: he will teach all his children (Isa. 54:13; John 6:45) that they may learn of him (cf. John 6:45). For if benefits were indiscriminately given, why would he have directed his Word to a few? To this corresponds the fact that the Evangelists commonly use the words "believers" and "disciples" as synonyms. This is especially Luke's usage in The Acts of the Apostles: indeed he extends this title even to a woman in Acts 9:36 (Acts 6:1–2, 7; 9:1, 10, 19, 25–26, 38; 11:26, 29; 13:52; 14:20, 28; 15:10; also chs. 16 to 21).

Therefore if faith turns away even in the slightest degree from this goal toward which it should aim, it does not keep its own nature, but becomes uncertain credulity and vague error of mind. The same Word is the basis whereby faith is supported and sustained; if it turns away from the Word, it falls. Therefore, take away the Word and no faith will then remain.

We are not here discussing whether a human ministry is necessary for the sowing of God's Word, from which faith may be conceived. This we shall discuss in another place. But we say that the Word itself, however it be imparted to us, is like a mirror in which faith may contemplate God. Whether, therefore, God makes use of man's help in this or works by his own power alone, he always represents himself through his Word to those whom he wills to draw to himself. And for this reason, Paul defines faith as that obedience which is given to the gospel (Rom. 1:5), and elsewhere praises allegiance to faith in Philippians (Phil. 1:3–5; cf. I Thess. 2:13). In understanding faith it is not merely a question of knowing that God exists, but also—and this especially—of knowing what is his will toward us. For it is not so much our concern to know who he is in himself, as what he wills to be toward us.

Now, therefore, we hold faith to be a knowledge of God's will toward us, perceived from his Word. But the foundation of this is a preconceived conviction of God's truth. As for its certainty, so long as your mind is at war with itself, the Word will be of doubtful and weak authority, or rather of none. And it is not even enough to believe that God is trustworthy (cf. Rom. 3:3), who can neither deceive nor lie (cf. Titus 1:2), unless you hold to be beyond doubt that whatever proceeds from him is sacred and inviolable truth.

7. Faith arises from God's promise of grace in Christ

But since man's heart is not aroused to faith at every word of God, we must find out at this point what, strictly speaking, faith looks to in the Word. God's word to Adam was, "You shall surely die" (Gen. 2:17). God's word to Cain was, "The blood of your brother cries out to me from the earth" (Gen. 4:10). But these words are so far from being capable of establishing faith that they can of themselves do nothing but shake it. In the meantime, we do not deny that it is the function of faith to subscribe to God's truth whenever and whatever and however it speaks. But we ask only what faith finds in the Word of the Lord upon which to lean and rest. Where our conscience sees only indignation and vengeance, how can it fail to tremble and be afraid? or to shun the God whom it dreads? Yet faith ought to seek God, not to shun him.

It is plain, then, that we do not yet have a full definition of faith, inasmuch as merely to know something of God's will is not to be accounted faith. But what if we were to substitute his benevolence or his mercy in place of his will, the tidings of which are often sad and the proclamation frightening? Thus, surely, we shall more closely approach the nature of faith; for it is after we have learned that our salvation rests with God that we are attracted to seek him. This fact is confirmed for us when he declares that our salvation is his care and concern. Accordingly, we need the promise of grace, which can testify to us that the Father is merciful; since we can approach him in no other way, and upon grace alone the heart of man can rest.

On this basis the psalms commonly yoke these two, mercy and truth, as if they were mutually connected (Ps. 89:14, 24; 92:2; 98:3; 100:5; 108:4; 115:1; etc.); for it would not help us at all to know that God is true unless he mercifully attracted us to himself. Nor would it have been in our power to embrace his mercy if he had not offered it with his word: "I have declared thy truth and thy salvation; I have not concealed thy goodness and thy truth. . . . Let thy goodness and thy truth . . . preserve me" (Ps. 40:10–11, Comm.). Another passage: "Thy mercy . . . extends to the heavens, thy truth to the clouds." (Ps. 36:5, Comm.) Likewise: "All the ways of Jehovah are kindness and truth to those who keep his covenant." (Ps. 25:10, Comm.) "For his mercy is multiplied upon us, and the truth of the Lord endures forever." (Ps. 117:2; 116:2, Vg.; cf. Comm.) Again, "I will sing thy name for thy mercy and thy truth." (Ps. 138:2.) I pass over what we read in the Prophets along the same line, that God is kind and steadfast in his promises. For it will be rash for us to decide that God is well disposed toward us unless he give witness of himself, and anticipate us by his call, that his will may not be doubtful or obscure. But we have already seen that the sole pledge of his love is Christ, without whom the signs of hatred and wrath are everywhere evident.

Now, the knowledge of God's goodness will not be held very important unless it makes us rely on that goodness. Consequently, understanding mixed with doubt is to be excluded, as it is not in firm agreement, but in conflict, with itself. Yet far indeed is the mind of man, blind and darkened as it is, from penetrating and attaining even to perception of the will of God! And the heart, too, wavering as it is in perpetual hesitation, is far from resting secure in that conviction! Therefore our mind must be otherwise illumined and our heart strengthened, that the Word of God may obtain full faith among us. Now we shall possess a right definition of faith if we call it a firm and certain knowledge of God's benevolence toward us, founded upon the truth of the freely given promise in Christ, both revealed to our minds and sealed upon our hearts through the Holy Spirit.

(Various unacceptable significations of the term "faith," 8–13)

8. *"Formed" and "unformed" faith*

But before we proceed farther, some preliminary remarks will be necessary to explain difficulties that could otherwise offer a stumbling block to our readers. First, we must refute that worthless distinction between formed and unformed faith which is tossed about the schools. For they imagine that people who are touched by no fear of God, no sense of piety, nevertheless believe whatever it is necessary to know for salvation. As if the Holy Spirit, by illumining our hearts unto faith, were not the witness to us of our adoption! And yet they presumptuously dignify that persuasion, devoid of the fear of God, with the name "faith" even though all Scripture cries out against it. We need no longer contend with their definition; our task is simply to explain the nature of faith as it is set forth in the Word of God. From this it will be very clear how ignorantly and foolishly they shout rather than speak about it.

I have already touched upon part; I shall later insert the rest in its proper place. I now say that nothing more absurd than their fiction can be imagined. They would have faith to be an assent by which any despiser of God may receive what is offered from Scripture. But first they ought to have seen whether every man attains faith by his own effort, or whether through it the Holy Spirit is witness of his adoption. Therefore they babble childishly in asking whether faith is the same faith when it has been formed by a superadded quality; or whether it be a new and different thing. From such chatter it certainly looks as if they never thought about the unique gift of the Spirit. For the beginning of believing already contains within itself the reconciliation whereby man approaches God. But if they weighed Paul's saying, "With the heart a man believes unto righteousness" (Rom. 10:10), they would cease to invent that cold quality of faith.

If we possessed only this one reason, it would have been sufficient to end the dispute: that very assent itself—as I have already partially suggested, and will reiterate more fully—is more of the heart than of the brain, and more of the disposition than of the understanding. For this reason, it is called "obedience of faith" (Rom. 1:5), and the Lord prefers no other obedience to it—and justly, since nothing is more precious to him than his truth. To this truth believers set their seal as if they have affixed their signatures, as John the Baptist testifies (John 3:33). Since there is no doubt about the matter, we establish in one word that they are speaking foolishly when they say that faith is "formed" when pious inclination is added to assent. For even assent rests upon such pious inclination—at least such assent as is revealed in the Scriptures!

But another much clearer argument now offers itself. Since faith embraces Christ, as offered to us by the Father (cf. John 6:29)—that is, since he is offered not only for righteousness, forgiveness of sins, and peace, but also for sanctification (cf. I Cor. 1:30) and the fountain of the water of life (John 7:38; cf. ch. 4:14)—without a doubt, no one can duly know him without at the same time apprehending the sanctification of the Spirit. Or, if anyone desires some plainer statement, faith rests upon the knowledge of Christ. And Christ cannot be known apart from the sanctification of his Spirit. It follows that faith can in no wise be separated from a devout disposition.

9. I Corinthians 13:2—a proof of the difference between "formed" and "unformed" faith

They are accustomed to urge Paul's words: "If anyone has all faith so as to remove mountains, but has not love, he is nothing" (I Cor. 13:2 p.). By this they would de-form faith by depriving it of love. They do not consider what the apostle means by "faith" in this passage. For after he has discussed in the preceding chapter the various gifts of the Spirit —including the divers kinds of tongues, powers, and prophecy (I Cor. 12:4–10)—and has exhorted the Corinthians to "seek after the better of these gifts," thereby to render greater benefit and advantage to the whole body of the church, he adds that he will show "a still more excellent way" (I Cor. 12:31). All such gifts, however excellent they may be in themselves, are still to be considered as nothing unless they serve love. For they were given for the edification of the church, and unless they contribute to this they lose their grace. To prove this, Paul elaborates by repeating those same gifts which he had enumerated before, but under other names. Moreover, he uses the terms "powers" and "faith" for the same thing, that is, for the ability to work miracles. This power or faith, therefore, is a special gift of God, which any impious man can brag about and abuse, as the gift of tongues, as prophecy, as the other graces. No wonder, then, if it be separated from love! But the whole error of these men lies in that, although the meanings of "faith" are diverse, they do not observe the diversity of the thing signified therein, but dispute as if the acceptation of the word were everywhere the same. The passage of James (James 2:21) that they bring forward in support of the same error will be discussed elsewhere.

Although we concede, for the purpose of instruction, that there are divers forms of faith. But, while we wish to show what kind of knowledge of God can exist among the impious —we nevertheless recognize and proclaim that there is only one kind of faith among the pious—as Scripture teaches. Of course, most people believe that there is a God, and they consider that the gospel history and the remaining parts of the Scripture are true. Such a judgment is on a par with the judgments we ordinarily make concerning those things which are either narrated as having once taken place, or which we have seen as eyewitnesses. There are, also, those who go beyond this, holding the Word of God to be an indisputable oracle; they do not utterly neglect his precepts, and are somewhat moved by his threats and promises. To such persons an ascription of faith is made, but by misapplication, because they do not impugn the Word of God with open impiety, or refuse or despise it, but rather pretend a certain show of obedience.

10. What is called "unformed" faith is only an illusion of faith

But this shadow or image of faith, as it is of no importance, does not deserve to be called faith. It will soon be seen more fully how far removed from the solid reality of faith it is, yet nothing prevents this from being briefly indicated now. [Simon] is said to have had faith attributed to him, we do not understand, [he] nevertheless betrayed his unbelief (Acts 8:18). When he is said to have had faith attributed to him, we do not understand the statement as do some, who hold that he pretended in words a faith that he did not have in his heart. Rather, we consider that, conquered by the majesty of the gospel, he showed a certain sort of faith, and thus recognized Christ to be the author of life and salvation, so that he willingly enlisted under him. In the same way, in the Gospel of Luke they are said to believe for a while (Luke 8:13), in whom the seed of the Word is choked before it bears fruit, or immediately withers and dies even before it takes any root (Luke 8:6–7).

We do not doubt that such persons, prompted by some taste of the Word, greedily seize upon it, and begin to feel its divine power; so that they impose a false show of faith not only upon the eyes of men but even upon their own minds. For they persuade themselves that the reverence that they show to the Word of God is very piety itself, because they count it no impiety unless there is open and admitted reproach or contempt of his Word. Whatever sort of assent that is, it does not at all penetrate to the heart itself, there to remain fixed. And although it seems sometimes to put down roots, they are not living roots. The human heart has so many crannies where vanity hides, so many holes where falsehood lurks, is so decked out with deceiving hypocrisy, that it often dupes itself. Yet let those who boast of such shadow-shapes of faith understand that in this respect they are no better than the devils! Surely those of the former class are far inferior to the devils, for they stupidly listen to and understand things the knowledge of which makes even the devils shudder (James 2:19). The others are like the devils in this respect, that whatever feeling touches them ends in dread and dismay.

11. "Faith" even among the reprobate?

I know that to attribute faith to the reprobate seems hard to some, when Paul declares it the result of election (cf. I Thess. 1:4–5). Yet this difficulty is easily solved. For though only those predestined to salvation receive the light of faith and truly feel the power of the gospel, yet experience shows that the reprobate are sometimes affected by almost the same feeling as the elect, so that even in their own judgment they do not in any way differ from the elect (cf. Acts 13:48). Therefore it is not at all absurd that the apostle should attribute to them a taste of the heavenly gifts (Heb. 6:4–6)— and Christ, faith for a time (Luke 8:13); not because they firmly grasp the force of spiritual grace and the sure light of faith, but because the Lord, to render them more convicted and inexcusable, steals into their minds to the extent that his goodness may be tasted without the Spirit of adoption.

Suppose someone objects that then nothing more remains to believers to assure themselves of their adoption. I reply: although there is a great likeness and affinity between God's elect and those who are given a transitory faith, yet only in the elect does that confidence flourish which Paul extols, that they loudly proclaim Abba, Father (Gal. 4:6; cf. Rom. 8:15). Therefore, as God regenerates only the elect with incorruptible seed forever (I Peter 1:23) so that the seed of life sown in their hearts may never perish, thus he firmly seals the gift of his adoption in them that it may be steady and sure.

But this does not at all hinder that lower working of the Spirit from taking its course even in the reprobate. In the meantime, believers are taught to examine themselves carefully and humbly, lest the confidence of the flesh creep in and replace assurance of faith. Besides this, the reprobate never receive anything but a confused awareness of grace, so that they grasp a shadow rather than the firm body of it. For the Spirit, strictly speaking, seals forgiveness of sins in the elect alone, so that they apply it by special faith to their own use. Yet the reprobate are justly said to believe that God is merciful toward them, for they receive the gift of reconciliation, although confusedly and not distinctly enough. Not that they are partakers of the same faith or regeneration with the children of God, but because they seem, under a cloak of hypocrisy, to have a beginning of faith in common with the latter. And I do not deny that God illumines their minds enough for them to recognize his grace; but he so distinguishes that awareness from the exclusive testimony he gives to his elect that they do not attain the full effect and fruition thereof. He does not show himself merciful to them, to the extent of truly snatching them from death and receiving them into his keeping, but only manifests to them his mercy for the time being. Only his elect does he account worthy of receiving the living root of faith so that they may endure to the end (Matt. 24:13). Thus is that objection answered: if God truly shows his grace, this fact is forever established. For nothing prevents God from illumining some with a momentary awareness of his grace, which afterward vanishes.

12. True and false faith

Also, although faith is a knowledge of the divine benevolence toward us and a sure persuasion of its truth, there is no wonder that the awareness of divine love vanishes in temporary things. Even if it is close to faith, it differs much from it. The will of God is unchangeable, I admit, and his truth ever remains in agreement with itself. Yet I deny that the reprobate proceed so far as to penetrate into that secret revelation which Scripture vouchsafes only to the elect. I deny, therefore, that they either grasp the will of God as it is immutable, or steadfastly embrace its truth, for they tarry in but a fleeing awareness. They are like a tree not planted deep enough to put down living roots. For some years it may put forth not only blossoms and leaves, but even fruits; nevertheless, it withers after the passage of time. To sum up, just as by the rebellion of the first man the image of God could be wiped out from his mind and soul, no wonder he illumines wicked persons with some rays of his grace, which he later allows to be quenched. Nor does anything prevent him from lightly touching some with a knowledge of his gospel, while deeply imbuing others. In the meantime we ought to grasp this: however deficient or weak faith may be in the elect, still, because the Spirit of God is for them the sure guarantee and seal of their adoption (Eph. 1:14; cf. II Cor. 1:22), the mark he has engraved can never be erased from their hearts; but on the wicked such light is shed as may afterward pass away. Yet, because he does not give life to the seed that lies in their hearts to keep it ever incorruptible as in the elect, it must not be supposed that the Holy Spirit is false.

Furthermore, although it is evident from the teaching of Scripture and daily experience that the wicked are sometimes touched by the awareness of divine grace, a desire to love one another must be aroused in their hearts. Thus, for a time in Saul there flourished a pious impulse to love God. For he knew God was as a father to him, and he was attracted by something delightful about His goodness (I Sam., chs. 9 to 11). But as a persuasion of God's fatherly love is not deeply rooted in the reprobate, so do they not perfectly reciprocate his love as sons, but behave like hirelings. For that Spirit of love was given to Christ alone on the condition that he instill it in his members. And surely that saying of Paul's is confined to the elect: "The love of God has been shed abroad in our hearts through the Holy Spirit, who has been given to us" (Rom. 5:5, cf. Vg.), that is, the love that generates the above-mentioned confidence that we can call upon him (cf. Gal. 4:6).

From the other side we see that God, while not ceasing to love his children, is wondrously angry toward them; not because he is disposed of himself to hate them, but because he would frighten them by the feeling of his wrath in order to humble their fleshly pride, shake off their sluggishness, and arouse them to repentance. Therefore, at the same time they conceive him to be at once angry and merciful toward them, or toward their sins. For they unfeignedly pray that his wrath be averted, while with tranquil confidence they nevertheless flee to him for refuge. Indeed, this evidence discloses that some are not pretending a faith, who nevertheless lack true faith; but while they are carried away with a sudden impulse of zeal, they deceive themselves in a false opinion. There is no doubt that indolence so fills them that they do not rightly examine their hearts as they should. It is likely that such are those to whom, according to John, Christ "did not trust himself," although they believed in him, "because he knew all men and . . . knew what was in man" (John 2:24–25). If many did not fall from the common faith (I call it "common" because there is a great likeness and affinity between transitory faith and living and permanent faith), Christ would not have said to his disciples, "If you continue in my word, you are truly my disciples, and you will know the truth, and the truth will make you free" (John 8:31–32). For he is addressing those who had embraced his teaching and is urging them to advance in faith, lest by their sluggishness they extinguish the light given them. Therefore, Paul attributes faith exclusively to the elect (Titus 1:1), meaning that many vanish because they have not taken living root. Christ says the same thing in the Gospel of Matthew: "Every tree that my Heavenly Father has not planted will be uprooted" (Matt. 15:13).

There is a grosser kind of lying in others, who are not ashamed to mock God and men. James inveighs against this type of men, who impiously profane faith on this deceitful pretext (James 2:14–26). And Paul would not require "a faith unfeigned" from the children of God (I Tim. 1:5), except that many boldly boast of what they do not have, and deceive others or even sometimes themselves with vain pretense. Therefore, he compares a good conscience to a chest

in which faith is kept. For many in falling from good conscience "have made shipwreck of their faith" (I Tim. 1:19;
cf. ch. 3:9).

13. Different meanings of the word "faith" in Scripture

We must understand that the meaning of the word "faith"
is ambiguous. Often faith means only sound doctrine of godliness, as in the passage we have just cited; and in the same
letter where Paul desires that deacons keep "the mystery of
faith in a pure conscience" (I Tim. 3:9). Likewise, when he
declares that some will fall away from faith (I Tim. 4:1).
But on the other hand, he says that Timothy had been
"nourished on the words of the faith" (I Tim. 4:6). Likewise, when he terms "godless chatter and contradictions of
what is falsely called knowledge," the cause why many fall
from faith (I Tim. 6:20–21; cf. II Tim. 2:16); elsewhere he
calls these "reprobate" in regard to faith (II Tim. 3:8).
Again, where he enjoins Titus, "Bid them" (Titus 2:2) "be
sound in the faith" (Titus 1:13), by the word "soundness"
Paul means simply purity of doctrine, easily rendered corrupt
and degenerate by men's fickleness. That is, because in Christ
whom faith possesses "are hidden all the treasures of knowledge and wisdom" (Col. 2:3), faith is rightly extended to
the whole sum of heavenly doctrine, from which it cannot
be separated.

On the other hand, it is sometimes confined to a particular
object, as when Matthew says that Christ saw the faith of
those who let the paralytic down through the tile roof (Matt.
9:2). And he exclaimed that even in Israel he had not found
so great faith as the centurion manifested (Matt. 8:10). Yet
it is probable that the centurion was wholly intent upon the
healing of his son (cf. John 4:47 ff.), whose cure occupied
his entire mind, because, content with only the nod and answer of Christ, he does not demand his bodily presence. On
account of this circumstance his faith is greatly commended.

A little while ago we taught that Paul takes "faith" as the
gift of performing miracles, a gift that certain ones possess
who have neither been regenerated by the Spirit of God nor
zealously worship him. Also, in another passage, he identi-
fies faith with the teaching whereby we are established in
faith. For when he writes that faith will pass away (I Cor.
13:10; cf. Rom. 4:14), he doubtless is referring to the minis-

try of the church, which today is useful for our weakness. Now, in these forms of speech there appears an analogy. When the term "faith" is improperly transferred to a false profession or a lying label, this misapplication of the term should seem no harsher than when vicious and perverted worship is termed "fear of God." For example, it is often stated in the Sacred History that the foreign tribes that had been transplanted to Samaria and neighboring districts feared false gods and the God of Israel (II Kings 17:24–41). This means, in so many words, that they mixed heaven and earth.

But now we ask, of what sort is that faith which distinguishes the children of God from the unbelievers, by which we call upon God as Father, by which we cross over from death into life, and by which Christ, eternal salvation and life, dwells in us? I believe that I have briefly and clearly explained the force and nature of faith.

(Detailed examination of what the definition of faith in paragraph 7 implies: the element of knowledge, 14–15)

14. Faith as higher knowledge

Now let us examine anew the individual parts of the definition of faith. After we have diligently examined it no doubt, I believe, will remain. When we call faith "knowledge" we do not mean comprehension of the sort that is commonly concerned with those things which fall under human sense perception. For faith is so far above sense that man's mind has to go beyond and rise above itself in order to attain it. Even where the mind has attained, it does not comprehend what it feels. But while it is persuaded of what it does not grasp, by the very certainty of its persuasion it understands more than if it perceived anything human by its own capacity. Paul, therefore, beautifully describes it as the power "to comprehend . . . what is the breadth and length and depth and height, and to know the love of Christ, which surpasses knowledge" (Eph. 3:18–19). He means that what our mind embraces by faith is in every way infinite, and that this kind of knowledge is far more lofty than all understanding. Nevertheless, the Lord has "made manifest to his saints" the secret of his will, which had been "hidden for ages and generations" (Col. 1:26; cf. ch. 2:2). For very good reason, then, faith is frequently called "recognition" (see Eph. 1:17;

4:13; Col. 1:9; 3:10; I Tim. 2:4; Titus 1:1; Philemon 6; II
Peter 2:21), but by John, "knowledge." For he declares that
believers know themselves to be God's children (I John
3:2). And obviously they surely know this. But they are more
strengthened by the persuasion of divine truth than instructed
by rational proof. Paul's words also point this out: "While
dwelling in this body, we wander from the Lord, for we
walk by faith, not by sight" (II Cor. 5:6–7). By these words
he shows that those things which we know through faith are
nonetheless absent from us and go unseen. From this we conclude that the knowledge of faith consists in assurance rather
than in comprehension.

15. Faith implies certainty

We add the words "sure and firm" in order to express a
more solid constancy of persuasion. For, as faith is not content with a doubtful and changeable opinion, so is it not
content with an obscure and confused conception; but requires full and fixed certainty, such as men are wont to have
from things experienced and proved. For unbelief is so
deeply rooted in our hearts, and we are so inclined to it,
that not without hard struggle is each one able to persuade
himself of what all confess with the mouth: namely, that
God is faithful. Especially when it comes to reality itself,
every man's wavering uncovers hidden weakness. And not
without cause the Holy Spirit with such notable titles ascribes
authority to the Word of God. He wishes to cure the disease
I have mentioned so that among us God may obtain full faith
in his promises. "The words of Jehovah are pure words,"
says David, "silver melted in an excellent crucible of earth,
purified seven times." (Ps. 12:6, cf. Comm. and Ps. 11:7,
Vg.) Likewise, "The Word of Jehovah is purified; it is a shield
to all those who trust in him." (Ps. 18:30, cf. Comm.)
Solomon, moreover, confirms this very idea in almost identical
words, "Every word of God is purified" (Prov. 30:5). But
because almost the entire 119th Psalm is taken up with
this proof, it would be superfluous to list more. Surely, as
often as God commends his Word to us, he indirectly rebukes us for our unbelief, for he has no other intention than
to uproot perverse doubts from our hearts.

Also, there are very many who so conceive God's mercy
that they receive almost no consolation from it. They are
constrained with miserable anxiety at the same time as they

are in doubt whether he will be merciful to them because
they confine that very kindness of which they seem utterly
persuaded within too narrow limits. For among themselves
they ponder that it is indeed great and abundant, shed upon
many, available and ready for all; but that it is uncertain
whether it will even come to them, or rather, whether they
will come to it. This reasoning, when it stops in mid-course,
is only half. Therefore, it does not so much strengthen the
spirit in secure tranquillity as trouble it with uneasy doubting. But there is a far different feeling of full assurance that
in the Scriptures is always attributed to faith. It is this
which puts beyond doubt God's goodness clearly manifested
for us (Col. 2:2; I Thess. 1:5; cf. Heb. 6:11 and 10:22).
But that cannot happen without our truly feeling its sweetness and experiencing it in ourselves. For this reason, the
apostle derives confidence from faith, and from confidence, in
turn, boldness. For he states: "Through Christ we have boldness and access with confidence which is through faith in
him" (Eph. 3:12 p., cf. Vg.). By these words he obviously
shows that there is no right faith except when we dare with
tranquil hearts to stand in God's sight. This boldness arises
only out of a sure confidence in divine benevolence and salvation. This is so true that the word "faith" is very often used
for confidence.

(Certainty of faith in relation to fear, 16–28)

16. Certainty of faith

Here, indeed, is the chief hinge on which faith turns: that
we do not regard the promises of mercy that God offers as
true only outside ourselves, but not at all in us; rather that we
make them ours by inwardly embracing them. Hence, at last
is born that confidence which Paul elsewhere calls "peace"
(Rom. 5:1), unless someone may prefer to derive peace from
it. Now it is an assurance that renders the conscience calm
and peaceful before God's judgment. Without it the conscience must be harried by disturbed alarm, and almost torn
to pieces; unless perhaps, forgetting God and self, it for the
moment sleeps. And truly for the moment, for it does not
long enjoy that miserable forgetfulness without the memory
of divine judgment repeatedly coming back and very violently rending it. Briefly, he alone is truly a believer who,
convinced by a firm conviction that God is a kindly and well-

disposed Father toward him, promises himself all things on the basis of his generosity; who, relying upon the promises of divine benevolence toward him, lays hold on an undoubted expectation of salvation. As the apostle points out in these words: "If we hold our confidence and glorying in hope, firm even to the end" (Heb. 3:7, cf. Vg.). Thus, he considers that no one hopes well in the Lord except him who confidently glories in the inheritance of the Heavenly Kingdom. No man is a believer, I say, except him who, leaning upon the assurance of his salvation, confidently triumphs over the devil and death; as we are taught from that masterly summation of Paul: I have confessed that "neither death nor life, nor angels, nor principalities, nor powers, nor things present, nor things to come . . . can separate us from the love of God which embraces us in Christ Jesus" (Rom. 8:38–39 p.). Thus, in the same manner, the apostle does not consider the eyes of our minds well illumined, except as we discern what the hope of the eternal inheritance is to which we have been called (Eph. 1:18). And everywhere he so teaches as to intimate that we cannot otherwise well comprehend the goodness of God unless we gather from it the fruit of great assurance.

17. Faith in the struggle against temptation

Still, someone will say: "Believers experience something far different: In recognizing the grace of God toward themselves they are not only tried by disquiet, which often comes upon them, but they are repeatedly shaken by gravest terrors. For so violent are the temptations that trouble their minds as not to seem quite compatible with that certainty of faith." Accordingly, we shall have to solve this difficulty if we wish the above-stated doctrine to stand. Surely, while we teach that faith ought to be certain and assured, we cannot imagine any certainty that is not tinged with doubt, or any assurance that is not assailed by some anxiety. On the other hand, we say that believers are in perpetual conflict with their own unbelief. Far, indeed, are we from putting their consciences in any peaceful repose, undisturbed by any tumult at all. Yet, once again, we deny that, in whatever way they are afflicted, they fall away and depart from the certain assurance received from God's mercy.

Scripture sets forth no more illustrious or memorable example of faith than in David, especially if you look at the whole course of his life. Yet with innumerable complaints he declares how unquiet his mind always was. From these plaints it will be enough to choose a few examples. When he reproaches his own soul for its disturbed emotions, with what else is he angry than with his own unbelief? "Why do you tremble," he says, "my soul, and why are you disquieted within me? Hope in God." (Ps. 42:5, 11; 43:5.) Surely, that very dismay was an open sign of unbelief, as if he thought himself forsaken by God. Elsewhere we read an even fuller confession: "I have said in my alarm, I am cast away from the sight of thine eyes" (Ps. 31:22, cf. Comm.). In another passage he also argues with himself in anxious and miserable perplexity; indeed, he starts a quarrel concerning the very nature of God: "Has God forgotten to be merciful? . . . Will he turn away forever?" (Ps. 77:9, 7; cf. Comm.). Even harsher is what follows: "And I said, to slay is mine, the changes of the right hand of the Most High" (Ps. 77:10, Comm.). In despair he condemns himself to death, and not only confesses himself to be troubled with doubt, but, as if he had fallen in the struggle, he feels that there is nothing left to him. For God has forsaken him, and has turned his hand, which was once his help, to his destruction. So, he justifiably urges his soul to return to its repose (Ps. 116:7) because he had experienced what it was to be tossed among stormy waves.

And yet—and this is something marvelous—amidst all these assaults faith sustains the hearts of the godly and truly in its effect resembles a palm tree (cf. Ps. 92:12, Vg.): for it strives against every burden and raises itself upward. So David, even when he might have seemed overwhelmed, in rebuking himself did not cease to rise up to God. He who, struggling with his own weakness, presses toward faith in his moments of anxiety is already in large part victorious. Thus we may infer from this statement and ones like it: "Wait for Jehovah, be strong; he will strengthen your heart. Wait for Jehovah!" (Ps. 27:14, cf. Comm.). David shows himself guilty of timidity, and, in repeating the same thought twice, confesses himself to be repeatedly subject to many troublesome emotions. In the meantime, he is not only displeased with himself for these weaknesses, but earnestly strives to correct them.

Surely, if we would duly weigh him in a fair balance with Ahaz, we shall find a great difference. Isaiah is sent to bring a remedy for the anxiety of the wicked and hypocritical king. He addresses him in these words: "Be on your guard, be still, fear not" (Isa. 7:4), etc. What does Ahaz do? It had previously been said that his heart was moved even as the trees of the forest are shaken by the wind (Isa. 7:2); thus though he has heard the promise, he does not cease to tremble. Here, then, is the proper reward and penalty of unbelief: so to tremble as to turn aside from God when one does not open the door for himself by faith. But, on the other hand, believers whom the weight of temptation bends down and almost crushes constantly rise up, although not without difficulty and trouble. And because they are aware of their own weak-mindedness, they pray with the prophet, "Take not the word of truth utterly out of my mouth" (Ps. 119:43, cf. Comm., and Ps. 118:43, Vg.). By these words we are taught that they sometimes become dumb as if their faith had been laid low; yet they do not fail or turn their backs, but persevere in their struggle. And by prayer they spur on their sluggishness, lest, at least, out of self-indulgence they become benumbed.

18. The conflict in the heart of the believer

In order to understand this, it is necessary to return to that division of flesh and spirit which we have mentioned elsewhere. It most clearly reveals itself at this point. Therefore the godly heart feels in itself a division because it is partly imbued with sweetness from its recognition of the divine goodness, partly grieves in bitterness from an awareness of its calamity; partly rests upon the promise of the gospel, partly trembles at the evidence of its own iniquity; partly rejoices at the expectation of life, partly shudders at death. This variation arises from imperfection of faith, since in the course of the present life it never goes so well with us that we are wholly cured of the disease of unbelief and entirely filled and possessed by faith. Hence arise those conflicts; when unbelief, which reposes in the remains of the flesh, rises up to attack the faith that has been inwardly conceived.

But if in the believing mind certainty is mixed with doubt, do we not always come back to this, that faith does not rest in a certain and clear knowledge, but only in an obscure and confused knowledge of the divine will toward us? Not at all. For even if we are distracted by various thoughts, we are not on that account completely divorced from faith. Nor if we are troubled on all sides by the agitation of unbelief, are we for that reason immersed in its abyss. If we are struck, we are not for that reason cast down from our position. For the end of the conflict is always this: that faith ultimately triumphs over those difficulties which besiege and seem to imperil it.

19. Even weak faith is real faith

To sum up: When first even the least drop of faith is instilled in our minds, we begin to contemplate God's face, peaceful and calm and gracious toward us. We see him afar off, but so clearly as to know we are not at all deceived. Then, the more we advance as we ought continually to advance, with steady progress, as it were, the nearer and thus surer sight of him we obtain; and by the very continuance he is made even more familiar to us. So we see that the mind, illumined by the knowledge of God, is at first wrapped up in much ignorance, which is gradually dispelled. Yet, by being ignorant of certain things, or by rather obscurely discerning what it does discern, the mind is not hindered from enjoying a clear knowledge of the divine will toward itself. For what it discerns comprises the first and principal parts in faith. It is like a man who, shut up in a prison into which the sun's rays shine obliquely and half obscured through a rather narrow window, is indeed deprived of the full sight of the sun. Yet his eyes dwell on its steadfast brightness, and he receives its benefits. Thus, bound with the fetters of an earthly body, however much we are shadowed on every side with great darkness, we are nevertheless illumined as much as need be for firm assurance when, to show forth his mercy, the light of God sheds even a little of its radiance.

20. The weakness and strength of faith

The apostle finely teaches both points in various passages. For when he teaches that "we know in part and prophesy in part" (I Cor. 13:9, 12), and "see in a mirror dimly" (I Cor. 13:12), he indicates what a tiny portion of that truly divine wisdom is given us in the present life. These words do not simply indicate that faith is imperfect so long as we groan under the burden of the flesh, but that, because of our own imperfection, we must constantly keep at learning. Nevertheless, he implies that the immeasurable cannot be comprehended by our inadequate measure and with our narrow capacities. Paul declares this also of the whole church: to each one of us his own ignorance is an obstacle and a hindrance, preventing him from coming as near as was to be desired.

But in another passage the same apostle shows what a sure and genuine taste of itself even a small drop of faith gives us when he declares that through the gospel, with uncovered face and no veil intervening, we behold God's glory with such effect that we are transformed into his very likeness (II Cor. 3:18). The greatest doubt and trepidation must be mixed up with such wrappings of ignorance, since our heart especially inclines by its own natural instinct toward unbelief. Besides this, there are innumerable and varied temptations that constantly assail us with great violence. But it is especially our conscience itself that, weighed down by a mass of sins, now complains and groans, now accuses itself, now murmurs secretly, now breaks out in open tumult. And so, whether adversities reveal God's wrath, or the conscience finds in itself the proof and ground thereof, thence unbelief obtains weapons and devices to overthrow faith. Yet these are always directed to this objective: that, thinking God to be against us and hostile to us, we should not hope for any help from him, and should fear him as if he were our deadly enemy.

21. The Word of God as the shield of faith

To bear these attacks faith arms and fortifies itself with the Word of the Lord. And when any sort of temptation assails us—suggesting that God is our enemy because he is unfavorable toward us—faith, on the other hand, replies that while he afflicts us he is also merciful because his chastisement arises out of love rather than wrath. When one is stricken by the thought that God is Avenger of iniquities, faith sets over against this the fact that his pardon is ready for all iniquities whenever the sinner betakes himself to the Lord's mercy. Thus the godly mind, however strange the ways in which it is vexed and troubled, finally surmounts all difficulties, and never allows itself to be deprived of assurance of divine mercy. Rather, all the contentions that try and weary it result in the certainty of this assurance. A proof of this is that while the saints seem to be very greatly pressed by God's vengeance, yet they lay their complaints before him; and when it seems that they will not at all be heard, they nonetheless call upon him. What point would there be in crying out to him if they hoped for no solace from him? Indeed, it would never enter their minds to call upon him if they did not believe that he had prepared help for them. Thus the disciples whom Christ rebuked for the smallness of their faith complained that they were perishing, and yet were imploring his help (Matt. 8:25–26). Indeed, while he reproves them for their little faith, he does not cast them out from the ranks of his disciples or count them among unbelievers, but urges them to shake off that fault. Therefore, we repeat what we have already stated: that the root of faith can never be torn from the godly breast, but clings so fast to the inmost parts that, however faith seems to be shaken or to bend this way or that, its light is never so extinguished or snuffed out that it does not at least lurk as it were beneath the ashes. And this example shows that the Word, which is an incorruptible seed, brings forth fruit like itself, whose fertility never wholly dries up and dies. The ultimate cause of despair for the saints is to feel God's hand in their ruin, taking into account things present. And yet Job declares that his hope will extend so far that even if God should slay him he will not for that reason cease to hope in him (Job 13:15). The matter stands thus: Unbelief does not hold sway within believers' hearts, but assails them from without. It does not mortally wound them with its weapons, but merely harasses them, or at most so injures them that the wound is curable. Faith, then, as Paul teaches, serves as our shield (Eph. 6:16). When held up against weapons it so receives their force that it either completely turns them aside or at least weakens their thrust, so that they cannot penetrate to our vitals. When, therefore, faith is shaken it is like a strong soldier forced by the violent blow of a spear to move his foot and to give ground a little. When faith itself is wounded it is as if the soldier's shield were broken at some point from the thrust of the spear, but not in such a manner as to be pierced. For the godly mind will always rise up so as to say with David, "If I walk in the midst of the shadow of death, I shall fear no evils, for thou art with me" (Ps. 22:4, Vg.; 23:4, EV). Surely it is terrifying to walk in the darkness of death; and believers, whatever their strength may be, cannot but be frightened by it. But since the thought prevails that they have God beside them, caring for their safety, fear at once yields to assurance. However great are the devices, as Augustine says, that the devil throws up against us, while he holds no lodgment in the heart, where faith dwells, he is cast out. Thus, if we may judge from the outcome, believers not only emerge safely from every battle, so that, having received fresh strength, they are shortly after ready to descend again into the arena; but besides, what John says in his canonical letter is also fulfilled: "This is the victory that overcomes the world, your faith" (I John 5:4 p.). And he affirms that our faith will be victor not only in one battle, or a few, or against any particular assault; but that, though it be assailed a thousand times, it will prevail over the entire world.

22. Right fear

There is another kind of "fear and trembling" (Phil. 2:12), one that, so far from diminishing the assurance of faith, the more firmly establishes it. This happens when believers, considering that the examples of divine wrath executed upon the ungodly as warnings to them, take special care not to provoke God's wrath against them by the same offenses; or, when inwardly contemplating their own misery, learn to depend wholly upon the Lord, without whom they see themselves more unstable and fleeting than any wind. For the apostle, by describing the chastisement with which the Lord of old punished the people of Israel, strikes terror into the Corinthians so that they should avoid entangling themselves in like misdeeds (I Cor. 10:11). In that way he does not weaken their confidence, but only shakes the sluggishness of their flesh, by which faith is commonly more destroyed than strengthened. And while he takes from the fall of the Jews the basis for his exhortation that "he who stands take heed lest he fall" (I Cor. 10:12 p.; Rom. 11:20), he is not bidding us to waver, as if we were unsure of our steadfastness. Rather, he is merely taking away arrogance and rash overconfidence in our own strength so that after the Jews have been rejected, the Gentiles, received into their place, may not exult more wildly. Yet, he there not only addresses believers but in his prayer includes also the hypocrites, who gloried only in outward show. And he does not admonish individual men, but makes a comparison between Jews and Gentiles; and he shows that the Jews in being rejected underwent the just punishments of their unbelief and ingratitude. He then also exhorts the Gentiles not to lose, through pride and self display, the grace of adoption, recently transferred to them. Just as in that rejection of the Jews some of them remained who had not fallen away from the covenant of adoption, so from the Gentiles some might arise who, without true faith, would only be puffed up with stupid confidence of the flesh, and thus, to their own destruction, would abuse God's generosity. But even if you take this statement to apply to the elect and believers, this will cause no discomfiture. For it is one thing to restrain presumption which sometimes creeps upon the saints from the vestiges of the flesh, in order that it may not play the wanton in vain confidence. It is another thing so to dishearten the conscience with fear that it cannot rest with full assurance in God's mercy.

23. *"Fear and trembling"*

Then, when the apostle teaches that we should "work out our own salvation in fear and trembling" (Phil. 2:12), he demands only that we become accustomed to honor the Lord's power, while greatly abasing ourselves. For nothing so moves us to repose our assurance and certainty of mind in the Lord as distrust of ourselves, and the anxiety occasioned by the awareness of our ruin. In this sense we must understand what is said by the prophet: "I, through the abundance of thy goodness, will enter thy temple; I will worship . . . in fear" (Ps. 5:7 p.). Here he fitly joins the boldness of faith that rests upon God's mercy with the reverent fear that we must experience whenever we come into the presence of God's majesty, and by its splendor understand how great is our own filthiness. Solomon, also, speaks truly when he declares that man blessed who is always afraid in his own heart, since by hardening it falls into evil (Prov. 28:14). But he means that fear which renders us more cautious—not the kind that afflicts us and causes us to fall—while the mind confused in itself recovers itself in God, cast down in itself is raised up in him, despairing of itself is quickened anew through trust in him.

Accordingly, nothing prevents believers from being afraid and at the same time possessing the surest consolation; according as they turn their eyes now upon their own vanity, and then bring the thought of their minds to bear upon the truth of God. How, someone will ask, can fear and faith dwell in the same mind? Indeed, in the same way that, conversely, sluggishness and worry so dwell. For while the impious seek freedom from pain for themselves that no fear of God may trouble them, yet the judgment of God so presses them that they cannot attain what they desire. Thus, nothing hinders God from training his own people in humility, that while fighting stoutly they may restrain themselves under the bridle of self-control. And from the context it is clear that this was the intention of the apostle where he assigns the cause of fear and trembling to God's good pleasure, whereby He gives to His people the capacity to will aright and to carry through valiantly (Phil. 2:12–13). In this sense we may rightly understand the prophet's saying: "The children of Israel shall fear the Lord and his goodness" (Hos. 3:5). For not only does piety beget reverence toward God, but the very sweetness and delightfulness of grace so fills a man who is cast down in himself ·with fear, and at the same time with admiration, that he depends upon God and humbly submits himself to his power.

24. The indestructible certainty of faith rests upon Christ's oneness with us

Yet we do not thus accept that most pestilent philosophy which certain half-papists are furtively beginning to fashion today. For because they cannot defend that rude doubt which has been handed down in the schools, they take refuge in another fiction: that they may make an assurance mingled with unbelief. Whenever we look upon Christ, they confess that we find full occasion for good hope in him. But because we are always unworthy of all those benefits which are offered to us in Christ, they would have us waver and hesitate at the sight of our unworthiness. In brief, they so set conscience between hope and fear that it alternates from one to the other intermittently and by turns. They so relate hope and fear that when the former is rising up the latter is oppressed; when the latter rises again, the former falls once more. Thus, when Satan once sees that those open devices with which he formerly had been wont to destroy the certainty of faith are now of no avail, he tries to sap it by covert devices. But what kind of confidence will that be, which now and again yields to despair? If, they say, you contemplate Christ, there is sure salvation: if you turn back to yourself, there is sure damnation. Therefore unbelief and good hope must alternately reign in your mind. As if we ought to think of Christ, standing afar off and not rather dwelling in us! For we await salvation from him not because he appears to us afar off, but because he makes us, ingrafted into his body, participants not only in all his benefits but also in himself. So I turn this argument of theirs back against them: if you contemplate yourself, that is sure damnation. But since Christ has been so imparted to you with all his benefits that all his things are made yours, that you are made a member of him, indeed one with him, his righteousness overwhelms your sins; his salvation wipes out your condemnation; with his worthiness he intercedes that your unworthiness may not come before God's sight. Surely this is so: We ought not to separate Christ from ourselves or ourselves from him. Rather we ought to hold fast bravely with both hands to that fellowship by which he has bound himself to us. So the apostle teaches us: "Now your body is dead because of sin; but the Spirit of Christ which dwells in you is life because of righteousness" (Rom. 8:10 p.). According to these men's trifles, he ought to have said: "Christ indeed has life in himself; but you, as you are sinners, remain subject to death and condemnation." But he speaks far otherwise, for he teaches that that condemnation which we of ourselves deserve has been swallowed up by the salvation that is in Christ. And to confirm this he uses the same reason I have brought forward: that Christ is not outside us but dwells within us. Not only does he cleave to us by an indivisible bond of fellowship, but with a wonderful communion, day by day, he grows more and more into one body with us, until he becomes completely one with us. Yet I do not deny what I stated above: that certain interruptions of faith occasionally occur, according as its weakness is violently buffeted hither and thither; so in the thick darkness of temptations its light is snuffed out. Yet whatever happens, it ceases not its earnest quest for God.

25. Bernard of Clairvaux on the two aspects of faith

Bernard of Clairvaux reasons similarly when he expressly discusses this question in his Fifth Sermon on the Dedication of a Church. "Now when I reflect upon my soul—which by the grace of God I sometimes do—it seems to me that I discover in it, so to speak, two opposite aspects. If I consider it in and of itself, I can say nothing more truly of it than that it is reduced to nothing (Ps. 72:22, Vg.). What need is there now to enumerate the individual miseries of the soul; how it is burdened with sins, enveloped in darkness, enslaved to pleasure, itching with lusts, subject to passions, filled with delusions, always prone to evil, bent to every sort of vice —in a word, full of shame and confusion? To be sure, if all our acts of righteousness, scrutinized in the light of truth, are found to be like 'the rag of a menstruous woman' (Isa. 64:6, Vg.), then to what will our unrighteous acts be compared? 'If then the light in us is darkness, how great will be the darkness!' (Matt. 6:23.) What then? Without doubt . . . 'Man has been made like unto vanity' (Ps. 143:4, Vg.; 144:4, EV). Man 'has been reduced to nothing' (Ps. 72: 22, Vg.). Man is nought. Yet how can he whom God magnifies be utterly nothing? How can he be nothing upon whom God has set his heart?

"Brethren, let us take heart again. Even if we are nothing in our own hearts, perchance something of us may be hidden in the heart of God. O 'Father of mercies' (II Cor. 1:3)! O Father of the miserable! How canst thou set thy heart upon us. . . . 'For where thy treasure is, thine heart is also.' (Matt. 6:21.) But how are we thy treasure if we are nothing? 'All the nations are as nothing before thee, they will be accounted by thee as nothing.' (Isa. 40:17 p.) So, indeed, *before* thee, not *within* thee: so in the judgment of thy truth, but not so in the intention of thy faithfulness. So, indeed, thou 'callest those things which are not as though they were' (Rom. 4:17). And they *are not*, therefore, because it is the things that are not that thou eallest, and they *are* at the same time because thou callest them. For although, as regards themselves, they are not, nevertheless with thee they are; but, as the apostle says, 'Not of their works' of righteousness, 'but of him who calls' (Rom. 9:11). Then he says that this connection between the two considerations is wonderful. Surely those things which are connected do not destroy one another!"

Also, in conclusion, he more openly declares this in these words: "Now if we diligently examine what we are, under these two considerations, or rather, if we examine how from the one point of view we are nothing, and from the other how magnified, . . . I believe our glorying will appear moderate, yet will perchance be greater and better founded than before, so that we glory not in ourselves but in the Lord (II Cor. 10:17). Surely if we think, 'If he has decreed to save us, we shall be immediately freed' (cf. Jer. 17:14); in this, then, we may take heart.

"But climbing up to a higher watchtower, let us seek the City of God, let us seek his temple, let us seek his house, let us seek his bride. I have not forgotten . . . , but with fear and reverence . . . I say: 'We, I say, are, but in the heart of God. We are, but by his dignifying us, not by our own dignity.'"

26. Fear of God and honor of God

Now, "the fear of the Lord"—to which all the saints give witness—and which is in some places called "the beginning of wisdom" (Ps. 111:10; Prov. 1:7), in other places "wisdom itself" (Prov. 15:33; Job 28:28)—although one, yet derives from a double meaning. For God has in his own right the reverence of a father and of a lord. Therefore, he who would duly worship him will try to show himself both an obedient son to him and a dutiful servant. The Lord, through the prophet, calls "honor" that obedience which is rendered to him as Father. He calls "fear" the service that is done to him as Lord. "A son," he says, "honors his father; a servant, his lord. If, then, I am a father, where is my honor? If I am a lord, where is my fear?" (Mal. 1:6). However he may distinguish them, you see how he fuses together the two terms. Therefore, let the fear of the Lord be for us a reverence compounded of honor and fear. No wonder if the same mind embraces both dispositions! For he who ponders within himself what God the Father is like toward us has cause enough, even if there be no hell, to dread offending him more gravely than any death. But also—such is the wanton desire of our flesh to sin without restraint—in order to check it by every means we must at once seize upon this thought: that the Lord, under whose power we live, abhors all iniquity. And they who, by living wickedly, provoke his wrath against themselves will not escape his vengeance.

27. Childlike and servile fear

John, moreover, says: "There is no fear in love, but perfect love casts out fear, for fear has to do with punishment" (I John 4:18). This does not clash with what we have said. For he is speaking of the dread arising from unbelief, far different from believers' fear. For the wicked fear God not because they are afraid of incurring his displeasure, if only they could do so with impunity; but because they know him

to be armed with the power to take vengeance, they shake
with fright on hearing of his wrath. And they so fear his
wrath because they think it hangs over them, because they
expect that at any moment it will fall upon their heads. But
believers, as has been said, both fear offending God more
than punishment, and are not troubled by fear of punishment, as if it hung over their necks. But they are rendered
more cautious not to incur it. So speaks the apostle when he
addresses believers: "Let no one deceive you, . . . for it is
because of this that the wrath of God comes upon the sons
of unbelief" (Eph. 5:6, Vg.; cf. Col. 3:6). He does not
threaten that God's wrath will descend upon them, but he
warns them to think on the wrath of the Lord, prepared for
the impious, on account of those wicked deeds which he had
recounted, lest they themselves also should wish to experience it. Yet it rarely happens that the wicked are aroused
by simple threats alone. Rather, whenever God thunders
with words from heaven, slow and sluggish in their hardness
they persist in their stubbornness. But once struck by his
hand, they are compelled, whether they will or not, to fear.
This fear men commonly call "servile" and contrast to it the
free and voluntary fear that befits children. Others subtly
interpolate an intermediate kind of fear because that
servile and constrained feeling sometimes so subdues men's
minds that they accede willingly to a proper fear of God.

28. Faith assures us not of earthly prosperity but of God's favor

Now, in the divine benevolence, which faith is said to
look to, we understand the possession of salvation and eternal
life is obtained. For if, while God is favorable, no good can
be lacking, when he assures us of his love we are abundantly
and sufficiently assured of salvation. "Let him show his face,"
says the prophet, "and we will be saved." (Ps. 80:3 p.; cf. Ps.
79:4, Vg.) Hence Scripture establishes this as the sum of our
salvation, that he has abolished all enmities and received us
into grace (Eph. 2:14). By this they intimate that when God
is reconciled to us no danger remains to prevent all things
from prospering for us. Faith, therefore, having grasped the
love of God, has promises of the present life and of that to
come (I Tim. 4:8), and firm assurance of all good things,
but of such sort as can be perceived from the Word. For faith
does not certainly promise itself either length of years or

honor or riches in this life, since the Lord willed that none of these things be appointed for us. But it is content with this certainty: that, however many things fail us that have to do with the maintenance of this life, God will never fail. Rather, the chief assurance of faith rests in the expectation of the life to come, which has been placed beyond doubt through the Word of God. Yet whatever earthly miseries and calamities await those whom God has embraced in his love, these cannot hinder his benevolence from being their full happiness. Accordingly, when we would express the sum of blessedness, we have mentioned the grace of God; for from this fountain every sort of good thing flows unto us. And we may commonly observe in the Scriptures that we are recalled to the love of the Lord whenever mention is made not only of eternal salvation but of any good we may have. For this reason, David sings of that divine goodness which, when felt in the godly heart, is sweeter and more desirable than life itself (Ps. 63:3).

In short, if all things flow unto us according to our wish, but we are uncertain of God's love or hatred, our happiness will be accursed and therefore miserable. But if in fatherly fashion God's countenance beams upon us, even our miseries will be blessed. For they will be turned into aids to salvation. So Paul heaps up all adverse things, but glories that we are not separated from God's love through them (Rom. 8:35, cf. v. 39), and always begins his prayers with God's grace, whence flows all prosperity; in like manner, against all terrors that disturb us David sets God's favor alone: "If I walk in the midst of the shadow of death, I shall fear no evils, for thou art with me" (Ps. 22:4, Vg.; 23:4, EV). And we always feel our minds wavering unless, content with God's grace, they seek their peace in it, and hold fixed deep within what is said in the psalm: "Blessed is the people whose God is Jehovah, and the nation he has chosen as his inheritance" (Ps. 33:12, cf. Comm.).

(Basis of faith the free promise, given in the Word, of grace in Christ, 29–32)

29. God's promise the support of faith

We make the freely given promise of God the foundation of faith because upon it faith properly rests. Faith is certain that God is true in all things whether he command or forbid, whether he promise or threaten; and it also obediently receives his commandments, observes his prohibitions, heeds his threats. Nevertheless, faith properly begins with the promise, rests in it, and ends in it. For in God faith seeks life: a life that is not found in commandments or declarations of penalties, but in the promise of mercy, and only in a freely given promise. For a conditional promise that sends us back to our own works does not promise life unless we discern its presence in ourselves. Therefore, if we would not have our faith tremble and waver, we must buttress it with the promise of salvation, which is willingly and freely offered to us by the Lord in consideration of our misery rather than our deserts. The apostle, therefore, bears this witness to the gospel: that it is the word of faith (Rom. 10:8). He distinguishes the gospel both from the precepts of the law and from the promises, since there is nothing that can establish faith except that generous embassy by which God reconciles the world to himself (cf. II Cor. 5:19–20). Thence, also, arises that frequent correlation of faith and gospel in the apostle, when he teaches that the ministry of the gospel is committed to him to further "obedience to the faith" (Rom. 1:5), that "it is the power of God for salvation to every believer; . . . in it the righteousness of God is revealed through faith for faith" (Rom. 1:16–17). And no wonder! Indeed, since the gospel is the "ministry of reconciliation" (II Cor. 5:18), no other sufficiently firm testimony of God's benevolence to us exists, the knowledge of which faith seeks.

Therefore, when we say that faith must rest upon a freely given promise, we do not deny that believers embrace and grasp the Word of God in every respect: but we point out the promise of mercy as the proper goal of faith. As on the one hand believers ought to recognize God to be Judge and Avenger of wicked deeds, yet on the other hand they properly contemplate his kindness, since he is so described to them as to be considered "one who is kind" (cf. Ps. 86:5, Comm.), "and merciful" (cf. Ps. 103:8, Comm.; 102:8, Vg.), "far from anger and of great goodness" (cf. Ps. 103:8, Comm.), "sweet to all" (Ps. 144:9, Vg.), "pouring out his mercy upon all his works" (cf. Ps. 145:9, Comm.).

30. Why faith depends solely on the promise of grace

And I do not tarry over the barkings of Pighius and dogs like him, when they attack this restriction, as if by tearing faith to pieces they might grab up a single piece. I admit, as I have already said, that God's truth is, as they call it, the common object of faith, whether he threaten or hold out hope of grace. Therefore, the apostle attributes to faith the fact that Noah feared the world's destruction when it was not as yet visible (Heb. 11:7). If fear of imminent punishment was the product of faith, then threats ought not to be excluded from the definition of it. This is indeed true. But our slanderers unjustly charge us with denying, as it were, that faith has regard to all parts of the Word of God. It is our intention to make only these two points: first, that faith does not stand firm until a man attains to the freely given promise; second, that it does not reconcile us to God at all unless it joins us to Christ. Both points are worth noting. We seek a faith that distinguishes the children of God from the wicked, and believers from unbelievers. If someone believes that God both justly commands all that he commands and truly threatens, shall he therefore be called a believer? By no means! Therefore, there can be no firm condition of faith unless it rests upon God's mercy. Now, what is our purpose in discussing faith? Is it not that we may grasp the way of salvation? But how can there be saving faith except in so far as it engrafts us in the body of Christ? Accordingly, when we define it there is no absurdity in our thus emphasizing its particular effect and, as a distinction, subordinating to the class that special mark which separates believers from unbelievers. In short, in this doctrine the malicious have nothing to carp at without implicating Paul in the same censure with us, who rightly calls the gospel "the word of faith" (Rom. 10:8).

31. The significance of the Word for faith

Hence, we again infer what had been explained before: that faith needs the Word as much as fruit needs the living root of a tree. For no others, as David witnesses, can hope in God but those who know his name (Ps. 9:10). But this knowledge does not arise out of anyone's imagination, but only so far as God himself is witness to his goodness. This the prophet confirms in another place: "Thy salvation according to thy word" (Ps. 119:41). Likewise, "I have hoped in thy word; make me safe." (Ps. 119:42, 40, 94.) Here we must first note the relation of faith to the Word, then its consequence, salvation.

Yet in the meantime we do not exclude God's power in re-

spect to which, unless faith sustains itself, it can never render
to God the honor due him. Paul seems to apply to Abraham
a barren commonplace: that he believed God, who had
promised him blessed offspring, to be mighty (Rom. 4:21).
Likewise, he says elsewhere concerning himself: "I know
whom I have believed, and I am sure that he is mighty to
guard until that day what has been entrusted to me" (II
Tim. 1:12). But if anyone considers in himself how many
doubts concerning the power of God often creep in, he will
sufficiently recognize that they who magnify it as it deserves
have made no slight progress in faith. All of us will confess
that God is able to do whatever he wills; but when the slightest temptation strikes us down in fear and stuns us with fright,
from this it is plain that we detract from God's might, preferring to it the threatening of Satan against His promises.
This is the reason why Isaiah, when he wishes to impress
the certainty of salvation upon the hearts of the people, so
grandly discusses God's boundless power (Isa. 40:25 ff., and
often in Isa., chs. 40 to 45). It often seems that, when he
begins to speak concerning the hope of pardon and reconciliation, he turns to something else and wanders through
long and superfluous mazes, recalling how wonderfully God
governs the frame of heaven and earth together with the
whole order of nature. Yet there is nothing here that does
not serve the present circumstance. For unless the power of
God, by which he can do all things, confronts our eyes, our
ears will barely receive the Word or not esteem it at its true
value.

Besides this, his effectual might is here declared, since
piety—as has appeared elsewhere—always adapts God's might
to use and need; and especially sets before itself the works of
God by which he has testified that he is the Father. Hence
comes the very frequent mention of redemption in the Scriptures, from which the Israelites could learn that God, who
had once for all been the Author of salvation, was to be its
eternal guardian. By his example David, also, reminds us that
those benefits which God bestows individually upon each
man serve to confirm faith in him for the future. Indeed,
when it seems that he has deserted us we must stretch our
thoughts farther, that his former benefits may revive us, as is
said in another psalm: "I remember the days of old, I have
meditated on all thy deeds . . ." (Ps. 143:5; 142:5, Vg.).
Likewise, "I will remember the works of the Lord . . . and
his wonders from the beginning." (Ps. 77:11, Comm.)

But because whatever we conceive concerning God's might and works is fleeting without the Word, we declare with good reason that there is no faith until God illumines it by the testimony of his grace.

Yet here it would be possible to raise the question What should we think of Sarah and Rebecca? both of whom, it seems, were fired with a zealous faith and went beyond the limits of the Word. Sarah, passionately desiring the promised offspring, yielded her maidservant to her husband (Gen. 16:2, 5). We must not deny that she sinned in many ways; but I am now dealing with her failure, when carried away with zeal, to confine herself within the limits of God's Word. Yet it is certain that that desire arose out of faith. Rebecca, assured by divine oracle of the choice of her son Jacob, obtains the blessing for him by a wicked subterfuge (Gen. 27:9): She deceives her husband, the witness and minister of God's grace. She compels her son to lie. She corrupts God's truth by various guiles and deceits. In short, in scorning his promise, she destroys it as far as she can (Gen., ch. 27).

Yet this act, although a failing and deserving of rebuke, was not devoid of faith. For it was necessary that she overcome many little obstacles that she might stoutly strive after something that offered no hope of earthly benefit, and was teeming with huge troubles and dangers. In the same way, we do not regard the patriarch Isaac as entirely devoid of faith for the reason that, admonished by the same oracle concerning the honor transferred to his younger son, he still did not cease to be inclined to his first-born son, Esau. These examples surely teach that errors are often mingled with faith, yet in such a way that when it is a true faith it always holds the upper hand. For just as Rebecca's particular error did not render void the effect of the blessing, so it did not render void her faith, which generally held mastery in her mind and was the beginning and cause of that action. Nonetheless, Rebecca betrayed in this how slippery are the turnings of the human mind, as soon as it relaxes its control in the slightest degree. But even though man's default and weakness obscure faith, they do not extinguish it. In the meantime, they warn us how carefully we ought to wait upon God's voice; and at the same time they confirm what we have taught: that faith vanishes unless it is supported by the Word. The minds of Sarah and Isaac and Rebecca would have vanished in their devious shiftings if they had not been kept in obedience to the Word by God's secret bridle.

32. *The promise of faith fulfilled in Christ*

Again, it is not without cause that we include all the promises in Christ, since the apostle includes the whole gospel under the knowledge of him (cf. Rom. 1:17), and elsewhere teaches that "however many are the promises of God, in him they find their yea and amen" (II Cor. 1:20 p.). The reason for this fact is at hand; for if God promises anything, by it he witnesses his benevolence, so that there is no promise of his which is not a testimony of his love. Nor does it make any difference that, while the wicked are plied with the huge and repeated benefits of God's bounty, they bring upon themselves a heavier judgment. For they neither think nor recognize that these benefits come to them from the Lord's hand; or if they do recognize it, they do not within themselves ponder his goodness. Hence, they cannot be apprised of his mercy any more than brute animals can, which, according to their condition, receive the same fruit of God's liberality, yet perceive it not. Nothing prevents them, in habitually rejecting the promises intended for them, from thereby bringing upon themselves a greater vengeance. For although the effectiveness of the promises only appears when they have aroused faith in us, yet the force and peculiar nature of the promises are never extinguished by our unfaithfulness and ingratitude. Therefore, since the Lord, by his promises, invites man not only to receive the fruits of his kindness but also to think about them, he at the same time declares his love to man. Hence we must return to the point: that any promise whatsoever is a testimony of God's love toward us.

But it is indisputable that no one is loved by God apart from Christ: "This is the beloved Son" (Matt. 3:17; 17:5 p.), in whom dwells and rests the Father's love. And from him it then pours itself upon us, just as Paul teaches: "We receive grace in the beloved" (Eph. 1:6 p.). It must therefore derive and reach us when he himself intercedes. Consequently, the apostle in one passage calls him "our peace" (Eph. 2:14); in another, Paul puts him forward as the bond whereby God may be found to us in fatherly faithfulness (cf. Rom. 8:3 ff.). It follows that we should turn our eyes to him as often as any promise is offered to us. And Paul rightly teaches us that all God's promises are confirmed and fulfilled in him (Rom. 15:8).

Some instances disagree with this. When, for example,

Naaman the Syrian inquired of the prophet as to the proper way of worshiping God, it is not likely that he was instructed concerning the Mediator. Still, his piety is praised (II Kings 5:1–14; Luke 4:27). Cornelius, a Gentile and a Roman, could scarcely grasp what was known only obscurely to the Jews, and not to all of them. Yet his alms and his prayers were acceptable to God (Acts 10:31). And Naaman's sacrifice was approved by the prophet's response (II Kings 5:17–19). Neither could have occurred except by faith. The same reasoning applies to the eunuch to whom Philip was brought: unless he had been endowed with some faith, he would not have undertaken the labor and expense of a difficult journey in order to worship (Acts 8:27). Yet we see that when asked by Philip, he showed his ignorance of the Mediator (Acts 8:31). And I even confess that their faith was in some part implicit, not only with respect to the person of Christ, but also with respect to the power and office enjoined upon him by the Father. In the meantime, it is certain that they were instructed in principles such as might give them some taste, however small, of Christ. This ought not to seem strange, for the eunuch would not have hastened to Jerusalem from a far-off region to worship an unknown God; and certainly Cornelius, having once embraced the Jewish religion, did not spend much time without becoming acquainted with the rudiments of true doctrine. As far as Naaman was concerned, it would have been too absurd, when Elisha instructed him concerning small things, to have been silent on the principal point. Therefore, although the knowledge of Christ was obscure among them, it is inconceivable to suppose that there was none at all; because they practiced the sacrifices of the law, which by their very end—that is, Christ—should be distinguished from the false sacrifices of the Gentiles.

(*Faith revealed in our hearts by the Spirit, 33–37*)

33. *The Word becomes efficacious for our faith through the Holy Spirit*

And this bare and external proof of the Word of God should have been amply sufficient to engender faith, did not our blindness and perversity prevent it. But our mind has such an inclination to vanity that it can never cleave fast to the truth of God; and it has such a dullness that it is always blind to the light of God's truth. Accordingly, without the illumination of the Holy Spirit, the Word can do nothing. From this, also, it is clear that faith is much higher than human understanding. And it will not be enough for the mind to be illumined by the Spirit of God unless the heart is also strengthened and supported by his power. In this matter the Schoolmen go completely astray, who in considering faith identify it with a bare and simple assent arising out of knowledge, and leave out confidence and assurance of heart. In both ways, therefore, faith is a singular gift of God, both in that the mind of man is purged so as to be able to taste the truth of God and in that his heart is established therein. For the Spirit is not only the initiator of faith, but increases it by degrees, until by it he leads us to the Kingdom of Heaven. "Let each one," says Paul, "guard the precious truth . . . entrusted by the Holy Spirit who dwells in us." (II Tim. 1:14 p.) We can with no trouble explain how Paul teaches that the Spirit is given by the hearing of faith (Gal. 3:2). If there had been only one gift of the Spirit, it would have been absurd of Paul to call the Spirit the "effect of faith," since he is its Author and cause. But because he proclaims the gifts with which God adorns his church and brings it to perfection by continual increase of faith, it is no wonder if he ascribes to faith those things which prepare us to receive them! This, indeed, is considered most paradoxical: when it is said that no one, unless faith be granted to him, can believe in Christ (John 6:65). But this is partly because men do not consider either how secret and lofty the heavenly wisdom is, or how very dull men are to perceive the mysteries of God; partly because they do not have regard to that firm and steadfast constancy of heart which is the chief part of faith.

34. Only the Holy Spirit leads us to Christ

But if, as Paul preaches, no one "except the spirit of man which is in him" (I Cor. 2:11) witnesses the human will, what man would be sure of God's will? And if the truth of God be untrustworthy among us also in those things which we at present behold with our eyes, how could it be firm and steadfast when the Lord promises such things as neither eye can see nor understanding can grasp (cf. I Cor. 2:9)? But here man's discernment is so overwhelmed and so fails that the first degree of advancement in the school of the Lord is to renounce it. For, like a veil cast over us, it hinders us from attaining the mysteries of God, "revealed to babes alone" (Matt. 11:25; Luke 10:21). "For flesh and blood does not reveal this" (Matt. 16:17), "but the natural man does not perceive the things that are of the Spirit"; rather, God's teaching is "foolishness to him . . . because it must be spiritually discerned" (I Cor. 2:14, cf. Vg.). Therefore, the support of the Holy Spirit is necessary, or rather, his power alone thrives here. "There is no man who has known the mind of God, or has been his counselor." (Rom. 11:34 p.) But "the Spirit searches everything, even the depths of God." (I Cor. 2:10.) It is through the Spirit that we come to grasp "the mind of Christ" (I Cor. 2:16). "No one can come to me," he says, "unless the Father who has sent me draw him." (John 6:44.) "Everyone who has heard from the Father and has learned, comes." (John 6:45.) Not that anyone has ever seen the Father but him who was sent by God (John 1:18 and 5:37, conflated). Therefore, as we cannot come to Christ unless we be drawn by the Spirit of God, so when we are drawn we are lifted up in mind and heart above our understanding. For the soul, illumined by him, takes on a new keenness, as it were, to contemplate the heavenly mysteries, whose splendor had previously blinded it. And man's understanding, thus beamed by the light of the Holy Spirit, then at last truly begins to taste those things which belong to the Kingdom of God, having formerly been quite foolish and dull in tasting them. For this reason, Christ, in clearly interpreting the mysteries of his Kingdom to two disciples (Luke 24:27), still makes no headway until "he opens their minds to understand the Scriptures" (Luke 24:45). Although the apostles were so taught by his divine mouth, the Spirit of truth must nevertheless be sent to pour into their minds the same doctrine that they had perceived with their ears (John 16:13). Indeed, the Word of God is like the sun, shining upon all those to whom it is proclaimed, but with no effect among the blind. Now, all of us are blind by nature in this respect. Accordingly, it cannot penetrate into our minds unless the Spirit, as the inner teacher, through his illumination makes entry for it.

35. *Without the Spirit man is incapable of faith*

In another place, when we had to discuss the corruption of nature, we showed more fully how unfit men are to believe. Accordingly, I shall not weary my readers with repeating the same thing. Let it suffice that Paul calls faith itself, which the Spirit gives us but which we do not have by nature, "the spirit of faith" (II Cor. 4:13). He therefore prays that in the Thessalonians "God . . . may fulfill with power all his good pleasure . . . and work of faith" (II Thess. 1:11, cf. Vg.). Here Paul calls faith "the work of God," and instead of distinguishing it by an adjective, appropriately calls it "good pleasure." Thus he denies that man himself initiates faith, and not satisfied with this, he adds that it is a manifestation of God's power. In the letter to the Corinthians he states that faith does not depend upon men's wisdom, but is founded upon the might of the Spirit (I Cor. 2:4–5). He is speaking, indeed, of outward miracles; but because the wicked, being blind, cannot see these, he includes also that inner seal which he mentions elsewhere (Eph. 1:13; 4:30). And God, to show forth his liberality more fully in such a glorious gift, does not bestow it upon all indiscriminately, but by a singular privilege gives it to those to whom he will. We have above cited testimonies of this. Augustine, the faithful interpreter of them, exclaims: "Our Savior, to teach us that belief comes as a gift and not from merit, says: 'No one comes to me, unless my Father . . . draw him' (John 6:44 p.), and '. . . it be granted him by my Father' (John 6:65 p.). It is strange that two hear: one despises, the other rises up! Let him who despises impute it to himself; let him who rises up not arrogate it to himself." In another passage he says: "Why is it given to one and not to another? I am not ashamed to say: 'This is the depth of the cross.' Out of some depth or other of God's judgments, which we cannot fathom, . . . comes forth all that we can do. . . . I see what I can do; I do not see whence I can do it—except that I see this far: that . . . it is of God. But why one and not the other? This means much to me. It is an abyss, the depth of the cross. I can exclaim in wonder; I cannot demonstrate it through disputation." To sum up: Christ, when he illumines us into faith by the power of his Spirit, at the same time so engrafts us into his body that we become partakers of every good.

36. Faith as a matter of the heart

It now remains to pour into the heart itself what the mind has absorbed. For the Word of God is not received by faith if it flits about in the top of the brain, but when it takes root in the depth of the heart that it may be an invincible defense to withstand and drive off all the stratagems of temptation. But if it is true that the mind's real understanding is illumination by the Spirit of God, then in such confirmation of the heart his power is much more clearly manifested, to the extent that the heart's distrust is greater than the mind's blindness. It is harder for the heart to be furnished with assurance than for the mind to be endowed with thought. The Spirit accordingly serves as a seal, to seal up in our hearts those very promises the certainty of which it has previously impressed upon our minds; and takes the place of a guarantee to confirm and establish them. After "you believed" (the apostle declares), "you were sealed with the Holy Spirit of promise, who is the guarantee of our inheritance" (Eph. 1:13–14, Comm.). Do you see how Paul teaches that the hearts of believers have, so to speak, been sealed with the Spirit; how, for this reason, Paul calls him the "Spirit of promise," because he makes firm the gospel among us? In like manner, he says in the letter to the Corinthians: "He who . . . has anointed us, is God; who has also sealed us, and given the guarantee of the Spirit in our hearts" (II Cor. 1:21–22, KJV). And, in another passage, when Paul speaks of confidence and boldness of hope, he lays as its foundation the guarantee of the Spirit (II Cor. 5:5).

37. Doubt cannot smother faith

And I have not forgotten what I have previously said, the memory of which is repeatedly renewed by experience: faith is tossed about by various doubts, so that the minds of the godly are rarely at peace—at least they do not always enjoy a peaceful state. But whatever siege engines may shake them, they either rise up out of the very gulf of temptations, or stand fast upon their watch. Indeed, this assurance alone nourishes and protects faith—when we hold fast to what is said in the psalm: "The Lord is our protection, our help in tribulation. Therefore we will not fear while the earth shakes, and the mountains leap into the heart of the sea" (Ps. 46:2–3, cf. Comm.). Another psalm, also, extols this very sweet repose: "I lay down and slept; I awoke again, for the Lord sustained me" (Ps. 3:5). Not that David always dwelt in a tranquil and happy state! But to the extent that he tasted God's grace, according to the measure of faith, he boasts that he fearlessly despises everything that could trouble his peace of mind. For this reason, Scripture, meaning to urge us to faith, bids us be quiet. In Isaiah: "In hope and in silence shall your strength be" (ch. 30:15, Vg.). In the psalm: "Be still before Jehovah and wait . . . for him" (Ps. 37:7, Comm.). To these verses corresponds the apostle's statement in The Letter to the Hebrews "For you have need of patience," etc. (ch. 10:36).

(Refutation of Scholastic objections to this, 38–40)

38. Scholastic error concerning the assurance of faith

Hence we may judge how dangerous is the Scholastic dogma that we can discern the grace of God toward us only by moral conjecture, according as every man regards himself as not unworthy of it. Indeed, if we should have to judge from our works how the Lord feels toward us, for my part, I grant that we can in no way attain it by conjecture. But since faith ought to correspond to a simple and free promise, no place for doubting is left. For with what sort of confidence will we be armed, I pray, if we reason that God is favorable to us provided our purity of life so merit it? But because I have reserved a suitable place to treat these matters, I will not for the present pursue them any longer; especially since it is abundantly clear that there is nothing more averse to faith than either conjecture or anything else akin to doubt.

The Schoolmen most wickedly twist the testimony of Ecclesiastes, which they have continually on their lips: "No one knows whether he deserves hate or love" (Eccl. 9:1, Vg.). For, to pass over how this passage is erroneously translated in the Vulgate, even children cannot miss what Solomon means by these words. That is, if anyone would judge by the present state of things, which men God pursues with hatred and which ones he embraces in love, he labors in vain and troubles himself to no profit, "since all things happen alike to righteous and impious, . . . to those who sacrifice victims and to those who do not sacrifice" (Eccl. 9:2, cf. Vg.). From this it follows that God does not everlastingly witness his love to those for whom he causes all things to prosper, nor does he always manifest his hate to those whom he afflicts. And he does this to prove the innate folly of humanity, since among things so necessary to know it is grasped with such great stupidity. As Solomon had written a little before, one cannot discern how the soul of a man differs from the

soul of a beast because both seem to die in the same way
(Eccl. 3:19). If any man would infer from this that the opinion that we hold concerning the immortality of souls rests
upon conjecture alone, should we not justly consider him
insane? Are they sane men who infer—since we can comprehend nothing by the physical beholding of present things—
that there is no certainty of God's grace?

39. The Christian rejoices in the indwelling of the Spirit

But they contend that it is a matter of rash presumption
for us to claim an undoubted knowledge of God's will. Now
I would concede that point to them only if we took upon ourselves to subject God's incomprehensible plan to our slender
understanding. But when we simply say with Paul: "We
have received not the spirit of this world, but the Spirit that is
from God . . . ," by whose teaching "we know the gifts bestowed on us by God" (I Cor. 2:12), how can they yelp
against us without abusively assaulting the Holy Spirit? But
if it is a dreadful sacrilege to accuse the revelation given by
the Spirit either of falsehood or uncertainty or ambiguity,
how do we transgress in declaring its certainty?

But they cry aloud that it is also great temerity on our part
that we thus dare to glory in the Spirit of Christ. Who would
credit such stupidity to those who wish to be regarded as
the schoolmasters of the world, that they so shamefully trip
over the first rudiments of Christianity? Surely, it would not
have been credible to me, if their extant writings did not
attest it. Paul declares that those very ones "who are led by
the Spirit of God are sons of God . . ." (Rom. 8:14). And
these men would have it that those who are the children of
God are moved by their own spirit, but empty of God's
Spirit. Paul teaches that God is called "Father" by us at the
bidding of the Spirit, who alone can "witness to our spirit
that we are children of God" (Rom. 8:16). Even though
these men do not keep us from calling upon God, they withdraw the Spirit, by whose leading he ought to have been
duly called upon. Paul denies that those who are not moved
by the Spirit of Christ are servants of Christ (cf. Rom. 8:9).
These men devise a Christianity that does not require the
Spirit of Christ. He holds out no hope of blessed resurrection
unless we feel the Spirit dwelling in us (Rom. 8:11). These
men invent a hope devoid of such a feeling.

Yet perchance they will answer that they do not deny we

ought to be endowed with the Spirit; but that it is a matter of modesty and humility not to be sure of it. What, then, does he mean when he bids the Corinthians examine themselves whether they are in the faith, to prove themselves whether they have Christ? Unless one knows that Christ dwells in him, he is reprobate (II Cor. 13:5). "Now we know," says John, "that he abides in us from the Spirit whom he has given us." (I John 3:24; 4:13.) And what else do we do but call Christ's promises into question when we wish to be accounted God's servants apart from his Spirit, whom he has declared he would pour out upon all his own people? (Isa. 44:3; cf. Joel 2:28.) What else is it, then, than to do injury to the Holy Spirit if we separate faith, which is his peculiar work, from him? Since these are the first beginnings of piety, it is a token of the most miserable blindness to charge with arrogance Christians who dare to glory in the presence of the Holy Spirit, without which glorying Christianity itself does not stand! But, actually, they declare by their own example how truly Christ spoke: "My Spirit was unknown to the world; he is recognized only by those among whom he abides" (John 14:17).

40. The alleged uncertainty as to whether we will persevere to the end

Not content with trying to undermine firmness of faith in one way alone, they assail it from another quarter. Thus, they say that even though according to our present state of righteousness we can judge concerning our possession of the grace of God, the knowledge of final perseverance remains in suspense. A fine confidence of salvation is left to us, if by moral conjecture we judge that at the present moment we are in grace, but we know not what will become of us tomorrow! The apostle speaks far otherwise: "I am surely convinced that neither angels, nor powers, nor principalities, nor death, nor life, nor things present, nor things to come . . . will separate us from the love by which the Lord embraces us in Christ" (Rom. 8:38–39 p.). They try to escape with a trifling solution, prating that the apostle had his assurance from a special revelation. But they are held too tightly to escape. For there he is discussing those benefits which come to all believers in common from faith, not those things which he exclusively experiences. Now the same apostle, in another place, puts us in fear by speaking of our weak-mindedness and inconstancy: "Let him who stands well," Paul says, "take heed lest he fall" (I Cor. 10:12 p.). It is true; but not such a fear as to put us to confusion, but such that we may learn to humble ourselves under God's mighty hand, as Peter explains it (I Peter 5:6).

Then, how absurd it is that the certainty of faith be limited to some point of time, when by its very nature it looks to a future immortality after this life is over! Since, therefore, believers ascribe to God's grace the fact that, illumined by his Spirit, they enjoy through faith the contemplation of heavenly life, such glorying is so far from arrogance that if any man is ashamed to confess it, in that very act he betrays his extreme ungratefulness by wickedly suppressing God's goodness, more than he testifies to his modesty or submission.

(Relation of faith to hope and love, 41–43)

41. Faith according to Heb. 11:1

The nature of faith could, seemingly, not be better or more plainly declared than by the substance of the promise upon which it rests as its proper foundation. Consequently, when that promise is removed, it will utterly fall, or rather vanish. Therefore, we have taken our definition from this fact. Yet this does not at all differ from the apostle's definition, or rather the description he applies to his discourse, where he teaches that "faith is the substance of things to be hoped for, the indication of things not appearing" (Heb. 11:1, cf. Vg.). Now, by the word "hypostasis," which he uses, he means a sort of support upon which the godly mind may lean and rest. It is as if he were to say that faith itself is a sure and secure possession of those things which God has promised us, unless someone prefers to understand "hypostasis" as confidence! This does not displease me, although I accept what is more commonly received. On the other hand, Paul intended to signify that even to the last day, when "the books shall be opened" (Dan. 7:10), the things pertaining to our salvation are too high to be perceived by our senses, or seen by our eyes, or handled by our hands; and that in the meantime we do not possess these things in any other way than if we transcend all the limits of our senses and direct our perception beyond all things of this world and, in short, surpass ourselves. Therefore he adds that this assurance of possession is of those things which lie in hope, and are therefore not seen. "Whatsoever," as Paul writes, "is visible, is not hope; nor do we hope for what we see." (Rom. 8:24 p.) When he calls it an "indication" or "proof"—or, as Augustine has often translated it, "a conviction of things not present" (the word for "conviction" is ἔλεγχος in Greek (Heb. 11:1)) —Paul speaks as if to say that faith is an evidence of things not appearing, a seeing of things not seen, a clearness of things obscure, a presence of things absent, a showing forth of things hidden. The mysteries of God, and especially those which pertain to our salvation, cannot be discerned in themselves, or as it is said, in their own nature. But we contemplate them only in his Word, of the truth of which we ought to be so persuaded that we should count whatever he speaks as already done and fulfilled.

(Faith and love)

But how can the mind be aroused to taste the divine goodness without at the same time being wholly kindled to love God in return? For truly, that abundant sweetness which God has stored up for those who fear him cannot be known without at the same time powerfully moving us. And once anyone has been moved by it, it utterly ravishes him and draws him to itself. Therefore, it is no wonder if a perverse and wicked heart never experiences that emotion by which, borne up to heaven itself, we are admitted to the most hidden treasures of God and to the most hallowed precincts of his Kingdom, which should not be defiled by the entrance of an impure heart.

For the teaching of the Schoolmen, that love is prior to faith and hope, is mere madness; for it is faith alone that first engenders love in us. How much more rightly Bernard states: "I believe that the testimony of the conscience, which Paul calls 'the glory of the pious,' (II Cor. 1:12) consists of three things. First of all, it is necessary to believe that you cannot have forgiveness of sins apart from God's mercy. Second, you can have no good work at all unless he gives it. Finally, you cannot merit eternal life by any works unless that is also given free." Shortly thereafter he adds that these things are not enough, but are a beginning of faith; because in believing that sins cannot be forgiven except by God, we ought at the same time to believe that they are forgiven, so long as we are persuaded also by the testimony of the Holy

Spirit that salvation is stored up for us. And because God himself forgives sins, gives merits, and gives back rewards, we must also believe that we cannot take a firm stand in this beginning. But these and other matters will have to be discussed in their place. Now, let us be content merely to grasp what faith itself is.

42. *Faith and hope belong together*

Yet, wherever this faith is alive, it must have along with it the hope of eternal salvation as its inseparable companion. Or rather, it engenders and brings forth hope from itself. When this hope is taken away, however eloquently or elegantly we discourse concerning faith, we are convicted of having none. For if faith, as has been said above, is a sure persuasion of the truth of God—that it can neither lie to us, nor deceive us, nor become void—then those who have grasped this certainty assuredly expect the time to come when God will fulfill his promises, which they are persuaded cannot but be true. Accordingly, in brief, hope is nothing else than the expectation of those things which faith has believed to have been truly promised by God. Thus, faith believes God to be true, hope awaits the time when his truth shall be manifested; faith believes that he is our Father, hope anticipates that he will ever show himself to be a Father toward us; faith believes that eternal life has been given to us; hope anticipates that it will some time be revealed; faith is the foundation upon which hope rests, hope nourishes and sustains faith. For as no one except him who already believes His promises can look for anything from God, so again the weakness of our faith must be sustained and nourished by patient hope and expectation, lest it fail and grow faint. For this reason, Paul rightly sets our salvation in hope (Rom. 8:24). For hope, while it awaits the Lord in silence, restrains faith that it may not fall headlong from too much haste. Hope strengthens faith, that it may not waver in God's promises, or begin to doubt concerning their truth. Hope refreshes faith, that it may not become weary. It sustains faith to the final goal, that it may not fail in midcourse, or even at the starting gate. In short, by unremitting renewing and restoring, it invigorates faith again and again with perseverance.

And we shall better see in how many ways the support of hope is necessary to establish faith if we ponder how many forms of temptation assail and strike those who have embraced the Word of God. First, the Lord by deferring his promises often holds our minds in suspense longer than we would wish. Here it is the function of hope to carry out what the prophet bids: "That, if they should tarry, we wait for them" (Hab. 2:3 p.). Occasionally he not only allows us to faint but exhibits open indignation toward us. Here it is much more necessary for hope to help us, that, according to another prophet's statement, we may "wait for the Lord who hid his face from . . . Jacob" (Isa. 8:17). Scoffers also rise up, as Peter says (II Peter 3:3), asking: "Where is the promise of his coming? Since the fathers fell asleep, all things continue as they were from the beginning of creation" (II Peter 3:4, Vg.). Indeed, the flesh and the world whisper these same things to us. Here we must keep our faith buttressed by patient hope, so fixed upon the contemplation of eternity as to reckon a thousand years as one day (Ps. 90:4; II Peter 3:8).

43. Faith and hope have the same foundation: God's mercy

Because of this connection and kinship, Scripture sometimes uses the words "faith" and "hope" interchangeably. For when Peter teaches that we are "guarded by God's power through faith until salvation is revealed" (I Peter 1:5 p.), he attributes to faith something that corresponds to hope. And not unjustly, since we have already taught that hope is nothing but the nourishment and strength of faith.

Sometimes they are joined together, as in the same letter: "So that your faith and hope are in God" (I Peter 1:21). But in the letter to the Philippians, Paul derives expectation from hope because by hoping patiently we suspend our own desires until God's appointed time is revealed (Phil. 1:20). This whole matter can be better understood from the eleventh chapter of Hebrews, which I have already cited (v. 1). In another passage, although speaking inexactly, Paul means the same thing by these words: "Through the Spirit, by faith, we wait for the hope of righteousness" (Gal. 5:5). That is, because, embracing the testimony of the gospel concerning freely given love, we look for the time when God will openly show that which is now hidden under hope.

It is now clear how foolishly Peter Lombard lays two foundations of hope: grace of God and merit of works. Hope can have no other goal than faith has. But we have already explained very clearly that the single goal of faith is the mercy of God—to which it ought, so to speak, to look with both eyes. But it behooves us to hear what a cogent reason Lombard brings forward: "If," he says, "you dare to hope for anything without merit, that ought not to be called 'hope' but rather 'presumption.'" Who, dear reader, will not justly despise such beasts, who declare that a man is acting rashly and presumptuously if he trust that God is true? For, though the Lord wills that we await all things from his goodness, they say that it is presumption to lean and rest upon it. A master indeed—worthy of such pupils as he found in the mad schools of wranglers! But for our part, when we as sinners see that we are commanded by the oracles of God to conceive of hope of salvation, let us so willingly presume upon his truth that, relying upon his mercy alone, abandoning reliance upon works, we dare to have good hope. He will not deceive, who said, "According to your faith be it done to you" (Matt. 9:29).

BOOK III, CHAPTER XI

JUSTIFICATION BY FAITH: FIRST THE DEFINITION OF
THE WORD AND OF THE MATTER

(Justification and regeneration, the terms defined, 1–4)

1. Place and meaning of the doctrine of "justification"

I believe I have already explained above, with sufficient care, how for men cursed under the law, there remains, in faith, one sole means of recovering salvation. I believe I have also explained what faith itself is, and those benefits of God which it confers upon man, and the fruits it brings forth in him. Let us sum these up. Christ was given to us by God's generosity, to be grasped and possessed by us in faith. By partaking of him, we principally receive a double grace: namely, that being reconciled to God through Christ's blamelessness, we may have in heaven instead of a Judge a gracious Father; and secondly, that sanctified by Christ's spirit we may cultivate blamelessness and purity of life. Of regeneration, indeed, the second of these gifts, I have said what seemed sufficient. The theme of justification was therefore more lightly touched upon because it was more to the point to understand first how little devoid of good works is the faith, through which alone we obtain free righteousness by the mercy of God; and what is the nature of the good works of the saints, with which part of this question is concerned. Therefore we must now discuss these matters thoroughly. And we must so discuss them as to bear in mind that this is the main hinge on which religion turns, so that we devote the greater attention and care to it. For unless you first of all grasp what your relationship to God is, and the nature of his judgment concerning you, you have neither a foundation on which to establish your salvation nor one on which to build piety toward God. But the need to know this will better appear from the knowledge itself.

2. The concept of justification

But that we may not stumble on the very threshold—and this would happen if we should enter upon a discussion of a thing unknown—first let us explain what these expressions mean: that man is justified in God's sight, and that he is justified by faith or works. He is said to be justified in God's sight who is both reckoned righteous in God's judgment and has been accepted on account of his righteousness. Indeed, as iniquity is abominable to God, so no sinner can find favor in his eyes in so far as he is a sinner and so long as he is reckoned as such. Accordingly, wherever there is sin, there also the wrath and vengeance of God show themselves. Now he is justified who is reckoned in the condition not of a sinner, but of a righteous man; and for that reason, he stands firm before God's judgment seat while all sinners fall. If an innocent accused person be summoned before the judgment seat of a fair judge, where he will be judged according to his innocence, he is said to be "justified" before the judge. Thus, justified before God is the man who, freed from the company of sinners, has God to witness and affirm his righteousness. In the same way, therefore, he in whose life that purity and holiness will be found which deserves a testimony of righteousness before God's throne will be said to be justified by works, or else he who, by the wholeness of his works, can meet and satisfy God's judgment. On the contrary, justified by faith is he who, excluded from the righteousness of works, grasps the righteousness of Christ through faith, and clothed in it, appears in God's sight not as a sinner but as a righteous man.

Therefore, we explain justification simply as the acceptance with which God receives us into his favor as righteous men. And we say that it consists in the remission of sins and the imputation of Christ's righteousness.

3. Scriptural usage

There are many clear testimonies of Scripture to confirm this fact. First, it cannot be denied that this is a proper and most customary meaning of the word. But because it would take too long to collect all the passages and to compare them, let it suffice to have called them to our readers' attention, for they will readily observe such of themselves. I shall bring forward only a few, where this justification of which we are speaking is expressly treated.

First, when Luke relates that the people, having heard Christ, justified God (Luke 7:29), and when Christ declares that "wisdom is justified by . . . her children" (Luke 7:35), Luke in the former passage (v. 29) does not mean that they confer righteousness. For righteousness always remains undivided with God, although the whole world tries to snatch it away from him. Nor does he, in v. 35, intend to justify the doctrine of salvation, which is righteous of itself. Rather, both expressions have the same force—to render to God and his teaching the praise they deserve. On the other hand, when Christ upbraids the Pharisees for justifying themselves (Luke 16:15), he does not mean that they acquire righteousness by well-doing but that they ambitiously seize upon a reputation for righteousness of which they are devoid. Those skilled in the Hebrew language better understand this sense: where not only those who are conscious of their crime but those who undergo the judgment of damnation are called "wicked." For when Bathsheba says that she and Solomon will be wicked (I Kings 1:21), she does not acknowledge any offense. But she complains that she and her son are going to be put to shame, to be counted among the wicked and condemned. Yet from the context it readily appears that this word, even when it is read in Latin, cannot otherwise be understood than relatively, but not so as to signify any quality.

But, because it pertains to the present case, when Paul says that Scripture foresaw that God would justify the Gentiles by faith (Gal. 3:8), what else may you understand but that God imputes righteousness by faith? Again, when he says that God justifies the impious person who has faith in Christ (Rom. 3:26 p.), what can his meaning be except that men are freed by the benefit of faith from that condemnation which their impiety deserved? This appears even more clearly in his conclusion, when he exclaims: "Who will accuse God's elect? It is God who justifies. Who will condemn? It is Christ who died, yes, who rose again . . . and now intercedes for us" (Rom. 8:33–34 p.). For it is as if he had said: "Who will accuse those whom God has absolved? Who will condemn those whom Christ defends with his protection?" Therefore, "to justify" means nothing else than to acquit of guilt him who was accused, as if his innocence were confirmed. Therefore, since God justifies us by the intercession of Christ, he absolves us not by the confirmation of our own innocence but by the imputation of righteousness, so that we who are not righteous in ourselves may be reckoned as such in Christ. Thus it is said in Paul's sermon in the thirteenth chapter of The Acts: Through Christ is forgiveness of sins announced to you, and everyone who believes in him is justified of all things from which the law of Moses could not justify him (Acts 13:38–39). You see that, after forgiveness of sins, this justification is set down, as it were, by way of interpretation. You see that it is plainly understood as absolution, you see that it is separated from the works of the law. You see it as the mere benefit of Christ, and you see that it is received by faith. You see finally that a satisfaction is introduced where he says that we are justified from our sins through Christ. Thus, when the publican is said to have gone down from the Temple justified (Luke 18:14), we cannot say that he achieved righteousness by any merit of works. This, therefore, is what is said: after pardon of sins has been obtained, the sinner is considered as a just man in God's sight. Therefore, he was righteous not by approval of works but by God's free absolution. Ambrose has, accordingly, fitly expressed it when he calls the confession of sins a lawful justification.

4. Justification as gracious acceptance by God and as forgiveness of sins

And to avoid contention over a word, if we look upon the thing itself as described to us, no misgiving will remain.

For Paul surely refers to justification by the word "acceptance" when in Eph. 1:5–6 he says: "We are destined for adoption through Christ according to God's good pleasure, to the praise of his glorious grace by which he has accounted us acceptable and beloved" (Eph. 1:5–6 p.). That means the very thing that he commonly says elsewhere, that "God justifies us freely" (Rom. 3:24). Moreover, in the fourth chapter of Romans he first calls justification "imputation of righteousness." And he does not hesitate to include it within forgiveness of sins. Paul says: "That man is declared blessed by David whom God renders acceptable or to whom he imputes righteousness apart from works, as it is written: 'Blessed are they whose transgressions have been forgiven'" (Rom. 4:6–7 p.; Ps. 32:1). There he is obviously discussing not a part of justification but the whole of it. Further, he approves the definition of it set forth by David when he declares those men blessed to whom free pardon of sins is given (Ps. 32:1–2). From this it is clear that the righteousness of which he speaks is simply set in opposition to guilt. But the best passage of all on this matter is the one in which he teaches that the sum of the gospel embassy is to reconcile us to God, since God is willing to receive us into grace through Christ, not counting our sins against us (II Cor. 5:18–20). Let my readers carefully ponder the whole passage. For a little later Paul adds by way of explanation: "Christ, who was without sin, was made sin for us" (II Cor. 5:21), to designate the means of reconciliation (cf. vs. 18–19). Doubtless, he means by the word "reconciled" nothing but "justified." And surely, what he teaches elsewhere—that "we are made righteous by Christ's obedience" (Rom. 5:19 p.)—could not stand unless we are reckoned righteous before God in Christ and apart from ourselves.

(*Refutation of Osiander's doctrine of "essential righteousness," 5–12*)

5. Osiander's doctrine of essential righteousness

But Osiander has introduced some strange monster of "essential" righteousness by which, although not intending to abolish freely given righteousness, he has still enveloped it in such a fog as to darken pious minds and deprive them of a lively experience of Christ's grace. Consequently, before I pass on to other matters, it behooves me to refute this wild dream.

First, this speculation arises out of mere feeble curiosity. Indeed, he accumulates many testimonies of Scripture by which to prove that Christ is one with us, and we, in turn, with him—a fact that needs no proof. But because he does not observe the bond of this unity, he deceives himself. Now it is easy for us to resolve all his difficulties. For we hold ourselves to be united with Christ by the secret power of his Spirit.

That gentleman had conceived something bordering on Manichaeism, in his desire to transfuse the essence of God into men. From this arises another fiction of his, that Adam was formed to the image of God because Christ had already been destined as the prototype of human nature before the Fall. But because I am striving after brevity, I must concentrate on the present matter.

He says that we are one with Christ. We agree. But we deny that Christ's essence is mixed with our own. Then we say that this principle is wrongly applied to these deceptions of his: that Christ is our righteousness because he is God eternal, the source of righteousness, and the very righteousness of God. My readers will pardon me if I now only touch upon what my teaching plan demands that I defer to another place. Although he may make the excuse that by the term "essential righteousness" he means nothing else but to meet the opinion that we are considered righteous for Christ's sake, yet he has clearly expressed himself as not content with that righteousness which has been acquired for us by Christ's obedience and sacrificial death, but pretends that we are substantially righteous in God by the infusion both of his essence and of his quality. For this is the reason why he contends so vehemently that not only Christ but also the Father and the Holy Spirit, dwell in us. Although I admit this to be true, yet I say that it has been perversely twisted by Osiander; for he ought to have considered the manner of the indwelling—namely, that the Father and Spirit are in Christ, and even as the fullness of deity dwells in him (Col. 2:9), so in him we possess the whole of deity. Therefore, all that he has put forward separately concerning the Father and the Spirit tends solely to seduce the simple-minded from Christ.

Then he throws in a mixture of substances by which God—transfusing himself into us, as it were—makes us part of himself. For the fact that it comes about through the power of the Holy Spirit that we grow together with Christ, and he becomes our Head and we his members, he reckons of almost no importance unless Christ's essence be mingled with ours. But in his treatment of the Father and the Holy Spirit he more openly, as I have said, brings out what he means: namely, that we are not justified by the grace of the Mediator alone, nor is righteousness simply or completely offered to us in his person, but that we are made partakers in God's righteousness when God is united to us in essence.

6. Osiander erroneously mixes forgiveness of sins with rebirth

Suppose he had only said that Christ, in justifying us, by conjunction of essence becomes ours, not only in that in so far as he is man is he our Head, but also in that the essence of the divine nature is poured into us. Then he would have fed on these delights with less harm, and perhaps such a great quarrel on account of this delusion would not have had to arise. But inasmuch as this principle is like the cuttlefish, which by voiding its black and turbid blood hides its many tails, unless we would knowingly and willingly allow that righteousness to be snatched from us which alone gives us the confidence to glory in our salvation, we must bitterly resist. For in this whole disputation the noun "righteousness" and the verb "to justify" are extended in two directions; so that to be justified is not only to be reconciled to God through free pardon but also to be made righteous, and righteousness is not a free imputation but the holiness and uprightness that the essence of God, dwelling in us, inspires. Secondly, he sharply states that Christ is himself our righteousness, not in so far as he, by expiating sins as Priest, appeased the Father on our behalf, but as he is eternal God and life.

To prove the first point—that God justifies not only by pardoning but by regenerating—he asks whether God leaves as they were by nature those whom he justifies, changing none of their vices. This is exceedingly easy to answer: as Christ cannot be torn into parts, so these two which we perceive in him together and conjointly are inseparable—namely, righteousness and sanctification. Whomever, therefore, God receives into grace, on them he at the same time bestows the spirit of adoption (Rom. 8:15), by whose power he remakes them to his own image. But if the brightness of the sun cannot be separated from its heat, shall we therefore say that the earth is warmed by its light, or lighted by its heat? Is there anything more applicable to the present matter than this comparison? The sun, by its heat, quickens and fructifies the earth, by its beams brightens and illumines it. Here is a mutual and indivisible connection. Yet reason itself forbids us to transfer the peculiar qualities of the one to the other. In this confusion of the two kinds of grace that Osiander forces upon us there is a like absurdity. For since God, for the preservation of righteousness, renews those whom he freely reckons as righteous, Osiander mixes that gift of regeneration with this free acceptance and contends that they are one and the same. Yet Scripture, even though it joins them, still lists them separately in order that God's manifold grace may better appear to us. For Paul's statement is not redundant: that Christ was given to us for our righteousness and sanctification (I Cor. 1:30). And whenever he reasons—from the salvation purchased for us, from God's fatherly love, and from Christ's grace—that we are called to holiness and cleanness, he clearly indicates that to be justified means something different from being made new creatures.

When it comes to Scripture, Osiander completely corrupts every passage he cites. In Paul's statement that "faith is reckoned as righteousness" not for the "one who works" but for the "one who believes in him who justifies the ungodly" (Rom. 4:4–5 p.), Osiander explains "justify" as "to make righteous." With the same rashness he corrupts that whole fourth chapter of Romans. And he does not hesitate to tinge with the same deceit a passage that we have recently cited: "Who will accuse God's elect? It is God who justifies" (Rom. 8:33). There it is plain that the question is simply one of guilt and acquittal, and the meaning of the apostle depends on this antithesis. Therefore, both in that reason and in citing Scriptural evidence, Osiander proves himself an incompetent interpreter.

Also, he discusses the term "righteousness" no more correctly, holding that the faith of Abraham was imputed to him as righteousness after he, having embraced Christ—who is the righteousness of God and God himself—had excelled in singular virtues. From this it appears that he has incorrectly made one corrupt statement out of two sound ones. For righteousness, of which mention is there made, does not extend throughout the whole course of Abraham's calling.

Rather, the Spirit testifies—although the excellence of the virtues of Abraham was outstanding, and by persevering in them for a long time he at length increased them—that he pleased God only when he received in faith the grace offered in the promise. From this it follows that, as Paul skillfully contends, there is in justification no place for works.

7. The significance of faith for justification

I willingly concede Osiander's objection that faith of itself does not possess the power of justifying, but only in so far as it receives Christ. For if faith justified of itself or through some intrinsic power, so to speak, as it is always weak and imperfect it would effect this only in part; thus the righteousness that conferred a fragment of salvation upon us would be defective. Now we imagine no such thing, but we say that, properly speaking, God alone justifies; then we transfer this same function to Christ because he was given to us for righteousness. We compare faith to a kind of vessel; for unless we come empty and with the mouth of our soul open to seek Christ's grace, we are not capable of receiving Christ. From this it is to be inferred that, in teaching that before his righteousness is received Christ is received in faith, we do not take the power of justifying away from Christ.

Yet, in the meantime, I do not admit the distorted figures of this Sophist when he says that "faith is Christ"—as if an earthen pot were a treasure because gold is hidden in it. For the reasoning is similar: namely, that faith, even though of itself it is of no worth or price, can justify us by bringing Christ, just as a pot crammed with money makes a man rich. Therefore, I say that faith, which is only the instrument for receiving righteousness, is ignorantly confused with Christ, who is the material cause and at the same time the Author and Minister of this great benefit. Now we have disposed of the problem as to how the term "faith" ought to be understood when justification is under consideration.

8. Osiander's doctrine that Christ is, according to his divine nature, our righteousness

In the receiving of Christ, Osiander goes farther: that the inner word is received by the ministry of the outer word. By this he would lead us away from the priesthood of Christ and the person of the Mediator to his outward deity. Now we do not divide Christ but confess that he, who, reconciling us to the Father in his flesh, gave us righteousness, is the eternal Word of God, and that the duties of the Mediator could not otherwise have been discharged by him, or righteousness acquired for us, had he not been eternal God. But Osiander's opinion is that, since Christ is God and man, he is made righteousness for us with respect to his divine nature, not his human nature. Yet if this properly applies to divinity, it will not be peculiar to Christ but common with the Father and the Spirit, inasmuch as the righteousness of one differs not from the righteousness of the other. Then, because he was by nature from eternity, it would not be consistent to say that he was "made for us." But even though we should grant that God was made· righteousness for us, how will this harmonize with what Paul interposes: that Christ was made righteousness by God (I Cor. 1:30)? This is surely peculiar to the person of the Mediator, which, even though it contains in it the divine nature, still has its own proper designation by which the Mediator is distinguished from the Father and the Spirit.

Osiander absurdly gloats over one word of Jeremiah, where he promises that Jehovah will be our righteousness (Jer. 51:10; cf. chs. 23:6; 33:16). But from this he shall deduce nothing but the fact that Christ, who is our righteousness, is God manifested in flesh (cf. I Tim. 3:16). Elsewhere we have quoted from Paul's sermon: "With his blood God purchased the church for himself" (Acts 20:28 p.). If anyone should infer from this that the blood whereby sins have been expiated is divine and of the divine nature, who could bear such a foul error? Yet Osiander thinks that he has obtained all things by this very childish cavil; he swells up, exults, stuffs many pages with his bombast—while there is a simple and ready explanation of the words that Jehovah, when he should become the offspring of David, would be the righteousness of the godly. But Isaiah teaches in what sense this is so: "By knowledge of himself shall the righteous one, my servant, make many to be accounted righteous" (Isa. 53:11).

Let us note that it is the Father who is speaking; that he assigns to the Son the office of justifying; that he adds the reason—that he is righteous; and that he has lodged the mode and means, as they say, in the teaching whereby Christ becomes known. For it is more fitting to take the word דעת as a passive. Hence I gather that Christ was made righteousness when "he took upon him the form of a servant" (Phil. 2:7); secondly, that he justifies us in that he has shown himself obedient to the Father (Phil. 2:8). Therefore he does this for us not according to his divine nature but in accordance with the dispensation enjoined upon him. For even though God alone is the source of righteousness, and we are righteous only by participation in him, yet, because we have been estranged from his righteousness by unhappy disagreement, we must have recourse to this lower remedy that Christ may justify us by the power of his death and resurrection.

9. Justification as the work of the Mediator

If Osiander should object that this work, by its very excellence, surpasses human nature, and for this reason can be ascribed only to divine nature, I grant the first point; in the second I say that he is grossly deluded. For even though Christ if he had not been true God could not cleanse our souls by his blood, nor appease his Father by his sacrifice, nor absolve us from guilt, nor, in sum, fulfill the office of priest, because the power of the flesh is unequal to so great a burden, yet it is certain that he carried out all these acts according to his human nature. For if we ask how we have been justified, Paul answers, "By Christ's obedience" (Rom. 5:19 p.). But did he obey in any other way than in taking the form of a servant (Phil. 2:7)? From this we conclude that in his flesh, righteousness has been manifested to us. Similarly in other words—I am surprised that Osiander is not ashamed to cite that so often—Paul has established the source of righteousness in the flesh of Christ alone. "Him who knew no sin he made to be sin for us that we might be the righteousness of God in him." (II Cor. 5:21 p.) At the top of his lungs Osiander extols God's righteousness, and sings a song of triumph as if he had confirmed that ghost of his of "essential righteousness." Yet the words express something far different, that we are made righteous through the atonement wrought by Christ. Every schoolboy should know that God's righteousness is to be understood as that righteousness which is approved of God, as in the Gospel of John where God's glory is compared with men's glory (John 12:43, RV; 5:44). I know that it is sometimes called the righteousness of God because God is its author and bestows it upon us. But discerning readers will recognize without my saying anything that this

expression means only that we stand, supported by the sacrifice of Christ's death, before God's judgment seat.

And the word is not very important, provided Osiander
agrees with us, that we are justified in Christ, in so far as he
was made an atoning sacrifice for us: something that does
not comport with his divine nature. For this reason also, when
Christ would seal the righteousness and salvation that he has
brought us, he sets forth a sure pledge of it in his own flesh.
Now he calls himself "the bread of life" (John 6:48), but,
in explaining how, he adds that "his flesh is truly meat, and
his blood truly drink" (John 6:55). This method of teaching
is perceived in the sacraments; even though they direct our
faith to the whole Christ and not to a half-Christ, they teach
that the matter both of righteousness and of salvation resides
in his flesh; not that as mere man he justifies or quickens by
himself, but because it pleased God to reveal in the Mediator
what was hidden and incomprehensible in himself. Accordingly, I usually say that Christ is, as it were, a fountain, open
to us, from which we may draw what otherwise would lie
unprofitably hidden in that deep and secret spring, which
comes forth to us in the person of the Mediator. In this
way and sense, I do not deny that Christ, as he is God and
man, justifies us; and also that this work is the common task
of the Father and the Holy Spirit; finally, that righteousness
of which Christ makes us partakers with himself is the eternal righteousness of the eternal God—provided Osiander accept the firm and clear reasons that I have brought forward.

10. What is the nature of our union with Christ?

Now, lest Osiander deceive the unlearned by his cavils, I
confess that we are deprived of this utterly incomparable
good until Christ is made ours. Therefore, that joining together of Head and members, that indwelling of Christ in
our hearts—in short, that mystical union—are accorded by us
the highest degree of importance, so that Christ, having been
made ours, makes us sharers with him in the gifts with which
he has been endowed. We do not, therefore, contemplate
him outside ourselves from afar in order that his righteousness
may be imputed to us but because we put on Christ and are
engrafted into his body—in short, because he deigns to make
us one with him. For this reason, we glory that we have fellowship of righteousness with him. Thus is Osiander's slander

refuted, that by us faith is reckoned righteousness. As if we were to deprive Christ of his right when we say that by faith we come empty to him to make room for his grace in order that he alone may fill us! But Osiander, by spurning this spiritual bond, forces a gross mingling of Christ with believers. And for this reason, he maliciously calls "Zwinglian" all those who do not subscribe to his mad error of "essential righteousness" because they do not hold the view that Christ is eaten in substance in the Lord's Supper. I consider it the highest glory to be thus insulted by a proud man, and one entangled in his own deceits; albeit he attacks not only me but world-renowned writers whom he ought modestly to have respected. It makes no difference to me, for I am not pleading my own private cause. I am the more sincerely pleading this case for the reason that I am free from all perverted motives.

The fact, then, that he insists so violently upon essential righteousness and essential indwelling of Christ in us has this result: first, he holds that God pours himself into us as a gross mixture, just as he fancies a physical eating in the Lord's Supper; secondly, that he breathes his righteousness upon us, by which we may be really righteous with him, since according to Osiander this righteousness is both God himself and the goodness or holiness or integrity of God.

I shall not labor much in refuting the Scriptural proofs that he brings forward, which he wrongly twists from the heavenly life to the present state. "Through Christ," says Peter, "were granted to us precious and very great promises . . . that we might become partakers of the divine nature." (II Peter 1:4 p.) As if we now were what the gospel promises that we shall be at the final coming of Christ! Indeed, John then reminds us we are going to see God as he is because we shall be like him (I John 3:2). I only wanted to give a small sample to my readers. Consequently, I purposely pass over these trifles. Not that it would be difficult to refute them, but I do not want to elaborate tediously and superfluously.

11. Osiander's doctrine of the essential righteousness nullifies the certainty of salvation

But more poison lurks in the second phase, where Osiander teaches that we are righteous together with God. I have already sufficiently proved, I think, that this doctrine—even though it were not so pestilent, yet because it is cold and barren and is dissipated in its own vanity—ought rightly to be unsavory for intelligent and pious readers. To enfeeble our assurance of salvation, to waft us above the clouds in order to prevent our calling upon God with quiet hearts after we, assured of expiation, have laid hold upon grace—to do all this under pretense of a twofold righteousness is an utterly intolerable impiety.

Osiander laughs at those men who teach that "to be justified" is a legal term; because we must actually be righteous. Also, he despises nothing more than that we are justified by free imputation. Well then, if God does not justify us by acquittal and pardon, what does Paul's statement mean: "God was in Christ, reconciling the world to himself, not imputing men's trespasses against them" (II Cor. 5:19)? "For our sake he made him to be sin who had done no sin so that we might be the righteousness of God in him." (V. 21 p.) First, I conclude that they are accounted righteous who are reconciled to God. Included is the means: that God justifies by pardoning, just as in another passage justification is contrasted with accusation. This antithesis clearly shows that the expression was taken from legal usage. Anyone moderately versed in the Hebrew language, provided he has a sober brain, is not ignorant of the fact that the phrase arose from this source, and drew from it its tendency and implication. Where Paul says that righteousness without works is described by David in these words, "Blessed are they whose transgressions are forgiven" (Ps. 32:1; 31:1, Vg.; Rom. 4:7), let Osiander answer me whether this be a full or half definition. Surely, Paul does not make the prophet bear witness to the doctrine that pardon of sins is part of righteousness, or merely a concomitant toward the justifying of man; on the contrary, he includes the whole of righteousness in free remission, declaring that man blessed whose sins are covered, whose iniquities God has forgiven, and whose transgressions God does not charge to his account. Thence, he judges and reckons his happiness because in this way he is righteous, not intrinsically but by imputation.

Osiander objects that it would be insulting to God and contrary to his nature that he should justify those who actually remain wicked. Yet we must bear in mind what I have already said, that the grace of justification is not separated from regeneration, although they are things distinct. But because it is very well known by experience that the traces of sin always remain in the righteous, their justification must be very different from reformation into newness of life (cf. Rom. 6:4). For God so begins this second point in his elect, and progresses in it gradually, and sometimes slowly, throughout life, that they are always liable to the judgment of death before his tribunal. But he does not justify in part but liberally, so that they may appear in heaven as if endowed with the purity of Christ. No portion of righteousness sets our consciences at peace until it has been determined that we are pleasing to God, because we are entirely righteous before him. From this it follows that the doctrine of justification is perverted and utterly overthrown when doubt is thrust into men's minds, when the assurance of salvation is shaken and the free and fearless calling upon God suffers hindrance— nay, when peace and tranquillity with spiritual joy are not established. Thence Paul argues from contraries that the inheritance does not come from the law (Gal. 3:18), for in this way "faith would be nullified" (Rom. 4:14, cf. Vg.). For faith totters if it pays attention to works, since no one, even of the most holy, will find there anything on which to rely.

This distinction between justification and regeneration, which two things Osiander confuses under the term "double righteousness," is beautifully expressed by Paul. Speaking of his own real righteousness, or of the uprighteous that had been given him, which Osiander labels "essential righteousness," he mournfully exclaims: "Wretched man that I am! Who will deliver me from the body of this death?" (Rom. 7:24). But fleeing to that righteousness which is founded solely upon God's mercy he gloriously triumphs over both life and death, reproaches and hunger, the sword and all other adverse things. "Who will make accusation against God's elect," whom he justifies (Rom. 8:33 p.)? For I am surely convinced that nothing "will separate us from his love in Christ" (Rom. 8:38–39 p.). He clearly proclaims that he has a righteousness which alone entirely suffices for salvation before God, so that he does not diminish his confidence in glorying, and no hindrance arises from the miserable bondage, consciousness of which had a moment before caused him to bemoan his lot. This diversity is sufficiently known, and so familiar to all the saints who groan under the burden of iniquities and yet with victorious confidence surmount all fears.

But Osiander's objection that this is out of accord with God's nature topples back upon him. For, even though he clothed the saints with this "double righteousness," like a furred garment, he is still compelled to confess that no one can please God without forgiveness of sins. But if this is true, let him at least grant that those who are not intrinsically righteous are reckoned righteous according to the fixed proportion of imputation, as they say. But how far will a sinner parcel out this free acceptance which stands in place of righteousness? By the pound or by the ounce? Assuredly, he will hang uncertainly, wavering to this side and to that, for he will not be allowed to assume in himself as much righteousness as he needs for assurance. It is well that he who would lay down a law for God is not the judge of this case. But this saying will stand fast: "So that thou mayest be justified in thy words and mayest overcome when thou art judged" (Ps. 50:6, Vg.; cf. Ps. 51:4, EV).

How great presumption is it to condemn the supreme Judge when he freely absolves, so that this answer may not have full force: "I will show mercy on whom I will show mercy"? (Ex. 33:19.) And yet Moses' intercession, which God restrains in these words, was not to the effect that he should spare no one but that he should wipe away the charge against them even though they were guilty, and absolve them all equally. And on this account, indeed, we say that those who were lost have their sins buried and are justified before God because, as he hates sin, he can love only those whom he has justified. This is a wonderful plan of justification that, covered by the righteousness of Christ, they should not tremble at the judgment they deserve, and that while they rightly condemn themselves, they should be accounted righteous outside themselves.

12. Refutation of Osiander

Yet my readers ought to be warned to pay careful attention to that mystery which Osiander boasts he does not wish to hide from them. For first he contends long and verbosely that we attain favor with God not by imputation of Christ's righteousness alone, because it would be impossible (I use his words) for him to regard as just those who are not just. In the end, he concludes that Christ has been given to us as righteousness, not in respect to his human but to his divine nature. And although this can be found only in the person of the Mediator, still it is not a righteousness of man but of

God. Now he does not weave his rope from the two kinds of righteousness but obviously deprives Christ's human nature of the office of justifying. Moreover, it behooves us to understand how he fights. In the same place it is said that Christ has become wisdom for us (I Cor. 1:30), but this applies only to the eternal word. Therefore Christ the man is not righteousness. I reply: the only-begotten Son of God was indeed his eternal wisdom, but in a different way this name is applied to him in Paul's letters, for in him "are hid all the treasures of wisdom and knowledge" (Col. 2:3). What he had with the Father (cf. John 17:5) he revealed to us. Hence what Paul says applies not to the essence of the Son of God but to our use, and rightly fits Christ's human nature. For even though the light shone in the darkness before he assumed flesh (John 1:5), yet the light was hidden until Christ came forth in the nature of man, the Sun of Righteousness, and he therefore calls himself "the light of the world" (John 8:12).

Osiander also stupidly objects that the power of justifying is far above both angels and men, inasmuch as this depends not upon the dignity of any creature but upon God's appointment. If the angels should wish to make satisfaction to God, they would achieve nothing, for they are not destined for this end. But this especially belonged to the man Christ, as he submitted to the law to redeem us from its curse (Gal. 3:13; cf. ch. 4:4).

Also, those who deny that Christ is our righteousness according to his divine nature are by Osiander very basely accused of leaving only one part of Christ and—what is worse—making two Gods. For even though they confess that God dwells in us, they still claim that we are not righteous by the righteousness of God. For if we call Christ the author of life, seeing that he underwent death "that . . . he might destroy him who had the power of death" (Heb. 2:14 p.), we do not thereby deprive the whole Christ of this honor, as he is God manifested in the flesh. Rather, we are only making clear how God's righteousness comes to us that we may enjoy it. On this point Osiander has fallen into abominable error. We do not deny that what has been plainly revealed to us in Christ derives from God's secret grace and power, nor do we contend over the fact that the righteousness Christ bestows upon us is the righteousness of God, which proceeds from him. But we steadfastly hold that in Christ's death and resurrection there is righteousness and life for us. I leave out that shameful heap of passages with which, without discrimination and even without common sense, he burdened his readers, to the effect that whenever righteousness is mentioned one ought to understand it as "essential righteousness." For example, when David calls upon God's righteousness to help him, even though he does so more than a hundred times, Osiander does not hesitate to corrupt as many passages.

The other objection is not a whit stronger: that righteousness is properly and correctly defined as that by which we are moved to act rightly, but that "God alone is at work in us both to will and to perfect" (Phil. 2:13 p.). I do not deny that God reforms us by his Spirit into holiness and righteousness of life. First, however, it must be seen whether he does this of himself and directly or through the hand of his Son, to whom he has entrusted the whole fullness of the Holy Spirit in order that by his abundance he may supply what is lacking in his members. Then, although righteousness comes forth to us from the secret wellspring of his divinity, it does not follow that Christ, who in the flesh sanctified himself for our sake (John 17:19), is righteousness for us according to his divine nature.

What he adds is no less absurd: that Christ himself was righteous by divine righteousness; for unless the will of the Father had impelled him not even he would have fulfilled the tasks enjoined upon him. For even though it was elsewhere said that all the merits of Christ himself flow solely from God's good pleasure, this adds nothing to the fantasy wherewith Osiander bewitches his own eyes and those of the simple-minded. For who allows anyone to infer that because God is the source and beginning of our righteousness we are righteous in essence, and the essence of God's righteousness dwells in us? In redeeming the church, says Isaiah, God "put on his own righteousness as a breastplate" (Isa. 59:17). Did he do this to deprive Christ of the armor that he had given him so that Christ might not be the perfect Redeemer? But the prophet only meant that God borrowed nothing outside himself, nor had he any help to redeem us. Paul has briefly indicated this in other words, saying, that he gave us salvation to show his righteousness (Rom. 3:25). But this in no way contradicts what he teaches elsewhere: that "we are righteous by the obedience of one man" (Rom. 5:19 p.). In short, whoever wraps up two kinds of righteous-

ness in order that miserable souls may not repose wholly in
God's mere mercy, crowns Christ in mockery with a wreath
of thorns (Mark 15:17, etc.).

13. Righteousness by faith and righteousness by works

But a great part of mankind imagine that righteousness is
composed of faith and works. Let us also, to begin with, show
that faith righteousness so differs from works righteousness
that when one is established the other has to be overthrown.
The apostle says that he "counts everything as dross" that he
"may gain Christ and be found in him, . . . not having a
righteousness of (his) own, based on law, but one that is
through faith in Jesus Christ, the righteousness from God
through faith" (Phil. 3:8–9 p.). You see here both a comparison of opposites and an indication that a man who wishes
to obtain Christ's righteousness must abandon his own righteousness. Therefore, he states elsewhere that this was the
cause of the Jews' downfall: "Wishing to establish their own
righteousness, they did not submit to God's righteousness"
(Rom. 10:3 p.). If by establishing our own righteousness we
shake off the righteousness of God, to attain the latter we
must indeed completely do away with the former. He also
shows this very thing when he states that our boasting is not
excluded by law but by faith (Rom. 3:27). From this it follows that so long as any particle of works righteousness remains some occasion for boasting remains with us. Now, if
faith excludes all boasting, works righteousness can in no
way be associated with faith righteousness. In this sense he
speaks so clearly in the fourth chapter of Romans that no
place is left for cavils or shifts: "If Abraham," says Paul,
"was justified by works, he has something to boast about."
He adds, "Yet he has no reason to boast before God" (Rom.
4:2). It follows, therefore, that he was not justified by works.
Then Paul sets forth another argument from contraries. When
reward is made for works it is done out of debt, not of grace
(Rom. 4:4). But righteousness according to grace is owed to
faith. Therefore it does not arise from the merits of works.
Farewell, then, to the dream of those who think up a righteousness flowing together out of faith and works.

14. Likewise, the works of the regenerated can procure no justification

The Sophists, who make game and sport in their corrupting of Scripture and their empty caviling, think they have a subtle evasion. For they explain "works" as meaning those which men not yet reborn do only according to the letter by the effort of their own free will, apart from Christ's grace. But they deny that these refer to spiritual works. For, according to them, man is justified by both faith and works provided they are not his own works but the gifts of Christ and the fruit of regeneration. For they say that Paul so spoke for no other reason than to convince the Jews, who were relying upon their own' strength, that they were foolish to arrogate righteousness to themselves, since the Spirit of Christ alone bestows it upon us not through any effort arising from our own nature. Still they do not observe that in the contrast between the righteousness of the law and of the gospel, which Paul elsewhere introduces, all works are excluded, whatever title may grace them (Gal. 3:11–12). For he teaches that this is the righteousness of the law, that he who has fulfilled what the law commands should obtain salvation; but this is the righteousness of faith, to believe that Christ died and rose again (Rom. 10:5, 9).

Moreover, we shall see afterward, in its proper place, that the benefits of Christ—sanctification and righteousness—are different. From this it follows that not even spiritual works come into account when the power of justifying is ascribed to faith. The statement of Paul where he denies that Abraham had any reason to boast before God—a passage that we have just cited—because he was not righteous by his works, ought not to be restricted to a literal and outward appearance of virtues or to the effort of free will. But even though the life of the patriarch was spiritual and well-nigh angelic, he did not have sufficient merit of works to acquire righteousness before God.

15. The Roman doctrine of grace and good works

Somewhat too gross are the Schoolmen, who mingle their concoctions. Yet these men infect the simple-minded and unwary with a doctrine no less depraved, cloaking under the disguise of "spirit" and "grace" even the mercy of God, which

alone can set fearful souls at rest. Now we confess with Paul
that the doers of the law are justified before God; but, because we are all far from observing the law, we infer from
this that those works which ought especially to avail for righteousness give us no help because we are destitute of them.

As regards the rank and file of the papists or Schoolmen,
they are doubly deceived here both because they call faith
an assurance of conscience in awaiting from God their reward
for merits and because they interpret the grace of God not
as the imputation of free righteousness but as the Spirit helping in the pursuit of holiness. They read in the apostle:
"Whoever would draw near to God must first believe that he
exists and then that he rewards those who seek him" (Heb.
11:6). But they pay no attention to the way in which he is
to be sought. It is clear from their own writings that in using
the term "grace" they are deluded. For Lombard explains
that justification is given to us through Christ in two ways.
First, he says, Christ's death justifies us, while love is aroused
through it in our hearts and makes us righteous. Second,
because through the same love, sin is extinguished by which
the devil held us captive, so that he no longer has the where-
withal to condemn us. You see how he views God's grace
especially in justification, in so far as we are directed through
the grace of the Holy Spirit to good works. Obviously, he
intended to follow Augustine's opinion, but he follows it at a
distance and even departs considerably from the right imitation of it. For when Augustine says anything clearly, Lombard obscures it, and if there was anything slightly contaminated in Augustine, he corrupts it. The schools have gone
continually from bad to worse until, in headlong ruin, they
have plunged into a sort of Pelagianism. For that matter,
Augustine's view, or at any rate his manner of stating it, we
must not entirely accept. For even though he admirably deprives man of all credit for righteousness and transfers it to
God's grace, he still subsumes grace under sanctification, by
which we are reborn in newness of life through the Spirit.

16. Our justification according to the judgment of Scripture

But Scripture, when it speaks of faith righteousness, leads
us to something far different: namely, to turn aside from the
contemplation of our own works and look solely upon God's
mercy and Christ's perfection. Indeed, it presents this order

of justification: to begin with, God deigns to embrace the
sinner with his pure and freely given goodness, finding nothing in him except his miserable condition to prompt Him to
mercy, since he sees man utterly void and bare of good
works; and so he seeks in himself the reason to benefit man.
Then God touches the sinner with a sense of his goodness
in order that he, despairing of his own works, may ground the
whole of his salvation in God's mercy. This is the experience
of faith through which the sinner comes into possession of
his salvation when from the teaching of the gospel he acknowledges that he has been reconciled to God: that with
Christ's righteousness interceding and forgiveness of sins accomplished he is justified. And although regenerated by the
Spirit of God, he ponders the everlasting righteousness laid
up for him not in the good works to which he inclines but in
the sole righteousness of Christ. When these things are pondered one by one, they will give a clear explanation of our
opinion. However, they might be arranged in another order,
better than the one in which they have been set forth. But it
makes little difference, provided they so agree among themselves that we may have the whole matter rightly explained
and surely confirmed.

17. Faith righteousness and law righteousness according to Paul

Here we should recall to mind the relation that we have
previously established between faith and the gospel. For faith
is said to justify because it receives and embraces the righteousness offered in the gospel. Moreover, because righteousness is said to be offered through the gospel, all consideration
of works is excluded. Paul often shows this elsewhere but
most clearly in two passages. For in comparing the law and
the gospel in the letter to the Romans he says: "the righteousness that is of the law" is such that "the man who practices these things will live by them" (Rom. 10:5). But the
"righteousness that is of faith" (Rom. 10:6) announces salvation "if you believe in your heart and confess with your
mouth that Jesus is Lord and that the Father raised him from
the dead" (Rom. 10:9 p.). Do you see how he makes this
the distinction between law and gospel: that the former attributes righteousness to works, the latter bestows free righteousness apart from the help of works? This is an important
passage, and one that can extricate us from many difficulties

if we understand that that righteousness which is given us through the gospel has been freed of all conditions of the law. Here is the reason why he so often opposes the promise to the law, as things mutually contradictory: "If the inheritance is by the law, it is no longer by promise" (Gal. 3:18); and passages in the same chapter that express this idea.

Now, to be sure, the law itself has its own promises. Therefore, in the promises of the gospel there must be something distinct and different unless we would admit that the comparison is inept. But what sort of difference will this be, other than that the gospel promises are free and dependent solely upon God's mercy, while the promises of the law depend upon the condition of works? And let no one here snarl at me that it is the righteousness which men, of their own strength and free will, would obtrude upon God that is rejected—inasmuch as Paul unequivocally teaches that the law, in commanding, profits nothing (cf. Rom. 8:3). For there is no one, not only of the common folk, but of the most perfect persons, who can fulfill it. To be sure, love is the capstone of the law. When the Spirit of God forms us to such love, why is it not for us a cause of righteousness, except that even in the saints it is imperfect, and for that reason merits no reward of itself?

18. Justification not the wages of works, but a free gift

The second passage is this: "It is evident that no man is justified before God by the law. For the righteous shall live by faith (cf. Hab. 2:4). But the law is not of faith; rather, the man who does these things shall live in them" (Gal. 3:11–12, Comm., cf. Vg.). How would this argument be maintained otherwise than by agreeing that works do not enter the account of faith but must be utterly separated? The law, he says, is different from faith. Why? Because works are required for law righteousness. Therefore it follows that they are not required for faith righteousness. From this relation it is clear that those who are justified by faith are justified apart from the merit of works—in fact, without the merit of works. For faith receives that righteousness which the gospel bestows. Now the gospel differs from the law in that it does not link righteousness to works but lodges it solely in God's mercy. Paul's contention in Romans is similar to this: that Abraham had no occasion to boast, for faith was reckoned as righteousness for him (Rom. 4:2–3); and he adds as confirmation that the righteousness of faith has a place in circumstances where there are no works for which a reward is due. "Where," he says, "there are works, wages are paid as a debt; what is given to faith is free." (Rom. 4:4–5 p.) Indeed, the meaning of the words he uses there applies also to this passage. He adds a little later that we on this account obtain the inheritance from faith, as according to grace. Hence he infers that this inheritance is free, for it is received by faith (cf. Rom. 4:16). How is this so except that faith rests entirely upon God's mercy without the assistance of works? And in another passage he teaches, doubtless in the same sense, that "the righteousness of God has been manifested apart from law, although it is attested by the Law and the Prophets" (Rom. 3:21 p.). For, excluding the law, he denies that we are aided by works and that we attain righteousness by working; instead, we come empty to receive it.

19. Through "faith alone"

Now the reader sees how fairly the Sophists today cavil against our doctrine when we say that man is justified by faith alone (Rom. 3:28). They dare not deny that man is justified by faith because it recurs so often in Scripture. But since the word "alone" is nowhere expressed, they do not allow this addition to be made. Is it so? But what will they reply to these words of Paul where he contends that righteousness cannot be of faith unless it be free (Rom. 4:2 ff.)? How will a free gift agree with works? With what chicaneries will they elude what he says in another passage, that God's righteousness is revealed in the gospel (Rom. 1:17)? If righteousness is revealed in the gospel, surely no mutilated or half righteousness but a full and perfect righteousness is contained there. The law therefore has no place in it. Not only by a false but by an obviously ridiculous shift they insist upon excluding this adjective. Does not he who takes everything from works firmly enough ascribe everything to faith alone? What, I pray, do these expressions mean: "His righteousness has been manifested apart from the law" (Rom. 3:21 p.); and, "Man is freely justified" (Rom. 3:24 p.); and, "Apart from the works of the law" (Rom. 3:28)?

Here they have an ingenious subterfuge: even though they have not devised it themselves but have borrowed it from Origen and certain other ancient writers, it is still utterly silly.

They prate that the ceremonial works of the law are excluded, not the moral works. They become so proficient by continual wrangling that they do not even grasp the first elements of logic. Do they think that the apostle was raving when he brought forward these passages to prove his opinion? "The man who does these things will live in them" (Gal. 3:12), and, "Cursed be every one who does not fulfill all things written in the book of the law" (Gal. 3:10 p.). Unless they have gone mad they will not say that life was promised to keepers of ceremonies or the curse announced only to those who transgress the ceremonies. If these passages are to be understood of the moral law, there is no doubt that moral works are also excluded from the power of justifying. These arguments which Paul uses look to the same end: "Since through the law comes knowledge of sin" (Rom. 3:20), therefore not righteousness. Because "the law works wrath" (Rom. 4:15), hence not righteousness. Because the law does not make conscience certain, it cannot confer righteousness either. Because faith is imputed as righteousness, righteousness is therefore not the reward of works but is given unearned (Rom. 4:4–5). Because we are justified by faith, our boasting is cut off (Rom. 3:27 p.). "If a law had been given that could make alive, then righteousness would indeed be by the law. But God consigned all things to sin that the promise might be given to those who believe." (Gal. 3:21–22 p.) Let them now babble, if they dare, that these statements apply to ceremonies, not to morals. Even schoolboys would hoot at such impudence. Therefore, let us hold as certain that when the ability to justify is denied to the law, these words refer to the whole law.

20. "Works of the law"

If anyone should wonder why the apostle, not content with naming works, uses such a qualification, there is a ready explanation. Though works are highly esteemed, they have their value from God's approval rather than from their own worth. For who would dare recommend works righteousness to God unless God himself approved? Who would dare demand a reward due unless he promised it? Therefore, it is from God's beneficence that they are considered worthy both of the name of righteousness and of the reward thereof. And so, for this one reason, works have value, because through them man intends to show obedience to God. Therefore, to prove that Abraham could not be justified by works, the apostle declares in another place that the law was given fully four hundred and thirty years after the covenant was made (Gal. 3:17). The ignorant would laugh at this sort of argument, on the ground that before the promulgation of the law there could have been righteous works. But because he knew that works could have such great value only by the testimony and vouchsafing of God, he took as a fact that previous to the law they had no power to justify. We have the reason why he expressly mentions the works of the law when he wants to take justification away from them, for it is clearly because a controversy can be raised only over them.

Yet he sometimes excepts all works without any qualification, as when on David's testimony he states that blessedness is imparted to that man to whom God reckons righteousness apart from works (Rom. 4:6; Ps. 32:1–2). Therefore no cavils of theirs can prevent us from holding to the exclusive expression as a general principle.

Also, they pointlessly strive after the foolish subtlety that we are justified by faith alone, which acts through love, so that righteousness depends upon love. Indeed, we confess with Paul that no other faith justifies "but faith working through love" (Gal. 5:6). But it does not take its power to justify from that working of love. Indeed, it justifies in no other way but in that it leads us into fellowship with the righteousness of Christ. Otherwise, everything that the apostle insists upon so vigorously would fall. "Now to him who works the pay is not considered a gift but his due," says he. (Rom. 4:4.) "But to one who does not work but believes in him who justifies the ungodly, his faith is reckoned as righteousness." (Rom. 4:5.) Could he have spoken more clearly than in contending thus: that there is no righteousness of faith except where there are no works for which a reward is due? And then that faith is reckoned as righteousness only where righteousness is bestowed through a grace not owed?

(*Sins are remitted only through the righteousness of Christ, 21–23*)

21. *Justification, reconciliation, forgiveness of sins*

Now let us examine how true that statement is which is spoken in the definition, that the righteousness of faith is reconciliation with God, which consists solely in the forgive-

ness of sins. We must always return to this axiom: the wrath
of God rests upon all so long as they continue to be sinners.
Isaiah has very well expressed it in these words: "The Lord's
hand is not shortened, that it cannot save, or his ear dull,
that it cannot hear; but your iniquities have made a separation between you and your God, and your sins have hid his
face from you lest he hear" (Isa. 59:1–2). We are told that
sin is division between man and God, the turning of God's
face away from the sinner; and it cannot happen otherwise,
seeing that it is foreign to his righteousness to have any deal-
ings with sin. For this reason, the apostle teaches that man
is God's enemy until he is restored to grace through Christ
(Rom. 5:8–10). Thus, him whom he receives into union with
himself the Lord is said to justify, because he cannot receive
him into grace nor join him to himself unless he turns him
from a sinner into a righteous man. We add that this is done
through forgiveness of sins; for if those whom the Lord has
reconciled to himself be judged by works, they will indeed
still be found sinners, though they ought, nevertheless, to be
freed and cleansed from sin. It is obvious, therefore, that
those whom God embraces are made righteous solely by the
fact that they are purified when their spots are washed away
by forgiveness of sins. Consequently, such righteousness can
be called, in a word, "remission of sins."

22. Scriptural proof for the close relation between justification and forgiveness of sins

Paul's words, which I have already quoted, express both of
these points very beautifully: "God was in Christ reconciling
the world to himself, not counting men's trespasses against
them, and has entrusted to us the word of reconciliation"
(II Cor. 5:19, cf. Comm. and Vg.). Then Paul adds the
summation of Christ's embassy: "Him who knew not sin he
made to be sin for us so that we might be made the righteousness of God in him" (II Cor. 5:21). Here he mentions
righteousness and reconciliation indiscriminately, to have us
understand that each one is reciprocally contained in the
other. Moreover, he teaches the way in which this righteousness is to be obtained: namely, when our sins are not counted
against us. Therefore, doubt no longer how God may justify
us when you hear that he reconciles us to himself by not
counting our sins against us. Thus, by David's testimony Paul
proves to the Romans that righteousness is imputed to man

apart from works, for David declares that man "blessed whose transgressions are forgiven, whose sins are covered, to whom the Lord has not imputed iniquity" (Rom. 4:6–8; Ps. 32:1–2). Undoubtedly, he there substitutes blessedness for righteousness; since he declares that it consists in forgiveness of sins, there is no reason to define it differently. Accordingly, Zechariah, the father of John the Baptist, sings that the knowledge of salvation rests in the forgiveness of sins (Luke 1:77). Paul followed this rule in the sermon on the sum of salvation that he delivered to the people of Antioch. As Luke reports it, he concluded in this way: "Through this man forgiveness of sins is proclaimed to you, and every one that believes in him is justified from all things from which you could not be justified by the law of Moses" (Acts 13:38–39 p.). The apostle so connects forgiveness of sins with righteousness that he shows them to be exactly the same. From this he duly reasons that the righteousness that we obtain through God's kindness is free to us.

And this ought not to seem an unusual expression, that believers are made righteous before God not by works but by free acceptance, since it occurs so often in Scripture, and ancient writers also sometimes speak thus. So says Augustine in one place: "The righteousness of the saints in this world consists more in the forgiveness of sins than in perfection of virtues." Bernard's famous sentences correspond to this: "Not to sin is the righteousness of God; but the righteousness of man is the grace of God." And he had previously declared: "Christ is our righteousness in absolution, and therefore those alone are righteous who obtain pardon from his mercy."

23. Righteous—not in ourselves but in Christ

From this it is also evident that we are justified before God solely by the intercession of Christ's righteousness. This is equivalent to saying that man is not righteous in himself but because the righteousness of Christ is communicated to him by imputation—something worth carefully noting. Indeed, that frivolous notion disappears, that man is justified by faith because by Christ's righteousness he shares the Spirit of God, by whom he is rendered righteous. This is too contrary to the above doctrine ever to be reconciled to it. And there is no doubt that he who is taught to seek righteousness outside himself is destitute of righteousness in himself. Moreover, the apostle most clearly asserts this when he writes: "He who knew not sin was made the atoning sacrifice of sin for us so that we might be made the righteousness of God in him" (II Cor. 5:21 p.).

You see that our righteousness is not in us but in Christ, that we possess it only because we are partakers in Christ; indeed, with him we possess all its riches. And this does not contradict what he teaches elsewhere, that sin has been condemned for sin in Christ's flesh that the righteousness of the law might be fulfilled in us (Rom. 8:3–4). The only fulfillment he alludes to is that which we obtain through imputation. For in such a way does the Lord Christ share his righteousness with us that, in some wonderful manner, he pours into us enough of his power to meet the judgment of God. It is quite clear that Paul means exactly the same thing in another statement, which he had put a little before: "As we were made sinners by one man's disobedience, so we have been justified by one man's obedience" (Rom. 5:19 p.). To declare that by him alone we are accounted righteous, what else is this but to lodge our righteousness in Christ's obedience, because the obedience of Christ is reckoned to us as if it were our own?

For this reason, it seems to me that Ambrose beautifully stated an example of this righteousness in the blessing of Jacob: noting that, as he did not of himself deserve the right of the first-born, concealed in his brother's clothing and wearing his brother's coat, which gave out an agreeable odor (Gen. 27:27), he ingratiated himself with his father, so that to his own benefit he received the blessing while impersonating another. And we in like manner hide under the precious purity of our first-born brother, Christ, so that we may be attested righteous in God's sight. Here are the words of Ambrose: "That Isaac smelled the odor of the garments perhaps means that we are justified not by works but by faith, since the weakness of the flesh is a hindrance to works, but the brightness of faith, which merits the pardon of sins, overshadows the error of deeds."

And this is indeed the truth, for in order that we may appear before God's face unto salvation we must smell sweetly with his odor, and our vices must be covered and buried by his perfection.

BOOK III, CHAPTER XIV

THE BEGINNING OF JUSTIFICATION AND ITS

CONTINUAL PROGRESS

(Man in his natural state dead in sins and in need of redemption, 1–6)

1. Four classes of men with regard to justification

To make this matter clearer, let us examine what kind of righteousness is possible to man through the whole course of his life; let us, indeed, make a fourfold classification of it. For men are either (1) endowed with no knowledge of God and immersed in idolatry, or (2) initiated into the sacraments, yet by impurity of life denying God in their actions while they confess him with their lips, they belong to Christ only in name; or (3) they are hypocrites who conceal with empty pretenses their wickedness of heart, or (4) regenerated by God's Spirit, they make true holiness their concern.

In the first instance, when they are to be judged according to their natural gifts, not one spark of good will be found in them from the top of their heads to the soles of their feet, unless perhaps we would accuse Scripture of falsehood when it sets off all the sons of Adam with these titles: that they are wicked and inflexible of heart (Jer. 17:9); that the whole imagination of men's hearts is evil from their first years (Gen. 8:21); "that their thoughts are vain" (Ps. 94:11, cf. Comm.); that they have not the fear of God before their eyes (cf. Ex. 20:20); that "no one of them understands or seeks after God" (Ps. 14:2). In short, that they are flesh (Gen. 6:3). By this word are meant all those works which Paul lists: "fornication, impurity, immodesty, licentiousness, idolatry, sorcery, enmity, strife, jealousy, anger, quarreling, dissension, party spirit, envy, murder," and everything foul and abominable that can be imagined (Gal. 5:19–21, cf. Vg.). This, then, is the worth on which they should be proud to rely!

But if anyone among them excels in that decency of morals which has some appearance of holiness among men, still, because we know that God cares nothing for outward splendor, we must penetrate to the very source of the works if we should wish these to have any value for righteousness. We must investigate deeply, I say, from what disposition of the heart these works come forth. Now, although here a vast field for discussion lies open, still, because the matter can be disposed of in a very few words, I will be as brief as possible in what I teach.

2. *The virtues of unbelievers are God-given*

To begin with, I do not deny that all the notable endowments that manifest themselves among unbelievers are gifts of God. And I do not so dissent from the common judgment as to contend that there is no difference between the justice, moderation, and equity of Titus and Trajan and the madness, intemperance, and savagery of Caligula or Nero or Domitian, or between the obscene lusts of Tiberius and the continence of Vespasian, in this respect, and—not to tarry over individual virtues and vices—between observance and contempt of right and of laws. For there is such a great difference between the righteous and the unrighteous that it appears even in the dead image thereof. For if we confuse these things, what order will remain in the world? Therefore, the Lord has not only engraved such a distinction between honorable and wicked deeds in the minds of individual men but often confirms it also, by the dispensation of his providence. For we see that he bestows many blessings of the present life upon those who cultivate virtue among men. Not because that outward image of virtue deserves the least benefit of him; but it pleases him so to prove how much he esteems true righteousness, when he does not allow even external and feigned righteousness to go without a temporal reward. Hence, there follows what we just now acknowledged: that all these virtues— or rather, images of virtues—are gifts of God, since nothing is in any way praiseworthy that does not come from him.

3. *No true virtue without true faith*

Yet what Augustine writes is nonetheless true: that all who are estranged from the religion of the one God, however admirable they may be regarded on account of their reputation for virtue, not only deserve no reward but rather punishment, because by the pollution of their hearts they defile God's good works. For even though they are God's instruments for the preservation of human society in righteousness, continence, friendship, temperance, fortitude, and prudence, yet they carry out these good works of God very badly. For they are restrained from evil-doing not by genuine zeal for good but either by mere ambition or by self-love, or some other perverse motive. Therefore, since by the very impurity of men's hearts these good works have been corrupted as from their source, they ought no more to be reckoned among virtues than the vices that commonly deceive on account of their affinity and likeness to virtue. In short, when we remember the constant end of that which is right—namely, to serve God—whatever strives to another end already deservedly loses the name "right." Therefore, because they do not look to the goal that God's wisdom prescribes, what they do, though it seems good in the doing, yet by its perverse intention is sin. He therefore concludes that all Fabriciuses, Scipios, and Catos in their excellent deeds have sinned in that, since they lacked the light of faith, they did not apply their deeds to the end to which they ought to have applied them. Therefore, true righteousness was not in them, because duties are weighed not by deeds but by ends.

4. Without Christ there is no true holiness

Moreover, if what John says is true, that there is no life apart from the Son of God (I John 5:12), those who have no part in Christ, whatever they may be, whatever they may do or undertake, yet hasten all their lives to destruction and to the judgment of eternal death. In agreement with this idea is the statement of Augustine's: "Our religion distinguishes the just from the unjust not by the law of works but by that of faith, without which what seemed good works are turned into sins." He also beautifully expresses the same thought in another passage when he compares the zeal of such men to a runner off his course. For the more strenuously anyone runs who is off the path, the farther he gets from his goal, and the more pitiable he therefore becomes. Consequently, Augustine contends that it is better to limp on the path than to run outside it. Finally, since there is no sanctification apart from communion with Christ, it is evident that they are evil trees; they can bear fruits beautiful and comely to the sight, and even sweet to the taste, but not at all good. From this we easily discern that whatever a man thinks, plans, or carries out before he is reconciled to God through faith is accursed, not only of no value for righteousness, but surely deserving condemnation. Yet why do we argue over this as if it were something doubtful, when it has already been proved by the apostle's testimony that "without faith it is impossible for anyone to please God" (Heb. 11:6)?

5. Righteousness before God comes not from works, though ever so good, but from grace

But the proof will shine even clearer if we set the grace of God directly against the natural condition of man. For Scripture everywhere proclaims that God finds nothing in man to arouse him to do good to him but that he comes first to man in his free generosity. For what can a dead man do to attain life? Yet when he illumines us with knowledge of himself, he is said to revive us from death (John 5:25), to make us a new creature (II Cor. 5:17). In this metaphor we see that God's generosity toward us is often commended, especially by the apostle. "God," he says, "who is rich in mercy, out of the great love with which he loved us, even when we were dead through our sins, made us alive together with Christ," etc. (Eph. 2:4–5.) Elsewhere, in discussing under Abraham as type the general calling of believers, he says: "It is God who brings the dead to life and calls things that are not as though they were" (Rom. 4:17, cf. Vg.). If we are nothing, what, I ask, can we do? In the history of Job, therefore, the Lord strongly restrains this arrogance, in the words: "Who anticipates me, that I should repay him? For all things are mine" (Job 41:11 p.; cf. ch. 41:2, Vg.). Paul, explaining this statement (Rom. 11:35), draws the inference: let us not suppose that we bring anything to the Lord but the sheer disgrace of need and emptiness.

Therefore, in the passage cited above, to prove that we have attained the hope of salvation by his grace alone, not by works (cf. Eph. 2:8–9), he states that "we are his creatures, since we have been reborn in Christ Jesus for good works, which God prepared beforehand that we should walk in them" (Eph. 2:10, cf. Vg.). It is as if he said: Who of us can boast that he has appealed to God by his own righteousness when our first capacity for well-doing flows from regeneration? For, as we have by nature been created, oil will sooner be pressed from a stone than any good work from us. It is truly wonderful that man, condemned to such disgrace, dares still assume that he has anything left. Let us therefore admit, with this very great instrument of God, that the Lord "called us with a holy calling, not according to our works, but according to his purpose and . . . grace" (II Tim. 1:9 p.), and that "the generosity and love of God our Savior was manifested toward us, for he saved us, not because of deeds done by us in righteousness, but on account of his own mercy, . . . that we might be justified by his grace and be made heirs of eternal life" (Titus 3:4–5, 7 p.). By this confession we deprive man of all righteousness, even to the slightest particle, until, by mercy alone, he is reborn into the hope of eternal life, since if the righteousness of works brings anything to justify us, we are falsely said to be justified by grace. Obviously, the apostle was not forgetful when he declared justification free, since he proves in another passage that grace would no longer be grace if works availed (Rom. 11:6). And what else does the Lord mean when he says that he "came not to call the righteous but sinners" (Matt. 9:13)? If only sinners are admitted, why do we seek entry through feigned righteousness?

6. Man can contribute nothing to his own righteousness

The thought repeatedly returns to my mind that there is danger of my being unjust to God's mercy when I labor with such great concern to assert it, as if it were doubtful or obscure. But since our ill will is such that it never yields to God that which is his, unless it is powerfully compelled, I am obliged to dwell on this a little longer. Now as Scripture is sufficiently clear on this matter, I shall contend by means of its words rather than my own. Isaiah, when he has described the universal destruction of mankind, beautifully adds the order of restoration: "The Lord saw it, and it appeared evil in his sight. . . . He saw that there was no man, and wondered that there was no one to intervene; and he entrusted salvation to his own arm, and with his own righteousness strengthened himself" (Isa. 59:15–16 p.). Where are our righteous acts if what the prophet says is true: that there is no one who helps the Lord to recover his salvation? Thus another prophet, when he represents the Lord as acting to reconcile sinners to himself, says: "I will betroth you to me forever . . . in righteousness, judgment, grace, and mercy. . . . I will say to her who has not obtained mercy, you have attained mercy" (Hos. 2:19, 23 p.). If a covenant of this sort, which is clearly the first union of us with God, depends upon God's mercy, no basis is left for our righteousness.

And I should like to learn from those who pretend that man goes to meet God with some work righteousness whether they think there can be any other righteousness at all than that which is accepted by God. If it is mad to think so, what acceptable thing can come to God from his enemies, all of whom he spurns with all their doings? Truth testifies that all of us, I say, are mortal and open enemies of our God (cf. Rom. 5:10; Col. 1:21) until we are justified and received into friendship. If justification is the beginning of love, what righteousness of works will precede it? To turn aside that pestilent arrogance, John faithfully reminds us how we did not first love Him (I John 4:10). And the Lord had at an earlier time taught this very thing through his prophet. "I will love them with a willing love," he says, "for my anger has turned from them." (Hos. 14:4 p.) If his love has willingly inclined itself to us, surely it is not aroused by works.

But the ignorant mass of men suppose this to mean only that no one has deserved Christ's completion of our redemption but that in entering into possession of redemption we are aided by our own works. Nay, rather, however we may have been redeemed by Christ, until we are engrafted into his fellowship by the calling of the Father, we are both the heirs of darkness and death and the enemies of God. For Paul teaches that we are not cleansed and washed of our uncleanness by Christ's blood except when the Spirit works that cleansing in us (I Cor. 6:11). Peter, meaning to say the same thing, asserts that the sanctification of the Spirit is effectual "for obedience and for sprinkling with the blood of Christ" (I Peter 1:2). If we are sprinkled through the Spirit with the blood of Christ for purification, let us not think that before this cleansing we were anything other than is a sinner without Christ. Therefore let this be regarded as a fact: the beginning of our salvation is a sort of resurrection from death into life, because when it has been granted to us to believe in Christ for his sake (Phil. 1:29), then at last we begin to pass over from death into life.

(*Hypocrites and nominal Christians, under condemnation, 7–8*)

7. Righteousness is a thing of the heart!

Under this condition are included those who are listed as the second and third classes in the above-mentioned division. For impurity of conscience proves that both classes have not yet been regenerated by the Spirit of God. On the other hand, the absence of regeneration in them shows their lack of faith. From this it is clear that they have not yet been reconciled to God, not yet been justified in his sight, inasmuch as men attain these benefits only by faith. What can sinners, estranged from God, bring forth except what is hateful to his judgment? All ungodly men, and especially all hypocrites, are puffed up with this stupid assurance because, however much they recognize that their hearts teem with impurities, still if they bring forth any well-seeming works, they think these worthy not to be despised by God. Hence arises the pernicious error that, convicted of a wicked and evil mind, they still cannot be compelled to confess themselves empty of righteousness. Even when they acknowledge themselves unrighteous because they cannot deny it, they still claim for themselves some righteousness.

The Lord eloquently refutes this vanity through the prophet: "Ask," he says, "the priests to decide this question, 'If one carries holy flesh in the skirt of his garment . . . and touches . . . bread . . . or any other food, does it become holy?' The priests answered, 'No.' Then Haggai said, 'If one polluted in soul touches anything of these, does it not become unclean?' The priests replied, 'It will become unclean.' Haggai said, 'So it is with this people . . . before me, says the Lord, and so with every work of their hands, and everything that they offer me will be unclean'" (Hag. 2:11–14 p.). Would that this utterance could obtain credit with us, or duly lodge in our memory! For there is no one, howsoever wicked in his whole life, who can let himself be persuaded of what the Lord here clearly declares. As soon as any very wicked person has performed one or another of the duties of the law, he does not doubt that it will be accounted to him as righteousness; but the Lord proclaims that no sanctification can be acquired from this action unless the heart has first been well cleansed. And not content with this, he declares that all the works that come forth from sinners are contaminated with

impurity of heart. Take, then, the name of righteousness
from those works which are condemned as works of pollution
by the Lord's mouth! And with what a fitting comparison
does he demonstrate this! For the objection could have been
raised that what the Lord had commanded is inviolably holy.
But he takes the opposite position, that it is no wonder things
sanctified in the law of the Lord are contaminated by the
filth of the wicked. For by handling something sacred, the
unclean hand profanes it.

8. Person and work

He beautifully treats the same matter also in Isaiah, saying: "Bring no more vain offering; incense is an abomination
to me. . . . My soul hates your new moons and solemn
feasts; they have become a burden to me, I am weary of
bearing them. When you spread forth your hands, I will hide
my eyes from you; even though you multiply prayer, I will
not listen; for your hands are full of blood. Wash yourselves,
make yourselves clean, remove the evil of your thoughts . . ."
(Isa. 1:13–16 p.; cf. ch. 58:1–5). What does this mean, that
the Lord abominates the observance of his law? Surely, he
despises nothing that is of the genuine observance of the
law, the beginning of which he everywhere teaches to be a
true fear of his name. Once that is taken away not only are
all the things offered to him trifles but loathsome and abominable filth.

Now let the hypocrites go, and keeping wickedness
wrapped up in their hearts, let them try to win God's favor
by works! In this way they will more and more anger him.
For "the sacrifices of the wicked are an abomination to him,
but the prayer of the upright is acceptable to him" (Prov.
15:8 p.). We therefore hold to be beyond doubt what ought
to be a mere commonplace even to one indifferently versed
in the Scriptures, that in men not yet truly sanctified works
manifesting even the highest splendor are so far away from
righteousness before the Lord that they are reckoned sins.

Accordingly, they have spoken very truly who have taught
that favor with God is not obtained by anyone through works,
but on the contrary works please him only when the person
has previously found favor in his sight. And here we must
faithfully keep the order to which Scripture leads us by the
hand. Moses writes: "The Lord had regard for Abel and his
works" (Gen. 4:4 p.). Do you see that he points out how the

Lord is favorable to men before he has regard for their works?
Therefore, purification of heart must precede, in order that
those works which come forth from us may be favorably received by God. For the statement of Jeremiah is always in
force, that the eyes of God have regard for truth (Jer. 5:3).
That it is faith alone, moreover, by which men's hearts are
purified, the Holy Spirit has declared through the mouth of
Peter (Acts 15:9). From this it is evident that the first foundation lies in true and living faith.

*(Those who are regenerated, justified by faith alone,
9–11)*

9. Also, true believers do no good works of themselves

Now let us examine what righteousness is possessed by
those whom we have placed in the fourth class. We confess
that while through the intercession of Christ's righteousness
God reconciles us to himself, and by free remission of sins
accounts us righteous, his beneficence is at the same time
joined with such a mercy that through his Holy Spirit he
dwells in us and by his power the lusts of our flesh are each
day more and more mortified; we are indeed sanctified, that
is, consecrated to the Lord in true purity of life, with our
hearts formed to obedience to the law. The end is that our
especial will may be to serve his will and by every means to
advance his glory alone.

But even while by the leading of the Holy Spirit we walk
in the ways of the Lord, to keep us from forgetting ourselves
and becoming puffed up, traces of our imperfection remain
to give us occasion for humility. Scripture says: There is no
righteous man, no man who will do good and not sin (Eccl.
7:21, Vg.; cf. I Kings 8:46). What sort of righteousness will
they obtain, then, from their works? First, I say that the best
work that can be brought forward from them is still always
spotted and corrupted with some impurity of the flesh, and
has, so to speak, some dregs mixed with it. Let a holy servant
of God, I say, choose from the whole course of his life what
of an especially noteworthy character he thinks he has done.
Let him well turn over in his mind its several parts. Undoubtedly he will somewhere perceive that it savors of the rottenness of the flesh, since our eagerness for well-doing is never
what it ought to be but our great weakness slows down our
running in the race. Although we see that the stains that
bespatter the works of the saints are plainly visible, though

we admit that they are only the slightest spots, will they not offend God's eyes, before which not even the stars are pure (Job 25:5)? We have not a single work going forth from the saints that if it be judged in itself deserves not shame as its just reward.

10. He who thinks he has his own righteousness misunderstands the severity of the law

Next, even if it were possible for us to have some wholly pure and perfect works, yet, as the prophet says, one sin is enough to wipe out and extinguish every memory of that previous righteousness (Ezek. 18:24). James agrees with him: "Whoever," he says, "fails in one point, has become guilty of all" (James 2:10 p.). Now since this mortal life is never pure or devoid of sin, whatever righteousness we might attain, when it is corrupted, oppressed, and destroyed, by the sins that repeatedly follow, could not come into God's sight or be reckoned to us as righteousness.

In short, when it is a question of the righteousness of works, we must have regard not for the work of the law but for the commandment. Therefore, if righteousness is sought from the law we will in vain bring forward one work or another, but unceasing obedience to the law is necessary. Therefore, God does not, as many stupidly believe, once for all reckon to us as righteousness that forgiveness of sins concerning which we have spoken in order that, having obtained pardon for our past life, we may afterward seek righteousness in the law; this would be only to lead us into false hope, to laugh at us, and mock us. For since no perfection can come to us so long as we are clothed in this flesh, and the law moreover announces death and judgment to all who do not maintain perfect righteousness in works, it will always have grounds for accusing and condemning us unless, on the contrary, God's mercy counters it, and by continual forgiveness of sins repeatedly acquits us. Therefore, what I said at the beginning always holds good: if we are judged by our own worth, whatever we plan or undertake, with all our efforts and labors we still deserve death and destruction.

11. Believers' righteousness is always faith righteousness

We must strongly insist upon these two points: first, that there never existed any work of a godly man which, if examined by God's stern judgment, would not deserve condemnation; secondly, if such a work were found (something not possible for man), it would still lose favor—weakened and stained as it is by the sins with which its author himself is surely burdened.

This is the pivotal point of our disputation. For on the beginning of justification there is no quarrel between us and the sounder Schoolmen: that a sinner freely liberated from condemnation may obtain righteousness, and that through the forgiveness of sins; except that they include under the term "justification" a renewal, by which through the Spirit of God we are remade to obedience to the law. Indeed, they so describe the righteousness of the regenerated man that a man once for all reconciled to God through faith in Christ may be reckoned righteous before God by good works and be accepted by the merit of them. But on the contrary, the Lord declares that for Abraham he reckoned faith as righteousness (Rom. 4:3), not at the time when Abraham was as yet serving idols but after he had for many years excelled in holiness of life. Therefore, Abraham had long worshiped God with a pure heart, and kept such obedience to the law as can be kept by mortal man. Yet he still had a righteousness set in faith. From this we infer, according to Paul's reasoning, that it was not of works (Eph. 2:9). Similarly, when a prophet says, "The just shall live by faith" (Hab. 2:4), the statement does not apply to impious and profane persons, whom the Lord by turning them to faith may justify, but the utterance is directed to believers, and to them life is promised by faith. Paul also removes all doubt when, to confirm that idea, he takes this verse of David's: "Blessed are they whose transgressions are forgiven" (Ps. 32:1; 31:1, Vg.; cf. Rom. 4:7). It is certain that David is not speaking concerning the ungodly but of believers, such as he himself was. For he spoke from the prompting of his own conscience. Therefore, we must have this blessedness not just once but must hold to it throughout life. Finally, he testifies that the embassy of free reconciliation with God is published not for one day or another but is attested as perpetual in the church (cf. II Cor. 5:18–19). Accordingly, to the very end of life, believers have no other righteousness than that which is there described. For Christ ever remains the Mediator to reconcile the Father to us; and his death has everlasting efficacy: namely, cleansing, satisfaction, atonement, and finally perfect obedience, with which all our iniquities are covered. And

Paul does not say to the Ephesians that we have the beginning of salvation from grace but that we have been saved through grace, "not by works, lest any man should boast" (Eph. 2:8–9).

(Scholastic objections to justification by faith, and doctrine of the supererogatory merits of the saints examined and refuted, 12–21)

12. Evasions of opponents

The evasions that the Schoolmen seek here in order to escape do not help them out. They say: Good works are not as important in their intrinsic worth as to be sufficient to obtain righteousness, but their great value lies in "accepting grace." Accordingly, because they are compelled to admit that here works righteousness is always imperfect, they concede that as long as we live we need forgiveness of sins to supply the defect of works; but that the transgressions committed are compensated by works of supererogation.

I reply that "accepting grace," as they call it, is nothing else than his free goodness, with which the Father embraces us in Christ when he clothes us with the innocence of Christ and accepts it as ours that by the benefit of it he may hold us as holy, pure, and innocent. For Christ's righteousness, which as it alone is perfect alone can bear the sight of God, must appear in court on our behalf, and stand surety in judgment. Furnished with this righteousness, we obtain continual forgiveness of sins in faith. Covered with this purity, the sordidness and uncleanness of our imperfections are not ascribed to us but are hidden as if buried that they may not come into God's judgment, until the hour arrives when, the old man slain and clearly destroyed in us, the divine goodness will receive us into blessed peace with the new Adam. There let us await the Day of the Lord in which, having received incorruptible bodies, we will be carried into the glory of the Heavenly Kingdom (cf. I Cor. 15:45 ff.).

13. One who speaks of "supererogatory" works misunderstands the sharpness of God's demand and the gravity of sin

If these things are true, surely no works of ours can of themselves render us acceptable and pleasing to God; nor can even the works themselves please him, except to the extent that a man, covered by the righteousness of Christ, pleases God and obtains forgiveness of his sins. For God has not promised the reward of life for particular works but he only declares that the man who does them shall live (Lev. 18:5), leveling that well-known curse against all those who do not persevere in all things (Deut. 27:26; Gal. 3:10). The fiction of partial righteousness is abundantly refuted by these statements, where no other righteousness than the complete observance of the law is allowed in heaven.

Their usual loose talk about "works of supererogation" providing sufficient compensation is no sounder. Why? Do they not always return to the position from which they have already been driven, that he who partly keeps the law is to that extent righteous by works? What no one of sound judgment will concede to them they too shamelessly assume as a fact. The Lord often testifies that he recognizes no righteousness of works except in the perfect observance of his law. What perversity is it for us, when we lack righteousness, in order not to seem deprived of all glory—that is, utterly to have yielded to God—to boast of some little bits of a few works and try through other satisfactions to pay for what is lacking?

Satisfactions have already been effectively demolished, so that they ought not even to come to our minds in a dream. I say that those who talk such nonsense do not realize what an execrable thing sin is in God's sight. Truly, they should have understood that men's whole righteousness, gathered together in one heap, could not make compensation for a single sin. For we see that man was so cast away and abandoned by God for one transgression that he lost at the same time all capacity to recover his salvation (Gen. 3:17). Therefore, the capacity to make satisfaction was taken away. Those who preen themselves on it surely will never satisfy God, to whom nothing is pleasing or acceptable that comes forth from his enemies. Now God's enemies are all those to whom he determines to impute sins. Therefore, our sins must be covered and forgiven before the Lord recognizes any work of ours. From this it follows that forgiveness of sins is free, and those who thrust in any satisfactions wickedly blaspheme it. Let us therefore, after the apostle's example, "forgetting what lies behind and straining forward to what lies before us," run our race, pressing "on toward . . . the prize of the upward call" (Phil. 3:13–14 p.).

*14. Even the perfect fulfillment of our obligation would
bring us no glory; but this also is not at all possible!*

To boast about works of supererogation—how does this
square with the injunction laid upon us that, when we have
done whatever is commanded us, we call ourselves "unworthy servants," and say that "we have done no more than
we ought to have done" (Luke 17:10 p.)? To speak before
God is not to pretend or lie but to determine within yourself
what you hold for certain. Therefore, the Lord bids us sincerely perceive and consider within ourselves that we perform no unrequired duties for him but render him our due
service. And rightly! For we are servants obligated to render
so many services that we cannot perform them, even though
all our thoughts and all our members were turned to the
duties of the law. Consequently, his statement, "When you
have done whatever is commanded you," is as much as to
say that all the righteous acts of men—and more—belonged
to one alone. How dare we, then, since we, every one, are
very far away from this goal, boast that we have accumulated
something beyond the measure due?

Now there is no reason for any man to object that, though
he partly fails in the necessary duties, nothing prevents him
from extending his endeavor beyond them. This fact we must
accept completely: that there is nothing that can come to
mind which contributes to the honoring of God or the love of
neighbor that is not comprised within God's law. But if it is
a part of the law, let us not boast of voluntary liberality when
we are constrained by necessity.

*15. God is entitled to all that we are and have; hence
there can be no supererogatory works*

Now they improperly apply to this matter Paul's boasting
that among the Corinthians he voluntarily yielded his right,
which he could otherwise have used if he had wished; and
he devoted to them not only what he owed out of duty but
bestowed a free service beyond the bounds of duty (I Cor.
9:1 ff.). But they should have paid attention to the reason
there indicated, that his action might not become an offense
to the weak (I Cor. 9:12). For evil and deceitful workmen
recommended themselves by this false show of kindness in

order to gain favor for their dangerous doctrines and to breathe hatred upon the gospel, so that it was necessary for Paul either to imperil the doctrine of Christ or to oppose such devices. Well then, if for a Christian man it is a matter of indifference to give offense when he can abstain from it, I admit the apostle performed some work of supererogation for the Lord. But if this was duly required of a prudent steward of the gospel, I say that he did what he ought. Finally, even if such a reason is not apparent, this statement of Chrysostom is always true: all our belongings have the same status as the possessions of slaves, which by right belong to their master himself. And Christ did not conceal this in his parable, for he asks what thanks we shall give our servant when after a whole day of various tasks he returns to us at evening (Luke 17:7–9). Yet it can happen that he labored with greater industry than we would have dared demand. Granted. Still, he did nothing that was not required of the condition of servitude. For he with his whole capacity is ours.

I am not speaking of the sort of supererogations that such persons wish to display before God, for they are trifles that he never either commanded or approves, nor will he accept them when account of them is to be rendered before him. In this sense only, we agree that there are works of supererogation—namely, those of which it is said in the prophet: "Who has required this of your hands?" (Isa. 1:12, cf. Vg.). But let them remember what is said of them in another place: "Why do you spend your money, and not for bread; why do you use up your labor, and not for repletion?" (Isa. 55:2 p.). Indeed, it is not very laborious for these leisured rabbis to dispute these matters under the shade in easy chairs. But when that supreme Judge sits in his judgment seat such windy opinions will have to vanish. It is this that we had to seek: what confidence we can bring to his judgment seat in our defense, not what we can talk about in the schools and corners.

16. No trust in works and no glory in works!

In this respect there are two plagues that we must especially banish from our minds: we must not put any confidence in the righteousness of works, and we must not ascribe to works any glory.

In teaching that all our righteous deeds are foul in God's

sight unless these derive a good odor from Christ's innocence, Scripture consistently dissuades us from confidence. Works can only arouse God's vengeance unless they be sustained by his merciful pardon. Thus they leave us nothing but to implore our Judge for mercy with that confession of David's: that no one will be justified before him if he demands a reckoning from his servants (Ps. 143:2 p.). But when Job says: "If I have acted wickedly, woe to me! but if justly, I will not lift up my head" (Job 10:15 p.), although he is concerned with that highest righteousness of God, to which not even the angels answer, he at the same time shows that when it comes to God's judgment, nothing remains to all mortals but to keep silence. For it not only concerns the fact that Job prefers to yield willingly rather than to struggle perilously against God's severity but signifies that he did not experience any other righteousness in himself than what at the first moment would wither before God's face.

When confidence is banished, all glorying also must necessarily depart. For who would accord credit for righteousness to works, trust in which trembles at God's sight? We must therefore come whither Isaiah calls us: "In God all the seed of Israel shall triumph and glory" (Isa. 45:25 p.); for what he says elsewhere is very true, that we are "the planting of the glory of God" (Isa. 61:3 p.). The mind will then be duly cleansed when it does not in any respect settle back in the confidence, or exult in the glory, of works. But this error disposes stupid men to be puffed up with false and lying confidence because they always lodge in works the cause of their salvation.

17. In no respect can works serve as the cause of our holiness

The philosophers postulate four kinds of causes to be observed in the outworking of things. If we look at these, however, we will find that, as far as the establishment of our salvation is concerned, none of them has anything to do with works. For Scripture everywhere proclaims that the efficient cause of our obtaining eternal life is the mercy of the Heavenly Father and his freely given love toward us. Surely the material cause is Christ, with his obedience, through which he acquired righteousness for us. What shall we say is the formal or instrumental cause but faith? And John includes these three in one sentence when he says: "God so loved the world that he gave his only-begotten Son that everyone who believes in him may not perish but have eternal life" (John 3:16). As for the final cause, the apostle testifies that it consists both in the proof of divine justice and in the praise of God's goodness, and in the same place he expressly mentions three others. For so he speaks to the Romans: "All have sinned and lack the glory of God; moreover, they are justified freely by his grace" (Rom. 3:23–24; cf. Eph. 1:6, cf. Vg.). Here you have the head and primal source: that God embraced us with his free mercy. There follows: "Through the redemption which is in Christ Jesus" (Rom. 3:24). Here you have, as it were, the material cause by which righteousness is brought about for us. In the words "through faith in his blood" (Rom. 3:25 p.), is shown the instrumental cause whereby the righteousness of Christ is applied to us. Lastly, he adds the final cause when, to demonstrate his righteousness, he says, "In order that he himself may be righteous, and the justifier of him who has faith in Christ" (Rom. 3:26, Vg.). And to note also, by the way, that this righteousness stands upon reconciliation, he expressly states that Christ was given as reconciliation. Thus also in the first chapter of Ephesians he teaches that we are received into grace by God out of sheer mercy, that this comes about by Christ's intercession and is apprehended by faith, and that all things exist to the end that the glory of divine goodness may fully shine forth (Eph. 1:3–14). Since we see that every particle of our salvation stands thus outside of us, why is it that we still trust or glory in works? The most avowed enemies of divine grace cannot stir up any controversy with us concerning either the efficient or the final cause, unless they would deny the whole of Scripture. They falsely represent the material and the formal cause, as if our works held half the place along with faith and Christ's righteousness. But Scripture cries out against this also, simply affirming that Christ is for us both righteousness and life, and that this benefit of righteousness is possessed by faith alone.

18. The sight of good works, however, can strengthen faith

Now the saints quite often strengthen themselves and are comforted by remembering their own innocence and uprightness, and they do not even refrain at times from proclaiming it. This is done in two ways: either comparing their good cause with the evil cause of the wicked, they thence derive confidence of victory, not so much by the commendation of their own righteousness as by the just and deserved condemnation of their adversaries. Or, without comparison with others, while they examine themselves before God, the purity of their own conscience brings them some comfort and confidence.

We shall look at the first reason later. Now concerning the second, let us briefly explain how what we said above agrees with it: that under God's judgment we must not put any trust in works, or glory in any esteem of them. The agreement lies in this: that the saints, when it is a question of the founding and establishing of their own salvation, without regard for works turn their eyes solely to God's goodness. Not only do they betake themselves to it before all things as to the beginning of blessedness but they repose in it as in the fulfillment of this. A conscience so founded, erected, and established is established also in the consideration of works, so far, that is, as these are testimonies of God dwelling and ruling in us. Inasmuch, therefore, as this reliance upon works has no place unless you first cast the whole confidence of your mind upon God's mercy, it ought not to seem contrary to that upon which it depends. Therefore, when we rule out reliance upon works, we mean only this: that the Christian mind may not be turned back to the merit of works as to a help toward salvation but should rely wholly on the free promise of righteousness. But we do not forbid him from undergirding and strengthening this faith by signs of the divine benevolence toward him. For if, when all the gifts God has bestowed upon us are called to mind, they are like rays of the divine countenance by which we are illumined to contemplate that supreme light of goodness; much more is this true of the grace of good works, which shows that the Spirit of adoption has been given to us (cf. Rom. 8:15).

19. *Works as fruits of the call*

When, therefore, the saints by innocence of conscience strengthen their faith and take from it occasion to exult, from the fruits of their calling they merely regard themselves as having been chosen as sons by the Lord. Accordingly, the statement of Solomon: "In the fear of the Lord one has strong confidence" (Prov. 14:26), and the fact that in order to be heard by him the saints sometimes use this calling of God to witness that they have walked before him in uprightness and simplicity (cf. Gen. 24:40; II Kings 20:3) are matters that have no place in laying a foundation to strengthen the conscience but are of value only when taken a posteriori. For there is nowhere that fear which is able to establish full assurance. And the saints are conscious of possessing only such an integrity as intermingled with many vestiges of the flesh. But since they take the fruits of regeneration as proof of the indwelling of the Holy Spirit, from this they are greatly strengthened to wait for God's help in all their necessities, seeing that in this very great matter they experience him as Father. And they cannot do even this unless they first apprehend God's goodness, sealed by nothing else than the certainty of the promise. For if they begin to judge it by good works, nothing will be more uncertain or more feeble; for indeed, if works be judged of themselves, by their imperfection they will no less declare God's wrath than by their incomplete purity they testify to his benevolence.

In sum, they so proclaim God's benefits as not to turn away from God's freely given favor, in which, as Paul testifies, there is set "length, breadth, depth, and height" (Eph. 3:18). It is as if he said: "Wherever the minds of the godly turn, however high they mount up, however far and wide they extend, still they ought not to depart from the love of Christ but should apply themselves wholly to meditating upon it. For in itself it embraces all dimensions." Therefore, he says that it excels and overtops all knowledge, and that when we acknowledge how much Christ loved us we are "filled with all the fullness of God" (Eph. 3:19). As elsewhere, while Paul boasts that the godly are victors in every contest, he soon adds the reason: "on account of him who loved us" (Rom. 8:37 p.).

20. Works are God's gift and cannot become the foundation of self-confidence for believers

We now see that the saints have not a confidence in works that either attributes anything to their merit, since they regard them solely as gifts of God from which they may recognize his goodness and as signs of the calling by which they realize their election, or in any degree diminishes the free righteousness that we attain in Christ, since it depends upon this and does not subsist without it. Augustine expresses this idea in few words but elegantly when he writes: "I do not say to the Lord, 'Despise not the works of my hands.' (Ps. 138:8; cf. Ps. 137:8, Vg.) 'I have sought the Lord with my hands and am not deceived.' (Ps. 77:2; cf. Ps. 76:3, Vg.) But I do not commend the works of my hands, for I fear lest, when Thou lookest upon them, thou mayest find more sins than merits. This only I say, this I ask, this I desire: despise not the works of thy hands; see in me thy work, not mine. For if thou seest mine, thou wilt condemn it. If thou seest thine own, thou wilt crown it. For whatever good works are mine are from thee." He gives two reasons why he dared not vaunt his works before God: because if he has anything of good works, he sees in them nothing of his own; and secondly, because these are also overwhelmed by a multitude of sins. From this it comes about that his conscience feels more fear and consternation than assurance. Therefore, he would like God to look upon his good deeds only that, recognizing the grace of his own call in them, he may finish the work he has begun.

21. Sense in which good works are sometimes spoken of as a reason for divine benefits

The fact that Scripture shows that the good works of believers are reasons why the Lord benefits them is to be so understood as to allow what we have set forth before to stand unshaken: that the efficient cause of our salvation consists in God the Father's love; the material cause in God the Son's obedience; the instrumental cause in the Spirit's illumination, that is, faith; the final cause, in the glory of God's great generosity. These do not prevent the Lord from embracing works as inferior causes. But how does this come about? Those whom the Lord has destined by his mercy for the inheritance of eternal life he leads into possession of it, according to his ordinary dispensation, by means of good works. What goes before in the order of dispensation he calls the cause of what comes after. In this way he sometimes derives eternal life from works, not intending it to be ascribed to them; but because he justifies those whom he has chosen in order at last to glorify them (Rom. 8:30), he makes the prior grace, which is a step to that which follows, as it were the cause. But whenever the true cause is to be assigned, he does not enjoin us to take refuge in works but keeps us solely to the contemplation of his mercy. What sort of thing is this teaching of the apostle: "The wages of sin is death; the grace of the Lord, eternal life" (Rom. 6:23)? Why does he not contrast righteousness with sin, as he contrasts life with death? Why does he not make righteousness the cause of life, as he does sin that of death? For thus an antithesis would duly have been set up that is somewhat broken by this variation. But the apostle intended by this comparison to express what was true: namely, that death is owing to men's deserts but life rests solely upon God's mercy.

In short, by these expressions sequence more than cause is denoted. For God, by heaping grace upon grace, from the former grace takes the cause for adding those which follow that he may overlook nothing for the enrichment of his servants. And he so extends his liberality as to have us always look to his freely given election, which is the source and beginning. For, although he loves the gifts which he daily confers upon us, seeing that they proceed from that source, still it is our part to hold to that free acceptance, which alone can support our souls; and so to subordinate to the first cause the gifts of the Holy Spirit he then bestows, that they may nowise detract from it.

BOOK IV, CHAPTER XX

CIVIL GOVERNMENT

(*How civil and spiritual government are related, 1–2*)

1. Differences between spiritual and civil government

Now, since we have established above that man is under a twofold government, and since we have elsewhere discussed at sufficient length the kind that resides in the soul or inner man and pertains to eternal life, this is the place to say something also about the other kind, which pertains only to the establishment of civil justice and outward morality.

For although this topic seems by nature alien to the spiritual doctrine of faith which I have undertaken to discuss, what follows will show that I am right in joining them, in fact, that necessity compels me to do so. This is especially true since, from one side, insane and barbarous men furiously strive to overturn this divinely established order; while, on the other side, the flatterers of princes, immoderately praising their power, do not hesitate to set them against the rule of God himself. Unless both these evils are checked, purity of faith will perish. Besides, it is of no slight importance to us to know how lovingly God has provided in this respect for mankind, that greater zeal for piety may flourish in us to attest our gratefulness.

First, before we enter into the matter itself, we must keep in mind that distinction which we previously laid down so that we do not (as commonly happens) unwisely mingle these two, which have a completely different nature. For certain men, when they hear that the gospel promises a freedom that acknowledges no king and no magistrate among men, but looks to Christ alone, think that they cannot benefit by their freedom so long as they see any power set up over them. They therefore think that nothing will be safe unless the whole world is reshaped to a new form, where there are neither courts, nor laws, nor magistrates, nor anything which in their opinion restricts their freedom. But whoever knows how to distinguish between body and soul, between this present fleeting life and that future eternal life, will without difficulty know that Christ's spiritual Kingdom and the civil jurisdiction are things completely distinct. Since, then, it is a Jewish vanity to seek and enclose Christ's Kingdom within the elements of this world, let us rather ponder that what Scripture clearly teaches is a spiritual fruit, which we gather from Christ's grace; and let us remember to keep within its own limits all that freedom which is promised and offered to us in him. For why is it that the same apostle who bids us stand and not submit to the "yoke of bondage" (Gal. 5:1) elsewhere forbids slaves to be anxious about their state (I Cor. 7:21), unless it be that spiritual freedom can perfectly well exist along with civil bondage? These statements of his must also be taken in the same sense: In the Kingdom of God "there is neither Jew nor Greek, neither male nor female, neither slave nor free" (Gal. 3:28, Vg.; order changed). And again, "there is not Jew nor Greek, uncircumcised and circumcised, barbarian, Scythian, slave, freeman; but Christ is all in all" (Col. 3:11 p.). By these statements he means that it makes no difference what your condition among men may be or under what nation's laws you live, since the Kingdom of Christ does not at all consist in these things.

2. The two "governments" are not antithetical

Yet this distinction does not lead us to consider the whole nature of government a thing polluted, which has nothing to do with Christian men. That is what, indeed, certain fanatics who delight in unbridled license shout and boast: after we have died through Christ to the elements of this world (Col. 2:20), are transported to God's Kingdom, and sit among heavenly beings, it is a thing unworthy of us and set far beneath our excellence to be occupied with those vile and worldly cares which have to do with business foreign to a Christian man. To what purpose, they ask, are there laws without trials and tribunals? But what has a Christian man to do with trials themselves? Indeed, if it is not lawful to kill, why do we have laws and trials? But as we have just now pointed out that this kind of government is distinct from that spiritual and inward Kingdom of Christ, so we must know that they are not at variance. For spiritual government, indeed, is already initiating in us upon earth certain beginnings of the Heavenly Kingdom, and in this mortal and fleeting life affords a certain forecast of an immortal and incorruptible blessedness. Yet civil government has as its appointed end, so long as we live among men, to cherish and protect the outward worship of God, to defend sound doctrine of piety and the position of the church, to adjust our life to the society of men, to form our social behavior to civil righteousness, to reconcile us with one another, and to promote general peace and tranquillity. All of this I admit to be superfluous, if God's Kingdom, such as it is now among us, wipes out the present life. But if it is God's will that we go as pilgrims upon the earth while we aspire to the true fatherland, and if the pilgrimage requires such helps, those who take these from man deprive him of his very humanity. Our adversaries claim that there ought to be such great perfection in the church of God that its government should suffice for law. But they stupidly imagine such a perfection as can never be found in a community of men. For since the insolence of evil men is so great, their wickedness so stubborn, that it can scarcely be restrained by extremely severe laws, what do we expect them to do if they see that their depravity can go scot-free—when no power can force them to cease from doing evil?

(Necessity and divine sanction of civil government, 3–7)

3. The chief tasks and burdens of civil government

But there will be a more appropriate place to speak of the practice of civil government. Now we only wish it to be understood that to think of doing away with it is outrageous barbarity. Its function among men is no less than that of bread, water, sun, and air; indeed, its place of honor is far more excellent. For it does not merely see to it, as all these serve to do, that men breathe, eat, drink, and are kept warm, even though it surely embraces all these activities when it provides for their living together. It does not, I repeat, look to this only, but also prevents idolatry, sacrilege against God's name, blasphemies against his truth, and other public offenses against religion from arising and spreading among the people; it prevents the public peace from being disturbed; it provides that each man may keep his property safe and sound; that men may carry on blameless intercourse among themselves; that honesty and modesty may be preserved among men. In short, it provides that a public manifestation of religion may exist among Christians, and that humanity be maintained among men.

Let no man be disturbed that I now commit to civil government the duty of rightly establishing religion, which I seem above to have put outside of human decision. For, when I approve of a civil administration that aims to prevent the true religion which is contained in God's law from being openly and with public sacrilege violated and defiled with impunity, I do not here, any more than before, allow men to make laws according to their own decision concerning religion and the worship of God.

But my readers, assisted by the very clarity of the arrangement, will better understand what is to be thought of the whole subject of civil government if we discuss its parts separately. These are three: the magistrate, who is the protector and guardian of the laws; the laws, according to which he governs; the people, who are governed by the laws and obey the magistrate.

Let us, then, first look at the office of the magistrate, noting whether it is a lawful calling approved of God; the nature of the office; the extent of its power; then, with what laws a Christian government ought to be governed; and finally, how the laws benefit the people, and what obedience is owed to the magistrate.

4. The magistracy is ordained by God

The Lord has not only testified that the office of magistrate is approved by and acceptable to him, but he also sets out its dignity with the most honorable titles and marvelously commends it to us. To mention a few: Since those who serve as magistrate are called "gods" (Ex. 22:8, Vg.; Ps. 82:1, 6), let no one think that their being so-called is of slight importance. For it signifies that they have a mandate from God, have been invested with divine authority, and are wholly God's representatives, in a manner, acting as his vicegerents. This is no subtlety of mine, but Christ's explanation. "If Scripture," he says, "called them gods to whom the word of God came . . ." (John 10:35.) What is this, except that God has entrusted to them the business of serving him in their office, and (as Moses and Jehoshaphat said to the judges whom they appointed in every city of Judah) of exercising judgment not for man but for God (Deut. 1:16–17; II Chron. 19:6)? To the same purpose is what God's wisdom affirms through Solomon's mouth, that it is his doing "that kings reign, and counselors decree what is just, that princes exercise dominion, and all benevolent judges of the earth" (Prov. 8:14–16). This amounts to the same thing as to say: it has not come about by human perversity that the authority over all things on earth is in the hands of kings and other rulers, but by divine providence and holy ordinance. For God was pleased so to rule the affairs of men, inasmuch as he is present with them and also presides over the making of laws and the exercising of equity in courts of justice. Paul also plainly teaches this when he lists "ruling" among God's gifts (Rom. 12:8, KJV or RV), which, variously distributed according to the diversity of grace, ought to be used by Christ's servants for the upbuilding of the church. For even though Paul is there speaking specifically of a council of sober men, who were appointed in the primitive church to preside over the ordering of public discipline (which office is called in the letter to the Corinthians, "governments" (I Cor. 12:28)), yet because we see the civil power serving the same end, there is no doubt that he commends to us every kind of just rule.

But Paul speaks much more clearly when he undertakes a just discussion of this matter. For he states both that power is an ordinance of God (Rom. 13:2), and that there are no powers except those ordained by God (Rom. 13:1). Further, that princes are ministers of God, for those doing good unto praise; for those doing evil, avengers unto wrath (Rom. 13:3–4). To this may be added the examples of holy men, of whom some possessed kingdoms, as David, Josiah, and Hezekiah; others, lordships, as Joseph and Daniel; others, civil rule among a free people, as Moses, Joshua, and the judges. The Lord has declared his approval of their offices. Accordingly, no one ought to doubt that civil authority is a calling, not only holy and lawful before God, but also the most sacred and by far the most honorable of all callings in the whole life of mortal men.

5. Against the "Christian" denial or rejection of magistracy

Those who desire to usher in anarchy object that, although in antiquity kings and judges ruled over ignorant folk, yet that servile kind of governing is wholly incompatible today with the perfection which Christ brought with his gospel. In this they betray not only their ignorance but devilish arrogance, when they claim a perfection of which not even a hundredth part is seen in them. But whatever kind of men they may be, the refutation is easy. For where David urges all kings and rulers to kiss the Son of God (Ps. 2:12), he does not bid them lay aside their authority and retire to private life, but submit to Christ the power with which they have been invested, that he alone may tower over all. Similarly, Isaiah, when he promises that kings shall be foster fathers of the church, and queens its nurses (Isa. 49:23), does not deprive them of their honor. Rather, by a noble title he makes them defenders of God's pious worshipers; for that prophecy looks to the coming of Christ. I knowingly pass over very many passages which occur frequently, and especially in the psalms, in which the right of rulers is asserted for them all (Ps. 21; 22; 45; 72; 89; 110; 132). But most notable of all is the passage of Paul where, admonishing Timothy that prayers be offered for kings in public assembly, he immediately adds the reason: "That we may lead a

peaceful life under them with all godliness and honesty"
(I Tim. 2:2). By these words he entrusts the condition of
the church to their protection and care.

6. Magistrates should be faithful as God's deputies

This consideration ought continually to occupy the magistrates themselves, since it can greatly spur them to exercise
their office and bring them remarkable comfort to mitigate
the difficulties of their task, which are indeed many and burdensome. For what great zeal for uprightness, for prudence,
gentleness, self-control, and for innocence ought to be required of themselves by those who know that they have been
ordained ministers of divine justice? How will they have the
brazenness to admit injustice to their judgment seat, which
they are told is the throne of the living God? How will they
have the boldness to pronounce an unjust sentence, by that
mouth which they know has been appointed an instrument of
divine truth? With what conscience will they sign wicked decrees by that hand which they know has been appointed to record the acts of God? To sum up, if they remember that they
are vicars of God, they should watch with all care, earnest-
ness, and diligence, to represent in themselves to men some
image of divine providence, protection, goodness, benevolence,
and justice. And they should perpetually set before themselves
the thought that "if all are cursed who carry out in deceit
the work of God's vengeance" (Jer. 48:10 p.), much more
gravely cursed are they who deceitfully conduct themselves
in a righteous calling. Therefore, when Moses and Jehoshaphat wished to urge their judges to do their duty, they had
nothing more effective to persuade them than what we have
previously mentioned (Deut. 1:16): "Consider what you do,
for you exercise judgment not for man but for the Lord;
since he is beside you in giving judgment. Now then, let the
fear of the Lord be upon you. Take heed what you do,
for there is no perversity with the Lord our God" (II Chron.
19:6–7 p.). And in another place it is said: "God stood in the
assembly of the gods, and holds judgment in the midst of
the gods" (Ps. 82:1). This is to hearten them for their task
when they learn that they are deputies of God, to whom they
must hereafter render account of the administration of their
charge. And this admonition deserves to have great weight
with them. For if they commit some fault, they are not only
wrongdoers to men whom they wickedly trouble, but are also

insulting toward God himself, whose most holy judgments
they defile (cf. Isa. 3:14–15). Again, they have the means
to comfort themselves greatly when they ponder in themselves that they are occupied not with profane affairs or those
alien to a servant of God, but with a most holy office, since
they are serving as God's deputies.

7. The coercive character of magistracy does not hinder its recognition

Those who, unmoved by so many testimonies of Scripture,
dare rail against this holy ministry as a thing abhorrent to
Christian religion and piety—what else do they do but revile
God himself, whose ministry cannot be reproached without
dishonor to himself? And these folk do not just reject the
magistrates, but cast off God that he may not reign over
them. For if the Lord truly said this of the people of Israel
because they refused Samuel's rule (I Sam. 8:7), why will it
less truly be said today of these who let themselves rage
against all governments ordained by God? The Lord said to
his disciples that the kings of the Gentiles exercise lordship
over Gentiles, but it is not so among the disciples, where he
who is first ought to become the least (Luke 22:25–26); by
this saying, they tell us, all Christians are forbidden to take
kingdoms or governments. O skillful interpreters! There arose
a contention among the disciples over which one would excel
the others. To silence this vain ambition, the Lord taught
them that their ministry is not like kingdoms, in which one is
pre-eminent above the rest. What dishonor, I ask you, does
this comparison do to kingly dignity? Indeed, what does it
prove at all, except that the kingly office is not the ministry
of an apostle? Moreover, among magistrates themselves, although there is a variety of forms, there is no difference in
this respect, that we must regard all of them as ordained of
God. For Paul also lumps them all together when he says
that there is no power except from God (Rom. 13:1). And
that which is the least pleasant of all has been especially
commended above the rest, that is, the power of one. This,
because it brings with it the common bondage of all (except
that one man to whose will it subjects all things), in ancient
times could not be acceptable to heroic and nobler natures.
But to forestall their unjust judgments, Scripture expressly
affirms that it is the providence of God's wisdom that kings

reign (cf. Prov. 8:15), and particularly commands us to honor the king (Prov. 24:21; I Peter 2:17).

(*Forms of government, and duties of magistrates. Issues of war and taxation, 8–13*)

8. The diversity of forms of government

Obviously, it would be an idle pastime for men in private life, who are disqualified from deliberating on the organization of any commonwealth, to dispute over what would be the best kind of government in that place where they live. Also this question admits of no simple solution but requires deliberation, since the nature of the discussion depends largely upon the circumstances. And if you compare the forms of government among themselves apart from the circumstances, it is not easy to distinguish which one of them excels in usefulness, for they contend on such equal terms. The fall from kingdom to tyranny is easy; but it is not much more difficult to fall from the rule of the best men to the faction of a few; yet it is easiest of all to fall from popular rule to sedition. For if the three forms of government which the philosophers discuss be considered in themselves, I will not deny that aristocracy, or a system compounded of aristocracy and democracy, far excels all others: not indeed of itself, but because it is very rare for kings so to control themselves that their will never disagrees with what is just and right; or for them to have been endowed with such great keenness and prudence, that each knows how much is enough. Therefore, men's fault or failing causes it to be safer and more bearable for a number to exercise government, so that they may help one another, teach and admonish one another; and, if one asserts himself unfairly, there may be a number of censors and masters to restrain his willfulness. This has both been proved by experience, and also the Lord confirmed it by his authority when he ordained among the Israelites an aristocracy bordering on democracy, since he willed to keep them in best condition (Ex. 18:13–26; Deut. 1:9–17) until he should bring forward the image of Christ in David. And, as I freely admit that no kind of government is more happy than one where freedom is regulated with becoming moderation and is properly established on a durable basis, so also I reckon most happy those permitted to enjoy this state; and if they stoutly and constantly labor to preserve and retain it, I grant that they are doing nothing alien to this office. Indeed, the magistrates ought to apply themselves with the highest diligence to prevent the freedom (whose guardians they have been appointed) from being in any respect diminished, far less be violated. If they are not sufficiently alert and careful, they are faithless in office, and traitors to their country.

But if those to whom the Lord has appointed another form of government should transfer this very function to themselves, being moved to desire a change of government —even to think of such a move will not only be foolish and superfluous, but altogether harmful. However, as you will surely find if you fix your eyes not on one city alone, but look around and glance at the world as a whole, or at least cast your sight upon regions farther off, divine providence has wisely arranged that various countries should be ruled by various kinds of government. For as elements cohere only in unequal proportion, so countries are best held together according to their own particular inequality. However, all these things are needlessly spoken to those for whom the will of the Lord is enough. For if it has seemed good to him to set kings over kingdoms, senates or municipal officers over free cities, it is our duty to show ourselves compliant and obedient to whomever he sets over the places where we live.

9. Concern for both Tables of the Law

Now in this place we ought to explain in passing the office of the magistrates, how it is described in the Word of God and the things in which it consists. If Scripture did not teach that it extends to both Tables of the Law, we could learn this from secular writers: for no one has discussed the office of magistrates, the making of laws, and public welfare, without beginning at religion and divine worship. And thus all have confessed that no government can be happily established unless piety is the first concern; and that those laws are preposterous which neglect God's right and provide only for men. Since, therefore, among all philosophers religion takes first place, and since this fact has always been observed by universal consent of all nations, let Christian princes and magistrates be ashamed of their negligence if they do not apply themselves to this concern. And we have already shown that these duties are especially enjoined upon them by God; and it is fitting that they should labor to protect and assert the honor of him whose representatives they are, and by whose grace they govern.

Also, holy kings are greatly praised in Scripture because they restored the worship of God when it was corrupted or destroyed, or took care of religion that under them it might flourish pure and unblemished. But on the contrary, the Sacred History places anarchies among things evil: because there was no king in Israel, each man did as he pleased (Judg. 21:25).

This proves the folly of those who would neglect the concern for God and would give attention only to rendering justice among men. As if God appointed rulers in his name to decide earthly controversies but overlooked what was of far greater importance—that he himself should be purely worshiped according to the prescription of his law. But the passion to alter everything with impunity drives turbulent men to the point of wanting all vindicators of violated piety removed from their midst.

As far as the Second Table is concerned, Jeremiah admonishes kings to "do justice and righteousness," to "deliver him who has been oppressed by force from the hand of the oppressor," not to "grieve or wrong the alien, the widow, and the fatherless" or "shed innocent blood" (Jer. 22:3, cf. Vg.). The exhortation which we read in Ps. 82 has the same purpose: that they should "give justice to the poor and needy, rescue the destitute and needy, and deliver the poor and needy from the hand of the oppressor" (Ps. 82:3–4). And Moses commands the leaders whom he had appointed as his representatives to "hear the cases between their brethren, and judge . . . between a man and his brother, and the alien" and "not recognize faces in judgment, and hear small and great alike, and be afraid of no man, for the judgment is God's" (Deut. 1:16–17 p.). But I pass over such statements as these: that kings should not multiply horses for themselves; nor set their mind upon avarice; nor be lifted up above their brethren; that they should be constant in meditating upon the law of the Lord all the days of their life (Deut. 17:16–19); that judges should not lean to one side or take bribes (Deut. 16:19)—and like passages which we read here and there in Scripture. For in explaining here the office of magistrates, it is not so much my purpose to instruct the magistrates themselves as to teach others what magistrates

are and to what end God has appointed them. We see, therefore, that they are ordained protectors and vindicators of
public innocence, modesty, decency, and tranquillity, and
that their sole endeavor should be to provide for the common
safety and peace of all. Of these virtues David professes that
he will be a pattern: when he has been elevated to the royal
throne, he will not consent to any crimes, but will detest the
impious, slanderers, and the proud, and will seek out from
everywhere upright and faithful counselors (Ps. 101, esp. vs.
4, 5, 7, 6).

But since they cannot perform this unless they defend
good men from the wrongs of the wicked, and give aid and
protection to the oppressed, they have also been armed with
power with which severely to coerce the open malefactors
and criminals by whose wickedness the public peace is
troubled or disturbed (cf. Rom. 13:3). For from experience
we thoroughly agree with the statement of Solon that all
commonwealths are maintained by reward and punishment;
take these away and the whole discipline of cities collapses
and is dissolved. For the care of equity and justice grows
cold in the minds of many, unless due honor has been prepared for virtue; and the lust of wicked men cannot be restrained except by severity and the infliction of penalties.
And the prophet has included these two functions, when he
bids kings and other rulers execute judgment and justice (Jer.
22:3; cf. ch. 21:12). Justice, indeed, is to receive into safekeeping, to embrace, to protect, vindicate, and free the innocent. But judgment is to withstand the boldness of the
impious, to repress their violence, to punish their misdeeds.

10. The magistrates' exercise of force is compatible with piety

But here a seemingly hard and difficult question arises: if
the law of God forbids all Christians to kill (Ex. 20:13; Deut.
5:17; Matt. 5:21), and the prophet prophesies concerning
God's holy mountain (the church) that in it men shall not
afflict or hurt (Isa. 11:9; 65:25)—how can magistrates be
pious men and shedders of blood at the same time?

Yet if we understand that the magistrate in administering
punishments does nothing by himself, but carries out the
very judgments of God, we shall not be hampered by this
scruple. The law of the Lord forbids killing; but, that murders

may not go unpunished, the Lawgiver himself puts into the hand of his ministers a sword to be drawn against all murderers. It is not for the pious to afflict and hurt; yet to avenge, at the Lord's command, the afflictions of the pious is not to hurt or to afflict. Would that this were ever before our minds —that nothing is done here from men's rashness, but all things are done on the authority of God who commands it; and while his authority goes before us, we never wander from the straight path! Unless perhaps restraint is laid upon God's justice, that it may not punish misdeeds. But if it is not right to impose any law upon him, why should we try to reproach his ministers? They do not bear the sword in vain, says Paul, for they are ministers of God to execute his wrath, avengers of wrongdoers (Rom. 13:4). Therefore, if princes and other rulers recognize that nothing is more acceptable to the Lord than their obedience, let them apply themselves to this ministry, if, indeed, they are intent on having their piety, righteousness, and uprightness approved of God (cf. II Tim. 2:15).

Moses was impelled by this desire when, realizing that he had been destined by the Lord's power to be liberator of his people, he laid his hand upon the Egyptian (Ex. 2:12; Acts 7:24). This was the case again, when, by slaying three thousand men in one day, he took vengeance upon the people's sacrilege (Ex. 32:27–28). David also, when at the end of his life he ordered his son Solomon to kill Joab and Shimei (I Kings 2:5–6, 8–9). Accordingly, he also includes this among kingly virtues: to destroy the wicked of the land, that all evildoers may be driven out of the city of God (Ps. 101:8). To this also pertains the praise which is given to Solomon: "You have loved righteousness and hated iniquity" (Ps. 45:7; 44:8, Vg.).

How does Moses' gentle and peaceable nature flame up into such savageness that, sprinkled and dripping with the blood of his brethren, he dashes through the camp to new carnage? How can David, a man of such great gentleness throughout life, as he breathes his last, make that bloody testament, that his son should not allow the hoary heads of Joab and Shimei to go in peace to the grave (I Kings 2:5–6, 8–9)? But both men, by executing the vengeance ordained of God, hallowed by cruelty their hands, which by sparing they would have defiled. "It is an abomination among kings," says Solomon, "to do iniquity, for the throne is established in righteousness." (Prov. 16:12.) Again: "A king who sits on the throne of judgment casts his eyes upon every evildoer" (Prov. 20:8 p.). Again: "A wise king scatters the evildoers and turns them upon the wheel" (Prov. 20:26 p.). Again: "Remove the dross from the silver, and a vessel will come forth to the metal caster; remove the impious from the king's sight, and his throne will be established in righteousness" (Prov. 25:4–5, cf. Geneva). Again: "He who justifies the wicked and he who condemns the righteous are both alike an abomination to the Lord" (Prov. 17:15). Again: "A rebel seeks evil for himself, and a cruel messenger is sent to him" (Prov. 17:11 p.). Again: "He who says to the wicked, 'You are righteous,' will be cursed by peoples . . . and nations" (Prov. 24:24 p.). Now if their true righteousness is to pursue the guilty and the impious with drawn sword, should they sheathe their sword and keep their hands clean of blood, while abandoned men wickedly range about with slaughter and massacre, they will become guilty of the greatest impiety, far indeed from winning praise for their goodness and righteousness thereby!

Begone, now, with that abrupt and savage harshness, and that tribunal which is rightly called the reef of accused men! For I am not one either to favor undue cruelty or think that a fair judgment can be pronounced unless clemency, that best counselor of kings and surest keeper of the kingly throne (as Solomon declares) (Prov. 20:28) is always present—clemency, which by a certain writer of antiquity was truly called the chief gift of princes.

Yet it is necessary for the magistrate to pay attention to both, lest by excessive severity he either harm more than heal; or, by superstitious affectation of clemency, fall into the cruelest gentleness, if he should (with a soft and dissolute kindness) abandon many to their destruction. For during the reign of Nerva it was not without reason said: it is indeed bad to live under a prince with whom nothing is permitted; but much worse under one by whom everything is allowed.

11. On the right of the government to wage war

But kings and people must sometimes take up arms to execute such public vengeance. On this basis we may judge wars lawful which are so undertaken. For if power has been given them to preserve the tranquillity of their dominion, to restrain the seditious stirrings of restless men, to help those forcibly oppressed, to punish evil deeds—can they use it more opportunely than to check the fury of one who disturbs both the repose of private individuals and the common tranquillity of all, who raises seditious tumults, and by whom violent oppressions and vile misdeeds are perpetrated? If they ought to be the guardians and defenders of the laws, they should also overthrow the efforts of all whose offenses corrupt the discipline of the laws. Indeed, if they rightly punish those robbers whose harmful acts have affected only a few, will they allow a whole country to be afflicted and devastated by robberies with impunity? For it makes no difference whether it be a king or the lowest of the common folk who invades a foreign country in which he has no right, and harries it as an enemy. All such must, equally, be considered as robbers and punished accordingly. Therefore, both natural equity and the nature of the office dictate that princes must be armed not only to restrain the misdeeds of private individuals by judicial punishment, but also to defend by war the dominions entrusted to their safekeeping, if at any time they are under enemy attack. And the Holy Spirit declares such wars to be lawful by many testimonies of Scripture.

12. Restraint and humanity in war

But if anyone object against me that in the New Testament there exists no testimony or example which teaches that war is a thing lawful for Christians, I answer first that the reason for waging war which existed of old still persists today; and that, on the other hand, there is no reason that bars magistrates from defending their subjects. Secondly, I say that an express declaration of this matter is not to be sought in the writings of the apostles; for their purpose is not to fashion a civil government, but to establish the spiritual Kingdom of Christ. Finally, that it is there shown in passing that Christ by his coming has changed nothing in this respect. For if Christian doctrine (to use Augustine's words) condemned all wars, the soldiers asking counsel concerning salvation should rather have been advised to cast away their weapons and withdraw completely from military service. But they were told: "Strike no man, do no man wrong, be content with your wages" (Luke 3:14 p.). When he taught them to be content with their wages, he certainly did not forbid them to bear arms.

But it is the duty of all magistrates here to guard particularly against giving vent to their passions even in the slightest degree. Rather, if they have to punish, let them not be carried away with headlong anger, or be seized with hatred, or burn with implacable severity. Let them also (as Augustine says) have pity on the common nature in the one whose special fault they are punishing. Or, if they must arm themselves against the enemy, that is, the armed robber, let them not lightly seek occasion to do so; indeed, let them not accept the occasion when offered, unless they are driven to it by extreme necessity. For if we must perform much more than the heathen philosopher required when he wanted war to seem a seeking of peace, surely everything else ought to be tried before recourse is had to arms. Lastly, in both situations let them not allow themselves to be swayed by any private affection, but be led by concern for the people alone. Otherwise, they very wickedly abuse their power, which has been given them not for their own advantage, but for the benefit and service of others.

Moreover, this same right to wage war furnishes the reason for garrisons, leagues, and other civil defenses. Now, I call "garrisons," those troops which are stationed among the cities to defend the boundaries of a country; "leagues," those pacts which are made by neighboring princes to the end that if any trouble should happen in their lands, they may come to one another's aid, and join forces to put down the common enemies of mankind. I call "civil defenses," things used in the art of war.

13. Concerning the right of the government to levy tribute

Lastly, I also wish to add this, that tributes and taxes are the lawful revenues of princes, which they may chiefly use to meet the public expenses of their office; yet they may similarly use them for the magnificence of their household, which is joined, so to speak, with the dignity of the authority they exercise. As we see, David, Hezekiah, Josiah, Jehoshaphat, and other holy kings, also Joseph and Daniel (according to the dignity of their office) were, without offending piety, lavish at public expense, and we read in Ezekiel that a very large portion of the land was assigned to the kings (Ezek. 48:21). There, although the prophet portrays the spiritual

Kingdom of Christ, he seeks the pattern for his picture from a lawful human kingdom.

But he does so in such a way that princes themselves will in turn remember that their revenues are not so much their private chests as the treasuries of the entire people (for Paul so testifies (Rom. 13:6)), which cannot be squandered or despoiled without manifest injustice. Or rather, that these are almost the very blood of the people, which it would be the harshest inhumanity not to spare. Moreover, let them consider that their imposts and levies, and other kinds of tributes are nothing but supports of public necessity; but that to impose them upon the common folk without cause is tyrannical extortion.

These considerations do not encourage princes to waste and expensive luxury, as there is surely no need to add fuel to their cupidity, already too much kindled of itself. But as it is very necessary that, whatever they venture, they should venture with a pure conscience before God, they must be taught how much is lawful for them, that they may not in impious self-confidence come under God's displeasure. And this doctrine is not superfluous for private individuals in order that they should not let themselves rashly and shamelessly decry any expenses of princes, even if these exceed the common expenditures of the citizens.

(*Public law and judicial procedures, as related to Christian duty, 14–21*)

14. *Old Testament law and the laws of nations*

Next to the magistracy in the civil state come the laws, stoutest sinews of the commonwealth, or, as Cicero, after Plato, calls them, the souls, without which the magistracy cannot stand, even as they themselves have no force apart from the magistracy. Accordingly, nothing truer could be said than that the law is a silent magistrate; the magistrate, a living law.

But because I have undertaken to say with what laws a Christian state ought to be governed, this is no reason why anyone should expect a long discourse concerning the best kind of laws. This would be endless and would not pertain to the present purpose and place. I shall in but a few words, and as in passing, note what laws can piously be used before God, and be rightly administered among men.

I would have preferred to pass over this matter in utter silence if I were not aware that here many dangerously go astray. For there are some who deny that a commonwealth is duly framed which neglects the political system of Moses, and is ruled by the common laws of nations. Let other men consider how perilous and seditious this notion is; it will be enough for me to have proved it false and foolish.

We must bear in mind that common division of the whole law of God published by Moses into moral, ceremonial, and judicial laws. And we must consider each of these parts, that we may understand what there is in them that pertains to us, and what does not. In the meantime, let no one be concerned over the small point that ceremonial and judicial laws pertain also to morals. For the ancient writers who taught this division, although they were not ignorant that these two latter parts had some bearing upon morals, still, because these· could be changed or abrogated while morals remained untouched, did not call them moral laws. They applied this name only to the first part, without which the true holiness of morals cannot stand, nor an unchangeable rule of right living.

15. Moral, ceremonial, and judicial law distinguished

The moral law (to begin first with it) is contained under two heads, one of which simply commands us to worship God with pure faith and piety; the other, to embrace men with sincere affection. Accordingly, it is the true and eternal rule of righteousness, prescribed for men of all nations and times, who wish to conform their lives to God's will. For it is his eternal and unchangeable will that he himself indeed be worshiped by us all, and that we love one another.

The ceremonial law was the tutelage of the Jews, with which it seemed good to the Lord to train this people, as it were, in their childhood, until the fullness of time should come (Gal. 4:3–4; cf. ch. 3:23–24), in order that he might fully manifest his wisdom to the nations, and show the truth of those things which then were foreshadowed in figures.

The judicial law, given to them for civil government, imparted certain formulas of equity and justice, by which they might live together blamelessly and peaceably.

Those ceremonial practices indeed properly belonged to the doctrine of piety, inasmuch as they kept the church of the Jews in service and reverence to God, and yet could be distinguished from piety itself. In like manner, the form of their judicial laws, although it had no other intent than how best to preserve that very love which is enjoined by God's eternal law, had something distinct from that precept of love. Therefore, as ceremonial laws could be abrogated while piety remained safe and unharmed, so too, when these judicial laws were taken away, the perpetual duties and precepts of love could still remain.

But if this is true, surely every nation is left free to make such laws as it foresees to be profitable for itself. Yet these must be in conformity to that perpetual rule of love, so that they indeed vary in form but have the same purpose. For I do not think that those barbarous and savage laws such as gave honor to thieves, permitted promiscuous intercourse, and others both more filthy and more absurd, are to be regarded as laws. For they are abhorrent not only to all justice, but also to all humanity and gentleness.

16. Unity and diversity of laws

What I have said will become plain if in all laws we examine, as we should, these two things: the constitution of the law, and the equity on which its constitution is itself founded and rests. Equity, because it is natural, cannot but be the same for all, and therefore, this same purpose ought to apply to all laws, whatever their object. Constitutions have certain circumstances upon which they in part depend. It therefore does not matter that they are different, provided all equally press toward the same goal of equity.

It is a fact that the law of God which we call the moral law is nothing else than a testimony of natural law and of that conscience which God has engraved upon the minds of men. Consequently, the entire scheme of this equity of which we are now speaking has been prescribed in it. Hence, this equity alone must be the goal and rule and limit of all laws.

Whatever laws shall be framed to that rule, directed to that goal, bound by that limit, there is no reason why we should disapprove of them, howsoever they may differ from the Jewish law, or among themselves.

God's law forbids stealing. The penalties meted out to

thieves in the Jewish state are to be seen in Exodus (Ex. 22:1–4). The very ancient laws of other nations punished theft with double restitution; the laws which followed these distinguished between theft, manifest and not manifest. Some proceeded to banishment, others to flogging, others finally to capital punishment. False testimony was punished by damages similar and equal to injury among the Jews (Deut. 19:18–21); elsewhere, only by deep disgrace; in some nations, by hanging; in others, by the cross. All codes equally avenge murder with blood, but with different kinds of death. Against adulterers some nations levy severer, others, lighter punishments. Yet we see how, with such diversity, all laws tend to the same end. For, together with one voice, they pronounce punishment against those crimes which God's eternal law has condemned, namely, murder, theft, adultery, and false witness. But they do not agree on the manner of punishment. Nor is this either necessary or expedient. There are countries which, unless they deal cruelly with murderers by way of horrible examples, must immediately perish from slaughters and robberies. There are ages that demand increasingly harsh penalties. If any disturbance occurs in a commonwealth, the evils that usually arise from it must be corrected by new ordinances. In time of war, in the clatter of arms, all humaneness would disappear unless some uncommon fear of punishment were introduced. In drought, in pestilence, unless greater severity is used, everything will go to ruin. There are nations inclined to a particular vice, unless it be most sharply repressed. How malicious and hateful toward public welfare would a man be who is offended by such diversity, which is perfectly adapted to maintain the observance of God's law?

For the statement of some, that the law of God given through Moses is dishonored when it is abrogated and new laws preferred to it, is utterly vain. For others are not preferred to it when they are more approved, not by a simple comparison, but with regard to the condition of times, place, and nation; or when that law is abrogated which was never enacted for us. For the Lord through the hand of Moses did not give that law to be proclaimed among all nations and to be in force everywhere; but when he had taken the Jewish nation into his safekeeping, defense, and protection, he also willed to be a lawgiver especially to it; and—as became a wise lawgiver—he had special concern for it in making its laws.

17. Christians may use the law courts, but without hatred and revenge

It now remains for us to examine what we had set in the last place: what usefulness the laws, judgments, and magistrates have for the common society of Christians. To this is also joined another question: how much deference private individuals ought to yield to their magistrates, and how far their obedience ought to go. To very many the office of magistrate seems superfluous among Christians, because they cannot piously call upon them for help, inasmuch as it is forbidden to them to take revenge, to sue before a court, or to go to law. But Paul clearly testifies to the contrary that the magistrate is minister of God for our good (Rom. 13:4). By this we understand that he has been so ordained of God, that, defended by his hand and support against the wrongdoing and injustices of evil men, we may live a quiet and serene life (I Tim. 2:2). But if it is to no purpose that he has been given by the Lord for our defense unless we are allowed to enjoy such benefit, it is clear enough that the magistrate may without impiety be called upon and also appealed to.

But here I have to deal with two kinds of men. There are very many who so boil with a rage for litigation that they are never at peace with themselves unless they are quarreling with others. And they carry on their lawsuits with bitter and deadly hatred, and an insane passion to revenge and hurt, and they pursue them with implacable obstinacy even to the ruin of their adversaries. Meanwhile, to avoid being thought of as doing something wrong, they defend such perversity on the pretense of legal procedure. But if one is permitted to go to law with a brother, one is not therewith allowed to hate him, or be seized with a mad desire to harm him, or hound him relentlessly.

18. The Christian's motives in litigation

Such men should therefore understand that lawsuits are permissible if rightly used. There is right use, both for the plaintiff in suing and for the accused in defending himself, if the defendant presents himself on the appointed day and with such exception, as he can, defends himself without bitterness, but only with this intent, to defend what is his by right, and if on the other hand, the plaintiff, undeservedly oppressed either in his person or in his property, puts himself in the care of the magistrate, makes his complaint, and seeks what is fair and good. But he should be far from all passion to harm or take revenge, far from harshness and hatred, far from burning desire for contention. He should rather be prepared to yield his own and suffer anything than be carried away with enmity toward his adversary. On the other hand, where hearts are filled with malice, corrupted by envy, inflamed with wrath, breathing revenge, finally so inflamed with desire for contention, that love is somewhat impaired in them, the whole court action of even the most just cause cannot but be impious. For this must be a set principle for all Christians: that a lawsuit, however just, can never be rightly prosecuted by any man, unless he treat his adversary with the same love and good will as if the business under controversy were already amicably settled and composed. Perhaps someone will interpose here that such moderation is so uniformly absent from any lawsuit that it would be a miracle if any such were found. Indeed, I admit that, as the customs of these times go, an example of an upright litigant is rare; but the thing itself, when not corrupted by the addition of anything evil, does not cease to be good and pure. But when we hear that the help of the magistrate is a holy gift of God, we must more diligently guard against its becoming polluted by our fault.

19. Against the rejection of the judicial process

As for those who strictly condemn all legal contentions, let them realize that they therewith repudiate God's holy ordinance, and one of the class of gifts that can be clean to the clean (Titus 1:15); unless, perchance, they wish to accuse Paul of a shameful act, since he both repelled the slanders of his accusers, exposing at the same time their craft and malice (Acts 24:12 ff.), and in court claimed for himself the privilege of Roman citizenship (Acts 16:37; 22:1, 25), and, when there was need, appealed from the unjust judge to the judgment seat of Caesar (Acts 25:10–11).

This does not contradict the fact that all Christians are forbidden to desire revenge, which we banish far away from Christian courts (Lev. 19:18; Matt. 5:39; Deut. 32:35; Rom. 12:19). For if it is a civil case, a man does not take the right path unless he commits his cause, with innocent simplicity, to the judge as public protector; and he should think not at all of returning evil for evil (Rom. 12:17), which is the passion for revenge. If, however, the action is brought for some capital or serious offense, we require that the accuser be one who comes into court without a burning desire for revenge or resentment over private injury, but having in mind only to prevent the efforts of a destructive man from doing harm to society. For if you remove a vengeful mind, that command which forbids revenge to Christians is not broken.

But, some will object, not only are they forbidden to desire revenge, but they are also bidden to wait upon the hand of the Lord, who promises that he will be present to avenge the oppressed and afflicted (Rom. 12:19); while those who seek aid from the magistrate, either for themselves or for others, anticipate all the vengeance of the Heavenly Protector. Not at all! For we must consider that the magistrate's revenge is not man's but God's, which he extends and exercises, as Paul says (Rom. 13:4), through the ministry of man for our good.

20. The Christian endures insults, but with amity and equity defends the public interest

We are not in any more disagreement with Christ's words in which he forbids us to resist evil, and commands us to turn the right cheek to him who has struck the left, and to give our cloak to him who has taken away our coat (Matt. 5:39–40). He indeed wills that the hearts of his people so utterly recoil from any desire to retaliate that they should rather allow double injury to be done them than desire to pay it back. And we are not leading them away from this forbearance. For truly, Christians ought to be a kind of men born to bear slanders and injuries, open to the malice, deceits, and mockeries of wicked men. And not that only, but they ought to bear patiently all these evils. That is, they should have such complete spiritual composure that, having received one offense, they make ready for another, promising themselves throughout life nothing but the bearing of a perpetual cross. Meanwhile, let them also do good to those who do them harm, and bless those who curse them (Luke 6:28; cf. Matt. 5:44), and (this is their only victory) strive to conquer evil with good (Rom. 12:21). So minded, they will not seek an eye for an eye, a tooth for a tooth, as the Pharisees taught their disciples to desire revenge, but, as we are instructed by

Christ, they will so suffer their body to be maimed, and their possessions to be maliciously seized, that they will forgive and voluntarily pardon those wrongs as soon as they have been inflicted upon them (Matt. 5:38 ff.).

Yet this equity and moderateness of their minds will not prevent them from using the help of the magistrate in preserving their own possessions, while maintaining friendliness toward their enemies; or zealous for public welfare, from demanding the punishment of a guilty and pestilent man, who, they know, can be changed only by death. For Augustine truly interprets the purpose of all these precepts. The righteous and godly man should be ready patiently to bear the malice of those whom he desires to become good, in order to increase the number of good men—not to add himself to the number of the bad by a malice like theirs. Secondly, these precepts pertain more to the preparation of the heart which is within than to the work which is done in the open, in order that patience of mind and good will be kept in secret, but that we may openly do what we see may benefit those whom we ought to wish well.

21. Paul condemns a litigious spirit, but not all litigation

But the usual objection—that Paul has condemned lawsuits altogether—is also false (I Cor. 6:5–8). It can easily be understood from his words that there was an immoderate rage for litigation in the church of the Corinthians—even to the point that they exposed to the scoffing and evilspeaking of the impious the gospel of Christ and the whole religion they professed. Paul first criticized them for disgracing the gospel among believers by the intemperateness of their quarrels. Secondly, he rebuked them also for contending in this way among themselves, brethren with brethren. For they were so far from bearing wrongs that they greedily panted after one another's possessions, and without cause assailed and inflicted loss upon one another. Therefore, Paul inveighs against that mad lust to go to law, not simply against all controversies.

But he brands it a fault or weakness for them not to accept the loss of their goods, rather than to endeavor to keep them, even to the point of strife. That is, when they were so easily aroused by every loss, and dashed to the court and to lawsuits over the least causes, he speaks of this as proof that their minds are too prone to anger, and not enough disposed to patience. Christians ought indeed so to conduct themselves that they always prefer to yield their own right rather than go into a court, from which they can scarcely get away without a heart stirred and kindled to hatred of their brother. But when any man sees that without loss of love he can defend his own property, the loss of which would be a heavy expense to him, he does not offend against this statement of Paul, if he has recourse to law. To sum up (as we said at the beginning), love will give every man the best counsel. Everything undertaken apart from love and all disputes that go beyond it, we regard as incontrovertibly unjust and impious.

(*Obedience, with reverence, due even unjust rulers, 22–29*)

22. *Deference*

The first duty of subjects toward their magistrates is to think most honorably of their office, which they recognize as a jurisdiction bestowed by God, and on that account to esteem and reverence them as ministers and representatives of God. For you may find some who very respectfully yield themselves to their magistrates and desire somebody whom they can obey, because they know that such is expedient for public welfare; nevertheless, they regard magistrates only as a kind of necessary evil. But Peter requires something more of us when he commands that the king be honored (I Peter 2:17); as does Solomon when he teaches that God and king are to be feared (Prov. 24:21). For Peter, in the word "to honor" includes a sincere and candid opinion of the king. Solomon, yoking the king with God, shows that the king is full of a holy reverence and dignity. There is also that famous saying in Paul: that we should obey "not only because of wrath, but because of conscience" (Rom. 13:5, cf. Vg.). By this he means that subjects should be led not by fear alone of princes and rulers to remain in subjection under them (as they commonly yield to an armed enemy who sees that vengeance is promptly taken if they resist), but because they are showing obedience to God himself when they give it to them; since the rulers' power is from God.

I am not discussing the men themselves, as if a mask of dignity covered foolishness, or sloth, or cruelty, as well as wicked morals full of infamous deeds, and thus acquired for vices the praise of virtues; but I say that the order itself is worthy of such honor and reverence that those who are rulers are esteemed among us, and receive reverence out of respect for their lordship.

23. Obedience

From this also something else follows: that, with hearts inclined to reverence their rulers, the subjects should prove their obedience toward them, whether by obeying their proclamations, or by paying taxes, or by undertaking public offices and burdens which pertain to the common defense, or by executing any other commands of theirs. "Let every soul," says Paul, "be subject to the higher powers. . . . For he who resists authority, resists what God has ordained." (Rom. 13:1–2, Vg.) "Remind them," he writes to Titus, "to be subject to principalities and powers, to obey magistrates, to be ready for every good work." (Titus 3:1, cf. Vg.) And Peter says, "Be subject to every human creature (or rather, as I translate it, ordinance) for the Lord's sake, whether it be to the king, as supreme, or unto governors who are sent through him to punish evildoers, but to praise doers of good." (I Peter 2:13–14.) Now, in order that they may prove that they are not pretending subjection, but are sincerely and heartily subjects, Paul adds that they should commend to God the safety and prosperity of those under whom they live. "I urge," he says, "that supplications, prayers, intercessions, and thanksgivings be made for all men, for kings, and all that are in authority, that we may lead a quiet and peaceable life, with all godliness and honesty." (I Tim. 2:1–2, cf. Vg.)

Let no man deceive himself here. For since the magistrate cannot be resisted without God being resisted at the same time, even though it seems that an unarmed magistrate can be despised with impunity, still God is armed to avenge mightily this contempt toward himself.

Moreover, under this obedience I include the restraint which private citizens ought to bid themselves keep in public, that they may not deliberately intrude in public affairs, or pointlessly invade the magistrate's office, or undertake anything at all politically. If anything in a public ordinance requires amendment, let them not raise a tumult, or put their hands to the task—all of them ought to keep their hands bound in this respect—but let them commit the matter to the judgment of the magistrate, whose hand alone here is free. I mean, let them not venture on anything without a command. For when the ruler gives his command, private citizens receive public authority. For as the counselors are commonly called the ears and eyes of the prince, so may one reasonably speak of those whom he has appointed by his command to do things, as the hands of the prince.

24. Obedience is also due the unjust magistrate

But since we have so far been describing a magistrate who truly is what he is called, that is, a father of his country, and, as the poet expresses it, shepherd of his people, guardian of peace, protector of righteousness, and avenger of innocence—he who does not approve of such government must rightly be regarded as insane.

But it is the example of nearly all ages that some princes are careless about all those things to which they ought to have given heed, and, far from all care, lazily take their pleasure. Others, intent upon their own business, put up for sale laws, privileges, judgments, and letters of favor. Others drain the common people of their money, and afterward lavish it on insane largesse. Still others exercise sheer robbery, plundering houses, raping virgins and matrons, and slaughtering the innocent.

Consequently, many cannot be persuaded that they ought to recognize these as princes and to obey their authority as far as possible. For in such great disgrace, and among such crimes, so alien to the office not only of a magistrate but also of a man, they discern no appearance of the image of God which ought to have shone in the magistrate; while they see no trace of that minister of God, who had been appointed to praise the good, and to punish the evil (cf. I Peter 2:14, Vg.). Thus, they also do not recognize as ruler him whose dignity and authority Scripture commends to us. Indeed, this inborn feeling has always been in the minds of men to hate and curse tyrants as much as to love and venerate lawful kings.

25. The wicked ruler a judgment of God

But if we look to God's Word, it will lead us farther. We are not only subject to the authority of princes who perform their office toward us uprightly and faithfully as they ought, but also to the authority of all who, by whatever means, have got control of affairs, even though they perform not a whit of the princes' office. For despite the Lord's testimony that the magistrate's office is the highest gift of his beneficence to preserve the safety of men, and despite his appointment of bounds to the magistrates—he still declares at the same time that whoever they may be, they have their authority solely from him. Indeed, he says that those who rule for the public benefit are true patterns and evidences of this beneficence of his; that they who rule unjustly and incompetently have been raised up by him to punish the wickedness of the people; that all equally have been endowed with that holy majesty with which he has invested lawful power.

I shall proceed no farther until I have added some sure testimonies of this thing. Yet, we need not labor to prove that a wicked king is the Lord's wrath upon the earth (Job 34:30, Vg.; Hos. 13:11; Isa. 3:4; 10:5; Deut. 28:29), for I believe no man will contradict me; and thus nothing more would be said of a king than of a robber who seizes your possessions, of an adulterer who pollutes your marriage bed, or of a murderer who seeks to kill you. For Scripture reckons all such calamities among God's curses.

But let us, rather, pause here to prove this, which does not so easily settle in men's minds. In a very wicked man utterly unworthy of all honor, provided he has the public power in his hands, that noble and divine power resides which the Lord has by his Word given to the ministers of his justice and judgment. Accordingly, he should be held in the same reverence and esteem by his subjects, in so far as public obedience is concerned, in which they would hold the best of kings if he were given to them.

26. Obedience to bad kings required in Scripture

First, I should like my readers to note and carefully observe that providence of God, which the Scriptures with good reason so often recall to us, and its special operation in distributing kingdoms and appointing what kings he pleases. In Daniel, the Lord changes times and successions of times, removes kings and sets them up (Dan. 2:21, 37). Likewise: "to the end that the living may know that the Most High rules the kingdom of men, and gives it to whom he will" (Dan. 4:17; cf. ch. 4:14, Vg.). Although Scripture everywhere abounds with such passages, this prophecy particularly swarms with them. Now it is well enough known what kind of king Nebuchadnezzar was, who conquered Jerusalem—a strong invader and destroyer of others. Nevertheless, the Lord declares in Ezekiel that He has given him the land of Egypt for the service he had done him in devastating it (Ezek. 29:19–20). And Daniel said to him: "You, O king, are a king of kings, to whom the God of heaven has given the kingdom, powerful, mighty, and glorious; to you, I say, he has given also all lands where the sons of men dwell, beasts of the forest and birds of the air: these he has given into your hand and made you rule over them" (Dan. 2:37–38, cf. Vg.). Again, Daniel says to Nebuchadnezzar's son Belshazzar: "The Most High God gave Nebuchadnezzar, your father, kingship and magnificence, honor and glory; and because of the magnificence that he gave him, all peoples, tribes, and tongues were trembling and fearful before him" (Dan. 5:18–19, cf. Vg.). When we hear that a king has been ordained by God, let us at once call to mind those heavenly edicts with regard to honoring and fearing a king; then we shall not hesitate to hold a most wicked tyrant in the place where the Lord has deigned to set him. Samuel, when he warned the people of Israel what sort of things they would suffer from their kings, said: "This shall be the right of the king that will reign over you: he will take your sons and put them to his chariot to make them his horsemen and to plow his fields and reap his harvest, and make his weapons. He will take your daughters to be perfumers and cooks and bakers. Finally, he will take your fields, your vineyards, and your best olive trees and will give them to his servants. He will take the tenth of your grain and of your vineyards, and will give it to his eunuchs and servants. He will take your menservants, maidservants, and asses and set them to his work. He will take the tenth of your flocks and you will be his servants" (I Sam. 8:11–17, with omissions; cf. Hebrew). Surely, the kings would not do this by legal right, since the law trained them to all restraint (Deut. 17:16 ff.). But it was called a right in relation to the people, for they had to obey it and were not allowed to resist. It is as if Samuel had said: The willfulness of kings will run to excess, but it will not be your part to restrain it; you will have only this left to you: to obey their commands and hearken to their word.

27. The case of Nebuchadnezzar in Jer., ch. 27

But in Jeremiah, especially, there is a memorable passage, which (although rather long) it will not trouble me to quote because it very clearly defines this whole question. "I have made the earth and men, says the Lord, and the animals which are upon the face of the earth, with my great strength and outstretched arm; and I give it to him who is pleasing in my eyes. Now, therefore, I have given all these lands into the hand of Nebuchadnezzar . . . my servant. . . . All the nations and great kings shall serve him . . . , until the time of his own land comes. . . . And it shall be that any nation and kingdom that will not serve the king of Babylon, I shall visit that nation with sword, famine, and pestilence. . . . Therefore, serve the king of Babylon and live." (Jer. 27:5–8, 17, cf. Vg.) We see how much obedience the Lord willed to be paid to that abominable and cruel tyrant for no other reason than that he possessed the kingship. But it was by heavenly decree that he had been set upon the throne of the kingdom and assumed into kingly majesty, which it would be unlawful to violate. If we have continually present to our minds and before our eyes the fact that even the most worthless kings are appointed by the same decree by which the authority of all kings is established, those seditious thoughts will never enter our minds that a king should be treated according to his merits, and that it is unfair that we should show ourselves subjects to him who, on his part, does not show himself a king to us.

28. General testimonies of Scripture on the sanctity of the royal person

It is vain for anyone to object that that command was peculiar to the Israelites. For we must note with what reason the Lord confirms it: "I have given," he says, "the kingdom to Nebuchadnezzar" (Jer. 27:6, cf. Vg.). "Therefore, serve him and live." (Jer. 27:17, cf. Vg.) Let us not doubt that we ought to serve him to whom it is evident that the kingdom has been given. And when once the Lord advances any man to kingly rank, he attests to us his determination that he would have him reign. For there are general testimonies of Scripture concerning this. Solomon, in the twenty-eighth chapter of The Proverbs, says: "Because of the iniquity of the land there are many princes" (Prov. 28:2 p.). Likewise, the twelfth chapter of Job: "He takes away subjection from kings, and girds them again with a girdle" (Job 12:18 p.). Once this has been admitted, nothing remains but that we should serve and live.

In Jeremiah the prophet, there is also another command of the Lord by which he enjoins his people to seek the peace of Babylon, where they have been sent as captives, and to pray to the Lord on its behalf, for in its peace will be their peace (Jer. 29:7). Behold, the Israelites, divested of all their possessions, driven from their homes, led away into exile, and cast into pitiable bondage, are commanded to pray for the prosperity of their conqueror—not as we are commanded in other passages to pray for our persecutors (cf. Matt. 5:44), but in order that his kingdom may be preserved safe and peaceful, that under him they too may prosper. So David, already designated king by God's ordination and anointed with his holy oil, when he was persecuted by Saul without deserving it, still regarded the head of his assailant as inviolable, because the Lord had sanctified it with the honor of the kingdom. "The Lord forbid," he said, "that I should do this thing before the Lord, to my lord, the Lord's anointed, to put forth my hand against him, since he is the Lord's anointed." (I Sam. 24:6, cf. Vg.) Again: "My soul has spared you; and I have said, 'I shall not put forth my hand against my lord, for he is the Lord's anointed'" (I Sam. 24:11, cf. Vg.). Again: "Who will put forth his hand against the anointed of the Lord and be innocent? . . . The Lord lives; unless the Lord strike him, or the day come for him to die, or he fall in battle, the Lord forbid that I should put forth my hand against the Lord's anointed" (I Sam. 26:9–11, cf. Vg.).

29. *It is not the part of subjects but of God to vindicate the right*

We owe this attitude of reverence and therefore of piety toward all our rulers in the highest degree, whatever they may be like. I therefore the more often repeat this: that we should learn not to examine the men themselves, but take it as enough that they bear, by the Lord's will, a character upon which he has imprinted and engraved an inviolable majesty.

But (you will say) rulers owe responsibilities in turn to their subjects. This I have already admitted. But if you conclude from this that service ought to be rendered only to just governors, you are reasoning foolishly. For husbands are also bound to their wives, and parents to their children, by mutual responsibilities. Suppose parents and husbands depart from their duty. Suppose parents show themselves so hard and intractable to their children, whom they are forbidden to provoke to anger (Eph. 6:4), that by their rigor they tire them beyond measure. Suppose husbands most despitefully use their wives, whom they are commanded to love (Eph. 5:25) and to spare as weaker vessels (I Peter 3:7). Shall either children be less obedient to their parents or wives to their husbands? They are still subject even to those who are wicked and undutiful.

Indeed, all ought to try not to "look at the bag hanging from their back," that is, not to inquire about another's duties, but every man should keep in mind that one duty which is his own. This ought particularly to apply to those who have been put under the power of others. Therefore, if we are cruelly tormented by a savage prince, if we are greedily despoiled by one who is avaricious or wanton, if we are neglected by a slothful one, if finally we are vexed for piety's sake by one who is impious and sacrilegious, let us first be mindful of our own misdeeds, which without doubt are chastised by such whips of the Lord (cf. Dan. 9:7). By this, humility will restrain our impatience. Let us then also call this thought to mind, that it is not for us to remedy such evils; that only this remains, to implore the Lord's help, in whose hand are the hearts of kings, and the changing of kingdoms (Prov. 21:1 p.). "He is God who will stand in the assembly of the gods, and will judge in the midst of the gods." (Ps. 82:1 p.) Before His face all kings shall fall and be crushed, and all the judges of the earth, that have not kissed his anointed (Ps. 2:10–11), and all those who have written unjust laws to oppress the poor in judgment and to do violence to the cause of the lowly, to pray upon widows and rob the fatherless (Isa. 10:1–2, cf. Vg.).

(*Constitutional magistrates, however, ought to check the tyranny of kings; obedience to God comes first, 30–31*)

30. When God intervenes, it is sometimes by unwitting agents

Here are revealed his goodness, his power, and his providence. For sometimes he raises up open avengers from among his servants, and arms them with his command to punish the wicked government and deliver his people, oppressed in unjust ways, from miserable calamity. Sometimes he directs to this end the rage of men who intend one thing and undertake another. Thus he delivered the people of Israel from the tyranny of Pharaoh through Moses (Ex. 3:7–10); from the violence of Chusan, king of Syria, through Othniel (Judg. 3:9); and from other servitudes through other kings or judges. Thus he tamed the pride of Tyre by the Egyptians, the insolence of the Egyptians by the Assyrians, the fierceness of the Assyrians by the Chaldeans; the arrogance of Babylon by the Medes and Persians, after Cyrus had already subjugated the Medes. The ungratefulness of the kings of Judah and Israel and their impious obstinancy toward his many benefits, he sometimes by the Assyrians, sometimes by the Babylonians, crushed and afflicted—although not all in the same way.

For the first kind of men, when they had been sent by God's lawful calling to carry out such acts, in taking up arms against kings, did not at all violate that majesty which is implanted in kings by God's ordination; but, armed from heaven, they subdued the lesser power with the greater, just as it is lawful for kings to punish their subordinates. But the latter kind of men, although they were directed by God's hand whither he pleased, and executed his work unwittingly, yet planned in their minds to do nothing but an evil act.

31. Constitutional defenders of the people's freedom

But however these deeds of men are judged in themselves, still the Lord accomplished his work through them alike when he broke the bloody scepters of arrogant kings and when he overturned intolerable governments. Let the princes hear and be afraid.

But we must, in the meantime, be very careful not to despise or violate that authority of magistrates, full of venerable majesty, which God has established by the weightiest decrees, even though it may reside with the most unworthy men, who defile it as much as they can with their own wickedness. For, if the correction of unbridled despotism is the Lord's to avenge, let us not at once think that it is entrusted to us, to whom no command has been given except to obey and suffer.

I am speaking all the while of private individuals. For if there are now any magistrates of the people, appointed to restrain the willfulness of kings (as in ancient times the ephors were set against the Spartan kings, or the tribunes of the people against the Roman consuls, or the demarchs against the senate of the Athenians; and perhaps, as things now are, such power as the three estates exercise in every realm when they hold their chief assemblies), I am so far from forbidding them to withstand, in accordance with their duty, the fierce licentiousness of kings, that, if they wink at kings who violently fall upon and assault the lowly common folk, I declare that their dissimulation involves nefarious perfidy, because they dishonestly betray the freedom of the people, of which they know that they have been appointed protectors by God's ordinance.

32. Obedience to man must not become disobedience to God

But in that obedience which we have shown to be due the authority of rulers, we are always to make this exception, indeed, to observe it as primary, that such obedience is never to lead us away from obedience to him, to whose will the desires of all kings ought to be subject, to whose decrees all their commands ought to yield, to whose majesty their scepters ought to be submitted. And how absurd would it be that in satisfying men you should incur the displeasure of him for whose sake you obey men themselves! The Lord, therefore, is the King of Kings, who, when he has opened his sacred mouth, must alone be heard, before all and above all men; next to him we are subject to those men who are in authority over us, but only in him. If they command anything against him, let it go unesteemed. And here let us not be concerned about all that dignity which the magistrates possess; for no harm is done to it when it is humbled before that singular and truly supreme power of God. On this consideration, Daniel denies that he has committed any offense against the king when he has not obeyed his impious edict (Dan. 6:22–23, Vg.). For the king had exceeded his limits, and had not only been a wrongdoer against men, but, in lifting up his horns against God, had himself abrogated his power. Conversely, the Israelites are condemned because they were too obedient to the wicked proclamation of the king (Hos. 5:13). For when Jeroboam molded the golden calves, they, to please him, forsook God's Temple and turned to new superstitions (I Kings 12:30). With the same readiness, their descendants complied with the decrees of their kings. The prophet sharply reproaches them for embracing the king's edicts (Hos. 5:11). Far, indeed, is the pretense of modesty from deserving praise, a false modesty with which the court flatterers cloak themselves and deceive the simple, while they deny that it is lawful for them to refuse anything imposed by their kings. As if God had made over his right to mortal men, giving them the rule over mankind! Or as if earthly power were diminished when it is subjected to its Author, in whose presence even the heavenly powers tremble as suppliants! I know with what great and present peril this constancy is menaced, because kings bear defiance with the greatest displeasure, whose "wrath is a messenger of death" (Prov. 16:14), says Solomon. But since this edict has been proclaimed by the heavenly herald, Peter—"We must obey God rather than men" (Acts 5:29)—let us comfort ourselves with the thought that we are rendering that obedience which the Lord requires when we suffer anything rather than turn aside from piety. And that our courage may not grow faint, Paul pricks us with another goad: That we have been redeemed by Christ at so great a price as our redemption cost him, so that we should not enslave ourselves to the wicked desires of men—much less be subject to their impiety (I Cor. 7:23).

GOD BE PRAISED

V

Three Forms of Exposition

SHORT TREATISE
ON THE HOLY SUPPER
OF OUR LORD JESUS CHRIST[1]

[*Written in French in 1540 in Strassbourg, and later translated into Latin, the treatise is intended as a single, straight-
forward account of the meaning of the Lord's Supper. Unlike
the later tracts in which the debates on the Supper are
polemic, this document is conciliatory in dealing with the
alternatives. Melanchthon's son-in-law reported that Luther,
picking up the book, applauded what he saw.*]

1. REASON WHY MANY WEAK CONSCIENCES
REMAIN IN SUSPENSE AS TO THE TRUE
DOCTRINE OF THE SUPPER

As the holy sacrament of the Supper of our Lord Jesus
Christ has long been the subject of several important errors,
and in these past years been anew enveloped in diverse opinions and contentious disputes, it is no wonder if many weak

---

[1] [Reprinted from *Tracts, Continuing Treatises on the Sacraments, Catechism of the Church of Geneva, Forms of Prayer, and
Confessions of Faith*, Volume II, translated from the original Latin
and French by Henry Beveridge (Edinburgh: Printed for the Calvin Translation Society, 1849), pp. 164–98.]

consciences cannot fairly resolve what view they ought to take of it, but remain in doubt and perplexity, waiting till all contention being laid aside, the servants of God come to some agreement upon it. However, as it is a very perilous thing to have no certainty on an ordinance, the understanding of which is so requisite for our salvation, I have thought it might be a very useful labour to treat briefly and, nevertheless, clearly deduce a summary of what is necessary to be known of it. I may add that I have been requested to do so by some worthy persons, whom I could not refuse without neglecting my duty. In order to rid ourselves of all difficulty, it is expedient to attend to the order which I have determined to follow.

2. THE ORDER TO BE OBSERVED IN
THIS TREATISE

First, then, we will explain to what end and for what reason our Lord instituted this holy sacrament.

Secondly, What fruit and utility we receive from it, when it will likewise be shown how the body of Jesus Christ is given to us.

Thirdly, What is the legitimate use of it.

Fourthly, We will detail the errors and superstitions with which it has been contaminated, when it will be shown how the servants of God ought to differ from the Papists.

Lastly, We will mention what has been the source of the discussion which has been so keenly carried on, even among those who have, in our time, brought back the light of the gospel, and employed themselves in rightly edifying the Church in sound doctrine.

3. AT BAPTISM GOD RECEIVES US INTO HIS
CHURCH AS MEMBERS OF HIS FAMILY

In regard to the first article—Since it has pleased our good God to receive us by baptism into his Church, which is his house, which he desires to maintain and govern, and since he has received us to keep us not merely as domestics, but as his own children, it remains that, in order to do the office of a good father, he nourish and provide us with every thing necessary for our life. In regard to corporal nourishment, as it is common to all, and the bad share in it as well as the good, it is not peculiar to his family. It is very true that we have an evidence of his paternal goodness in maintaining our bodies, seeing that we partake in all the good things which he gives us with his blessing. But as the life into which he has begotten us again is spiritual, so must the food, in order to preserve and strengthen us, be spiritual also. For we should understand, that not only has he called us one day to possess his heavenly inheritance, but that by hope he has already in some measure installed us in possession; that not only has he promised us life, but already transported us into it, delivering us from death, when by adopting us as his children, he begot us again by immortal seed, namely, his word imprinted on our hearts by the Holy Spirit.

4. THE VIRTUE AND OFFICE OF THE WORD OF GOD IN REGARD TO OUR SOULS

To maintain us in this spiritual life, the thing requisite is not to feed our bodies with fading and corruptible food, but to nourish our souls on the best and most precious diet. Now all Scripture tells us, that the spiritual food by which our souls are maintained is that same word by which the Lord has regenerated us; but it frequently adds the reason, viz., that in it Jesus Christ, our only life, is given and administered to us. For we must not imagine that there is life any where than in God. But just as God has placed all fulness of life in Jesus, in order to communicate it to us by his means, so he ordained his word as the instrument by which Jesus Christ, with all his graces, is dispensed to us. Still it always remains true, that our souls have no other pasture than Jesus Christ. Our heavenly Father, therefore, in his care to nourish us, gives us no other, but rather recommends us to take our fill there, as a refreshment amply sufficient, with which we cannot dispense, and beyond which no other can be found.

5. JESUS CHRIST THE ONLY SPIRITUAL
NOURISHMENT OF OUR SOULS

We have already seen that Jesus Christ is the only food by which our souls are nourished; but as it is distributed to us by the word of the Lord, which he has appointed an instrument for that purpose, that word is also called bread and water. Now what is said of the word applies as well to the sacrament of the Supper, by means of which the Lord leads us to communion with Jesus Christ. For seeing we are so weak that we cannot receive him with true heartfelt trust, when he is presented to us by simple doctrine and preaching, the Father of mercy, disdaining not to condescend in this matter to our infirmity, has been pleased to add to his word a visible sign, by which he might represent the substance of his promises, to confirm and fortify us by delivering us from all doubt and uncertainty. Since, then, there is something so mysterious and incomprehensible in saying that we have communion with the body and the blood of Jesus Christ, and we on our part are so rude and gross that we cannot understand the least things of God, it was of importance that we should be given to understand it as far as our capacity could admit.

6. THE CAUSE WHY OUR LORD INSTITUTED
THE SUPPER

Our Lord, therefore, instituted the Supper, first, in order to sign and seal in our consciences the promises contained in his gospel concerning our being made partakers of his body and blood, and to give us certainty and assurance that therein lies our true spiritual nourishment, and that having such an earnest, we may entertain a right reliance on salvation. Secondly, in order to exercise us in recognising his great goodness toward us, and thus lead us to laud and magnify him more fully. Thirdly, in order to exhort us to all holiness and innocence, inasmuch as we are members of Jesus Christ; and specially to exhort us to union and brotherly charity, as we are expressly commanded. When we shall have well considered these three reasons, to which the Lord had respect in ordaining his Supper, we shall be able to understand, both what benefit accrues to us from it, and what is our duty in order to use it properly.

7. THE MEANS OF KNOWING THE GREAT
BENEFIT OF THE SUPPER

It is now time to come to the second point, viz., to show how the Lord's Supper is profitable to us, provided we use it profitably. Now we shall know its utility by reflecting on the indigence which it is meant to succour. We must necessarily be under great trouble and torment of conscience, when we consider who we are, and examine what is in us. For not one of us can find one particle of righteousness in himself, but on the contrary we are all full of sins and iniquities, so much so that no other party is required to accuse us than our own conscience, no other judge to condemn us. It follows that the wrath of God is kindled against us, and that none can escape eternal death. If we are not asleep and stupified, this horrible thought must be a kind of perpetual hell to vex and torment us. For the judgment of God cannot come into our remembrance without letting us see that our condemnation follows as a consequence.

8. THE MISERY OF MAN

We are then already in the gulf, if God does not in mercy draw us out of it. Moreover, what hope of resurrection can we have while considering our flesh, which is only rottenness and corruption? Thus in regard to the soul, as well as the body, we are more than miserable if we remain within ourselves, and this misery cannot but produce great sadness and anguish of soul. Now our heavenly Father, to succour us in this, gives us the Supper as a mirror, in which we may contemplate our Lord Jesus Christ, crucified to take away our faults and offences, and raised again to deliver us from corruption and death, restoring us to a celestial immortality.

9. THE SUPPER INVITES US TO THE PROMISES
OF SALVATION

Here, then, is the singular consolation which we derive
from the Supper. It directs and leads us to the cross of Jesus
Christ and to his resurrection, to certify us that whatever
iniquity there may be in us, the Lord nevertheless recognises
and accepts us as righteous—whatever materials of death may
be in us, he nevertheless gives us life—whatever misery may
be in us, he nevertheless fills us with all felicity. Or to explain
the matter more simply—as in ourselves we are devoid of all
good, and have not one particle of what might help to procure salvation, the Supper is an attestation that, having been
made partakers of the death and passion of Jesus Christ,
we have every thing that is useful and salutary to us.

10. ALL THE TREASURES OF SPIRITUAL GRACE
PRESENTED IN THE SUPPER

We can therefore say, that in it the Lord displays to us all
the treasures of his spiritual grace, inasmuch as he associates
us in all the blessings and riches of our Lord Jesus. Let us
recollect, then, that the Supper is given us as a mirror in
which we may contemplate Jesus Christ crucified in order
to deliver us from condemnation, and raised again in order
to procure for us righteousness and eternal life. It is indeed
true that this same grace is offered us by the gospel, yet as
in the Supper we have more ample certainty, and fuller enjoyment of it, with good cause do we recognise this fruit as
coming from it.

11. JESUS CHRIST IS THE SUBSTANCE OF
THE SACRAMENTS

But as the blessings of Jesus Christ do not belong to us
at all, unless he be previously ours, it is necessary, first of

all, that he be given us in the Supper, in order that the things which we have mentioned may be truly accomplished in us. For this reason I am wont to say, that the substance of the sacraments is the Lord Jesus, and the efficacy of them the graces and blessings which we have by his means. Now the efficacy of the Supper is to confirm to us the reconciliation which we have with God through our Saviour's death and passion; the washing of our souls which we have in the shedding of his blood; the righteousness which we have in his obedience; in short, the hope of salvation which we have in all that he has done for us. It is necessary, then, that the substance should be conjoined with these, otherwise nothing would be firm or certain. Hence we conclude that two things are presented to us in the Supper, viz., Jesus Christ as the source and substance of all good; and, secondly, the fruit and efficacy of his death and passion. This is implied in the words which were used. For after commanding us to eat his body and drink his blood, he adds that his body was delivered for us, and his blood shed for the remission of our sins. Hereby he intimates, first, that we ought not simply to communicate in his body and blood, without any other consideration, but in order to receive the fruit derived to us from his death and passion; secondly, that we can attain the enjoyment of such fruit only by participating in his body and blood, from which it is derived.

12. HOW THE BREAD IS CALLED THE BODY, AND THE WINE THE BLOOD OF CHRIST

We begin now to enter on the question so much debated, both anciently and at the present time—how we are to understand the words in which the bread is called the body of Christ, and the wine his blood. This may be disposed of without much difficulty, if we carefully observe the principle which I lately laid down, viz., that all the benefit which we should seek in the Supper is annihilated if Jesus Christ be not there given to us as the substance and foundation of all. That being fixed, we will confess, without doubt, that to deny that a true communication of Jesus Christ is presented to us in the Supper, is to render this holy sacrament frivolous and useless—an execrable blasphemy unfit to be listened to.

13. WHAT IS REQUISITE IN ORDER TO LIVE IN JESUS CHRIST

Moreover, if the reason for communicating with Jesus Christ is to have part and portion in all the graces which he purchased for us by his death, the thing requisite must be not only to be partakers of his Spirit, but also to participate in his humanity, in which he rendered all obedience to God his Father, in order to satisfy our debts, although, properly speaking, the one cannot be without the other; for when he gives himself to us, it is in order that we may possess him entirely. Hence, as it is said that his Spirit is our life, so he himself, with his own lips, declares that his flesh is meat indeed, and his blood drink indeed. (John 6:55.) If these words are not to go for nothing, it follows that in order to have our life in Christ our souls must feed on his body and blood as their proper food. This, then, is expressly attested in the Supper, when of the bread it is said to us that we are to take it and eat it, and that it is his body, and of the cup that we are to drink it, and that it is his blood. This is expressly spoken of the body and blood, in order that we may learn to seek there the substance of our spiritual life.

14. HOW THE BREAD AND WINE ARE THE BODY OF JESUS CHRIST

Now, if it be asked whether the bread is the body of Christ and the wine his blood, we answer, that the bread and the wine are visible signs, which represent to us the body and blood, but that this name and title of body and blood is given to them because they are as it were instruments by which the Lord distributes them to us. This form and manner of speaking is very appropriate. For as the communion which we have with the body of Christ is a thing incomprehensible, not only to the eye but to our natural sense, it is there visibly demonstrated to us. Of this we have a striking example in an analogous case. Our Lord, wishing to give a visible appearance to his Spirit at the baptism of Christ, presented him under the form of a dove. St. John the Baptist, narrating the fact, says, that he saw the Spirit of God descending. If we look more closely, we shall find that he saw nothing but the dove, in respect that the Holy Spirit is in his essence invisible. Still, knowing that this vision was not an empty phantom, but a sure sign of the presence of the Holy Spirit, he doubts not to say that he saw it, (John 1:32,) because it was represented to him according to his capacity.

15. THE SACRAMENT IS REPRESENTED BY
VISIBLE SIGNS

Thus it is with the communion which we have in the body and blood of the Lord Jesus. It is a spiritual mystery which can neither be seen by the eye nor comprehended by the human understanding. It is therefore figured to us by visible signs, according as our weakness requires, in such manner, nevertheless, that it is not a bare figure but is combined with the reality and substance. It is with good reason then that the bread is called the body, since it not only represents but also presents it to us. Hence we indeed infer that the name of the body of Jesus Christ is transferred to the bread, inasmuch as it is the sacrament and figure of it. But we likewise add, that the sacraments of the Lord should not and cannot be at all separated from their reality and substance. To distinguish, in order to guard against confounding them, is not only good and reasonable, but altogether necessary; but to divide them, so as to make the one exist without the other, is absurd.

16. THE PROPER BODY AND BLOOD OF
JESUS CHRIST RECEIVED ONLY
BY FAITH

Hence when we see the visible sign we must consider what it represents, and by whom it has been given us. The bread is given us to figure the body of Jesus Christ, with command to eat it, and it is given us of God, who is certain and immutable truth. If God cannot deceive or lie, it follows that it accomplishes all which it signifies. We must then truly receive in the Supper the body and blood of Jesus Christ, since

the Lord there represents to us the communion of both. Were
it otherwise, what could be meant by saying, that we eat the
bread and drink the wine as a sign that his body is our meat
and his blood our drink? If he gave us only bread and wine,
leaving the spiritual reality behind, would it not be under
false colours that this ordinance had been instituted?

17. THE INTERNAL SUBSTANCE IS CONJOINED
WITH THE VISIBLE SIGNS

We must confess, then, that if the representation which
God gives us in the Supper is true, the internal substance of
the sacrament is conjoined with the visible signs; and as the
bread is distributed to us by the hand, so the body of Christ
is communicated to us in order that we may be made partakers of it. Though there should be nothing more, we have
good cause to be satisfied, when we understand that Jesus
Christ gives us in the Supper the proper substance of his
body and blood, in order that we may possess it fully, and
possessing it have part in all his blessings. For seeing we
have him, all the riches of God which are comprehended in
him are exhibited to us, in order that they may be ours. Thus,
as a brief definition of this utility of the Supper, we may say,
that Jesus Christ is there offered to us in order that we may
possess him, and in him all the fulness of grace which we can
desire, and that herein we have a good aid to confirm our
consciences in the faith which we ought to have in him.

18. IN THE SUPPER WE ARE REMINDED OF
OUR DUTY TOWARDS GOD

The second benefit of the Supper is, that it admonishes
and incites us more strongly to recognise the blessings which
we have received, and receive daily from the Lord Jesus, in
order that we may ascribe to him the praise which is due. For
in ourselves we are so negligent that we rarely think of the
goodness of God, if he do not arouse us from our indolence,
and urge us to our duty. Now there cannot be a spur which
can pierce us more to the quick than when he makes us, so
to speak, see with the eye, touch with the hand, and dis-

tinctly perceive this inestimable blessing of feeding on his own substance. This he means to intimate when he commands us to show forth his death till he come. (1 Cor. 11:26.) If it is then so essential to salvation not to overlook the gifts which God has given us, but diligently to keep them in mind, and extol them to others for mutual edification; we see another singular advantage of the Supper in this, that it draws us off from ingratitude, and allows us not to forget the benefit which our Lord Jesus bestowed upon us in dying for us, but induces us to render him thanks, and, as it were, publicly protest how much we are indebted to him.

19. THE SACRAMENT A STRONG INDUCEMENT
TO HOLY LIVING AND BROTHERLY LOVE

The third advantage of the Sacrament consists in furnishing a most powerful incitement to live holily, and especially observe charity and brotherly love toward all. For seeing we have been made members of Jesus Christ, being incorporated into him, and united with him as our head, it is most reasonable that we should become conformable to him in purity and innocence, and especially that we should cultivate charity and concord together as becomes members of the same body. But to understand this advantage properly, we must not suppose that our Lord warns, incites, and inflames our hearts by the external sign merely; for the principal point is, that he operates in us inwardly by his Holy Spirit, in order to give efficacy to his ordinance, which he has destined for that purpose, as an instrument by which he wishes to do his work in us. Wherefore, inasmuch as the virtue of the Holy Spirit is conjoined with the sacraments when we duly receive them, we have reason to hope they will prove a good mean and aid to make us grow and advance in holiness of life, and specially in charity.

20. WHAT IT IS TO POLLUTE THE HOLY SUPPER.
—THE GREAT GUILT OF SO DOING

Let us come to the third point which we proposed at the commencement of this treatise, viz., the legitimate use, which consists in reverently observing our Lord's institution. Whoever approaches the sacrament with contempt or indifference, not caring much about following when the Lord calls him, perversely abuses, and in abusing pollutes it. Now to pollute and contaminate what God has so highly sanctified, is intolerable blasphemy. Not without cause then does St. Paul denounce such heavy condemnation on all who take it unworthily. (1 Cor. 11:29.) For if there is nothing in heaven nor on earth of greater price and dignity than the body and blood of the Lord, it is no slight fault to take it inconsiderately and without being well prepared. Hence he exhorts us to examine ourselves carefully, in order to make the proper use of it. When we understand what this examination should be, we shall know the use after which we are inquiring.

21. THE MANNER OF EXAMINING OURSELVES

Here it is necessary to be well on our guard. For as we cannot be too diligent in examining ourselves as the Lord enjoins, so, on the other hand, sophistical doctors have brought poor consciences into perilous perplexity, or rather into a horrible Gehenna, requiring I know not what examination, which it is not possible for any man to make. To rid ourselves of all these perplexities, we must reduce the whole, as I have already said, to the ordinance of the Lord, as the rule which, if we follow it, will not allow us to err. In following it, we have to examine whether we have true repentance in ourselves, and true faith in our Lord Jesus Christ. These two things are so conjoined, that the one cannot subsist without the other.

22. TO PARTICIPATE IN THE BLESSINGS
OF CHRIST, WE MUST RENOUNCE ALL
THAT IS OUR OWN

If we consider our life to be placed in Christ, we must acknowledge that we are dead in ourselves. If we seek our strength in him, we must understand that in ourselves we are weak. If we think that all our felicity is in his grace, we must understand how miserable we are without it. If we have our rest in him, we must feel within ourselves only disquietude and torment. Now such feelings cannot exist without producing, first, dissatisfaction with our whole life; secondly, anxiety and fear; lastly, a desire and love of righteousness. For he who knows the turpitude of his sin and the wretchedness of his state and condition while alienated from God, is so ashamed that he is constrained to be dissatisfied with himself, to condemn himself, to sigh and groan in great sadness. Moreover, the justice of God immediately presents itself and oppresses the wretched conscience with keen anguish, from not seeing any means of escape, or having any thing to answer in defence. When under such a conviction of our misery we get a taste of the goodness of God, it is then we would wish to regulate our conduct by his will, and renounce all our bygone life, in order to be made new creatures in him.

23. THE REQUISITES OF WORTHY COMMUNION

Hence if we would worthily communicate in the Lord's Supper, we must with firm heart-felt reliance regard the Lord Jesus as our only righteousness, life, and salvation, receiving and accepting the promises which are given us by him as sure and certain, and renouncing all other confidence, so that distrusting ourselves and all creatures, we may rest fully in him, and be contented with his grace alone. Now as that cannot be until we know how necessary it is that he come to our aid, it is of importance to have a deep-seated conviction of our own misery, which will make us hunger and thirst after him. And, in fact, what mockery would it be to go in search of food when we have no appetite? Now to have a good appetite it is not enough that the stomach be empty, it must also be in good order and capable of receiving its food. Hence it follows that our souls must be pressed with famine and have a desire and ardent longing to be fed, in order to find their proper nourishment in the Lord's Supper.

24. SELF-DENIAL NECESSARY

Moreover, it is to be observed that we cannot desire Jesus Christ without aspiring to the righteousness of God, which consists in renouncing ourselves and obeying his will. For it is preposterous to pretend that we are of the body of Christ, while abandoning ourselves to all licentiousness, and leading a dissolute life. Since in Christ is nought but chastity, benignity, sobriety, truth, humility, and such like virtues, if we would be his members, all uncleanness, intemperance, falsehood, pride, and similar vices must be put from us. For we cannot intermingle these things with him without offering him great dishonour and insult. We ought always to remember that there is no more agreement between him and iniquity than between light and darkness. If we would come then to true repentance, we must endeavour to make our whole life conformable to the example of Jesus Christ.

25. CHARITY ESPECIALLY NECESSARY

And while this must be general in every part of our life, it must be specially so in respect of charity, which is, above all other virtues, recommended to us in this sacrament: for which reason it is called the bond of charity. For as the bread which is there sanctified for the common use of all is composed of several grains so mixed together that they cannot be distinguished from each other, so ought we to be united together in indissoluble friendship. Moreover, we all receive there one body of Christ. If then we have strife and discord among ourselves, it is not owing to us that Christ Jesus is not rent in pieces, and we are therefore guilty of sacrilege, as if we had done it. We must not, then, on any account, presume to approach if we bear hatred or rancour against any man living, and especially any Christian who is in the unity of the Church. In order fully to comply with our Lord's injunction, there is another disposition which we must bring. It is to confess with the mouth and testify how much we are indebted to our Saviour, and return him thanks, not only that his name may be glorified in us, but also to edify others, and instruct them, by our example, what they ought to do.

26. ALL MEN IMPERFECT AND BLAMEWORTHY

But as not a man will be found upon the earth who has made such progress in faith and holiness, as not to be still very defective in both, there might be a danger that several good consciences might be troubled by what has been said, did we not obviate it by tempering the injunctions which we have given in regard both to faith and repentance. It is a perilous mode of teaching which some adopt, when they require perfect reliance of heart and perfect penitence, and exclude all who have them not. For in so doing they exclude all without excepting one. Where is the man who can boast that he is not stained by some spot of distrust? that he is not subject to some vice or infirmity? Assuredly the faith which the children of God have is such that they have ever occasion to pray,—Lord, help our unbelief. For it is a malady so rooted in our nature, that we are never completely cured until we are delivered from the prison of the body. Moreover, the purity of life in which they walk is only such that they have occasion daily to pray, as well for remission of sins as for grace to make greater progress. Although some are more and others less imperfect, still there is none who does not fail in many respects. Hence the Supper would be not only useless, but pernicious to all, if it were necessary to bring a faith or integrity, as to which there would be nothing to gainsay. This would be contrary to the intention of our Lord, as there is nothing which he has given to his Church that is more salutary.

27. IMPERFECTION MUST NOT MAKE US CEASE TO HOPE FOR SALVATION

Therefore, although we feel our faith to be imperfect, and our conscience not so pure that it does not accuse us of many vices, that ought not to hinder us from presenting ourselves at the Lord's holy table, provided that amid this infirmity we feel in our heart that without hypocrisy and dissimulation we hope for salvation in Christ, and desire to live according to the rule of the gospel. I say expressly, provided there be no hypocrisy. For there are many who deceive themselves by vain flattery, making themselves believe that it is enough if they condemn their vices, though they continue to persist in them, or rather, if they give them up for a time, to return to them immediately after. True repentance is firm and constant, and makes us war with the evil that is in us, not for a day or a week, but without end and without intermission.

28. THE IMPERFECTIONS OF BELIEVERS SHOULD
RATHER INCLINE THEM TO USE THE SUPPER

When we feel within ourselves a strong dislike and hatred of all sin, proceeding from the fear of God, and a desire to live well in order to please our Lord, we are fit to partake of the Supper, notwithstanding of the remains of infirmity which we carry in our flesh. Nay, if we were not weak, subject to distrust and an imperfect life, the sacrament would be of no use to us, and it would have been superfluous to institute it. Séeing, then, it is a remedy which God has given us to help our weakness, to strengthen our faith, increase our charity, and advance us in all holiness of life, the use becomes the more necessary the more we feel pressed by the disease; so far ought that to be from making us abstain. For if we allege as an excuse for not coming to the Supper, that we are still weak in faith or integrity of life, it is as if a man were to excuse himself from taking medicine because he was sick. See then how the weakness of faith which we feel in our heart, and the imperfections which are in our life, should admonish us to come to the Supper, as a special remedy to correct them. Only let us not come devoid of faith and repentance. The former is hidden in the heart, and therefore conscience must be its witness before God. The latter is manifested by works, and must therefore be apparent in our life.

29. TIMES OF USING THE SUPPER.—PROPRIETY
OF FREQUENT COMMUNION

As to the time of using it, no certain rule can be prescribed for all. For there are sometimes special circumstances which excuse a man for abstaining; and, moreover, we have no express command to constrain all Christians to use a specified day. However, if we duly consider the end which our Lord has in view, we shall perceive that the use should be more frequent than many make it: for the more infirmity presses, the more necessary is it frequently to have recourse to what may and will serve to confirm our faith, and advance us in purity of life; and, therefore, the practice of all well ordered churches should be to celebrate the Supper frequently, so far as the capacity of the people will admit. And each individual in his own place should prepare himself to receive whenever it is administered in the holy assembly, provided there is not some great impediment which constrains him to abstain. Although we have no express commandment specifying the time and the day, it should suffice us to know the intention of our Lord to be, that we should use it often, if we would fully experience the benefit which accrues from it.

30. IMPROPRIETY OF ABSTAINING ON FRIVOLOUS GROUNDS.—PRETENDED UNWORTHINESS IN OURSELVES

The excuses alleged are very frivolous. Some say that they do not feel themselves to be worthy, and under this pretext, abstain for a whole year. Others, not contented with looking to their own unworthiness, pretend that they cannot communicate with persons whom they see coming without being duly prepared. Some also think that it is superfluous to use it frequently, because if we have once received Jesus Christ, there is no occasion to return so often after to receive him. I ask the first who make a cloak of their unworthiness, how their conscience can allow them to remain more than a year in so poor a state, that they dare not invoke God directly? They will acknowledge that it is presumption to invoke God as our Father, if we are not members of Jesus Christ. This we cannot be, without having the reality and substance of the Supper accomplished in us. Now, if we have the reality, we are by stronger reason capable of receiving the sign. We see then that he who would exempt himself from receiving the Supper on account of unworthiness, must hold himself unfit to pray to God. I mean not to force consciences which are tormented with certain scruples which suggest themselves, they scarcely know how, but counsel them to wait till the Lord deliver them. Likewise, if there is a legitimate cause of hindrance, I deny not that it is lawful to delay. Only I wish to show that no one ought long to rest satisfied with abstaining on the ground of unworthiness, seeing that in so doing he deprives himself of the communion of the Church, in which all our wellbeing consists. Let him rather contend against all the impediments which the devil throws in his way, and not be excluded from so great a benefit, and from all the graces consequent thereupon.

31. ABSTAINING BECAUSE OF PRETENDED
UNWORTHINESS IN OTHERS

The second class have some plausibility. The argument they use is, that it is not lawful to eat common bread with those who call themselves brethren, and lead a dissolute life —*a fortiori*, we must abstain from communicating with them in the Lord's bread, which is sanctified in order to represent and dispense to us the body of Christ. But the answer is not very difficult. It is not the office of each individual to judge and discern, to admit or debar whom he pleases; seeing that this prerogative belongs to all the Church in general, or rather to the pastor, with the elders, whom he ought to have to assist him in the government of the Church. St. Paul does not command us to examine others, but each to examine himself. It is very true that it is our duty to admonish those whom we see walking disorderly, and if they will not listen to us, to give notice to the pastor, in order that he may proceed by ecclesiastical authority. But the proper method of withdrawing from the company of the wicked, is not to quit the communion of the Church. Moreover, it will most frequently happen, that sins are not so notorious as to justify proceeding to excommunication; for though the pastor may in his heart judge some man to be unworthy, he has not the power of pronouncing him such, and interdicting him from the Supper, if he cannot prove the unworthiness by an ecclesiastical judgment. In such case we have no other remedy than to pray God that he would more and more deliver his Church from all scandals, and wait for the last day, when the chaff will be completely separated from the good grain.

32. EXCUSE, THAT HAVING ALREADY RECEIVED
CHRIST, IT IS UNNECESSARY TO RETURN OFTEN
TO RECEIVE HIM

The third class have no semblance of plausibility. The spiritual bread is not given us to eat our fill of it all at once, but rather, that having had some taste of its sweetness, we may long for it the more, and use it when it is offered to us. This we explained above. So long as we remain in this mortal life, Jesus Christ is never communicated in such a way as to satiate our souls, but wills to be our constant nourishment.

33. FOURTH GENERAL DIVISION.—ERRORS ON THE SUPPER

We come to the fourth principal point. The devil knowing that our Lord has left nothing to his Church more useful than the holy sacrament, has after his usual manner laboured from the beginning to contaminate it by errors and superstitions, in order to corrupt and destroy the benefit of it, and has never ceased to pursue this course, until he has as it were completely reversed the ordinance of the Lord, and converted it into falsehood and vanity. My intention is not to point out at what time each abuse took its rise and at what time it was augmented; it will be sufficient to notice articulately the errors which the devil has introduced, and against which we must guard if we would have the Lord's Supper in its integrity.

34. FIRST ERROR

The first error is this—While the Lord gave us the Supper that it might be distributed amongst us to testify to us that in communicating in his body we have part in the sacrifice which he offered on the cross to God his Father, for the expiation and satisfaction of our sins—men have out of their own head invented, on the contrary, that it is a sacrifice by which we obtain the forgiveness of our sins before God. This is a blasphemy which it is impossible to bear. For if we do not recognise the death of the Lord Jesus, and regard it as our only sacrifice by which he has reconciled us to the Father, effacing all the faults for which we were accountable to his justice, we destroy its virtue. If we do not acknowledge Jesus Christ to be the only sacrifice, or, as we commonly call it, priest, by whose intercession we are restored to the Father's favour, we rob him of his honour and do him high injustice.

35. THE SACRAMENT NOT A SACRIFICE

The opinion that the Supper is a sacrifice derogates from that of Christ, and must therefore be condemned as devilish. That it does so derogate is notorious. For how can we reconcile the two things, that Jesus Christ in dying offered a sacrifice to his Father by which he has once for all purchased forgiveness and pardon for all our faults, and that it is every day necessary to sacrifice in order to obtain that which we ought to seek in his death only? This error was not at first so extreme, but increased by little and little, until it came to what it now is. It appears that the ancient fathers called the Supper a sacrifice; but the reason they give is, because the death of Christ is represented in it. Hence their view comes to this—that this name is given it merely because it is a memorial of the one sacrifice, at which we ought entirely to stop. And yet I cannot altogether excuse the custom of the early Church. By gestures and modes of acting they figured a species of sacrifice, with a ceremony resembling that which existed under the Old Testament, excepting that instead of a beast they used bread as the host. As that approaches too near to Judaism, and does not correspond to our Lord's institution, I approve it not. For under the Old Testament, during the time of figures, the Lord ordained such ceremonies, until the sacrifice should be made in the person of his well-beloved Son, which was the fulfilment of them. Since it was finished, it now only remains for us to receive the communication of it. It is superfluous, therefore, to exhibit it any longer under figure.

36. THE BREAD IN THE SUPPER ORDAINED TO BE EATEN, NOT SACRIFICED.—ERRORS OF THE MASS

And such is the import of the injunction which Jesus Christ has left. It is not that we are to offer or immolate, but to take and eat what has been offered and immolated. However, though there was some weakness in such observance, there was not such impiety as afterwards supervened. For to the

Mass has been wholly transferred what was proper to the death of Christ, viz., to satisfy God for our sins, and so reconcile us to him. Moreover, the office of Christ has been transferred to those whom they name priests, viz., persons to sacrifice to God, and in sacrificing, intercede to obtain for us grace, and the pardon of our offences.

37. ATTEMPTED DEFENCE OF THE SACRIFICE OF THE MASS

I wish not to keep back the explanations which the enemies of the truth here offer. They say that the Mass is not a new sacrifice, but only an application of the sacrifice of which we have spoken. Although they colour their abomination somewhat by so saying, still it is a mere quibble. For it is not merely said that the sacrifice of Christ is one, but that it is not to be repeated, because its efficacy endures for ever. It is not said that Christ once offered himself to the Father, in order that others might afterwards make the same oblation, and so apply to us the virtue of his intercession. As to applying to us the merit of his death, that we may perceive the benefit of it, that is done not in the way in which the Popish Church has supposed, but when we receive the message of the gospel, according as it is testified to us by the ministers whom God has appointed as his ambassadors, and is sealed by the sacraments.

38. ERRORS CONNECTED WITH THE ABOMINATION OF THE MASS

The common opinion approved by all their doctors and prelates is, that by hearing Mass, and causing it to be said, they perform a service meriting grace and righteousness before God. We say, that to derive benefit from the Supper, it is not necessary to bring any thing of our own in order to merit what we ask. We have only to receive in faith the grace which is there presented to us, and which resides not in the sacrament, but refers us to the cross of Jesus Christ as proceeding therefrom. Hence there is nothing more contrary to the true meaning of the Supper, than to make a sacrifice of it. The effect of so doing is to lead us off from recognising the death of Christ as the only sacrifice, whose virtue endures for ever. This being well understood, it will be apparent that all masses in which there is no such communion as the Lord enjoined, are only an abomination. The Lord did not order that a single priest, after making his sacrifice, should keep himself apart, but that the sacrament should be distributed in the assembly after the manner of the first Supper, which he made with his apostles. But after this cursed opinion was forged, out of it, as an abyss, came forth the unhappy custom by which the people, contenting themselves with being present to partake in the merit of what is done, abstain from communicating, because the priest gives out that he offers his host for all, and specially for those present. I speak not of abuses, which are so absurd, that they deserve not to be noticed, such as giving each saint his mass, and transferring what is said of the Lord's Supper to St. William and St. Walter, and making an ordinary fair of masses, buying and selling them with the other abominations which the word sacrifice has engendered.

39. TRANSUBSTANTIATION

The second error which the devil has sown to corrupt this holy ordinance, is in forging and inventing that after the words are pronounced with an intention to consecrate, the bread is transubstantiated into the body of Christ, and the wine into his blood. First of all, this falsehood has no foundation in Scripture, and no countenance from the Primitive Church, and what is more, cannot be reconciled or consist with the word of God. When Jesus Christ, pointing to the bread, calls it his body, is it not a very forced construction to say, that the substance of the bread is annihilated, and the body of Christ substituted in its stead? But there is no cause to discuss the thing as a doubtful matter, seeing the truth is sufficiently clear to refute the absurdity. I leave out innumerable passages of Scripture and quotations from the Fathers, in which the sacrament is called bread. I only say that the nature of the sacrament requires, that the material bread remain as a visible sign of the body.

40. FROM THE NATURE OF A SACRAMENT THE
SUBSTANCE OF THE VISIBLE SIGN MUST REMAIN

It is a general rule in all sacraments that the signs which we see must have some correspondence with the spiritual thing which is figured. Thus, as in baptism, we are assured of the internal washing of our souls when water is given us as an attestation, its property being to cleanse corporal pollution; so in the Supper, there must be material bread to testify to us that the body of Christ is our food. For otherwise how could the mere colour of white give us such a figure? We thus clearly see how the whole representation, which the Lord was pleased to give us in condescension to our weakness, would be lost if the bread did not truly remain. The words which our Lord uses imply as much as if he had said: Just as man is supported and maintained in his body by eating bread, so my flesh is the spiritual nourishment by which souls are vivified. Moreover, what would become of the other similitude which St. Paul employs? As several grains of corn are mixed together to form one bread, so must we together be one, because we partake of one bread. If there were whiteness only without the substance, would it not be mockery to speak thus? Therefore we conclude, without doubt, that this transubstantiation is an invention forged by the devil to corrupt the true nature of the Supper.

41. FALSE OPINION OF THE BODILY PRESENCE
OF CHRIST IN THE SUPPER

Out of this fantasy several other follies have sprung. Would to God they were only follies, and not gross abominations. They have imagined I know not what local presence and thought, that Jesus Christ in his divinity and humanity was attached to this whiteness, without paying regard to all the absurdities which follow from it. Although the old doctors of Sorbonne dispute more subtilely how the body and blood are conjoined with the signs, still it cannot be denied that this opinion has been received by great and small in the Popish Church, and that it is cruelly maintained in the present day by fire and sword, that Jesus Christ is contained under these signs, and that there we must seek him. Now to maintain that, it must be confessed either that the body of Christ is without limit, or that it may be in different places. In saying this we are brought at last to the point, that it is a mere phantom. To wish then to establish such a presence as is to enclose the body within the sign, or to be joined to it locally, is not only a reverie, but a damnable error, derogatory to the glory of Christ, and destructive of what we ought to hold in regard to his human nature. For Scripture everywhere teaches us, that as the Lord on earth took our humanity, so he has exalted it to heaven, withdrawing it from mortal condition, but not changing its nature.

42. THE BODY OF OUR SAVIOUR IN HEAVEN
THE SAME AS THAT WHICH HE HAD ON EARTH

We have two things to consider when we speak of our Lord's humanity. We must neither destroy the reality of the nature, nor derogate in any respect from his state of glory. To do so we must always raise our thoughts on high, and there seek our Redeemer. For if we would place him under the corruptible elements of this world, besides subverting what Scripture tells us in regard to his human nature, we annihilate the glory of his ascension. As several others have treated this subject at large, I refrain from going farther. I only wished to observe, in passing, that to fancy Jesus Christ enclosed under the bread and wine, or so to conjoin him with it as to amuse our understanding there without looking up to heaven, is a diabolical reverie. We will touch on this in another place.

43. OTHER ABUSES ARISING OUT OF AN
IMAGINARY BODILY PRESENCE

This perverse opinion, after it was once received, engendered numerous other superstitions. First of all comes that carnal adoration which is mere idolatry. For to prostrate ourselves before the bread of the Supper, and worship Jesus Christ as if he were contained in it, is to make an idol of it rather than a sacrament. The command given us is not to adore, but to take and eat. That, therefore, ought not to have been presumptuously attempted. Moreover, the practice always observed by the early Church, when about to celebrate the Supper, was solemnly to exhort the people to raise their hearts on high, to intimate, that if we would adore Christ aright, we must not stop at the visible sign. But there is no need to contend long on this point when the presence and conjunction of the reality with the sign (of which we have spoken, and will again speak) is well understood. From the same source have proceeded other superstitious practices, as carrying the sacrament in procession through the streets once a-year; at another time making a tabernacle for it, and keeping it to the year's end in a cupboard to amuse the people with it, as if it were a god. As all that has not only been invented without authority from the word of God, but is also directly opposed to the institution of the Supper, it ought to be rejected by Christians.

44. REASON WHY THE PAPISTS COMMUNICATE
ONLY ONCE A YEAR

We have shown the origin of the calamity which befell the Popish Church—I mean that of abstaining from communicating in the Supper for the whole period of a year. It is because they regard the Supper as a sacrifice which is offered by one in the name of all. But even while thus used only once a year, it is sadly wasted and as it were torn to pieces. For instead of distributing the sacrament of blood to the people, as our Lord's command bears, they are made to believe that they ought to be contented with the other half. Thus poor believers are defrauded of the gift which the Lord Jesus had given them. For if it is no small benefit to have communion in the blood of the Lord as our nourishment, it is great cruelty to rob those of it to whom it belongs. In this we may see with what boldness and audacity the Pope has tyrannized over the Church after he had once usurped domination.

45. THE POPE HAS MADE EXCEPTIONS TO
THE GENERAL RULES LAID DOWN BY
OUR LORD

Our Lord having commanded his disciples to eat the bread sanctified in his body, when he comes to the cup, does not say simply, "drink," but he adds expressly, that all are to drink. Would we have any thing clearer than this? He says that we are to eat the bread without using an universal term. He says that we are *all* to drink of the cup. Whence this difference, but just that he was pleased by anticipation to meet this wickedness of the devil? And yet such is the pride of the Pope that he dares to say, Let not all drink. And to show that he is wiser than God, he alleges it to be very reasonable that the priest should have some privilege beyond the people, in honour of the sacerdotal dignity; as if our Lord had not duly considered what distinction should be made between them. Moreover, he objects dangers which might happen if the cup were given in common to all. Some drop of it might occasionally be spilt; as if our Lord had not foreseen that. Is not this to accuse God quite openly of having confounded the order which he ought to have observed, and exposed his people to danger without cause?

46. FRIVOLOUS REASONS FOR WITHHOLDING
THE CUP

To show that there is no great inconvenience in this change, they argue, that under one species the whole is comprised, inasmuch as the body cannot be separated from the blood: as if our Lord had without reason distinguished the one from the other. For if we can leave one of the parts behind as superfluous, what folly must it have been to recommend them separately. Some of his supporters, seeing that it was impudence to maintain this abomination, have wished to give it a different colour, viz., that Jesus Christ, in instituting, spoke only to his apostles whom he had raised to the sacerdotal order. But how will they answer what St. Paul said, when he delivered to all the people what he had received of the Lord—that each should eat of this bread and drink of this cup? Besides, who told them that our Lord gave the Supper to his apostles as priests? The words import the opposite, when he commands them to do after his example. (Luke 22:19.) Therefore he delivers the rule which he wishes to be always observed in his Church; and so it was anciently observed until Antichrist, having gained the upper hand, openly raised his horns against God and his truth to destroy it totally. We see then that it is an intolerable perversion thus to divide and rend the sacrament, separating the parts which God has joined.

47. THE BUFFOONERY OF THE POPE IN REGARD TO THE SUPPER

To get to an end, we shall embrace under one head what might otherwise have been considered separately. This head is, that the devil has introduced the fashion of celebrating the Supper without any doctrine, and for doctrine has substituted ceremonies partly inept and of no utility, and partly dangerous, having proved the cause of much mischief. To such an extent has this been done, that the Mass, which in the Popish Church is held to be the Supper, is, when well explained, nothing but pure apishness and buffoonery. I call it apishness, because they there counterfeit the Lord's Supper without reason, just as an ape at random and without discernment imitates what he sees done.

48. THE WORD OUGHT ALWAYS TO ACCOMPANY THE SACRAMENTS

The principal thing recommended by our Lord is to celebrate the ordinance with true understanding. From this it follows that the essential part lies in the doctrine. This being taken away, it is only a frigid unavailing ceremony. This is not only shown by Scripture, but attested by the canons of the Pope, (Can. Detrahe. 1:4, 1,) in a passage quoted from

St. Augustine, (Tract 80, in Joan.) in which he asks—"What is the water of baptism without the word but just a corruptible element? The word (he immediately adds) not as pronounced, but as understood." By this he means, that the sacraments derive their virtue from the word when it is preached intelligibly. Without this they deserve not the name of sacraments. Now so far is there from being any intelligible doctrine in the Mass, that, on the contrary, the whole mystery is considered spoiled if every thing be not said and done in whispers, so that nothing is understood. Hence their consecration is only a species of sorcery, seeing that by muttering and gesticulating like sorcerers, they think to constrain Jesus to come down into their hands. We thus see how the Mass, being thus arranged, is an evident profanation of the Supper of Christ, rather than an observance of it, as the proper and principal substance of the Supper is wanting, viz., full explanation of the ordinance and clear statement of the promises, instead of the priest standing apart and muttering to himself without sense or reason. I call it buffoonery, also, because of mimicry and gestures, better adapted to a farce than to such an ordinance as the sacred Supper of our Lord.

49. THE CEREMONIES OF THE ANCIENT LAW, WHY APPOINTED.—THOSE OF THE PAPISTS CENSURABLE

It is true, indeed, that the sacrifices under the Old Testament were performed with many ornaments and ceremonies, but because there was a good meaning under them, and the whole was proper to instruct and exercise the people in piety, they are very far from being like those which are now used, and serve no purpose but to amuse the people without doing them any good. As these gentry allege the example of the Old Testament in defence of their ceremonies, we have to observe what difference there is between what they do, and what God commanded the people of Israel. Were there only this single point, that what was then observed was founded on the commandment of the Lord, whereas all those frivolities have no foundation, even then the difference would be large. But we have much more to censure in them.

50. THE JEWISH CEREMONIES HAVING SERVED
THEIR PURPOSE, THE IMITATION OF
THEM ABSURD

With good cause our Lord ordained the Jewish form for a time, intending that it should one day come to an end and be abrogated. Not having then given such clearness of doctrine, he was pleased that the people should be more exercised in figures to compensate for the defect. But since Jesus Christ has been manifested in the flesh, doctrine having been much more clearly delivered, ceremonies have diminished. As we have now the body, we should leave off shadows. To return to the ceremonies which are abolished, is to repair the veil of the temple which Jesus Christ rent by his death, and so far obscure the brightness of his gospel. Hence we see, that such a multitude of ceremonies in the Mass is a form of Judaism quite contrary to Christianity. I mean not to condemn the ceremonies which are subservient to decency and public order, and increase the reverence for the sacrament, provided they are sober and suitable. But such an abyss without end or limit is not at all tolerable, seeing that it has engendered a thousand superstitions, and has in a manner stupified the people without yielding any edification.

51. THE DEATH AND PASSION OF OUR LORD
THE PERFECT AND ONLY SACRIFICE

Hence also we see how those to whom God has given the knowledge of his truth should differ from the Papists. First, they cannot doubt that it is abominable blasphemy to regard the Mass as a sacrifice by which the forgiveness of sins is purchased for us; or rather, that the priest is a kind of mediator to apply the merit of Christ's passion and death to those who purchase his mass, or are present at it, or feel devotion for it. On the contrary, they must hold decidedly that the death and suffering of the Lord is the only sacrifice by which the anger of God has been satisfied, and eternal righteousness procured for us; and, likewise, that the Lord Jesus has entered into the heavenly sanctuary in order to appear there for us, and intercede in virtue of his sacrifice. Moreover, they will readily grant, that the benefit of his death is communicated to us in the Supper, not by the merit of the act, but because of the promises which are given us, provided we receive them in faith. Secondly, they should on no account grant that the bread is transubstantiated into the body of Jesus Christ, nor the wine into his blood, but should persist in holding that the visible signs retain their true substance, in order to represent the spiritual reality of which we have spoken. Thirdly, they ought also to hold for certain, that the Lord gives us in the Supper that which he signifies by it, and, consequently, that we truly receive the body and blood of Jesus Christ. Nevertheless they will not seek him as if he were enclosed under the bread, or attached locally to the visible sign. So far from adoring the sacrament, they will rather raise their understandings and their hearts on high, as well to receive Jesus Christ, as to adore him.

52. VIEW OF ENLIGHTENED CHRISTIANS IN REGARD TO THE SUPPER

Hence they will despise and condemn as idolatrous all those superstitious practices of carrying about the sacrament in pomp and procession, and building tabernacles in which to adore it. For the promises of our Lord extend only to the uses which he has authorized. Next, they will hold that to deprive the people of one of the parts of the sacrament, viz., the cup, is to violate and corrupt the ordinance of the Lord, and that to observe it properly it must be administered in all its integrity. Lastly, they will regard it as a superfluity, not only useless but dangerous, and not at all suitable to Christianity, to use so many ceremonies taken from the Jews contrary to the simplicity which the Apostles left us, and that it is still more perverse to celebrate the Supper with mimicry and buffoonery, while no doctrine is stated, or rather all doctrine is buried, as if the Supper were a kind of magical trick.

53. LAST DIVISION.—RECENT DISPUTES ON
THE SUPPER

To have done, it is necessary to come to the last principal point, viz., the contention which has arisen in our time in regard to this matter. Now, as it is an unhappy business—the devil, no doubt, having stirred it up to impede, nay altogether to interrupt the course of the gospel—so far am I from taking pleasure in referring to it, that I could wish the remembrance of it were altogether abolished. Nevertheless, as I see many good consciences troubled, because they do not know to what side to turn, I shall only say as much as may seem necessary to show them how they ought to decide.

54. GOD SOMETIMES ALLOWS HIS OWN PEOPLE
TO FALL INTO ERROR

First, I beseech all believers, in the name of God, not to be too much scandalized at the great difference which has arisen among those who ought to be a kind of leaders in bringing back the light of truth. For it is no new thing for the Lord to leave his servants in some degree of ignorance, and suffer them to have debate among themselves—not to leave them for ever, but only for a time to humble them. And indeed had every thing till now turned out to a wish without any disturbance, men might possibly have forgotten themselves, or the grace of God might have been less known than it ought. Thus the Lord has been pleased to take away all ground of glorying from men, in order that he might alone be glorified. Moreover, if we consider in what an abyss of darkness the world was when those who have shared this controversy began to bring back the truth, we shall not wonder that they did not know every thing at the beginning. The wonder rather is, that our Lord in so short a time enlightened them that they were themselves able to escape and draw others out of that sink of error in which they had been so long immersed. But no better course can be taken than to show how matters have proceeded, because this will make it appear that people have not so much cause to be scandalized at it as is commonly supposed.

55. HISTORY OF THE CONTROVERSY ON THIS SUBJECT AMONG THE REFORMERS.—LUTHER

When Luther began to teach, he took a view of the subject which seemed to imply, that in regard to the corporal presence in the Supper he was willing to leave the generally received opinion untouched; for while condemning transubstantiation, he said that the bread was the body of Christ, inasmuch as it was united with him. Besides, he added similitudes which were somewhat harsh and rude; but he was in a manner compelled to do so, as he could not otherwise explain his meaning. For it is difficult to give an explanation of so high a matter without using some impropriety of speech.

56. VIEWS OF ZUINGLIUS AND ŒCOLOMPADIUS

On the other hand arose Zuinglius [Zwingli] and Œcolompadius, who, considering the abuse and deceit which the devil had employed in establishing such a carnal presence of Christ as had been taught and held for more than six hundred years, thought it unlawful to disguise their sentiments, since that view implied an execrable idolatry, in that Jesus Christ was worshipped as enclosed in the bread. Now, as it was very difficult to remove this opinion, which had been so long rooted in the hearts of men, they applied all their talents to bring it into discredit, showing how gross an error it was not to recognise what is so clearly declared in Scripture touching the ascension of Jesus Christ, that he has been received in his humanity into heaven, and will remain there until he descend to judge the world. Meantime, while engrossed with this point, they forgot to show what presence of Jesus Christ ought to be believed in the Supper, and what communion of his body and blood is there received.

57. LUTHER IMPUGNS THEIR VIEWS

Luther thought that they meant to leave nothing but the bare signs without their spiritual substance. Accordingly he began to resist them to the face, and call them heretics. After the contention was once begun it got more inflamed by time, and has thus continued too bitterly for the space of fifteen years or so without the parties ever listening to each other in a peaceful temper. For though they once had a conference, there was such alienation that they parted without any agreement. Instead of meeting on some good ground, they have always receded more and more, looking to nothing else than to defend their own view and refute the opposite.

58. ATTEMPTED RECONCILIATION.—CAUSE

OF FAILURE

We thus see wherein Luther failed on his side, and Zuinglius and Œcolompadius on theirs. It was Luther's duty first to have given notice that it was not his intention to establish such a local presence as the Papist's dream; secondly, to protest that he did not mean to have the sacrament adored instead of God; and lastly, to abstain from those similitudes so harsh and difficult to be conceived, or have used them with moderation, interpreting them so that they could not give rise to any scandal. After the debate was moved, he exceeded bounds as well in declaring his opinion, as in blaming others with too much sharpness of speech. For instead of explaining himself in such a way as to make it possible to receive his view, he, with his accustomed vehemence in assailing those who contradicted him, used hyperbolical forms of speech very difficult to be borne by those who otherwise were not much disposed to believe at his nod. The other party also offended, in being so bent on declaiming against the superstitious and fanatical opinion of the Papists, touching the local presence of Jesus Christ within the sacrament, and the perverse adoration consequent upon it, that they laboured more to pull down what was evil than to build up what was good; for though they did not deny the truth, they did not teach it so clearly as they ought to have done. I mean that in their too great anxiety to maintain that the bread and wine are called the body of Christ, because they are signs of them, they did not attend to add, that though they are signs, the reality is conjoined with them, and thus protest, that they had no intention whatever to obscure the true communion which the Lord gives us in his body and blood by this sacrament.

59. DUTY OF THE SERVANTS OF GOD IN REGARD
TO THE ADVANCEMENT OF TRUTH

Both parties failed in not having the patience to listen to each other in order to follow the truth without passion, when it would have been found. Nevertheless, let us not lose sight of our duty, which is not to forget the gifts which the Lord bestowed upon them, and the blessings which he has distributed to us by their hands and means. For if we are not ungrateful and forgetful of what we owe them, we shall be well able to pardon that and much more, without blaming or defaming them. In short, since we see that they were, and still are, distinguished for holiness of life, excellent knowledge, and ardent zeal to edify the Church, we ought always to judge and speak of them with modesty, and even with reverence; since at last God, after having thus humbled them, has in mercy been pleased to put an end to this unhappy disputation, or at least to calm it preparatory to its final settlement. I speak thus, because no formulary has yet been published in which concord is fixed, as is most expedient. But this will be when God will be pleased to assemble those who are to frame it in one place.

60. FRATERNAL CONCORD AMONG
THE CHURCHES

Meanwhile it should satisfy us, that there is fraternity and communion among the churches, and that all agree in so far as is necessary for meeting together, according to the commandment of God. We all then confess with one mouth, that on receiving the sacrament in faith, according to the ordinance of the Lord, we are truly made partakers of the proper substance of the body and blood of Jesus Christ. How that is done some may deduce better, and explain more clearly than others. Be this as it may, on the one hand, in order to exclude all carnal fancies, we must raise our hearts upwards to heaven, not thinking that our Lord Jesus is so debased as to be enclosed under some corruptible elements; and, on the other hand, not to impair the efficacy of this holy ordinance, we must hold that it is made effectual by the secret and miraculous power of God, and that the Spirit of God is the bond of participation, this being the reason why it is called spiritual.

COMMENTARY UPON THE ACTS
OF THE APOSTLES[1]

[*Material from this commentary, completed in 1560, is used as a sample of Calvin's exegetical and technical work. The particular passages here printed include the sermon text of a sermon on Pentecost, so that the commentary and the sermonic form may be compared. Moreover, this text is particularly appropriate, given Calvin's strong sense of the authenticating role of the Spirit.*]

CHAPTER II

1. *And when the day of Pentecost was fulfilled, they were all with one accord gathered together:*
2. *And there was made from heaven suddenly a sound, as it were when a violent wind breaketh in, and it filled all the house where they sat:*
3. *And they saw cloven tongues, as it were of fire, and it sat upon every one of them.*
4. *And they were all filled with the Holy Ghost, and they began to speak with strange tongues, even as the Spirit gave them to speak.*

1. *And when. To be fulfilled* is taken in this place for *to come.* For Luke beareth record again of their perseverance, when he saith that they stood all in one place until the time which was set them. Hereunto serveth the adverb, *with one accord.* Furthermore, we have before declared why the Lord did defer the sending of his Spirit a whole month and a half.

[1] [Reprinted by permission of the publisher from *Commentary Upon the Acts of the Apostles*, Vol. I, edited from the original English translation of Christopher Fetherstone by Henry Beveridge (Grand Rapids: Wm. B. Eerdmans Publishing Company, 1949), pp. 72–92.]

But the question is, why he sent him upon that day chiefly. I will not refute that high and subtle interpretation of Augustine, that like as the law was given to the old people fifty days after Easter, being written in tables of stone by the hand of God, so the Spirit, whose office it is to write the same in our hearts, did fulfil that which was figured in the giving of the law as many days after the resurrection of Christ, who is the true Passover. Notwithstanding, whereas he urgeth this his subtle interpretation as necessary, in his book of Questions upon Exodus, and in his Second Epistle unto Januarius, I would wish him to be more sober and modest therein. Notwithstanding, let him keep his own interpretation to himself. In the mean season, I will embrace that which is more sound.

Upon the feast day, wherein a great multitude was wont to resort to Jerusalem, was this miracle wrought, that it might be more famous. And truly by means hereof was it spread abroad, even unto the uttermost parts and borders of the earth. For the same purpose did Christ oftentimes go up to Jerusalem upon the holy days, (John 2, 5, 7, 10, 12,) to the end those miracles which he wrought might be known to many, and that in the greater assembly of people there might be the greater fruit of his doctrine. For so will Luke afterward declare, that Paul made haste that he might come to Jerusalem before the day of Pentecost, not for any religion's sake, but because of the greater assembly, that he might profit the more, (Acts 20:16.) Therefore, in making choice of the day, the profit of the miracle was respected: First, that it might be the more extolled at Jerusalem, because the Jews were then more bent to consider the works of God; and, secondly, that it might be bruited abroad, even in far countries. They called it the fiftieth day, beginning to reckon at the first-fruits.

2. *And there was made.* It was requisite that the gift should be visible, that the bodily sense might the more stir up the disciples. For such is our slothfulness to consider the gifts of God, that unless he awake all our senses, his power shall pass away unknown. This was, therefore, a preparation that they might the better know that the Spirit was now come which Christ had promised. Although it was not so much for their sake as for ours, even as in that the cloven and fiery tongues appeared, there was rather respect had of us, and of all the whole Church in that, than of them. For

God was able to have furnished them with necessary ability to preach the gospel, although he should use no sign. They themselves might have known that it came to pass neither by chance, neither yet through their own industry, that they were so suddenly changed; but those signs which are here set down were about to be profitable for all ages; as we perceive at this day that they profit us. And we must briefly note the proportion of the signs. The violence of the wind did serve to make them afraid; for we are never rightly prepared to receive the grace of God, unless the confidence (and boldness) of the flesh be tamed. For as we have access unto him by faith, so humility and fear setteth open the gate, that he may come in unto us. He hath nothing to do with proud and careless men. It is a common thing for the Spirit to be signified by wind, (or a blast,) (John 20:22.) For both Christ himself, when he was about to give the Spirit to his apostles, did breathe upon them; and in Ezekiel's vision there was a whirlwind and wind, (Ezek. 1:4.) Yea, the word Spirit itself is a translated word; for, because that *hypostasis*, or person of the Divine essence, which is called the Spirit, is of itself incomprehensible, the Scripture doth borrow the word of the wind or blast, because it is the power of God which God doth pour into all creatures as it were by breathing. The shape of tongues is restrained unto the present circumstance. For as the figure and shape of a dove which came down upon Christ, (John 1:32,) had a signification agreeable to the office and nature of Christ, so God did now make choice of a sign which might be agreeable to the thing signified, namely, that it might show such effect and working of the Holy Ghost in the apostles as followed afterward.

The diversity of tongues did hinder the gospel from being spread abroad any farther; so that, if the preachers of the gospel had spoken one language only, all men would have thought that Christ had been shut up in the small corner of Jewry. But God invented a way whereby it might break out, when he divided and clove the tongues of the apostles, that they might spread that abroad amongst all people which was delivered to them. Wherein appeareth the manifold goodness of God, because a plague and punishment of man's pride was turned into matter of blessing. For whence came the diversity of tongues, save only that the wicked and ungodly counsels of men might be brought to nought? (Gen. 11:7.) But God doth furnish the apostles with the diversity of tongues now, that he may bring and call home, into a blessed unity, men which wander here and there. These cloven tongues made all men to speak the language of Canaan, as Isaiah foretold, (Isa. 19:18.) For what language soever they speak, yet do they call upon one Father, which is in heaven, with one mouth and one spirit, (Rom. 15:6.) I said that that was done for our sake, not only because the fruit came unto us, but because we know that the gospel came unto us not by chance, but by the appointment of God, who to this end gave the apostles cloven tongues, lest any nation should want that doctrine which was committed unto them; whereby is proved the calling of the Gentiles; and, secondly, hereby their doctrine doth purchase credit, which we know was not forged by man, seeing that we hear that the Spirit did dwell in their tongues.

Now, it remaineth that we declare what the *fire* meaneth. Without all doubt, it was a token of the (force and) efficacy which should be exercised in the voice of the apostles. Otherwise, although their sound had gone out into the uttermost parts of the world, they should only have beat the air, without doing any good at all. Therefore, the Lord doth show that their voice shall be fiery, that it may inflame the hearts of men; that the vanity of the world being burnt and consumed, it may purge and renew all things. Otherwise they durst never have taken upon them so hard a function, unless the Lord had assured them of the power of their preaching. Hereby it came to pass that the doctrine of the gospel did not only sound in the air, but pierce into the minds of men, and did fill them with an heavenly heat (and burning.) Neither was this force showed only in the mouth of the apostles, but it appeareth daily. And, therefore, we must beware lest, when the fire burneth, we be as stubble. Furthermore, the Lord did once give the Holy Ghost under a visible shape, that we may assure ourselves that his invisible and hidden grace shall never be wanting to the Church.

3. *And it sat.* Because the number is suddenly changed, it is to be doubted whether he speaketh of the fire. He said that there appeared tongues as it had been of fire. It followeth by and by, *and it sat upon them.* Notwithstanding, I refer it unto the Spirit. For the Hebrews use commonly to express the substantive of the verb in the second member, which they did omit in the former. Wherefore we have an example in this place: *It sat* upon them, and they were all filled with the Holy Ghost. And we know that although Luke did write in Greek, yet is he full of those phrases which the

Hebrews use. Now, whereas he calleth the tongues the Holy Ghost, it is according to the custom of the Scripture. For John calleth the dove by the same name, (John 1:32,) because the Lord would testify and declare the presence of his Spirit by some such sign. If it were a vain sign, it should be an absurd naming (to call the sign by the name of the thing signified;) but where the thing is annexed, the name of the thing is fitly given to the sign which offereth the same unto our senses to be perceived. The fulness of the Spirit, wherewith he saith every one was replenished, doth not express the (an) equal measure of gifts in every one, but that excellence which should be meet for such a calling.

4. *They began to speak.* He showeth that the effect did appear presently, and also to what use their tongues were to be framed and applied. But because Luke setteth down shortly after, that strangers out of divers countries did marvel, because that every one of them did hear the apostles speaking in their own tongue, some think that they spake not in divers tongues, but that they did all understand that which was spoken in one tongue, as well as if they should hear their natural tongue. Therefore, they think that one and the same sound of the voice was diversely distributed amongst the hearers. Another conjecture they have, because Peter made one sermon in the audience of many gathered together out of divers countries, who could not understand his speech (and language,) unless another voice should come unto their ears than that which proceeded out of his mouth. But we must first note that the disciples spake indeed with strange tongues; otherwise the miracle had not been wrought in them, but in the hearers. So that the similitude should have been false whereof he made mention before; neither should the Spirit have been given so much to them as to others. Again, we hear how Paul giveth thanks to God, that he speaketh with divers tongues, (1 Cor. 14:18.) Truly he challengeth to himself both the understanding, and also the use thereof. Neither did he attain to this skill by his own study and industry, but he had it by the gift of the Spirit. In the same place he affirmeth that it is an especial gift, wherewith all men are not endued. I suppose that it doth manifestly appear hereby that the apostles had the variety and understanding of tongues given them, that they might speak unto the Greeks in Greek, unto the Italians in the Italian tongue, and that they might have true commu-

nication (and conference) with their hearers. Notwithstanding, I leave it indifferent, whether there was any second miracle wrought or no, so that the Egyptians and Elamites did understand Peter speaking in the Chaldean tongue, as if he did utter divers voices. For there be some conjectures which persuade me thus to think, and yet not so firm but that they may be refuted. For it may be that they spake with divers tongues, as they light upon this man or that, and as occasion was offered, and as their languages were diverse. Therefore, it was a manifest miracle, when they saw them ready to speak divers languages. As touching Peter's sermon, it might be understood of the greater part of men wheresoever they were born; for it is to be thought that many of those which came to Jerusalem were skilful in the Chaldean tongue. Again, it shall be nothing inconvenient, if we say that he spake also in other tongues. Although I will not much stand about this matter; so that this be out of doubt, that the apostles changed their speech.

5. *And there were at Jerusalem Jews abiding, godly men, out of every nation of those which are under heaven.*

6. *And when this was noised abroad, the multitude came together, and was astonished: because every one heard them speak in his own tongue.*

7. *And they wondered all, and marvelled, saying amongst themselves, Behold, are not all these which speak men of Galilee?*

8. *And how do we every one hear them speaking in his own language, wherein we were born?*

9. *Parthians, and Medes, and Elamites, and inhabiters of Mesopotamia, Judea, and Cappadocia, of Pontus and Asia,*

10. *And of Phrygia and Pamphylia, of Egypt, and of the parts of Libya towards Cyrene, and strangers of Rome;*

11. *Jews and Proselytes, Cretes and Arabians, we hear them speaking in our tongues the wonderful works of God.*

12. *Therefore they were all amazed, and marvelled, saying one to another, What meaneth this? Others mocking, said, They are full of sweet wine.*

5. *And there were at Jerusalem.* When he calleth them godly or religious men, he seemeth to give us to understand

that they came to Jerusalem that they might worship God; like as God, in all ages, after the scattering abroad, did gather together into that city some seed which remained, having, as it were, set up his banner, because as yet the temple did serve to some use. Yet, nevertheless, he showeth, by the way, who those be which profit by those miracles, whereby God doth declare his power. For wicked and profane men do either laugh at them, or else pass (care) not for them, as we shall see by and by. Furthermore, he meant to cite those as witnesses, which may the better be believed for their religion and godliness. When he said, *out of every nation,* he meaneth out of divers countries, whereof one is far from another. For he doth also afterwards reckon up those lands whereof one was far distant from another, of which sort are Libya and Pontus, Rome and Parthia, and Arabia, and such like. This serveth to increase the greatness of the thing. For the Cretians and men of Asia, dwelling so near together, might have some likelihood and agreement in speech; but the same could not be betwixt the Italians and the men of Cappadocia, betwixt the Arabians and those of Pontus. Yea, this was also a work of God worthy to be remembered and wondered at, that in so huge and horrible a scattering abroad of the people, he did always reserve some relics, yea, he caused certain strangers to adjoin themselves unto a people which was in such misery, and, as it were, quite destroyed. For although they lived here and there in exile in far countries, and being one far from another, did, as it were, inhabit divers worlds, yet did they hold among themselves the unity of faith. Neither doth he call them unadvisedly, and without good consideration, godly men, and men fearing God.

6. *When this was noised abroad.* Luke saith thus in Greek, *This voice being made;* but his meaning is, that the fame was spread abroad, whereby it came to pass that a great multitude came together. For if one after another in divers places, and at divers times, had heard the apostles speaking in divers tongues, the miracle had not been so famous; therefore they come altogether into one place, that the diversity of tongues may the better appear by the present comparison. There is a further circumstance also here to be noted, that the country (and native soil) of the apostles was commonly known, and this was also commonly known, that they never went out of their country to learn strange tongues. Therefore, forasmuch as one speaketh Latin, another Greek, another the

Arabian tongue, as occasion was offered, and that indifferently, and every one doth also change his tongue, the work of God appeareth more plainly hereby.

11. *The wonderful works of God.* Luke noteth two things which caused the hearers to wonder; first, because the apostles being before ignorant and private persons, born in a base corner, did, notwithstanding, intreat profoundly of divine matters, and of heavenly wisdom. The other is, because they have new tongues given them suddenly. Both things are worth the noting, because to huddle out (utter) words unadvisedly and foolishly, should not so much have served to move their minds; and the majesty of the things ought the more to have moved them to consider the miracle. Although they give due honour to God, in that they are astonished and amazed, yet the principal fruit of the miracle is expressed in this, that they inquire, and thereby declare that they are prepared to learn; for otherwise their amazedness and wondering should not have done them any great good. And certainly we must so wonder at the works of God, that there must be also a consideration, and a desire to understand.

12. *Others mocking.* Hereby it appeareth how monstrous as well the sluggishness, as also the ungodliness of men is, when Satan hath taken away their mind. If God should openly (and visibly) descend from heaven, his majesty could scarce more manifestly appear than in this miracle. Whosoever hath any drop of sound understanding in him must needs be stricken with the only hearing of it. How beastly, then, are those men who see it with their eyes, and yet scoff, and go about with their jests to mock the power of God? But the matter is so. There is nothing so wonderful which those men do not turn to a jest who are touched with no care of God; because they do, even upon set purposes, harden themselves in their ignorance in things most plain. And it is a just punishment of God, which he bringeth upon such pride, to deliver them to Satan, to be driven headlong into blind fury. Wherefore, there is no cause why we should marvel that there be so many at this day so blind in so great light, if they be so deaf when such manifest doctrine is delivered, yea, if they wantonly refuse salvation when it is offered unto them. For if the wonderful and strange works of God, wherein he doth wonderfully set forth his power, be subject to the mockery of men, what shall become of doc-

trine, which they think tasteth of nothing but of that which is common? Although Luke doth signify unto us that they were not of the worst sort, or altogether past hope, which did laugh (and mock;) but he meant rather to declare how the common sort was affected when they saw this miracle. And truly it hath been always so in the world, for very few have been touched with the true feeling of God as often as he hath revealed himself. Neither is it any marvel; for religion is a rare virtue, and a virtue which few men have; which is, indeed, the beginning of understanding. Nevertheless, howsoever the more part of men, through a certain hard stiffneckedness, doth reject the consideration of the works of God, yet are they never without fruit, as we may see in this history.

14. *But Peter, standing with the eleven, lift up his voice, and spake unto them, Ye men of Judea, and all ye which dwell at Jerusalem, let this be known unto you, and with your ears hear my words.*
15. *For these men are not drunk as ye suppose; for it is the third hour of the day.*
16. *But this is that which was spoken by the prophet Joel,*
17. *And it shall be in the last days, saith God, I will pour out my Spirit upon all flesh; and your sons and your daughters shall prophesy, and your young men shall see visions, and your elders shall dream dreams:*
18. *Verily, I will pour out of my Spirit in those days upon my servants, and upon mine handmaids, and they shall prophesy.*
19. *And I will show wonders in heaven above, and signs upon the earth beneath, blood and fire, and vapour of smoke.*
20. *The sun shall be turned into darkness, and the moon into blood, before the great and notable day of the Lord do come.*
21. *And it shall come to pass, that whosoever shall call upon the name of the Lord he shall be saved.*

14. *And Peter, standing.* By this word *standing* he did signify, that there was a grave sermon made in the assembly; for they did rise when they spake unto the people, to the end they might be the better heard. The sum of this sermon is this, he gathereth that Christ is already revealed and given by the gift of the Holy Ghost, which they saw.

Yet, first, he refuteth that false opinion, in that they thought that the disciples were drunk. This refutation consisteth upon a probable argument; because men use not to be drunk betimes in the morning. For, as Paul saith, "Those which are drunk are drunk in the night," (1 Thess. 5:7.) For they flee the light for shame. And surely so great is the filthiness of this vice, that for good causes it hateth the light. And yet this argument were not always good; for Esaias doth inveigh in his time against those which did rise early to follow drunkenness. And at this day there be many who, like hogs, so soon as they awake, run to quaffing. But because this is a common custom amongst men, Peter saith, that it is no likely thing. Those which have but even small skill in antiquity do know that the civil day, from the rising of the sun until the going down thereof, was divided into twelve hours; so that the hours were longer in summer, and shorter in winter. Therefore, that which should now be the ninth before noon in winter, and in summer the eighth, was the third hour amongst the old people. Therefore, whereas Peter doth only lightly remove the opinion of drunkenness, he doth it for this cause, because it had been superfluous to have stood about any long excuse. Therefore, as in a matter which was certain and out of doubt, he doth rather pacify those which mocked, than labour to teach them. And he doth not so much refute them by the circumstance of time, as by the testimony of Joel. For when he saith that that is now come to pass which was foretold, he toucheth briefly their unthankfulness, because they do not acknowledge such an excellent benefit promised unto them in times past, which they now see with their eyes. And whereas he upbraideth the fault of a few unto all, he doth it not to this end, that he may make them all guilty of the same fault; but because a fit occasion was offered by their mocking to teach them altogether, he doth not foreslow the same.

17. *It shall be in the last days.* By this effect he proveth that the Messiah is already revealed. Joel, indeed, doth not express the last days, (Joel 2:29;) but for as much as he intreateth of the perfect restoring of the Church, it is not to be doubted but that that prophecy belongeth unto the last age alone. Wherefore, that which Peter bringeth doth no whit dissent from Joel's meaning; but he doth only add this word for exposition sake, that the Jews might know that the Church could by no other means be restored, which was

then decayed, but by being renewed by the Spirit of God. Again, because the repairing of the Church should be like unto a new world, therefore Peter saith that it shall be in the last days. And surely this was a common and familiar thing among the Jews, that all those great promises concerning the blessed and well-ordered state of the Church should not be fulfilled until Christ, by his coming, should restore all things. Wherefore, it was out of all doubt amongst them, that that which is cited out of Joel doth appertain unto the last time. Now, by the last days, or fulness of time, is meant the stable and firm condition of the Church, in the manifestation or revealing of Christ.

I will pour out my Spirit. He intendeth to prove, (as we have already said,) that the Church can be repaired by no other means, saving only by the giving of the Holy Spirit. Therefore, forasmuch as they did all hope that the restoring drew near, he accuseth them of sluggishness, because they do not once think upon the way and means thereof. And when the prophet saith, "I will pour out," it is, without all question, that he meant by this word to note the great abundance of the Spirit. And we must take *I will pour out of my Spirit* in the same sense, as if he had said simply, I will pour out my Spirit. For these latter words are the words of the prophet. But Peter followed the Grecians, who translate the Hebrew word חֵ (*cheth,*) απο. Therefore, some men do in vain more subtilely play the philosophers; because, howsoever the words be changed, yet must we still retain and keep the prophet's meaning. Nevertheless, when God is said to pour out his Spirit, I confess it must be thus understood, that he maketh manifold variety and change of gifts to flow unto men from his Spirit, as it were out of the only fountain, the fountain which can never be drawn dry. For, as Paul doth testify, there be divers gifts, and yet but one Spirit, (1 Cor. 12:4.) And hence do we gather a profitable doctrine, that we can have no more excellent thing given us of God than the grace of the Spirit; yea, that all other things are nothing worth if this be wanting. For, when God will briefly promise salvation to his people, he affirmeth that he will give them his Spirit. Hereupon it followeth that we can obtain no good things until we have the Spirit given us. And truly it is, as it were, the key which openeth unto us the door, that we may enter into all the treasures of spiritual good things; and that we may also have entrance into the kingdom of God.

Upon all flesh. It appeareth, by that which followeth, of what force this generality is; for, first, it is set down generally, *all flesh;* after that the partition is added, whereby the prophet doth signify that there shall be no difference of age or kind, but that God admitteth all, one with another, unto the partaking of his grace. It is said, therefore, *all flesh,* because both young and old, men and women, are thereby signified; yet here may a question be moved, why God doth promise that unto his people, as some new and unwonted good thing, which he was wont to do for them from the beginning throughout all ages; for there was no age void of the grace of the Spirit. The answer of this question is set down in these two sentences: "I will pour out," and, "Upon all flesh;" for we must here note a double contrariety between the time of the Old and New Testament; for the pouring out (as I have said) doth signify great plenty, when as there was under the law a more scarce distribution; for which cause John also doth say that the Holy Ghost was not given until Christ ascended into heaven. *All flesh* doth signify an infinite multitude, whereas God in times past did vouchsafe to bestow such plenty of his Spirit only upon a few.

Furthermore, in both comparisons we do not deny but that the fathers under the law were partakers of the selfsame grace whereof we are partakers; but the Lord doth show that we are above them, as we are indeed. I say, that all godly men since the beginning of the world were endued with the same spirit of understanding, of righteousness, and sanctification, wherewith the Lord doth at this day illuminate and regenerate us; but there were but a few which had the light of knowledge given them then, if they be compared with the great multitude of the faithful, which Christ did suddenly gather together by his coming. Again, their knowledge was but obscure and slender, and, as it were, covered with a veil, if it be compared with that which we have at this day out of the gospel, where Christ, the Sun of righteousness, doth shine with perfect brightness, as it were at noon day. Neither doth that any whit hurt or hinder that a few had such an excellent faith, that peradventure they have no equal at this day. For their understanding did nevertheless smell or savour of the instruction and schoolmastership of the law. For that is always true, that godly kings and prophets have not seen nor heard those things which Christ hath revealed by his coming. Therefore, to the end the prophet Joel may commend the excellency of the New Testament, he affirmeth and foretelleth that the grace of the Spirit shall be more plentiful in time thereof; and, again, that it shall come unto more men, (Matth. 13:17; Luke 10:24.)

And your sons shall prophesy. By the word *prophesy* he meant to note the rare and singular gift of understanding. And to the same purpose tendeth that partition which followeth afterwards, *"your young men shall see visions, and your old men shall dream dreams;"* for we gather out of the twelfth chapter of Numbers, that these were the two ordinary ways whereby God did reveal himself to the prophets. For in that place, when the Lord exempteth Moses from the common sort of prophets, he saith, "I appear unto my servants by a vision, or by a dream; but I speak unto Moses face to face," (Numb. 12:6.) Therefore, we see that two kinds are put after the general word for a confirmation; yet this is the sum, that they shall all be prophets so soon as the Holy Ghost shall be poured out from heaven. But here it is objected, that there was no such thing, even in the apostles themselves, neither yet in the whole multitude of the faithful. I answer, that the prophets did commonly use to shadow under tropes most fit for their time, the kingdom of Christ. When they speak of the worship of God, they name the altar, the sacrifices, the offering of gold, silver, and frankincense. Notwithstanding, we know that the altars do cease, the sacrifices are abolished, whereof there was some use in time of the law; and that the Lord requireth some higher thing at our hands than earthly riches. That is true, indeed; but the prophets, whilst they apply their style unto the capacity of their time, comprehend under figures (wherewith the people were then well acquainted) those things which we see otherwise revealed and showed now, like as when he promiseth elsewhere that he will make priests of Levites, and Levites of the common sort of men, (Isaiah 66:21,) this is his meaning, that under the kingdom of Christ every base person shall be extolled unto an honourable estate; therefore, if we desire to have the true and natural meaning of this place, we must not urge the words which are taken out of the old order of the law; but we must only seek the truth without figures, and this is it, that the apostles, through the sudden inspiration of the Spirit, did intreat of the heavenly mysteries prophetically, that is to say, divinely, and above the common order.

Therefore, this word *prophesy* doth signify nothing else

save only the rare and excellent gift of understanding, as if Joel should say, Under the kingdom of Christ there shall not be a few prophets only, unto whom God may reveal his secrets; but all men shall be endued with spiritual wisdom, even to the prophetical excellency. As it is also in Jeremiah, "Every man shall no longer teach his neighbour; because they shall all know me, from the least unto the greatest," (Jeremiah 31:34.) And in these words Peter inviteth the Jews, unto whom he speaketh, to be partakers of the same grace. As if he should say, the Lord is ready to pour out that Spirit far and wide which he hath poured upon us. Therefore, unless you yourselves be the cause of it, ye shall receive with us of this fulness. And as for us, let us know that the same is spoken to us at this day which was then spoken to the Jews. For although those visible graces of the Spirit be ceased, yet God hath not withdrawn his Spirit from his Church. Wherefore he offereth him daily unto us all, by this same promise, without putting any difference. Wherefore we are poor and needy only through our own sluggishness; and also it appeareth manifestly, that those are wicked and sacrilegious enemies of the Spirit which keep back the Christian common people from the knowledge of God; and forasmuch as he himself doth not only admit, but also call by name unto himself, women and men, young and old.

18. *Upon my servants.* In these words the promise is restrained unto the worshippers of God. For God doth not profane his Spirit; which he should do, if he should make the same common to the unbelieving and despisers. It is certain that we are made the servants of God by the Spirit; and that, therefore, we are not, until such time as we have received the same; but, first, whom God hath adopted to be of his family, and whom he hath framed by his Spirit to obey him, those doth he furnish with new gifts afterward. Again, the prophet did not respect that order of time, but his meaning was to make this grace proper to the Church alone. And forasmuch as the Church was only among the Jews, he calleth them honourably the servants and handmaids of God. But after that God did gather unto himself on every side a Church, the wall of separation being pulled down, so many as are received into the society of the covenant are called by the same name. Only let us remember, that the Spirit is appointed for the Church properly.

19. *And I will show wonders.* We must first see what is
meant by this great day of the Lord. Some do expound it
of the former coming of Christ in the flesh; and others refer
it unto the last day of the resurrection; I do allow neither
opinion. For, in my judgment, the prophet comprehendeth
the whole kingdom of Christ. And so he calleth it the *great
day*, after that the Son of God began to be revealed in the
flesh, that he may lead us into the fulfilling of his kingdom.
Therefore, he appointeth no certain day, but he beginneth
this day at the first preaching of the gospel, and he extendeth
the same unto the last resurrection. Those which restrain it
unto the time of the apostles are moved with this reason,
because the prophet joineth this member and that which
goeth next before together. But in that there is no absurdity
at all, because the prophet doth assign the time when
these things began to come to pass, howsoever they have a
continual going forward even until the end of the world.
Furthermore, whereas he saith that the sun shall be turned
to darkness, and the moon into blood, they are figurative
speeches, whereby he doth give us to understand thus much,
that the Lord will show tokens of his wrath through the
whole frame of the world, which shall bring men even to
their wit's end, as if there should be some horrible and fearful change of nature wrought. For as the sun and moon are
unto us witnesses of God's fatherly favour towards us, whilst
that by course they give light to the earth; so, on the other
side, the prophet saith, that they shall be messengers to fore-
show God's wrath and displeasure. And this is the second
member of the prophecy. For after that he had intreated of
the spiritual grace which should be abundantly poured out
upon all flesh, lest any man should imagine that all things
should be quiet and prosperous together, therewithal he
addeth that the estate of the world shall be troublesome,
and full of great fear under Christ; as Christ himself doth
more fully declare, Matth. 24 and Luke 21.

But this serveth greatly to the setting forth of grace, that
whereas all things do threaten destruction, yet whosoever
doth call upon the name of the Lord is sure to be saved. By
the darkness of the sun, by the bloody streaming of the moon,
by the black vapour of smoke, the prophet meant to declare,
that whithersoever men turn their eyes, there shall many
things appear, both upward and downward, which may make
them amazed and afraid, as he hath already said. Therefore,
this is as much as if he should have said, that the world was

never in a more miserable case, that there were never so many and such cruel tokens of God's wrath. Hence may we gather how inestimable the goodness of God is, who offereth a present remedy for so great evils; and again, how unthankful they are towards God, and how froward, which do not flee unto the sanctuary of salvation, which is nigh unto them, and doth meet them. Again, it is out of all doubt, that God meaneth by this so doleful a description, to stir up all godly men, that they may with a more fervent desire seek for salvation. And Peter citeth it to the same end, that the Jews may know that they shall be more miserable unless they receive that grace of the Spirit which is offered unto them. Yet here may a question be asked, how this can hang together, that when Christ is revealed, there should such a sea of miseries overflow and break out therewithal? For it may seem to be a thing very inconvenient, that he should be the only pledge of God's love toward mankind, in whom the heavenly Father doth lay open all the treasure of his goodness, yea, he poureth out the bowels of his mercy upon us, and that yet, by the coming of the same, his Son, his wrath should be more hot than it was wont, so that it should, as it were, quite consume both heaven and earth at once.

But we must first mark, that because men are too slow to receive Christ, they must be constrained by divers afflictions, as it were with whips. Secondly, forasmuch as Christ doth call unto himself all those which are heavy laden and labour, (Matth. 11:28,) we must first be tamed by many miseries, that we may learn humility. For through great prosperity men do set up the horns of pride. And he cannot but despise Christ fiercely, whosoever he be, that seemeth to himself to be happy. Thirdly, because we are, more than we ought, set upon the seeking of the peace of the flesh, whereby it cometh to pass that many tie the grace of Christ unto the present life, it is expedient for us to be accustomed to think otherwise, that we may know that the kingdom of Christ is spiritual. Therefore, to the end God may teach us that the good things of Christ are heavenly, he doth exercise us, according to the flesh, with many miseries; whereby it cometh to pass that we do seek our felicity without the world. Moreover, men do bring miseries upon themselves through their unthankfulness; for the servant which knoweth his master's will, and doth not obey, is worthy of greater and more stripes, (Luke 12:47.) The more familiarly that God doth communicate with us in Christ, the more doth our ungodliness grow and break out into open contumacy, so that it is no marvel if, when Christ is revealed, there appear many tokens of God's vengeance on the other side, forasmuch as men do hereby more grievously provoke God against them, and kindle his wrath through wicked contempt. Surely, in that the day of Christ is fearful, it is an accidental thing; whether God will correct our slothfulness, to bring us under, which (who) are yet unapt to be taught, or whether he will punish our unthankfulness. For it bringeth with it of itself nothing but that which is pleasant; but the contempt of God's grace doth provoke him to horrible anger not without cause.

21. *Whosoever shall call upon.* An excellent place. For as God doth prick us forward like sluggish asses, with threatenings and terrors to seek salvation, so, after that he hath brought darkness upon the face of heaven and earth, yet doth he show a means whereby salvation may shine before our eyes, to wit, if we shall call upon him. For we must diligently note this circumstance. If God should promise salvation simply, it were a great matter; but it is a far greater when as he promiseth the same amidst manifold dungeons of death. Whilst that (saith he) all things shall be out of order, and the fear of destruction shall possess all things, only call upon me, and ye shall be saved. Therefore, howsoever man be swallowed up in the gulf of miseries, yet is there set before him a way to escape. We must also note the universal word, *whosoever.* For God admitteth all men unto himself without exception, and by this means doth he invite them to salvation, as Paul gathereth in the tenth chapter to the Romans, and as the prophet had set it down before, "Thou, Lord, which hearest the prayer, unto thee shall all flesh come," (Psalm 65:2.)

Therefore, forasmuch as no man is excluded from calling upon God, the gate of salvation is set open unto all men; neither is there any other thing which keepeth us back from entering in, save only our own unbelief. I speak of all unto whom God doth make himself manifest by the gospel. But like as those which call upon the name of the Lord are sure of salvation, so we must think that, without the same, we are thrice miserable and undone. And when as our salvation is placed in calling upon God, there is nothing in the mean season taken from faith, forasmuch as this invocation is grounded on faith alone. There is also another circumstance no less worthy the noting; in that the prophet doth signify, that the calling upon God doth properly appertain and agree unto the last days. For although he would be called upon in all ages, notwithstanding, since that he showed himself to be a Father in Christ, we have the more easy access unto him. Which thing ought both the more to embolden us, and to take from us all sluggishness. As he himself doth also reason, that by this privilege our forwardness to pray is doubled to us: "Hitherto have ye asked nothing in my name; ask, and ye shall receive;" as if he should say, Heretofore, although I did not yet appear to be a mediator and advocate in the flesh, yet did ye pray; but now, when you shall have me to be your patron, with how much more courage ought ye to do that?

FIRST SERMON ON PENTECOST[1]

[This sermon, as indicated previously, is on a text included in the Commentary Upon the Acts of the Apostles.]

FIRST SERMON ON PENTECOST

Of the Descent of the Holy Spirit upon the Apostles, Delivered on the Day of Pentecost, on which is celebrated the Holy Supper of the Lord.

> *And when it came to the day of Pentecost they were all of one spirit in the same place. And suddenly there was a sound from heaven, as if a mighty wind were raised, which filled all the house where they were seated. And parted tongues as of fire appeared to them and rested on each of them. And all were filled with the Holy Spirit, and began to speak other languages, just as the Spirit gave them to speak.*
>
> —ACTS 2:1–4

We are by nature so inclined to unbelief that the truth of God must be sealed in our hearts in an authentic manner so that we may receive it and be entirely decided about it. True it is that God stamps it on the heart of every believer by His Holy Spirit, and that is also why He is named the Seal of the Gospel. But those who were to proclaim this teaching through all the world must have been sealed in the first place, and God must have governed them in such a way that now we are assured in full certainty of the teaching which they have published to us, that we do not receive it from them as

---

[1] [Reprinted by permission of the publisher from *The Deity of Christ and Other Sermons,* translated from the French and Latin by LeRoy Nixon (Grand Rapids: Wm. B. Eerdmans Publishing Company, 1950), pp. 243–57.]

from mortal creatures, but that God is the real author of it. For we know that our faith would have too weak a foundation if we had only the authority of men. We would be, then, always shaky unless our spirits were raised above the world and were founded in God, knowing that it is from Him that this Word of salvation has proceeded which is daily preached to us. And that is why this account has been set down for us in writing, so that whenever we read or hear the Word of God, this comes before us, that men have not invented what is contained in the Old and New Testaments, but God by a visible sign has testified, even as there was need, that men were organs solely of His Holy Spirit. As for Moses and all the Prophets—they have had the approval of being sent by God, so that if their teaching is held in doubt by us, that must be imputed to us and to our ingratitude and malice.

Now it is said to us that before the Apostles had published the Gospel to all the world God made His Holy Spirit descend upon them, so that we might know that they have put forward nothing of their own, but that they have faithfully delivered that which was commanded to them by God. We see, then, how this account ought to serve us. For if we were not assured that the Apostles were as new creatures and that God had given them a certain mark to show that they were approved and authorized by Him, what would become of our faith? It would be only a fleeting opinion. We could say, "I think so; so it seems to me," but that we should be entirely persuaded to have a proper firmness and constancy—it would be impossible. For what is man? Since there is nothing but vanity here below, we must put out our anchor even as far as heaven, as also the Apostle says in the Epistle to the Hebrews. And then we can sustain all whirlwinds and tempests, and the world and the devil can gain no hold on us, however they may plot. But our faith will be always firm and will not give way when we hold this basic principle: that God is He Who leads us onward, Who calls us to Himself, and that the teaching which is preached to us is His pure and infallible truth. This, then, is how we must summarize what we have read: that when there arose a great disturbance like a rushing wind, God wished to show by a visible sign that He had chosen the twelve Apostles to carry the message of salvation here and there. It is true that for the time being there were only eleven, but the number of twelve was not allowed to remain forever broken, because in the place of Judas, Matthias was sent. And that is how the number was repaired that had been formerly destroyed; and this interruption was only for a little time, as St. Luke records later.

There are, then, the twelve Ambassadors of our Lord Jesus Christ, who had already been chosen and marked by Him. However, they had to be furnished with gifts which were required for a charge so difficult and so lofty. They must, then, be fashioned from on high, and God had to work in them in a strange and admirable manner which surpasses all human capacity. Now with respect to a wind and disturbing whirlwind which was there, it was to show that the Holy Spirit descended upon the Apostles not only to make them sharers in His gifts, but also in order that all the world might be disturbed by it. For it had been said by the Prophet Haggai, " 'Yet a little while and I will shake heaven and earth,' says the Lord." Now that was fulfilled in the preaching of the Gospel. We see, then, when the Holy Spirit descended, that it was not only for a little handful of people, but in order that this might reach all the ends and extremities of the world. For otherwise this narrative would be very cold to us, if we were not well persuaded that it was for us and for the building up of our faith that God sent once for all His Holy Spirit. Besides, God could surely have sent the Holy Spirit in a more gentle manner. But let us note that this impetuosity was to beat down all pride of the flesh, and on the other hand, to wake us up, since we are too drowsy and slow. There are two very great vices in us, which hinder us from feeling the power of the Spirit of God, to throw in our lot with the Gospel. One is that we are haughty and full of presumption. Now all that must be put down and in humility we must learn, both great and small, to do such homage to God, that we be emptied of everything, and that we consider our life as coming from Him and from His pure grace. It is needful, then, that this pride which is rooted in our nature be reproved, even in a violent manner, because we are too hardened in it. On the other hand, each one feels in himself an earthly sluggishness, so that we are preoccupied and wrapped up in this world. Briefly, we are almost stupid, so that we can taste neither the Word of God nor the power of His Holy Spirit, unless we are awakened, as it were, by force. That then is what is here narrated means, that a whirlwind was raised, like an impetuous wind. Now in the first place we see that the descent of the Holy Spirit was to move all the world and to make all mankind tremble, so that God might be adored with common accord and that men might be subject to Him. However, we must be awakened, since we are too stupid, and we must also be led to obey God, being stripped of all presumption, knowing well that there is only all misery in us, that we are only mud and rottenness, indeed, even that there is only corruption in our souls until God has renewed us.

Besides, when the Holy Spirit descended in such a form, that is, in *parted tongues and as of fire*, it was to better express how God wished to work through the preaching of the Gospel. If a man speaks, his voice is dispersed in the air and it is a dead thing. Now it is said that the Gospel is the power of God unto salvation to all those who believe. How so? Can a sound which flies into the air and which is dispersed lead us to the Kingdom of heaven? Nobody by himself knows how to create even a little fly. It is necessary that the image of God be repaired in us, that we receive this incorruptible seed to reach the heavenly glory, to be companions of Angels, to be transfigured even into the glory and immortality of our Lord Jesus Christ, and to be sharers in His Divine nature, as St. Peter speaks of it. And can this be done by the voice of a man? Certainly not, but it is then said especially that the Holy Spirit is joined in the same place with the word which is preached. For why did He take this figure of tongues? It is certain that there is always some likeness between the visible signs and the truth which is represented by them. We must, then, see why the Holy Spirit appeared in the form of tongues. It is to show that he would be in the mouths of the Apostles, and that He would give to them what was required to execute their office and their commission, and indeed, that He would make their labor profitable that it might not be useless. For also, in the first place, we know that even the most clever man to be found would not know how to pronounce a single word unless he were governed by the Holy Spirit. By this God shows us our condition, since we would not be able to open our mouths to say a single word to His glory, which would be appropriate, unless He had given it to us. It was, then, very necessary that the Apostles were governed by the Spirit of God, or else they would have become mutes. We see also what crudeness there was in them, for they might have had much more active and keen spirits, except that God by their crudeness wished to show us, as in a mirror, our condition unless we are illuminated by

His grace. It is true, when the Apostles went about with our Lord Jesus, they held Him to be their Master, they were subject in all modesty to His doctrine; yet what did they know about it? We see that they were poor beasts, so that, considering how little they learned in such a good school, we must be ashamed of their slowness. But that serves us well. For there they are! Changed in a minute, so that the grace of God has all the brighter a luster, since we see that they speak of the secrets of God so loudly as being wonders, and everyone is astonished by it, and previously there was nothing. Further let us consider what their virtue and constancy was. They had all been weakened. It seemed that their faith was dead and extinct. There was Peter who was, as it were, the leader, who so shabbily renounced his Master, and yielded like a slave of Satan. It was very necessary, then, that God put down His hand. For from man's side there was no possible remedy. So, let us note that not without cause the Spirit of God appeared under the form of tongues, to show that by this means the doctrine of the Gospel was approved and sealed by God, in order that we might receive it in all reverence and humility, and that there might not be any dispute at all about where it came from; since God displayed His arm and declared that He was the author of it.

Besides, it is not without cause that the tongues are parted and of fire. For we know how the human race was divided in itself as well as being alienated from God. And the plot that was made to build the tower of Babel was the reason why men were barbarians to one another, so that there was no longer any communication. But it seemed that God dispersed them, as it were, in spite. How then were the Apostles, having always been isolated as foolish and unlearned people in this corner of Judea, able to publish the Gospel to all the world, unless God accomplished what He had previously promised: namely, that He would be known by all tongues and by all nations? It is true that it is said that all will speak the Hebrew language in order to join in a true faith, but the truth is better declared to us when it is said that all believers, from whatever region they may be, will cry, "Abba, Father," invoking God with one accord; although there may be diversity of language. That, then, is how the Spirit of God wished to display His power in these tongues, in order that the Name of God might be invoked by all and that we might together be made partakers of this covenant of salvation which belonged only to the Jews until the wall was torn down.

By that we see the wonderful goodness of our God, when He changed evil into good. For if we seek the reason why there are different languages in the world, we must come to the conclusion that it is on account of a curse from God. Yet here appeared His goodness and fatherly mercy, when the message of life was brought into all tongues. That is how God converted evil into good. All the more have we to magnify and bless His Holy Name, knowing that difference of languages did not hinder Him from declaring through all the world that He wished to receive those who previously were estranged from Him, and to gather them all, as it were, into His bosom, until they are received into the inheritance of heaven.

So much for one item. But it would not be enough that the Gospel be preached, and that God by this means might be known by all the world, unless this doctrine had more and more power to touch hearts to the quick, and to draw men into obedience. That is also why the tongues appeared like fire. For in the first place we need to be purged, since there are only corruption and filth in us. If one scans all our affections and desires, he will find that there is stench everywhere. We have to be made over, and God must purge us in a strange fashion. Then, on the other hand, we are as cold as we could be. We need, then, to be set on fire with the love of God. Instead of being all wrapped up in the things of earth, He must raise us on high, which He does by means of His Word.

Now we see, in summary, how this account serves us today. In the first place, to the end that we might receive the doctrine of the gospel as a certain and infallible truth it bears the mark of God and it is sealed by His Holy Spirit and is an excellent witness of our adoption. That, then, is how we are brought into obedience, seeing how God has given approval to His Gospel, both to be assured in order that our faith may no longer be variable, and that we be not always liable to change our words and our opinions, but that we walk always without swerving from the good path, until we have finished our course. That is how in the power of the Spirit of God our faith will be victorious over the world. For if it were a matter of limiting ourselves to the wisdom of men, where would we be? But when we have as a foundation the Spirit of God, that is how we are never shaken. However, we have to think of ourselves, in order that God may today make us partakers of that which we have just now declared, that is, that we in-

voke Him with true accord (I say, although we are separated
by tongues) and then that we be renewed by the doctrine
which is preached to us, in such a way that we know that
there has to be fire to change us, and to cleanse both our
senses, and our spirits, and our hearts of all corruptions of
this world. For although the elect of God are made submis-
sive by means of the Gospel, yet on the other hand we see
that the enemies of truth become more proud and more rebellious, so that it puts the world into combat, as experience
today shows. For as long as the Gospel was not preached all
the world was without care and at rest. There were neither
arguments nor disputes. And why not? The devil reigned
without contradiction. But when our Lord Jesus Christ appeared with the pure doctrine of the Gospel the skirmishes
got closer and closer. And we see today the combats among
those who are called Christians. All the more ought we to
pray to God that He may make us to experience why the
Holy Spirit descended upon the Apostles and that He may
give us the grace that with entire obedience we may render
testimony that it was to gather us, where as previously we
were scattered, and that we may be joined together under
our Lord Jesus Christ, that we may be members of His body
and that truly He may be our Head.

Besides, to succeed in it, we have to pray to Him that He
may give us such a firmness that there may be only fire, instead of the coldness which is in our hearts, that also He may
remake us so that we may cast off all the corruptions of our
nature, that we may be so renewed that we are separated
from the world. We shall see often how the word of God is a
fire; indeed, but it is of another kind, to consume all who
contradict; as the Prophet Jeremiah speaks of it, showing
that even to the people of Israel it came thus, that they were,
as it were, straw and stubble to be burned by the Word of
God, because of their malice and rebellion. And today, how
many are there who are made inexcusable since they fight
against God, like enraged beasts, who foam at the mouth,
and perhaps other things, who are mockers and profane people, who defy God, attributing neither authority nor honor
to His Holy Word? Now it is true that such people will not
render the Word of God useless or without power, but that
they will have to experience it as a consuming fire, to be
reduced to ashes and completely crushed. Let us learn, then,
to note why God wished that His Holy Spirit appeared in
tongues of fire. It was so that believers might know that they

needed to be touched to the quick, even in such a manner that God change them and renew them. That, then, is what we have to bear in mind, in summary, to properly apply this account to our use.

Furthermore, let us note the two principal parts of faith, and then let us come to ourselves to know what we would be unless God cared for us. In faith there is first knowledge or certainty, and then there is firmness and constancy. Now when God speaks we are deaf to what He says, because we are already preoccupied with this world, and even all the wisdom contained in the Gospel will be foolishness to us until God has enlightened us. In the first place, then, God must open the way for us to know Him and to cling to this truth, or else we shall be deaf to His word, we shall be stupid and without any comprehension. So much for one item. For the second, we need to persevere against the assaults which Satan stirs up against us, and against so many skirmishes; for those we must be armed and equipped. Now how shall we be thus armed until God extends His hand? Only the power of the Holy Spirit can suffice for that. When, then, we shall have been taught a hundred times by the Gospel, yet since we are fickle and unsteady, we shall be soon turned away from it, unless God confirms us in it. Even today, when there are so many perils and threats, poor believers cannot open their mouths to call upon God, unless death is right next to them; they cannot make confession of their faith, unless fire is kindled to abolish all memory of our Lord Jesus Christ. When then there is such a resistance, and those who ought to maintain the Christian faith are inflamed by Satan to ruin everything, if it were possible for them, must not God be at work here? Yet we are today invited by the experience, and warned of what need we have to practice what is contained in this account, and beyond that to call upon God and to pray to Him that, since He wished to give testimony when the Gospel came into the world, inasmuch as He was at work there by the power of His Holy Spirit, we also may experience Him, each one in his place. Since we must be persuaded and resolved that the word which is preached to us does not proceed from men, also it is not to be interpreted through anyone's cleverness, as St. Peter shows. For he connects these two points. (1) Since the Holy Spirit of God has spoken by His holy Prophets, (2) we also on our part, when we wish to understand what is declared by their doctrine, each one must put away his natural senses, and must not bring here his speculations, saying, "so it seems to me; thus I presume"; but we must come with soberness and modesty, asking God that He may govern us and introduce us by His Holy Spirit into the understanding of His Word, of which He is author. So much, then, for one item.

Since today we see that the devil has refilled the world with so many sects, that there are many heretics who do not cease to upset all purity of the Gospel, and even that there are so many despisers of God, and mastiff dogs who no longer have either faith or religion in them; all the more do we need always to present ourselves to God in order that He may enlighten us by His truth, and that we may be so united to our Lord Jesus Christ that nothing may be able to separate us from Him. On the other hand, may He give us a Spirit of power and of constancy until the end; in order that, however much the enemies of truth may be animated, we may persist nevertheless, and that Satan by this means may be conquered. And we ought not only to have concern for ourselves, but we ought to think with concern for others. It is here very easy for us today to make confession of our faith; we do not see the fires kindled like our poor brothers, we do not experience the storms which fall upon their heads; yet we surely must be united in one body. For why are we assembled, unless in order that we may have true brotherhood together, since God through His infinite goodness has adopted us for His children, and He daily testifies to us that He wishes to be our Father? It is, then, very fitting that our solicitude should extend to those who are, as it were, in the snare of wolves, who experience new troubles daily; that we may have such pity for them, that we may pray to God that He may help them and that He may strengthen them for the battles, according to their need; that He may never permit them to remain confounded, but, though Satan may plot from all sides to ruin their faith, that nevertheless they may persist until the end. Even we need to be admonished of how things are today; for if ever there was persecution prepared, it is now; especially, is there a place where the rage of the enemies of God flared up for a whole week, so that they have more occasion than was ever seen to execute their cruelty against poor believers. Also it is seen how these miserable tyrants are possessed by Satan, and that there is such a frenzy in them that there is no longer any hope of bending them in any manner whatever. Now our poor brothers are there exposed as prey, they are watched and spied upon;

and it is apparent that the greatest preparations were made
in unthinkable rage and cruelty, and that the obstinacy of
wicked men against God is greater than ever. It is, then, well
for us, while God gives us leisure, to think carefully about
this, and to practice this account which we see: namely, since
the Holy Spirit descended upon those who were of one accord, may we learn to assemble ourselves, and although we
are far from the front lines, nevertheless may we be joined
with those who do battle, and may we help them in combat
by our prayers with mouth and heart; so that the Spirit of
God may be in charge of everything, and that He may inflame us with such a zeal that we may be ardent to call upon
our God, instead of being too cold. As for our brothers who
need to be confirmed in such assaults as they have to sustain,
may the good God show that it is He Who has worked in
them, and that He leads and governs them.

Besides we must still note the word "consent" or "accord,"
to lead us to the Head, Who is our Lord Jesus Christ. For it
will be seen how the Gospel is preached today; but if a
census is taken of the believers, the number will be found to
be very small and obviously scattered; for there are hardly
any places where the pure doctrine is preached, and even
where there is Church, there are many despisers of God,
dissolute and profane people, who are there to infect the
remainder, if God did not preserve it by His power. Others
will remain always in their brutishness. There are so many
today who have not in twenty or twenty-five years advanced
a single pace in the knowledge of God; they have no more
idea of faith or reverence than beasts. Others, although they
have intelligence enough, yet lose courage and are entirely
asleep, and no longer take account either of God or of His
Word, so that the number of sheep and true lambs is very
small. However, we see how through all Europe the devil is
popular, that lies, snares, and delusions are received, and that
the world is so bewitched that there is no means to reduce
it. It is seen that men not only provoke God and knowingly
blaspheme against Him, but they are so inflamed by madness that it seems that they ought to pull the sun out of the
sky and to take away its brightness. When, then, we see that,
we need to commit ourselves to our Head, our Lord Jesus
Christ. For what cause is such scorn and impiety seen everywhere in the world, and so many rebellions and mockeries,
unless that grace is not given to all to be led under the
sovereign Shepherd Who was given for us by God His

Father? We know that those who are in His keeping will never perish, as He has pronounced. Thus, then, let us take the side of our Lord Jesus Christ, if we wish to experience to our salvation the profit and the fulfilment of what is here narrated by St. Luke: namely, not only may God speak to our ears, and may His doctrine pierce our hearts, may we be inflamed, may we be remade and renewed, in such a way that the corruptions of this world may be put down, and, as we wish to be owned and acknowledged as His people, may we be able to claim in truth our God in the Name of our Lord Jesus Christ, to Whom we are joined in order that He may unite us in perfection to God His Father.

That is also why this Holy Table is now prepared for us. For, as I have already said, we cannot communicate any grace from the Holy Spirit without being members of our Lord Jesus Christ. How can we arrive at that condition unless He presents Himself to us and He lives with us in such a manner that everything that is His belongs to us, and we enjoy the benefits which have been given to Him in our name? It is said in the eleventh chapter of Isaiah that the Spirit of God has rested upon Him, but not for any necessity He had of it, nor for His private use; it was for the profit of all of His body, that is to say, of all of the Church. So then, let us recognize, when now the Supper is offered to us, that our Lord Jesus wishes that we might find all our good in Him, He draws near to us through His goodness. It is true that He does not leave His heavenly glory, He need not descend here below (as the Papists imagine) to communicate to us His body and His blood, but although we are far away from Him, yet He does not cease to feed us with His body and His blood. Also we shall not cease to be united to Him, in entire perfection, indeed, as much as it will be needed. That is why I call that "perfection," although He comes to us little by little. For though that may be, we shall not cease to be joined to Him. Indeed, let us recognize that He did not wish to disappoint us when He declared that He is our Head and that we are His members, and that, if we let ourselves be governed by Him, we shall experience that He will be our good and sure Guide, and that the power of His Holy Spirit is infinite in order to sustain us. In the first place, then, when we come to this holy table, let us recognize that it is a secret which surpasses all our senses, and yet we must here give place to faith. Let us know that what cannot be conceived of by men is accomplished, nevertheless, by the secret and invisible grace of the Holy Spirit; for this is how we are made partakers of the body and of the blood of Jesus Christ.

Besides, when He dwells in us and we are truly His body, let us not doubt that all that is said in Isaiah of the gifts of the Spirit belong to us and are appropriated by us. It is true that we do not receive the Holy Spirit in complete perfection, for there is the measure of the gift, as St. Paul says, and we must believe more and more. Also it is not without cause that our Lord distributes them thus to us by certain portions and degrees; for His strength needs to be made perfect in our weakness, in order that we may depend always upon Him, that we may be solicitous to call upon Him; and also that we may be humbled, recognizing that there is still much to find fault with in us. That, then, is how we shall know that it is not in vain that Jesus Christ dwells in us, for He will give us testimony through the fact that His Holy Spirit will display His power to strengthen us in Him, to draw us toward Him, and to withdraw us from this world. It is said in this passage from Isaiah that the Spirit of wisdom rested upon Him, to show that there is only darkness in us, that we are poor blind people, and that to the extent that we presume to be clever and artful, we shall always pervert and falsify the truth of God, until He has enlightened us, and He has given us heavenly brightness, which we have not by birth nor by heritage. Then it is said that He has also the Spirit of fear of God, because our desires are so many rebellions against the will of God, until they are reformed, even entirely changed. Next it is said that He has as well the Spirit of power, in order that we may recognize our weakness, and that we cannot do otherwise than fail, unless we are strengthened from on high. We shall experience, then, all these things when we shall come to receive the testimony which is here given to us, and when we shall be persuaded that, as mortal men distribute the bread and the wine, our Lord Jesus Christ will work, since it is done by His authority and in His Name, and that it is not a thing which men have contrived in their brains, but that Jesus Christ is the author of it. That, then, is the purpose to which we must apply this account.

Besides, let us be so united under our Head, that we may adore God with one heart and with one mouth, and so may we be joined together. For it is not said that the Apostles were joined with everybody in one accord. They had all the city of Jerusalem for an enemy, and yet they did not cease, although they were small in number, although they were despised people, to persist and to be there united and gathered together under the sign of God in the Name of Jesus Christ. So now, seeing that so many mastiff dogs bark against us, seeing that the devil raises up so many troubles and in various manners, may we be all the more joined and in greater firmness, and may the cord of our agreement be unbreakable, so that we may defy Satan and all his minions by this means. It is true that we ought to seek peace in general with all without exception; we ought to love those who hate us and persecute us, we ought to desire their salvation, although they are not worthy of it; all the same we must be enemies to them, or else we would separate ourselves from Jesus Christ. Let us despise, then, all the world, and let us recognize even that we must leave ourselves to be joined to the Son of God, and that we are not wicked because the rage of unbelievers is stirred up against us, when we try to agree together among ourselves and to be united in the Name of Jesus Christ. Let us recognize that He acknowledges our agreement, although we are only a handful of people, let us defy boldly all the world and all those who are governed by Satan and are at all rebels against God. Although then, we are nothing in comparison with them, let us not doubt that God acknowledges us, and that He dwells in our midst. At the time which St. Luke described here they offered sacrifices in the Temple as previously, and the Priest was there with great dignity; he was there in his pontificate. There was as well the "common order" which had luster, so that it seemed that God was attached to that people. Now the Holy Spirit was only over a house, indeed over a room where the disciples were inclosed, like poor frightened people, like poor trembling lambs, seeing themselves surrounded by wolves. It surely seemed that the condition of such people was miserable; however, the Holy Spirit appeared there to this little company. So then, today, although we are despised by the world, and though we are not a great crowd, yet let us not doubt: that the Son of God displays the power of His Holy Spirit over us, that He makes us to experience His gifts, according to our need; and let us content ourselves with this inestimable benefit, so that we may not be at all envious of the prosperity of wicked men and enemies of God; that it will do us no harm to be rejected by the world, and to be considered rotten members; that this is all one to us, by means of which we may remain joined together, indeed, in this union which we have by means of the Gospel, and by means of Jesus Christ, Who is the Fountain of every benefit and of life and Who has in Himself all perfection of joy.

Now let us bow in humble reverence before the majesty of our God.

SELECTED BIBLIOGRAPHY
FOR FURTHER READING

I. WRITINGS OF CALVIN

God and Political Duty, ed. by J. T. McNeill, Little Library of Liberal Arts, New York: The Liberal Arts Press, 1950
Institutes of the Christian Religion, ed. by J. T. McNeill, Library of Christian Classics, trs. by Ford Lewis Battles, Philadelphia: Westminster Press, 1960
Instruction in Faith, trs. by P. T. Fuhrmann, Philadelphia: Westminster Press, 1949
Theological Treatises, trs. and ed. by J. K. S. Reid, Library of Christian Classics, Philadelphia: Westminster Press, 1954
Tracts and Treatises, Vols. I–III, republications of the Calvin Translation Society, by Wm. B. Eerdmans and Oliver & Boyd

For Commentaries, Letters and Sermons, reference is made to the following:
Calvin: Commentaries (Selections), newly trs. and ed. by J. Haroutunian in collaboration with L. P. Smith, Philadelphia: Westminster Press, 1958
Commentaries of Calvin, Published by Wm. B. Eerdmans and Oliver & Boyd
Letters of John Calvin, by Jules Bonnet, Vols. I–IV, Philadelphia: Presbyterian Board of Education (19th Century —not in print)
Sermons—Limited editions by Wm. B. Eerdmans and Oliver & Boyd

II. WRITINGS ABOUT CALVIN

Battles, F. L., *New Light on Calvin's Institutes,* a supplement to the McNeill-Battles trs., Hartford: Hartford Seminary Foundation, 1966

Biéler, A., *The Social Humanism of Calvin*, trs. by Paul T. Fuhrmann, Richmond: John Knox Press, 1964

Breen, Quirinus, "John Calvin and the Rhetorical Tradition," in his volume *Christianity and Humanism*, Grand Rapids: Wm. B. Eerdmans, 1968

Cadier, J., *The Man God Mastered*, trs. by O. R. Johnston, London: Inter-Varsity Fellowship, 1964

Davies, R. E., *The Problem of Authority in the Continental Reformers*, London: The Epworth Press, 1946

Dowey, Jr., E. A., *The Knowledge of God in Calvin's Theology*, New York: Columbia University Press, 1952

Duffield, G. E. [ed.], *John Calvin*, Courtenay Studies in Reformation Theology I, Appleford, Abingdon, Berkshire: The Sutton Courtenay Press, 1966

Forstmann, H. Jackson, *Word and Spirit*, Stanford: Stanford University Press, 1962

Gerrish, B. A. [ed.], *Reformers in Profile*, Philadelphia: Fortress Press, 1967

Hall, Basil, *John Calvin—Humanist and Theologian*, London: London Historical Society, 1967

Henderson, R. W., *The Teaching Office in the Reformed Tradition*, Philadelphia: The Westminster Press, 1962

Higman, F. M., *The Style of John Calvin in His French Polemical Treatises*, New York: Oxford University Press, 1967

Hoogland, Marvin P., *Calvin's Perspective on the Exaltation of Christ in Comparison with the Post Reformation Doctrine of the Two States*, Holland, Kampen: H. H. Kok, 1966

Hoogstra, Jacob T. [ed.], *John Calvin—Contemporary Prophet, A Symposium*, Philadelphia: Presbyterian and Reformed Publishing Co., 1959

Jansen, J. F., *Calvin's Doctrine of the Work of Christ*, London: James Clarke & Co., 1956

McDonnell, K., *John Calvin, the Church, and the Eucharist*, Princeton: Princeton University Press, 1967

McNeill, J. T., *The History and Character of Calvinism*, New York: Oxford University Press, 1954

Monter, E. William, *Calvin's Geneva*, New York: John Wiley & Sons, Inc., 1967

Monter, E. William, *Studies in Genevan Government*, Geneva: Librairie Droz, 1964

Mueller, W. A., *Church and State in Luther and Calvin*, New York: Doubleday (Anchor), 1954

Niesel, W., *The Theology of Calvin*, trs. by Harold Knight, London: Lutterworth Press, 1956

Nixon, LeRoy, *John Calvin, Expository Preacher*, Grand Rapids: Wm. B. Eerdmans Publishing Co., 1950

Nixon, LeRoy, *John Calvin's Teachings on Human Reason*, New York: Association Press, 1960

Parker, T. H. L., *The Oracles of God*, London: Lutterworth Press, 1947

Parker, T. H. L., *Portrait of Calvin*, London: S.C.M. Press (no date given)

Parker, T. H. L., *The Doctrine of the Knowledge of God*, Edinburgh: Oliver & Boyd, 1952

Quistorp, H., *Calvin's Doctrine of Last Things*, trs. by Harold Knight, London: Lutterworth Press, 1955

Reid, J. K., *The Authority of Scripture*, New York: Barnes & Noble, 1957

Schmidt, Albert M., *John Calvin and the Calvinist Tradition*, trs. by Ronald Wallace, New York: Harper & Brothers, 1960

Stickelberger, Emanuel, *Calvin: A Life*, London: James Clarke & Co., 1959

Stuermann, W. E., *A Critical Study of Calvin's Concept of Faith*, Tulsa: Thesis for University of Chicago, 1952

Torrance, T. F., *Calvin's Doctrine of Man*, London: Lutterworth Press, 1952

Torrance, T. F., *Kingdom and Church, A Study in the Theology of the Reformation*, London: Oliver & Boyd, 1956

Van Buren, Paul, *Christ in our Place*, London: Oliver & Boyd, 1957

Wallace, R. S., *Calvin's Doctrine of the Christian Life*, London: Oliver & Boyd, 1959

Wallace, R. S., *Calvin's Doctrine of the Word and Sacrament*, London: Oliver & Boyd, 1953

Wendel, F., *Calvin—The Origins and Development of His Religious Thought*, trs. by Philip Mairet, New York: Harper & Row, 1963

Whitney, H. J., *The Teaching of Calvin for Today*, Grand Rapids: Zondervan Publishing House, 1959

Willis, E. David, *Calvin's Catholic Christology*, London: E. J. Brill, 1966

III. BIBLIOGRAPHICAL SURVEYS

Dowey, Jr., Edward A., "The Continental Reformation; Studies in Calvin and Calvinism since 1948," *Church History*, 1955. "Studies in Calvin and Calvinism since 1955," *Church History*, 1960

McNeill, John T., "Fifty Years of Calvin Study," in Williston Walker, *John Calvin*, New York: Schocken Books, 1969, pp. xvii–lxxvii. Part I appeared in *Church History* (1968); Part II is new. The Walker volume otherwise is a reprint of the 1906 edition

Niesel, Wilhelm, *Calvin Bibliographie, 1901–1959*, Munich: Chr. Kaiser Verlag, 1961

Index of Names

Aaron, 363, 365
Abel, 459
Abraham, 151, 160, 171, 175, 206, 287, 292, 322, 350, 351, 362, 364, 408, 430, 441, 445, 448, 455, 462
Acatus (physician), 77
Adam, 14, 134, 159, 161, 204, 268, 285, 293, 297, 323, 337, 350, 379, 452
Ahab, King, 188
Ahaz, King, 393, 394
Aix, Archbishop of, 123
Alciati, Andrea, 2
Ambrose, St., 92, 155, 204, 219, 312, 426, 451
Ameux, Pierre, 7
Anderson, Rev. James, 21
André, James, 66
Antiochus, King, 368, 369
Aratus, 336
Aristophanes, 124
Aristotle, 337, 361, 367
Arius, 280–81, 282
Asellus (papal legate), 142
Augustine, St., 17, 92, 99, 120, 146, 147, 153, 155, 161–63, 167–70, 174–76, 178, 190, 194–96, 204, 208, 209, 217, 219, 243, 356–57, 369, 372, 373, 414, 420, 443, 450, 453, 454, 470–71, 486, 487, 495, 534
Basil, St., 92
Bathsheba, 425
Battles, Ford Lewis, 318
Bernard of Clairvaux, St., 103, 175, 200, 227, 401–3, 420, 450
Berthelier, 7
Beveridge, Henry, 81, 119, 245, 507, 542
Beza, Theodore, 10, 34, 37, 40, 42, 65, 66, 73–74, 79
Blandrata, Giorgio, 8
Bolsec, Jerome, 7
Boniface, Pope, 142, 196
Bonnet, Dr. Jules, 34, 45
Bordese, James, 37
Brentz, Johann, 65, 77
Bucer, Martin, 5, 22, 28–29, 45–49, 50, 51
Budé, 66
Bullinger, Heinrich, 65–67, 73–77, 79–80
Bure, Idelette de, 5
Cadier, Jean, 11

Caligula, Emperor, 327, 453
Calvin, Anna, 36
Calvin, Anthony, 36
Calvin, Antoine, 8
Calvin, David, 36
Calvin, Dorothy, 36
Calvin, John (nephew), 36
Calvin, Samuel, 36
Calvin, Susanna, 36
Capito, Wolfgang, 45
Carlostadt, 48, 50, 51
Castalio, 71–72
Castellio, Sebastianus, 6–7, 8
Catharinus, Ambrosius, 135–36
Charles V, Emperor, 3
Chauvet, Raymund, 37
Chenalat, Peter, 34–35, 37
Chusan, King of Syria, 504
Cicero, 137, 138, 140, 328, 361, 367
Clement, Pope, 84
Colladon, Nicholas, 37
Condé, Prince of, 76
Constans, Charles, 36
Cop, Michael, 37
Cop, Nicholas, 2
Cornelius, Bishop, 137–38
Cornelius the Gentile, 411
Courant, 41
Crispin, 64, 68
Cyprian, St., 17, 92, 136, 216
Cyrus, King, 366, 504
Daniel, 367, 477, 487, 500
Dathan, 364
David, King, 21, 25–26, 29, 31–33, 39, 92, 148–49, 163, 164, 171, 173, 178, 179, 190, 289, 313, 330, 335, 343, 353, 362, 366, 368, 390, 392, 393, 397, 405, 407, 415, 427, 432, 436, 440, 448–50, 462, 467, 477, 480, 483, 484, 487, 502
Demosthenes, 361
Diagoras the Atheist, 328
Dicer, Michael, 66
Dionysius, 328
Domitian, Emperor, 453
Elijah (prophet), 313, 322
Elisha (prophet), 411
Enoch, Lewis, 37
Epicurus, 324, 337
Erasmus, Desiderius, 9, 150
Etienne, Robert, 53
Eugenius, Pope, 103
Ezekiel, 129, 130, 367, 487, 500, 544

Index of Subjects